UNEQUAL RELATIONS

AN INTRODUCTION TO RACE, ETHNIC, AND ABORIGINAL DYNAMICS IN CANADA

FIFTH EDITION

AUGIE FLERAS
University of Waterloo

JEAN LEONARD ELLIOTT
Late, of Dalhousie University

PEARSON

Prentice
Hall

Toronto

To Jim Curtis (1942–2005)—dear friend, brilliant colleague, and cherished mentor.

Library and Archives Canada Cataloguing in Publication

Fleras, Augie, 1947–
  Unequal relations : an introduction to race and ethnic dynamics
in Canada / Augie Fleras and Jean Leonard Elliott. — 5th ed.

Authors' names in reverse order on 1st ed.
Includes bibliographical references and index.
ISBN 0-13-197755-5

  1. Canada—Race relations—Textbooks. 2. Canada—Ethnic relations—Textbooks.
3. Multiculturalism—Canada—Textbooks. I. Elliott, Jean Leonard, 1941– II. Elliott,
Jean Leonard, 1941– Unequal relations III. Title.

FC104.F55 2006   305.8'00971   C2006-900888-4

ISBN 0-13-197755-5

Vice President, Editorial Director: Michael J. Young
Senior Acquisitions Editor: Ky Pruesse
Executive Marketing Manager: Judith Allen
Assistant Editor: Emily Jardeleza
Production Editors: Jennie Warden, Avivah Wargon
Copy Editing: DiacriTech
Proofreader: Karen Alliston
Production Coordinator: Sharlene Ross
Composition: Laserwords
Art Director: Julia Hall
Cover Design: Anthony Leung
Cover Image: Masterfile

1 2 3 4 5   11 10 09 08 07

Printed and bound in the United States of America.

Contents

Preface viii

Part 1—Conceptualizing Race, Ethnic, and Aboriginal Relations 1

Chapter 1—Race, Ethnic, and Aboriginal Relations: Patterns, Policies, Perspectives 4

Debate—Official Multiculturalism in Canada: Putting It Under the Microscope 4

Introduction: The Good, the Bad, and the In-Between 6

Inter-Group Dynamics: Models of Race, Ethnic, and Aboriginal Relations 8

Case Study—The Politics of Genocide: Never Again or Yet Again? 10

Case Study—From Segregation to Integration to "Re-separation" 16

Explaining Race, Ethnic, and Aboriginal Relations: Sociological Models of Society 19

Debate Revisited—Re-evaluating the Relationships of an Official Multiculturalism to Canada 23

Chapter 2—The Politics of Race 27

Debate—The Racialization of Sports 27

Introduction: Race Matters 28

The Race Concept: The Power of an Illusion 30

Rethinking Race as Racialization 31

FYI—Racialization 31

Insight—Numbers Don't Lie, or Do They? Criminalizing Race; Racializing Crime 32

The Race Concept: Biological Reality or Social Construct? 34

The Historical Roots of Race 37

Putting Race to Work: Justifying Colonial Capitalism 38

Doctrines of Racial Superiority 39

Taking Race Seriously 42

Insight—Whiteness as Race Privilege 43

Debate Revisited—Black Success: Race or Opportunity? 46

Chapter 3—Unmasking Racism 50

Debate—Racial Rashomon: Putting Police Racial Profiling to the Test 50

Introduction: The Toxicity of Racism 53

Theorizing Racism 56

Defining Racism 58

Constituents of Racism 60

Types of Racism 64

Explaining Racism 70

Insight—Is Canada a Racist Society? 72

Anti-Racism 75

Debate Revisited— A Few Bad Apples or a Rotten Institutional Barrel? 78

Chapter 4—The Ethnicity Experience: Politics and Power 83

Debate—Is Whiteness an Ethnicity? 83

Introduction: Global Implosion/Ethnicity Explosion 84

Insight—Ethnic Diversity in Canada 87

Defining Ethnicity 87

Components of Ethnicity 89

Insight—Ethnicity and Religion: Taking Religion Seriously 90

Why Ethnicity? 91

Expressions of Ethnicity 95

Case Study—Growing Up South-Asian Canadian: Walking the Postmodern Tightrope of Multiple Identities 100

Insight—White Nationalism: Separation or Supremacy? 106

Depoliticizing Ethnicity: Canada-Building 107

Debate Revisited—Is Canadian an Ethnicity? 109

Chapter 5—Racialized Inequality 113

Debate—Employment Equity: A Solution in Search of a Problem? 113

Introduction: Canada's Racialized Inequality 116

Case Study—From Ethnicity to Race: A New Vertical Mosaic 118

A Racialized Mosaic 119

Insight—Are African-Americans Closing the Gap? 125

Explaining Racialized Inequality 128

Rethinking Racialized Inequality 130

Insight—Employment Equity: Reframing Inequality 131

Toward an Equity-Based Equality 132

Debate Revisited—Employment Equity: Reverse Discrimination or
Reversing Discrimination? 134

Chapter 6—Gender Diversity/Gendered Inequality 138

Debate—Is Multiculturalism Biased Against Women? The Politics of Sharia 138

Introduction: Minorities Are Women, Too 140

Gender Diversity as Gendered Inequality 141

Case Study—The Politics of Hijab: Laicité vs. Diversité? 147

Explaining Gendered Inequality: Intersecting Exclusions 153

Intersectional Analysis: Gender x Race x Ethnicity x Class 154

Debate Revisited—Sharia—Inclusiveness or Intersectional Exclusion? 155

Part 2—Canada's Diversity Model: Peoples, Nations, and Minorities 161

Chapter 7—Aboriginal Peoples in Canada: Re-priming the Relationship 164

Debate—Nisga'a Self-Government: "More Like 'Us'" or "Less Like You"? 164

Introduction: Rethinking the "Social Contract" 166

Canada's Aboriginal Peoples: Diversity in Inequality 169

Case Study—The Kasechewan Water Crisis: First Nations or
Third World Nation? 175

Canada's Aboriginal Policy: "No More Indians" 178

Rethinking the Relationship: Toward a New Social Contract 186

Insight—What Will Keep Us Together: Assimilationism? Autonomism?
Or Inbetweenism? 188

Self-Determining Autonomy Through Self-Governance 190

Speedbumps on the Roadmap for Remaking Canada 196

Unblocking the Impasse: Constructive Engagement 200

Toward a Post-Colonial Canada 203

Debate Revisited—Living Together Separately: Inclusiveness or Apartheid? 204

Chapter 8—The Quebec Question, A Canada Quandary 208

Debate—Official Bilingualism: Society-Building or Yet More Solitude? 208

Introduction: Two Solitudes or Scorpions in a Bottle? 211

Quebec: Province or Peoples? 214

Case study—Duelling Nationalisms/Intersecting Sovereignties 216

The Politics of Brinkmanship: Bluff or Reality? 219

Toward a Flexible (Asymmetrical) Federalism 223

Debate Revisited—Official Bilingualism: A Canadian Covenant? 225

Chapter 9—Immigrants and Immigration: Getting In, Settling Down, Fitting In, Moving Up 229

Debate—The Refugee Determination Process: Is It Working? 229

Introduction: The Paradox of Immigration 232

Diversity in Canada 236

Getting In: Canada's Immigration Laws, Policies, Programs, and Practices 237

Case Study—Chinese Immigration to Canada: Yellow Peril or
    White Xenophobia? 240

Immigration Programs: Who Gets In? 247

Insight—Processing Refugee Claimants 250

FYI—Immigration and Refugee Board 251

Costs and Benefits of Immigration: Problem or Solution? 252

Insight—Immigration to Canada: Keeping the Dialogue Open 254

"Settling Down, Fitting In, Moving Up" 256

Case Study—Being Discredited/Getting Accredited 259

Debate Revisited—Refugee Determination Process: System or Dysfunction? 263

Part 3—Multiculturalism as Canada-Building 269

Chapter 10—Multiculturalism in Canada: "Living Together with Differences" 272

Debate—The Politics of Multiculturalism: Drawing the Line 272

Living Together with Differences: Puzzles and Prospects 274

Theorizing Multiculturalism 276

Multiculturalism in Canada 279

Public Perceptions / Critical Reactions 288

Critiquing Multiculturalism 289

Insight—Europe's Retreat from Multiculturalism and Immigration Versus Canada's
Continued Acceptance 293

Multiculturalism: Doing It the Canadian Way 295

Debate Revisited—Cultural Defence or Multiculturally Offensive? 297

Chapter 11—Putting Multiculturalism into Practice: Policing, Media, and Education 302

Debate—Processing Aboriginality: Criminal Injustice System 302

Introduction: Putting Multiculturalism to Work 303

Institutional Inclusiveness: Principles and Practice 305

Policing in a Multicultural Milieu 307

Insight—Crisis in Policing Minority Youth 309

Bridging the Gap: Community Policing 312

Barriers to Community Policing 313

Media and Minorities: A Contested Site 315

Portraying Minority Women and Men 316

Accounting for the Problem 320

Multiculturalizing the Media 322

Couched in Compromise 323

Multicultural and Anti-Racist Education 324

Monocultural Education 325

Multicultural Education 326

Case Study—Schooling with a Difference 328

Anti-Racist Education 330

Debate Revisited—Restoring Aboriginal Justice 331

Chapter 12—This Adventure Called Canada 335

Debate—Rethinking Citizenship: Universal or Differentiated? 335

Introduction: New Game, New Rules, New Adventures 338

Canada: A Work in Progress 340

Insight—Contesting Human Rights 341

Canada's Diversity Model: The Canadian Way 344

Toward a Post-National Canada 346

Debate Revisited—Toward an Inclusive Citizenship: Belonging
   Together Differently 349

Glossary 354
References 365
Index 408

PREFACE

Canada is a society of paradox. Paradoxes prevail because Canada is rapidly changing and increasingly diverse, yet seemingly gridlocked into preferences and paradigms from the past without a definitive blueprint for the future. Such an assessment is especially applicable to the domain of race, ethnic, and Aboriginal relations, where the politics of diversity are proving more complex and contradictory than many had imagined. Every enlightened move forward for engaging diversity is matched by a corresponding slip backwards, with the result that diversity politics transcend the simplistic categories of "good" or "bad," but, paradoxically, hover in between these oppositional poles. Any study of race, ethnic, and Aboriginal relations must incorporate the politics of paradox as a framework for analysis, with the result that the likelihood of consensus and co-operation is sharply compromised.

Consider the contradictions: On one side, Canada remains a remarkably open society with a commitment to justice, inclusiveness, and tolerance that is widely admired and occasionally copied. Possibly no other country has had to cope with the conflicting demands of such a deeply divided and multi-layered society. But rather than imploding as might have been expected, Canadian society has been transformed by a much-ballyhooed model (the Canadian Diversity Model) for living together with our differences. On the other side, racial politics and ethnic conflicts continue to perplex or provoke. Aboriginal peoples and racialized minorities must contend with conditions and conventions that, frankly, are an embarrassment to Canada's lofty reputation as a beacon of enlightenment. Paradoxes abound because of this reality gap, most noticeably in the contrast between the lives we lead (reality) and the way we want to see ourselves (self-esteem) or have others see us (professed ideal)—as the following contradictions clearly demonstrate:

- Race continues to matter at a time when most Canadians think it shouldn't (Chan and Mirchandani 2002).

- Racism has proven much more pervasive and tenacious than many would have predicted because of new and virulent forms that are increasingly difficult to detect or eradicate (Bishop 2005).

- References to ethnicity are increasingly directed at competition, conflicts, and "cleansings" rather than at cuddly attachments for display in festivals and food courts (Taras and Ganguly 2002).

- No amount of multicultural gloss can mask the obvious: Minority women and men continue to experience inequities in power, income, and privilege, despite values and ideals to the contrary (Elabor-Idemudia 2005; Pendakur 2005).

- Aboriginal peoples are increasingly at the forefront of national political developments, including a right to confer with first ministers at constitutional talks, yet remain Canada's foremost human rights concern.

- Mantras about "unity within diversity," notwithstanding, the politics of Québécois and Aboriginal nationalism evoke a Canada so politically fragmented that it may eventually exist only on paper (Venne 2001).

- Constitutional guarantees for gender equality are commendable, but minority women (including Aboriginal women, women of colour, and immigrant/refugee women) continue to experience intersecting patterns of exclusion and discrimination that differ in kind from those experienced by non-racialized (white) women or racialized minority males (Folson 2004; Zawilski and Levine-Rasky 2005).

- With the exception of Aboriginal peoples, all Canadians are immigrants or descendants of immigrants; curiously, however, Canadians remain "reluctant hosts" (Avery 2000). Proof? The paradox of foreign-trained professionals driving taxis in Toronto is so common as to border on a cliché (Yelaja 2005).

- Canada may be the world's first and only example of official Multiculturalism; nevertheless, Multiculturalism remains one of the more politically charged battlegrounds of our era (James 2005).

- Canadians take pride in being tolerant, yet many are intolerant of those multicultural differences that incur cost or inconvenience, thus reinforcing perceptions of multiculturalism as a kind of "polite racism" or "assimilation in slow motion" (Aguiar et al. 2005).

- The commitment to inclusiveness is widely proclaimed and actively pursued, yet continues to be undermined by institutional structures that remain unmistakably "pale male" in composition, process, and outcomes (Kobayashi 2005).

- Both the "Canadian Way" and "Canada's Diversity Model" are attracting attention as principled blueprints for living together with differences, but proving difficult to implement because of systemic barriers (Kymlicka 2001).

The evidence seems inescapable: Canada is an enigma because of the paradoxes for living together differently in an era both astonishing and bewildering—in some ways the best of times (to paraphrase Charles Dickens), but also the worst of times. In theory, the health of Canada's race, ethnic, and Aboriginal relations should be getting better (whatever that might mean); in reality, it is not (however difficult that might be to measure). Instead of answers, Canadians are swamped with more questions. Rather than certainty and resolution, confusion prevails. Debates revolve around the politics of diversity: How much diversity can be tolerated? What kind? Who says so and why? How much unity must be imposed for societal survival? Should differences because of race or ethnicity or aboriginality be ignored in defining who gets what? Or should these differences be taken into account for full and equal participation? The fact that Canadians rarely agree on a framework for constructively engaging diversity is perplexing in its own right. More enigmatic still is a growing awareness that the very dynamic that captures Canada's strength and greatest pride—its diversity—may also prove its weakness and downfall.

The fifth edition of *Unequal Relations* is designed to confront these lacunae in our knowledge. This introductory text addresses the challenge of living together with differences in a multi-layered and deeply divided Canada by exploring the politics of race, ethnic, and Aboriginal relations. Four themes prevail—inequality, social construction, contestation, and power. First, we focus on explaining why race, ethnic, and Aboriginal relations have evolved into relationships of inequality (Teelucksingh and Galabuzi 2005); how these inequities of power, privilege, and property are created, expressed, and sustained, as well as challenged and transformed by way of government policy, institutional reform, and minority assertiveness. Second, we devote attention to race, ethnic, and Aboriginal relations as social constructs. Race, ethnic, and Aboriginal relations neither originate in a political vacuum nor unfold outside a wider context. On the contrary, they constitute conventions created by individuals who make choices and take chances—albeit within broader contexts beyond their control. Third, we direct our focus to a contestation perspective. Canada is portrayed as a contested site involving inter-group competition over scarce resources as each major ethnic category struggles to define priorities, secure interests, and impose agendas. Fourth, we explore how the pervasiveness of power is critical in driving the dynamics of diversity. Power is to society as energy is to physics; without it, nothing happens. Certain groups dominate not because of genetic superiority, but because the powerful can invariably define and control. Subdominant groups are subordinate not because of race but because they lack access to institutionalized power. The resulting imbalance of power generates those tensions that animate and inform the politics of race, ethnic, and Aboriginal relations.

The content and organization of *Unequal Relations* subscribe to the adage of "continuity in change." Much is retained in this fifth edition, including the basic chapter outline, the content in terms of concepts and applications to Canadian society, and the theme of race, ethnic, and Aboriginal relations as socially constructed and fundamentally unequal. Every effort was made to revise language, update the material, introduce new case studies, and keep the material fresh by way of synthesis and reinterpretation. The text continues to be organized around three thematic sections: theory, application, and practice. A certain logic underpins the rationale behind the sequence of topics: Concepts appear before application; theory before practice; abstractions before the concrete. Each section builds upon the other without necessarily precluding the possibility of alternative sequences.

- The first part (Chapters 1 to 6) provides a *theoretical* framework for the study of race, ethnicity, and aboriginality. Emphasis converges on the constructs and perspectives employed by sociologists for sorting out inter-group relations. Topics for discussion include models of race, Aboriginal, and ethnic relations; the theorizing of race, racism, and anti-racist strategies; the ethnicity experience; and social inequality as it applies to minority women and men.

- The second part (Chapters 7 to 9) *applies* many of these concepts to the emergent realities of a diversifying Canadian society. State policies and the politics of government–minority interaction are organized around the classification of Canadian society into three major diversities: namely, Aboriginal peoples, charter groups (descendants of the French- and English-speaking colonizers), and multicultural minorities (immigrants and descendents of immigrants). Each of these "diversities" claims a unique constitutional status in Canadian society, with corresponding differences in aspirations, entitlements, problems, and solutions.

- The third part (Chapters 10 to 12) draws attention to the *demands* of living together with differences in a multicultural society. Multiculturalism in Canada is examined at the levels of fact, ideology, policy, practice, and critique, with particular emphasis on recent developments in official Multiculturalism. Also discussed are multicultural initiatives for advancing inclusiveness at institutional levels, including the media, policing, social services, and education. The book closes with a discussion of the challenges that confront Canada as it grapples with the foundational principles that historically informed the constitutional agenda for race, ethnic, and Aboriginal relations.

Finally, the core of the text remains as unwavering as ever: to foster "diversity-literacy." The challenge lies in encouraging readers to critically reflect on the nature and dynamics of diversity politics—not by examining the issues and debates in the abstract, but by "painting oneself into the picture" of a diverse and changing Canada (James 1999).

Of course, the fifth edition of this text is not without changes—as might be expected in a domain where the mix of social patterns and conventional wisdom is rarely constant, often contested, and subject to changes. The usual amendments are in evidence, including revisions, updates, deletions, and additions where necessary. Terms like "racialization" and "racial profiling" are highlighted not because they are fashionable, but because they involve new ways of thinking about the politics of race, ethnic, and Aboriginal relations. Many new case studies and insight boxes have replaced those in earlier editions. Several substantial changes are in evidence, including new sections on ethnicity and religion and ethnic conflict, plus a new end-of-chapter "Links and Recommendations" section that lists recommended books, films and websites. Of particular note is the increased focus on the intersecting inequities of race, class, and gender that confront racialized women and men, limiting choices and closing opportunities.

What can the reader expect from this text? *Unequal Relations* is about many things, including an introduction to the politics of race, ethnic, and Aboriginal relations in Canada. The book provides a synthesis of existing and sometimes obscure research that would otherwise be inaccessible to most students. But there are also several things the book is not. The book eschews descriptions of minority groups and Canadian ethnic lifestyles except in a highly politicized sense. It rarely provides a literary platform for minority "voices" or stories by minority authors, although there is much to gain from such an approach (Fong Bates 2004).

The big picture prevails: Priority is assigned to a macro-sociological study of institutional dynamics and power politics rather than micro-models of individual behaviour, personal attitudes, or life experiences. The focus on government policy is constant throughout, as might be expected of a macro-sociological approach, yet the text avoids regurgitating both blatant government propaganda and ethnic posturing, without dismissing the rationale that propelled these dynamics in the first place. To the extent that history is employed, it is history as it relates to the present not the past, about the "is" rather than the "was" (Walker 2001); after all, as E.M. Forster once reminded us, "unless we remember, we cannot understand" (cited in Baker 2005:279).

Finally, this introduction to the politics of race, ethnic, and Aboriginal dynamics does not pretend to have all the answers. Too much reliance on answers assumes a discoverable objective reality that unlocks its "truth" to the privileged observer. But in a postmodern world that denies the existence of truth, only discourses about truths whose so-called truthfulness reflects a person's social location in terms of race, ethnicity, gender, class, and age, it is not the answers that are important but the asking of questions.

The fifth edition of *Unequal Relations* comes at a critical juncture in Canadian history. The boundaries of "being Canadian" are being buffeted by the deep diversities and radical ethnicities of a society in the throes of transformative change. Ours is the age of diversity, not simply in the descriptive or celebratory sense, but because an increasingly politicized diversity is flexing its muscles in the competition for scarce resources. Traditional images and conventional assumptions about Canada are no longer applicable. Proposed instead are new mindsets for embracing a postmodern Canada that is shifting away from stability, tradition, uniformity, and deference to one that endorses flexibility, innovation, diversity, and defiance of convention (Samuel and Schachhuber 1998).

Such transformations do not come easily or without costs. The interplay of conflict with confusion invariably inflames passions by provoking people's complacency over identity and self-esteem, core cultural values, the legitimacy of conventional authority, and taken-for-granted privileges. Not surprising, pressure is mounting to isolate and eliminate those structures that erect walls and create enclosures rather than build bridges for living together differently. To be sure, Canada is not alone in rising to the challenges of managing diversity. Other countries have also introduced policies and programs geared toward the removal of discriminatory barriers while promoting cultural diversity and social equality. But Canada is proving a pacesetter in taking a principled approach to coping with the concurrent demands of a multicultural and multi-national society in ways that are workable, necessary, and fair. It is precisely this *principled* approach for constructively engaging diversity that secures the rationale for this new edition of *Unequal Relations*.

In Memoriam

Jean Leonard Elliott (1941–1995)

First-time readers should be reminded that the "we" in *Unequal Relations* is meant in a metaphorical sense. *Unequal Relations* is a jointly authored text in name only—collaborative in spirit rather than process. Jean's untimely death in 1995 brought to a close an all too brief but productive partnership that never flinched from tackling tough issues without ever abandoning the playfulness of collegiality. May the fifth edition stand as testimony to a much-loved colleague and friend whose commitment to social justice and disdain for inequality continue to infuse the spirit of *Unequal Relations*.

ACKNOWLEDGMENTS

Thanks go to the following reviewers who took the time to comment on an earlier draft of this text: Sara Abraham, University of Toronto; Parin Dossa, Simon Fraser University; Tim Epp, Redeemer University College; Cynthia Levine-Rasky, Queen's University; and Ronald McGivern, Thompson Rivers University.

Thanks also to the team at Pearson: Patty Riediger, Acquisitions Editor, Ky Preusse, Senior Acquisitions Editor, and Emily Jardeleza, Assistant Editor. Thanks to Production Editors Jennie Warden and Avivah Wargon for their patience and thoroughness, and to Avivah for her warmth and humanity, which shone through what in most cases is a coldly analytical exercise and businesslike exchange.

CONCEPTUALIZING RACE, ETHNIC, AND ABORIGINAL RELATIONS

It has been said that this "adventure" called Canada resembles an enigma wrapped around a mystery inside a riddle. How can a deeply divided and multi-layered Canada continue to survive and even flourish under conditions that would topple lesser societies? In many ways, Canada has no business even existing, given the vagaries of its geography, history, and demographics, yet it now stands as the world's third oldest federal system (behind Switzerland and the United States). Another aphorism follows from this: Canada is accused of being a "solution" in search of a "problem" (as one ambassador to Canada aptly put it). Translation: Canada remains one of the world's best places to live—a society so blessed with physical resources and human resourcefulness that it literally has to "invent" problems that others might dismiss or ignore. The extent that Canadians dwell on the negative at the expense of the positive, even though we have much to be thankful for, may say more about being pampered than having problems.

But the prospect of "living together with differences" remains a perplexing and provocative challenge. The world we inhabit is rapidly changing and sharply diverse, with the result that confusion and uncertainty often prove the rule rather than the exception. Just as scholars have had to rethink those social moorings that conventionally secured Canada, so too must Canadians grapple with a host of diversity issues beyond their comprehension or control. Conventional wisdom for living together no longer resonates as the rules of the game twist and shift.

Consider the following challenges: Aboriginal peoples claim to be relatively autonomous political communities with rights to self-determining autonomy over land, identity, and political voice—up to and including sovereignty. National minorities such as the Québécois are seeking to transform Canada's constitutional arrangements in hopes of constructing a new social compact based on the principles of partnership, peoplehood, and power sharing. And multicultural minorities (immigrants and their descendants) have become increasingly politicized in hopes of establishing a more inclusive Canada. The challenge of coping with each of these dynamics—and doing so in a principled way—poses both a grave risk and a splendid opportunity for Canada in advancing the benchmarks for living together with differences.

Part 1 of *Unequal Relations* addresses these challenges by providing a conceptual map for deconstructing the politics of Canada's race, ethnic, and Aboriginal relations against the backdrop of diversity, change, and uncertainty. A chapter breakdown reveals the scope of coverage:

- Chapter 1 begins by exploring the concept of inter-group relations as it applies to race, ethnicity, and aboriginality. The chapter emphasizes how these constructed and unequal relationships are (1) patterned and predictable, (2) evolving and unique to specific historical circumstances, and (3) amenable to study from different sociological paradigms (or theories) of society (or social reality). Various concepts, definitions, theories, models, and perspectives are introduced that advance a more complex and nuanced understanding of race, ethnic and Aboriginal relations.

- Chapter 2 addresses the politics of race in contemporary society. The concept of race may lack biological validity or scientific justification. Nevertheless, as a social construct that is real and powerful in establishing hierarchies of inequality, race continues to matter not only as a lived reality and key organizing principle, but also in defining "who gets what"—proving yet again the brilliance of W.I. Thomas' insight: Phenomena do not have to be real to have very real consequences.

- Chapter 3 is concerned with unmasking the many faces of racism in Canada. Racism is examined in terms of definitions, properties, diverse types, constituent units, impact, and implications. The chapter also addresses anti-racist initiatives in advancing the goal of living together equitably.

- Chapter 4 examines ethnicity as a powerful force in Canadian society. By capitalizing on its many dimensions, the concept of ethnicity is discussed at the level of community, identity, and social movement. Ethnicity is discussed not only as a key explanatory variable in articulating minority identities and collective action, but also as a key idiom by which people live their lives, organize their activities, arrange themselves in relationship to others, and align themselves around politicized movements (nationalism).

- Chapter 5 looks at social inequality as it affects racialized minorities. Many perceive Canada to be an open and egalitarian society; nevertheless, hierarchies of subdomination continue to mar the lives and life chances of minority women and men. In that terms such as "equality" and "inequality" are undergoing a conceptual shift in response to social, political, demographic, and intellectual changes, the chapter promises to enlighten.

- Chapter 6 focuses on the increasingly contested domain of gender inequality. Minority women (including Aboriginal women, women of colour, and immigrant and refugee women) are known to experience patterns of inequality differently than do white women or minority men. The chapter discusses how gender is superimposed on race, ethnicity, and social class to generate interlocking patterns of inequality or exclusion that amplify as they intersect.

The challenge in exploring each of these issues is neither for the timid nor for the politically correct. A commitment to critically informed thinking is crucial in adjusting to the realities of a post-9/11 world—with its warning to expect the unexpected, to think the unthinkable, and to cope with the uncontrollable. By clarifying and rethinking perennial debates in this field, *Unequal Relations* hopes to avoid sloppy reasoning, mindless clichés, lazy over-simplifications, and common-sense assumptions at odds with hard-hitting analysis.

To be sure, Canadians have become adept at "talking the walk" about race, ethnic, and Aboriginal relations. Canada's diversity landscape is peppered with sometimes sanctimonious talk about "tolerance," "inclusion," or "partnership." But many Canadians are less enthralled with "walking the talk"—putting principles into practice—in part because confusion over concepts contributes to a kind of inertia known as "paralysis by analysis." Canadians play fast and loose with popular expressions such as "multiculturalism." Keywords are stretched to mean everything yet nothing, without much concern for precision and clarity (Kymlicka 2001). Concepts intended to enlighten and clarify—including notions of "race," "ethnicity," and "aboriginality"—are normatively and ideologically loaded because of a tendency toward ambiguity, misuse, and inconsistent application. The challenges of navigating such a conceptual minefield are daunting, and this section hopes to ground these "free-floating concepts" in ways that inform rather than inflame, enlighten rather than confuse, and empower rather than depress.

RACE, ETHNIC, AND ABORIGINAL RELATIONS: PATTERNS, POLICIES, PERSPECTIVES

DEBATE	Official Multiculturalism in Canada: Putting It Under the Microscope

To define Canada as multicultural is typically considered an understatement. References to **multiculturalism** in Canada range from the descriptive to the prescriptive, with the politics of policy in between. Canada's population is known to be multiculturally diverse; Canadians generally subscribe to the multicultural values of openness and **tolerance**; and both minority and political elites are known to play multicultural politics to advance vested interests (Lupul 2006). Canada is also multicultural because of its commitment to an official Multiculturalism (note use of upper case "M" to denote official government policy; otherwise lower case "m"). Entrenchment of Multiculturalism in the *Constitution Act* of 1982, followed by the passage of the world's first and only *Multiculturalism Act* in 1988, has further secured Canada's status as a trailblazer in managing **diversity**. Finally, there is widespread support for an official Multiculturalism as a principled approach for living together with differences, although agreement over practices or implementation remains elusive (Fleras 2002).

Despite its pervasiveness and popularity, Canadians express a love–hate relationship with an **official Multiculturalism**. Those who embrace Multiculturalism as the solution to Canada's problems of diversity are dismissive of those who dismiss it; conversely, those who pounce on Multiculturalism as an evil incarnate are no less contemptuous of its supporters. Some Canadians are justifiably proud of a homegrown initiative that many regard as Canada's foremost contribution to world peace. Other Canadians lack conviction about its usefulness or are openly critical of its weaknesses (Gregg 2006; Abu Laban 2002; Bannerji 2000). Still others are unsure of how to assess official Multiculturalism. Costs and consequences are acceptable in principle, but not if they (1) entail inconveniences or sacrifices, (2) make excessive demands, (3) undermine Canada's social cohesiveness, or (4) erode core Canadian values. There are yet others who acknowledge its paradoxes. Official Multiculturalism is proving to be contradictory because of its significance and impact as a site of contestation. On the one hand are liberal views of tolerance and inclusiveness. On the other is the tendency for Multiculturalism to deny what it sets out to affirm—diversity—while reinforcing what it hopes to eliminate—inequality. In addition there is political pressure for a shared national unity—neither embracing differences at the expense of unity nor denying them because of commonalities (Kivisto and Ng 2005).

Canadians are no less divided over objectives and outcomes. For some, official Multiculturalism is about consensus, conformity, and co-operation. For others, it should be about challenge, resistance, and transformation. For others still, it is largely a hoax imposed on Canadians, designed to convey the impression, rather than the reality, of inclusiveness and justice. Yet others believe that multiculturalism can mean whatever people want it to mean. The lack of consensus complicates any easy assessment of Multiculturalism as a basis for living together with our differences.

Does Canada's official Multiculturalism contribute to or detract from society-building? Is Multiculturalism a good or a bad thing for Canada, or, is it simultaneously a benefit as well as a cost, as might be expected of any political experiment in social engineering? How potent a force is official Multiculturalism? Is it a powerful force that hides behind soothing clichés to disguise its transformative dynamic? Or is Canada's Multiculturalism essentially a toothless tiger whose roar is more menacing than its bite? In other words, should official Multiculturalism be interpreted as no more than a docile sheep masquerading in wolf's clothing—all bluster but no substance? Or is it more cautiously approached as a predatory wolf disguised in the innocence of sheep's clothing?

Possible responses to these questions will be addressed at the end of the chapter. Different answers are possible because of the difficulties in deciding on the criteria for assessment, with the result that any reference to the "good" or the "bad" may say more about the evaluator and her agenda than about the evaluated or assessed. Nor can debates over Multiculturalism be divorced from the central theme of the text. In that Canada's race, ethnic, and Aboriginal relations are unequal relations, what role does official Multiculturalism play in creating and sustaining as well as challenging and changing these patterns of inequality? As we shall see, any evaluation of Canada's official Multiculturalism will depend on the model of society proposed by functionalists, conflict theorists, and interactionists.

INTRODUCTION: THE GOOD, THE BAD, AND THE IN-BETWEEN

Canada is widely admired for its many qualities; two, however, appear foremost. People around the world marvel at Canada's ability to resist the pressures of absorption as the fifty-first state of the world's most powerful melting pot. How, they ask, can Canada keep the American colossus at bay and yet pursue a relatively independent course of action at home and abroad? That Canadians have managed to secure a "true north, strong and free" is a testimony to the resilience of its people.

People overseas are no less astonished by Canada's resourcefulness in weaving a remarkably united and distinct society from the strands of diversity. How do Canadians manage to keep a lid on those ethnic tensions that have fractured other societies into warring factions? How can we explain the relatively smooth transformation of the once stodgy Victorian-era cities such as Toronto and Vancouver into the most cosmopolitan and diverse of any in the world without experiencing paralyzing strife (Ibbitson 2005)? To be sure, the potential for unravelling Canada's social fabric is a reminder that we need to constantly "stand on guard for" Canada. But while other countries are groping for solutions to "accommodate" diversity, Canada is embarking on a promising if unprecedented quest for "living together with differences" along principled lines. How does this assessment stand up to scrutiny?

A sense of perspective is helpful. First, compared to its historical past, Canada's engagement with race, ethnicity, and aboriginality has come a long way. Canada's historical past left much to be desired: Canada originated in the dispossession of Aboriginal peoples and their lands—by "hook," "crook," or the "book." Canada-building had as its foundations policies and practices that routinely excluded or exploited racialized minorities, and included xenophobic attitudes and racist political responses to Chinese and East Indian immigrants (Li 2003); the internment and dispossession of Japanese-Canadians during World War II (Maki 2004); the enslavement of black people and their segregation from mainstream institutions until the 1950s (Walker 1985; Calliste 2005); and the pervasive anti-Semitism of the 1920s and 1930s, which culminated in the rejection of Jewish émigrés from Nazi Germany (Penslar 2005).The extent to which this racism went beyond the perversions of a few misguided bigots says a lot about its institutionalization within Canadian society.

Times have changed. Evidence of Canada's historical advancement can be gleaned from a list of global firsts in the diversity sweepstakes. Canada's *Citizenship Act* of 1947 was the first in the world to disregard any distinction between immigrants and native-born citizens. The *Immigration Act* of 1967 was one of the first to abolish all quotas or preferences on the basis of race or ethnicity, with the result that Canada's enlightened immigration policies may well prove to be its greatest achievement (Ibbitson 2005). Canada was the first country to receive the United Nations–sponsored Nansen Medal in 1986 for its humanitarian response to the global refugee problem. In 1982 Canada became the first country to constitutionally enshrine Aboriginal and treaty rights. Furthermore, Canada remains the first and only country to constitutionally endorse official Multiculturalism as a principled framework for engaging diversity. This lofty reputation is further secured by Canada's consistent high placement in quality-of-life surveys—including its ranking for eight consecutive years (between 1993 and 2000) as the world's best place to live according to a human development index that takes into account the wealth, education, and longevity of each country's population.

Consider global comparisons. Compared with other societies that routinely tolerate **human rights** abuses, ranging from ethnic cleansing and mass expulsion to exploitation and forced assimilation, Canada possesses an enviable reputation as a paragon of virtue, toler-ance, and compassion. The "management" of Canada's race, Aboriginal, and ethnic relations is widely acknowledged within global circles as a model to emulate. People applaud Canada's moxie in forging unity from the fragments of diversity, without sacrificing a commitment to prosperity or capitulating to chaos. Paradoxically, however, Canada's lofty status makes it vulnerable to criticism. Even the smallest infractions, which would barely rate a mention in many foreign countries, tend to be amplified in Canada because of its exacting standards. Not surprisingly, Canadians appear perplexed and angry when international bodies criticize Canada for relatively "minor" human rights violations while rogue societies are allowed to get away with "bloody murder."

In short, Canada looks good by comparison. But Canada also falls short of its estab-lished benchmarks with respect to the ideals of tolerance, openness, and a commitment to inclusiveness. Relations between racialized minorities and the rest of Canada tend to waver uneasily between grudging acceptance and qualified accommodation, with the spectre of public backlash ever present. Discrimination and racism are not simply relics from the past, but are so deeply embedded in the present that there seems little chance of their disappear-ing in the foreseeable future (Razack 2004). To be sure, racism is no longer blatant; never-theless, more subtle forms of racism exert an equally powerful negative impact. Anti-Semitism persists, albeit in different guises (Weinfeld 2005; Schoenfeld 2004); white supremacist groups proliferate because of access to the Internet; and racialized minorities continue to do poorly because of institutional barriers to access, participation, and equity (Henry and Tator 2006). The fact that highly skilled immigrants find it difficult to secure appropriate employ-ment exposes a gap between the ideals of immigration and the realities of multiculturalism (Teelucksingh and Galabuzi 2005; Pendakur 2005). Even the UN Human Rights Committee has issued a stinging indictment of Canada's treatment of vulnerable minorities, citing anti-terrorist legislation that is too broad and imprecise and the issuing of security certificates to arrest, detain, or expel immigrants without due process (Goar 2005). Of particular dismay as the country's most egregious human rights violation is the continued mistreatment of Aboriginal peoples. The uproar over the water contamination crisis in a remote James Bay reserve of Kashechewan (see case study in Chapter 7), coupled with the awareness that similar Kashechewans prevailed elsewhere, confirmed what some had suspected: In that Aboriginal communities remain politically repressed, economically depressed, and cultur-ally oppressed, Canada's reputation as a beacon for diversity management needs deflation (Frideres and Gadacz 2005).

This admittedly selective overview paints a discordant picture of Canadian race, Aboriginal, and ethnic relations. From a distance, Canada looks idyllic; up close, however, the picture is smudged, and one can see a country that has had little to boast about in the mismanage-ment of race, ethnic, and Aboriginal relations. That discord suggests the possibility of a third interpretation—that Canada is positioned somewhere in between the extremes of good and bad. Neither a paragon of virtue nor the fountainhead of all evils, Canada's status in engaging diversity probably falls somewhere in the middle. In comparison to the past or to other coun-tries, Canada soars, but when compared to the ideals that many Canadians espouse, Canada misses the mark. Initiatives for "managing" race, ethnicity, and aboriginality are at times enlightened, yet at other times callously expedient, especially as Canadians strive to balance "national interests" with the rights of minority women and men (see Kymlicka 2001). Considering that Canada still has a long way to go in meeting the ideals espoused under its Diversity Model (see Chapter 12), its people have no room for smugness or complacency.

This chapter aims to deconstruct the paradoxes and puzzles in Canada's race, ethnic, and Aboriginal relations record by cutting through the conceptual clutter that conceals as much as it reveals, confuses as it clarifies, and distorts as it enlightens. Such an ambitious undertaking is not without personal cost to the reader. Debates over diversity—how much, what kind, who says so, and on what grounds—often pose a threat to people's sense of what it means to live in Canada or be a Canadian (see also Dion 2005). Most have been taught to think of Canada as a "kinder, gentler" society of good and just people who disapprove of racism and racially based exploitation. Few, however, have been taught to challenge the myths of Canada as "a society without racism" (Razack 2004). Fewer still are capable of seeing how the privilege of whiteness contributes to the dis-privileging of Aboriginal peoples and disempowering of racialized minorities. That this and other chapters strive to shatter these misconceptions indicates the scope of the challenge before us: We have the choice of acquiescing to the status quo, and thereby propagating it, or working to advance a just and inclusive Canada through critically informed activism.

INTER-GROUP DYNAMICS: MODELS OF RACE, ETHNIC, AND ABORIGINAL RELATIONS

Canada is widely acknowledged as a remarkably diverse society. Yet, it is hardly alone in this regard. The contemporary world comprises many societies that are generally polyethnic or multinational in composition. Of the approximately 200 countries recognized by the United Nations, all but a dozen or so are defined as ethnically diverse. In most of these countries, one ethnic group tends to be dominant, insofar as both national governance and social institutions are organized around its agenda and priorities. By contrast, **subdominant minority groups**' members are disadvantaged in the competition for power or privilege. The corresponding tension between competing interests transforms each of these societies. A competitive struggle involving opposing groups ensues: On the one hand, the dominant sector will do everything at its disposal to preserve its lofty status; on the other, **subdominant groups** demand a more equitable distribution of power and privilege. The ensuing interplay of interests reinforces a key theme of this text: As long as race, ethnic, and Aboriginal relations are unequal relations, initiatives to reinforce or to challenge these inequities will activate the dynamics that animate inter-group relations.

What exactly is meant by the dynamics of race, ethnic, and Aboriginal relations? What should be included in a study of race, ethnicity, and aboriginality (see Banton 2005; also Solomos and Bulmer 2005)? For some, the study of race, ethnic, and Aboriginal relations is concerned with inter-group relations over time and across space (Marger 2001). These relations exist because individuals with a shared culture and similar ancestral backgrounds continue to identify (or are identified by others) with each other and engage in behaviour that protects or promotes their interests (Kivisto and Ng 2005). For others, pure racial, ethnic, and Aboriginal groups do not exist per se, although a significant racial, ethnic, and Aboriginal component may inform the dynamics of inter-group relations (Taras and Ganguly 2002). Co-operation or competition between groups may be driven by political or economic concerns; nonetheless, references to race or ethnicity may be invoked to (1) mobilize like-minded individuals into action; (2) justify patterns of action or inaction toward groups; and (3) provide a convenient label to simplify otherwise complex inter-group relations. For still others, the focus is on how inter-group relations become racialized (or ethnicized) around power politics. The interplay of meaningful choices by way of negotiated interaction reinforces the fluid and imprecise nature of inter-group dynamics, but also reflects the centrality of human agency in the social construction of reality.

How do race, ethnic, and Aboriginal relations arise? A limited number of contact situations may account for various inter-group relations in ethnically mixed societies. First, a **dominant group** incorporates or annexes a foreign territory by force or "rights of (European) discovery." The British conquest of the French on the Plains of Abraham in 1759 provides an example that, for some, rankles even today. Second, colonization and frontier expansion result in the acquisition of land or resources through diplomatic channels. Territories may be acquired by purchase or through treaties such as those between Canada's Aboriginal peoples and the Crown. Forced migration is a third possibility that involves a foreign population being forcibly brought into the country for essentially exploitative purposes. The importation of Africans for slave labour into the United States—and into Canada on a more limited basis—is a classic example. Fourth, voluntary migration from overseas entails some degree of choice in moving from one country to another. It stands to reason that the interests of "voluntary migrants" will differ from the interests of those who have been forcibly incorporated through annexation or colonization.

Sustained contact between and among groups invariably leads to a patterned set of inter-group relations. Ranging in scope from hostility to acceptance, with varying levels of indifference or tolerance in between, the exact nature of the relationship will vary with the quality of the contact situation—its duration, timing, conflicts of interest, magnitude, and intensity. Interaction based on these relationships gives rise to a limited number of patterned responses that can be conceptualized as models of inter-group relations, namely, *genocide, assimilation, segregation, integration*, and *pluralism*. In theory, each of the "models" contains its own set of assumptions about the status of diversity in society, including both prescriptions for "managing" race, ethnic, and Aboriginal relations and proposed outcomes for society-building. In reality, however, these models of inter-group relations are not strictly separate from each other. Overlap is the rule rather than the exception because reality itself is contextual rather than categorical. These models are not always explicitly articulated or codified into law. But, in many cases, they do attain official policy status, and this text tends to interpret these models of inter-group relations from the perspective of official government (or state) policies for managing diversity.

Genocide

Genocide may be the most serious of punishable crimes under international law, and one of the few crimes for which UN military intervention is permitted (Saunders 2005). Despite (or perhaps because of) its magnitude, genocide proves difficult to define. Generally speaking, most definitions include the notion of deliberate and systematic mass killings of a despised domestic minority that dwells in a territory controlled by another group—often government-backed killers (Taras and Ganguly 2002). Many see intent, including the idea of state involvement by openly condoning or tacitly accepting violence against its own citizens, as the key factor (Rummel 2005). Others prefer a more expansive definition that includes the unintended yet genocidal consequences of seemingly well-intentioned initiatives (Deak 2002).

The concept of genocide encompasses a broad range of actions. According to the UN-based convention of 1948, genocide can include five classes of action: (1) members of a group are slaughtered with the intent of bringing about their disappearance as a people;

(2) conditions are created that foster the dispersal of the group by destroying the essential foundations of community life; (3) intense psychological abuse or physical discomfort is inflicted, culminating in the dissolution of the group; (4) children are transferred from one group to another, thus bringing about the demise of the culture; and (5) births are prevented through involuntary sterilization, birth control, or abortion, in the process pushing remnants of the population to an edge from which recovery is difficult. Such a range of activities complicates the search for a definition (Caplan 2005).

For some, very few calamities meet UN criteria for genocide—the extermination of the German Jews (and other "undesirables") and Rwandan Tutsi (and moderate Hutu) are clear-cut examples. For others, history is replete with genocidal purges of dehumanized minorities—whether deliberate or unintentional. In asserting colonial control over a land they saw as *terra nullius*, European settlers openly stalked and killed Australia's aboriginal populations. Likewise, Aboriginal peoples such as the Beothuk in Newfoundland became extinct because of disruptive contact with early European colonialists. The twentieth-century killing fields were no less punitive: Ukrainians suffered massive losses in famines engineered by Stalinist purges. The Armenians accused the Turkish regime of genocide during World War I. The blatant mistreatment of indigenous populations by Brazilian settlers and miners in the Amazonian rainforest appears no less genocidal (Chagnon 1998). Even the proselytizing work of missionaries is deemed genocidal, in consequence if not necessarily by intent, according to Napoleon Chagnon. Also widely viewed as genocidal were the **"ethnic cleansing"** campaigns by Serbs against Muslim populations in Bosnia and Albanians in Kosovo. But nothing in recent memory exceeds the murderous rampages in Rwanda and currently those in the Darfur region of Sudan.

CASE STUDY	**The Politics of Genocide: Never Again or Yet Again?**

As dawn breaks, pandemonium breaks loose. The silence of a sleepy village is shattered by helicopters whose guns punctuate the air with explosions and flames. People flee their burning huts, as hundreds of men on horseback gallop into the village, their automatic rifles firing, killing everyone in sight. Eventually, only the men and boys are singled out to be shot to death, while the women are rounded up and marched toward the church. Gunmen seize the male children and throw them into the burning buildings—with mothers forced to watch their excruciating deaths in agonizing silence. Once inside the church, the women are forced to undress, and are raped repeatedly, often for days on end. Some women, children, and men have managed to escape into the surrounding forests, but the men on horseback relentlessly pursue the escapees, and, as a lesson to others, will rape, torture, and kill the unlucky ones in front of everyone. The so-called lucky ones finally emerge from their hiding places after several days only to discover that their homes are burnt to the ground, possessions confiscated, livestock taken, wells poisoned, and the surviving women either infected with disease or impregnated by the rapists. What other choice is there except a forced flight to squalid refugee camps? Along the way the survivors learn that the same thing has happened in thousands of villages, with the result that everyone is homeless and on the run in a vast desert region the size of France (adapted from Saunders 2005; for details see **www.ohchr.org/english/darfur.htm).**

Genocide? Ethnic cleansing? Crime against humanity? Human rights atrocity? Darfur now ranks as the world's most serious humanitarian crisis since the frenzy that claimed nearly a million lives in Rwanda a decade ago. The scope of the mass killings of black farmers by marauding Arab militias known as Janjaweed with the support of helicopter gunships and Antonov bombers from the regime at Khartoum is beyond human comprehension (Kumar and Kelly 2005). Nearly 200 000 have died from fighting, disease, or starvation since 2003. Another 2 million have been displaced from their homes—in a country that with 4 million already has the world's largest number of internally displaced persons, with another 500 000 refugees in bordering countries (Kilgour 2005). Adding to the misery is the widespread rape of women and children, the forced movement of people off the land, and a paralyzing realization that possibly one half of Sudan's population of 7 million is on the verge of starvation.

International outrage over these atrocities is slowly mounting. The international community has voiced widespread frustration over the United Nations' failure to intervene, the slow pace of intervention by the peacekeeping African Union force in "looking after their own," and the dearth of meaningful media coverage to galvanize international outrage over the carnage. Canada's reaction remains long on rhetoric but short on action—a delay all the more remarkable in light of Canada's endorsement of the "Responsibility to Protect" principle, which holds that the international community has a responsibility to protect a country's citizens—even to the point of armed humanitarian intervention—when governments are unwilling or unable to do so (Heinbecker and Axworthy 2005). How else can we explain Canada's meagre commitment of 100 minimally armed peacekeepers

to a land the size of Texas? (In all fairness, Canada has nearly 1000 troops stationed in Afghanistan, and another nearly 1000 troops in Bosnia and 1400 in Kosovo to staunch the ethnic cleansings in those regions.) Why such indifference? Does it stem from a lack of political will, a lack of intervention resources to deploy, ignorance, fear of involvement in tribal wars, or blatant racism (Kilgour 2005)?

More frustrating still is a reluctance to define as genocide the slaughter of Darfuri men, women, and children, reminiscent of similar slaughters in Rwanda. The conflict in Darfur is so complicated and has gone on for so long that few international powers really care who is killing whom as long as their strategic interests are safeguarded. The United Nations is unwilling to define the situation in Darfur as genocide, because such a declaration would necessitate international intervention. Anti-genocide conventions that go back to 1948 call upon participant members of the international community to intervene in jurisdictions where the state is either incapable of curbing gross human rights violations, or complicit in the slaughter of innocents. Much of the problem is based on semantics, namely, a high burden of proof for the word "intent." According to the United Nations, there is no conclusive proof of intent to destroy an ethnic group, only a campaign to kill those males whom the marauders regard as rebels while expelling the population from arable land (Saunders 2005). The Western powers concede that this is genocidal in effect, but not intent, and without intent there is no legal mandate for foreign powers to get involved in a country that strategically has little to offer in compensation.

The irony of such inaction in the face of gross provocation is unmistakable: In May of 2005, Europe commemorated the sixtieth anniversary to mark the end of the Nazi genocide of Jews and other so-called undesirables, although there was barely any reference to the humanitarian crisis in

Darfur. Paradoxically, two countries that suffered greatly from the genocidal fascism of Germany—France and Russia—continue to support Khartoum's crime against humanity because of commercial interests (Gurwitz 2005). No less silent—despite an initial labelling of the crisis as genocide—was the president of the United States who has delivered military support in order to secure the rights of oppressed people in strategically placed parts of the world. How sadly ironic: Rather than *never again*, as promised after World War II, the pampered and powerful are *yet again* closing their eyes to atrocities in Darfur, just as they did a decade ago in Rwanda.

Common to many genocides is a pattern of barbarism. As people are hacked, bludgeoned, raped, or shot to death, this violence often comes across as random and uncontrollable, involving high levels of spontaneity and irrationality. But appearances can be deceiving. This mass liquidation process is indeed a process—not an isolated nor unintentional act by poorly disciplined militia. The killing fields are neither an unfortunate by-product of dormant tribal hatred nor a spontaneous spasm of uncontrolled primeval rage. To the contrary, genocide represents a calculated political decision to achieve political goals in a politically acceptable manner. For example, the Darfur conflict erupted over competition for scarce resources, as African farmers and nomadic Arab herders competed for what little land there was in the face of creeping desertification, followed by a fierce government crackdown of Darfurian insurgents who attacked a government outpost (Wrzesnewskyj 2005). An orchestrated campaign of terror that sanctions the dehumanization and destruction of the "other" is activated to remove competitors or silence opponents. What may look like mindless aggression is often a ruthless strategy to defend a sacred ideal; to destroy a group perceived as a threat to the ruling regime; to diminish those who are hated or envied; to transform the ideological basis of society; to eliminate foreign elements from society; to consolidate elite advantage; or to secure economic gain (Rummell 2005; also Koenigsberg 2004).

In short, genocide does not necessarily erupt because of natural differences or pent-up hostilities. Outside of local outbursts that may spiral out of control, genocide originates in the manipulation of these differences by cynical elites who will stop at nothing to retain power, achieve advantage, secure political support, conceal economic difficulties, and distract from internal squabbles (Ignatieff 1995). Even the victims and victimizers fall into a gendered pattern, with young males often the perpetrators and victims, but increasingly women as targets for rape and infections (Jones 2004). To be sure, not all genocides are blunt or direct. The process of genocide can encompass varying strategies: from those that explicitly seek to exterminate "troublesome minorities" to those well-intentioned initiatives that, however inadvertently, have had the effect (rather than intent) of eliminating the "other." Annihilation of this magnitude may be accomplished directly through military means, or indirectly through the spread of disease, loss of livelihood, or compulsory re-socialization.

The resurgence of genocide in recent years is as disconcerting as it is disturbing: disconcerting, because many thought we had put that part of history behind us; disturbing, because of the intensity and savagery that accompanies the killings (Caplan 2005). Why have such crimes against humanity proven so common in recent years—despite inhumane consequences that invariably lead to suffering and death? How and why do neighbours who share social and cultural space suddenly morph into murderous enemies (Ward 2004)? This lust for killing compels us to rethink our understanding of human nature. Are humans naturally good but twisted by social circumstances beyond their control? Are genocides exceptions to the rule of natural goodness—even if many humans may be capable of unspeakable crimes against humanity under specific circumstances (Caplan 2005)? Or are people naturally evil in the Hobbesian sense of living lives that are "nasty, brutish, and short"—with the result that genocides reflect our hard-wiring as a species? If true, should we be asking ourselves if, in fact, the rules of law and reason are contrary to human nature, and secured only by an unremitting struggle that "goes against the grain" of fundamental instincts (Ignatieff 1994)?

Assimilation

Assimilation has been referred to as a one-way process of absorption. It involves a process whereby the dominant sector imposes its culture, authority, values, and institutions on subdominant sectors with a corresponding loss of their distinctiveness because of exposure to these conformity pressures. The concept was taken from biology (absorption through digestion), and reflects a largely scientific belief that social life could be better understood by drawing upon simplified analogies with the natural world (Jaret 1995). Rather than something simple and straightforward, however, assimilation is a complex and multi-dimensional process that unscrolls at a varying pace, sometimes deliberately but often unconsciously, involves different intensities of absorption, ranges in scope from cultural to institutional, and entails varying degrees of conformity (Zhou 1997).

In the past, assimilation was endorsed as an official government policy in defining majority–minority relations. Under assimilation, all minorities would be expected to adopt the cultural values and social practices of the ruling majority. Yet, assimilationist policies were rarely intended to transform minorities in their entirety. The complete absorption of everybody was neither attainable nor always desirable; after all, few majorities possessed either the resources or the political will to enforce wholesale conformity. Endorsed instead was a commitment to dominant-conformity (or **anglo-conformity** in areas under British control). A dominant-conformity model required outward compliance with dominant values and practices. Select elements of a subdominant lifestyle were tolerated as long as they (1) were restricted to the private or personal realm, (2) involved only the "cultural" (aesthetic) realm, (3) conformed to majority commercial, political, or ideological interests, and (4) did not violate moral principles or the law.

Assimilation emerged as an "enlightened" social policy for its time, especially when compared with alternatives such as forced separation or genocide. A commitment to assimilation informed a government framework for managing indigenous peoples in settler societies (Pearson 2001). At times this commitment was tacitly assumed as a guideline for government–indigenous people relations; at other times, it was explicitly articulated as official government policy. Through assimilation, the dominant element sought to (1) undermine the cultural basis of indigenous societies, (2) expose individuals to dominant norms as normal and acceptable, (3) convert them into patriotic, productive, and God-fearing citizens; and (4) facilitate their entry and transition into the mainstream. Dominant values, beliefs, and social patterns were valorized as inevitable or desirable; conversely, differences were demonized as inferior or irrelevant. Such Eurocentrism proved both paternalistic and patronizing.

Those singled out for assimilationist treatment were often portrayed as children in need of discipline under the ever-vigilant eye of a judicious parent.

Assimilation no longer prevails as an explicit policy principle. There is little inclination to openly support an agenda that once dismissed group differences as a liability to be overcome through assimilation. In its place is an official commitment to diversity, not as a weakness to be suppressed, but as a strength to be nurtured, especially as a gateway "language" to global markets. Yet appearances can be deceiving: Although publicly scorned and officially rebuked as a model for managing diversity, assimilation as a process continues to play a prominent role in shaping inter-group relations. Even in Canada where diversity under official Multiculturalism is the rule, new Canadians are expected to conform to the cultural and normative standards if they hope to succeed here (Li 2003). Moreover, as racialized minorities become increasingly involved in the mainstream, assimilation is proving the rule rather than the exception—in large part because of the often unintended consequences of choices made by individuals who are looking to settle down, fit in, and move up. Assimilation may unfold informally as well: Consider how the offspring of immigrants intermarry, live in ethnically mixed neighbourhoods, are employed in all economic sectors, including "white-collar" jobs, and share comparable levels of education and income with other groups (Denton and Tolnay 2002). Finally, assimilation can also be inferred as the logic underlying all government actions. The logical consequences of even seemingly progressive initiatives to assist racialized minorities (for instance, employment equity initiatives) may have the effect of drawing them deeper into the "system."

Segregation and Separation

The concept of **segregation** provides yet another model of inter-group relations. Segregated societies are segmented into relatively autonomous dominant and subdominant groups. Both the dominant and subordinate groups live apart, sharply divided and largely incompatible. When used as a policy model for managing diversity within unequal contexts, the role of central authorities or governments is critical. In cases of *de jure* segregation, the government deliberately keeps the races apart, thus stigmatizing and handicapping the vulnerable by confining them to inferior facilities. A *de facto* segregation results in the government tacitly condoning forced segregation by not actively intervening to dismantle the social architecture of forced separation (Kennedy 1996).

Segregation involves a forced and physical separation. Contact between the "races" is kept to an absolute minimum, except in contexts of obvious benefit to the controlling sector. What little interaction exists is conducted primarily in the marketplace ("selective incorporation"), where the dominant group exercises monopolistic control over the economy and distribution of wealth. Compliance in unequal contexts is rarely secured by value consensus or social norms, but instead by physical force. In the absence of any morally legitimate basis to govern, the dominant group must rely on physical threats to compel obedience. Yet segregation goes beyond a physical separation of unequal groups. Also implicated is a social relationship involving patterns of power and domination (Jaret 1995). The dominant group defines itself as superior because of technological prowess, military might, and moral superiority. "Others" are dismissed as inferior or irrelevant, or a threat, to the society-building process.

History is rife with patterns of interaction that segregate groups from one another. Few cases of segregation have been as highly profiled as that of apartheid in South Africa. A comprehensive set of segregationist laws and practices compartmentalized blacks and whites into separate groups at social, economic, and political levels. Canada's reserve system for the status of Aboriginal peoples may also be interpreted as segregation—at least in consequence if not intent—given the government's longstanding commitment to "no more Indians" as a solution to the so-called "Indian problem." No less segregationist was the colour bar that existed in both the United States and Canada (Horton and Horton 2004). Whites were segregated from blacks at institutional, occupational, interactional, and residential levels, in large part because of the power of the Ku Klux Klan that terrorized the American South (see case study below).

Segregation as a policy model is usually generated from the top down. But as a model for inter-group behaviour, segregation can also be generated from "below" by groups who prefer voluntary separation from a society for lifestyle or strategic purposes. Voluntary separation is not the same as segregation or apartheid, despite similarities in appearance and structure. Racialized minorities, indigenous peoples, and religious groups may prefer to isolate themselves from the mainstream to preserve their independence and identity. For example, the Hutterites of western Canada and other communal religious sects have voluntarily divorced themselves from the outside world through expressions of religion, language, communal lifestyle, dress, and social interaction. Aboriginal peoples in Canada are casting about for aboriginal models of self-determining autonomy as a basis for living together separately (Maaka and Fleras 2005). Insurgent ethnicities such as Québécois nationalism are proliferating as well in exploring new arrangements within existing state systems. Part 2 of this text will further explore the politics of separation in Canada.

Integration

Integration represents a fourth model for race, ethnic, and Aboriginal relations. Generally speaking, the concept of integration stands in opposition to that of segregation. Segregation is defined as the forced separation of people who live apart from each other, socially and geographically. **Integration**, by contrast, refers to a process whereby individuals interact with each other at all institutional levels (Jaret 1995). A distinction between desegregation and integration is also useful. Desegregation entails removing physical or social barriers to achieve formal equality, while integration involves unifying disparate parts into a co-operative and functioning whole.

Two variations underlie the integration theme. First, integration represents a two-way process by which the dominant and subdominant sectors are brought together in a single comprehensive lifestyle, without either losing its distinctiveness. Each is expected to contribute to the construction of the new reality, yet retain a distinct presence within the framework of a new configuration. A second variant involves a process by which the dominant and the subdominant groups merge together like different colours of paint in a bucket. The result of this "blending" process is a new cultural entity comprising constituent elements of this mixture. This fusion of the "modern" with the "traditional" into a relatively homogeneous entity is metaphorically captured by the concept of the **melting pot**, an image that is often invoked to describe, and prescribe, American race and ethnic relations. Keep in mind that metaphors such as "melting pot" or "the mosaic" are useful yet problematic shorthands because they simplify complex matters (Kivisto and Ng 2005). Under a melting pot paradigm, all immigrants can be transformed into new Americans—a cultural alloy forged in the crucible of democracy, freedom, and civic responsibility (Booth 1998).

A commitment to integration emerged as a preferred policy model for managing diversity after World War II. The impetus for change reflected a growing disillusionment with assimilation as a workable model for living together. Resentment over segregation increased because of international conventions that sought to protect human rights through removal of discriminatory barriers. Another impetus in demolishing segregationist structures was the mounting assertiveness by blacks and Aboriginal peoples who bristled over second-class treatment in a country that had gone to war to protect individual freedom. Despite great fanfare and high expectations, a commitment to integration did not necessarily translate into a *de facto* equality, as the next case study on black–white relations in the United States demonstrates.

CASE STUDY | **From Segregation to Integration to "Re-separation"**

All "men" may be created equal according to the American Constitution. But some women and men are born more equal than others, and neither the *Declaration of Independence* nor the Civil War did much to improve the legal and socio-economic status of African-Americans (Horton and Horton 2004). Blacks and whites were unequal and separated by law and custom prior to the Civil Rights movement of the 1950s and 1960s. Both *de jure* and *de facto* segregations were enforced in restaurants, public transport, and major social institutions such as hospitals, churches, and schools. The labour force was racially stratified. Interracial marriages were prohibited in many states. The colour bar led to uneven levels of development among black people, thereby intensifying patterns of discrimination against a segregated population.

The Civil Rights movement established a pathway to integration. The movement was largely a struggle for racial equality by dismantling the openly discriminatory features of a segregated social order that had entrenched white supremacy (Estes 2005; Goldberg 2005). Desegregation was expected to undo segregation by eliminating legal and social prohibitions, while integration sought to improve the overall participation of African-Americans within the society. Integration guaranteed all Americans formal equality before the law by expressly prohibiting discrimination on the basis of race. The promise of integration was predicated on a relatively simple premise: Whites will discriminate in favour of themselves if there is a separation of races. With integration, however, whites cannot self-discriminate without favourably assisting black people in the process. In short, the best way of guaranteeing black children a good education was by linking their fate with that of white children through integrated schools, even if forced busing had to be mandated (Kennedy 1996).

The commitment to integration held out much promise. The advancement of black people was driven by the 1954 Supreme Court decision to ban separate but equal public school facilities. By striking down the separate but equal concept that had segregated whites from blacks, the Civil Rights Act of 1961 outlawed racial discrimination in employment and accommodation, while the Voters Rights Act of 1965 improved black political participation by eliminating all qualifying tests for voter registration (Horton and Horton 2004). But theory was one thing, reality quite another. The legal and social progress since the Civil Rights movement notwithstanding, many African-Americans continue to be plagued by the aftermath of segregation (Shapiro 2004).

They continue to be confined to economic and residential ghettoes, primarily because most lack the wealth (assets like home equity or savings) to break the cycle of poverty. Worse still, whites continue to hide behind a "wall of ignorance" that eliminated from public discourse the bitter legacy of slavery and those racial injustices that continue to haunt and to hinder (Assante 2003).

Not surprisingly, the Civil Rights movement gave way to the Black Pride movement that, in turn, spawned Black Power militants. The shift from "Negro" to "black" as a term of self-description symbolized this rejection of the Civil Rights integrationist ideals. In making this shift from the politics of distribution ("Civil Rights") to the politics of recognition ("identity politics") (Morning and Sabbagh 2005), Black Pride evolved into an identity-building movement that sought to promote a "Black Is Beautiful" image by politicizing the concept of indigenous ghetto culture as the basis for black unity (Spencer 1994). A demand for affirmative action replaced a commitment to formal equality, as it was no longer sufficient to remove only legal barriers to black advancement but also those social impediments that precluded full and equal participation.

Put bluntly, America continues to be a society with sometimes very different sets of histories, experiences, and aspirations: On one side of the narrative is a white majority that sees America as a land of promise and opportunity. For many whites, racism is a thing of the past, synonymous with lynching, cross burning, and segregated facilities, and at worst restricted to a few bad apples (Gerstle 2003). On the other narrative side, a black minority is consigned to the margins of the wilderness (Assante 2003). Many blacks continue to experience racism in everyday life—from police encounters to limited employment opportunities and glaring disparities in health and socio-economic status. In other words, integration does not appear to be working, as many had hoped, and this belief that blacks and whites cannot integrate— on the assumption that applying equal treatment to unequal contexts tends to perpetuate the inequities—has shattered Martin Luther King's dream of the United States as an integrated country of goodwill and equality. Even the National Association for the Advancement of Colored People (NAACP), founded in 1908 by W.E.B. DuBois to combat discrimination, appears to be abandoning the principle of integration in the face of mounting black nationalism for separating the races as a basis for cooperative coexistence (Maxwell 1997).

Reaction to integration as a policy or process is mixed. Some associate integration with the attainment of equality and participation; others conjure up images of unwanted conformity. In theory, a commitment to integration differs from assimilation. Assimilation endorses a one-way process of absorption in which minority identities are collapsed into the mainstream. By contrast, integration upholds a two-way system of synthesis that proposes a unique cultural fusion. In practice, however, the outcomes of both integration and assimilation may be indistinguishable. The subdominant group is incorporated into the basic framework as defined by the dominant sector. For example, although immigrants to the United States are expected to create a new amalgam by melting into the American pot, this cauldron remains irrefutably "pale male" in composition and control. Any restructuring of American society is recast along the lines and priorities of the prevailing institutional framework, while the subdominant sector simply adds a "dash of spice" to an otherwise monocultural stew.

Pluralism

Many countries are seeking to come to terms with the diversity of their populations (Rex 2004). Yet, governments of these countries find themselves in a structural contradiction. On the one hand, the nation-state has historically been grounded on the attainment of a culturally and linguistically homogeneous population, resulting in a deliberate rejection of diversity; on the other, government policies that once diminished the value of diversity for society-building are now conceding ground to more inclusive models of race, ethnic, and Aboriginal relations. Acceptance of diversity as a basis for governance within a national framework is called **pluralism**. Pluralism goes beyond a simple existence of racial or ethnic minorities in society. It implies a belief that not only acknowledges the possibility of constructing a unified society from (or despite) diversity, but also endorses diversity as a valued component of an egalitarian society. Not surprisingly, some degree of government intervention may be required to address minority needs by reaffirming individual rights, rectifying past injustices, reducing social inequities by removing discriminatory barriers, providing positive actions through employment equity programs, and ensuring protection of traditional language and culture.

Both colour/culture blind and colour/culture conscious variants of pluralism can be discerned. For some, a pluralistic society is one that ignores differences by ensuring that everyone is equal before the law regardless of race or culture, with the result that no minority group receives special treatment. In other words, a society of many cultures is possible as long as people's cultural differences do not get in the way of full and equal participation. For others, a pluralistic society is one that recognizes the need to take differences seriously by incorporating diversity as a basis for entitlement and recognition (Fleras 2002). A culture-conscious model embraces the idea that a society of many cultures is possible if people's cultural differences, when necessary to ensure equality and inclusiveness, are taken into account. As we shall see, Canada's official Multiculturalism appears to incorporate both these principles as a pluralistic framework for living together with differences.

Pluralism can be expressed in diverse ways, including multiculturalism, biculturalism, and multinationalism. Each will be discussed more thoroughly in later parts of this book. Canada's pluralistic commitments are enshrined in the concept of an official Multiculturalism. With Multiculturalism, Canada endorses the legitimacy of ethnic diversity as different yet equal by creating institutional space where all Canadians can interact without fear of ethnic entanglements. The United States has also experienced a multicultural turn in recent years (Glazer 1997), with a critical, even insurgent, style of multiculturalism that differs sharply from Canada's consensus-oriented integrative multiculturalism (Goldberg 1994; Fleras 2001). Biculturalism resembles multiculturalism in many ways, but is focused on the relationship between two major groups or peoples, each of which stands in a relationship of partnership with the other. For example, biculturalism describes the relationship between the indigenous Maori peoples and the non-Maori in New Zealand/Aotearoa (Fleras and Spoonley 1999). To the extent that it persists, Canada's biculturalism is expressed at the level of Quebec–Ottawa relations. Finally, multinationalism implies the existence of multiple nations or peoples who see themselves as political communities—both autonomous ("sovereign") in their own right, yet sharing in the sovereignty of society (Asch 1997; Maaka and Fleras 2005). Canada is increasingly described as a multinational coalition comprising Aboriginal peoples, the Québécois, and the English-speaking sectors, including immigrants and descendants of immigrants.

TABLE 1.1	Managing Diversity: Inter-group Models of Race, Ethnic, and Aboriginal Relations		
Definition	**Objectives**	**Means**	**Outcomes**
Genocide	annihilation	violence	minority cleansed
Assimilation	absorption	undermining the culture	one people
Segregation	forced separation	threat of force	separate and unequal groups
Integration	desegregation/fusion	reincorporation	formal equality
Pluralism	living together	inclusiveness	"mosaic"

To summarize, recurrent responses and patterned outcomes occur when competitively different groups come into sustained contact. A network of patterned relations is established, many of which become formalized into explicit government policy for managing diversity. Policy outcomes vary, and may include those that deny differences (assimilation), reject minorities (segregation), and demonize out-groups (genocide), as well as those that espouse formal equality (integration) and positively engage diversity (pluralism). To be sure, some degree of overlap and duplication is inevitable in making the distinction, as social reality cannot possibly be carved into static and exclusive categories. Moreover, while definitions are critical for analysis and assessment, they do run the risk of simplifying, essentializing, or rigidifying what in reality is complex, shifting, and contextual (Castles 2000). Table 1.1 highlights some of the key features of each model by comparing definitions, objectives, means, and outcomes.

EXPLAINING RACE, ETHNIC, AND ABORIGINAL RELATIONS: SOCIOLOGICAL MODELS OF SOCIETY

Sociology as a discipline is often defined as the scientific study of human society. Society can be differently defined, but most profitably as a complex, contested, and evolving network of relations in the broadest sense of the term, ranging from the interpersonal to the international, with inter-group dynamics occupying an intermediate position. Both society and inter-group relations are amenable to study from different sociological models. Each of the sociological models, including **functionalism**, **conflict**, and **interactionism**, offers different ways of explaining the relationship of inter-group dynamics to society (see Banton 2005).

Briefly, a functionalist perspective tends to emphasize stability by focusing on the orderly incorporation of racial, ethnic, and Aboriginal groups into a dominant culture. For functionalists, race, ethnic, and Aboriginal relations are essentially co-operative relations because of mutual interests instilled through a process of assimilation. Functionalists, then, emphasize assimilation as a key to a smoothly functioning and stable society. Opposed to functionalism are conflict perspectives that focus on inequalities because of the barriers that preclude full minority participation. For conflict theorists, the centrality of inequality ensures that race, ethnic, and Aboriginal relations are ultimately unequal because of power differentials in society. Interactionists (or, alternatively, symbolic interactionism) focus on race, ethnic, and Aboriginal relations as a dynamic and socially constructed process involving meaningful interaction within the broader framework of society. For interactionists, emphasis is on human agency—how individuals and groups define situations related to race, ethnicity, and aboriginality, and use these definitions as a basis for the ongoing social construction of race, ethnic, and Aboriginal relations.

Functionalism

Functionalist paradigms remain enduring and durable approaches to the study of race, ethnic, and Aboriginal relations. For functionalists, society is viewed as a complex and integrated whole comprising interrelated parts that collectively contribute to maintenance and survival. Society is compared to a living organism; like any life form, it consists of parts that mesh for effective functioning, resist disruptive changes, and react to any invasion by isolating or removing the disruption to ensure stability and the status quo. Under optimal conditions, all elements of a society operate smoothly to enhance success. But tensions and conflicts associated with rapid social change may unravel these relationships to a point of temporary disarray. Corrective measures are activated to remove potentially disruptive situations, thus restoring society to its natural state of equilibrium and order.

For functionalism, consensus, co-operation, and control are the keys to a successful society. To achieve this highly desired state, all members of society (but especially minorities) must internalize core beliefs and values. Not surprisingly, functionalists endorse assimilation (or integration) as the preferred model for race, ethnic, and Aboriginal relations. Failure to assimilate diversity is viewed as a potential threat to society. For example, the arrival of immigrants to Canada has proven beneficial to its economic and cultural well-being. Immigrants often provide a valuable source of labour to meet the needs of an expanding economy, while enriching Canadian society through the diversity of their cultural heritages. Yet, according to functionalists, their entry into Canada may be problematic because of costs of settlement or disruptions to the status quo. To thwart any potential conflicts while facilitating the entry and settlement of new Canadians, measures are introduced for damage control and conflict management. On one side are assimilationist agencies, such as education and mass media; on the other, initiatives such as official Multiculturalism for fostering consensus and shared values; on yet another side are employment equity programs calculated to improve the process of fitting in, settling down, and moving up. The end result? A smoothly functioning society that defuses any disruptive potential as a basis for living together.

Conflict Theory

A conflict model of society differs sharply from a functionalist perspective. Whereas functionalists espouse a normative theory of society by emphasizing consensus and equilibrium, conflict perspectives prefer to emphasize contradiction, confrontation, and changes. A conflict perspective portrays society as a complex and unstable site of unequal yet competing groups in perpetual competition over scarce and valued resources. Dominant groups will rely on peaceful or violent methods to preserve privilege, property, and power. Subdominant sectors are more likely to challenge the status quo through different strategies of resistance, ranging from outright confrontation to passive resistance.

For **conflict theorists**, the normal state of society resonates with conflict and change. Instead of consensus or stability, society is held together by force or the threat of force because of inequities in opportunity or outcomes. To be sure, a conflict perspective does not posit a perpetual state of conflict and confrontation. Of interest to conflict theorists is what happens in between clashes. Certain techniques are employed to maintain and legitimize a fundamentally unequal order without resorting to heavy-handed tactics. At times, the dominant group is powerful enough to defuse the potential for overt conflict. At other times, even opposing groups find it mutually advantageous to put aside their differences in pursuit of common interests. This "double-edgedness" suggests that conflict and co-operation are strategically different dimensions of a single struggle.

With their focus on inequality and power, conflict models have proven valuable in explaining the politics of diversity. A variant of conflict theory incorporates **Marxist** approaches. Marxist conflict theory positions the concept of class at the heart of all exploitation and conflict. Marxists argue that the fundamental contradiction in any complex society entails two social classes: the working and the ruling class. The ruling class profits by owning the means of production; the working class can survive only by selling its labour to the ruling class. The ruling class will do anything to facilitate the flow of profits, in part by shaving the costs of labour through creating split labour markets (paying some workers more than others), in part by fomenting internal divisions that pit worker against worker in the competition for valued resources, thus reducing their ability to act in unison against the source of the exploitation, namely, the owners. In recent years, Marxist thinking has moved away from strict economic determinism, without discarding the importance of class relations to group dynamics. That is, with ideas and ideals as critical in shaping outcomes, while acknowledging that people matter as well, inter-group relations are shaped *only in the first instance* by economic forces rather than in the final analysis. In short, minority women and men are seen as active subjects in solving problems, defending interests, and mobilizing into action groups—albeit in contexts and within structures beyond their control—rather than as passive objects that are victimized by impenetrable social forces.

Yet another variation of the conflict models is an **internal colonialism** model. This approach argues that not all inequities are created the same. Indigenous peoples, such as the Aboriginal peoples in Canada or even the Québécois, are not just another ethnic minority. Rather, they are a peoples or nations whose experience of oppression compares with those victimized by overseas ("saltwater") colonialism (Hechter 1975). Both groups of indigenous peoples are forcibly incorporated into the broader system, and thereby robbed of their independence as relatively autonomous political communities. As their access to land, culture, and identity are undermined, they are pushed to the periphery. A cultural division of labour evolves in which the indigenes occupy the most menial occupations. Indirect rule and control are facilitated by the co-optation of indigenous elites or through establishment of a bureaucracy such as the Department of Indian Affairs in Canada. The net result is a colonialist relationship that is every bit as oppressive as the exploitative relationships within "saltwater" colonies.

Interactionism

Both functionalist and conflict perspectives define society as taken-for-granted. Society is portrayed as durable and real, existing above and beyond the individual, yet exerting vast leverage over people's behaviour. By contrast, interactionist perspectives begin with the notion of society as an ongoing human accomplishment. Instead of something "out there" and determinative, society is perceived as socially constructed through meaningful interaction. According to this outlook, people do not live in a predetermined world of mechanistic outcomes. Rather, reality is constructed by applying provisional meanings to a variety of situations. Once a situation has been defined and redefined, jointly linked lines of action are developed. Society—as the sum total of these personal and group interactions—emerges from the interplay of these joint linkages at a given point in time and place. Not surprisingly, inter-group dynamics are couched in the framework of constant flux, dynamic tension, mutual adjustment, negotiated compromise, and ongoing movement.

A similar line of reasoning applies to race, ethnic, and Aboriginal relations. Inter-group relations are not defined by system needs or class conflict but assume diverse forms as social constructions within specific contexts. Race, ethnicity, and aboriginality are treated as resources in defining situations and acting out on the basis of these definitions to create jointly linked patterns of interaction. In attempting to make sense of the world they live in, group-specific identities are activated as a basis for collective action, especially when there is a competitive advantage to group affiliation. Patterned interaction is thus generated and sustained by opposing elements that compete for definitional control of the situation to attract constituencies and promote interests. From a minority point of view, the question revolves around the benefits of working either within the system or outside of it. From a majority perspective the question is no less perplexing: Should minorities be allowed into the mainstream, or is it better to exclude them from meaningful involvement? These interactional styles and outcomes are not mutually exclusive, but intersect to create diverse group dynamics.

One variation of interactionism is known as **collective definition** (Blumer and Duster 1980). A collective definition approach emphasizes the process by which intra- and inter-group relations are formulated and reformulated because of opposing tendencies **(dualisms)** that coexist within all groups. Both the dominant and subdominant groups may be internally divided into competing factions or "dualisms." Within the dominant sector are at least two factions: On one side are those who support the inclusion (assimilation or integration) of minorities, especially if there is something to be gained by doing so; on the other side are those who prefer the status quo (and prevailing distribution of power, privilege, and property) by excluding minorities from full and equal participation. The subdominant sector is no less bifurcated. On one side are those factions that insist on assimilation into the dominant sector as a solution to their problems; on the other are those that endorse separation through the creation of parallel institutions and independent power bases as the preferred option.

The pull and push of these factional dualities, both within and between, generate the dynamics in inter-group relations. Dualities *within* the dominant and subdominant sectors give rise to an inner dynamic that may elicit mixed messages and contradictory positions. Another set of social dynamics is created by the interaction *between* dominant and subdominant sectors. The interplay of these dualistic oppositions helps to explain the diverse range of subdominant responses and dominant reactions. These dual responses—inclusion or exclusion/assimilation or segregation—are neither mutually exclusive nor fixed in perpetuity. They tend to vary over time and across space, as any one of these dualisms may gain ascendancy or decline in response to local, national, or international developments. Admittedly, the division of dominant and subdominant sectors into two factions is too simplistic to capture the complexities and fluidity of human group life. Nevertheless, a collective definition approach does provide insights into the dynamics that propel inter-group relations.

To sum up: Sociological paradigms such as functionalism, conflict theory, and interactionism provide distinctly different ways of looking at the dynamics of race, ethnic, and Aboriginal relationships within the broader framework of society. No perspective is inherently more correct than the other. Rather, each draws attention to some aspects of social reality, but away from others. One way of evaluating the benefits and costs of each sociological model of society is by putting Canada's official Multiculturalism to the perspectival test.

DEBATE REVISITED	Re-evaluating the Relationships of an Official Multiculturalism to Canada

At the beginning of the chapter, public and political reaction to Canada's Multiculturalism was shown to be extremely varied. For some, official Multiculturalism is perceived as good in securing benefits; for others, multiculturalism is bad because of controlling properties; for still others, it is good or bad depending on the criteria; and for others yet, it is both good and bad because of the context (Fleras 2002). Who is right, and on what grounds? How can sociological paradigms help in the sorting out process?

A functionalist model acknowledges the role of official Multiculturalism in creating a coherent and prosperous Canada. Multiculturalism is perceived as a conflict management device, whose function is to foster harmony by making both the majority and minority more comfortable with each other. According to a functionalist interpretation of official Multiculturalism, a society of many cultures is possible as long as people's ethnic differences do not stand in the way of full and equal participation. Under multiculturalism, ethnocultural differences are de-politicized, that is, "neutered" of any potential to provoke or divide, in part by ensuring that all Canadians are treated equally as a matter of course, in part by taking their differences into account when the need arises. The removal of prejudicial and discriminatory barriers under multiculturalism further secures its status as a conflict resolution device that acknowledges the attainment of national

unity *despite* (rather than because of) diversity.

A conflict paradigm disagrees with this positive spin. While functionalists point to the role of multiculturalism in contributing to the stability and order of society, conflict models of society focus on its role in preserving or advancing vested interests. According to conflict theorists, multiculturalism is a calculated tactic employed by the ruling elites to secure consent in defence of the prevailing distribution of power, privilege, and property. As an elite scheme for controlling minorities, a commitment to multiculturalism tends to foster a false consciousness: It camouflages the real sources of exploitation in society by suggesting cultural solutions to structural problems. Alternatively, recourse to multiculturalism creates the illusion of radical change behind a smokescreen of "assimilation in slow motion." For conflict theorists, the end result is entirely predictable: Members of the subordinate classes are co-opted into a system that enriches and empowers some at the expense of many.

Interactionists differ in focus from functionalists or conflict theorists. Rather than assessing it on a scale of good to bad, multiculturalism is defined by interactionists as a socially constructed dynamic process. People define situations in terms of their perception of multiculturalism and then respond on the basis of these definitions. Multiculturalism itself becomes a site in which different interests interact to impose their definition of the situation at the expense of others. Within the dominant sector, multiculturalism may be endorsed by some as a basis for social stability or a cultural gateway to a global marketplace. It may be rejected by others as a recipe for disaster that inadvertently reinforces ethnic divisions and inter-group conflicts. Conversely, the subdominant sector may support multiculturalism as a window of opportunity in levelling the playing field, or, alternatively, repudiate it as a hegemonic device for co-opting minorities into the mainstream. The interplay of these factions contributes to the ongoing and socially constructed dynamic at the heart of a multicultural Canadian society.

Each of these models of society casts a different spin on official Multiculturalism. Advocates of each approach selectively emphasize those aspects of reality that enhance their respective standpoints, while downplaying those inconsistent with the model. Each paradigm reflects a particular vision of society, and the status of diversity and the role of multiculturalism in advancing this vision. Multiculturalism is seen as "functional" in bolstering the collective sentiments upon which order and stability are conveyed; in "conflict" terms for fostering the illusion of progressive change without really disrupting the status quo; and in "interactional" terms as part of a broader process in socially constructing the reality we live in.

None of the perspectives is inherently superior to the other. Insofar as there is no consensus over how multiculturalism should be defined or employed, together they provide a more complex and multi-dimensional view (Gilroy 2004). In the final analysis, preference for one perspective over another is rarely a case of right or wrong. Rather, the real issue is in acknowledging the multi-dimensionality of multiculturalism as powerful yet weak: Official Multiculturalism has proven both potent (i.e., more powerful than skeptics give it credit for, hence a "wolf in sheep's clothing") and impotent (less powerful than its boosters propose, hence "a sheep in wolf's clothing"). The push and pull of this paradox culminates in the sometimes fiercely contested politics of diversity.

CHAPTER HIGHLIGHTS

- Sociological interest in race, ethnic, and Aboriginal relations focuses on the social dimensions of inter-group dynamics within the contexts of power, inequality, and politics, with particular emphasis on the evolving relationship of race, ethnicity, and aboriginality to society and to Canada-building.

- Canada's race, ethnic, and Aboriginal relations record requires a working perspective. Compared to the past, Canada has come a long way in managing diversity more equitably; compared to human rights violations in other countries, Canada is indeed a beacon of enlightenment; however, compared to the ideals that Canadians espouse, we still have a long way to go.

- Race, Aboriginal and ethnic relations are defined as relationships of inequality. Emphasis is on how these unequal relations of power, privilege, and property are constructed, expressed, and supported, as well as challenged and transformed by way of government practices, institutional reform, and minority resistance.

- Certain types of interactional patterns, namely, genocide, integration, assimilation, segregation, and pluralism, result when racially and culturally different groups come into sustained contact and compete over scarce resources.

- Various perspectives for the study of racial and ethnic relations exist, with particular emphasis on functionalism, conflict, and interactionism. Functionalist models are concerned with controlling, correcting, or eliminating diversity. Conflict models envision society as a site of competition for scarce resources between ethnically different groups. Interactionist models emphasize the socially constructed nature of minority–majority interaction.

- The contested notion of official Multiculturalism as good, bad, good or bad, or good and bad provides insights into a key sociological truism: What you understand about society depends on which sociological paradigm is applied as an explanatory framework.

KEY TERMS

anglo-conformity

assimilation

collective definition

conflict theory

diversity

dominant group

dualism

ethnic cleansing

functionalism

genocide

human rights

integration

interactionism

internal colonialism

Marxism

melting pot

minority group

multiculturalism

official Multiculturalism

pluralism

segregation

subdominant group

tolerance

REVIEW QUESTIONS

1. What is meant by the concept of race, Aboriginal, and ethnic relations?

2. Briefly compare and contrast the concepts of genocide, assimilation, integration, segregation, and cultural pluralism as strategies for "managing" race, Aboriginal, and ethnic relations.

3. Select any issue or incident involving racial, ethnic, or Aboriginal groups. Analyze the issue or incident from one or all three sociological perspectives. For guidelines, use the sections "Debate: Multiculturalism in Canada," and "Debate Revisited: Re-evaluating Multiculturalism."

4. Canada's record in engaging with racial, ethnic, and Aboriginal peoples can be summed up by the expression "the good, the bad, and the in-between." Indicate what is meant by this expression. Do you agree or disagree with this assessment? Why?

LINKS AND RECOMMENDATIONS

Films

Hotel Rwanda (2004)

> Based on a true story of a hotelier who saved hundreds of people from the machetes of Hutu extremists, the first half of the film provides a chilling example of how hatred is mobilized to justify the genocidal killing of friends and neighbours. Also recommended is the equally powerful *Sometimes in April*.

Shake Hands with the Devil (2004)

> A different slant on the Rwandan genocide, this widely acclaimed documentary explores the wider issue of global indifference through the perceptions and experiences of Roméo Dallaire, the Canadian general who commanded a woefully inadequate UN peacekeeping force that was powerless to stop the rampage.

Rabbit-Proof Fence (2002)

> An Australian film that captures the notion of genocide in slow motion through forced assimilation. No one can be unmoved by the pluck of three young Aborigine children who manage to escape boarding school and return to their community over 2100 kilometres away (twice no less) by following a fence that was built to keep out rabbits.

Books

> *Slavery and the Making of America* by James Horton and Lois Horton (2004). An immensely interesting and lavishly illustrated (both prints and photos) book on slavery, its impact and significance for building an American society, and its continuing legacy in contemporary society.

> *Americans All: Race and Ethnic Studies in Historical, Structural, and Comparative Perspectives,* Second Edition, by Peter Kivisto and Wendy Ng (2005). A useful introduction for those who like to see how the topic of race, ethnic and aboriginal relations are addressed in the United States.

Websites

For more on genocide, there is the ever accessible Wikipedia article:

> **http://en.wikipedia.org/wiki/genocide**

Or you may prefer access to a clearinghouse of information that has compiled information on how to end this senseless slaughter of human beings.

> **www.genocidewatch.org**

An overview of multiculturalism in Canada is provided by this government site.

> **www.canadianheritage.gc.ca/progs/multi/index_e.cfm**

A wealth of general information on race and ethnic relations is provided by the English server.

> **www.eserver.org/race**

Google provides a web directory that assists in searching for articles on race and ethnicity and religion.

> **www.directory.google.com/Top/Society/Issues/Race-Ethnic-Religious_Relations**

2

THE POLITICS OF RACE

| DEBATE | The Racialization of Sports |

Many rely on the concept of race to explain differences and similarities. Race-based explanations possess a certain appeal. They are simple and direct, conform to common-sense logic, tap into prevailing stereotypes, and provide a convenient excuse to exclude or control others. However widespread the popularity of race-based thinking—and there never seems to be a shortage of proponents for it—a commitment to accuracy is not one of its strengths. Reference to race as an excuse or explanation not only plays fast and loose with scientific evidence, but also downplays the social, cultural, and historical dimensions of inter-group relations.

The controversial link between race and sport is a case at hand. In the late 1940s, black people did not participate in professional North American team sports. The colour bar kept white from black in professional baseball until 1947, when Jackie Robinson joined the Brooklyn Dodgers, after a minor league stint with the Montreal Royals. The Boston Red Sox were the last major league ball team to integrate when they signed infielder Pumpsie Green in 1959. Neither professional football nor basketball accepted black athletes until the late 1940s, although two blacks did play for now-defunct football teams during the 1920s. The last major league sport to integrate was professional hockey when Willy O'Ree signed with the Boston Bruins of the National Hockey League in 1958. To be sure, black people could participate as athletes at the professional level, but only in the minors or in segregated "Negro" leagues. Owners and players steadfastly refused to integrate teams for fear of alienating sponsors or scaring off audiences.

By the early twenty-first century, a radically different picture had appeared. African-Americans dominated three of the nation's most popular spectator sports. Although comprising about 13 percent of America's population, black people constitute about three-quarters of the gridiron personnel in the National Football League, over four-fifths of hoopsters in the National Basketball Association, and about one-sixth of the major league ball players (another one-quarter are Latin American). Black people also account for approximately half of all basketball and football players in the NCAA Division 1A (Lapchick 2000). At international levels, sprinting and long-distance running are dominated by African blacks and African-Americans, while West African–descended blacks hold the 200 fastest 100-metre times, all under 10 seconds—a standard rarely matched by any white, Asian, or East African runner (Entine 2000).

How do we explain this astonishing pattern? Are black people as a race inherently more athletic than other races? Do black athletes possess anatomical features that predispose them to success? Does black culture encourage athletic achievement? Is athletic success one of the few opportunity structures that is available to black youth? Responses to these questions will be addressed at the end of the chapter.

INTRODUCTION: RACE MATTERS

Few will dispute the significance of **race** in shaping inter-group dynamics (Brace 2005). References to race not only rationalized nineteenth-century European colonization, but also conferred a pseudo-scientific legitimacy for arbitrarily pigeonholing people into mutually exclusive categories. The classification of colonized peoples into racialized "others" secured a simple yet self-serving explanation of human diversity during the era of European exploration, capitalistic expansion, and imperialistic dispossession (McCalla and Satzewich 2002). Race "mattered" for various reasons, but primarily as (1) a tool for justifying control and inequality, (2) an excuse for doing the inexcusable, (3) a framework for explaining human differences, and (4) a rationalization for salving guilty consciences. The race concept may have been little more than a fiction—a fabrication in defence of white domination—but its capacity to wreak destruction was anything but fictional.

That race "mattered" in the historical past is beyond dispute. In both the United States and Canada, few disputed an essentialized vision of race as natural and static, universal and immutable (Dalmage 2004). But many are dismayed that race continues to matter at a time when we should know better (Frederico and Luks 2005). The fact that race continues to "matter" for precisely the same reasons as in the past—to explain or rationalize for purposes of control or exploitation—should indeed be cause for concern. Race "matters" not because groups of people are biologically inferior as proclaimed by the narrow-minded or politically incorrect. Rather, it "matters" because people perceive others to be racially distinct, and rely on these perceptions of difference to discriminate or differentiate. Race in a racialized society represents a tainted status that is deeply discrediting and shameful—a stigma or badge of incompetence—that justifies who gets what. And as long as racism and racialized inequality persist in a society, race will continue to "matter" in privileging some and disempowering others (Cose 1997; Morris and Cowlishaw 1997).

The conclusion seems inescapable: Instead of being banished to the dustbins of history, as might be expected of such a blemished notion, the seemingly antiquated concept of race persists and continues to provoke (Sarich and Miele 2004). Consider how race mattered in the aftermath of Hurricane Katrina, when the predominantly black and poorer parts of New Orleans were most affected by the devastating floods. Such persistence raises an interesting if perplexing question: Why has a biological concept of minimal scientific worth exerted such a punishing impact in shaping the course of history? Why, indeed, does a largely discredited concept enjoy such enduring power in a multicultural Canada that aspires to colour-blind coexistence? Divergent opinions fuel a range of responses. Some believe race is real and must be taken into account in explaining social reality. Others believe race should never enter public discourse, because races do not exist, it is only the differences that have been racialized. Still others see race as a social construction that is politically significant in shaping identities and relationships. And from yet another perspective, the reality of race is rejected, but because people perceive it to be real, they act accordingly—in effect reaffirming W.I. Thomas's prescient notion that "things do not have to be real to be real in their consequences."

Canadians display a degree of ambivalence toward the concept of race. In a merit-based and achievement-oriented society such as ours, references to race are thought to be awkward or offensive, especially if the value of a person is equated with the colour of their skin—a stigma beyond one's control but still a key predictor of "who gets what." Consider the contradictions: Race may reflect an accident of birth, yet it profoundly shapes a person's life or life chances; race may be skin deep, but it appears to provide a quick indicator of the worth of an individual or group; race should never justify unequal treatment, yet it is increasingly assigned a role in reversing discrimination by way of Employment Equity initiatives; Canadians explicitly reject the race concept, yet they implicitly condone a race-based status quo. A sense of ambiguity is captured by this declaration at the 2002 meeting of the American Sociological Association:

> [T]hose who favor ignoring race as an explicit administrative matter, in a hope that it will cease to exist as a social concept, ignore the weight of a vast body of sociological research that shows that racial hierarchies are embedded in the routine practices of social groups and institutions. (cited in the *New Zealand Herald*, 22 March 2004)

Finally, a focus on race challenges the tenets of liberal universalism. According to these principles, what we have in common as rights-bearing and morally autonomous individuals is more important for purposes of recognition or reward than what divides us as members of racially distinct groups.

In short, race "matters." Race matters not because it is real, but because people tend to act *as if* it were real, with shockingly real consequences. Race matters even though it should not, but because it constitutes a lived experience for many, the issue of race must be confronted squarely. After all, as sociologists have long known, where a person is socially located in terms of how race is perceived will influence the way people see them, think about them, and relate to them. And race matters because concepts of race are so deeply ingrained in many Canadians that dislodging them from mindsets and frameworks will prove a tricky affair (see Foster 2005). Ken Wiwa (2001) concedes as much when reviewing L. Hill's book *Black Berry, Sweet Juice: On Being Black and White in Canada*:

> Race is just about the trickiest topic to write about with any measure of objectivity, and only brave men or fools should try. Anyone who wants to walk the minefield of race should invest in a thick skin with chameleon-like pigment . . . Because the trouble with race is that there are black and white and a kaleidoscope of shades in between.

The politics of race represents one of the most bewildering dilemmas in contemporary society. The race concept has changed and will continue to change over time and across space, while the concept itself may mean different things to different groups (Blank et al. 2004). Questions are many, and answers few. This chapter attempts to engage these questions by exploring the politics of race in the past and at present. The chapter examines the race concept with respect to (1) meaning and content, (2) genesis and rationale, (3) impact and implications, and (4) validity and value. The chapter also emphasizes those social forces that advanced the race concept as a misguided yet powerful explanatory tool. Key questions provide coverage for this chapter: Why did this compulsion to pigeon-hole people into predetermined categories arise in the first place? Why do pockets of openly race-based thinking persist in the present? Is there any empirical justification for the race concept? How does race continue to justify entitlement and rules of engagement? What are the consequences of racializing the concept of race? Emphasis throughout the chapter is not on the analysis of race traits *per se*, but on the politics of race in defining "who gets what, and why" (McCalla and Satzewich 2002). In focusing on race as a social construction without any scientific justification, emphasis is on framing race as a process for labelling people or activities rather than a thing with a corresponding set of traits (Chan and Mirchandani 2002).

THE RACE CONCEPT: THE POWER OF AN ILLUSION

The politics of race have proven both explosive and divisive in shaping the dynamics of inter-group relations. No matter how often it is discredited as intellectually dead, race continues to bounce back as a politically charged marker of differences and discrimination. Often used unconsciously, race remains a potent element in everyday life and encounters, with untapped potential for conflict and misunderstanding (Holdaway 1996). Reactions to race vary because of responses that invariably invite scorn or criticism, regardless of the position taken. Those who endorse the race concept tend to be dismissed as little more than "knuckle-dragging Neanderthals." Conversely, those who dismiss race as a fiction may be accused of compromising a people's identity by trampling on social history, group solidarity, or cultural aspirations. Or consider the challenge of writing about an idea that paradoxically

> . . . can be seen as nothing but a phantom invented to justify a myriad of power relationships but, on the other hand, is one of history's most instrumental agencies of social composition? How does one write about the most potent instrument of taxonomy ever imposed on humankind without giving added credence to the idea of race as a viable organizing tool? (Hall 2000:120)

A compromise is proposed for reconciling these opposing viewpoints. References to race must stay clear of dismissing it as purely an "illusion," without falling into the trap of **essentializing** race as a fixed and objective category. Race may not be real in the empirical sense of the word; nevertheless, people perceive it to be real, and act upon this perception to create very real consequences. Under these circumstances, we would do well to remember that, when it comes to race, perception *is* reality—even when largely unfounded by empirical evidence—because, even if race is a fiction, it is a powerful fiction that impacts profoundly on social reality (Picard 2005). George Sefa Dei (2004) nails it succinctly when he explains:

> Race has powerful material, political, and economic currency in our society. Rather than dismiss race, we ought to be honest about it and spend time reflecting on it through critical discussion, instead of sweeping it under the carpet and hope that this will settle everything. Racial categories such as "black," "white," and "brown," etc., no matter how imperfect, are not the problem in

themselves. The reality is that these categories organize our society. Rather than deny them, we must challenge the interpretations attached to them.

RETHINKING RACE AS RACIALIZATION

Definitions of race have proven elusive (Biddiss 1979). There is much value in Ellis Cose's (1997:1) reference to race ". . . as a strange and flexible concept, with an endless capacity to confound." Part of the problem reflects the multi-dimensionality of race as a concept. Race is a historically grounded social construction, dynamic and shifting as well as contradictory and ambiguous, but never far from the thrust and parry of privilege and power (Brace 2005). People are classified into categories on the basis of preconceived attributes involving innate characteristics that shape thought or action. With race, each group is defined as different by virtue of predetermined properties that are seen as fixed and permanent. And finally, race invariably invokes a system of evaluation in which clusters of differences are ranked higher than others in an ascending/descending scale of worth.

But the concept of race has shifted in recent years. Where once defined as a thing—a tangible object that could be isolated and measured as a fixed biological entity—race is now conceptualized as a process involving the imposition of racially linked meanings by the powerful on those less powerful. In shifting the focus from race to racialization—from race as a thing to race as a social construction—attention is moving away from both the physical attributes of minority groups and their presumed inferiority. In its place is an emphasis on the perceptions and motivations of those powerful enough to impose these labels that control or restrict opportunities (Chan and Mirchandani 2002). The implications of this shift influence people's perceptions of race relations. Put simply, there is no such thing as race relations in the sense of a "race" of people who stand in a relationship to another "race." Existing instead are relations that have been defined by reference to race, that is, "racialized." To the extent that the race concept has no empirical justification except in the perceptual sense, it is more accurate to speak of relationships that have been "racialized" than race relations *per se* (Bonilla-Silva 1996).

FYI	**Racialization**

Racialization has emerged as a central concept in the study of race, ethnic, and Aboriginal relations. Yet the concept remains poorly theorized because of its indiscriminate use—ranging from "the racialization of whiteness" to "the racialization of crime" and "living in a racialized world" (Murji and Solomos 2005). In some cases, *racialization* is used interchangeably with *race*. For example, consider the division of the world's population into races to explain and justify European exploration and exploitation. In other cases, racialization is defined as the opposite of race. Race has no biological basis *per se*, but it reflects how biological significance is attached to the people who are stigmatized because of negative racial attributes. In other words, racialization refers to the process and power by which race-based meanings are attached to issues, activities, or groups of people, with the result that race becomes a key factor in how reality is defined, organized, and lived (James 2005).

To sum up: The proper study of race seeks to explain why some relationships or activities are racially linked and devalued accordingly (Holdaway 1996; 1997). In reflecting, reinforcing, and advancing relationships of power and politics, reference to race says more about those constructing and imposing the labels than about those who are racialized—as the next case study demonstrates.

INSIGHT	**Numbers Don't Lie, or Do They?**
	Criminalizing Race; Racializing Crime

Racialized minorities and Aboriginal peoples have long been accused of excessive criminal behaviour. From the Irish and Chinese of the nineteenth century to twentieth-century Italians, Jews, and African Canadians, certain groups have been vilified as inherently criminal and in need of constant supervision and control. Recent incidents in major Canadian urban centres have again singled out racialized minorities for special attention. Although black people constitute a relatively small proportion of urban Canada's population, they (especially young black males) are disproportionately found in statistics related to victims or suspects. For example, in a year-long study of non-casual police stops in Kingston between October 2003 and September 2004, about 15 percent of a black population of less than 700 was stopped, compared to about 5 percent of the white population (Wortley 2005—see case study in chapter 3). Aboriginal peoples may comprise just over 4 percent of Canada's population, but they occupy 18 percent of the federal penitentiary space and about 21 percent of provincial and territorial jails, including an astonishing 75 percent of the inmates in Saskatchewan prisons (see *The Daily*, Statistics Canada, 3 June 2005).

These figures raise an important question: How to account for the "over-representation of racialized minorities and aboriginal people in Canada's criminal justice statistics"? (Roberts 2002). Is a tendency toward criminality inherent within certain races, a race–crime link, with the result that any so-called overrepresentation is consistent with higher levels of offending? Do certain social conditions—from poverty to powerlessness—put some minorities at greater risk? Or do racialized minorities attract disproportionate attention from the police? Is crime racial? Does race cause crime? Or is it more accurate to say that crime is racialized because of a police bias toward some groups rather than others? How does race become criminalized as particular crimes become attributed to particular groups? In turn, how does crime become racialized, as specific groups are perceived as prone to committing particular crimes (Jiwani 2002)? Not surprisingly, there are renewed demands for keeping track of crime rates by racial origins of the perpetrators. Others are not so sure: Of what value are crime-rate statistics involving racialized minorities? Is it possible to measure the relationship between race and crime, or do the measurements say more about the measuring and the measurer rather than the measured?

The Kingston police may have been one of the first forces to collect data on police–community relations (but see Fleras et al. 1989), a decision that was not without controversy. The debate over race-based crime statistics revolves around two opposing questions: To what extent will access to this information reinforce bigotry, stereotypes, and excessive policing? Or will these data be employed to foster tolerance, remove discrimination, and improve quality of life for Canadians of colour (Roberts 2002)? Those who support the collection of race statistics argue that problem areas need to be identified: to raise awareness, to define the problem, to customize solutions, and to allocate resources appropriately (Simon 2005). Analyses of crime statistics by race would produce profiles of suspected criminals, and the kind of crimes they commit and contexts behind this criminal behaviour, as well as proposed solutions and recommendations for the prevention of future occurrences. In other words, supporters of racially based crime statistics are not necessarily racist in assuming that certain groups are predisposed to commit certain types of reported crime. Rather, they may be anxious to see if patterns can be discerned in order to apply solutions. Besides, the harm done by statistics may be overstated:

> The truth is, statistics do not stigmatize minorities more than they are labeled by segments of the larger society. Those who engage in this racist practice do not need any statistics to back them up. (Dei 2004)

Those against the routine collection of racial crime statistics argue that such data are impossible to collect, subject to abuse and manipulation, and risk reinforcing stereotypes (Cryderman et al. 1998). In an era of quantification, statistical data confer an air of authenticity and objectivity that may be unwarranted because of flaws in collection or interpretation. Statistics reflect incidents of crime that are reported *by* or *to* the police rather than actual rates of criminal offence. Statistical information may say more about those collecting the data than about the world. If police create a statistical profile that results in more intensive monitoring, they will gravitate toward the suspects they are looking for. Police will then conclude that they were justified in conducting more intense surveillance or selective

searches (James 1998). In a culture where blackness is synonymous with criminality, the police and the public may be inclined to assume a black susceptibility to violence or criminal acts (Flynn 1998). Furthermore, consider the possible detrimental impact of disseminating these data. However inadvertently, the circulation of this information may (1) reinforce stereotypes and legitimize a racist mindset, (2) promote ulterior motives and hidden agendas, (3) distract attention from the real sources of the problem, namely, poverty and powerlessness, and (4) strengthen the intrusive powers of police.

In short, the collection of race–crime statistics is problematic for a variety of reasons, both technical and political (see also Roberts 2002; Chan and Mirchandani 2002):

- Only a small proportion of individuals within any community is likely to engage in criminal behaviour.
- Repeat offences by the same person may grossly inflate the scope of criminality within a community.
- Many crimes are never reported to the police.
- The process of racial identification is itself riddled with inconsistencies: Who decides on the appropriate racial category—the victim, the suspect, the police officer? The high level of subjectivity in making the classification undermines any degree of reliability.
- Racial categories themselves are excessively broad to the point of meaninglessness. The end result is the stigmatizing of an entire community of law-abiding citizens who have little in common except skin colour.

In between the critics and supporters are those who accept the relevance of such data but insist on safeguards to prevent abuse. In collecting and analyzing *any* type of information it is important to know who is gathering the data, how this information will be collected, who wants to know and why, and how the data are to be utilized. Are the police properly trained and sufficiently impartial to impose labels? Do the police want this information in order to improve the quality of policing, or do they want it as an excuse to use more invasive surveillance powers within racialized communities? Do politicians hope to look tough on crime by the collection of such data? Will the availability of statistics spur an effort to weed out the criminal element within minority communities? What crimes should be included in the count? Will the inclusion of "white collar" crime and other types of underreported crime provide a more balanced picture of what really happens? Until answers are forthcoming, cautionary discretion is advised.

There is yet another reason for exercising caution in this area. No matter how accurate the survey or sound the interpretations, a causal relation between race and crime can never be proven. Race is not a cause of crime (Roberts 2002). To the contrary, the causes of crime are social and cultural rather than biological or race specific. Crime does not correlate with certain races, but cuts across all groups of people. Its detection, however, may be racially motivated. These distinctions make it doubly important to acknowledge the social dimensions of

crime-related behaviour, including poverty, unemployment, hopelessness, police harassment, racism, dysfunctional families, disregard for the law, and absence of meaningful employment opportunities (Jiwani 2002; Hylton 2002). Structural barriers that inhibit minority life chances may magnify minority encounters with the criminal justice system. Downward poverty enhances the possibility of crime; crime, in turn, may intensify poverty by discouraging business initiatives, thus inflating minority unemployment (Loury 1997). And, finally, both cultural values and social patterns may generate public behaviour that is more likely to attract police attention.

In short, there is no empirical justification for correlating race with crime. Race cannot account for crime but only public perceptions about "who's committing what." Race matters, to be sure, but not because some races carry a crime gene. Rather, race matters because people believe it does, and act accordingly by assigning moral force to spurious statistics. Yet, statistics can only measure levels of enforcement against targeted minorities. These and related incidents should sound alarm bells. They remind us that race does matter in Canada, not because race is real, but because a belief in the reality of race may well prove a self-fulfilling prophesy.

THE RACE CONCEPT: BIOLOGICAL REALITY OR SOCIAL CONSTRUCT?

The completion of the Human Genome Project in 2000 revealed what many had suspected: Human beings belong to a single biological species *(Homo sapiens)* within a larger grouping or genus *(Homo)*. Humans as a species are 99.9 percent genetically identical with just 0.1 percent of genetic material accounting for human diversity. The term "species" is used in the genetic sense of a breeding population whose members possess the capacity to naturally produce fertile offspring. Within the human species numerous populations exhibit genetically diverse frequencies. These gene frequencies are manifest in readily observable characteristics including skin colour *(phenotypes)* in addition to less discernible attributes such as blood types *(genotypes)*. Biologically speaking, then, the race concept refers to this distribution of genes based on clusters of phenotypes or genotypes between populations. It also may refer to a subpopulation of the species in which certain hereditary features appear more frequently in some population pools than others because of relative reproductive isolation (Jaret 1995).

On the surface, it might appear as if human diversity is too broad for humans to qualify as a single species. But appearances can be deceiving. Judging by our capacity to propagate with each other, and produce healthy, fertile offspring, all individuals qualify as members of the human "race" (or, more accurately, human species). Human beings constitute a single intrabreeding species with phenotypic and genotypic variation, but this variation generally exists only at the most superficial level. In that sense, humans resemble other floral and faunal species that are equally defined by varying gene frequencies and distributions. Anatomical differences exist, of course, and span the spectrum from phenotypical features such as skin colour and consistency of ear wax (moist or crumbly) to genotypical attributes such as blood chemistry (A, B, O, AB), metabolic rates, and physiological functions such as susceptibilities to disease (Jaret 1995). Most differences reflect adaptations to environmental niches in accordance with conventional evolutionary principles of mutation and natural selection. These differences presumably contributed to our collective survival as relatively distinct population clusters.

There is no dearth of initiatives to study human diversity within a race-based framework. This preoccupation with classifying humans into categories of race reflected an Enlightenment-era quest for unitary schemes to explain the totality of human experience (Goldberg 1993). Just as early anthropologists devised a host of unilinear evolutionary schemes to explain the coexistence of civilization with barbarism and savagery, so too did social theorists resort to race as an all-encompassing framework for understanding human differences and similarities (Biddiss 1979). With the race concept, the world was divided into a fixed and finite number of permanent categories, each with a distinctive assemblage of physical and behavioural characteristics. Based largely on measurement and quantification as proof of fundamental differences, a slew of classificatory schemes (or **typologies**) evolved from the eighteenth century onwards, with the most common and widely known system of classification consisting of a threefold division of humanity into Caucasoid (white), Negroid (black), and Mongoloid (Asian or Oriental) (see Brace 2005). Each of these categories was distinguished from the others by common physical features such as skin colour, hair form (fuzzy, wavy, or straight), shape of the eyelid, and so on. Each was also thought to have evolved (or to have had divinely bestowed on it) its own unique and fixed bundles of characteristics. These characteristics could be arranged hierarchically in a cascading order of inferiority and superiority based on their cultural or biological proximity to European stock.

These typologies continue to elicit interest. A professor of psychology from the University of Western Ontario, Philippe Rushton, unleashed a storm of controversy when his 1994 book, *Race, Evolution, and Behavior: A Life History Perspective*, promoted a theory of racialized evolution to account for human differences across a broad range of domains. Rushton argued that separate races, namely, "Oriental," "Caucasoid," and "Negroid" (Rushton's terminology), evolved distinctive packages of physical, social, and mental characteristics because of different reproductive strategies in diverse environments. High reproductive strategies (many offspring, low nurturing) evolved in tropical climates; low reproductive strategies (few offspring, intense nurturing) in temperate climates. A racial pecking order resulted: "Orientals" (Rushton's terminology) are deemed superior to "Caucasoids" on a range of sociobiological factors. "Caucasoids" are in turn ranked superior to

"Negroids" (also Rushton's word) on the grounds of measurements involving skull size, intelligence, strength of sex drive and genital size, industriousness, sociability, and rule-following. For Rushton, "Orientals" as a group have the biggest brains, the smallest genitals, and the least promiscuity; they also are more intelligent, more family focused, and more law abiding than "Negroids," who have the smallest brains, the biggest genitals and most testosterone, the lowest IQs, and the highest crime rates. Caucasoids, Rushton concluded, fall in between.

How valid is the race concept as an explanatory tool? Most social scientists have rejected the validity of the race concept as germane to the understanding of human diversity (Brace 2005; but see Sarich and Miele 2004). Racial types and typologies have been discredited as pseudo-science and dangerous politics, without any redeeming scientific value or empirical merit. Arguments against race thinking are numerous; the most common include the following:

1. Reference to race cannot explain reality because discrete and distinct categories of racially pure people do not exist. The intermingling effect of migration with intermarriage has made it impossible to draw a line around human populations, with certain characteristics on one side, but not on the other (Martin and Franklin 1973). According to the Human Genome Project, humans share 99.9 percent of the same genetic material; not surprisingly, genetic differences within the so-called races are larger than those between races (Gee 2001). Explicit boundaries between racial groups are non-existent (unlike political boundaries, which are fixed at some point in time). Instead, populations with variable characteristics merge into one another, thus forming gradients (or clines). This makes any division between races a somewhat arbitrary exercise that reflects the whims of the investigator rather than anything intrinsic to reality itself. For example, picture the composition of populations from the north of Europe to the Mediterranean and across to Africa. Where do we draw the line between white, brown, and black populations? Any proposed demarcation is open to dispute as light-skinned northwestern Europeans merge into relatively darker Mediterranean populations and into progressively darker black-skinned populations in Africa. Ultimately, such a division is a subjective decision on the part of the investigator.

2. The integrity of racial typologies is open to question because of high rates of internal variation. Just as physical differences exist among persons who are categorized as Caucasoid ("Nordic, Alpine, Mediterranean, and Indo-Pakistani"), so too equally significant diversity exists within the Asian and Black categories. Such internal diversity would appear to invalidate the credibility of any system of classification that strives for universality and consistency. The options are lose–lose: Either an awkwardly large number of distinct categories are created to account for this diversity, or a restricted number of classifications overlook the rich diversity within the human species. Yet, no system of classification—large or small—can possibly include those that invariably fall between the cracks.

3. A tendency to confuse the race concept with human variation. Social scientists do not reject the reality of biogenetic differences between individuals or among groups (populations). Anatomical variations do exist and may help to account for differences in human behaviour, such as sport ability. Nor do social scientists deny the validity of studying these differences in an objective and scholarly fashion. Specific traits can be classified, for example, but groups of people cannot, as all populations represent bundles of different combinations of traits (Rensberger 1994). Problems can arise when valid scholarly pursuits that seek to

explore human differences harden into an obsession about racial classifications as an explanatory framework. In short, differences exist; what do *not* exist are racially discrete populations with fixed inventories of shared characteristics that can be ranked in ascending and descending orders.

4. A biological determinism that links biology with culture and behaviour. There is no evidence to suggest that some groups (or races) are inherently smarter or faster or more criminal. Human behaviour is a complex, adaptive, and evolving process, involving an interplay of genes with culture and social structure.

5. References to a racial hierarchy represent one of the more odious consequences of the race concept. With race, a doctrine emerges that upholds the proposed superiority of one race over another. On the grounds that races do not exist, it becomes pointless to devote countless studies to the notions of "racial superiority"when reality fails to conform with the units under study (Banton 1987).

To sum up, the concept of race has no biological or scientific justification (Brace 2005). Rather it represents a social construct that reflects human interests rather than anything inherent or self-evident within reality (Miles 1982; also Achenbach 2004). The consequences of this shift in thinking are significant in rethinking inter-group relations. Race relations are not about relations between races but rather about relations that have been racialized by those with power. Race relations are not biological relations, but constitute relations of inequality in which minorities are racialized as inferior or irrelevant (i.e., racialized minorities). The racialization of relationships confirms the sociological axiom that socially constructed phenomena do not have to be real, to be real in their consequences—as the next section makes painfully clear.

THE HISTORICAL ROOTS OF RACE

There is in the world a hierarchy of races . . . [Some] will direct and rule the others, and the lower work of the world will tend in the long run to be done by the lower breeds of men. This much we of the ruling colour will no doubt accept as obvious. (Murray 1900; cited in Banton 1987:vii)

For many, the race concept has outlived its utility as an explanatory framework. The concept itself originated with European expansion, conquest, and settlement, including the expansion of the cross-Atlantic slave trade, slave abolition movements, the appearance of human and biological sciences (with their focus on comparative anatomy), and international competition (Brace 2005). European expansion in regions with culturally diverse populations spawned a global division of labour in which "races" were assigned particular economic functions based on their physical appearance, local resources, power to resist, geographical location, and cultural proximity to Europe (Walker 1998). European imaginations were intrigued by sustained contact with highly diverse populations whose appearances and cultures stimulated amusement, fascination, and repulsion.

The intellectual climate proved receptive to race thinking. Reference to race was consistent with Enlightenment philosophies that extolled the virtues of human progress and individual perfectibility. Exposure to diversity encouraged a system of explanation that imposed a framework of coherence and order. The classification of diverse peoples into ranked race categories secured a "common sense" framework for explaining human differences beyond simple references to climate or history. This concept was also invoked to explain why non-Western populations seemingly lacked the techno-military prowess of imperialistic Europeans. Far from being the product of irrationality or hate, the race concept reflected an Enlightenment commitment to classifying the diversity of the world's plants, animals, and peoples into a single grand scheme (Goldberg 1993).

To be sure, references to race prevailed prior to European exploration and expansion. Embryonic forms of race thinking existed among the Chinese and Arabs in the late Middle Ages (Goldberg 1993). Ancient peoples possessed an intense aversion to those who were different. But this antipathy toward others was anchored in superstition or ignorance rather than in comprehensive theories rooted in a quasi-scientific commitment to quantification and measurement (Jaret 1995). Europeans, too, had long relied on other criteria for demonizing those beyond the pale of Christianity. For instance, the world of the Middle Ages was divided into Christian and non-Christian sectors. Non-Christians were viewed as wild and untamed pagans who had crawled out from beneath the flat world to test Christian patience. Heathens were dispatched to the lower rungs of the ladder of creation—a stable and static hierarchy that relegated lesser beings to one end and Christians to the other. Primitives and savages were fortunate to have occupied the realms in between.

The magnitude and impact of the dichotomy between Christian and non-Christian should not be underestimated. The intensity and cruelty of the violence espoused by the Crusades, the Inquisition, and the Protestant Reformation—all in the name of God—verify this. Still, these earlier patterns of exclusion were no match for the ruthless destruction carried out in the name of race. Disparaging non-Westerners as worthless and unsalvageable except for proselytizing purposes was one thing. It was quite another to construct elaborate classificatory schemes that invoked crypto-scientific explanations to legitimize worldwide exploitation and domination. The European "races" defined themselves as the ruling class and assumed a superior status, while relegating others to an inferior status with race and colour as badges of social inferiority. Of course, not all of Europe was awash with racists who relished every opportunity to disparage and exploit distant peoples (Biddiss 1979). Concern and compassion surely existed. But Europeans were among the first to popularize the race concept as a quantifiable formula for explaining away human diversity in an expansionist era.

PUTTING RACE TO WORK: JUSTIFYING COLONIAL CAPITALISM

It has been suggested that Europeans manipulated the concept of race as one way of domesticating human diversity. The proliferation of racial doctrines or dogmas fed into the racial mindset. Racial doctrines originated to condone the negative treatment of non-Western populations who were perceived as irrelevant or inferior. Under the sway of these dogmas, Europeans embarked on civilizing crusades that served as a cloak for the exploitation and attendant disregard for the human rights of inhabitants (Hommel 2001). Admittedly, the race concept did not originate to justify European control or domination of others; nevertheless, the unintended impact of the associated doctrines had a controlling effect on racialized minorities. When sanctioned by human and biological sciences, these classifications made group differences appear more comprehensive, more entrenched, and more scientifically valid (Stocking Jr. 1968; Stepan 1982). When harnessed to military prowess and technological advances, the effects proved fatal to many.

The nineteenth century is often regarded as the age of imperialism. It represented a period of time when various European nations (as well as Russia and the United States) assumed an inalienable right to conquer, colonize, and exploit overseas territories. The requirements of an expanding capitalist system reflected a need for new foreign markets, investment opportunities, cheap labour, and accessible resources. In addition, European imperialist expansion intensified an obsession with accumulating foreign territories for nationalistic, decorative, or strategic reasons. This fascination with colonial empires may also have been perpetuated for no other reason than "one-upmanship" in an ever-spiralling game of tit for tat, which no side could realistically hope to win except at the expense of the other.

This predatory approach toward global relations exposed a paradox. First, how could the so-called civilized and Christian nations rationalize and justify the blatant exploitation of others? Second, how could colonialist exploitation be sustained without contradicting the image of Europeans as a sophisticated and enlightened people with a moral duty to civilize and convert? Answers to these uncomfortable questions inspired an ideology that condoned the mistreatment of others as natural or normal—even necessary. The contradiction between Christian ideals and exploitative practices was masked and mediated by the racist conviction that lower ranked races would benefit from servitude and close supervision (Lerner 1997). This ideology not only rationalized the sorting of populations along racial lines but also set the tone for asserting absolute European supremacy at the expense of those most vulnerable. As Martin and Franklin (1973:71) write,

> [The] advent [of race] seemed to be due in large measure to the need for a rationalization of the exploitation of certain groups . . . This proposition was also advanced to justify the imperialism and colonialism that flourished . . . Racism became a convenient ideological defense for social practices which patently and flagrantly violated basic social and institutional principles.

In short, racial doctrines arose to "soften" the impact of imperialist encounters throughout Central and South America, the Caribbean, Africa, Australia, and New Zealand. By dismissing overseas races as inferior or subhuman, Europeans could exploit and oppress "inferior stocks" with impunity and without remorse or guilt. And because racial differences were ingrained as fixed and immutable, Europeans were absolved of any responsibility for improving the plight of the less fortunate. With consciences salved, they were free to do whatever was expedient to expand or safeguard white privilege.

DOCTRINES OF RACIAL SUPERIORITY

As noted by many, race emerged as an eighteenth-century concept to label, describe, and classify large groups of people by reference to immutable traits such as the colour of the skin. Doctrines of racial superiority began to appear once racial types were assigned a fixed moral value—that is, prescribed by nature as a superior or inferior colour and backed by the unquestioned authority of science. Only a minimal cognitive shift was required to move from racial types to their placement on rank orderings of superiority and inferiority (Biddiss 1979). These hierarchies were intrinsically racist in that they employed the authority of science to confirm the superiority of some groups over others (Stepan 1982). Their impact was devastating despite the arbitrariness of the criteria or classification. In justifying inequality between races, the doctrines endorsed the commodification of races as objects for exploitation or control, as targets of pity or contempt, and as victims of progress. The most notorious doctrines included social Darwinism, eugenics, and scientific racism.

Social Darwinism evolved into a widely acceptable doctrine of racial superiority toward the end of the nineteenth century. The doctrine borrowed a number of Darwin's biological propositions, then reworked them to further the aims of overseas exploitation. Foremost were the notions of a "struggle for survival" and "survival of the fittest" on a global scale. Social Darwinism portrayed the social world as a gladiatorial arena where populations were locked in mortal combat over scarce and valuable resources. Those who were better adapted to compete in this ongoing struggle prospered and progressed to the apex of the evolutionary ladder. Those with less adaptive attributes were left behind in the competitive struggle for evolutionary survival. A race-based pecking order was established that justified spoils to the victor; for the vanquished, however, it meant a life of servitude and suffering.

Social Darwinist philosophies provided a philosophical justification for Western colonialism. The subjugation of colonized peoples was condoned on grounds consistent with the laws of nature. In the words of Nancy Stepan (1982:83),

> Evolutionism provided a new emotionally charged, yet ostensibly scientific language with which to express old prejudices . . . [T]he "lower races" were now races that had "evolved" least far up the evolutionary ladder, had lost out in the "struggle for survival" and were "unfit" for the competition between tribes. Or they represented the evolutionary "childhood" of the white man.

These doctrines exonerated the colonialists of responsibility in the colonization of African blacks, East Asian populations, Aboriginal peoples, and Polynesian Islanders. Racial ideologies not only explained European superiority and justified outgroup exploitation but also endorsed the virtues and inevitability of capitalism as the engine room of human progress and social enlightenment.

With **eugenics**, racist doctrines assumed even more sinister proportions. At the turn of the twentieth century, in countries like the United States, Britain, Russia, and Japan, eugenics proposed the idea that the social, mental, and behavioural qualities of the human "race" could be improved by selective manipulation of its hereditary essence (Kevles 1995). Fortified by the discovery of hereditary laws, the eugenics movement collectively advocated the improvement of human stock by purging the species of undesirables through selective breeding procedures. Eugenics operated on the assumption that the genetically unfit were a threat to society. Defectives such as racial minorities, the congenitally deformed, and the "retarded" would be sterilized in hopes of curbing the further "bastardization" of the human species (Banton 1967). By contrast, racially superior stocks were encouraged to freely propagate to ensure the proliferation of the "fittest" (Stepan 1982).

Eugenicists in the United States were instrumental in restricting immigration from less "fit" countries in Eastern and Southern Europe. They promoted sterilization laws in 31 states that disproportionately targeted lower-income groups (Kevles 1995). In Canada, the 1928 *Sexual Sterilization Act* in Alberta condoned the sterilization of 2822 women, most of them poor or Aboriginal, before being repealed in 1972 (Caulfield and Robertson 1996). Eugenics as an ideological movement culminated with the compulsory sterilization and mass destruction of millions of undesirables under the Nazi genocide machine. In time, however, eugenics fell out of favour as a doctrine. Prominent American anthropologists such as Franz Boas, Ruth Benedict, and Margaret Mead played a significant role in demolishing the validity of biological reductionist arguments, proposing, instead, the relevance of social and cultural forces in explaining human behaviour or diversity. Nevertheless, the idea of eugenics has persisted into the present, albeit in diverse and somewhat more disguised forms, and without the backing of an openly receptive social climate.

Racial dogmas under the umbrella of **scientific racism** became especially marked in the United States. The existence of an indigenous native population, a more mobile black population, and the ongoing influx of European immigrants transformed the United States into a fiercely contested site. The movement of black people from the south to the north further intensified competition in urban areas where black people competed with white immigrants for jobs and housing (van den Berghe 1967). In light of such social turmoil, American whites were clearly receptive to any scientific support for putting racialized minorities back into place. The most popular of these was the intelligence quotient (IQ) test, which even today continues to fascinate some, but repel others.

Scientific racism was built on the premise that racial capacities between populations could be measured and evaluated by statistical means. The introduction of the IQ test proved invaluable in supporting a link between race and intelligence. The IQ test itself, called the Stanford–Binet test, was designed at Stanford University by French psychologist Alfred Binet to assist in the discovery of deficiencies in French pupils' cognitive skills. American interests co-opted the test, which had never been intended to measure the amount of intelligence a person possessed, and applied it indiscriminately. A notable application took place during the latter stages of World War I, when it was used as a means of sorting raw recruits into officer rank or foot soldier. As black people, for a variety of reasons, were more likely to perform poorly on these tests, the IQ test quickly established itself as an instrument for racializing "cannon fodder."

Repeated testings revealed that black people on average scored about 15 percentage points less than white people on the IQ test. This gap was taken as proof that black people were inherently intellectually inferior. With few exceptions, many believed this biogenetic gap could never be bridged, even with environmental improvements and enrichment programs. But in their hurry to promote white intellectual supremacy at the expense of black people, the advocates of the IQ test took some unwarranted liberties with the results. For example, while blacks scored consistently lower than whites as a group, the range of variation between black and white scores was comparable. The highest and the lowest scores within each category were approximately the same. Also relevant but widely ignored were variations in group averages. Whereas blacks on an average scored about 15 percent lower than whites, 15 percent of the blacks scored higher than the average score for whites—implying by inference that some blacks were intellectually superior to many whites. Furthermore, both the social environment and the test's cultural bias were ignored as possible explanations.

Debates about the relevance of race to explaining differences in intelligence persist. According to the authors of *The Bell Curve: Intelligence and Class Structure in American Life*, Charles Murray and Richard J. Herrnstein (1994), the relatively low levels of intelligence exhibited by certain races such as blacks are (1) real, (2) measurable by IQ tests, (3) inherited, (4) predictive, and (5) resistant to modification. Low levels of intelligence, in turn, are responsible for social problems such as poverty, lawlessness, and dysfunctional families. And in a June 2005 issue of the journal *Psychology, Public Policy, and Law*, co-authors

Philippe Rushton and Arthur Jensen continue to assert that genes explain 50 percent of the differences in IQ between different races, with Asians ranked higher than whites and whites higher than blacks in intelligence.

Many social scientists sharply dispute this line of thinking (Alland Jr. 1996). Individual variation in intelligence is one thing; a race-based theory of fixed intelligence is quite another and is repudiated by most social scientists. Low IQ scores do not create social problems; rather, social problems that stem from conditions of poverty and powerlessness are likely to foster lower IQ scores. Social inequality cannot be directly reduced to differences in cognitive ability; differences in cognition may reflect responses to social inequality. To be sure, (1) intelligence may be partly inherited and measurable; (2) heredity and environment may interact in diverse ways to create intelligence; (3) environments can strongly influence a person's intelligence regardless of heredity; and (4) genetic and environmental factors are impossible to separate (Sternberg and Grigorenko 1997). But because the concept of intelligence varies across time and space, there is not much value in positing that a constant (race) can explain a variable (intelligence).

Two reasons may account for the tenacity of scientific racism. First, if intelligence is biologically innate and largely impervious to environmental modification, then the mainstream cannot be held responsible for the plight of racialized minority groups. The results of these tests can be used to justify the negative treatment of minorities, ranging from segregated facilities to inferior programs. These results can also be employed to pre-empt progressive change as there is little hope for improvement. Second, IQ tests are an effective device for explaining away differences through their logical presentation of "facts" and simple causal explanations (Mirza 1998). They possess an aura of scientific validity that is substantiated by the "hocus pocus" of quantification and measurement. The halo effect associated with science can also create the impression that race is a respectable intellectual position with a legitimate place in the national agenda (Naureckas 1995).

TAKING RACE SERIOUSLY

That race matters in the United States may be taken as self-evident. Critics point to a country riddled with a historical legacy of slavery and segregation as well as lynchings and the Ku Klux Klan. American racism was animated by a belief in the innate differences between people as a basis for justifying unequal treatment. Even today, the race subtext is unmistakable in public discourses about crime, poverty, and urban decay. Social problems are framed as black or white issues, with the result that everything from welfare to income is refracted through the prism of skin colour (Mitchell 1998). Public debates take place in which welfare mothers, inner-city violence, urban decay, and hard drugs are essentially code terms for "blackness." Statistical evidence confirms how race matters when it comes to distinguishing the "haves" from the "have-nots." The status for many African-Americans continues to deteriorate in the aftermath of the Civil Rights revolution (Assante 2003). The real median household income for black people has declined, while an increasing number of black households and children hover below the federal poverty line. Even for middle-class black people race matters, as many are rebuked for acting too white or too black, depending on the context. Conversely, race matters for whites, because their whiteness is the norm that confers the privilege of being everything, yet nothing.

INSIGHT	**Whiteness as Race Privilege**

There is a paradox at play in contemporary race debates. Many believe that race shouldn't matter for two reasons: first, the concept itself has no empirical validity or biological reality; second, how can skin colour (shorthand for race) be relevant in a merit-based society rooted in the colour-blind principles of liberal universalism? And yet, in a white-dominated society, a paradox prevails: As Henry and Tator (1993) remind us, the colour of a person's skin may be the single most important factor in determining his or her dignity, identity, self-esteem, and opportunities. Or put in slightly more sociological terms, where one is socially located in society with respect to skin colour (or race) will profoundly influence a person's life (experiences), self-image (identity), and life chances (opportunities).

Most Canadians will admit that certain minorities are disadvantaged because of skin colour. Many are also willing to concede that minority disadvantages do not always reflect individual failure. No less important are restricted opportunity structures because of colour-conscious barriers. But few Canadians are prepared to concede how whiteness may privilege some while disprivileging others (Wise 2005). They are reluctant to acknowledge "whiteness" as a category of race, just as many prefer to exclude men from the category of gender. In other words, whites will see "others" as "races," but view themselves as beyond race—as a neutral and colourless norm that manages to be everything yet nothing, everywhere yet nowhere. Yet whites are "raced" just as men are "gendered," and failure to acknowledge this reality does not bode well for understanding how the racializing of Canadian society has rendered people of colour simultaneously visible yet, paradoxically, invisible (Deake and Ray 2001).

Just as whiteness is taken for granted, so too are the privileges associated with whiteness (McIntosh 1988). Being white means one can purchase a home in any part of town without being "blacklisted" or "redlined" by the local real estate market. Being white allows one to go strolling around shopping malls without the embarrassment of being "blackballed" (e.g., followed, frisked, monitored, or fingerprinted). Being white ensures one the freedom to drive anything, anywhere, and anytime, without being pulled over by the police for "driving while black" ("DWB"). Being white allows one to take a stand on a variety of topics without someone disputing one's objectivity or second-guessing one's motives. Being white means one's misdeeds are not judged by—or made excuses for—what others in one's community do. Or as an Australian aboriginal woman once put it, "If a whitefella does something wrong, he's wrong; if a blackfella does something wrong, we're all wrong" (cited in Morris and Cowlishaw 1997).

Put bluntly, whiteness is a privilege that is taken for granted yet largely unearned—an accident of birth. Stamped into one's skin, whiteness is a kind of "passport" that opens doors and unlocks opportunities just as identity cards in South Africa once defined who got what based on the lightness or darkness of skin colour. Not surprisingly, there is a booming market for skin whiteners in parts of the world such as South Asia where whiteness is equated with beauty, success, and popularity (McPhate 2005). Yet, whites rarely acknowledge the privileges associated with whiteness, arguing that they personally have had nothing to do with the disprivileging of "others"—a denial that manifests itself as a form of privilege because no social consequences are suffered as a result of denying another person's reality (Wise 2005). This privilege of whiteness is neither openly articulated nor logically deserved, but assumed and universalized as normal and natural, and beyond scrutiny or criticism. For many whites, whiteness is the "natural" way of being human; whites are unaware of their whiteness in the same way that fish are unaware of their "wetness" because they are so immersed in water. As Judith Levine (1994:22) puts it in equating the experience of whiteness as raceless and thus the norm:

> Whiteness purports to be nothing and everything. It is the race that need not speak its name. Yet it defines itself as no less than whatever it chooses to exclude. To grow up white is to be the ground zero from which everything else differs . . .

Herein, then, lies the "genius" of white privilege. Whiteness is everything yet nothing: everything, because it is perceived by whites to be nothing in particular; nothing, because whiteness is the normative standard by which everything else is judged (Mackey 1998). Conversely, those without the privilege of whiteness are stigmatized as the "other" and demonized accordingly. Blackness represents the antithesis of whiteness in terms of privilege or entitlement—a highly visible stigma (or marked category) that denies, excludes, or exploits. Unlike whites who rarely experience whiteness, people of colour have little choice except to confront blackness on a daily basis. No aspect of existence, no moment of the day, no contact, no relationship, no response is exempt from the stigma of blackness in a racialized society (Philip 1996).

In short, skin colour really matters in defining "who gets what," whether we like it or not, approve or disapprove. Whiteness shapes people's lives by symbolizing

(1) dominance rather than subdomination, (2) normativity rather than marginality, and (3) privilege rather than disadvantage. To be sure, not everyone views whiteness as an unmarked vehicle of privilege. White supremacist groups have cleverly transformed whiteness into victimhood—in much the same way as some men's movements have depicted males as victims of radical feminism, equity initiatives, and political correctness. Whiteness is valorized as the hallmark of an endangered or persecuted race, one that is, according to supremacists, under threat and challenge by minorities because of quotas or "reverse discrimination" (see Ferber 1998). Yet, these challenges to "whiteness" need to be put into context. True, whites no longer possess the exclusive power and privilege of the past. But moves toward inclusiveness have hardly resulted in any significant shift in institutional power or white privilege.

Two final questions: First, are whites a race? Technically no, but in a world of perceptions, everybody is racially located or perceived to be—whether they are aware of it or not (see Hall 1996). That alone makes it doubly important to foster awareness of whiteness *as if* it were a "race" in alignment with other races. Moreover, to exclude whiteness as an unmarked race category that stands outside history or convention is to redouble its privilege by naturalizing it (Bell 1996). Second, is whiteness inherently racist? No, not in the sense of racial hatred. But yes, to the extent that whiteness is secured as culturally normative space, as a relationship of power, and as a standpoint by which to understand the world by way of cultural practices that are largely unmarked, unnamed, and invisible (Frankenburg 1993; Mackey 1998). The racism implicit within whiteness reflects a stubborn refusal to appreciate its largely unearned privileges and advantages. It reflects the ethnocentric tendency to interpret reality from a white point of view as natural and normal, while non-white viewpoints are dismissed as irrelevant or inferior. Finally, whiteness may be systemically racist, in that white privilege inheres within the system without people's awareness of its presence or consequences. Whiteness may not set out to control, but the systemic bias of white rules and "pale male" agendas may have a controlling effect in perpetuating a racialized status quo.

The politics of race continue to perplex. On one side, the so-called race card may be routinely invoked to instill public fears or to manipulate legal decisions that adversely affect minority women and men. On the other side, references to race may be used to advance rewards and entitlements, while garnering sympathy for the plight of racialized minorities. On yet another side, racially based distinctions that formerly stigmatized individuals as inferior or irrelevant are now invoked as criteria for promotion or admission. The logic behind race-conscious programs such as employment equity is relatively straightforward: If race contributed to the problem of inequality and exploitation, then race must be included as part of the solution. The idea of black-focus schools is justified on grounds that young blacks are at a risk of underperforming in the public system (which may be interpreted as white-focus schools). Proposed instead is an "Afro-centred" curriculum and pedagogy that reflects, reinforces, and advances black experiences, realities, and aspirations. "Black Rage" defence strategies are predicated on the principle that the social context in which racialized minorities find themselves has contributed to a state of mind that may induce criminal behaviour (Harris 1997). Finally, race serves as a distinguishing marker for oppressed groups who are transforming the stigma of oppression into a mark of pride, identity, or resistance (Lerner 1997).

Does race matter in Canada? Canadians and Americans are often perceived as poles apart when it comes to race relations. Compared to the United States, Canadians appear cool to the notion that race matters or that it should matter (James 1994:47). Canada is widely applauded for emphasizing achievement and merit rather than skin colour as the basis for recognition, reward, and relationships. Canadians exult in the myth that we have a deep aversion to judging others by the colour of their skin. Discussions about race tend to be muted, often employing circumlocutions, such as visible minorities or ethnicity, for fear of inflaming public passions (Mitchell 1998). A quick reality check suggests otherwise.

Canada's history is organized around a perception of itself as a "white man's society." Its immigration policy rested on racial factors; immigrants with darker skins were less desirable than those with lighter skins (Avery 2000). Perceptions of Aboriginal peoples as an inferior race simplified the task of divesting the original occupants of their land and resources. Race continues to affect contemporary Canada. Racialized minorities bear the brunt of negative treatment, ranging from local snubs to half-hearted service delivery. People of colour continue to be employed as cheap and disposable labour in often menial tasks. Foreign-born racialized minorities tend to earn less than whites even when educational levels are held constant (Pendakur 2005; Galabuzi 2006). Participation and decision-making are influenced by prevailing stereotypes and racial prejudices, whereas social rewards are allocated on the basis of racial affiliation. Minority women and men with professional degrees find it difficult to get jobs consistent with their credentials. Even the emergence of race-conscious state policies such as the *Employment Equity Act* to ameliorate disadvantage have endured criticism as tokenistic or divisive (see Chapter 5 for case study).

In short, race matters not because it is real, but because people respond as if it were real. Race matters not because people are inherently different or unequal, but because perceived differences may be manipulated to achieve desired outcomes. Race matters not because of biological differences, but because an exclusive preoccupation with biology detracts from scrutinizing those opportunity structures that are largely responsible for unequal relations. And finally, race matters because reference to race has a controlling effect on those who are racially devalued. But nowhere does race matter more than in the persistence of racism in Canada—as the next chapter will demonstrate.

DEBATE REVISITED   **Black Success: Race or Opportunity?**

There is no scarcity of biologically grounded explanations for black success in certain sports (Entine 1999). A popular explanation is derived from the "theory" of black anatomical advantages. Black athletes perform well because of natural (biological) factors including bone structure, stamina, strength, coordination, and size. Anatomical differences include (1) leg and calf structures more suitable for jumping, (2) faster twitch muscles (muscle fibres that rapidly burn cell glycogen) for sprinting, (3) more sweat glands (more body surface) for dissipating excess body heat, (4) less subcutaneous fat on arms and legs, (5) faster patellar tendon reflex, (6) higher levels of plasma testosterone, and (7) darker eye colours for excelling at reactive sports (Jaret 1995).

However "valid" each of these factors, biological differences in anatomy do not mean that black people are racially superior in sports. While superficially appealing, the notion that blacks as a race are racially better endowed than whites cannot stand up to scrutiny. For example, blacks may excel in certain sports, from boxing to basketball, but not at others such as tennis, golf, and swimming. Of course well-known exceptions exist, including Tiger Woods in golf and the Williams sisters in tennis, but the attention these athletes receive tends to prove the rule. Nor can the race concept explain the absence of blacks from professional team sports until after World War II—unless one reverts to some wildly implausible genetic displacement in an impossibly short time span. That leaves social and cultural factors as alternative explanatory frameworks to account for these shifting patterns.

First, professional sports is one of the few opportunity structures open to African-Americans (Edwards 1971; 2000). Not only do black people focus on sports to escape the poverty of the inner city but they also gravitate to sports as a legitimate avenue for power, privilege, and wealth. Success itself creates role models that provide additional incentive for youth. Second, American sports is a big business that extols winning at all costs. This post-war commitment put a premium on attracting the best athletes—regardless of colour or race. Black athletes were able to overcome discrimination by pursuing those sports whose performance levels could be evaluated objectively by way of statistics. Thus, highly quantifiable performances among black athletes (such as pass-catching yardage or batting average) proved pivotal in dismantling barriers. Third, entry occurred in team-oriented sports where black excellence could be diffused among white teammates and rationalized as integral to team success. Fourth, blacks did not excel in all sports. They tended to gravitate toward sports that were relatively inexpensive, did not require special equipment, and were easily accessible regardless of socio-economic status.

Yet, black success in sport is "skin deep." Blacks may do well in team numbers, but they are not randomly distributed across the playing field. Black players tend to cluster around certain positions in a phenomenon known as stacking. In the NFL, for example, blacks predominate in positions such as running back or wide receiver on offence, and cornerback and safety at defence. Black quarterbacks were a rarity until recently; few black college-level quarterbacks ever made it to the NFL in that position (usually they were converted to defensive backs), with the first being James Harris of the Los Angeles Rams in 1975. Whites, in turn, prevail at quarterback and kicking on offence, and the more central positions on defence. Similarly, stacking occurs in baseball where pitchers and catchers are overwhelmingly white, with blacks predominantly in the outfield. And management positions remain stacked in favour of whites, notwithstanding modest changes. Of the 411 major league baseball managers since 1900, according to *Baseball Weekly,* 10 March 1999, 402 have been white.

This racialized pattern is not entirely accidental. It reflects a view that whites should monopolize the thinking positions, whereas blacks should concentrate on those that can capitalize on their natural talents. The racial subtext is clear: Whites succeed as athletes through perseverance, brain power, and strategic reasoning; black athletes are successful because of raw genetic prowess rooted in speed and power. The end result is to reinforce widely held presumptions of innate black athletic superiority yet intellectual inferiority (Edwards 2000). Not surprisingly, racial tensions have mounted in the professional leagues, especially in basketball, where blacks who are selected for aggressiveness and transformed into instant millionaires invariably come into conflict with authority figures—from coaches to managers to owners—most of whom are white.

In short, the racialization of sport reinforces the theme that race matters. Blacks are overrepresented in certain sports and positions, underrepresented in others, excluded from the spatial centre of team formations, and denied leadership positions both on and off the field (Smith and Leonard II 1997). To be sure, biological factors are not irrelevant in explaining success. Biology is known to intersect with culture and society in ways that are real but have yet to be determined. Nor is there anything racist in admitting that blacks are better in some sports rather than others because of evolution or genes—even though such an admission runs the risk of opening the floodgates that link brain size with crime or intelligence. But references to genetic or anatomical variations should not be confused with race-based typologies. Race matters when it comes to sports—not because one race has more natural talent than another, but because people believe it does—thus creating the conditions for a self-fulfilling prophecy.

CHAPTER HIGHLIGHTS

- The politics of race are explored by looking at its value as an explanatory framework to account for human differences and disadvantages related to intelligence or crime, the role of racial doctrines as instruments of colonialist expansion and contemporary control, and the status of race in the construction of human reality.

- The key theme of this chapter can be quickly grasped: Human differences exist, race does not, although people act as if it does.

- Race and crime do not necessarily correlate. Race cannot explain crime (crime transcends racial groupings) while race-based crime statistics do not measure crime but rates of minority apprehension by law enforcement.

- The race concept is primarily a social construct, without any biological basis or scientific validity. As a social construct, the race concept implies not only a belief in innate differences as unequal, determinative of behaviour, and resistant to change, but also a division of humanity into discrete groups that can be hierarchically arranged.

- Race matters. Race may be a social construction; nevertheless, it is a social fiction with material consequences—thus confirming that phenomena such as race do not have to be real to be real in their consequences.

- Technically speaking, whites are not a race, as there is no such thing as races. Nevertheless, the privileges that are associated with whiteness compel us to approach whites as if they were a race.

KEY TERMS

colonialism
essentializing
eugenics
race

racialization
racial typologies
scientific racism
social Darwinism

REVIEW QUESTIONS

1. Race has little to do with genes or biological reality, but everything to do with perceptions about genes and biology. Explain this assertion that race is not about biology but about society.

2. Why did racial doctrines emerge in nineteenth-century Europe, and why do they persist into the twenty-first century?

3. What do we mean by the statement that there is no such thing as race relations, only relationships that have been "racialized"? Include reference to the concept of racialization.

4. Race matters not because race is real, but because people believe it to be real, and act according to this belief, with often very real consequences. Explain what this means, and provide an example.

5. Indicate whether there is any validity to the collection of crime statistics by race.

LINKS AND RECOMMENDATIONS

Films

A Japanese Story (2003)

A story of an interracial affair that shows how love conquers all, but that there is always a price to pay. Set in Australia, and involving a Japanese businessman and an Australian geologist, the film captures the complexities of a relationship between differently racialized persons.

Crash (2005)

Directed by Paul Haggis, this Oscar-winning film by Lions Gate Entertainment (not to be confused with David Cronenberg's quirky film of the same title) consists of a series of vignettes that take place across two days in L.A. The storyline follows a series of characters whose lives are informed by race and interconnected because of racism.

Books

C. Loring Brace. 2005. *"Race" is a Four-Letter Word: The Genesis of the Concept.* New York: Oxford University Press.

Vincent Sarich and Frank Miele. 2004. *Race: The Reality of Human Differences.* Boulder, CO: Westview Press.

Websites

Canada's foremost site for issues pertaining to race and discrimination. Provides access to news, events, research, and publications.

www.crr.ca

Urban Alliance on Race Relations. Canada's only journal that deals exclusively with race-related articles and research.

www.tgmag.ca/magic/uarr.html

An excellent site that focuses on exploring the characteristics and consequences of race as a powerful illusion.

www.pbs.org/race/000_General/000_00-Home.htm

A splendid clearing house of information pertaining to issues of race.

http://racerelations.about.com

So you think you haven't got a racist bone in your body. Take the Implicit Association Test to see if there are some racialized residues lurking in the recesses of your mind.

http://implicit.harvard.edu

Chapter

UNMASKING RACISM

3

DEBATE Racial Rashomon: Putting Police Racial Profiling to the Test

Both sociologists and filmmakers have long known what postmodernists claim to have invented. People see the world differently because of who they are, what they own, how they work, and where they stand. Japanese film director Akira Kurosawa explored this multi-perspectival theme in his brilliantly conceived film *Rashomon*. This 1951 epic focuses on the competing perceptions of those implicated in a brutal incident involving a woman, her husband, and a bandit, with a peasant as eyewitness. Each of the incumbents interprets the death of the husband and the rape of his wife differently, albeit in a manner that reflects favourably on them. In presenting this viewpoint, Kurosawa tapped into the postmodernist belief that there is no such thing as truth (or reality), only discourses about truth, whose "truthfulness" reflects a person's social location in society. The process by

which divergent and self-serving interpretations define the same incident—that what we see depends on where we stand—has come to be known as the "Rashomon effect."

The radical relativism implicit in the Rashomon effect may help to untangle a paradox in race relations. That is, why do some believe that racism in Canada is under control while others think it is out of control? At one end of this debate are those who usually underestimate the scope and impact of racism. Many prefer to see racism as the random and aberrant act of a dysfunctional individual (bad apple) whose unfortunate actions are at odds with an open and tolerant society. At the other end are those who emphasize the spiralling magnitude and corrosive effect of racism. Racism is deemed to be institutionalized, deeply embedded within the structures and culture of a racialized society, resistant to change because of systemic barriers, and reflective of a society that is fundamentally rotten to the core, with the bad apples simply a manifestation of the creeping rot (Gosine 2003). A perceptual divide is apparent. Minority discourses criticize Canada as an essentially racist society in need of transformation from the top down. For the mainstream, however, Canada is basically sound with a few misguided racists to spoil an otherwise healthy brew. Such a perceptual gap is not without its consequence: How can we expect to live together differently if there is no agreement regarding the nature and magnitude of the forces that confuse or divide?

Reference to the Rashomon effect exposes the polarities and paradoxes behind the police racial profiling crisis. Do police profile? Do they engage in a criminal profiling that is based on race (Wortley 2005)? Who says so? If so, why? Do data support this allegation? Is an expensive car stopped because it is speeding and swerving, or because the driver is a young black male? Do police have reasonable and clearly expressed cause for the stop, or do they use race to detain someone (Ibbitson 2005)? Evidently, yes: On the basis of data collected from police reports over a five-year period (1996–2001), a major newspaper outlet accused the Toronto police of racial profiling. The *Toronto Star* concluded that black people charged with simple drug possession were treated more harshly than white people with the same charge. The *Star* investigation also argued that a disproportionate number of black people were ticketed with offences that would only come to light after a traffic stop, such as driving under suspension or without insurance—a pattern of behaviour that the daily deemed to be consistent with racial profiling.

The highly contentious issue of police race profiling was put to the test when the Kingston Police Services released the results of a one-year study to determine if police did practise racial profiling. The project was designed to gather information on the nature of non-casual contacts between Kingston police officers and the general public. To determine whether the exercise of police discretion results in unequal treatment, each police officer was instructed to fill out a "contact card" that indicated the "race" (i.e., race as perceived by police officers) as well as the gender and age of those local residents who were stopped on a non-casual basis. A total of 10 114 incidents were eventually tabulated, with traffic stops accounting for about one-third of the stops, and pedestrian incidents for the remainder.

The results of the report, entitled *Bias Free Policing* and compiled by the University of Toronto criminologist Scot Wortley, proved to be both interesting and provocative, yet somewhat misleading. According to the data, some racialized minorities are stopped more often than others. Black people, who constitute 0.6 percent of Kingston's population, were stopped 2.2 percent of the time, yielding a stop ratio of 3.67, compared to white people who accounted for 92 percent of the stops, as well as 92 percent of the population, for a stop ratio of 0.99. Aboriginal peoples were overrepresented in police stops, according to the report; but this overrepresentation was eliminated by controlling for individuals who were stopped on multiple occasions. South Asians, who comprise 2.5 percent of Kingston's population, accounted for 1.3 percent of the stops for a stop ratio of 0.5 while Asians with 1.3 percent of the population accounted for 0.9 percent of the stops for a stop ratio of about 0.8. Or consider the number of stops per 1000 of a race (keeping in mind that small population bases can distort ratios): black males 213/1000; black females 74/1000; West Asian males 105/1000; West Asian females 23/1000; Hispanic males 83/1000; Hispanic females 10/1000; white males

75/1000; white females 29/1000; South Asian males 63/1000; South Asian females 19/1000; Aboriginal males 51/1000; Aboriginal females 35/1000; Asian males 42/1000; Asian females 16/1000.

What do these data tell us? For some, the fact that black people are disproportionately stopped by the police is overwhelming proof of "anti black racism." According to Karen Mock of the Canadian Race Relations Foundation and Dudley Laws of Toronto's Black Action Defence Committee (cited in Freeze 2005), police are clearly guilty of racial profiling because of who they stop rather than why the stop. Both local and regional media headlines appeared to endorse this conclusion: "Kingston proves race bias," "Activists pounce on police race study," "Kingston police apologize after racial bias study." These headlines were consistent with statements in *The Report of the Commission on Systemic Racism in the Ontario Criminal Justice System* (1995) when it concluded ". . . police stops for the purpose of control are racialized" (p. 88).

Others disagreed: As far as Toronto Police Association president David Wilson was concerned, the report "proves nothing," much less the existence of systemic racism within the police services. An editorial in a major Toronto paper was equally dismissive: Do the data point to anti-black bias by police? Or is it the case that young black males are more likely to engage in unlawful or suspicious behaviour? Or are black people more likely to attract police attention because of their visibility and preference for public spaces? Another Toronto paper was no less critical of the conclusion. If racial profiling exists why do police not direct this bias at Asians? Paradoxically, an anti-white bias could be inferred from the results, as Asian and South Asian groups are stopped less frequently per 1000 of a race than white people. Age and gender were strongly

associated with police stops: Is there a sexist bias (gender profiling) in light of the three to one ratio of male stops to female stops? Do the data point to an anti-youth bias (age profiling)? After all, only 7 percent of stops involved those over 55 years, compared to 35 percent for those between 15 and 24 years of age. In short, there is only one definitive conclusion from the data: Young black males experience more stops than other demographic groups.

Who is right in this interpretive divide? Strictly speaking, the data cannot prove anything except group disparities in police stops. It is obvious—and many studies confirm this—that the problem involves the police and young black males rather than black people in general. Even this conclusion may be challenged because of flaws in the methods; for example, a small number of individuals who are frequently stopped may inflate the overall stop rate. Or difficulties may arise when police officers are asked to slot individuals into racial categories based on impressionistic evidence. The methodology is no less questionable: The use of contact cards may lack validity, that is, the study may not prove what it sets out to prove. Do the data show high levels of suspicious behaviour by black people or high levels of police racial bias? Comparing this study with actual crime rates in Kingston may provide a control for comparison. However, even statistics on crime are not infallible as they do not necessarily measure actual crime rates, but only crimes that come to police attention.

In short, certain groups are more likely to be stopped and questioned by police. But to make inferences about racism and profiling, both systemic and personal, cannot be warranted from the available data. A racial divide can be discerned—a kind of Racial Rashomon (the notion that what you see depends on where you stand). Those who are least likely to experience racism usually react in two ways: they attack the methods or methodology, or they dismiss the broader implications of any study. By contrast, those racialized persons who may encounter racial discrimination tend to "assume the worst." Still, to dismiss the study because of weaknesses is a classic case of throwing out the baby with the proverbial bathwater. The project may be unable to conclusively prove the existence of systemic racial profiling within Kingston police, but it does reveal perceptual disparities that cannot be casually discarded. And that in its own right is troubling because, when it comes to policing, perception *is* reality, and perceptions of unfairness must be addressed for justice to be seen to be done.

INTRODUCTION: THE TOXICITY OF RACISM

From a distance, Canada strikes many as a paragon of racial tranquility. Racism may loom as the single most explosive and divisive force in other countries, including the United States, but surely not in Canada, where racism is publicly scorned and officially repudiated. In contrast with the United States where racism is thought to divide or destroy, Canada's racism is perceived as relatively muted, isolated to fringe circles, a survival from the past, and or the work of a twisted few. Laws are in place that criminalize racism and **discrimination**. Brazen racists such as white supremacists are routinely charged and convicted for disseminating hate propaganda. Race riots are virtually unheard of except, perhaps, in history books, while blatant forms of racial discrimination are illegal and socially unacceptable. The popularity of terms such as "multiculturalism," "inclusiveness," and "equity" provides proof that Canadians have learned to "talk the walk."

To their credit, Canadians are learning to "walk the talk" as well. No longer are Aboriginal peoples out of relevance as political actors in the constitutional mainstream (Ponting and Gibbins 1980), but are clearly in ascendancy in reclaiming some degree of self-determining autonomy as the "nations within" (Fleras and Elliott 1992; Maaka and Fleras 2005). As proof, consider the "watershed" conference that brought together both the First Ministers and five national Aboriginal organizations at the First Nations Summit in November of 2005 at Kelowna, B.C. The situation is similar with the Québécois, who, for all intents and purposes, function as a distinct society. Another positive indicator is the demographic revolution that has transformed once staunchly anglocentric cities such as Vancouver and Toronto into vibrant, cosmopolitan centres. So too is the institutionalization of multiculturalism, which has catapulted Canada into the global spotlight as a bluep rint for "living together with differences." The fact that the United Nations had ranked Canada as the country of choice for eight consecutive years (currently fourth) must surely say something about its enlightened commitments.

Up close, however, the image shatters. Canadians could be smug about their enlightened status if racism were a mere blip on Canada's social and historical landscape. This, sadly, is far from the truth. Racism is no stranger to Canadian society, but was deeply embedded in its history, culture, law, and institutions (see Satzewich 1998; Walker 1998). Canada was founded on the colonization of its indigenous peoples, the appropriation of their land and resources, the exploitation of immigrant labour for Canada-building purposes, and a preferential treatment toward white European settlers. Minority women and men were racialized as inferior or irrelevant, and then arranged into a hierarchy of acceptance or rejection based on their proximity to the French and English as the primary reference groups. Even that most quintessential of American racist institutions, slavery, appears to have flourished in Canada (Cooper 2006)—at least judging by this advertisement:

> TO BE SOLD, A BLACK WOMAN, named Peggy, aged about forty years; and a black boy her son, named JUPITER, aged about fifteen years, both of them the property of the subscriber. The woman is a tolerable Cook and washerwoman and perfectly understands making Soap and Candles. The Boy is tall and strong of his age, and has been employed in Country Business, but brought up principally as a House Servant—They are each of them Servants for life. The Price for the Wowan [sic] is one hundred and fifty Dollars—for the Boy two hundred Dollars, payable in three years with Interest from the day of Sale and to be properly secured by Bond &c—But one fourth less will be taken in ready Money. PETER RUSSELL. York, Feb. 10th 1806. (adapted from Bristow et al. 1993)

The legacy of racialized woes goes on. Racism furnished the ideological life support for capitalism at large, for society-building in general, and the exploitation of racialized minorities in particular (Bolaria and Li 1988; Bishop 2005). Hate and fear compelled authorities to intern thousands of ethnic minorities, including the placement of 5000 Ukrainians in concentration camps during World War I—at great personal cost to themselves and to their families. An equally spiteful internment was inflicted on Japanese-Canadians in British Columbia. Most were rounded up like Jews in Nazi Germany, their property confiscated and civil rights suspended, then confined to labour internment camps. Restrictions were not lifted until 1949. Black people in Canada were no less denied and excluded because of segregation at schools, housing, and public venues such as movie theatres. Contrary to public opinion, the Ku Klux Klan assumed a major profile during the 1920s and 1930s in central and western Canada. The "Kanadian Klan" aimed its racist bile at black people as well as at Catholics, French-Canadians, and Asians.

The present may be equally if not more quietly racist, at least in consequence if not always in intent. Critics charge that racism is alive and well in Canada, with only its worst effects camouflaged by a Teflon veneer of tolerance and politeness (Henry and Tator 2006; Satzewich 1998). Such an accusation may puzzle the reader; after all, at a cognitive level, many have internalized the values of tolerance, equality, and justice. But racism remains at subconscious levels of prejudice, while institutions continue to deny and exclude because of rules and protocols that exert a discriminatory impact. Racism is so naturalized in history and society that it constantly finds new and complex forms of expression by making itself more invisible. Or in the words of Senator David Oliver, racism is

> . . . not something readily discernable by the senses: you cannot see it, hear it, smell it, touch it, but it does exist. It is subtle, invisible, and ethereal. (cited in a report by Conference Board of Canada 2004)

Yet, brazen expressions have not altogether vanished. Consider this incident in Quebec at one of Canada's largest commercial vegetable farms located southwest of Montreal where a Tribunal awarded a compensation package of between $10 000 and $15 000 in damages to each of four black plaintiffs because of racial discrimination. In 2001, it was pointed out, day labourers, most of whom were black, were not allowed in the regular (white) cafeteria but were segregated in a "black people only" cafeteria without a heater, running water, refrigeration, or proper toilets (Patriquin 2005; see also Woodward 2005).

In short, racism assumes many different forms, ranging from the failure of institutions to remove discriminatory barriers, including reports that visible minority nurses face a backlash from co-workers and administrators if they don't accept additional workloads or extra shift work (Keung 2005), to the violence of racially motivated crimes, including anti-Semitic vandalism in Toronto and Montreal in the spring of 2004. Rather than improving as might be expected because of laws, human rights legislation, and an official Multiculturalism, the situation appears to be deteriorating: According to the B'nai B'rith, 857 anti-Semitic incidents were reported in 2004—an increase of 47 percent over 2003 and the highest total ever in the history of the audit (Fraser 2005). People of colour continue to be politely denied equitable access to housing, employment, media, education, policing, and social services (Henry and Tator 2006). Not surprisingly, one in six adult Canadians report being victims of racism, in a survey of 1001 randomly selected individuals (March 12–15, 2005) conducted by Ipsos-Reid and the Dominion Institute. Even Canada's much-lauded attempts to "engage" diversity under an official Multiculturalism have been questioned as racism in disguise (Thobani 1995; Bannerji 2000). That Canada has managed to be largely free of race riots and cross burning is commendable in its own right. Yet, such a fortuitous state of affairs may reflect exceptional good fortune and a powerful myth-making machine instead of enlightened policies or public goodwill.

Canada in the twenty-first century must confront an inescapable paradox. On the one hand, Canadians, at the cognitive level, have rejected notions of biological inferiority, while internalizing a commitment to tolerance, justice, and equality. On the other hand, they also continue to rely on racially based prejudices at subconscious levels, while institutions are known to discriminate against minorities because of rules that when equally applied have the seemingly unintended effect of excluding or exploiting. At one end, Canada remains at the forefront in fighting racism at individual, institutional, and ideological levels. And at the other, awareness is mounting that racism is an everyday reality for many Canadians of colour, that racist practices affect individuals in very real ways, and that racism is not some relic from the past, but is dynamically invasive and socially toxic. Which picture is more accurate? Is Canada as racist to the core as critics say? Or is Canada essentially an open and tolerant society, with only isolated and random incidences of racism? Is Canada a society where individuals are rewarded on the basis of merit, where no group is singled out for negative treatment, and where race is deemed to be irrelevant in determining a person's status? Or is Canada as racist as the next country but prefers to mask this racism behind a mythology of racelessness by concealing it under a blanket of whiteness (Backhouse 1999; Kobayashi 2003)? The Ontario Human Rights Commission (2005:1) pulls no punches in pointing out the reality yet denial of racism and racial discrimination (but see Loney 2005):

> Racialized persons experience disproportionate poverty, over-representation in the prison population, underrepresentation in the middle and upper layers of political, administrative, economic, and media institutions, and barriers to accessing employment, housing, and health care to name just a few. Courts have recognized that racism exists in Canada. It's all too easy for those who do not experience it to deny the reality of racism. This is counterproductive and damaging to our social fabric. Racial discrimination and racism must be acknowledged as a pervasive and continuing reality as a starting point . . .

Or is it more accurate to say that racism in Canada falls somewhere in between the naïveté of the optimists and the cynical pessimism of the sceptics? In other words, Canada is home to a baffling blend of hard-core racists and resolute anti-racists, with most individuals aligned along this continuum of extremes. Accordingly, it makes no more sense to exaggerate the magnitude of racism in Canada than to underestimate its tenacity and sting in privileging some and disprivileging others.

The face of racism is shifting in response to a changing and diverse society. Rather than performing the vanishing act or staying pat, racism is proving a moving target both difficult to pin down or to put away (Frederickson 2002). A growing realization that there are many racisms rather than a single racism makes it doubly important to unmask this complex and evolving dynamic. This chapter will explore racism in Canada as a concept for analysis as well as a reality for many Canadians. The different dimensions of racism are analyzed by reference to definitions of racism as (1) biology, (2) culture, (3) ideology, (4) structure, and (5) power. The concept of racism is dissected into its component elements, namely, prejudice (from ethnocentrism to stereotyping) and discrimination (including harassment). The different types of racism are also compared: from the interpersonal (including hate and polite) to the institutional (including the systematic and systemic), and to the ideological (including normative and subliminal). Also explored in this chapter are the reasons why racism continues to persist even though "we should know better." Finally, **anti-racism** strategies are addressed at different action levels. The concept of a holistic (or integrative) anti-racism strategy underscores a key theme of this chapter. Is it possible for people in a multi-layered and deeply divided Canada to live together with their differences when confronted by persistent and pervasive racisms?

THEORIZING RACISM

Liberal racism, aversive racism, "friendly" racism, racism without race, colour-blind racism, experiential racism, democratic racism, reverse racism, enlightened racism, cultural racism, the new racism, and deliberative racism: Judging by the proliferation of terms and references, the profile of racism has expanded exponentially, implying that racism may be the defining issue of contemporary times (Gwyn 2001). Yet prolonged exposure has not translated into consensus. Insofar as references to racism can mean everything, yet nothing—a kind of floating signifier full of sound and sizzle signifying everything yet nothing—efforts to theorize racism will prove to be challenging.

References to racism can span a spectrum, from the openly defamatory to those systemic patterns that unobtrusively confer institutional advantage to some but not others. Racism also includes those subtle and discreet forms that generally escape detection except when experienced by victims (Solomos and Back 1996). Certain types of racism are spontaneously expressed in isolated acts at irregular intervals because of individual impulse or insensitivity. Other expressions of racism are neither spontaneous nor sporadic but systemic and structural, and manifest through discriminatory patterns that inadvertently exclude or exploit. Certain actions are unmistakably racist, others are labelled racist to shut down debate, and still others are defined as racist because of context or consequence. Some see racism as something that individuals do, while others claim racism involves what people don't do. Exaggerating people's difference when irrelevant may be racist, yet ignoring their differences when necessary may prove equally racist. Both infuriating and disorienting, such a range of references can only play havoc with consensus over (1) defining racism, (2) determining its magnitude and scope, and (3) finding effective solutions. Consider the following points of contention:

1. Are incidents of racism and racial conflict increasing across Canada? Or are Canadians more aware of racism and human rights, with a growing willingness to report violations to proper authorities?

2. Is racism a recent introduction into Canada? Or is racism historically and deeply embedded in Canadian history and institutional structures?

3. To what extent is racism a case of individual ignorance or fear? Or should racism be interpreted as a complex array of practices and discourses that are historically defined, embedded within institutional structures, reflective of patterns of power, and woven into an ideological fabric?

4. How valid is the charge that Canada is a racist society? What constitutes a racist society—the existence of racism or a refusal to prevent racism and deal with it when it happens?

5. In what way is racism a "thing" out there? Is it a process involving relationships of inequality? Or is racism an attribute applied to an action after the fact, depending on the context or consequence?

6. Is it possible for individuals to be colour-blind yet stand accused of racism? For some, the taking of differences seriously is critical to challenging racism. For others, the idea of taking differences into account is fundamentally racist.

7. Is there a danger of overusing the word "racism"? Can constant repetition of the "r" word have the effect of trivializing its meaning, specificity, and impact for those who routinely suffer from its presence?

8. Is any criticism directed at people of colour a form of racism by definition? Or is a reluctance to criticize minorities a kind of racism in its own right by implying minority actions are beyond reproach or immune to criticism?

9. Is racism rational or irrational? Many regard racism as essentially irrational in discriminating against others on the basis of physical or cultural characteristics. Others see racism as a "rational" strategy employed by vested interests in competing for scarce resources. Which stance is right?

10. Do all minorities experience racism in the same way, or is racism differently understood and experienced by, say, Asians than black people? Do white people who rarely experience racism see it differently than racialized minorities?

11. Can racism be isolated and analyzed independently? Or must it be seen as constitutive of other forms of exclusion related to class, gender, ethnicity, or sexual preference in ways that intersect and amplify?

Conceptual difficulties are compounded by an indiscriminate use of the word itself. Critical comments directed at Aboriginal peoples or racialized minorities are assumed to be racist. But such thoughtless remarks may more accurately reflect a combination of bad manners, fear, laziness, or ignorance (Wieseltier 1989; Satzewich 1998). Blaming racism for everything when race is irrelevant may be racist in its own right, in part because attention is deflected away from the root causes of minority problems. Used as a smokescreen, racism can foreclose debate by silencing others or diverting attention from the issues at hand.

Such open-endedness in conceptualizing racism reinforces what many already know: Racism refuses to go away even though we should know better or would like it to. Instead, racism has proven notoriously resistant and adaptive—intellectually dead, as many have noted, but never quite interred, and ever primed to reappear during times of stress or anxiety. Racism is proving to be a "scavenger" ideology that parasitically pounces on the most unlikely of sources, bobbing and bending to escape detection, and losing its precision when used loosely and unreflectively to describe a dislike of others (Frederickson 2002). Racism does exist, to be sure, but consensus is elusive and divisive. Certain actions are unmistakably racist; others are labelled racist for political or social reasons; and still other actions become defined as racist because of context, criterion or consequences. Racism has become so expansive in scope and application, with such an array of meanings from context to context, that it no longer conveys a meaning in the conventional sense of a single understood definition (Winant 1998). Accordingly, racism can mean whatever people want it to mean and, while such breadth may prove insightful or empowering, it can also confuse and provoke.

DEFINING RACISM

Definitions of racism have varied and multiplied over time and place. Older theories tended to link racism with a specific set of beliefs and actions, with clearly defined victims and perpetrators. This racism-as-a-thing approach has been replaced by an analysis that increasingly acknowledges the complexity of racism as a contradictory and contingent dynamic (Banton 2000). References to racism are multi-dimensional rather than singular or monolithic (Winant 1998), and this multi-dimensionality is captured by looking at the different ways to define racism. While numerous definitions exist, and it would be exhausting to review even a small portion, definitions of racism can be classified on the basis of key dimensions: as biology, ideology, culture, structure, and power. Phrased differently, definitions of racism have historically revolved around five major themes that can be categorized accordingly: (1) dislike of others because of who they are (racism as biology); (2) dislike of others because of a particular world view (as ideology); (3) dislike of people for what they do (as culture); (4) denial of others that is institutional and institutionalized (as structure); and (5) domination and control over others (as power). To be sure, many definitions incorporate several of these dimensions; after all, references to reality are contextual rather than categorical. Nevertheless, these distinctions may be analytically separated for conceptual purposes.

Racism as Biology: Many definitions of racism are anchored in the root, "race," with its attendant notion that biology is destiny (Jakubowicz et al. 1994). References to *racism as biology* entail a belief in innate differences as socially significant in two ways. First, racism is defined as any belief that links behaviour with biology (biological determinism). Discriminatory treatment of others is then justified on the grounds of innate differences that are natural and fixed. As one prominent scholar in this field has noted in correlating racism with biology:

> [R]acism is an ideology which considers a group's unchangeable physical characteristics to be linked in a direct causal way to psychological or intellectual characteristics, and which on this basis distinguishes between superior and inferior racial groups. (van den Berghe 1967)

Second, racism can be defined as any treatment—either negative or positive—directed at others, solely because of race (or skin colour). To deny or exclude others because of race may be defined as racism. To provide preferential assistance to others because of race is no less racist. In both cases, individuals are singled out for different treatment on the basis of who they are rather than what they need or are entitled to.

Racism as Ideology: Strictly speaking, the concept of race is concerned with perceived differences. Racism, by contrast, transforms these differences into a relatively coherent ideology that justifies the superiority of one group over another. According to race ideology, the human world can be partitioned into a set of fixed and discrete categories of population known as race. Each of these racial categories embraces a distinctive and inherited assemblage of physical, cultural, and psychological characteristics that can be arranged in ascending or descending order of acceptance or desirability. From this emerges an ideology of intellectual or moral superiority—a hierarchy of superior and inferior races that unjustly diminishes others and justifies this discrimination by reference to race. Ideologies in themselves are not necessarily evil or destructive; nevertheless, when wedded to institutionalized power relations, they can inflict injury, including the purging of six million "undesirables" under a Nazi Germany.

Racism as Culture: In recent years, the definitional focus of racism has shifted: References to cultural inferiority are replacing a preoccupation with race (biology) as a basis for definition. Racism is no longer defined as a universal discourse of dominance over racial inferiors as was the case with colonialism. The objective then was to destroy the other as an impediment, to exploit them for gain, or to assimilate them in the name of progress. The issue is no longer about biological dominance, although culture and biology may be fused to essentialize differences within or between groups, but about the danger that foreign cultural practices pose to citizenship, patriotism, and mainstream heritage (Fleras 2004). Dominant sectors are not defined as racially superior but as culturally normal and preferred over those cultural differences that pose a threat to a secular and liberal society. Accordingly, the new colour-blind but culture-conscious racism can be defined as the dislike of the other not only because of who they are, but also because of what they do. In that cultural differences are vilified as dangerous, irrelevant, or inferior, the racialization of culture through claims of cultural superiority is every bit as powerful as racial ideologies in obstructing or excluding.

Racism as Structure: Another set of definitions focuses on racism as structure. This broader definition goes beyond racism as a set of ideas or individual actions, despite the tendency for many to equate racism with extreme acts that incite prejudice, hatred, or violence toward racialized minorities. While such acts are common, equally prevalent are those structural racisms embedded within the broader context of social processes and institutional practices. Reference to racism as structure emphasizes the arrangement of a system of practices and beliefs so that the perpetual disadvantage of one "race" of persons contributes to the privileges of another (Editorial, *Share,* 17 March 2005). This racial bias is wired into the very fabric of society, in effect becoming so normalized that people tend to think of it as natural or inevitable (Kobayashi 2001). Institutions are structured so that power and privilege are transmitted from one generation to the next without much disruption to the status quo. And the system is organized to ensure that even those racialized minorities who succeed confront enormous pressures to conform, with the result that the system becomes self-perpetuating even as the incumbents change.

Racism as Power: Definitions of racism increasingly emphasize the concept of **power**. Racism as power consists of virtually any type of exploitation or exclusion by which the dominant group institutionalizes its privilege at the expense of others (Al-Krenawi and Graham 2003). Power is monopolized by one group of individuals, resulting in the dominance and control over another through a system of ideas, laws, and practices that regulates the aspirations, actions, and livelihood of racialized minorities (Browne 2005). For example, the power differential inherent within an old white boys' network effectively screens out minorities by way of hiring and promoting practices that may unintentionally deny or exclude. Or, as deftly phrased by Christine Silverberg, former chief of the Calgary Police Services (2004):

> [R]acism is not just an overt act of discrimination, or even a series of such incidents, but rather the use of institutional power to deny or grant whole groups of people rights, respect, and representation based on their skin colour.

At its most fundamental, then, racism is about power, not pigmentation (Khayatt 1994). Racism goes beyond individual prejudice but focuses on the manipulation of power to differentiate, categorize, and exclude (Ochocka and Jantzen 2005). Racism is not about differences *per se* but about how those in positions of power can racialize these differences to protect ruling-class privilege. Racism is not about treating others differently because they are different, but the differential treatment of others within contexts of power that limit or oppress (Blauner 1972). Finally, racism is not about manipulating people's attitudes, but about the power to establish agendas regarding what is normal, necessary, desirable, or acceptable, thus reinforcing the superiority of one group over another. bell hooks (1995:154–55) puts racism into perspective by reinforcing the notion that racism is about power when she writes

> Why is it so difficult for many white folks to understand that racism is oppressive not because white folks have prejudicial feelings about black people . . . but because it is a system that promotes domination and subjugation.

One thing is clear from this overview of definitions of racism: Defining racism must go beyond a personal ideology based on race prejudice. Emphasis, instead, must focus on a system of disadvantage founded on institutional power, anchored in values and beliefs, and predicated on a supremacist mindset. Keeping these conditions in mind, we may define racism as *those ideas and ideals (ideology) that assert or imply the superiority of one social group over another because of physical or cultural differences, together with the institutional power to put these beliefs into practice in a way that controls, excludes, or exploits those defined as different or inferior.* This definition is critical in drawing attention to key attributes of racism, namely, its status as an ideology either articulated or implied; a corresponding set of practices that involves deliberate intent or reflects inadvertent consequences; and an impact that embraces both personal and institutional dimensions. Finally, the centrality of power is duly acknowledged. In that racism is about power, and because those with power rarely want to share it with those perceived as inferior, the profile of racism is unlikely to diminish in Canada's foreseeable future.

CONSTITUENTS OF RACISM

Racism does not exist as a monolithic reality. Rather, in a multicultural society, racism is a complex and multi-faceted dynamic constructed around different components. Each of the components or building blocks of racism—namely, prejudice (including ethnocentrism and stereotypes), **discrimination** (including harassment), and power—contributes to the totality of racism as an ideology and practice.

Prejudice

The concept of **prejudice** refers to negative, often unconscious, and preconceived notions about others. Prejudice arises because of a very normal tendency to prejudge persons or situations. As a precondition for processing information about the world out there, there is nothing inherently racist about prejudice. Everyone makes prejudgments when defining situations. Prejudice becomes a problem only when people use these prejudgments to deny or exclude others.

Prejudice consists of *pre+judgments* that are irrational and unfounded on grounds of existing or compelling evidence. A set of generalized attitudes is embraced that mistakenly encourages people to see and judge others without taking into account internal differences

(Holdaway 1996). According to psychologist Frances Aboud, prejudice provides a very simple way of seeing the world, and in a child's mind this craving for simplicity may be transformed into a preference for in-group members (cited in Abel 2001). Such ignorance may persist into adulthood; unlike ignorance, however, prejudice is inflexible and characterized by a refusal to modify beliefs when presented with contrary evidence.

Prejudices come in all shapes and forms. At times, expressions of prejudice are conscious but polite. At other times, individuals may not be aware of their prejudice except in those split second situations that expose dormant dislikes. Tests, such as the Implicit Association Test at **www.tolerance.org/hidden_bias/index.html,** suggest that the vast majority of people have unconscious prejudices that stand in sharp contrast to explicit values of egalitarianism (Banaji 2003; Dow 2003). Just as people don't always "speak their minds," so too do people not "know their minds," culminating in a gap between conscious and unconscious, belief and behaviour. Even those who are strongly committed to egalitarian values and struggle against their own personal prejudices may hold hidden and unconscious biases that may influence their thought and actions (see web link). This notion of prejudice as a kind of "mental residue" should not be discounted as trivial or inconsequential, given its potential to shape attitudes and actions without people being aware that their beliefs and behaviours are being changed (Blank et al. 2004).

Many regard prejudice as a psychological phenomenon with a corresponding set of rigid or authoritarian personality traits (Adorno et al. 1950; Allport 1954). Others link these prejudgments with a visceral and deep-seated fear of those whose appearances, values, or practices threaten a cherished and comfortable status quo. In that prejudice may involve a projection of fear or displacement of anxieties upon others, such beliefs may say more about the perpetrator than the perpetrated (Curtis 1997). Still others define prejudice as unmistakably social. Prejudices neither materialize out of nowhere nor necessarily reflect a warped personality. Rather, prejudice arises from group interaction within unequal contexts. Prejudices are socially constructed as a means for controlling others in contexts involving a competition for scarce resources. Whether intended or not, the social consequences of prejudices have the potential to perpetuate a racialized system that privileges some, while disprivileging others.

Ethnocentrism can be defined as a belief in the superiority of one culture over another. Like prejudice, ethnocentrism is a normal and universal process, reflecting patterns of socialization that focus on generating in-group loyalty. In some cases, a belief in cultural superiority is openly articulated by comparing other cultures or cultural practices with one's own standards of right, acceptable, or desirable. In other cases, ethnocentrism involves the universal tendency to interpret reality from one's cultural perspective as natural and normal—and assume that others are doing so as well—while dismissing other perspectives as inferior or irrelevant.

There is nothing intrinsically wrong with endorsing one's cultural lifestyle as self-evident and preferable. Difficulties arise when these standards are used as a frame of reference for negatively evaluating others as backward, immoral, or irrational. Further problems appear when these ethnocentric judgments are manipulated to condone the mistreatment of others. In other words, ethnocentrism is a two-edged social phenomenon. Favouritism toward one's group may forge in-group cohesion and morale; it can also foster inter-group tension and hostility. And when those in positions of power put their ethnocentrism into practice, the results can get ugly.

Ethnocentrism often leads to a proliferation of stereotypes about out-group members. **Stereotypes** are essentially generalizations about others, both unwarranted and unfounded on the basis of available evidence. Stereotyping reinforces a universal tendency to reduce a complex phenomenon to simple (or simplistic) explanations that can be generalized to a whole category. It reflects an essentialized notion that all individuals within a certain category will act uniformly and predictably because of this membership (Essed 1991). Those who are stereotyped often live up to them, or down to them in the case of underperforming racialized minorities whose outcomes are stigmatized (Steele et al. 2005). Evidence also suggests that people tend to view out-groups as uniformly homogeneous, that is, individuals are lumped together as members of a devalued group rather than valued as individuals with skills and talents.

Like ethnocentrism, stereotypes in themselves are harmless. But problems arise when these preconceived mental images give way to discriminatory practices or generate self-fulfilling practices. And like prejudice, stereotypes are social. Stereotypes do not necessarily represent an error in perception, at least no more so than prejudice is a case of mistaken identity. More accurately, stereotyping is yet another instrument of social control for preserving the prevailing distribution of power and resources, while helping to justify unequal treatment in the past or at present. Consider how the dispossession of Aboriginal people's lands was facilitated through negative images of Aboriginal peoples as savages, cannibals, and brutes. Stereotypes of Eastern Europeans as untrustworthy subversives facilitated the internment of over 5000 Ukrainians in concentration camps during World War I. A pervasive "anti-orientalism" in British Columbia fostered hatred against Asian populations, thereby simplifying the task of expelling 22 000 Japanese-Canadians from the West Coast in 1942. And hostility toward Arab/Muslim-Canadians continues to fester in light of demeaning media stereotypes that portray them as (1) members of a devalued minority who come from "backward" countries, (2) colonized peoples without democratic traditions, and (3) terrorists and religious fanatics who are determined to bury the West (Karim 2002; Goldberg 2005).

All negative stereotypes are hurtful; nevertheless, not all negative portrayals have an equivalent impact. Context and consequence are critical in shaping different outcomes and responses. For example, members of a dominant group need not be unduly concerned with negative stereotyping about themselves; after all, as a group, they have control over a wide range of representations that flatter or empower. Negative stereotypes might cause discomfort for "pale males," yet men as a group possess both the political authority and economic clout to neutralize any damaging effect. In that power and privilege provide a protective buffer, even a constant barrage of negative images can be absorbed without harm or damage. But for minorities with specific vulnerabilities, stereotyping is a problem (Elmasry 1999). Each negative image or unflattering representation reinforces their peripheral status because of power imbalances within society.

Discrimination

The word "discrimination" can be employed in different ways. Non-evaluative meanings indicate a capacity to distinguish (e.g., a colour-blind person may not be able to discriminate [distinguish] between blue and green). Evaluative meanings of discrimination can be used positively (a discriminating palate) or negatively (narrow-mindedness). Section 15 of the *Canadian Charter of Rights and Freedoms* prohibits discrimination on the basis of race, ethnicity, or origins. Yet, the Charter concedes the possibility of seemingly "discriminatory" measures such as employment equity to assist historically disadvantaged minorities. Distinctions are not discriminatory, in other words, if they have a legitimate goal of levelling the playing field.

Discrimination is also permissible if demonstrated to be a bona fide occupational requirement. In brief, some forms of discrimination are acceptable—even essential—to the functioning of a complex and democratic society (MacQueen 1994).

Research, including the Ethnic Diversity Survey (2002) and Statistics Canada census data, points to the reality of discrimination in Canada (Government of Canada, 2005). Up to 36 percent of racialized minorities indicate they have experienced discrimination because of their race or ethnicity, including 50 percent of black people and 33 percent of South Asian and Chinese respondents. This discrimination may be differently expressed—blatant or oblique, individualized or institutionalized, or deliberate or unintended—with the result that motivation behind the act is less important than its effect on the victim (Rusk 2005). Direct discrimination aimed at an entire group represents an open bias that is no longer acceptable, although it may be directed primarily at members of those devalued groups who refuse to assimilate into the mainstream (Yoshino 2006). By contrast, indirect discrimination arises when the outcomes of rules or procedures that apply equally to everybody have the unintended yet controlling effect of denying or excluding others through no fault of their own. The applying of similar rules to unequal contexts may inadvertently but systemically perpetuate discrimination by failing to take differences and disadvantages into account (see also systemic racism). Combining these components—that is, differential treatment and differential effects because of race—produces a working definition along lines proposed by the United Nations (see Editorial, *Share,* 17 March 2005; also Blank et al. 2004): *Discrimination can be defined as any restrictive act, whether deliberate or not, that has the intent or the effect of adversely affecting ("denying" or "excluding") others on grounds other than merit or ability.*

Is there a relationship between prejudice and discrimination? Often "yes," sometimes "no." Prejudice refers to attitudes and beliefs; by contrast, *discrimination* entails a process by which these prejudgments are put into practice. But such a distinction or relationship is neither clear-cut nor causal. Discrimination can exist without prejudice, especially when negative treatment of racialized minorities is deeply and systemically embedded. Thus, institutions can operate on discriminatory grounds even if the individuals themselves are free of prejudice (what is called systemic bias). Conversely, prejudice may flourish without its expression in discrimination. Individuals may be prejudiced, and yet compartmentalize these attitudes by refusing to act in a discriminatory manner for fear of losing face or facing retaliation (what is called polite racism). In brief, prejudice and discrimination are analytically distinct if mutually related concepts can vary independently under certain conditions.

Harassment is commonly appraised as a type of discrimination. Racial harassment consists of persistent and unwelcome actions of a racially oriented nature by those who ought to reasonably know better. In the words of Monique Shebbeare (McGill 1994:6), harassment involves

> [t]he abusive, unfair, or demeaning treatment of a person or group of persons that has the effect or purpose of unreasonably interfering with a person's or group's status or performance or creating a hostile or intimidating working or educational environment. . . .

Like discrimination, harassment constitutes an abuse of institutional power. Seemingly minor and isolated incidents may amount to harassment when viewed over time or within an institutionalized context. The creation of a chilly climate or "poisoned environment" because of harassment can also have an adverse effect on work, study, involvement, or well-being. For some, harassment is ultimately defined from the perspective of the victim who determines what distinguishes offence from harassment, consensual conduct from an abuse of power. Others disagree, and insist on making a principled distinction between harassment and causing offence. Harassment should be restricted to speech or behaviour that habitually targets a particular individual or group in a way that prevents full and equal participation. Merely offending someone because of random ethnic jokes or thoughtless remarks may have the effect of expanding harassment to include everything, yet nothing.

To sum up: There is much to commend in the popular equation—Racism = Prejudice + Discrimination + Power. Racism consists of a complex interplay of ideas and actions, involving a mix of prejudice (stereotyping and ethnocentrism) with discrimination (harassment). Racism also encompasses an ideology with a patterned set of responses that secures the unequal treatment of minorities through political exclusion, economic exploitation, or social segregation. The key element in this equation is power. Those with access to institutional power possess the ability to transform prejudicial attitudes into discriminatory actions. When combined with power, the interplay of prejudice and discrimination creates fertile grounds for racism to thrive.

TYPES OF RACISM

Racism is not a uniform concept that reflects a singular experience or common reality. On the contrary, different types of racism can be discerned that vary in intent, levels of awareness, magnitude and scope, depth of intensity, and consequences. These variations have led to the proliferation of diverse types of racism: (1) interpersonal (including "hate" and "polite"), (2) institutional (including "systematic" and "systemic"), and (3) ideological (including "normative" and "subliminal") (see Table 3.1). Unmasking each of these admittedly ideal types will expose the complex and multi-dimensional nature of racism as theory and practice. Envisaging racism as a rope of many strands should also alert us to the complexity of anti-racist solutions.

Interpersonal

Interpersonal racism entails a pattern of dislike that occurs at the level of interpersonal relations. This dislike is directed at the "other" because of who he is or what she stands for. Two types of interpersonal racism can be discerned: hate and polite.

Hate racism is the kind of racism that most commonly comes to mind. It refers to the old-fashioned (red-necked) hatred of the racialized "other" that once prevailed in the past and continues to exist in the present among a handful of the reactionary or defiant. Intrinsic to hate racism is its explicit and highly personalized character. Hate racism is expressed through sharply personal attacks on those who are perceived as culturally or biologically inferior. These personalized attacks often consist of derogatory slurs and minority name-calling—but physical abuse may also be involved as well as destruction of property through vandalism.

Even a cursory glance over Canada's past exposes the stain of hate racism (Walker 1998). This may come as a shock to many readers. Certain myths are deeply entrenched in

TABLE 3.1	Types of Racism	
Interpersonal	**Institutional**	**Ideological**
hate	systematic	normative
polite	systemic	subliminal

our collective memories, especially those that extol Canada's progressive status, the absence of American-style race riots and prolonged slavery, and the entrenchment of multicultural and human rights principles. Close scrutiny suggests otherwise. Canada's treatment of racial, Aboriginal, and ethnic minorities, since Confederation, has left much to be desired (Backhouse 1999). Chinese, Japanese, Indo-Pakistanis, First Nations, Jews, and black people have been and continue to be the object of dislike or aversion. Laws and practices were invoked that segregated people of colour, especially black people, from full and equal participation in Canadian societies until the 1950s and 1960s (Walker 1998). Racist groups such as the Ku Klux Klan have also relied on naked violence to cultivate an environment of fear and hatred against minorities throughout the United States and Canada (Barrett 1987).

Hate racism continues to flourish in Canada. A hatred of others is perpetuated by white supremacist groups ranging from the White Aryan Nation and Western Guard movements to neo-Nazi skinheads in urban areas (Kinsella 1994; Barkun 1994). Admittedly, there is no way of gauging the number of hard-core supremacists in Canada; nonetheless, even a small number of racist ideologues have the potential to destabilize a society where prejudice is pervasive and the economy is sputtering (Lauder 2002). These groups are committed to an ideology of racial supremacy that asserts the superiority of white people over other races. On the surface, white supremacists may not be explicitly anti-minority, but rather see themselves as white Christians, fusing race and religion in a single nationalist crusade against the forces of evil (Jaret 1995). Toward that end, they are prepared to transform society along white supremacist lines by seeking out converts to their racist cause (Li 1995). Disaffected youth are an obvious target because of perceived government indifference to their plight in a changing and diverse world. The combination of music, pamphlets, disinformation by telephone hotlines, and the Internet (from chat rooms to web sites that offer unique ways of spreading hate (Rajagopal 2006) concocts a poisonous but appealing mishmash of neo-Nazi philosophies, KKK folklore, pseudo-Nordic mythology, and anti-government slogans (Wood 1998; Kinsella 2001).

Polite Racism: Few people at present will tolerate the open expression of racism. Compare this with the past when racism was openly tolerated and socially acceptable. There was no need for pretence; everything was upfront and openly visible (Griffin 1996). The passage of constitutional guarantees such as the *Canadian Charter of Rights and Freedoms* and human rights codes has eroded the legitimacy of hate racism from public discourse. But while blatant forms of racism have dissipated to some extent, less candid expressions of bigotry and stereotyping remain in force. Instead of disappearing in the face of social reprisals and legal sanctions as might have been expected, racism is increasingly couched in a way that allows people to conceal their dislike of others by way of coded language (Wetherell and Potter 1993). In short, racism in Canada tends to be unobtrusive, obliquely couched in the language of political correctness, and coded to confuse.

Polite racism can be defined as a contrived attempt to disguise a dislike of others through behaviour that outwardly is non-prejudicial in appearance. These politely aversive feelings are not expressed through outright hostility or hate, but entail discomfort or unease, often leading to patterns of avoidance rather than intentionally destructive behaviour. It may consist of the "look" that "otherizes" racialized minorities as different and inferior, and out of place in Canadian society. It often manifests itself in the use of coded or euphemistic language (those people) to mask inner feelings behind a facade of gentility (Blauner 1994). This politeness is especially evident when racialized minorities are ignored or turned down for jobs, promotions, or accommodation. For example, when approached by an undesirable applicant, an employer may claim a job is filled rather than admit "no black people need apply." "Sorry, the apartment is rented," when the apartment in question is, in truth, still vacant, is another polite way of rejecting undesirable tenants. Polite racism may appear to be a more sophisticated version than its hate equivalent; nevertheless, the effect on the victims is no less debilitating:

> In some ways I prefer to live in a society where they just say "You're Black, we don't like you." Here in Canada, people are hiding behind a mask. (Kolawole Sofowora, cited in the *Toronto Star*, 2 May, 1999)

Institutional

Other types of racism go beyond the interpersonal in terms of scope, style, and impact. Racism at the institutional level represents such a shift in expression. It is predicated on the assumption that rather than neutral sites that are devoid of agendas or consequences, institutions consist of beliefs and practices that are loaded with cultural assumptions that inadvertently favour some at the expense of others. **Institutional racism** refers to the process by which organizational practices and procedures adversely penalize minority women and men through those rules, procedures, rewards, and practices that have the intent (systematic) or effect (systemic) of excluding or exploiting minorities.

Systematic racism speaks of a racism that directly and deliberately prevents minorities from full and equal institutional involvement. This institutionalized racism appears when discriminatory practices are legally sanctioned by the institution (or the state). This exclusion or exploitation of others is expressed by employees who act on behalf of the organization and with its approval (Milloy 2001). Systematic institutional racism flourished in societies that endorsed racial segregation. The regime of apartheid in South Africa was a classic example, as was the pre–Civil Rights United States. Canada was also tarnished by institutionally racist practices that openly and deliberately denied or excluded. Institutions at present can no longer openly discriminate against minorities, lest they attract negative publicity, face legal action, or incite consumer resistance. Nevertheless, systematic institutional racism continues to exist through discriminatory actions that the corporate culture discreetly endorses. Or organizations may deliberately manipulate rules or procedures to deny or exclude racialized minorities who are seen as bad for business. The revelation that both Denny's Restaurant chain (USA) and Texaco went out of their way to discriminate against African-Americans points to the persistence of systematic racism. The fact that Coca-Cola is being hit with a US$1.5 billion lawsuit for mistreatment of black workers (*National Post,* 16 June 2000) provides additional proof that the more things change, the more they stay the same.

Systemic Racism: There is another type of institutional racism that is impersonal and unconscious, without much awareness of its presence or consequences except, of course, by those who are targeted. Systemic racism is predicated on the belief that institutional rules and procedures can be racist in design, by practice, or in their effects, even if the actors are themselves free of prejudicial discrimination (Canadian Race Relations Foundation 2005). Unlike other forms of racism that are seen as departures from the norm, systemic racism is situated within normal institutional functions. Institutional rules, expectations, and rewards may appear to be universally applicable and ostensibly colour-blind; nevertheless, such a one-size-fits-all neutrality may have a discriminatory impact on those who are different or disadvantaged through no fault of their own. Treating everyone the same when people's differences and disadvantages need to be recognized has the unintended effect of inadvertently excluding those with different needs, goals, and values.

With systemic racism, neither intent nor awareness counts. The context and the consequences are critical as even seemingly neutral policies and programs can have an adverse effect. Institutional rules, priorities, and practices may not be inherently racist or deliberately discriminatory. That is, institutions do not go out of their way to exclude or deprive minorities. But once entrenched within institutions, racism no longer requires intent but is perpetuated by seemingly benign practices and programs (ERACE Racism, 2005). In that disadvantages are inherent within the system because the system itself is socially constructed by those with power and privilege, institutional rules that are evenly applied may have a discriminatory effect when they ignore how organizational practices reflect and reinforce white experiences as normal and necessary. Alternatively, systemic bias may arise because of the logical consequences of well-intentioned policies and initiatives that are based on faulty assumptions, ignore cultural differences, or fail to take context into account (Shkilnyk 1985).

How do mainstream institutions exert a systemic bias against minority women and men? For years, a number of occupations, for example, the police, firefighters, and mass transit drivers, retained minimum weight, height, and educational requirements for job applicants. In retrospect, these criteria may be interpreted as systemically discriminatory because they favoured males over females and white applicants over people of colour. Valid reasons may have existed to justify these restrictions; nevertheless, the imposition of these qualifications inflicted a set of unfair entry restrictions, regardless of intent or rationale. No deliberate attempt was made to exclude anyone; after all, equal standards were uniformly applied. But these criteria have had a controlling effect of excluding racialized minorities who, as a group, lacked the criteria for entry or success *through no fault of their own*. Or consider the systemic bias experienced by migrant agricultural workers from Mexico and the Caribbean who qualify under Canada's Seasonal Agricultural Workers Program. Like all Canadian workers, migrant workers must pay premiums under the *Employment Insurance Act*. However, unlike Canadian workers who don't have to leave the country upon completion of their authorized work terms, migrant workers cannot claim unemployment benefits or sick leave benefits because the Act stipulates that a claimant must be physically in Canada and available for work to receive benefits. In other words, the established rules of the *Employment Insurance Act* when evenly applied to both categories of workers have the effect of excluding migrant workers through no fault of their own. Other examples of systemic racism may include the following: an insistence on Canadian-only experience for new Canadians in search of work; the devaluation of minority experiences and credentials as a precondition for professional employment; unnecessarily high educational standards for entry into certain occupations; entry exams that do not take a candidate's cultural or racial background into account; and other demanding qualifications that discourage membership in professional bodies. Proposals by the Supreme Court of Canada to ban male circumcision as cruelty to male children would be construed as a form of systemic bias by many Jewish people based on the consequences of such a ban for Jewish identity (Weinfeld 2005).

Ideological

Ideological racism constitutes that level of racism that pervades the general functioning of society. Ideological racism points to the prevalence of cultural values and communication patterns in advancing dominant interests as natural and normal at the expense of those who are defined as irrelevant and inferior. In that an ideological racism is controlling, its hegemonic role by way of consensus rather than coercion—by changing people's attitudes without their awareness of these changes—deserves scrutiny. A distinction between the normative and subliminal components of ideological racism is useful. Normative (or everyday) racism consists of unconscious speech habits and everyday actions that have the cumulative effect of demeaning minority women and men. Subliminal (or cultural) racism reflects a largely unconscious bias that cloaks a dislike of others on principled grounds.

Contemporary racism is no longer directly expressed. Instead, more culturally acceptable ways that achieve the same effect without attracting negative attention are preferred (Sirna 1998; also Jonas 2006). Certain ideas and ideals are widely circulated that explicitly or implicitly assert the superiority of some people at the expense of others. **Normative racism** consists of those racist practices that infiltrate everyday life by becoming part of what is accepted as normal by society (Essed 1991). With normative racism, a dislike of others is created and reconstructed through daily actions that are repetitive or routine.

The role of language in perpetuating normative racism is widely recognized (Essed 1991; Wetherell and Potter 1993; Blauner 1994). Many think of language as equivalent to a postal system, namely, a relatively neutral system of conveyance between sender and receiver for the transmission of messages created independently through a process called thinking. In reality, language is intimately bound up with our experiences of the world followed by our efforts to convey that experience to others. Rather than a passive or mechanical transmitter of information, words are "loaded" with values and preferences that define some aspects of reality as normal and acceptable while drawing attention away from other aspects. Words are not neutral; rather they have a political dimension by virtue of conveying negative images beyond what is intended. Ideas and ideals are "trapped inside" language, in effect influencing patterns of thought and behaviour without our awareness. The two-edged nature of language is unmistakable. On the one hand, language can be used to enlighten and inform; and on the other, it can be employed to control, conceal, evade issues, draw attention, or dictate agendas.

Language can be readily manipulated to express intolerance. It possesses the potency to socially construct reality by highlighting differences, enlarging distance, and sanctioning normalcy (Sirna 1998). It may be used to degrade or ridicule minorities, as Robert Moore (1992) demonstrates in his oft-quoted article on racism in the English language, by way of obvious bigotry, colour symbolism (black = bad), loaded terms (Indian massacres), and seemingly neutral phrases that are infused with hidden anxieties (waves of immigrants). Negative meanings may infiltrate everyday speech, as the following passage from Robert Moore (1992) demonstrates:

> Some may blackly (angrily) accuse me of trying to blacken (defame) the English language, to give it a black eye (mark of shame) by writing such black words (hostile) . . . by accusing me of being black-hearted (malevolent), of having a black outlook (pessimistic; dismal) on life, of being a blackguard (scoundrel) which would certainly be a black mark (detrimental fact) against me.

To be sure, the racism implicit in words and metaphors may not be intentional or deliberate. Nor will the occasional use of derogatory words explode into full-blown racism. But while it is inaccurate to say that language determines our reality, it provides a cultural frame of reference for defining what is desirable and important. Language, in short, represents an ideal vehicle for expressing intolerance by highlighting differences or sanctioning inequality through invisible yet real boundaries (Sirna 1998).

A second type of ideological racism—**subliminal racism**—also operates at an unconscious level. Subliminal racism entails a largely unconscious process that reflects a gap between what people say and what they do—between what values they profess to endorse and those they prefer to practice. Subliminal racism is found among that class of persons who openly abhor discriminatory treatment of minorities. Yet, despite ideals, these same individuals are incapable of escaping those biasing blinkers that foster a principled dislike of others because of how they act or what they want. With subliminal racism, individuals may endorse a commitment to the principle of equality; nevertheless, they oppose measures that would remedy the problem of inequality by way of excuses, principles, or values (Henry et al. 2000; Augoustinos and Reynolds 2001). Even those who profess egalitarian attitudes and a commitment to racial equality may not escape contradiction if they don't act on this commitment. After all, the cost of doing nothing to bring about progressive change is not neutrality, but a tacit acceptance of a status quo that is unequal and racialized.

What is distinctive in the expression of subliminal racism? Rather than being directly expressed (hate) or indirectly expressed (polite), subliminal racism is couched in a dislike of others that cloaks this dislike on principled grounds. A general principle is invoked to deny the legitimacy of specific instances (e.g., people may agree with the principle of workplace diversity but reject any special measures to achieve this goal on grounds that it violates Canada's merit principle). The opposition is coded in terms that politely skirt the issue by justifying criticism of minorities or government policy on lofty grounds that appeal to a higher sense of fair play, equality, and justice. To be sure, criticism of racialized minorities is not necessarily racist, and it would be unfair to label critics as such, but the unintended consequences of such criticism may end up reinforcing those very inequality structures that many want eradicated (hooks 1995).

Several examples of subliminal racism come to mind. While Jewish people have long been targets of hate, a new strain of anti-Semitism is increasingly directed not at Jews *per se*, given the social unacceptability of such blatant dislike. The acceptable face of anti-Semitism is aimed not at their perceived wealth or suspect loyalties but at criticism of Israel's policy toward Palestinians, with the result that animus toward Israel may serve as a surrogate for traditional anti-Jewishness (Weinfeld 2005; Endelman 2005; Bunzl 2005). Or consider how Canadians generally are sympathetic toward refugees in distress, but less enamoured with those who are seen as breaking the rules. So-called bogus refugee claimants are not condemned in blunt racist terminology; rather their landed entry into Canada is criticized on procedural, that is, principled grounds like "jumping the queue." Employment equity initiatives may be endorsed in principle but rejected in practice as unfair to the majority (reverse discrimination). Individuals may support a commitment to inclusiveness as a matter of principle, yet disapprove of its implementation because it violates the principle of meritocracy. Support for the principle of equality for minorities may be widely endorsed in principle, but there is deep-seated resentment at the prospect of doing something about it by moving over and making space, especially if it involves costs or inconvenience, or special treatment.

How then to explain the subliminality of this "love–hate" relation toward minorities? Cynics would argue that Canadians are hypocrites whose deep-seated racism is candy-coated by platitudinous pieties. Coded opposition to multiculturalism or immigration is perceived as more acceptable than brazen expressions of intolerance (Palmer 1996). A subliminal racism allows a dislike of others a veneer of respectability by adopting the sombre tones of Canadian values or the phony language of "racial separatism" or "reverse discrimination" (Ansley 2004). Yet, subliminal racism differs from polite racism precisely because it involves a clash of competing values. The paradox is palpable: On one side, belief in the innate inferiority of minorities is eroding because of growing support for the principle of racial and ethnic inequality. On the other side, there remains a reluctance to support policies and programs for equality despite growing inequities (see also Brezina and Winder 2003). The lack of support for "closing the gaps" is rationalized on principled grounds, a rationalization that exposes a disconnect between core values. Two apparently conflicting value systems are at play. One is rooted in the egalitarian virtues of justice and fairness, including preferential treatment for those disadvantaged through no fault of their own. The other is rooted in an equalitarian belief that, because everyone is equal before the law, everyone should play by the same rules applied equally to everyone with no exception. The conflict between these cultural values—a principled gap between what people say and what they are willing to do—puts subliminal racism in a distinct category (Katz et al. 1986; Henry and Tator 2006).

To sum up: That racism in one form or another exists in Canada is surely beyond debate at this point in our history. With the benefit of some prodding and sharp reminders, Canadians are increasingly facing up to our checkered past, with its bewildering mixture of tolerance and repression. Canada was founded on racist principles and continues to be racialized in consequence if not intent, despite a tendency toward collective denial and historical amnesia (Razack 2004). Some forms of racism are now widely condemned and detested, even by those who are indifferent toward diversity. Other varieties of racism continue to be endemic to Canada, with few signs of easing up or disappearing. The threat of social condemnation may have propelled racism to go underground or redefine itself in seemingly more innocuous ways.

EXPLAINING RACISM

Racism costs all Canadians: An environment is fostered where existing prejudices are articulated, legitimized, and defended as a basis for white privilege (McKenna 1994). Mixed messages are conveyed that often contradict the ideals of a socially progressive society, in part by perpetuating inequality despite Canada's constitutionally protected human rights code. As well, racism diminishes the number of people who can contribute to Canada, whilst useless energy is expended that otherwise could be funnelled into more productive channels. Finally, institutions that cannot capitalize on a diverse workforce because of racism are destined to lose their competitive edge in the global marketplace. The end result is nothing less than a blot upon Canadian society because of the capacity of racism to squander our potential and reputation as a progressive and prosperous country.

The costs of racism are absorbed unevenly across society, with some capitalizing on racism as a basis for preserving privilege or power while others suffer (Bonnett 2000). Racialized minorities live in perpetual fear of physical retaliation; they experience a loss of personal security that, in turn, intensifies isolation and self-defensive behaviours. They endure a restricted set of economic and social opportunities, and their self-worth is diminished by a constant barrage of negative media messages. Exposure to racism may contribute to the poor health of minority women and men—with corresponding pressure on Canada's much beleaguered health care system (Maioni 2003; Picard 2005). Similarly, in the United States, the stress, physical illnesses, and other injuries associated with racism constitute a serious public health problem for black people whose life expectancy remains seven years less than an American born white (Feagin 2005).

Why, then, does racism exist if it comes with such costs? What are its causes? Do we look to biology, culture, social structure, or personality as the major sources? Should it be defined as a disease, a bad habit, a conspiratorial plot, a cultural blind spot, a structural flaw, a historical act, or a relic from the past? Why does it persist despite widespread disapproval of a practice at odds with the realities of a modern society? How to explain its persistence in the face of government initiatives to condemn, curb, and control? Is it because of fear, greed, ignorance, or arrogance? Is it because of societal inertia or public disinterest, irrespective of its dysfunctional effects on society, or is it because racism is so embedded within the institutional structures of society that trying to eradicate it may prove unlikely?

Some attribute the pervasiveness of racism to our biogenetic hardwiring from an evolutionary past. A fear of outsiders elicited a survival response in uncertain environments that continues to operate in the present so that recoiling from what is different seems only natural. This visceral dislike of out-groups may explain the universality of racism. Others see racism as the by-product of ignorance of the unknown because of improper socialization. Improving people's knowledge about diversity will gradually diminish the spectre of racism. Others believe that racism persists because of its psychological benefits. Racism has a way of making the mainstream feel good about itself in part by bolstering a collective self-image of superiority. This notion of racism as "functional" for white people is captured in these words by Julian Bond of the NAACP (National Association for the Advancement of Colored People) when referring to the tenacity of white supremacist racism (White 1999:25):

> It's still white supremacy. It still means so much to those who practice it. It defines who they are. It makes them feel that they are better than others. It ensures them positions in employment and college admissions they otherwise might not have. It still puts a lid on the dreams of black people.

Each of these explanations of racism is partially valid. But reference to racism as a function of biology or psychology cannot be divorced from sociological analyses. With the possible exception of sociobiologists (see van den Berghe 1981), most sociologists would argue that individuals are not biologically programmed to act in a racist manner. There are no genes that express themselves in racial discrimination. No compelling reason exists to believe that people are genetically hardwired with a propensity to hate. Nor does racism exist solely in the minds of poorly socialized individuals. Rather than an error of perception or belief, people are conditioned to be racist by environments that foster ethnocentrism, out-group antipathy, and racism. They are conditioned to be racist as part of a broader process of social control for preserving the status quo in complex societies. Racism, in short, provides simple but effective explanations to justify why people get what they deserve or deserve what they get.

For many, racism is rooted in the material conditions of social life (Bolaria and Li 1988; Satzewich 1998). Neither a transient phenomenon nor an anomalous and unpredictable feature, racism in Canada is deeply rooted in Canada's historical and economic development, embedded within the institutional structures of an unequal society, endemic to core Canadian values, and integral to Canada-building. Historically, Canada's economic well-being and standard of living were facilitated by a racism toward those that helped build the railways, settle the west, extract timber and mineral resources, and work the assembly lines. Canada's quality of life continues to be supported by racialized minorities who are employed in low-paying jobs to ensure cheaper goods and services (Bishop 2005). Racialized minorities are expected to provide low-wage labour and work in unsafe conditions because of our demand for cheap goods and inexpensive services. Exploitation of such a magnitude makes it doubly important for the privileged to examine their role in advancing advantage for themselves at the expense of others.

In short, racism originated and continues to persist within a capitalist Canada because of its usefulness in advancing class interests (Bolaria and Li 1988). Racist ideologies were and continue to be employed for securing ready access to a cheap and disposable labour supply; to destabilize labour movements by undermining any potential show of unity or strength; and to justify intrusive devices for controlling troublesome minorities. The conclusion seems inescapable: Racism flourishes because of its controlling functions in support of ruling-class interests. Rather than a departure from the norm, racism persists because it supports a system designed to augment prevailing patterns of power and privilege. However unconsciously, those in positions of power will do anything to preserve privilege in the competition for scarce resources. Sowing the seeds of racism provides this advantage without drawing unnecessary attention to the contradictions and dysfunctions within the system (Galabuzi 2006).

The evidence is compelling: Racism is not a departure from society and its ideals—a kind of irrational or dysfunctional feature of an otherwise rational and sound system—but a true expression of them. Not surprisingly, explanations of the origins and persistence of racism continue to miss the mark. Instead of asking, "Why does racism exist?" we should ask, "Why shouldn't racism exist in light of societal and institutional pressures for preserving privilege, power, and property?" Rephrasing the question in this way not only alters our approach to solutions, but also confirms that racism cannot be understood apart from the social, cultural, economic, and political context in which it is embedded and nourished. That, in turn, raises the question of whether Canada is a racist society.

| INSIGHT | Is Canada a Racist Society? |

Is Canada a racist society? If so, what constitutes a racist society? Who says so, why, and on what grounds? Are Canadians racist? Is a racist society the same as a society of racists? How attainable is a non-racist society? Answers to these questions are complex and problematic, yet must be confronted in advancing the ideal of "erasing" racism. Coming to grips with the nature and magnitude of racism in Canada is hardly an idle intellectual exercise, but a sense of perspective is required. It has been said that the smallest misdemeanour in a society of saints would be sufficient to inflict capital punishment (Levitt 1997). In societies where hatred toward others is the norm, even the most egregious forms of racial violence often go unnoticed or unpunished. In a society such as Canada, where racism and racial intolerance are socially and legally unacceptable, the slightest provocation is cause for public remorse or vigorous rebuke. And it is precisely these high standards that complicate any assessment.

For some, Canada is an inherently racist society in design and outcomes, with a thin veneer of tolerance that camouflages a pervasive white superiority complex (Lian and Matthews 1998; Alfred 1999). A highly respected academic and activist from Queen's University has also claimed that "we live in a racist society" (cited in the *Kingston Whig-Standard,* 13 June 2003). For others, Canada is a fundamentally sound society with a few bad apples to spoil the barrel. Raymond Chan, the former Minister of State for Multiculturalism, has described Canada as the least racist society in the world, although not perfect by any stretch of the imagination (Canadian Press, 15 March 2005; also Seiler 2002). For still others, perceptions of racism in Canada depend on where one stands in the wider scheme of things. While many white people are inclined to see racism as an irrational aberration from the normal functioning of society, racialized minorities tend to see racism as institutionalized within Canada's existing framework. And others argue still that references to racism depend on how the concept is defined.

Which interpretation is more correct? Responses are more difficult than appearances suggest. Consider some of the difficulties in making this assertion. First, what is meant by the word "racism" when applied to Canadian society? Is racism about race, biology, culture, ideology, structure, or power? Is racism manifest at interpersonal, institutional, or ideological levels? Is racism about treating people differently or treating everyone the same regardless of their differences? Is a racist someone who openly inflicts harm on minorities, or a person whose passivity and indifference reinforce the marginality of minority women and men? Is a racist someone who proudly vilifies the other as inferior or irrelevant, or a person who claims to be colour blind yet uncritically embraces "whitestream" point of view as necessary and normal, while dismissing others? Some would even say that all mainstream Canadians are racist by virtue of being normal in a racialized society. Disproportional benefits are derived from simple involvement in institutions, values, and structures that systemically exclude some, but privilege others.

Second, how do we measure the concept of "a racist society" (Fleras and Spoonley 1999)? Is a racist society based on a minimum number of racial incidents per year, or should we look more closely at systemic biases that inadvertently perpetuate a racialized social order? Too much of what constitutes a so-called racist society is based on surveys that measure racially related incidents. But surveys and statistical measures have inherent drawbacks (Blank et al. 2004). Surveys cannot reveal the ratio of reported to unreported acts. Increases in the number of reported acts may not reflect more incidents, but rather a greater public awareness of racism, along with an increased willingness to do something about it by pressing charges or utilizing a hate-crime hotline with an 800 number. Statistical measures have additional weaknesses. Pollsters are cautious about drawing sweeping conclusions from a few survey questions on racism. According to Donald Taylor of McGill University, polls are a crude measure of public attitudes because of their superficiality in diagnosing complex problems. Intolerance is difficult to measure because of the responders' reluctance to answer truthfully for fear of blowing their cover.

Third, what constitutes a "racist society"? Logic suggests a racist society is one in which racism is institutionalized insofar as it is (1) supported by cultural values, (2) expressed through widely accepted norms, (3) tacitly approved by the state or government, (4) intrusive in many interpersonal relations, (5) codified into laws that openly discriminate against minorities, and (6) prone to exclude minorities from equal participation as part of the normal functioning of society (Aguirre and Turner 1995). With a racist society, prejudice toward others is institutionally entrenched, while formal boundaries are drawn around racialized groups to ensure the separation of the haves from the have-nots. Finally, racist societies are those that do nothing to prevent the outbreak of racist incidents at individual or institutional levels; even less is done to deal with these violations when they occur.

According to these criteria, South Africa would have qualified as a racist society.

Under an official apartheid, a system of race-based segregation was introduced that separated white people from black people, including an archipelago of homelands that surrounded South Africa. Black people were cruelly exploited as miners or domestics, thereby securing power and privilege for the white ruling class. As well, both the United States and Canada could have been defined as racist societies prior to the mid-1950s, thanks to the colour bars that segregated black people to ensure the preservation of white privilege (Horton and Horton 2004). At present, however, the situation is much different. Canada possesses human rights legislation, criminal codes against racial hatred, and sentencing procedures that more severely punish hate crimes. It is also committed to the principles of a multicultural and inclusive society, including a $56 million anti-racism action plan to be applied to the departments of Labour, Immigration, Justice, and Multiculturalism (Government of Canada 2005). Of course, racism exists in Canada, both at the individual level and institutionally, as well as openly and covertly. But saying there is racism and there are racists in Canada is not the same as saying that Canada is a racist society. On these grounds, Canada can no longer be regarded as a racist society, as was once the case in our not-too-distant past. But is that the entire story?

However enlightened and empowering this assessment, it might be a bit premature to uncork the celebratory champagne. Canadians may not be racists in the blatant sense of unfurling swastikas and burning crosses. Rather, racism in Canadian society is increasingly covert, embedded in normal operations of institutions, and beyond the direct discourse of racial terminology. The language, values, and institutions that predominate in Canada have a distinctly racial connotation that makes them exclusionary, synonymous with whiteness, and racist in consequences (see also Gilroy 2004). Racism in Canada may be entrenched within the foundational principles whose unquestioned assumptions continue to govern Canada's colonial constitutional order (Maaka and Fleras 2005). As Sandra Lipsitz Bem (1994) observes, just as female differences are transformed into female disadvantages in a male-centred world, so too are minority differences defined as disadvantageous in a white-o-centric world. The society we live in is designed and organized (both deliberately and inadvertently) in a way that reflects, reinforces, and advances white experiences and mainstream interests, thus transforming racialized differences into minority disadvantage. For instance, Canada's espousal of liberal universalism constitutes a foundational principle that privileges **Eurocentric** values and institutions as natural and superior rather than seeing them for what they really are: white standards and mainstream norms that masquerade as colour-blind principles. Finally, Canada may be defined as a racist society because its racism is deeply embedded in Canada's colonial history, embodied in those institutional rules and practices that normalize "pale male" privilege, and woven into the language, laws, and rules of Canadian society—each of which may have the unwitting effect rather than deliberate intent of perpetuating a racially based (racialized) status quo. Inasmuch as mainstream values and institutions may "inadvertently" advantage some as normal, necessary, and superior, while minority experiences and alternatives are dismissed accordingly, references to Canada as a racist society cannot be casually dismissed.

ANTI-RACISM

> Power concedes nothing without a demand, it never did, and it never will. Find out just what people will submit to, and you have found the exact amount of injustice and wrong, which will be imposed upon them; and these will continue until they are resisted with either words or blows, or with both. The limits of tyrants are prescribed by the endurance of those whom they oppress.
> (Frederick Douglas, Abolitionist Leader and Former Slave, 1857)

Most Canadians are no longer racists in the classic sense of blatantly vilifying minority women and men. The days are gone of openly denying and excluding others because of appearances. These "bad old days" are unlikely to return in light of numerous checks and balances to prevent a repeat of such an occurrence in Canada. Yet, racism continues to exist in unobtrusive ways, deliberately or unconsciously, by way of action or inaction. Racism is rarely experienced in immediate and obvious ways, but through constant and cumulative impact of demeaning incidents that quietly accumulate day by day into a "ton of feathers." That knowledge alone puts the onus on Canadians to do something about it (Bishop 2005). As Tim Wise (1999:17), a renowned American anti-racism educator, puts it:

> [T]hose persons called "white" have a particular obligation to fight racism because it's *ours* [emphasis added], created in its modern form by us, for the purpose of commanding power over resources and opportunities at the expense of people of color. Furthermore all whites . . . have to address the internalized beliefs about white supremacy from which we all suffer. No one is unaffected by the daily socialization to which we are all subjected—specifically with regard to the way we are taught to think about persons of color in this society.

Most of us would agree: To do something to someone because of their skin colour is racism and something should be done about it. But doing nothing to confront racial discrimination may be no less racist; after all, fence-sitting (through inactivity or silence) is not impartiality or neutrality but tacit acceptance of a racialized and unequal status quo. The only option is to do something; otherwise one may be accused of being part of the problem rather than part of the solution.

The range of activities that openly challenge racism fall under the broad category of anti-racism. **Anti-racism** can be defined as the process that challenges racism through direct action (see also Dei 1996; Bonnett 2000). Anti-racism entails active involvement in changing those cultural values, personal prejudices, discriminatory behaviour, and institutional structures of society that perpetuate racism. Two levels of anti-racist strategy can be discerned: interpersonal and institutional. One is concerned with modifying individual behaviour through law, education, or interaction; the other with removal of discriminatory structural barriers by challenging the structural and systemic roots of racism. Combining both creates the possibility of a more holistic anti-racism.

Individual Anti-Racism

Taken at its most obvious level, racism is normally envisaged as a personal problem of hatred or ignorance. There is an element of truth to this assertion. Racism is often expressed through the thoughts and actions of individuals who dislike others because they are different or threatening. Thus anti-racist strategies tend to focus on modifying defective attitudes related to prejudice, ethnocentrism, and stereotyping. Three of the more common personal anti-racist strategies for improvement are *interaction, education,* and *law.*

Learning through contact and interaction represents one technique for individual anti-racism change. Interaction with others is proposed for removing barriers that stem from ignorance or fear. Lack of knowledge is replaced with mutually reinforcing understanding. But contact in its own right is not necessarily beneficial. It is doubtful whether racism is reduced by the thousands of tourists who escape to the Caribbean each winter. Improvement is unlikely in contexts where interactional patterns tend to reinforce the gap between the haves and have-nots. Under these potentially degrading circumstances, the degree of resentment and contempt escalates in tune with the reconstituting of colonialist patterns of servitude and deference.

Reducing racism through interaction varies with the quality of the interactional setting. For any positive effect, interaction must be conducted between individuals who are relatively equal in status, who collaborate on a common endeavour in a spirit of trust and respect, whose interaction receives some degree of institutional and societal support, and who derive mutual benefit from co-operation of sufficient frequency and duration to foster a working relationship (Jaret 1995). Interaction between unequals outside a supportive context simply upholds the status quo by perpetuating stereotypes in a negatively charged environment.

It is widely assumed that education can reduce racism. According to this line of thinking, racism arises when individuals are locked into ignorance or irrational beliefs; thus the cure lies in educating people to realize the errors of their ways. Once aware of their mistakes, people are deemed sufficiently rational to make the appropriate adjustments. This notion of enlightenment through learning has put schools in the vanguard of institutions for challenging racism. Milder versions of multicultural education propose modifying individual attitudes through exposure to diversity. Yet, there are difficulties in defending the transformative properties of education in challenging racism. Gloria Yamato (2001) captures the futility of quick-fix solutions to a problem that has taken centuries to grow, take root, invade space, and morph into variations:

> Many believe that racism can be dealt with effectively in one hellifying workshop, or one hour long heated discussion . . . I've run into folks who really think that we can beat this devil, kick this habit, be healed of this disease in a snap. In a sincere blink of a well-intentioned eye, presto—poof—racism disappears. "I've dealt with my racism . . . (envision a laying on of hands) . . . Hallelujah! Now I can go to the beach." Well fine, go to the beach.

Harder versions of multicultural education encourage individuals to look inside themselves, to examine their own racism and privileged positions, to see how the dominant sector exercises power over racialized minorities, and to take responsibility for the disempowerment of others (McIntosh 1988). Admittedly, most white people can see and sympathize with victims of racism, yet most are incapable of seeing the benefits and advantages associated with whiteness. They are equally reluctant to see how their privilege is directly and structurally connected with the disempowerment and exploitation of those at the wrong end of racism (Bishop 2005). In other words, people need to be educated about whiteness as the engine that drives racism, and Yamato (2001:153) provides some hard-hitting educational guidelines for white folk in the anti-racism struggle when she writes:

> You can educate yourself via research and observation rather than rigidly, arrogantly relying solely on interrogating people of color. Do not expect that people of color should teach you how to behave non-oppressively . . . Know that you'll make mistakes and commit yourself to correcting them and continuing on as an ally, no matter what. Don't give up.

Recourse to law is sometimes upheld as an effective personal deterrent. Laws exist in Canada that prohibit the expression of racial discrimination against vulnerable minorities. The scope of these laws is broad. Some legal measures consist of protection for identifiable minorities through restrictions on majority behaviour. For example, the Supreme Court of Canada has ruled repeatedly that prohibition of hate literature is a justifiable and reasonable limitation on the freedom of speech. Other measures are aimed at removing discriminatory barriers that preclude minority participation within society. On the assumption that most individuals are law abiding because of the threat of punishment or social ostracism, passage of anti-racist laws focuses on outward compliance with the letter of the law—if not personal conviction. Passage of these and related laws is not intended to alter people's attitudes, at least not in the short run. A democratic society such as ours entitles people to their own private thoughts, however repugnant or anti-social. Over time, however, people may realign their beliefs to match behaviour in hopes of reducing the dissonance between thought and action.

Institutional Anti-Racism

There is room for cautious optimism when discussing the effectiveness of individually tailored anti-racist programs. But are these initiatives of sufficient scope to erase racism? Racism may be expressed in and through people (who may be regarded as precipitating causes), but individuals are merely the conduits of racial antipathy. It is the social context that counts. Are the structures of society amenable to reform through personal transformation? Personal solutions such as anti-racist training are comparable to applying a bandage to a cancerous growth—compassionate and humane to be sure, but ultimately self-defeating in light of the magnitude of the disease.

With individual anti-racism, the symptoms are addressed, not the cause or source. Racism can be resolved only by attacking it at its source, namely, within the institutional structures that support a capitalist society. Racism is not just about individuals with regressive beliefs or dormant prejudices. It is rooted in institutional structures that provide justifying ideologies and practices in those contexts where the social order is organized (racialized) around the placement of minorities in racial categories (Bonilla-Silva 1996). The problem of racism must be addressed within the wider confines of political domination and economic control. This institutional approach will entail a different set of assumptions and tactics than those focusing on personal initiatives. Tactics may include fighting racist hate groups, direct action through protest or civil disobedience, boycotts, litigation, or legislation (Jaret 1995).

Toward a Holistic Anti-Racism

It is relatively easy to define racism as a personal problem. Common sense dictates that people are the cause of racism. As individuals, people must reflect critically upon our degree of complicity in perpetuating racism through daily actions. But it is equally tempting to situate racism within a system of vast and impersonal forces that are largely beyond individual control. Such an approach runs the risk of absolving individuals of any responsibility. Neither of these positions is entirely correct. Individuals may not be the root cause of racism; nevertheless, racism is located within and carried by the person. Systems may generate root causes; nonetheless, institutions do not exist apart from individuals who interact to create, support, maintain, and transform patterns of racism. Each of us must be held accountable for our actions, no matter how powerful the social context in which we find ourselves.

Only a holistic anti-racism approach can deliver the goods with any hope of success. Holistic anti-racist strategies acknowledge as source and solution the interplay of social forces and individual experiences. In rejecting an either/or approach for a both/and perspective with its embrace of contextuality, connectedness, and simultaneity of unequal relations, an integrative anti-racism acknowledges the interplay of structure with agency (Dei 2005). A holistic anti-racism also recognizes the interlocking nature of racism (Bishop 2005). Racialized minorities do not find themselves excluded because of race or class or gender. Rather each of these "jeopardies" intersects with the other to amplify overlapping patterns of exclusion and denial. As well, a holistic approach accepts the importance of looking at racism within the broader context of globalization and global capitalism (Sivanandan 2005). What can we conclude? The interdependence of race, class, and gender as intertwined strands of a wider, more complex, and self-perpetuating system of privilege and power makes it abundantly clear: The purging of racism must be confronted holistically if we want to create an inclusive society based on the principle of "living together differently."

DEBATE REVISITED	**A Few Bad Apples or a Rotten Institutional Barrel?**

Reactions to allegations of police racial profiling have varied: Some said no, never; others said yes, always; and still others said maybe, but only occasionally. Police authorities at both local and provincial levels vehemently denied the existence of racial **profiling**—either as principle or practice (Perkel 2002). As far as the police are concerned, only criminal behaviour is profiled regardless of skin colour (Di Matteo 2002). If black people are over-represented in crime statistics, according to this line of thinking, it is because they engage in actions that are more likely to bring them into contact with the law. For example, black people may comprise only 8 percent of Toronto's population, but they are charged with 27 percent of the violent offences in the city (Blatchford 2002). Moreover, insofar as profiling persists, critics argue, it represents a necessary if unfortunate by-product of sensible policing. After all, police are in the business of stopping people, and all modern police work is grounded on the principle of preventing crime through proactive policing, including more extensive surveillance of people's movements in high crime areas (Closs 2003). The fact that police are trained to use their intuition and experience in enforcing the law enhances the likelihood of targeting those perceived as the "usual suspects."

Opposed to this denial was the reaction of academics (Henry and Tator 2002), anti-racist organizations, and members of the black community (Smith 2004; Brown 2004), including an ad hoc coalition of organizations and individuals named the African Canadian Community Coalition against Racial Profiling. Each supported the findings of the *Toronto Star* as consistent with what black male youth have long proclaimed: *Police tend to stop who they see rather than what they see* (Hurst 2003). Similarly, parents in Montreal have complained that the police are criminalizing race, youth, and poverty disproportionately because of a zero-tolerance policy against incivilities, with its disproportionate adverse impact on black and brown men. In the words of one anguished and angry parent, "There is no greater pain or anger than seeing your son being treated like an animal by the very people who are paid by your tax dollars to serve and protect you" (Press release, Mothers United against Racism, 16 May 2005).

On too many occasions, crime and race are linked because of profiling. The real danger occurs when profiling goes beyond personal prejudice to form the basis for public policy—from an undesirable social practice to infringing the civil rights of specific populations (Muharrar 2005). Once a problem is racialized by profiling, it encourages suspicion, and typically induces a stigmatizing of a racial group for punitive treatment. Too many police presume that people with dark skin colour are more likely to be criminals (or worth checking out), resulting in selective police stops and searches that can prove an embarrassing inconvenience for some or humiliating experiences for others (Stone 2005). This projection is consistent with a kind of social blindness that judges racialized groups by the unlawful conduct of a small number of wrongdoers who call attention to themselves, while ignoring the vast majority who conduct themselves lawfully (Coyle 2004). For black people, then, racism is a lot worse than what many white people believe. Racism is such a pervasive reality in their daily lives that Hon. Lincoln Alexander, former lieutenant governor of Ontario and chair of a police-minority summit meeting, observed, "Racism is everywhere." "There's racism all over the bloody place" (cited in Duncanson 2003:A16).

So what is going on, and who is right (Wortley 2005)? Put bluntly, the police deny they racially profile; racialized minorities believe they do on a regular basis. This perceptual gap was nicely captured by one senior police official who proclaimed, "You think we profile, we think we don't"

(cited in Hurst 2003). Each racialized group not only sees different types of racisms, but the magnitude and scope varies as well, with white people acknowledging the possibility of a "few bad apples" while minorities define discrimination as "rotten to the core" with the bad apples a sign of the rot in progress. Reference to the Rashomon effect may explain the disparity in police and black responses to the crisis. According to the Rashomon effect, one's social location in society will shape what you see, think, or experience, in addition to how others will relate to you on the basis of their perceptions. For example, senior police officials who rarely encounter any discrimination because of their whiteness, power, and affluence tend to underestimate the magnitude and scope of racism. Their privileged status diminishes the possibility of being discriminated against because of race or ethnicity. Not surprisingly, those unlikely to be victims tend to underrate the scope and pervasiveness of racism, restricting its presence to a "few bad apples" who can be rehabilitated through sensitivity training.

By contrast, black people and minorities may emphasize the extent and intensity of racism because of their visibility, powerlessness, and poverty. Police racism is institutional and part of the structure of the "whole rotten barrel" because of routine practices that draw attention to some aspects of reality, but not others. In generating arrests from random stops, strips, and searches, this racism amounts to little more than institutionalized harassment as police use their authority to "over-police" those street crimes where visibility becomes a factor. To the extent that those with less power may read situations more "accurately" because their survival depends on better understanding and assessment of a situation (Bishop 2005), there is much of value in this perspective.

What to do? The rightness or wrongness of each position is less relevant than the need to address minority perceptions. If the police are to regain the trust of disaffected minority youth, they must acknowledge perceptual realities by going beyond denial or trivialization (Closs 2003). Or as put by Kingston Police Chief Bill Closs (2003), in urging officers to better understand the implications of pulling over a person of colour,

> Visible minorities may have been victims of racism and discrimination in the past, so police training must foster an understanding that, when members of visible minorities are stopped and interrogated of crime they did not commit, the police should anticipate that police motives may be questioned.

Such an assertion does not imply that police are racist. Nevertheless, the perception of police profiling must be addressed since perceptions *are* reality when it comes to justice and fairness (i.e., justice must be seen to be done). The reality of perceptions creates such a climate of distrust toward police that minority communities become unpoliceable, thus fostering those very conditions that justify an even more invasive police presence. Nor does reference to a Rashomon effect exonerate police services of blame. Just because senior management rejects the practice of police profiling, there is no guarantee of compliance by the rank and file. Racism exists because race is frequently a factor in making discretionary judgments; only its scale and kind is open to debate. As the Ontario Court of Appeal concluded, the attitude underlying police profiling may be largely unconscious, that is, police officers are not necessarily openly racist as their conduct may reflect unconscious racial stereotyping (Canadian Press, 20 April 2003).

The analysis of the problem is one thing. Doing something about it is a lot tougher as solutions must connect with a problem definition. If the problem of profiling is the result of a few maverick officers, then the focus must be on attitude change through consciousness raising. If the problem is organizational, then institutional changes are necessary that focus on rules, priorities, and agendas. If the problem is a function of the job, it may be time to rethink the very concept of policing in a multicultural society. Policing in the twenty-first century may not be conducive to a "thin blue line" mindset (us vs. them) and militaristic structure and culture. Or perhaps the problem is societal? Race is not a determining factor in accounting for criminal activity. Rather the real culprits are social problems beyond the scope of policing, including poverty, powerlessness, dysfunctional families, derelict housing, availability of guns and drugs, inadequate supports, cultural values, lifestyle habits, and immigration patterns that separate parents from children over long periods of time (James 2002).

The last word belongs to Royson James, a columnist with the *Toronto Star* who put racial profiling into a perspective that many Canadians can relate to. When he watches his son or daughter drive a car, the parent in him worries that his son might get into trouble for no other reason than driving while black (DWB). If stopped, the police may prove more of a trigger than a tonic by making a bad situation even worse. I too worry when our sons drive off. But as a white parent my gut reaction is quite the opposite: Should they get into trouble with the law because of their misjudgments, I naturally assume the police are there to help. The Rashomon effect could not be more forcefully profiled.

CHAPTER HIGHLIGHTS

- Racism exists and has always existed in Canada, although its magnitude and scope as well as depth and intensity have varied over time. Unmasking the many faces of racism, both past and present, is the central theme of the chapter.
- Racism is not only about individual prejudice but is also a structural feature of society in which power, privilege and resources are distributed unequally among socially different groups.
- Definitions of racism fall into five main categories: racism as race, racism as ideology, racism as culture, racism as structure, and racism as power.
- In addition to prejudice, racism includes a behavioural component involving discriminatory practices that deny or exclude. Power underpins all forms of racism: without it, racism is indistinguishable from a host of negative attitudes and practices.
- The many faces of racism include (1) interpersonal (hate, polite), (2) institutional (systematic, systemic), and (3) ideological (normative, subliminal). The different types of racism can be compared on the basis of intent, awareness, and intensity.
- A variety of social and psychological explanations may account for the pervasiveness of racism in Canada. It is suggested that racism persists as it provides "positive" functions for some in a society organized around the principles of profit and white privilege.
- Anti-racism is concerned with the elimination of racism through direct action at personal and institutional levels.

KEY TERMS

anti-racism	polite racism
discrimination	power
ethnocentrism	prejudice
Eurocentric	profiling
harassment	stereotypes
hate racism	subliminal racism
ideological racism	systematic racism
institutional racism	systemic racism
normative racism	

REVIEW QUESTIONS

1. Compare and contrast the different types of racism that have been discussed in terms of degree of intent, level of awareness, and style of expression.
2. Discuss whether or not you think Canada is or is not a racist society. Use specific examples to support your answer.
3. It has been said that all white people are racists (and vice versa), and that if you are white and living in Canada or the United States the odds are that you are a racist regardless of your socio-economic status (Sue 2003). Explain the thinking behind this line of argument (include references to whiteness study). Do you agree or disagree? Why?
4. How do we explain the persistence of racism? Be sure to emphasize the social dimensions in your answer.
5. Compare the strategies of anti-racism at the personal level versus the institutional level in terms of underlying assumptions, means, and anticipated outcomes.

LINKS AND RECOMMENDATIONS

Films

The Birth of a Nation (1915)

A classic in filmmaking by D.W. Griffith, but disturbing in its content because it reflected widespread perceptions about race and racism during this era. The demeaning portrayal of black people is matched only by the triumphalist view of the Ku Klux Klan in rescuing the post–Civil War South from carpetbaggers and freed slaves.

Crash (2005)

The film pulls no punches: Everything and everybody is implicated in both polite and not-so-polite racism, either as victimized or victimizer. Riveting, especially in showing how racism is a lot more complex than many believe in a multicultural society.

American History X (1998)

A chilling look at urban racism and hate through the life of a person who drops in and drops out of a white supremacist movement in the United States.

Paperclips (2005)

A documentary based on the anti-racist activities of a middle school in small town Tennessee. To fathom some idea of the millions who died during the Nazi Holocaust, students collected paperclips as a tangible expression of the needless deaths.

Books

The Colour of Democracy 3/e (2006; Nelson) by Frances Henry and Carol Tator is pretty much the standard in the field. Highly recommended.

Also highly recommended is Vic Satzewich et al.'s book entitled *Racism and Social Inequality in Canada: Concepts, Controversies, and Strategies of Resistance* (1998; Thomson Publishing).

For an insightful and provocative look at racism and sexism, see Zillah Eisenstein's (1996) *Hatreds: Racialized and Sexualized Conflicts in the Twenty-first Century*.

Websites

The Canadian Ethnic Studies Association publishes a journal and news items pertaining to (among other related issues) race and racism.
> **www.ucalgary.ca/CESA**

For a recent survey on racism and racial discrimination in Canada:
> **www.dominion.ca/Downloads/IRracismSurvey.pdf**

For a general overview of racism at different levels and in different parts of the world:
> **www.globalissues.org/HumanRights/Racism.asp**

Another valuable site that includes numerous references to articles on racism:
> **www.debwewin.ca/racism.htm**

THE ETHNICITY EXPERIENCE: POLITICS AND POWER

4

| **DEBATE** | **Is Whiteness an Ethnicity?** |

It has been said that many academic arguments could be solved *a priori* if care was taken in defining terms (Tilley 1997). This principle is aptly demonstrated in the often animated debates over the concept of "whiteness" as an **ethnicity** (Bell 1996; Beddgood 1997). In popular usage, references to ethnicity are usually reserved for minorities. But in the social science literature, there is growing acknowledgement that everyone has ethnicity in the sense of group belonging, rootedness in somewhere, and identification with something (Castles and Miller 1998). However valid such an assessment, the perception of ethnicity depends on how it is defined, as evidenced by the following questions: Is whiteness an ethnicity? Are "whites" an ethnic group? Do white people have ethnicity? Is there such a thing as a Canadian ethnicity? Answers to these questions are

hardly academic but critical in defining who we are.

Everyone agrees that Canada is ethnically robust. The myriad **ethnic groups** and attachments attest to that. Yet, for many, ethnicity in Canada applies only under certain conditions, that is, if it (1) is ancestral or roots-based, (2) exudes an air of authenticity, (3) originates in some faraway homeland, and (4) applies to racialized minorities (see Howard-Hassmann 1999; also Foot 2000). Migrants from countries such as China and Somalia are generally perceived as having a distinctive ethnicity ("Chinese" or "Somalian"), as are Aboriginal communities across Canada. English-speaking Canadians might label the Québécois an ethnic group, even though both Quebecers and Aboriginal peoples prefer to define themselves as peoples rather than as **ethnic** minorities. The same English-speaking

Canadians, however, appear reluctant to define themselves as an ethnicity because, frankly, ethnicity is something that immigrants have. They prefer to conceal their "ethnicity-ness" by attributing ethnicity to "minorities," in effect implying "whiteness" as the tacitly accepted centre that masquerades as the norm around which everything revolves.

Debates over whiteness as an ethnicity are increasingly polarized. On one side are those who argue that mainstream white people lack an ethnicity because most are unaware of their shared identity as a conscious distinction. They just *are*, and labelling them as ethnic is inconsistent with commonly accepted definitions of ethnicity as shared awareness of one's distinctiveness and commonalities. On the other side are those who contend that everybody, including white people, is ethnically located, whether or not they are aware of it.

To be sure, the "whitestream" does not represent a classic case of ethnicity. But in a world where there is no position from nowhere, because everyone is from somewhere, whiteness qualifies as an ethnicity, regardless of approval or awareness (Hall 1996; Gillespie 1996). In between these poles are those who concede a potential for mainstream ethnicity. Emergence of a politicized ethnic consciousness among Quebec's English-speaking minority clearly reveals an ethnicity-in-waiting when confronting distressful conditions. Finally, there is a feeling that whiteness must be interpreted as an ethnicity for purposes of living together with differences. Only when white people acknowledge their embeddedness as part of the mosaic rather than a normative grout that consolidates and confines will a truly multicultural society emerge. So what is going on? Is whiteness an ethnicity or not?

INTRODUCTION: GLOBAL IMPLOSION/ETHNICITY EXPLOSION

Two distinct but seemingly contradictory dynamics are at play as the twenty-first century progresses. The interplay of these ostensibly opposing trends has proven perplexing and provocative, both conceptually and politically. On the one hand are the imploding forces of globalization: Nation-states are inexorably drawn into the vortex of a single global economy across increasingly porous national boundaries. The local and the national are conflated into a single world system that compresses and homogenizes because of mass communication, mass travel, mass corporatization (transnationals), and mass education. The distinctiveness that once flourished worldwide is threatened by the forces of globalization, with its diversity-dampening commitment to rationality, progress, achievement, universalism, individualism, and equality. Fears are growing over a trend toward a "McDonaldization" of societies—a kind of one-size-fits-all standardization in which differences are commodified as "ethnic chic." In short, ethnicity is being pushed to the folklorist margins of society because of globalization—little more than a residual category to fall back on as a default option (Hutchinson and Smith 1996).

On the other hand is an equally vibrant but opposing dynamic. The inward-leaning forces of globalization are confronting the centrifugal (outward) dynamics of ethnicity.

Minority women and men have become increasingly assertive in capitalizing on ancestral differences for expressive and instrumental purposes. The **politicization** of ethnicity has not only redefined conventional inter-group relations—often in ways that few could have confidently predicted—but the rhythms of an established global order have been disrupted as well. Where certainty and consensus once prevailed, the new global order is pervaded by uncertainty and confusion because of politicized ethnicities that relegate followers to a past that clashes with the present and may prove irrelevant for the future (Rosado 2005). Paradoxically, the surge in ethnicity may be directly related to globalization. That is, the greater the pressure for standardization because of global market economies, the greater the incentive for asserting ethnic differences (Behrens 1994; Fukuyama 1994). The very globalization that threatens ethnic distinctiveness may also spark a renewed interest in ethnic attachments in two ways: first, by creating new hybrid identities that oscillate between the "here" and the "there" without fear of contradiction (Hall 1996; Gillespie 1996; Wiwa 2003); second, by uncoupling ethnicity from place because of global population movements, resulting in vastly more fluid identities that are increasingly international in scope and definition (Pluss 2005). The corresponding diaspora has spawned a new set of "transnational" identities that challenge conventional notions of belonging, namely, place, identity, and borders (Anthias 1998; Cohen 1998).

Its centrality in shaping human behaviour and inter-group dynamics notwithstanding, reference to ethnicity as a social force has elicited mixed reaction (Yinger 1994). For some, ethnic experiences have proven "regressive" because of their capacity to unleash dormant hatreds for settling old scores. The cult of ethnicity is demonized as an inexcusable reversion to "tribalism" that panders to humanity's basest instincts. The "ethnification" (fragmentation) of society into squabbling ethnic communities is seen as incompatible with society-building, prompting some central authorities to dispose of this disruption by expulsion, extermination, cleansing, forced assimilation, or segregation (Taras and Ganguly 2002). For others, ethnicity can be "progressive" by virtue of providing like-minded individuals with a source of community, continuity, and connections in a highly competitive world. Ethnicity is endorsed as a positive contributor to global survival by emphasizing how differences rather than similarities constitute the definitive feature of the human species. Still others are resigned to ethnicity as a persistent presence in human affairs, with the potential to harm or help, depending on the circumstances. Societies that historically have championed ethnicity as an asset will flourish; conversely, those societies that haven't will struggle in balancing the particular with the universal. In that the preferred option lies in determining how ethnicity can be put to good use, without capitulating to a worst-case scenario of division or destruction, the challenge is deceptively simple. How can we make society safe *for* ethnicity as well as make it safe *from* ethnicity (Schlesinger Jr. 1992)?

Scholarly perceptions of ethnicity are also undergoing a conceptual shift. Ethnicity was once viewed as a category of belonging to a specific ancestral group whose shared distinctiveness set it apart from others. But ethnicity is no longer perceived as a cuddly security blanket for protection in times of stress or change. Nor is it framed as an anachronistic survivor from a bygone era. Rather than a relic from the past, ethnicity is now positioned as a powerful if enigmatic social dynamic capable of transformative changes that perplex yet illuminate, unite yet divide, empower yet enfeeble. Ethnicity has proven a key variable (i.e., a variable = a measurable difference that makes a difference) in shaping people's behaviour, influencing identities, negotiating relations, and defining who gets what.

It also provides an explanatory framework for answering the question of "who am I?" Rather than a separate state of being into which differences are slotted into pre-existing categories, ethnicity is increasingly viewed in non-essentialist terms as a fluid and flexible resource for coping with the demands of a diverse and changing society. The end result is nothing less than a fundamental shift in thinking. Static and homogeneous models of ethnicity that once embraced essentialized notions of identity are conceding ground to more dynamic and hybridic models of the ethnic experience.

In short, far from fading away into oblivion, ethnicity has catapulted to the forefront of social and political life. The so-called end of history has ushered in an era of explosive ethnic revivals across the globe that are proving disruptive at best, destructive at worst (Hutchinson and Smith 1996). Canada is no exception to this global dynamic. Recent years have witnessed a convergence of controversies and challenges linked with "ethnic" or "ethnicity." The politics of Aboriginal ethnicity have challenged the very foundational principles that govern Canada's constitutional order. Québécois ethnicity continues to provoke English-speaking Canadians, many of whom are perplexed or apoplectic over Quebec's political posturing. Multicultural minorities have been no less adamant in demanding ethnocultural space consistent with their constitutional rights to equality and inclusiveness. For minority Canadians, their ethnicity is embraced as a marker of personal identity or group pride rather than grounds for exclusion (Mendelsohn 2003). The interplay of these inter-group dynamics prompts a series of questions. Why do individuals and groups turn to ethnicity for expressive or instrumental goals? What is it about this powerful force that threatens to dismantle the conventional in exchange for the unorthodox? Why has ethnicity assumed such salience in shaping Canada's destiny? And how do the politics of ethnicity challenge Canada-building? Answers to these questions are necessarily complex, but the quality of our responses will determine how adroitly Canadians can finesse the politics of ethnicity.

This chapter explores the "ethnic experience" as a formidable dynamic in reshaping inter-group relations. The power of ethnicity strikes at the very heart of the politics of a divided society, with domestic ethnic conflicts displacing external state conflicts as the most destabilizing source of global disorder (see Huntington 1993). More specifically, the chapter directs attention to the politics and power of ethnicity when applied to a changing and diverse Canada. The chapter emphasizes ethnicity as an important macro-variable in explaining the dynamics of (1) intra-group behaviour, (2) inter-group dynamics, and (3) group differences and similarities. By contrast, a micro approach to ethnicity demonstrates how individuals go about negotiating their identities in a multicultural Canada. To address these issues, the chapter is organized accordingly: (1) what is ethnicity, (2) why does it exist, (3) how is it expressed, (4) what is its relation to inequality, and (5) what are its impact on and implications for Canada-building? Particular attention is devoted to the processes and outcomes associated with different levels of ethnicity as (1) group or community, (2) varied types of ethnic identities, including lived-in, symbolic, insurgent, and postmodern, and (3) social movements including **ethnic nationalism**. The chapter concludes by discussing ethnicity against the backdrop of Canada's official Multiculturalism. Like other chapters, this chapter is predicated on the notion that Canada's ethnic relations are relations of inequality—in effect prompting the question of how ethnicity contributes to the creation and maintenance of these inequities, and how ethnicity can be mobilized to challenge and change them. First, however, a brief overview of ethnic diversity in Canada (see Chapter 10 for more details).

| INSIGHT | **Ethnic Diversity in Canada** |

An ethnic diversity survey to discover information on the ethnic and cultural backgrounds of Canadians was conducted by Statistics Canada in partnership with the Department of Canadian Heritage from April to August of 2002, involving 42 500 respondents, aged 15 and over, who were interviewed by telephone in all ten provinces. Key findings included:

- Nearly 46 percent of Canada's population of 22.4 million (over the age of 15) report only British Isles (accounting for 21 percent of the total population), French, and/or Canadian ethnic and cultural origins.

- About 19 percent of the total population had only European ancestry (other than French or English).

- People of non-European descent (usually visible minorities) accounted for 13 percent of the total population, with Chinese and East Indian most common.

- In addition, 22 percent of the population reported mixed ethnic heritages or did not know their ethnic ancestry.

- Almost one quarter, or 23 percent, of Canada's population are first generation, i.e., born outside Canada. Seventeen percent are second generation,

i.e., born in Canada but of one parent who was born overseas. Fifty-eight percent are third plus generation, i.e., both they and their parents are Canadian born.

- One half of the total population aged 15 and over indicated a strong sense of belonging to their ethnic group, with a sense of belonging strongest among the first generation, especially relative newcomers, such as Filipinos with 78 percent saying yes, compared to only 33 percent for Germans and Ukrainians.

- Just over half of the total population (55%) said that Canadian was either their only ethnic identity or was reported in combination with another identity.

- The vast majority of Canadians (93%) said they never or rarely ever experienced discrimination because of their ethnicity. But nearly one-third of black respondents indicated they had sometimes or often experienced negative treatment because of their ethnicity.

The publication *Ethnic Diversity Survey: Portrait of a Multicultural Society* (89 593 IIE) is now available on the Statistics Canada website.

DEFINING ETHNICITY

Most societies are composed of racially and ethnically diverse groups (Isajiw 1999). The range of variation is almost limitless. Some societies are relatively homogeneous in terms of composition (Japan and Korea); others have a single dominant majority with numerous minorities in different stages of assimilation (United Kingdom); still others consist of dominant and subdominant groups that are locked in competition for power (Fiji); still others, including Australia and New Zealand, are constitutive of white settler colonies with immigrant populations superimposed on increasingly powerful indigenous nations (Fleras and Spoonley

1999). Finally, there is Canada, which is unique as a society, with its composition of immigrant populations, Aboriginal nations, and national minority of Quebec peoples.

On the surface it might appear hopeless to extract a pattern from this demographic disarray. Nevertheless, two patterns can be discerned. First, a dominant ethnic group prevails whose culture, language, values, and social patterns are privileged as normal and desirable. Those in control possess the power and resources to establish institutional arrangements and ideological systems consistent with their interests. Ethnocultural minorities have suffered as a result of this mistreatment, and many have reacted accordingly. Some have sought to diminish their marginalization by assimilation into the mainstream. Others have exaggerated ethnic differences in hopes of securing a strategic separation from the mainstream. And still others are looking for some kind of compromise in between the poles of assimilation and separatism in hopes of advancing the goal of living together with difference.

A second pattern involves the proliferation of ethnically diverse groups who are increasingly restive because of their marginal status. Options that may be open to these subdominant groups are limited and limiting. Many endure constant pressure to conform to prevailing values, norms, and institutions. Others are kept securely in place to ensure a reserve pool of largely exploited labour. And still others are encouraged to retain diversity, but find themselves penalized or ostracized as a result. Responses to these pressures have differed: On one side are those who want to preserve or promote their ethnicity at all costs; and on the other side are those who want to discard ethnicities regardless of the cost; and there are yet others who want to fully participate in society without rejecting what makes them meaningful and unique.

Not surprisingly, reference to the term "ethnicity" continues to baffle and confuse as well as to infuriate and inflame. Ethnicity has evolved into an imprecise mélange of contested meanings that can be stretched out to mean everything yet nothing, in the process acquiring the status of a cliché without much analytical substance. The term itself seems immune to rational analysis without collapsing under its own weight: How can a single term encompass everything from ethnocide in the Darfur region of Sudan to Québécois ethnic nationalism, to the contrived ethnicity of Kitchener-Waterloo's annual Oktoberfest celebration? What can be done with a word that people often use as a more polite substitute for "race"? Or how does one cope with a term that is increasingly restricted to those of European origins, while non-European immigrants are framed as races and racialized accordingly? Finally, the term is subject to additional overuse. For example, consider how reference to ethnic conflict is routinely employed to describe inter-group hostilities (usually in Africa, but never applied to American initiatives in Iraq or Afghanistan) even though ethnicity is but one component alongside political, economic, and cultural factors. In brief, reference to ethnicity provides a convenient and simplified shorthand that plays well with North American stereotypes of primitive life as nasty, brutish, and short (Taras and Ganguly 2002).

Still, any definition must reflect certain prerequisites. A working definition must be sufficiently broad to capture the expansion of ethnicity as principle and practice, yet not so sprawling as to lose this focus. A distinction between race and ethnicity provides a useful starting point. Whereas race connotes biological variation and genetic determinism, ethnicity emphasizes social and cultural differences, with greater emphasis on values, lifestyle, and world view (Durie 2005). Definitions must also be consistent with a sociological embrace of ethnicity as inter- and intra-group dynamics in unequal contexts, while acknowledging both subjective and objective dimensions at either individual or group levels. Or as Yinger (1994) notes, three components are required for ethnicity to prevail: (1) members of a so-called ethnicity see themselves as different; (2) others see them as different; and (3) they participate in shared activities with the intent of affirming their distinctiveness. Broadly speaking, then, **ethnicity** can be defined as a principle of *shared awareness of a people's ancestral linkages, including shared commonalities and group commitment as basis for recognition (identities), rewards (entitlements), or relationships (both internally and externally).* This definition captures the multi-dimensionality of ethnicity as (1) embodying a consciousness of being different because of tradition and transmission, (2) an awareness of differences as socially constructed yet grounded in historical and structural realities, (3) a recognition that a people may define themselves as different or be defined by others in this way, and (4) an acknowledgment of how these differences make a difference in terms of entitlement and engagement.

There is some value in distinguishing ethnicity from ethnic groups and ethnic minority. Ethnicity consists of those distinctive attributes that distinguish members of one category from another because of beliefs, values, emotions, and practices. With ethnicity, persons who are related by birth, loyalty, culture, or homeland are organized into goal-directed action groups in pursuit of instrumental or expressive ends. **Ethnic groups**, by contrast, refer to actual communities of people who are socially and culturally distinct, who see themselves and are seen by others as distinct from other communities, and who are separated from others by way of ancestries and boundaries. The extent to which ethnic groups maintain a strong consciousness among members will fluctuate too, that is, some ethnic groups seek rapid assimilation and are quickly accepted by the mainstream, while others may defend their identity because of mainstream rejection or desire for distinctiveness (Cornell and Hartman 1998). Finally, the concept of ethnic minority refers to a group of culturally distinct people who occupy (or are seen to occupy) a marginal status in society, even though they may outnumber those of the dominant sector. In other words, references to minority vs. majority—as well as dominant vs. subdominant—are about power and not about numbers.

COMPONENTS OF ETHNICITY

Canadian society was once envisioned as a mosaic of relatively durable and distinct ethnic entities whose totality was greater than the sum of its parts. Ethnicity embraced an objective and fixed compendium of cultural traits that identifies a person as belonging to "x" rather than "y." A set of appropriate symbols and artifacts was attached to a particular community of people. Other groups were defined and distinguished by a different catalogue of qualities. Explicit and unbending boundaries were drawn around designated ethnic groups, reflecting an inventory of values, language, religion, and culture. This focus on the objective dimension of ethnicity culminated in a "cookie-cutter" approach to the study of ethnicity.

This emphasis on objective ethnic content has waned in recent years. In its place has emerged an interest in the subjective experiences that embrace and the symbolic boundaries that encircle. A subjectivist orientation rejects the notion of ethnicity as a clearly articulated cultural category with an easily defined set of objective features. Ethnicity instead is informed by a shared "we feeling" that infuses a particular group with a sense of who they are and where they came from. Emphasis is focused on ethnicity as an intersubjective activity, that is, a largely fluid and flexible resource for crafting patterns of meaningful interaction in contexts of negotiation, conflict, or compromise (Barth 1969; Isajiw 1999). Emphasis is also on ethnicity as a key variable in explaining thought and behaviour; after all, where a person is ethnically located will profoundly influence their perception and response to the world, their personal and social identity, their norms and values for appropriate behaviour, and their limits to choices and opportunities (Gibb and Huang 2003). In acknowledging that people may manipulate ethnicity to adapt, gain or play, there is an unmistakable shift away from conventional notions that assume sameness in people's thought and behaviour because of their ethnicity.

But just as a laundry-list approach to ethnicity has proven inadequate, so too has an overemphasis on subjective experience. Ethnicity is more than a feeling of apartness or a sense of shared awareness. While ethnicity may be socially constructed, its constructedness is socially grounded around those visible cultural symbols deemed essential to group survival. Select tangible markers such as patterns of kinship, descent, and obligations are required to validate a sense of continuity, collectivity, and commitment. These distinguishing markers provide a rallying point around which to galvanize ethnically like-minded people by mobilizing them into action.

Of those characteristics that shine as indices of ethnicity, including everything from appearance to dietary preferences, the most prominent are birthright, homeland, and language. Birthright is critical: Only persons with proven (or perceived) descent from a common source can claim membership to a particular ethnicity. No less crucial is a powerful attachment to a territory or homeland that may have been lost or left behind. Instead of viewing land as a commodity for purchase and profit, ethnic homelands are valorized as an embodiment of the past whose value must be defended at all costs. Language often represents the quintessential component of group distinctiveness. As a powerful symbol of distinctiveness, cohesion, and integrity, language requires little additional value to perform its integrative and identifying functions. (Chapter 8 will pursue this argument more closely.)

To ensure ethnic distinctiveness, boundaries are required. Ethnic boundaries can be defined as socially constructed barriers that provide a protective barrier by regulating the degree of movement between ethnic groups (Barth 1969). Neither totally impenetrable nor excessively permeable, these boundaries can be likened to "membranes" that simultaneously inhibit yet permit the inter-flow of particles. In some cases, these boundaries are vigorously maintained as a way of keeping some people in, others out, especially when group members consider themselves under threat because of racist legislation, restricted economic opportunity, restrained cultural expression, and social rejection. In other cases, boundaries between these identities are fluid, contested, context-dependent, and increasingly complex (Cornell and Hartman 1998). But difficulties arise in maintaining a degree of bounded distinctiveness. Countries such as Canada, with their highly democratic and multicultural outlook, are particularly hard on maintaining ethnic boundaries. Under multiculturalism, the absence of government pressure or out-group hostility makes it difficult for ethnic minorities to avoid assimilating into the mainstream unless vigilance is constant (Weinfeld 2001).

| INSIGHT | **Ethnicity and Religion: Taking Religion Seriously** |

Religion and ethnicity as dimensions of diversity have much in common (Bramadat and Seljak 2005). Both provide followers with a sense of meaning and identity even if critics tend to dismiss both as relics from the past. Both have a moral capacity to empower and enlighten those who subscribe to their principles, yet an equally irrational power to disrupt and destroy those who

don't (Harris 2005). Both are often ignored for public policy purposes on grounds of maintaining a separation from the state, especially as religion-based ethnicities may be regarded as potentially incompatible with a secular and multicultural Canada (Seljak 2005). And following widespread predictions of their demise—the proverbial withering on the vine under the bright light of

TABLE 4.1	Ethnic Religions in Canada, 2001 and 2017	
Muslims	579 645	1.4 million (est)
Jews	329 995	375 000
Buddhists	300 345	400 000
Hindus	297 200	600 000
Sikhs	278 415	500 000

rational modernity—each has staged a remarkable comeback from the brink. This has been possible even if many believe these forces are thought best kept under wraps in private and the personal rather than in the forefront of defining, negotiating, and shaping public life, agendas, and outcomes (see Armstrong 2004).

What, then, is the nature of the complex relationship between religion and ethnicity in Canada? What is it about this relationship that gives it the potential to generate social conflict in Canada, replacing traditional causes like language conflicts, ethnic hatreds, and Aboriginal unrest (see *Negotiating Religious Pluralism,* 2005)? How does the interplay of religion with ethnicity advance the concerns and interests of faith-based ethnic communities? A sense of perspective is handy: Mainstream religions appear to be doing poorly, although appearances may be deceiving (Bibby 2002): According to Statistics Canada, 35 percent of the 25–44-year-olds in Canada say they have no religious affiliation, while weekly church attendance has dropped from 67 percent of the population in

1946 to 20 percent in 2001. By contrast, religious diversity remains an area of strong growth in Canada, as Table 4.1 demonstrates.

How do we account for this explosion of religiosity? Immigration patterns that reflect an emphasis on faith-based ethnicities are one factor. Another is how the pace of globalization continues to disrupt local cultures, thus reinforcing a return to religious identity as a bastion of personal and group solidarity in times of uncertainty, change, and diversity (Bibby 2002). And with integration into Canada proving more difficult than many imagined, individuals and communities will increasingly rely on religion to recapture a sense of rootedness, belonging, and attachment (Biles and Ibrahim 2005). Admittedly, ethnic minority religions are no more static, uniform, and rigid than their counterparts, ethnic cultures and identities. Ethnic religions are internally diverse, experience change over time, and are constantly adjusted for the evolving realities of Canadian life. Still, time will tell whether religion can be taken seriously enough to be re-incorporated into Canada's public domain.

WHY ETHNICITY?

Ethnicity is evolving into one of the world's more powerful dynamics. It has proven pivotal in defining, shaping, and advancing group relations within multicultural contexts such as Canada. Not surprisingly, many regard the challenge of making society safe for ethnicity, yet safe from ethnicity, as the quintessential twenty-first-century challenge. But such a lofty status was not always the case. The inevitable dissolution of ethnicity was widely predicted and anticipated as recently as a generation ago. Both socialism and liberalism attacked the particularist attachments associated with ethnicity as atavistic survivals at odds with universal progress and modernization. Ancient tribal hatreds would melt into memory because of a modernist belief in liberal universalism, with its attendant notion that what people have in common as individuals is more fundamental than what divides them because of membership in racial or ethnically distinct groups (Maaka and Fleras 2005). A Marxist perspective was no less dismissive of ethnic attachments. Class relations constituted the fundamental dynamic in society. Everything else, including ethnicity, was derivative or residual (Bell-Fialkoff 1993). To think or to act otherwise, namely, in terms of ethnicity, would not only perpetuate false consciousness but also postpone the inevitable demise of capitalism. In short, both functionalist and conflict theorists pounced on ethnicity as inferior, irrelevant, and an obstacle to progress and prosperity.

Predictions of the decline of ethnicity have been premature to say the least. Ethnicity has proven both resilient and tenacious, with no signs of easing up in the foreseeable future, despite powerful pressures to the contrary. Perpetuated at times by individuals as genuine culture (i.e., enjoyed for its own right) or as an impetus for mobilizing people into goal-directed action (i.e., employed as a means to a practical goal), the ethnicity "revolution" has profoundly redefined the notion of "what society is for." A powerful dynamic has evolved that elevates ethnicity as a cutting edge for collectively challenging the status quo (Nagel and Olzak 1982; See and Wilson 1988). People have turned to ethnicity as a means of protecting their immediate interests, especially when central authorities are unable or unwilling to regulate or control them. No longer are ethnic attachments dismissed as archaic survivals from the past—quaint and colourful, perhaps, but irrelevant to contemporary realities. To the contrary, this renewal of ethnic pride and identity has evolved into a formidable power, with the double-edged capacity to not only enhance or empower but also to destroy or dispossess.

The rejuvenation of ethnicity in Canada and elsewhere raises many questions. How do we account for the popularity and proliferation of ethnicity in contemporary societies? How is it manifested? With what impact? What are the immediate and long-term implications? How can the visceral appeal of ethnicity as identity possibly prevail over the cosmopolitan lure of a modern society? Why, indeed, do people prefer to affiliate along ethnic lines rather than associate with political parties or trade unions? Or why would anyone want to be thought of as a Québécois or Aboriginal or Vietnamese-Canadian when they have the opportunity to identify solely as non-hyphenated Canadians? Two major explanations help to isolate the factors that underscore the ethnicity experience as power and politics, namely: the primordial explanation and the constructivist explanation, including the identity thesis and the instrumentalist approach.

The **primordial explanation** argues that the boom in ethnicity is essentially an extension of powerful and immutable instincts that cannot be suppressed for any length of time. People appear to have a genuine preference for aligning themselves with closely related blood kin. Ethnicity represents an ancient and deep-rooted impulse that reflects a tendency to seek out others of your "own kind" by capitalizing on an inherent need for belonging with others who are similar. This genetic inheritance makes it only natural to exhibit such spontaneous feelings and emotional attachments as natural, normal, and necessary. Suppression of these instinctive impulses doesn't make ethnicity go away, but forces it underground, only to re-emerge in an often explosive rage when the lid is lifted.

People affiliate with one another because of a "primordial" urge to stick together. These bonds are primordial in the sense that they appear to have been hardwired by evolution into the human species for survival purposes. This intrinsic dimension may help to explain the intensity of passions and emotions associated with the ethnic experience. Consider this statement by a "Serbian-Canadian" in rationalizing his loyalties during the 1999 NATO-led bombings of Serbia: "I'm a Canadian by birth and a Serbian by blood. I think family values come ahead of values or loyalties to your country . . . It's not a question of loyalty to Canada or Serbia" (cited in Sarick 1999). The primordiality of ethnic attachments may also explain the popularity of staunchly ethnic social movements in advancing collective interests (Bell-Fialkoff 1993).

Within the primordialist camp are various biologically informed theories of ethnic bonding, the most popular of which is sociobiology. According to this perspective, ethnicity is biogenetically "wired" into the human species as a mechanism for maximizing the transmission of genes from one generation to the next. Pierre van den Berghe (1981), for example, traces the origins of ethnic bonding to an extension of kinship group solidarity. Any kinship group tends to act in a self-preservative manner by providing mutual aid and cooperation for those related because of a common ancestor. Involvement with related others ensures the long-term survival of the kin groups—albeit at some expense to any specific individual. It follows from this that even ostensibly altruistic actions that assist a people's kin have the effect of protecting and promoting the evolutionary survival of one's own ethnic kind.

There is something of value in sociobiological explanations of ethnicity. By situating ethnic feelings within our genetic and evolutionary past, reference to sociobiology conveys the tenacity and the intensely emotional appeal of ethnicity, especially when compared to alternative explanations for bonding (Brown 1989). But sociologists are divided over the merits of sociobiology as an explanatory framework, especially as many reject any minimizing of the social as the preferred causal framework. Many are unsettled by the political implications of reductionist arguments when they link biology with culture. True, we may be genetically "hardwired" to identify with our "own kind"; nevertheless, definitions of what constitutes our "own kind" will vary over time and across space. The fact that people are also free to choose otherwise, and that many have done so by repudiating their ethnic heritage, should caution against too uncritical an acceptance of primordiality.

In contrast to the primordial explanation, which sees ethnicity as natural and inevitable, a **constructivist explanation** focuses on the creation of ethnicity through meaningful interaction. For constructivists, ethnicity is constructed, but its construction cannot be understood outside the broader social and historical context (Binder 2000). Ethnicity reflects a socially constructed response to political and economic opportunities for reviving or securing group goals. Reference to the concept of social construction does not imply the phony, false, or fictional. Rather, the "construction" in a social constructivist position confirms that there is nothing natural or normal about the world we live in, despite continued efforts by vested interests to make it seem so. Social conventions that guide or organize are continually constructed and reconstructed through a process of meaningful human interaction. Similarly, ethnicity is not a natural feature of society, but a constructed response to material exclusion, a search for social meaning, a quest for identity, and a struggle for creating culturally safe space. Inasmuch as ethnicity represents a social construct, it is "imagined." But its effects on the lives and life chances of minority women and men are far from imaginary.

One of two constructivist explanations, the **identity thesis**, approaches ethnicity as a means to an end. According to the identity thesis, ethnicity persists because it provides a means for coping with the globalizing demands of contemporary urban society. An identity perspective points to ethnicity as a buffer for insulating individuals from the pressures of an impersonal and competitive world. A commitment to ethnicity secures a source of stability in a world of diversity, uncertainty, and change by restoring a measure of meaning in an increasingly meaningless world. Appeals to ethnicity foster a sense of relief, continuity, belonging, importance, and security—especially for those at the margins of society without alternative channels for coping with societal stress.

How do we account for this identification with ethnicity in times of change? Certainties once associated with the modern world are vanishing in the face of intense global competition, radicalized individualism, a disintegrating civil society, increasingly porous territorial borders and erosion of the nation-state as the primary source of legitimacy, and cultural upheavals created by the proliferation of computer-mediated technologies. The dissolution of the familiar and reassuring has undermined people's sense of social belonging, including a rootedness in traditional collectivities such as kinship or community. The confluence of uncertainty and change induces individuals to withdraw into ethnic enclaves that are familiar and emotionally satisfying (Littleton 1996). As Manuel Castells (1997:66) writes,

> When the world becomes too large to be controlled, social actors aim at shrinking it back to their size and reach. When networks dissolve time and space, people anchor themselves in places, and recall their historic memory.

Ethnic involvements, in other words, permit meaningful identity to be crafted when meanings are in short supply. A "quasi-kinship" community is sustained that provides a buffer against the backdrop of unremitting rationality, standardization, and central control (Scott 1998). This binding and bonding dimension also helps to explain the universal appeal of such affiliation when confronting the relentless pressures for conformity and consensus.

An **instrumentalist approach** views ethnicity as a resource for pursuit of diverse goals (Hutchinson and Smith 1996). One version refers to elite competition for scarce resources by manipulating ethnic symbols to secure mass support. A second version refers to a process by which both leaders and followers maximize preferences, in part because pooled resources provide a competitive advantage in advancing vested interests. An instrumentalist approach is firmly grounded in a sociology of group competition and rational choice theory, that is, ethnicity is designed to maximize in-group power by excluding others (Castles and Miller 1998). The drawing power of ethnicity provides a competitive edge in the struggle for scarce and valued resources by providing a major source of political and social mobilization as groups rely on their ethnic affinity to challenge and change. Especially in contexts where an ethnic division of labour persists (Hechter 1975; Gross 1996), dominant sectors tend to monopolize wealth and power at the expense of ethnically different subdominant groups, many of whom are locked into a position of inferiority because of their unskilled status. Resentment over this differential treatment boils over when expectations soar but the means to achievement are blocked, with the result that this system of ethnic stratification may buckle under pressure because of escalating ethnic activism (Nagel and Olzak 1982; See and Wilson 1988). Ethnic activism is further bolstered by the actions of opportunistic elites who may cloak personal concerns behind a facade of altruism.

Two questions arise from an instrumentalist approach to ethnicity: First, why do ethnically like-minded persons prefer to act collectively to achieve their goals rather than as individuals? Put simply, a collective basis is superior for coping with the demands of a complex and bureaucratized society. According to **resource mobilization theory,** large-scale social movements possess the human resources and critical mass to compete effectively at a national level by influencing central policy structures. Second, why are ethnic attachments important in securing the loyalty and commitment of members? What is the tactical advantage of relying on ethnicity as a basis for mobilizing people into groups? The best answer may be the most obvious. Recruitment by appealing to ethnicity is perceived as more natural and durable than the "artificial" linkages associated with political or economic ties. These bonds are consolidated by emotional involvement with persons of one's own kind, a kind of quasi-kinship that needs no justification beyond its own existence. These quasi-kinship ties also infuse the movement with the commitment for waging a protracted struggle against even seemingly insurmountable odds.

To sum up: Three distinct approaches account for the popularity and persistence of ethnicity when many thought it shouldn't or couldn't. Each of these approaches may be partially correct as far as explanatory frameworks go, including (1) ethnicity as an inherent affiliation that reflects an intrinsic need for belonging to one's kind (primordiality), (2) ethnicity as a constructed framework of social organization for securing meaning and continuity in a changing and uncertain world (identity), and (3) ethnicity as a constructed tool for rational attainment of goals (instrumentalist). To be sure, the constructivist approach has come under criticism. As minorities seek to recover and assert their ethnic distinctiveness, they endorse those elements that are perceived as most authentic—the apparent essences of their culture—not only as more than simply invented traditions but as ways of coping with the present for survival in the future (Alfred 2005; Maaka and Fleras 2005). Still, no one is suggesting that one approach is more accurate than the other. Each provides an insight into aspects of the ethnic experience that others prefer to ignore. That said, there is no reason why primordial explanations cannot be integrated with constructivist explanations to secure a multi-textured understanding of the ethnicity experience as power and politics.

EXPRESSIONS OF ETHNICITY

Ethnicity can be expressed in different ways. At one level, ethnicity is manifested in ethnic groups who live together in relatively self-sufficient communities. At another level, ethnicity manifests itself through different expressions of identity, including lived in, symbolic and situational, postmodern, and insurgent. At a third level, ethnicity is expressed as a social movement with nationalistic overtones. These different expressions of the ethnic experience—as *community, identity*, and *social movement*—may be analyzed separately. In reality, however, they tend to coexist, overlap, and intersect in complex ways.

Ethnicity as Community

Ethnicity refers to a principle of potential group formation. Persons with shared and felt identification may be classified into a category that mobilizes ancestrally related persons into action groups to advance individual or collective claims. Ethnicity also provides a basis for relatively permanent communities with clearly defined rules for living together. Preference for being with one's own kind may foster a commitment to community. Or pressures from the outside may also compel a closing of the ranks along community lines. The host society may impose a demeaning ethnic label on migrants who then fall back on community bonds to cope with unfriendly environments (Castles and Miller 1998).

Parts of urban Canada are composed of a mosaic of ethnic communities, including the widely celebrated Chinatowns in Vancouver and Toronto, South Asian communities in Brampton, and the relatively self-sufficient Hasidic Jews in Montreal. Or consider the borough of Markham just north of Toronto where 62 percent of the population of 208 615 in the 2001 Census identified as ethnic—including one ward with 95 percent self-identified as ethnic (Verma 2005). These ethnic communities can be conceptualized in different ways. They can be viewed as a cultural enclave with a distinctive set of values, traditions, and habits that have evolved over time. Institutions are established that offer a variety of political, economic, and cultural functions for individuals who are related by descent or kinship. A relatively high degree of "institutional completeness" (Breton 1964) provides ethnic minority members with mutual support, access to networks of goods and services, and a source of identity and meaning. Increasingly, these suburban enclaves are no longer residences of necessity as was often the case in the past, but are often chosen destinations for those new Canadians who could afford to live elsewhere if they wanted to, but who demonstrate a preference for their "own kind" (Yelaja and Keung 2005).

Ethnic communities can also be seen as complex systems of social relations. They consist of interpersonal and kinship relations for emotional and material support; they also entail a framework for collective activities. Recent immigrants may find economic and cultural refuge in ethnic communities by facilitating the transition from the society of origin to urban Canada. Ethnic community organizations may assist in the preservation of language and transmission of culture. They also establish a power base for advancing political consciousness and action. These organizations may attract resources and influence if local leaders can command community loyalty and deliver this "commodity" as electoral support for government initiatives. Still, internal tensions may threaten community solidarity or issue consensus. Despite a constructed facade of wholesome unity, political cleavages are readily apparent as people jockey for position, with a high potential for factional infighting because of differences in age, sex, income, education, and length of residence.

Blessing or curse? Social unity or detached coexistence? Enclave or ghetto? Mainstream fears over these self-contained enclaves are palpable. According to Ryerson professor Mohammed Qadeer and colleague Sandeep Kumar, who have tracked enclave growth in Greater Toronto, perceptions are mounting that new immigrants are refusing to integrate because of self-imposed isolation, thus diminishing a sense of shared values and Canadian commonality (see Yelaja and Keung 2005). Admittedly, these enclaves do provide racialized minorities with a high comfort level by providing them with a territorial unit where they can convene with their "own kind," where they can dress and act without explaining themselves, have proximity to shops and culturally relevant services, benefit from the creation of social networks, and improve chances of preserving their language and culture. And yes, this inwardness can foster old world mentalities among older immigrants who remain stuck in a time warp, often at the expense of generating intergenerational conflicts. Moreover, the spatial concentration of immigrants when combined with an explosive mix of poverty and powerlessness can lead to social exclusion (Papillon 2002). But there is no proof that younger immigrants are rejecting Canada, at least judging by the exceptionally high number of citizenships that are taken out each year (Kymlicka 2001). Still, with benefits outweighing costs, the enclavization of ethnic communities in urban Canada is likely to create a new spin on the meaning of living together with our differences.

Ethnicity as Identity

One of the identities open to Canadians is that of ethnicity. In a multicultural society such as ours, many individuals regard their ethnicity as important in defining "who I am" (Cornell and Hartmann 1998). Identity entails that part of the person that defines who they are, what they would like to be, and how they would like others to see them. (As we shall see in the next chapter, ethnicity also serves as a critical determinant of "who gets what," "what there is to get," and "in what amounts.") Ethnic identities can be broadly defined as personal attachments involving loyalty to a distinctive group (or tradition) based on commonalities with similar others (Driedger 1989). In certain cases, ethnic identities are imposed by outside sources; in others, they are voluntarily adopted on the basis of how individuals or groups feel about themselves. Some identities, such as "white ethnicity," are sharply contested, as people are not consciously aware of connectedness unless challenged to do so. Other identities may be active in that individuals are conscious of them and act accordingly to protect or promote. Still other identities are politicized in securing the basis for collective action to achieve goals. In all cases, identities are relational in that they are constructed through interaction and in opposition to others—in effect reinforcing a feeling of "in-groupness" at the expense of out-groups (Hall 1996).

Patterns of ethnic identities can be varied. Some Canadians reject their ethnic background except for special occasions, and want to be identified only as Canadians for purposes of recognition, relationships, and rewards. Others maintain a dual identity without much difficulty: Modern communication and transport technologies allow ethnic minorities to transcend national borders by participating in the internal affairs of the homeland without relinquishing a commitment to Canada. Such a dynamic makes it difficult to think of Canada as a collection of self-contained localities. Rather, the intensified transnational exchanges between localities and the homeland because of migration, globalization, and communication have altered how people think about identity, place, and borders (Papillon 2002). Still others thrive on multiple identities. They flit in and out of different ethnic identities without undergoing a crisis of confusion. Their identities are fluid and contextual—even contradictory—in coping with the many opportunities that a postmodern society has to offer, especially as individuals and groups are drawn into an ever-expanding nexus of networks and linkages (Handa 2003). And yet still others remain locked into an "old country" identity and can't wait to return "home." With such an array of possibilities, four expressions of ethnic identity can be discerned, at least for purposes of analysis, namely **lived-in, situational, postmodern**, and **insurgent**.

Lived-in ethnic identity: Individuals with common cultural values or religious beliefs may strongly identify with a particular ethnic group. Individuals are born into these primary groups, membership is irrevocably assigned at birth, and the group remains a virtually exclusive source of identity throughout an entire lifetime. An attachment to the norms, values, and institutions of the group constitutes a serious statement about personal affiliation. Anabaptist sects such as the Hutterites are ethnic communities governed by rules, values, and sanctions. Here, the principle of ethnicity is expressed in the organization of viable groups that retain a pervasive influence in shaping members' lives. These individuals admit that their identification with the cultural past makes a difference in how they think and behave. Involvement at this level presupposes a canopy of constraints, demands, and responsibilities that cannot be casually discarded as mood shifts or personality changes (Boldt 1985).

A lived-in ethnicity represents a difference that makes a difference in defining "who we are." There is no option or choice; either people conform or they are shunned or expelled. Not surprisingly, this "old-fashioned" style of ethnicity is disappearing, although there are signs of a renewal in larger urban centres (Yelaja and Keung 2005). Restricted largely to rural areas and certain urban enclaves of Canada, conventional ethnic groups have lost much of their moral authority as arbiters of correct human behaviour. Many of these groups can no longer supply a common set of shared values, enforce mutual obligations or responsibilities, offer incentives or impose sanctions, or secure compliance from members. A lived-in ethnicity no longer appeals to those who are anxious to derive full benefit from an achievement-oriented society. A more flexible and fluid identity arrangement has appeared instead.

Symbolic and situational ethnic identity: Ethnicity in a multicultural society takes on a different dynamic. Ethnic identities are often part-time, focused on symbols rather than substance, and situation-specific. The obligations of a lived-in identity are secondary to options and flexibility in identification through symbolic commitments and situational adjustments. This situationally specific and symbolically loaded identity often takes the form of a strategic personal resource that allows individuals to improve their life chances without rejecting their life sources. References to ethnic identities as situational or symbolic are not intended to trivialize or demean the ethnic experience as inauthentic or contrived. Emphasis instead is on their adaptiveness and resilience across time and place.

An ethnic identity based on situation and symbols reflects a process of adaptation by immigrants. Through involvement in their adopted country, incoming immigrants may become more and more estranged from participating in their cultural heritage—especially in terms of language use, friendship circles, and residential patterns—preferring instead to identify with the values and lifestyle of the host society. Ethnic attachments to the homeland culture become increasingly tentative as their commitments become both provisional and superficial, and lack conformist zeal. Involvement in ethnic organizations declines (except on isolated occasions or in favourable circumstances) to the point of insignificance—if measured by the frequency or intensity of institutional participation. Yet, many new Canadians may retain a strong emotional tie to the symbolic aspects of their cultural past when the situation is appropriate. In resisting the lure of wholesale assimilation, they reveal an affective attachment to the community as a reference group, but reject as unacceptable both the restrictions and responsibilities of lived-in ethnicity (Roberts and Clifton 1990).

The emergence of this "part-time" ethnicity is known as **situational** or **symbolic ethnic identity.** This ethnicity is situational because its expression is context-dependent; it is symbolic because identity is informed by an attachment to symbols rather than the substance of ethnicity. Ethnic salience is not measured by a person's degree of participation in ethnic clubs, knowledge of ethnic language, circle of friends, place of residence, and marital patterns. Of salience is a personal identification with the symbols of that ethnicity, with a corresponding willingness to activate and manipulate those symbols to achieve individual goals or advantage. Individuals do not so much belong to an ethnic group as they voluntarily affiliate with relevant cultural symbols as preferences dictate and situations demand. Ethnic minority members do not necessarily share a common culture; more accurately, they possess an attachment to ethnicity on the basis of perceived similarities and shared attachments. Not everyone, of course, has such a choice of options. The centrality and constraints of visibility make this option less applicable to people of colour who may find ethnic identities imposed on them against their will, rather than something they can opt into or out of when they want.

The situational and symbolic nature of ethnic identity provides answers to concerns about ethnicity. First, can distinct ethnic identities survive in situations where the traditional culture has disappeared? Second, can individuals continue to identify themselves as "ethnics" long after abandoning all involvement in group activities? According to the logic of situational and symbolic ethnicity, the answer to both questions is yes. The decline of a particular lifestyle will not necessarily diminish the validity of the ethnic experience. What is critical for ethnic identity is the identification with select aspects of that cultural lifestyle—not the scope or intensity of affiliation. Needless to say, this style of identity is relatively painless and voluntary, and its abstract and effortless style makes it well suited to the needs of an upwardly mobile society.

A third question is also of interest: Is a hyphenated Canadian a contradiction in terms? Is it possible to identify and participate as a Canadian, yet retain an affiliation with a certain ethnic heritage such as Lithuanian (or New Zealander or Tongan)? Again, the answer is in the affirmative. A hyphenated identity entitles people to compartmentalize their identities; in turn, the demands of a particular context will determine which identity is to be activated. Dual (even multiple) identities are not mutually exclusive; rather, they may complement each other in fulfilling diverse personal needs and goals. Nor does identification with select symbolic elements necessarily interfere with the business of making a living. As long as identification is restricted to the cognitive rather than the behavioural level, everyone can regard themselves as an "ethnic" without abdicating full and active participation within Canadian society. Access to the best of both worlds may help to explain the popularity and persistence of situational ethnicities.

Postmodern Ethnic Identity: Most perspectives on ethnicity reflect a modernist or "structuralist" approach. Structuralists see social groups or institutional arrangements as the fundamental building blocks of society, a primary source of human identity, a critical factor in shaping behaviour, and the key determinant of inter-group relations. According to structuralist thought, for each identifiable group there is a single ethno-culture with a unique and unchanging essence that can be grasped independently of context or without any reference to interaction with others (McHugh 1998). But the seemingly fixed, rigid, and locked-in identities of the modern era are eroding, giving way to the emergence of the **postmodern** self as relatively free floating and detached from conventional structures of identity. Individuals move in and out of so many different contexts and identities that the idea of categorizing them into stable ethnic groups no longer seems valid (Uitermark et al. 2005). People not only define themselves in terms of multiple national attachments, but also express themselves around identities both relational and contextual as well as fluid and contingent (Castells 1997; Parekh 2000). In short, ethnicities are increasingly evolving as hybrid identities that oscillate between the past and present, involving a multiplicity of crossovers in a world where people inhabit their paradoxes by inventing and reinventing their identities to fit an environment of fragmentation, plurality, and indeterminacy (Wiwa 2003; Giroux 1995; Hall 1996; Handa 2003).

Postmodern identities reflect the predicaments and opportunities of a contemporary era. The postmodern world we live in is a diasporic reality where (1) immigrants mingle with national minorities and indigenous peoples, (2) cultural boundaries are constantly invented, renegotiated, or hybridized, and (3) people politics assert innovative patterns of belonging based on intersecting lines of gender, sexual preferences, homeland, and ethnicity. Minority identities are continually changing and reinventing themselves by fusing with other ethnicities to create both unstable and provisional hybrids—neither stable nor coherent, much less fixed in some kind of essentialized past, but evolving, highly adaptive, and subject to the continuous play of context (Hall 1996; Modood 2000).

CASE STUDY	**Growing Up South Asian–Canadian: Walking the Postmodern Tightrope of Multiple Identities**

It is tough enough being an adolescent in a society that simultaneously if paradoxically reveres yet reviles youth (Anisef and Kilbride 2003). It is tougher still for second-generation immigrant youth who must confront the paradoxes of negotiating their way through Canadian society without trampling on parental tradition (Handa 2003; also Garroutte 2003; Biswas 2003). The process of identity formation is an especially vexing time for immigrant youth who confront a number of tensions that play themselves out at school, with family, friends, and peers, and in the labour market (Nazroo and Karlsen 2003). A juggling act comes into play because of the often conflicting challenges of fitting in and settling down within the context of a so-called culture clash. Admittedly, references to the concept of culture clash are misleading. What transpires is not a clash of cultures per se—such a model has a tendency to treat culture as fixed and static, and assumes the equivalence between cultures when clearly the reality of white Canadian power dynamics prevails. More accurately, what we have is a negotiated process involving a clash between selective aspects of modernity and tradition within contexts of power and politics (Handa 2003).

Youth Life on the Highwire

The oppositional tensions that youth confront are formidable. To one side, youth must balance the demands of home, family, and tradition with the challenges of performing well at school, forging healthy relations with peers and friends, developing a sense of belonging, and seeking employment opportunities. To the other, they are pushed to identify with the mainstream, thus compromising their relationship to parents

who may want them to become Western but not so Westernized as to lose respect for tradition and family values. Yet again, they must also resist, even rebel, against identifying too closely with the norms of mainstream society for fear of being accused of selling out to the "other" (Anisef and Kilbride 2003). Compounding the difficulties is the creation of diverse social strategies and psychological mechanisms for coping with disadvantage and discrimination in culturally appropriate ways (Ghuman 2003). For example, more time spent with one's "own ethnic kind" can provide a sense of security and belonging for youth because of shared perspectives on issues, experiences, and aspirations (Johal 2003). And yet too much of this in-group affiliation can prove a social death knell.

In short, immigrant youth confront some tough challenges (Desai and Subramanian 2003). They are seen by some as having problems because of adjustment difficulties and by others as creating problems because of a tendency toward anti-social or un-Canadian behaviour (Rathzel 2003). Problems also arise from conflicting expectations: Immigrant youth may want to maintain some connection with their parents and cultural tradition but not at the expense of precluding full participation in society. Conversely, most want to identify with mainstream Canada but not if this leads to wholesale abandonment of what makes them distinctive and authentic (Berry 2006).

Still tougher challenges await immigrant girls and young women—especially those from South Asian cultures. Not only do many often experience a conflicting set of standards compared to their brothers and boyfriends, but young immigrant girls and women are also expected to shoulder an unfair share of the burden in walking the highwire between "here" and "there." They are routinely framed as custodians of cultural tradition with an obligation to family honour yet, simultaneously, they must attend to the demands and expectations of living in the modern world outside the home. In walking the tightrope between modern and traditional, the parental and peer group, and community and culture, young second-generation women struggle to fashion an identity that reflects their experiences and realities of being Canadian in Canada (Handa 2003). For some, coping with the demands of opposing value systems is exciting and rewarding. For others, the perpetual tug between their immigrant roots and Canadian soil is confusing and frustrating; as aptly articulated by Puneet Parhar (cited in Ravinder Sandhu, 26 August 2003), "We grow up in the confusion of different morals, different values, and the fear of another culture."

Duelling Traditions: Navigating Bicultural Identities in a Multicultural Context

Consider the promises and perils of growing up Canadian for a South Asian youth whose parents migrated to Canada in search of opportunity. As often happens, second-generation South Asian youth are better off than their parents. Many are relatively free from those fears and frustrations that their parents had to endure, such as obligations to support family and relatives back home. They are also less likely to be ambivalent about the nature of their belonging to Canada, as the majority have no interest in returning to their parents' homeland. As explained by Riad Saloojee, Executive Director of the Council of America-Islam Relations in Canada, in acknowledging an emergent and positive Muslim-Canadian youth identity (cited in Martin 2004:42),

They see themselves as being firmly entrenched here. There are less emotional ties to the home country, in some cases none at all. They have a distinct Canadian and Muslim identity and many people see that as being perfectly compatible and harmonious.

Yet, unlike their parents, South Asian youth face a unique and equally baffling set of problems. Growing up in a multicultural society is fraught with pitfalls and paradoxes in negotiating answers to the question of "who am I" (Ghuman 2003). Their parents may be secure in their personal and social identities because of a rootedness in tradition, but the younger generation confront a bewildering set of options and choices as well as constraints and criticism. South Asian youth must constantly compare themselves to others in school in negotiating acceptance, yet worry about appeasing parents while saving face among peers at school (Johal 2003). What other choice do they have except to compartmentalize language and culture by speaking English to friends but reverting to their heritage language at home? For some, this code-switching is no problem; for others, the balancing act is as nerve-racking as life on a high wire.

Many of these challenges that confront young South Asians arise from tensions between competitively different value systems, namely those of home and community versus those of school and society at large. The former emphasizes religion, culture, and tradition of the sending society, while the latter not only emphasizes the opposing norms, beliefs, and values, but also possesses the power to reject or tolerate. One endorses customs and traditions such as extended family values, including the possibility of arranged marriages. The other promotes a competitive and freewheeling individualism—those very virtues that parents simultaneously reject yet endorse as keys to success in Canada. Contradictory demands are imposed on South Asian youth: ethnic emphasis vs. ethnic rejection; mainstream acceptance vs. mainstream resistance; ethnic and parental deference vs. peer group conformity. Also the paradox of obedience (parents want them to obey without losing the initiative to succeed); retention of parental culture against the backdrop of Canadian expectations and normative standards; and parental ambivalence toward success (be successful but not to the point of outgrowing their roots).

In short, South Asian youth are caught in a dilemma. They are confronted by the challenges of integration and full participation in the host culture; they are equally challenged by the prospect of losing their religious and cultural identities (see Alvi et al. 2003). They do not want to be left out of the "loop" and tend to see as rites of passage into the mainstream those very activities such as dating or parties that repulse their parents as diabolical and evil. Intergenerational conflicts between parents and offspring are inevitable. Parents are perceived as out of touch with the realities their children must confront on a daily basis. Children, by contrast, rarely take the time to understand the social, cultural, and economic pressures that parents must contend with in a secular and liberal Canada that often devalues their skills, culture, and values—leaving parents with little choice except to project their hopes for success on their children by making the appropriate sacrifices (Anisef and Kilbride 2003).

The end result is nothing short of confusing or infuriating. What constitutes proper behaviour is constantly compromised by mixed messages about irreconcilable differences between "the here" and "the over there" (Ghuman 2003). Youth identities must be negotiated in relation to "whiteness" as the normative reference point. South Asianness may be officially tolerated in Canada's multicultural matrix, but too much difference may compromise acceptance into the mainstream. As well, identity is negotiated in relationship to "South Asianness" as a reference point, yet excessive identification may run the risk of fostering stereotypes or social exclusion (Handa 2003). The challenge lies in finding a middle or hyphenated way, one in which there is a fusion or synthesis of two cultures (hybrids) without discarding the realities of both cultures.

Double Lives/Double Standards?

Not all South Asian youth confront the same problems. South Asian girls tend to experience additional difficulties in negotiating identities because of differences in gender expectations between "the home" in which they live and the wider society in which they participate (Ghuman 2003). Put bluntly, young South Asian women do not have as much freedom as their brothers and boyfriends because of double standards. South Asian families in Canada have tended to be more indulgent with sons, even to the point of overlooking social taboos related to dating, curfews, partying, drinking, food preferences, and dress codes. Yet, daughters and sisters are expected to conform religiously to the dictates of the culture. They are seen as symbols of tradition—custodians of culture and moral guardians—who must be protected from the polluting influence of the modern. Notions of women's sexuality—especially innocence, purity, and modesty in dress, behaviour, and body functions—are employed as a marker of virtue in marking the boundaries between the East and the West. Nor do young South Asian women have as much autonomy as their white classmates because of parental "paranoia." While dating and premarital sex may be routinely accepted by middle-class Canadian parents as part of the growing up process, South Asian families condemn such behaviour for fear of exposing their children to the risk of disease, sexual exploitation, and family dishonour in the case of unwanted pregnancies—not to mention the risk of not finding a suitable South Asian marital partner (Hai 2003).

The consequences of this protectiveness may prove highly awkward. To secure and negotiate their reputations, young South Asian women must create a generation space in which there is constant masking of truths as the price for upholding family and community honour in a sometimes hostile environment (Handa 2003). The codes of femininity and femalehood associated with South Asian cultures are so narrow that there is little wiggle room for crafting an identity that captures the complexities and nuances of living in a modern Canada. Yet, peer pressures are constantly mounting to "move with the times." As expressed by one young South Asian woman in dismissing the old-fashioned notion of saving virginity for marriage, "Sex is part of our culture now. Plus, there's a lot of pressure from the boys" (cited in Hai 2003).

Double standards complicate life for young South Asian women. No less complicating is the challenge of having to lead double lives by walking the tightrope of culture. They are under pressure to lead a double life that embraces being traditionally South Asian at home but a thoroughly modern Canadian against the backdrop of community scrutiny and parental restrictions. Young South Asian women must quickly learn what is acceptable for "good" daughters. They are aware that their behaviour, especially in sexual matters, will have an impact on how they and their families are viewed by the community, in that the community and relatives closely monitor their reputation and the family honour. Young South Asian women have little

recourse except to wear masks, safeguard secrets, tell "white" lies, protect reputations, and in general to engage in subterfuge of such daring and precision that a spy agency would be duly impressed (Hai 2003). Admittedly, there may be guilt about lying, but as one 18-year-old put it, "We live in fear of upsetting our parents, but we have to get on with life. We can't become isolated like your generation was" (cited in Hai 2003).

To say that young South Asian women are experiencing a crisis of identity is surely an understatement. They must learn to walk the tightrope of everyday life in constructing identities that balance the modern with the traditional within a predominantly white context of power, inequality, and racism. They must also learn to walk a cultural highwire in negotiating their reputation, as openness can inflict shame on the community, risk family criticism, or foster alienation from one's roots. Young South Asian women may have difficulty in balancing the impossible: On one side, belonging to a particular religion and culture; on the other side, a citizenship in a Canada that continues to harbour colonial perceptions about South Asia against the backdrop of extremism in the Muslim world (Alvi et al. 2003). Not surprisingly, tension and confusion are inevitable because of the double standards imposed on them by both parents and society at large. Of course, no one said that growing up South Asian in Canada was going to be easy. But some have it more difficult than others in navigating and negotiating the challenge of living within one's differences.

Insurgent Ethnic Identity: Both lived-in and situational ethnic identities appear to be relatively innocuous. Postmodern identities are equally "harmless" because of their preoccupation with the discourses of authenticity rather than the politics of power. With few exceptions, each of these identities upholds the multicultural axiom of "live and let live" by abiding by the slogan of "agreeing to disagree." But not all ethnic identities are so accommodating. Insurgent ethnic identities are much more assertive about what they believe is right or wrong, are highly politicized in terms of what they want, and are more aggressive in achieving their goals. Affiliation with insurgent ethnicity transcends mere identification or celebration. Insurgent ethnicity incorporates the notion of a shared attachment to a people, tradition, or territory by pushing this consciousness to the extreme. Ethnic identities become politicized and a primary focus of their politics in reaction to perceptions of rejection or marginalization (Nazroo and Karlsen 2003). In place of co-operative coexistence is a politicized assertion of peoplehood that establishes a new political order based on the principles of self-determining autonomy. An intense dislike of others may be actively fostered, especially when issues pertaining to religion, language, or homelands are factored into the competition. Such collectivities are willing to take whatever measures necessary to achieve their goals, including the revival of dormant grievances and recourse to violent measures (Taras and Ganguly 2002).

The playing out of insurgent ethnicities invariably leads to ethnic conflict. The exclusive, often essentialized, nature of insurgent ethnic identities is conducive to actions that pit one ethnicity against another in the competition for space or resources. Many of these conflicts have deep colonial roots. Consider Africa, where boundaries between states were created for political, military, economic, and diplomatic reasons, with little regard for ethnic differences and tribal borders. These artificially constructed and politically expedient nation-states are brittle and prone to fracture by tribal groups who seek a degree of autonomy at the expense of others. Ethnic conflicts inevitably arise from the clash of opposing principles, that is, the territorial integrity of the state versus the principle of national self-determination. This is especially seen in those countries where there is a lack of "fit" between the political borders of the state (a political organization) and the cultural borders of the nation (a politicized ethnic group). In this sense, the uncoupling of an ethnic nation from a political state is not an aberration but rather a politicized reaction to and rejection of dated nineteenth-century arrangements (Tishkov 2004). True, an insurgent ethnicity signals the undoing of centuries of colonial damage by breaking up the artificiality of nation-states established by colonial powers (Taras and Ganguly 2002). But an insurgent ethnicity transforms this defiance into a potent force for destabilizing a national or international order. Nowhere is this more evident than in the proliferation of highly politicized and ethnically driven social movements.

Ethnicity as a Social Movement

Ethnicity as a social movement entails the idea of peoples engaging in organized action to achieve the political goals of identity, voice, or land. Appeals to ethnicity provide a basis for mobilizing individuals into collective action; they also furnish the motivation and rationale to achieve ethnically defined goals. This surge of ethnic-based movements has come about for various reasons. The UN-based principle of national self-determination articulated a normative basis for making ethnically based political claims against the state. The collapse of superpower colonialism has also given rise to social formations that emphasized ethnic loyalties rather than the abstractions of citizenship (Ignatieff 1994). Tribal conflicts, once suppressed by colonialist control, have fuelled the revival of ancient cultural hatreds. Finally, the demise of the Cold War has created fertile conditions for ethnic conflict to flourish (Snyder 2001).

The dismantling of the Berlin Wall in 1989 was widely heralded as a defining moment in global history (Cooper 2003). Many saw its dismantling as a triumph of universalism and reason over the irrationalities of ideologues, rampant prejudices, and petty hostilities. But the promise proved short-lived; evident instead is an intensely parochial era in which the "key narrative of the new world order is the disintegration of nation states into warring factions. The key architects of that order are warlords; and the key language of our age is *ethnic nationalism*" (emphasis added) (Ignatieff 1994). With several exceptions, virtually all conflicts since 1990 have involved confrontations between ethnic groups within existing borders, largely because of the political vacuum created by collapsed states and stagnant economies (Gurr 2001; Taras and Ganguly 2002). Ancient animosities and dormant hatreds have been unleashed by these ethno-chauvinisms, and when twinned with religious intolerance, may invoke a passion and fury that has rattled an abiding faith in the decency of human nature (Behrens 1994; Kymlicka 1995; Tishkov 2004).

Nationalism constitutes the political expression of a nation whose peoples claim a common ancestry and shared destiny to govern themselves in a place they call a homeland (Wiebe 1996/97). The nineteenth century gave rise to nationalism in Europe, resulting in the birth of modern Germany, with its rallying cry of Germany for the Germans while being dismissive of Slavs, Jews, and Gypsies as unwelcome residue from past empires. In that the nation-state was defined by a shared language, culture, and identity (Smith 1999), all expressions of nationalism remain grounded in a simple ideal: namely, the idea of group exclusiveness, assertiveness of self-esteem and collective loyalty against outside threats (Rothchild and Groth 1995). As an ideological movement, the concept of nationalism asserts the divisibility of the world into fundamentally autonomous political communities by peoples who define themselves as a nation. They claim the status of an actual or potential nation, with corresponding rights to self-determination over homeland, identity, and political voice, either as self-governing entities (nation-states or countries) or as subunits within society (nations) (see also Pearson 2001). All nationalisms vest political sovereignty in a people's right to self-rule. In making this claim for self-determining autonomy, unity, and identity, nations are seeking to establish jurisdictional control over a defined homeland, in addition to reclaiming the sovereignty denied to them as a subject people (Graff 1994). To no one's surprise, the proliferation of nationalist movements poses a threat to the nation-state model that underpins a global world order (Kymlicka 2001).

Nationalist movements are frequently driven by the politics of exclusion. These nationalisms often involve the politicization of a conquered people who, because they have been involuntarily and forcibly incorporated into a nation-state, are now looking for a way out of this entrapment (Maaka and Fleras 2005). Unlike a **state**, which is essentially a political and administrative system, a **nation**(hood) consists of people who believe they are fundamentally different, insist on self-determination at social and cultural levels, and are deserving of political autonomy on those grounds (Snyder 2000). A moral community is proposed in which members feel themselves emotionally involved and responsible to each other, with a passionate attachment to a homeland as the site of pre-existing ethnic entitlements (Mead 1993). Membership is defined on the basis of birthright and descent from a common ancestry, with loyalty to the group or the homeland paramount over any commitment to the state or to social classes. The territorial rights, distinctive language, and shared ethnicity of this imagined political community must be defended from hostile interlopers, both internal and external, and by whatever means necessary.

Nationalisms can be classified by how they define who is entitled. Two patterns are discernible, in theory at any rate, based largely on divergent patterns of belonging as criteria for group membership, namely, civic and ethnic nationalism (Medrano and Koenig 2005). **Ethnic nationalisms** base their notion of a nation on largely ascriptive characteristics such as kinship ties, and use these criteria to include/exclude membership in a national group. Ethnic nationalism is aimed at building nationhood by strengthening a "peoples" (or nation) at the expense of others if necessary. With its focus on ascription, bloodlines, and descent, membership in the nationhood is restricted to those who can demonstrate common roots rather than shared attachments to key institutions and central values. By contrast, **civic nationalism** bases its appeal on loyalty to a set of political ideals, rule of law, the principle of inclusiveness, and institutions that are perceived as just and effective (Heath and Tilley 2005; Snyder 2000). Civic nationalism is concerned with society-building by strengthening the organization of the state. It maintains that society should be composed of all individuals, regardless of race or ethnicity, as long as they subscribe to the norms of this constructed community. This nationalism is called civic, Ignatieff observes, because it envisages society as a constructed community of equal rights-bearing citizens organized around a commitment to the rule of law (although some civic nationalisms have proven more ruthless than ethnic nationalism in advancing their goals). Ethnicity is largely irrelevant in determining belonging or inclusion, as membership is open to anyone who complies with core values and constitutional principles.

To be sure, the distinction between these nationalisms reflects ideal types rather than accurate reflections of reality. No nationalism is purely ethnic or civic. Ethnic nationalisms have proven more civic oriented than theory suggests; civic nationalisms, in turn, have proven more ethnically grounded than many give credit for (Neilson and Couture 1996/97; Resnick 2001; Kymlicka 2001; Vickers and de Seve 2000). The case of Quebec is instructive. To one side, Quebec's political aspirations were equated with ethnic nationalism because of a historical tendency to exclude those non-white francophones (Ignatieff 1994). To the other, Quebec's drive for autonomy within the Canadian state is defended as civic nationalism, that is, broad, tolerant, and inclusive of all who make the commitment to construct a modern political community without compromising its distinctiveness (see Editorial, *The Globe and Mail*, 16 December 2000). Is either position more correct than others, or are both correct in their own way—thus reflecting the emergence of a hybrid nationalism? Or perhaps we don't have a conceptual framework for a post-ethnic and non-racialized nationalism that is neither a defensive reaction nor an inclusive embrace (Kymlicka 2001).

INSIGHT	**White Nationalism: Separation or Supremacy?**

Nationalist movements are difficult to evaluate. Are they pro their own kind or anti the other? Does living with your own kind really create a better society with less conflict and more consensus? A new white racial advocacy movement has emerged in recent years that poses a robust challenge to the United States as an integrated melting pot (Swan 2002). Cultured and mannered, with impressive credentials from America's universities, in contrast to the hooded Klansmen of the past, the new white nationalists rely on the language of nationhood and national self-determination as well as the discourses of civil rights and ethnic identity politics to protect what they assert is their God-given right to a distinct white European society. Former white supremacists such as David Duke have reinvented themselves as white civil rights crusaders whose rhetoric taps into people's fears of an America swamped by supposedly inferior black and brown people with potentially catastrophic consequences in terms of diluting the culture and bloodlines that created America the great. As well, their identities as white people are gravely threatened by the emergence of multiculturalism, affirmative action programs, identity politics, racial intermarriage, and large-scale migration from non-white societies (see Ferber 1999).

White nationalists endorse a racialized view of the world, although they argue that they are neither racists nor white supremacists. They believe that race is a legitimate criterion for inclusion and entitlement within a community; after all, those societies that are dominated by a single race tend to be the least faction ridden and conflict prone (Levin 1998; Rushton 1995). Toward the creation of a neo apartheid, white nationalists want

to reclaim a part of America in which white people would be able to freely develop their culture and pursue their identities without hindrance from members of other racial groups—in a manner envisaged by the original fathers of Independence such as George Washington and Thomas Jefferson. The Pacific Northwest is touted as an ideal site for a white nation because of the current small numbers of migrants and minorities. Ironically, white nationalists have joined forces with black nationalists who too believe that integration cannot work and that racial separatism is the only solution (see Swan 2002).

DEPOLITICIZING ETHNICITY: CANADA-BUILDING

Ethnicity can no longer be dismissed as some primitive relic or primordial rage. Ethnicity is more than an obsessive craving to discover "roots" in the hopes of uncovering the past or collecting compensation. References to the irony of ethnic cleansing have seen to that. Nor should it be trivialized as a transient whimsy in a cultural backwater outside the path of rational progress and liberal democracy. Rather, ethnicity constitutes a socially constructed vehicle to advance collective interests and exploit economic and political opportunities (Gross 1996). Recourse to ethnicity provides a modicum of security in a highly impersonal and mechanized society by buffering the old from the new, the individual from society, and the familiar from the strange. Under the banner of ethnicity, individuals corroborate to maximize social advantage in a rational and calculated manner (Hechter 1975).

Ethnicity's potential for greatness or depravity is further magnified when coupled with the conflicting demands of a new global order. The new millennium is proving to be a bewildering place (Smith 1996; Fleras 2001). Gone are the global certainties of the past: The relatively simple verities of an established order have been superseded by a complex and multi-polar world whose moral ambivalence and political ambiguity both baffle and infuriate. Even the language has undergone changes to better describe new global realities because of rapid changes and a politicized ethnicity, with old words taking on new meanings while new words propose novel ways of thinking about what makes the world tick (Rosado 2005). With the obvious exception of the United States, no comparable political or military power has reclaimed the political vacuum created by the disintegration of the U.S.S.R., thus encouraging both intermediate powers and ethnic nationalisms to compete for vacated space. Not surprisingly, the very forces that many thought would reduce the risk of group conflicts have, paradoxically, increased inter-ethnic strife (Snyder 2000). The politics of ethnicity are here to stay, whether we like it or not, and, as postmodernity "bites" deeper, more ethnic conflicts are inevitable (Smith 1996).

Canada, as the world's third oldest federal system (behind the United States and Switzerland), is not unaffected by these political and cultural upheavals. Just as international relations are animated by a clash of competing and often incommensurable world views, so too does Canada's ethnicity agenda reflect both conflict and confusion (Kymlicka 2001). Rules that formerly defined right from wrong are openly challenged or deemed increasingly irrelevant. What once were defined as virtues are now vices, and vice versa. Aboriginal peoples are no longer willing to abide by colonial paradigms (Alfred 2005), the Québécois are looking for a foundationally different kind of partnership in association with the rest of Canada (Gibbins and Laforest 1998), and multicultural minorities want to re-contour Canada along inclusive lines (Fleras 2002). The politics of ethnicity are proving double-edged: Canada may be enriched by weaving national unity from the strands of diversity; alternatively, ethnic forces may ignite a chain reaction that could detonate Canada's society-building aspirations. That kind of paradox—how to make Canada safe from ethnicity, yet safe for ethnicity—raises the question of whether Canada can remain cohesive in the face of potentially divisive forces.

An official Multiculturalism represents Canada's answer to the politics of ethnicity. In advancing the then unorthodox notion that Canadians from all cultural backgrounds could fully contribute to Canada without the spectre of prejudice or discrimination, Canada's official Multiculturalism is premised on the belief that all citizens can find a place and protection for their identities, even multiple identities, without sacrificing integration into Canada's social, political, and economic framework (Jenson and Papillon 2001). Multiculturalism in Canada is premised on the notion that a Canada of many different cultures and diverse people can live together with their differences. This is possible in part by transcending the specifics of cultures to ensure that no one is excluded from full and equal participation in society because of their ethnicity; in part by acknowledging the legitimacy of ethnic differences as long as they stay within limits.

But protection and preservation of ethnocultural diversity as grounds for living differently together comes with a qualifier. Canada's multiculturalism is constructed around a narrow reading of ethnicity. Put bluntly, an official Multiculturalism is not concerned with promoting ethnic diversity or ethnic communities. Few societies could survive the strain of multiple competing groups with clearly demarcated political boundaries, a separate power base, and parallel institutions. Even fewer are equipped for addressing the society-busting demands of ethnic nationalism. Nowhere is this more evident than in Canada. Ethnicity within the framework of Canada's multicultural commitments is justified only when stripped of its potency to divide or incite. In place of a politicized ethnicity in the competition for scarce resources, multiculturalism endorses the symbols of differences at personal or private levels. Rather than taking differences seriously, the "pretend pluralism" endorsed by an official Multiculturalism accommodates the appearance (rather than the substance) of ethnicity without challenging the interconnectedness at the core of Canadian society (Fleras 2002).

In other words, an official Multiculturalism is not about promoting ethnic cultures as distinct and coherent lifestyles (Modood 1997). More accurately, it revolves around a **depoliticizing ("neutering") of ethnicity**. Under an official Multiculturalism, ethnicity is rendered tolerable as long as (1) people identify only with the symbols of their difference, (2) this identification is restricted to the personal and private rather than public realm, and (3) this affiliation does not violate the laws of the land, interfere with the rights of others, or conflict with core Canadian values and constitutional principles. Put bluntly, then, Canada's official

Multiculturalism does not exist to "celebrate" ethnicity. More to the point, official Multiculturalism is more concerned with neutering ethnicity as a framework for living together with what's left of our differences (consider the analogy: when your pet is neutered, it still looks like your pet but appearances are deceiving because Spot has lost a lot of its oomph). In a society of many cultures, in other words, no one should be denied or excluded because of their ethnic origins. By the same token, according to Canada's integrative multiculturalism, no one should be given special treatment because of their ethnic identity (Fleras 2003).

Herein, then, lies the appeal of postmodern and situational ethnic identities within a multicultural society. Promotion of ethnic identity at these levels comes across as relatively innocuous, as recognition does not fundamentally alter the political and economic status quo. In neutering the potential of ethnicity as a force for resistance and transformation, official Multiculturalism represents Canada's much debated response to the challenges of making society safe for ethnicity as well as safe from ethnicity (Fleras 1998). Time will tell whether Canada's multicultural response for engaging ethnicity will be sufficient for those minorities who are seeking to make ethnicity safe from society, yet safe for society.

DEBATE REVISITED | **Is Canadian an Ethnicity?**

The notion of white ethnicity is sharply contested. Some argue that whiteness is not an ethnicity, others say it is, and still others say it may depend on the context. To some extent, responses will depend on how ethnicity is defined. Implicit in most definitions of ethnicity is the notion of a shared awareness of common history and destiny as a basis for membership (engagement) or rewards (entitlements). Applying this ideal of ethnicity as consciousness would appear to exclude the "whitestream," except for pockets of active ethnicity at the extreme right of the political continuum. At best, then, whiteness may be defined as ethnicity, but this white people-as-ethnicity is properly described as hidden or dormant, with the potential to be activated when necessary or to assert itself when challenged.

Two points prevail in rethinking white ethnicity. First, definitions of ethnicity as a conscious awareness of differences may need to be modified to include the idea of "potential" awareness as a defining characteristic. The fact that nearly 39 percent of respondents (single and multiple responses) on the 2001 Census identified as Canadians suggests such a reading. Moreover, those white people who prefer to acknowledge a home-grown ethnicity (i.e., Canadianness) should not be regarded as any less ethnic than the hyphenated ethnicities associated with ancestral homelands (Howard-Hassmann 1999). Second, refusal to acknowledge white ethnicity may be more problematic than acknowledging it. Denial of white ethnicity may have the effect of elevating whiteness as the universal norm rather than just another manifestation of the human experience. This denial also has the consequence of privileging whiteness by making ethnicity synonymous with being a minority, with a corresponding trivializing of status or achievement. Refusal to "ethnicize" the dominant sector tends to privilege the mainstream as the hidden centre—the unmarked standard of normalcy—but at the cost of masking the socially constructed nature of "white-o-centric" society. The ethnically informed values that underpin the so-called neutral "whitestream" institutions are also marked.

How do we account for this denial? Why do minorities clearly see the privileged ethnicity of the mainstream yet the whitestream appears oblivious to its ethnicity? The dominant sector's inability or refusal to identify itself ethnically can be attributed to the quality of life enjoyed by those with power and privilege. Those in positions of advantage are rarely conscious of their advantages. After all, just as fish are unaware of their aquatic environment, so too are privileges, rather than handicaps or barriers, more likely to be taken for granted (McIntosh 1988). Not surprisingly, ethnicity for the mainstream plays little or no overt role in shaping thought or behaviour. Whitestream members are rarely reminded of their uniqueness on a day-to-day basis because (1) they are unlikely to have their ethnic identity challenged by mainstream institutions, (2) they are much less likely to have encountered prejudice, discrimination, or disadvantage because of ethnicity or race, and (3) they rarely find themselves in a position of having to defend a threatened ethnic identity (Doane 1997). By contrast, those in positions of disadvantage routinely and sharply experience the dynamics of being different, of having to defend their differences, and of being disadvantaged because of them.

The consequences of ignoring white ethnicity are contrary to healthy ethnic relations. Put candidly, to ignore white ethnicity runs the risk of redoubling its hegemony by naturalizing whiteness as normal and necessary (Spoonley 1993:57). The emergence of a Canadian ethnicity may have a useful "de-centring" effect. Attention is directed at mainstream Canada as part of the multicultural landscape rather than an unquestioned norm that is beyond judgment. Time will tell if mainstream Canadians can endorse the idea that they themselves are yet another tile in the multicultural mosaic rather than the all-defining grout. It also remains to be seen if a planetary model of multiculturalism as a basis for living together, with white people at the centre and minorities in orbit, will give way to a multiple helix model in which all strands are interwoven in mutual complementariness. The challenge would appear twofold: first to render visible the invisibility of the mainstream as an ethnicity and, second, to question the status of white-as-ethnicity as the normative standard by which to judge, compare, and criticize.

CHAPTER HIGHLIGHTS

- Sociologists tend to see ethnicity as a key variable in shaping what we think and do and how others respond to us. Ethnicity is also important as an explanatory framework in helping to explain patterns of behaviour at individual and group levels.

- Ethnicity can be defined as a shared awareness of ancestral differences as a basis for engagement or entitlement. Both subjective experiences and objective properties are integral for mobilizing individuals into action groups.

- The surge in ethnicity can be explained in primordialist and constructivist approaches (identity and instrumentalist terms).

- Ethnicity is manifested in three ways: ethnic communities, ethnic identities, and new social movements.

- Ethnicity can provide an important component of identification for many Canadians. Ethnic identities can be expressed at the level of lived-in, symbolic, postmodern, and insurgent.

- Especially when harnessed with a vibrant nationalism, ethnicity is a powerful political force and potent social movement. The politicization of ethnicity under an ethnic nationalism has grave consequences in disrupting the rhythm of an established order.

- Ethnically diverse countries confront a challenge with respect to national identity and unity. Initiatives such as Canada's official Multiculturalism are best seen as moves to depoliticize ethnicity as a precondition for Canada-building.

KEY TERMS

civic nationalism	lived-in ethnic identity
constructivist explanation	nation
depoliticizing ("neutering") of ethnicity	nationalism
ethnic	politicization
ethnic groups	postmodern ethnic identity
ethnicity	postmodern
ethnic nationalism	primordial explanation
identity politics	resource mobilization theory
identity thesis	situational (or symbolic) ethnic identity
instrumentalist approach	state
insurgent ethnic identity	symbolic ethnic identity

REVIEW QUESTIONS

1. Define ethnicity and demonstrate how and why both subjective and objective attributes should be part of the definition.

2. Two major approaches—primordialist and constructivist—have historically been utilized to explain the ethnic surge. Compare how each approaches the nature and extent of the ethnic experience.

3. Compare ethnic nationalism and civic nationalism as ideal types with respect to their underlying logic in creating a new society.

4. How is ethnicity expressed? Focus on the notions of community, identity, and social movement.

5. What are the impact and implications for ethnicity in Canada's continuing efforts to make the country safe for ethnicity as well as safe from ethnicity?

6. Ethnicity is seen by sociologists as a key variable that accounts for patterns of human behaviour. Explain, with examples.

LINKS AND RECOMMENDATIONS

Films

Several films capture some of the ethnic tensions between generations, including *Bollywood/Hollywood*; *Bend It Like Beckham*, and *Monsoon Wedding*.

A film called *The "N" Word* provides a wide-ranging discussion of the politics of the word "nigger" in everyday use.

Books

Peter Li (1998). *The Chinese in Canada*. 2nd Ed. Oxford University Press.

Morton Weinfeld (2001). *Like Everyone Else . . . But Different. The Paradoxical Success of Canadian Jews*. Toronto: CJS.

Reginald Bibby (2002). *Restless Gods. The Renaissance of Religion in Canada*. Toronto: Stoddart.

The following books provide excellent insights into the micro politics of identity when young people need to walk the tightrope between over here and over there:

Anisef Paul and Kenise Murphy Kilbride (eds.) (2003). *Managing Two Worlds: The Experiences and Concerns of Immigrant Youth in Ontario*. Toronto: Canadian Scholars Press.

Handa, Amita (2003). *Of Silk Saris and Mini Skirts: South Asian Girls Walk the Tightrope of Culture*. Toronto: Women's Press.

Journals

The fall 2005 issue of *Canadian Diversity* (vol. 4, no. 3) is devoted to *Negotiating Religious Pluralism: International Approaches*.

Websites

Canadian Ethnocultural Association.
  www.ethnocultural.ca

Canadian cultures—celebrating Canada's multicultural diversity.
  www.culturescanada.ca

Association for Canadian Studies. Numerous articles and research reports on ethnicity in Canada.
  www.acs-aec.ca

The Metropolis project is a global research "team" that explores issues of ethnicity and urbanization.
  www.metropolis.net

RACIALIZED INEQUALITY

Employment Equity: A Solution in Search of a Problem?

Canada is widely proclaimed as an egalitarian society whose commitment to inclusiveness is globally admired and occasionally emulated. Yet, Canada has proven to be a paradox in engaging diversity. On one side, nearly all major institutions, both private and public, have policies and programs in place to create a more inclusive institutional setting. Both the private sector and federally regulated institutions like telecommunication firms have incorporated diversity principles for doing business in the twenty-first century. No less active are banks such as Montreal and CIBC with a large number of women as senior managers. On the other side, the results of this social engineering are modest at best, dismal at worst, with many of the targeted groups still continuing to endure workplace discrimination (Galabuzi 2006). Institutional disparities at the level of the federal services are particularly worrying: While 13.4 percent of Canadians in 2001 self-identified as visible minorities, racialized populations occupied only 3 percent of the executive suites in the federal public services. Numbers are particularly low at senior levels, with racialized minorities constituting a mere 1.7 percent of directors on boards of organizations (Conference Board 2004). A similar situation exists in the United States (Associated Press 2005). In that Canada's federal service does not reflect the diversity of the public it serves, its motto as "merit based, non-partisan, and representative" appears at odds with the government's multicultural commitments. To overcome this potentially embarrassing situation, the federal government's Embracing Change policy has penciled in a target of "one in five" for the hiring, training, and promotion of visible minorities within the public service.

Several questions come to mind. How do we account for these disparities in a system committed to the principle of inclusiveness? Is the status quo acceptable? Is the current rate of improvement sufficient to bring about parity? What should be done to achieve a critical mass of racialized minorities within the workforce? Canada's response to this inequitous state of affairs involves a commitment to the principles and practices of Employment Equity. Yet, few issues have elicited as much admiration or hostility as this formal initiative for inclusiveness at institutional levels. For some, this exercise in preferential hiring is nothing less than "reverse" discrimination against white males that creates more problems than it solves; for others, it is seen as a bold venture in "**reversing discrimination**"; for still others, it can take on different meanings—"reverse" or "reversing"—depending, of course, on the frame of reference.

One way of cutting through this impasse is by making a key distinction. On the one hand the concept of employment equity can be interpreted as a philosophy for attainment of equality through institutional inclusiveness (see insight in this chapter). On the other hand, the *Employment Equity Act* represents an official government policy and program in place since 1986. The two are not the same, despite sounding alike (but note the upper case in reference to the official version), but reflect a distinction between ideals and practices. Nor does an endorsement of **employment equity as philosophy** automatically translate into support for **Employment Equity as official policy**. Failure to acknowledge this distinction can lead to misunderstanding and miscommunication.

The Employment Equity Act constitutes a legislated program with a formal set of practices for advancing mandated government goals. Employment Equity initiatives are aimed at proactively assisting those historically disadvantaged minorities who, through no fault of their own, have been excluded from full and equal workplace participation—even though workplace discrimination has been illegal since 1962. Good intentions informed the passage of the *Employment Equity Act* of 1986, which was updated in 1996 to include the federal public service:

> [E]quality in the workplace so that no person shall be denied employment opportunities or benefits for reasons unrelated to ability . . . by giving effect to the principle that employment equity means nothing more than treating persons in the same way but also requires special measures and the accommodation of differences.

Terms of the 1986/96 Act applied to all federally regulated employers (with 100 or more employees), public sector companies, and Crown corporations. These companies were obligated to file and submit annual reports on the composition of their workforce, with particular reference to the number and type of work performed by the four targeted groups, including women, visible (racialized) minorities, people with disabilities (differently able), and Aboriginal peoples. (for difficulties in defining visible minorities, see Pendakur 2005) Also falling under the Employment Equity provisions were federal contractors with at least 100 employees. Each had to sign a certificate of compliance in accord with **equity** provisions if they intended to bid on government goods or services contracts worth $200 000 or more.

As policy and program, Canada's *Employment Equity Act* bears some affinity to Affirmative Action in the United States. Both initiatives endorse the principle of hiring and promoting minorities in numbers commensurate with their proportion in the general workforce. Both are also bound by principle to remove discriminatory barriers for bringing about a more supportive institutional environment. Yet, differences can be discerned—at least in theory if not always in practice. Unlike Affirmative Action, Canada's *Employment Equity Act* rejects the idea of government-mandated quotas and deadlines, including the idea of an externally imposed system of fixed percentages to be achieved within a certain time frame. Under such a framework, American companies felt compelled to hire even unqualified personnel if only to comply with the law, to circumvent penalties, or to secure government contracts. By contrast, Canada's Employment Equity targets and timetables are much more flexible, involving "reasonable expectations" about hiring and promotion of individuals from qualified groups when and if available for employment. Targets are preferred over deadlines because it allows an employer to make a reasonable effort in creating a representative workforce. Finally, emphasis is proactively directed at improving workplace representation by reforming the processing of personnel for employment.

There is yet another similarity. Just as Affirmative Action invites widespread criticism (Sowell 2004), so too has Canada's *Employment Equity Act* triggered an avalanche of reactions, both supportive and dismissive. Consider the public outcry when the federal government advertised a $100 000-a-year senior public service job in British Columbia that insisted on visible minority applicants. Supporters endorsed this Employment Equity move as a necessary intervention to break the cycle of institutional exclusion that historically has compromised minority women and men. Critics disagree, and argue that decades of race-based equity programs in Canada and the United States have done more harm than good (Loney 1998; D'Angelo and Douglas 2005).

Reaction to Employment Equity appears to vary along political lines. On the right, Employment Equity is criticized as a violation of (1) the principle of equality and **merit**, (2) principles of liberal universalism, and (3) the right of corporations to conduct business as they see fit. On the left, critics attack Employment Equity as a Band-Aid strategy that fails to address the root causes of unequal distribution. Passage of the federal Employment Equity legislation twenty years ago may have sough to end workplace discrimination while providing the historically disadvantaged with some leverage to improve equity, access, and representation. Nevertheless, racialized groups and immigrants continue to confront numerous obstacles, including a "revolving door" that makes entry and access difficult, a "sticky floor" that limits opportunities for initial advancement, and a "glass ceiling" that precludes achievement of senior positions (Conference Board 2004).

In between the "yeas" and the "nays" are those who agree with the intent of Employment Equity but fear its backlash or unintended consequences. Many are puzzled by inherent contradictions. For example, as Canada becomes increasingly diverse, mainstream institutions are under increased pressure to standardize by adopting universal (colour and culture blind) standards that transcend the claims of any one constituent group except, of course, the hegemonic claims of the dominant group (Sowell 2004). Or consider this paradox: According to the principles of liberal universalism, all individuals are equally different, in part because our commonalities as morally autonomous and freewheeling individuals supersede our differences as group members—at least for purposes of recognition or reward. This refusal to take differences seriously may preclude the possibility of assisting the historically disadvantaged by way of racial preferences (Crawford 2003).

Which position is correct: "yes," "no," "maybe," or "it depends"? Responses can be rephrased around a series of questions. Is Employment Equity about giving minorities preference in competition for jobs or positions? Or does it involve redesigning institutional criteria to provide minority women and men with the same opportunities as all Canadians (see Holmes 2001)? Is it about changing the composition of the workforce by switching white incumbents for black and brown, or is Employment Equity aimed at transforming the "business as usual" mindset and "that's how it's done around here" structures that systemically deny or exclude? Should Employment Equity be restricted only to the historically disadvantaged who have suffered decades of deprivation or exclusion? Or should it be directed at anyone who is poor or marginalized, regardless of race or ethnicity? To what extent does Employment Equity help to right historical wrongs by "reversing" discrimination? Or is it really an exercise in political correctness that—despite good intentions—"reverses" discrimination against white people? Does it involve upholding the merit principle by expanding the pool of applicants, or does it violate the equality and fairness principle by privileging group membership over individual merit (Reyna et al. 2005)? Is it possible to create a better *Employment Equity Act* than the one in place at present? Should the focus be on targets and timetables, or on the removal of discriminatory barriers to ensure that real merit is recognized and rewarded (Samuel 1997)? The Debate Revisited at the end of the chapter will cast some additional light on this clearly vexing issue.

INTRODUCTION: CANADA'S RACIALIZED INEQUALITY

The test of a just society, a society organized around the principles of equality and human dignity, is how it treats the most vulnerable of its members—children, women, the elderly, the sick, refugees, minorities, and Aboriginals. We must aspire for a society in which no one is left behind, in which equality is not only an ideal but a constitutional norm, in which we extend a hand to those disadvantaged and discriminated against, in which we build bridges rather than erect walls in our multicultural mosaic. (Honourable Irwin Cotler addressing the annual meeting of the Canadian Bar Association, 16 August 2004; available at http://canada.justice.gc.ca/en/news/sp/2004/doc_31202.html)

Canada cherishes its image as a fundamentally egalitarian utopia. With supposedly few extremes in poverty or wealth, Canadians like to see themselves as a predominantly "race-less" society that disdains the evils of prejudice, discrimination, and **racism**. There is some truth to this collective self-perception. Compared to its racist and exclusionary past, Canada has evolved into a remarkably open and equitable society with a powerful commitment to equality before the law, regardless of a person's background or beliefs. Ideally, all the ethnic tiles in Canada's multicultural "mosaic" are envisaged as contributing equally to the whole. Each component is also viewed as deserving of a fair share of the entitlements and rewards. This bucolic portrayal is arguably true in a relative sense as well, given the magnitude of inequities and exploitation elsewhere.

But appearances are deceiving. Canada can be more accurately portrayed as an unequal and stratified society—a racialized, vertical, and "sticky" mosaic—with wealth concentrated in the hands of the few (Kunz et al. 2001; Teelucksingh and Galabuzi 2005). Income and opportunity gaps that privilege some while disempowering others have reinforced a pattern of racialized stratification that says a lot about the powers of self-deception. Racialized groups continue to be stratified unequally against a "mosaic" of raised (dominant) and lowered (subordinate) tiles (Tepper 1988). Pyramids of privilege exist that elevate the white "male stream" to the top of the heap and the racialized others to the bottom—in many cases through no fault of their own. Sadly, neither the inception of official Multiculturalism nor the introduction of Employment Equity initiatives have appreciably altered this arrangement, with some measures having had the somewhat perverse effect of perpetuating inequality. In other words, all the deeply ingrained myths in the country cannot disguise the obvious: Canada remains a racially stratified society where differences because of race and ethnicity continue to make a difference in terms of who gets what and how much (Pendakur 2005).

That Canada is stratified by race and ethnicity should come as no surprise. Racism is a deeply embedded and defining characteristic of Canadian history, despite mythologizing to the contrary, and the tenacious hold of white "suprema-centrism" has underscored the damaging legacy of a racially stratified inequality (Backhouse 1999). Some minorities do well because of or in spite of their ethnicity; others suffer, and may never recover; and still others do not appear adversely affected one way or the other (Breton et al. 1990). This observation raises a number of questions for discussion and debate. What causes **racialized inequality**? Who is responsible? If **racialized minorities** are doing poorly in the economy, is this evidence of discrimination, a lack of human capital (from education to work experience to language competence), or the play of market forces that limits economic opportunities (Hum and Simpson 2000)? Is the problem attributable to minority cultures and values that discourage coping and success? Or should the finger be pointed at mainstream structures that, wilfully or unintentionally, manage to create discriminatory barriers? Answers to these questions remain at the forefront of vigorous debate, with varied and contradictory responses that reflect different visions of Canada as a society.

This chapter is predicated on the assumption that racialized inequality is neither "natural" nor "healthy." Rather inequalities (namely the gap between rich and poor) are highly toxic because of their corrosive effect in fraying the social fabric of society (Wilkinson 2005). The devaluations and put downs associated with low social status, dominance hierarchies, and dysfunctional communities can prove extremely stressful, Richard Wilkinson writes, with devastating impacts on society, ranging from people's health and life expectancies to the erosion of social trust. No less an indictment of inequality and its effect on society is captured in this excerpt from a keynote address delivered by Kay McConney, Consul-general of Barbados, at the recent Harry Jerome Awards in Toronto:

> The prosperity of Canada, this province, this city, are inextricably bound to the prosperity of its constituent communities. Should communities . . . be left behind in the margins of Canada's economic prosperity, then that prosperity that enfranchises only a few will not withstand the explosive anger of upheaval by the discontented masses . . . (cited in Editorial, Equal Opportunity, Equal Justice For All, *Toronto Star,* 12 May 2005)

This chapter draws on these themes by exploring the inequitable relationship of racialized minority groups to society at large. Inequality in Canada is not randomly distributed but stratified around the poles of race and ethnicity even as each intersects with social **class** and gender to intensify crosscutting patterns of exclusion and exploitation. Racialized inequality is approached not as a personal defect of human nature, but as a social construct involving an interplay of structure and agency, thus making it amenable to criticism, challenge, and reform.

Such a macro perspective focuses on how these inequities are created, expressed, and sustained as well as challenged and transformed by way of government initiative, institutional reform, and minority assertiveness. The content of this chapter is organized around the racialization of inequality in Canada, exploring the relationship of race, ethnicity, and **class** to inequality and stratification. (The next chapter looks at gendered inequality.) Issues for discussion include (1) the nature of racialized inequality, (2) how this inequality is manifested, (3) why it exists, and (4) what can be done about it. The chapter begins by looking at the magnitude and scope of racialized inequality both in the past and at present. This is followed by a brief insight into the paradoxes of black socio-economic status in the United States. The concept of racialized inequality is examined next from a functionalist and conflict perspective, including a discussion of the relationship between race and class. The chapter concludes by pointing out how discourses about inequality and equality are undergoing revision in response to social, political, and demographic changes. References to the debates over employment equity as a philosophy and Employment Equity as a government program put these discursive shifts into perspective.

CASE STUDY	From Ethnicity to Race: A New Vertical Mosaic

John Porter's seminal book *The Vertical Mosaic* (1965) is widely regarded as the quintessential Canadian study of ethnicity and inequality. For Porter, Canada's tapestry of cultural differences was stratified vertically along ethnic lines, hence the expression "**vertical mosaic**." Porter argued that ethnic groups in Canada were arranged hierarchically, with the British and, to a lesser extent, the French monopolizing the role of gatekeeper in regulating entry into the corridors of power. Non-British and non-French immigrants occupied an inferior socio-economic status because of their lower entry status into Canada. Retention of ethnicity also hampered the upward mobility of ethnic minorities, leading to what Porter called an ethnic mobility trap. For immigrant groups, ethnicity and inequality proved a paradox. According to Porter, attainment of equality and success depended on rejecting their ethnic background and assimilating into the mainstream. But severing their ethnic ties also increased the risk of relinquishing an invaluable support system. Embracing their ethnicity was no solution

either: To the extent that racial and ethnic groups became trapped in self-contained communities, Porter claimed, social mobility would be compromised. Not surprisingly, Porter chided the Canadian government for its misguided efforts to encourage ethnicity by way of multiculturalism. That multiculturalism would entrench ethnic inequality by relegating ethnic minorities to a perpetual lower class status was bad enough. Even worse, he argued, the promotion of ethnicity at the expense of equal opportunity would also undermine national prosperity.

How accurate was Porter's assessment of Canada as a vertical mosaic? Do his conclusions stand up to the test of time (Helmes-Hayes and Curtis 1998)? Many have contested Porter's key arguments about the determinacy of ethnicity in shaping Canadian stratification (Lian and Matthews 1998). Consider how many European-based ethnics have adjusted to Canadian society as social equals, but without having to relinquish affiliation with selective elements of their traditional past (Weinfeld 2001). European ethnic minorities in Toronto, especially the

Germans and Ukrainians, have achieved a high level of incorporation into society as measured by economic rewards and socio-political acceptance (Breton et al. 1990).

But not all minority women and men are so "lucky." Racialized minorities continue to be stratified and subjected to denial, exclusion, or exploitation (Kunz et al. 2001; Finnie and Meng 2002; Teelucksingh and Galabuzi 2005). Canadians of Chinese, African, and Caribbean origins remain stuck near the bottom of the socio-economic heap. Even higher levels of educational achievement may fail to buffer them from poverty, under(un)employment, and income disadvantage (Pendakur 2000). The situation has improved, of course, thanks to the passage of human rights and multicultural legislation. Yet, both foreign-born and racialized minorities continue to be shunted into marginal employment ghettos with few possibilities for escape or advancement. Seasonal labourers from Mexico and the Caribbean are brought into Canada on a temporary basis for seasonal employment primarily in agricultural work, yet exposed to systemic biases including ineligibility for unemployment insurance. Domestic workers (nannies) from the Philippines are exploited by middle-class families who should know better (Simmie 2004). Working conditions for nannies are reported to be among the most demanding of any occupation, subject to abuse and emotional blackmail, with many domestic workers denied fundamental workers' rights because of discriminatory laws (Stasiulis and Bakan 1997).

In short, as Breton et al. (1990) concede, the vertical mosaic concept needs to be rethought. Certain ethnic groups have little or no trouble with integration into the mainstream, even while maintaining their ethnocultural identity. The same degree of mobility does not apply to those minority women and men who are racially visible. Put bluntly, the vertical mosaic of Porter has been displaced by a racialized mosaic that is both birth based and colour coded (Teelucksingh and Galabuzi 2005).

A RACIALIZED MOSAIC

Canada's involvement in multiculturalism, employment equity, and human rights deserves commendation. But national studies continue to expound on what many "intuitively" know: Not all Canadians are created equal when it comes to distributing the "goodies," with the result that Canada is characterized by layers of racialized inequality (Galabuzi 2006). Inequality can be defined as the unequal distribution of scarce resources. Access to the good things in life (from power and prestige to property) is not randomly distributed but patterned, persistent, and resistant to reform. Race has long proven a key variable (predictor) in shaping unequal outcomes. First, racialized groups may be singled out as inferior or irrelevant, and dismissed accordingly. Second, racialized groups are thought to possess social and cultural patterns not only at odds with the mainstream, but also at a disadvantage in the competition for scarce resources. Finally, an inequality that is racialized embraces the notion that inequities between racialized groups go beyond individual prejudice. Rather, they are embedded within the structures of society, namely, at institutional levels where hidden agendas and systemic biases are at play (Jiwani 2001).

Herein lies the gist of what is sociologically known as **racial(ized) stratification**. The term "stratification" can be employed in two ways (See and Wilson 1988). First, it refers to hierarchical systems in which scarce resources are unequally distributed among diverse minority groups. Second, it consists of highly segmented systems in which minority groups occupy specialized occupational statuses that reflect a racial(ized) division of labour. These ranked differences in occupation or valued resources are not randomly scattered across the population. Nor are they of a transitory nature, that is, reflecting the "costs" of initial adjustment. These differences are patterned and pervasive insofar as they are socially significant, deeply embedded, and have proven difficult to dislodge.

Income Differences

Canada too is highly stratified along racial(ized) lines despite claims to the contrary. Inequality remains a fact of life in Canadian society if income differences are measured (Pendakur 2005). Income measures have historically been used to measure inequality between groups, that is, to determine if there is labour market discrimination, by comparing the annual earnings of racialized minorities with those of white Canadians. Consider this study, presented in Table 5.1, involving average employment income, visibility of Canadians (racialized vs. all Canadians), and gender and age (see also Teelucksingh and Galabuzi 2005).

According to the data in Table 5.1 (Statistics Canada 2003), racialized women generally do more poorly than women in general and racialized men; racialized men do less well than men at all age levels; and older males and females, except for those in the retirement bracket, generally outperform younger men and women. Yet, there are dangers in making such simple income comparisons. Such studies are incomplete—perhaps even misleading—because they combine all racialized minorities into a single category without distinguishing between those born in Canada and those who are foreign-born but now residents of Canada (Hum and Simpson 2000). Consider how an important study by Jean Lock Kunz and associates (2001) for the Canadian Race Relations Foundation focused on the earning disparities between white people (or non-racialized groups) and visible minorities (racialized groups) with regard to average annual income, gender, and immigrant status (foreign-born), as set out in Table 5.2.

The table clearly demonstrates how labour market disadvantages exist for racialized immigrants (Hum and Simpson 2000). Canadian-born men, both racialized and non-racialized, outearn foreign-born racialized males but not foreign-born white people. Men across all categories do better than women regardless of visibility and place of birth; and Aboriginal peoples rank at the bottom for both genders. As well, regional differences across Canada are noticeable; as Table 5.3 reveals, with few exceptions foreign-born visible minorities and Aboriginal people are underperforming in relationship to the other categories—in the process reinforcing references to Canada as a racialized mosaic.

TABLE 5.1 Income, Visibility, Gender, and Age, 2000				
	Racialized Minorities		**All Canadians**	
Age of Persons*	**Men**	**Women**	**Men**	**Women**
15–24	$22 394	$20 707	$23 696	$19 634
25–44	$41 638	$32 462	$47 611	$35 048
45–64	$46 626	$33 664	$55 754	$37 407
65 and over	$41 568	$23 663	$44 661	$28 171
All over 14	$42 377	$32 143	$49 224	$34 892

* Includes only those in full-time, full-year employment (adapted from Statistics Canada 2003).

TABLE 5.2	Earnings* by Gender, Racialization, and Place of Birth (in $)		
	Male	**Female**	**Total**
Racialized minority (CB)	42 433	33 519	38 582
Racialized minority (FB)	35 329	27 075	31 829
White people (CB)	43 456	31 150	38 529
White people (FB)	46 457	31 627	40 854
Aboriginal peoples	32 369	26 361	29 290

* Full-time, full-year earnings for those aged 25 to 64.

CB—Canadian Born

FB—Foreign Born

Adapted from Kunz et al. 2001.

Source: 1996 Census, Public Use Microdata File

Paradoxically, higher education levels may not improve income levels of racialized minorities. Minorities, especially racialized immigrants, have generally higher education levels than white people or Aboriginal peoples based on postsecondary degrees held (but a larger percentage also possess less than grade 8 education). Yet highly educated racialized immigrants tend to trail behind Canadian-born white people and minorities with regard to employment, income, and access to professional/managerial jobs (Kunz et al. 2001). The irony is inescapable: Canada's foreign-born workforce may be becoming increasingly educated, yet racialized immigrants continue to experience difficulties in securing employment consistent with their qualifications or overseas experience. To the extent that discrimination and racism may account for these differences, such workplace bias is rarely openly expressed but tends to be subtle or systemic.

Not all minorities are doing poorly. Studies indicate that Canadian-born black people face a statistically significant wage gap, once other variables such as education are controlled (Hum and Simpson 2000; Jedwab 2004). Table 5.4 compares the average income of black people in Canada and non-racialized minorities, then provides a percentage difference between the

TABLE 5.3	Earnings* by Region and Racialized Groups (in $)				
	RM (Cb)	**RM (Fb)**	**W (cb)**	**W (Fb)**	**AP**
Canada	38 601	31 821	38 498	40 820	29 051
Atlantic Can	28 558	37 323	33 190	37 025	27 212
Quebec	31 705	28 892	35 939	37 287	30 563
Ontario	41 313	33 293	41 708	41 691	31 860
Prairies	35 648	27 799	36 423	39 144	25 995
BC	40 319	31 417	41 660	42 340	30 597

*Full-time, full-year earnings for ages 25 to 64.

RM = racialized minorities; W = white people; AP = Aboriginal peoples

Adapted from Kunz et al. 2001.

Source: 1996 Census, Public Use Microdata File

TABLE 5.4   Black and Non-Racialized Average Income for Canada and Provinces, 2001

	Average Income of Black People Born in Canada ($)	Average Income of Non-Racialized Minorities ($)	% Difference Between Black People and Non-Racialized Minorities
Canada	20 024	30 516	.69
NFLD/Labrador	20 360	22 546	.92
Quebec	16 339	27 574	.59
Ontario	20 993	34 228	.61
B.C.	23 772	31 254	.76
United States	14 437 (US)	23 918 (US)	.60

Adapted from Jedwab (2004).

two based on a total for Canada and select provinces. A comparison with the United States is also included for illustrative purposes.

The table indicates that black people in Canada earn about 69 percent of what white people (non-racialized) earn. Compare this figure with the United States, where black people earn about 60 percent. Provincial variations are no less evident, with a relatively small percentage gap in Newfoundland/Labrador but much larger disparities in Quebec and Ontario (Jedwab 2004).

To be sure, income as a measure of inequality tends to conceal as much as it reveals (Hum and Simpson 2000). Internal variations within the category of racialized minorities are glossed over. For example, multiple-origin visible minorities who are partly European confront smaller income differentials in labour market performance than single-origin visible minorities (Pendakur 2005). Averages don't tell the story of the range of disparities between the richest and the poorest. Annual wages don't tell us the number of hours that people have worked over the year. Inequities pertaining to power and privilege are ignored, as are those pertaining to ownership of wealth or assets in breaking the cycle of poverty (Shapiro 2004). Important variables that may account for the disparities between racialized and non-racialized Canadians may be excluded, including gender, place of birth, length of stay in Canada, levels of work experience, educational levels, language competence, and sample size (see Statistics Canada 2006). Still, income differences remain the index by default for measuring inequality.

Immigrant Wage Gaps

Among immigrants, there is an unexplained wage gap (Walters et al. 2006; Statistics Canada 2006). Immigrants appear to be losing ground in the income-earning sweepstakes both in initial income and income earnings over time. In 1980, Statistics Canada has revealed, immigrants who had lived in Canada for ten years earned about the same as Canadian-born workers. Males earned 100.4 percent of what a Canadian-born male earned while females earned 103.1 percent of what a Canadian-born female earned. In 2000, immigrants who had lived in Canada for ten years were making much less than Canadian-born workers. A male immigrant's earnings as a percentage of earnings of a Canadian-born male had dropped to 79.8 percent, while a female immigrant's earnings fell to 87.3 percent. Other data seem to support these figures. According to the 2001 Census, recent arrivals earned 30 percent less than Canadian-born counterparts, with little chance that these new immigrant cohorts will ever reach earning parity (Statistics Canada 2006).

In short, racialized immigrants start with a distinct earning disadvantage relative to the Canadian-born, a gap that narrows over time, but this initial earning gap has widened and the catch-up rate has slowed. Between 1996 and 2001, Canada witnessed a double-digit income gap between racialized and non-racialized populations, higher unemployment and lower participation rates, and occupational concentrations in the lower income occupations. This in spite of educational attainment and overseas experience being taken into account, which suggests continued barriers in converting international credentials and expertise into comparable occupational status and compensation (Teelucksingh and Galabuzi 2005). Human capital skills do not transfer well and are discounted once in Canada, with the result that one year of overseas experience may be valued at one-third of a year of domestic experience while foreign education is worth about 75 percent of an education for a Canadian-born (Finnie and Meng 2002). Others suggest a three-fold factor in the earning gaps: (1) changes in the characteristics of immigrants and their mother tongue with the shift in source countries since the 1960s; (2) declining returns to foreign work experiences and educational levels among non-European immigrants; and (3) a general decline in labour market outcomes for new labour entrants where immigrants are treated as new entrants (Aydemir and Skuterud 2004; Statistics Canada 2006).

Division of Labour

The labour market continues to be segmented along racial lines (Teeelucksingh and Galabuzi 2005). Racialized group members are overrepresented in low paying and insecure jobs—sewing machine operators (46 percent of the total workforce in this field), plastics processing (36.8 percent), and taxi and limo drivers (37.5 percent). They were underrepresented in better paying, more secure jobs, including senior management (8.2 percent), fire fighting (2 percent), legislation (2.2 percent), and oil and gas drilling (1.5 percent). One area in which racialized minorities excelled was in the information technology sector, headed by software engineers (36.3 percent) and computer programmers (27.8 percent).

Still, far too many university-educated immigrants fail to land employment, although 80 percent of new Canadians between the ages of 25 and 44 had found at least one job within two years of arrival in Canada. Among those that do, however, 60 percent end up working in areas other than those in which they are qualified (Statistics Canada 2005; Editorial, 12 March 2005). Failure to translate overseas work experience and educational qualifications into Canadian equivalents reflects bottlenecks in the licensing and accreditation process, a resistance to hiring those with international credentials, and an insistence on Canadian experience even when not job related (Galabuzi 2006).

Racializing Poverty

Poverty in Canada is becoming increasingly racialized. That is, patterns of poverty are not randomly distributed across all Canadians, but clustered around certain historically disadvantaged

TABLE 5.5	Rates of Poverty / Low Income for Select Groups, 2000 and 2001	
	United States (%)	**Canada (%)**
All	12.4	12.4
Greek	7.0	13.7
Irish	6.8	8.8
Lebanese	8.6	26.9
Haitian	20.2	37.2
Jamaican	13.4	24.3
Chinese	13.5	23.8
Black	24.8	32.5
Latin American	22.9	24.5
Japanese	9.7	10.3

Source: Adapted from Jedwab 2004.

minorities. Table 5.5 points out poverty rates for different groups in Canada, both racialized and non-racialized, and compares their poverty levels with those in the United States.
Keep in mind that this comparison is not without problems as the two countries use different methods of assessment (Jedwab 2004). American poverty is based on total family
income that falls below a threshold appropriate for that family. For example, a threshold
level in 2002 for a family of five is $22 007. Any household that falls below this figure
is defined as poor. Canada measures poverty by reference to a low-income cut-off line,
that is, any family that spends more than 70 percent of its income on basic necessities is
deemed to be living in straitened circumstances (the government does not like to use
the "p" word).

These results are dismaying if one persists in idolizing Canada as an egalitarian para-
dise compared to our American neighbours. First, with the exception of Japanese-
Canadians, there are striking variations between racialized and non-racialized minorities.
Second, the poverty rates for these groups appear to be more intense in Canada than in
the United States. In short, repeated references to Canada as multicultural and egalitarian have not translated into equal outcomes across the board when measured by statistical indicators such as income or poverty rates. There is a glaring gap between the haves
and have-nots, and this widening gap is becoming increasingly racialized and gendered.
In terms of income, employment, and poverty levels, racialized foreign-born minorities
are also underperforming compared to the rest (Hum and Simpson 2000; Teelucksingh
and Galabuzi 2005). The reasons for these disparities are numerous, but include (1)
racial discrimination, (2) discounting of education credentials and overseas experience,
(3) increased competition with the educational credentials of the Canadian-born, (4) the
shift in immigration sources, (5) a generally tightened labour market especially for
entry-level jobs, and (6) an immigration system that permits a large number of new
Canadians to bypass the point system meant to identify applicants with job-related skills
(Grubel 2005).

INSIGHT	Are African-Americans Closing the Gap?

How does the situation in Canada compare with that elsewhere? Studies clearly indicate similar patterns of exclusion and exploitation in New Zealand (Fleras and Spoonley 1999) and Australia (Vasta and Castles 1996). Here too, a multi-layered inequality has evolved, at least in terms of income, with white people at the top, indigenous peoples at the bottom, and visible minority immigrants and Pacific Islanders sandwiched in between. Patterns of racialized inequality and stratification prevail in the United States as well. Evidence points to growing gaps in the income status of white people and non-white people. Table 5.6 indicates both the income differences and poverty levels among major racialized groups in the United States.

According to the table, both Asian-Americans and white people are doing well in terms of median income and rates of poverty. By contrast, African-Americans continue to have poor performance indicators, as they do in Canada.

In 1903, W.E.B. DuBois predicted that the problem of the colour bar would be the key issue of the twentieth century. A Swedish observer of American politics, Gunnar Myrdahl (1944), reiterated this observation by declaring the race problem as the quintessential paradox in challenging American democracy. Nearly one hundred years after DuBois's prediction, the colour bar remains no less a central challenge for

the twenty-first century (Kozol 2005). The Civil Rights struggle that secured legal equality for black people achieved much. But it does not appear to have dismantled those stubborn inequalities seemingly immune to laws or affirmative action programs (Loury 1998). As a result, opinion is divided. Some say black people are better off than before; others say not. Some believe affirmative action has fostered racial progress; others disagree (Shipler 1997). Who is right, and on what grounds can this be proven?

For black people, the socio-economic figures are disturbing. Nearly 40 years after civil rights legislation and affirmative action programs, the colour bar continues to exact its toll—crime, drug addiction, family breakdown, imprisonment, welfare dependency, and community decay that are virtually unrivalled in scale and severity by anything in the industrial West (Loury 1998). The struggle for equal treatment and civil rights against the backdrop of a colour-blind society has not reaped dividends (Sleeper 1997). The corridors of power look much the same as before: 95 percent of senior corporate management remains white. Similar percentages apply to members of Congress, state governors, tenured faculty, daily newspaper editors, and TV news directors (Kivisto and Ng 2005). The annual income of African-Americans who are employed in

TABLE 5.6	Median Income and Poverty Rates, U.S., (2003)	
	Median Income ($)	**Poverty Rate (%)**
Asian-American	55 089	10
Whites	47 951	10
Native Americans	34 740	23
Latino/Latina	33 915	23
African-Americans	29 987	23

Adapted from the U.S. Census Bureau.

full-time jobs amounts to about 60 percent of that of white people. And while 40 percent of white households earn US$50 000 per year or more, only 21 percent of black families do. The black unemployment rate is double that of the whole nation; one-third of all black people, including one-half of all black children, live below the poverty line. Homicide is the leading cause of death for black males between the ages of 15 and 24, with the result that the life expectancy of 65 years for American black men is equivalent to that in some developing countries (D'Souza 1995).

Inequality is expressed through income differences. Yet, this emphasis on earnings may be misleading, as high expenditures can deplete the benefits of income. The possession of wealth or assets is a more reliable measurement of "inequality" (Oliver and Shapiro 1995; Shapiro 2004). For example, most university students living away from home may be income-poor and fall far short of the federally regulated poverty (low-income cut-off) line. Nonetheless, they are asset-rich because of the marketability of their pending degrees (and family background). The distinction between wealth and income is key: Income is what people earn from work or receive from government transfers for purchase of goods or services. Wealth is what people own (from investment in stocks and bonds to home ownership). Whether through inheritance or savings, wealth signifies command over financial resources that can be used to create opportunities, generate investment incomes, or enhance inheritance packages for children. In the explanation of racial disadvantage, then, wealth matters (Conley 1999).

Focusing on wealth rather than income also casts a new light on inequality and racial stratification. Minority women and men may possess similar levels of income compared with the mainstream. Yet, many are asset-poor, thus foreclosing opportunity structures.

As a result, America remains split along the racial lines of black and white people—and divided by the "colour of green"—with black families as a whole owning only 10 percent of wealth compared to white families (Associated Press, 18 January 2005). While 18.2 percent of white families owned $500 000 in net worth, according to the Federal Reserve, only 2.4 percent of black households did. Fewer black people than white people own their own homes, invest in the stock market, sit on corporate boards, or have much clout over the trillions of dollars circulating in the financial markets. Even adjusting for social class does not dramatically improve the picture. Middle-class American black people may earn about 70 percent of white middle-class incomes, but they own only about 25 percent of white middle-class wealth.

Black–white gaps have been variously explained. Those of a liberal persuasion tend to attribute the gap to a combination of white people's racism, racial segregation, black poverty, and inadequate funding of black schools. The causes of black poverty are both social and cultural, and solutions must focus on corresponding adjustments in preparing black people for the new economy (Gates Jr. 1998). The most common conservative explanations rely on genetic differences, the culture of poverty, single motherhood, and poor educational attainment because of negative peer pressure, preoccupation with money and consumerism, and disdain for conventional avenues of success (see Jencks and Phillips 1998; Hinsliff and Bright 2000). The distinction is useful if easily overstated. Whereas conservatives believe that success would follow if black people would only "get their acts together," liberals are more inclined to link black impoverishment with deeply rooted political, economic, and legal practices in American history. Radical **conflict theorists** point to **capitalism** as the cause, with black people rarely owning or controlling the means of production. Finally, for black nationalists, white domination is the problem (Marable 1998). Black nationalisms differ in details, but include a belief that African-Americans are an oppressed minority trapped inside a white society. The survival of black people in such a hostile environment must be based on becoming self-reliant by constructing their own institutions, supporting their own enterprises, establishing black homelands, and espousing black cultures and values.

However uneven, improvements are unmistakable even if the results are mixed and ambiguous (Shipler 1997). Social transformation in American race relations since 1945 has yielded positive outcomes. Official segregation and a caste system of domination have been eradicated; black demands for equal citizenship rights and equal opportunity are upheld by law and embraced by political institutions; and black participation in the economic and political life of the nation has expanded impressively (Loury 1998). Consider the contrasts: In 1940, 60 percent of employed black women worked as domestic servants in contrast to only 2.2 percent at present; today, a large percentage of black women hold white-collar jobs. The number of black college and university professors has doubled since 1970, the number of physicians tripled, the number of engineers almost quadrupled, and the number of attorneys has increased nearly sixfold. The shift in public attitudes is no less impressive. In 1958, 44 percent of white people said they would leave if a black family moved next door; today the figure is down to 1 percent. As recently as 1964, only 18 percent of white people claimed to have a black friend compared with 86 percent who say they do now (Thernstrom and Thernstrom 1998). According to a 1994 National Conference survey, white people feel that they have most in common with black people who, paradoxically, feel that they have little in

common with white people (conversely, Latinos feel they have most in common with white people, but this feeling is not reciprocated) (Hochschild 1998).

It would be misleading to fixate exclusively on this divide. An equally distinctive and widening rift can be discerned between a downward-spiralling black underclass and an increasingly upwardly mobile black middle class. On one hand, over 40 percent of black people now consider themselves to be middle class; 42 percent own their own homes (75 percent if only black married couples are included); 33 percent live in the suburbs; and black two-parent families earn only 13 percent less than white people (Thernstrom and Thernstrom 1998). In short, middle-class black people have never had it so good, argues Henry Louis Gates Jr. (1998). On the other hand, there is the curious plight of the black underclass. Both media and government have stereotyped and stigmatized them because of their purported criminality, sexual excesses, and intellectual deficiencies, to the point of being objects of public derision and cast into a pariah status (Loury 1998). But both public and media preoccupation with ghetto culture, hip-hop, and gangsta rap conveys the impression of the black underclass as the "essence" of black America (Thernstrom and Thernstrom 1998). Conversely, those who achieve success in the "whitestream" are seen as selling out—in effect dismissing the achievements of those middle-class Uncle Toms who have hurdled the colour bar.

In short, the colour bar may be real, but its reality should not blind us to the fact that black people are no less heterogeneous than white people when it comes to socioeconomic status. There is a growing disparity between the top fifth and the bottom fifth of African-Americans with respect to income, education, victimization by violence, occupational status, and electoral involvement (Hochschild 1998). Interestingly, a similar situation exists in post-apartheid South Africa

where the income gap between black people and white people is narrowing, but
widening within the black population
(Roberts 2000). True, the Civil Rights movement has created a more positive social and
political climate for black Americans.

Nevertheless, abolishing legal racism has
proven insufficient in advancing meaningful equality without a corresponding move
to remedy the disadvantages inherited from
the past as well as create the conditions for
success in the future.

EXPLAINING RACIALIZED INEQUALITY

Sociological perspectives on explaining the cause of and solutions to racialized inequality vary widely. Some regard inequality of any sort as a social problem in need of a solution; others believe inequality is necessary and desirable. For some, inequality is a
regrettable component of a modern complex system; for others, inequality is inevitable but
only in regimes that pivot around profit and private property. A few see inequality as the
culmination of individual shortcomings; many tend to see inequality as structurally embedded within society. To what extent are racialized inequities the result of race? Or class? Or
ethnicity? Or gender? Are group conflicts in Canada the result of racial tensions or class
confrontations? For example, did nineteenth-century Chinese immigrants experience discrimination because of a pervasive anti-Orientalism? Or did the treatment of the Chinese
reflect their occupational status as essentially disposable labour for Canadian nation-
building purposes? Answers to these questions may be couched within the framework of
two sociological theories of society, namely, functionalism and conflict. Both functionalist
and conflict theorists differ in analyzing and assessing the causes of racialized inequality.
Each also advocates a different set of solutions.

Functionalist Perspectives

The economic division of labour is the starting point for functionalist models. For society to operate smoothly, functionalists argue, positions in the economic structure must be
filled with suitable personnel. As these jobs differ in skill and importance, people need to
be rewarded appropriately for doing tasks of differing complexity. The occupational prestige hierarchy is the result of these differential rewards. We accept as "natural" that physicians are compensated more for their services than plumbers even though, arguably, both
are crucial for our well-being (Davis and Moore 1945). Leading sports figures are paid
more than common labourers (in the United States the average major league baseball player
earned about US$2.4 million per year in 2005), while the average child-care worker earns
minimum wage. This discrepancy arises not because one is more important to society. Salary
and status gaps exist because certain skills are in short supply compared with the demand.
Those skills that can generate more wealth for their owners are in shorter supply still, and
rewarded handsomely.

Functionalists acknowledge the existence of minority inequities. Four explanations prevail: personal prejudice, legal barriers, cultural deficits, and misguided government policies (see Velez 1998). According to functionalist perspectives, the failure of minorities to
penetrate the market may reflect a lack of expertise or credentials. Efforts to boost their
"human capital" would focus on improving minority "skills" consistent with competitive
labour force needs. In turn, prejudicial or racial considerations will be rendered superfluous

when employers overcome bias in hiring the brightest and the best on the basis of ability—regardless of race or ethnicity. A commitment to "colour-blindness" is critical to the bottom line as such a commitment can capitalize on the entire spectrum of brainpower for competing in a global market economy.

In sum, functionalists distinguish "good" (functional) inequality from "bad" (dysfunctional) inequality (Fleras 2001). Inequality is "good" when achieved "fair and square," that is, on the basis of merit, credentials, and equal opportunities; it is "bad" if unfairly achieved. Functionalists recognize and decry inequality when based on excluding others because of irrelevant ascriptive attributes (such as race) outside a person's control. To be sure, a degree of inequality is inevitable, as people are not equally endowed. Functionalists may accept the inevitability of innate differences, not necessarily in a racial way but in terms of the skills an individual brings to the marketplace. In that sense, functionalists argue, inequality is necessary and desirable in a merit-based, openly competitive society.

Conflict Perspectives

Conflict theorists share with functionalists the view that complex societies are differentiated by inequality. They differ in their assessment of inequality as process and outcome. The inevitability of inequality—a basic tenet of functionalism—is anathema to conflict theory. For conflict theorists, society is envisaged as a site of inequality involving competitively different groups in a struggle for valued resources like power, privilege, and property. Society (including institutions, values, and relations) is designed and organized in a way that reflects, reinforces, and advances the interests and experiences of the rich and the powerful. For specific conflict theorists such as Karl Marx, gaping patterns of inequality are neither natural nor normal, but rather "naturalized" or "normalized" in those societies organized around the rational pursuit of profit. Inequities stem from different locations that groups of people occupy—owners vs. workers—in relationship to the means of production. The ruling class does everything in its power to secure its power and privilege, including sowing the seeds of dissension to destabilize the working classes, while the working classes struggle to redefine the status quo.

Conflict theories of racialized inequality emphasize the centrality of class relations (Velez 1998). The primacy of class is anchored in Marxist analysis of capitalist relations. Shared experiences notwithstanding, the working class is neither homogeneous in composition nor uniform in outlook. It is internally divided inasmuch as some workers are more exploited than others because of gender or race. For example, white male workers often are better paid than non-white workers. Males in general earn more than females from all racialized groups. In addition to income differentials, males generally have access to more secure types of employment with greater opportunities for promotion and power. These class factions can also be manipulated to foster what Marx termed "false consciousness." Instead of directing their hostility at the source of their exploitation and domination (i.e., the capitalists), workers misplace their antagonism toward each other. In other words, race and ethnicity is manipulated by the ruling class to distract oppressed classes, mask the underlying relations of production, and conceal or mystify the primary source of exploitation. Fomenting racial prejudice and out-group hostility helps to perpetuate the status quo, prevents the formation of worker solidarity, improves capital formation, destabilizes countermovements, militates against the development of class consciousness, and justifies the exploitation of a cheap and disposable labour force by stigmatizing groups as inferior (Velez 1998). This infighting also has the effect of eroding workers' ability to "unite and throw off their chains."

Under conflict models, the salience of race and ethnicity reflects their importance for capitalist relations of production. The focus is on structural arrangements whose profitability depends on defining minorities as inferior or irrelevant. Nevertheless, class relations remain at the root of this conflict. Exploitation arising from capitalist systems rather than ethnicity or race is the true source of racialized inequality. Racial differences and confrontations are simply aspects of the wider struggle between classes. Minority concerns merely complicate the issue by distorting the reality of domination and cause of exploitation. Thus, conflicts between racial groups are ultimately conflicts within and between classes—whether people are aware of it or not (see Farley 2005). In that this text begins with the premise that race, ethnic, and Aboriginal relations are essentially unequal relations, a conflict perspective provides a richer insight into how these racialized inequalities are constructed and maintained or challenged and changed.

RETHINKING RACIALIZED INEQUALITY

Two perspectives help to explain racialized inequality and stratification. Whereas functionalists tend to blame race and ethnicity for the inequality problem (the ethnicity paradigm), conflict models see the problem as more deeply embedded within institutional and opportunity structures (the equity paradigm). A shift toward structures as key explanatory frameworks reflects a rethinking of racialized inequality, its origins, nature, and outcomes. A generation ago references to racial(ized) stratification were couched within the discursive framework of an ethnicity paradigm (Fleras 1993). Canadian society was envisaged as an open and competitive marketplace in which individuals competed as equals and were rewarded because of their skills or production. Individual success or failure reflected a person's amount of human capital: namely, those people with training, skills, and education succeeded; those without did not. Ethnic differences were pivotal. On one side, ethnic minorities had to discard the debilitating aspects of their ethnicity that precluded participation. On the other side, those in charge also had to discard those prejudgments that precluded inclusiveness. The introduction of a multiculturalism policy in 1971 sought to remove prejudice from the workplace by making sure that people's differences did not get in the way of who got what. It also sought to depoliticize ethnicity by eliminating its salience as a basis for public recognition and reward. Institutions were transformed into culturally neutral public spaces, thus ensuring equal treatment irrespective of ethnicity and without the threat of messy entanglements (Breton 1998).

The concept of inequality underwent a shift in emphasis from the 1980s onward (Agocs and Boyd 1993). Emphasis shifted from a focus on individual attributes such as prejudice and ethnicity as the source of the problem to a growing concern with discriminatory barriers and racism. This cognitive shift was driven by a dramatic increase in immigrants from developing countries. Multicultural commitments that focused on ethnicity no longer resonated with the language of relevance. Proposed instead were new equity discourses based on institutional inclusion, removal of discriminatory barriers at structural levels, and racism that precluded full and equal participation. References to inequality shifted accordingly, from individuals to structure, from ethnicity to race, from equality of opportunity to equal outcomes, and from a commitment to formal (abstract) equality to that of **substantive equality (equity)**—as demonstrated in Table 5.7.

A new paradigm was proposed to explain institutional discrimination of racialized women and men. According to an equity paradigm, the problem did not rest with individuals or attitudes

TABLE 5.7 Competing Paradigms for Explaining Inequality	
The Ethnicity Paradigm	**The Equity Paradigm**
Root cause = individuals	Root cause = institutional structures
Expression = prejudice	Expression = racism
Problem = attitudinal	Problem = discriminatory barriers
Cause = blaming the victim	Cause = blaming the system
Focus of solution = human capital	Focus of solution = institutional inclusion
Outcome = formal equality	Outcome = substantive equity
Solution = treat everyone the same	Solution = customize everyone differently
Context of solution = market forces	Context of solution = gov't intervention

per se. Rather, the source of the problem was rooted in the institutional *structures* of society. Inequality and barriers to advancement reflected structural constraints that were largely systemic in advancing "pale male" interests. In applying the metaphor of a competitive footrace with staggered starting blocks, it was obvious that not all contestants were equally positioned to compete in the labour market. The race was rigged because of ascribed characteristics that handicapped some because of skin colour or gender differences, while privileging others for precisely the same reasons. In short, the onus lay on the government to remove discriminatory barriers through legislation to create a more level playing field.

| INSIGHT | **Employment Equity: Reframing Inequality** |

Employment equity as a philosophy is organized around the principle of "institutional inclusion." It embraces the principle that all persons, regardless of colour and gender, should be treated equally and equitably. That is, each person should be recruited, hired, promoted, trained, and rewarded on the basis of merit and credentials—assuming the person is qualified for any position that is available. As a philosophy then, employment equity consists of the following priorities:

- Ensure proportional representation of designated groups throughout all occupational and income levels at numbers consistent with their percentage in the regional workforce (Jain and Hackett 1989). If discriminatory employment barriers did not exist, the argument goes, minority

women and men would be evenly distributed along all occupational and income levels in accordance with their numbers in the population (allowing, of course, for individual and cultural pressures, which may restrict occupational choices).

- Identify and remove employment practices that systematically or systemically discriminate against identifiable and devalued groups. Racially discriminatory barriers do not arise from personal fear, ignorance or self-interest. Institutional structures from hidden agendas to systemic biases are prime causes that may inadvertently distort the recruitment, retention, and reward process.

- Remedy adverse effects of past discrimination through positive programs for the entry, selection, promotion, and training of minorities. Temporary colour-conscious initiatives may be required on the assumption that race problems respond only to racial solutions, structural problems to structural solutions, and institutional problems to institutional solutions.

- Ensure reasonable progress in meeting numerical targets and timetables as proof of a more inclusive workplace (Jain 1988). The goal is to achieve a workplace environment where differences are seen as a natural and normal aspect—as well as a legitimate and valued component—of a business-as-usual mindset.

Three additional premises underscore employment equity as a philosophy of inclusiveness. First, employment equity is concerned with moving over and making institutional space through the removal of discriminatory barriers that deny or exclude minority women and men through no fault of their own. Historically advantaged minorities are not the problem, according to employment equity principles, but institutions are, particularly those traditionally pale male occupations such as firefighting or the police services. Second, employment equity is premised on the belief that, left to their own, institutions will tend to reproduce discriminatory patterns unless an outside force is applied to break the circularity. Otherwise, like will hire like largely because it is easier, safer, and more comfortable. That puts the onus on changing the hiring mindset to ensure that everyone is taken seriously as a candidate. Third, employment equity is predicated on the premise that minorities suffer from a strict commitment to equal opportunity. The universality implicit in merit-based hiring penalizes minority women and men. Treating everyone the same when differences need to be taken into account conspires against those whose experiences, interests, and concerns fall outside the "pale male stream." Treating people alike in situations of inequality also has the effect of freezing the racialized status quo—in effect confirming the motto that treating people as equals may require taking their differences into account.

TOWARD AN EQUITY-BASED EQUALITY

That most minorities aspire to social and economic equality is surely beyond dispute or debate. Many Canadians would also agree that equality is to be preferred over an inequality that is unfairly achieved. But the concept of "equality" is itself subject to diverse interpretations. Mutually opposed definitions may be endorsed by different groups, by different individuals across the spectrum of society, or by competing factions within the group. The situation is further complicated by concurrent versions at a given point in time in response to changing circumstances. This proliferation of definitions has led to confusion and misunderstanding over the issue of who should get what and why.

The concept of equality is employed in three different ways: as abstract, as equivalence, and as equity (or substantive). For some, equality is used as synonymous with sameness. Everyone is treated the same regardless of background or circumstances because true equality is based on acknowledging our common humanity. No one is explicitly accorded special privileges in a market system designed around the principles of equal opportunity, equality before the law, and credential-based merit. For others, equality is used in the sense of numerical, or "proportional," equivalence. Under systems of preferential hiring and promotion, each group is allocated positions according to their numbers in society or the workforce. For yet others, the concept of equality is aimed at the principle of "equity." References to equality as equity acknowledge the need to take seriously those differences that create a disadvantage. The unique circumstances of a person or group are taken into account to ensure "customized" treatment by way of institutional adjustments. Emphasis is on the attainment of equal outcomes (or conditions) rather than the abstract principle of equal opportunity.

Consider, for example, the "special" treatment that is extended to individuals with disabilities. Concessions such as wheelchair ramps, closed-caption TV, and designated parking spots are common enough. But these concessions can hardly be thought of as special or preferential; rather, removing disability barriers ensures equality of opportunity by providing reasonable accommodation. Likewise, historically disadvantaged minorities with racially prescribed characteristics will encounter barriers as real and as debilitating as physical impediments. But just as building on-ramps for the wheelchair bound creates a more level playing field, so too does a similar line of reasoning apply to racialized minorities. In both cases, those with socially defined disabilities require different treatment if only to ensure their right to equality of opportunity. A commitment to "reversing" discrimination by way of "customized" treatment makes it doubly important to treat unequals differently. To do otherwise, that is, treat everyone the same in contexts of inequality, is tantamount to freezing the status quo.

Each of these perspectives on equality differs from the other in terms of objectives and scope. **Formal equality** is concerned with mathematical equivalence and a market-driven means for establishing who gets what. Any measure that rewards individuals on grounds other than merit or competition is criticized as unfair or counterproductive. More substantive versions of equality (or equity) disagree. Equity-based equality argues that seemingly neutral rules applied evenly and equally may exert an adverse if unintended impact on certain minority groups. A one-size-fits-all mentality can produce unequal results and perpetuate group-based inequities, according to the Ontario Human Rights Commission annual reports, especially when everyone is treated as asexual, deracialized, and classless without a history or context for purposes of reward (McIntyre 1993). Or consider how the Supreme Court contends that discrimination may arise when racialized minorities must comply with a mainstream standard unless, of course, the standards can be shown to be necessary and reasonable (Lawton 1999). Insofar as treating everyone the same regardless of circumstances is not equality but a privileging of a racialized and unequal status quo, social policies must be judged by the actual effect they have on individuals rather than by strict adherence to abstract legal principles (Cohen 1999).

The distinction between equality and equity is captured by the debate over equivalence-based equality vs. equity-based equality (Table 5.8). Equal opportunity focuses on the rights of individuals to be free from discrimination when competing for the good things in life. By contrast, equitable outcomes concentrate on the rights of historically disadvantaged individuals to a fair and equitable share of the goods and services in society. A commitment to equal opportunity openly advocates competition, inequality, and hierarchy as a natural and healthy way of allocating rewards and entitlements. An equal-outcome perspective is concerned with controlled distribution and egalitarian conditions for members of a disadvantaged group. This perspective recognizes the need for collective considerations over individual rights when the situation demands it. It also endorses the principle of social intervention for true equality, as equal outcomes are unlikely under competitive market forces. Finally, differences should be taken into account when the situation demands it, but people should be treated the same as a matter of course.

TABLE 5.8 Comparing Paradigms of Equality	
Equivalence-Based Equality	**Equity-Based Equality**
Formal (abstract and mathematical equivalent)	Substantive (context and consequences)
Everyone is or must be the same	Differences must be taken into account
Pretend pluralism	Taking differences seriously
Same treatment as a matter of course	Customized treatment when situation arises
Equal opportunity	Equitable outcomes
Discipline of the market	Government intervention
Human capital = solution	Institutional inclusiveness = solution

Which version of equality should prevail? Is one more important than the other, or is it a case of one serving as a necessary if insufficient precondition for the other? By themselves, equal opportunity structures cannot overcome the debilitating effects of systemic discrimination and institutional racism. Additional treatment is required over and above that available to the general population for true equality to take root. Context and consequences are as important as abstract principles in righting the wrongs. References to equal opportunity sound good in theory but rarely stand up to scrutiny when the playing field is tilted and the game is rigged. Taking context into consideration may mean the necessity for differential treatment in some cases to achieve an equality of outcome. Taking consequences into account suggests that intent and awareness are less important than the effects of practices in fostering unequal results. The unintended consequences of even seemingly neutral practices may lead to the exclusion of qualified personnel, regardless of motive or consciousness.

In short, equity-based equality hinges on the principle that treating everyone the same is not equality or justice. This outcome-based equity is not opposed to equal opportunities in defining equality. On the contrary, it acknowledges a commitment to the principle of equal opportunity as a necessary first step in overcoming entrenched racism and discrimination. But ultimately such a commitment cannot achieve a fair and just equality in contexts where the competition is "rigged" in favour of a "pale male stream." Only a dual commitment to equitable outcomes and equal opportunities can create an equitable equality. Put differently, for an equity-based equality, people must be treated the same as a matter of course, but they must also be treated differently when the situation arises. To what extent, then, do employment equity initiatives help or hinder the achievement of this goal of "reversing" discrimination?

DEBATE REVISITED	**Employment Equity: Reverse Discrimination or Reversing Discrimination?**

The philosophy of employment equity and Canada's Employment Equity policy have one thing in common: an aversion to racial discrimination and a commitment to remove discriminatory barriers in hopes of improving access, equity, and representation. Yet, critics argue that Employment Equity initiatives are less about removing discriminatory barriers than about replacing "pale males" with quotas of racialized minorities (Loney 1998). Not surprisingly, the Act has come under criticism for creating more problems than solutions. By encouraging a "reverse" discrimination, Equity programs are criticized for discriminating against white, able-bodied males—either deliberately or through the unintended consequence of initiatives that have the inadvertent effect of excluding whiteness and maleness from the exercising of rights. If it is unfair to discriminate against minorities, critics say, it is just as wrong to give preference to minorities by penalizing white people unfairly. All distinctions based on race, gender, or ethnicity are discriminatory and wrong, according to this line of thinking, especially when the discrimination is government endorsed under the guise of fairness or equity.

Others disagree: Reference to context and consequences is important in evaluating Employment Equity. Employment equity measures may appear discriminatory on the surface. In reality, rather than exclusion because of discrimination, employment equity is aimed at "reversing" discrimination through the removal of discriminatory barriers. The removal of these barriers is intended to expand the pool of qualified but formerly excluded applicants in the competition for employment rather than to explicitly exclude "white guys." In the final analysis, "reversing discrimination" fosters a workplace culture that is both inclusive and equitable, as well as progressive and productive. Canadians place a high value on inclusiveness, and Employment Equity appears to be consistent with core values. Canadians also value the principles of merit, equality before the law, and individualism. As a result, references to Employment Equity that seem to present a model that assigns value to colour, race, or gender are likely to elicit strong reaction. This clash between competing values may explain why Employment Equity is seen by some as a solution in search of a problem, and by others as more of a problem than a solution.

CHAPTER HIGHLIGHTS

- The relationship between inequality and racialized minority groups is a complex and evolving one, but generally speaking, Canada remains stratified by race and ethnicity, judging by persistence gaps in income, employment, and poverty levels.

- Functionalists tend to see ethnic inequality as necessary and normal in a complex society. Conflict theorists prefer to think of inequality as inevitable only in securing the foundations of exploitative societies.

- The colour bar remains in effect in the United States, where African-Americans continue to bear the brunt of inequality, despite impressive gains by a rapidly emerging middle class.

- The notion of racialized inequality is currently under reconsideration. The emphasis on ethnocultural differences and individual attitudes as the source of the problem (the ethnicity paradigm) is shifting toward structural factors as they relate to institutional rules, processes, and outcomes. With the emergence of the equity paradigm, the focus on structures as the problem has altered government solutions, with growing emphasis on institutional inclusion through removal of discriminatory barriers.

- Employment equity can be interpreted as a solution to the structural problem of inequality. A distinction needs to be made between employment equity as a principle (which many accept) and its application as a government program (which many reject).

KEY TERMS

capitalism	merit
class	racialized inequality
conflict theory	racialized minorities
employment equity	racial stratification
employment equity as philosophy	racism
Employment Equity as policy	reversing discrimination
equity	substantive equality
formal equality	vertical mosaic

REVIEW QUESTIONS

1. How would you explain the kind of income differences that characterize race and ethnic minorities in Canada? Compare and contrast the approaches of conflict versus functionalist theory as a means for explaining inequality and social stratification.

2. Point out how race and class offer different explanations for the source of group inequality. Which do you think is correct?

3. Our thinking on inequality has evolved in recent years. The equity paradigm (the new vertical mosaic) is replacing the ethnicity paradigm implicit within the old vertical mosaic. Explain what has happened and why.

4. The concept of equality can mean different things. Discuss the different meanings of equality as they pertain to race and ethnicity.

5. Stanley Fish has posed an interesting question: White people once set themselves apart from minorities and claimed privileges while denying them to others because of race or colour. Now, on the basis of race and employment equity, people of colour are claiming special status and reserving for themselves privileges that they deny to others. Not surprisingly, employment equity has been described as both "reverse" discrimination as well as a case of "reversing" discrimination. Expand by focusing on whether employment equity promotes racial equality and minority representation or promotes quotas and political correctness at the expense of merit, fairness, and qualifications.

LINKS AND RECOMMENDATIONS

Books

For a useful introduction to theories of social inequality, consult Edward Grab's *Theories of Social Inequality,* 4th Ed. (Harcourt/Nelson, 2002).

For an insightful anthology of key writings on the relationship of race and class (and gender) (mostly American sources), see Margaret Andersen and Patricia Collins, *Race, Class, and Gender,* 4th Ed. (Wadsworth, 2001).

Many excellent articles on inequality and race are found in Peter Li's *Race and Ethnic Relations in Canada*, 2nd Ed. (Oxford University Press, 1999).

Websites

Canadian Metropolis
http://canada.metropolis.net

An excellent site that covers material on immigration and inequality.

The Fraser Institute
www.fraserinstitute.ca

Provides an often different slant on economic inequality and diversity in Canada.

Each of the following websites produces reports of value for information about ethnicity and inequality in Canada:

Centre for Research and Information Canada
www.cric.ca

Canadian Council for Social Development
www.ccsd.ca

Center for Social Justice
www.socialjustice.org

Conference Board of Canada
www.conferenceboard.ca

GENDER DIVERSITY/ GENDERED INEQUALITY

DEBATE	**Is Multiculturalism Biased Against Women? The Politics of Sharia**

Multiculturalism is widely regarded as a politically acceptable framework for engaging diversity. With multiculturalism, individuals are allowed to affiliate with the cultural tradition of their choice (within limits), without having to forfeit their right to full and equal participation in society. Yet, not all individuals are equal beneficiaries of an official Multiculturalism. For minority women, a commitment to Multiculturalism may condone cultural practices that systemically exclude them from the full and equal exercise of their rights (Okin 1999). This is particularly true in those contexts where the principle of gender equality clashes with the claims of those racialized groups who assert their collective right to preserve culture and identity over individual rights, including the rights of women (Reitman 2005). These competing claims

raise an interesting question regarding the relationship between **feminism** and multiculturalism. Can societies endorse multiculturalism policies of tolerance and inclusiveness while at the same time pursuing a commitment to gender equality?

Such a challenge is sharply pronounced in Canada, where debates over inclusiveness are inextricably linked with the politics of an official Multiculturalism, constitutional protection of individual rights, and a commitment to equality before the law. But the challenge of "drawing the line" has taken on new resonance in Ontario because of proposals to formalize Islamic family law ("sharia" or "shariah"— loosely translated as a religious path that defines how a Muslim should live) as the basis for arbitration tribunals. For some, the sharia is dismissed as a centuries-old body of archaic Islamic law embedded in a medieval psychology. For others, the sharia is synonymous with Islam (as well as state law in many Muslim countries such as Sudan or Saudi Arabia) and must be applied in exactly the same way as in the past. For still others, the problem is not the sharia per se as an informal agreement to arbitrate disputes; rather it is its proposed formalization as part of Ontario's legal system that is the key issue. Not surprisingly, opponents and supporters have squared off, with one side implying that a truly inclusive multiculturalism will embrace Muslim moves to establish conflict resolution according to Islamic religious precepts. As noted by some, sharia is open to a wide range of interpretations and can be interpreted positively by rereading the Koran, putting scriptures into context, or disentangling versions stemming from tribalism (Coleman 2006). By contrast, the other side claims that the institutionalization of sharia law exposes the dark side of multiculturalism. A commitment to sharia not only hinders women's abilities to settle marital, family, property, and civil disputes because of the power of male-dominated religious authorities, but also compromises their rights to equitable divorce, child custody, and inheritance (Reitman 2005).

How does this dispute relate to broader issues? Family disputes in Ontario have been open to formal arbitration since the passage of the *Arbitration Act* in 1991. The Act was designed to alleviate pressure from an overburdened court system by allowing faith-based groups (and secular groups such as businesses) to settle civil disputes more quickly and cheaply than would recourse to courts. With the Act, aggrieved individuals have an opportunity to voluntarily opt for an alternative dispute resolution process with reduced procedural and evidentiary safeguards. The status of this faith-based arbitration to resolve civil and family-law disputes is mixed: On one side, arbitration results are enforceable by the provincial courts; and on the other side, Ontario's courts have the power to override those rulings that infringe on the rights of women and children. In other words, arbitration remains subordinate to secular law, especially in those cases where the parties in question are unhappy with the arbitration results.

There is nothing new in the use of religious laws to settle family disputes, including issues of divorce, child custody, and property division. By utilizing the guiding principles of religion for settling private family disputes, Orthodox Jews, Catholics, and Ishmaeli Muslims have long settled disputes through arbitration, and these judgments are enforced by provincial courts. Rulings are binding, to be sure, but must be consistent with Canadian laws, human rights codes, and the *Charter of Rights and Freedoms*. Additional restrictions that apply include (1) criminal cases cannot go to arbitration; (2) both parties must voluntarily give consent to the process while agreeing upon a common set of legal ground rules, such as the choice of an arbiter who theoretically is conversant with Islamic and Canadian law; (3) either party can abandon the process at any point by taking their case to court; (4) each party is bound by the adjudicator's rulings, but all decisions can be appealed to the courts; and (5) arbitration outcomes must take into account a child's best interest, including sufficient support. With these kinds of safeguards in place, why is the sharia turning into such a hot political potato at provincial levels?

INTRODUCTION: MINORITIES ARE WOMEN, TOO

The concepts of race, ethnicity, and class are proven indicators of social differentiation. Each of these indicators provides a framework by which to interpret both individual and group identities, with respect to "who am I/are we?" "How do others see me/us?" and "what is my/our place in the broader scheme of things?" These indicators also serve as "variables" to account for "who owns what" and "why." To be sure, these indicators of inequality rarely remain unchallenged. As inequities coalesce along the lines of race, class, and ethnicity, minority groups have become more politically engaged and increasingly articu-late about righting historical wrongs (see Muszynski 2000). That minority assertiveness often clashes with the prevailing status quo should come as no surprise, but it does say a lot about the challenges of "living together with differences."

Gender is no less critical an indicator in shaping negative outcomes (Nelson 2006). Women of colour, immigrant and refugee women, and Aboriginal women have experienced denial and exclusion because of gender stereotypes, double standards, glass ceilings, and sticky floors. This marginalization may not be deliberate or conspiratorial, reflecting instead the log-ical consequences of possibly well-meaning initiatives that are grounded on "androcentric" assumptions. Or inequality may reflect the inevitable consequences of living in a society that is constitutionally governed by the principles of capitalism, democracy, and patriarchy. The cumulative effect of such a patricentric bias is punitive. A pattern of gender stratification is established that perpetuates prevailing distributions of "pale male" power and privil-ege while reinforcing a racialized and gendered social order.

Few sociologists would deny the asymmetry of gender relations in Canada. Women continue to be "put down" because of institutional and systemic bias, "put in their place" by way of outright violence or harassment, or "put out of sight" as inferior or irrelevant (Rothenberg 2001). Many are denied equality in the workplace or deprived of the human capital to compete equitably with men in the corporate boardroom. In some cases, this mistreatment is deliberate; in other cases, inequities are the logical consequence of a sys-tem designed around the foundational principles that promote pale-male interests at the expense of others. Minority women continue to be denied or exploited because of their location within a predominantly male world. On-site discrimination may account for the gen-dered disparity. However, a more plausible reason is related to the much narrower range of occupations that are open to minority women, most of which are lower paid with fewer chances for promotion. Even highly accredited persons may be forced to accept demean-ing labour if they are without the requisite amount of Canadian experience or credentials. This situation is compounded by the marginality of class status. After all, to be poor in a soci-ety that values wealth is marginalizing. To be poor and different—and a woman—intensifies the marginalization.

That minority women and men endure both exclusion and exploitation because of race, ethnicity, and social class is widely acknowledged (Satzewich 1998; Henry and Tator 2006). But minority women (including women of colour, immigrant women, and Aboriginal women) are additionally disadvantaged because of their gender. Minority women are often confronted by gender barriers that are uniquely related to their circumstances and experi-ences. Yet, the literature on gender and inequality—at least compared with that on race and class—was neither well established nor taken seriously (Nelson 2006). Academics often fell into the trap of approaching minorities as if they were a homogeneous category of people—regardless of age, socio-economic status, origins, or gender. When gender was acknowledged, all minority women tended to be indiscriminately lumped together into a single encompassing category. Such reductionism had a controlling effect in underscoring the invisibility of minority women at the expense of their contributions to society. Studies were further unhinged by a lack of analytical sophistication. Instead of seeing gender in terms of its interplay with race, ethnicity, and class, each of these indicators of inequality was separately analyzed in a mechanical and additive fashion (see Stasiulis 1990, 1999). Such an approach made it difficult to acknowledge how gender intersected with other indicators of inequality to amplify the exclusion or exploitation of minority women.

The invisibility of gender in the study of race, ethnic, and Aboriginal relations is no longer the case. Women are minorities too, or so the slogan goes, and excluding minority women from analysis diminishes our understanding of race, ethnic, and Aboriginal relations—in the same way that excluding men from gender studies is no less diminishing. This chapter hopes to take advantage of this conceptual shift by exploring the relationship of gender diversity to **gendered inequality**. Race, ethnic, and Aboriginal relations are not gender-neutral, but are deeply and fundamentally structured in a way that uniquely disadvantages minority women. Inasmuch as the gendered basis of group relations reflects a separate dynamic, with its own history, rationale, and expression, minority women and men experience a fundamentally different world. Conversely, minority women experience gender differently than do white women because of race and ethnicity. These "categories" are not only interrelated but also mutually constitutive, insofar as they reinforce the class privilege of elite women, the race privileges of white women, and cultural privileges of women of dominant groups (Lerner 1997).

The objective of this chapter is doubly articulated: (1) to examine race, ethnic, and Aboriginal relations through the conceptual framework of gender and (2) to examine gender by filtering it through the prism of race, ethnicity, and aboriginality. The chapter begins by looking at the concept of gender diversity. The varied experiences of so-called minority women are divided into the categories of aboriginal women, refugee and immigrant women, and women of colour/racialized women. The dynamics of gendered inequality are examined next, by focusing on their impact on minority women's lives and life chances. Gender relations are ultimately unequal relations, and that fact alone reinforces a focus on how these gendered inequalities are constructed, expressed, and maintained, in addition to how they are challenged and transformed by way of government policy, protest movements, and institutional reform. The chapter also attempts to explain the unequal status of minority women by reference to how gender is superimposed on and intersects with race, class, and ethnicity to differentially shape realities and outcomes for minority women. The chapter concludes by pointing out how patterns of resistance among minority women create identities and equalities consistent with their realities and experiences. In short, instead of looking at women as variables or a control group, women are increasingly seen as active agents in constructing their world—as subjects rather than objects—in coping with the sometimes competing demands of community and Canada.

GENDER DIVERSITY AS GENDERED INEQUALITY

The concerns of minority women and men often converge with those of Canadians in general. Minority women and men are looking to put down roots in Canada without forsaking all continuities with their cultural past, an end to discrimination in housing, employment, education, and delivery of social services, protection of their fundamental human rights without having to put up with excessive bureaucratic interference, and the best for their children without loss of their cultural heritage. In this sense, minority women and men are similar to the "mainstream" in terms of wants, needs, concerns, and ambitions (see also Suarez-Orozco and Suarez-Orozco 2001).

But what minority women and men want is not necessarily what they get. Minorities routinely endure denial or exclusion because of their race, ethnicity, and social class as obstacles to equality (Galabuzi 2006). For many, visibility continues to compound their integration while compromising full and equal participation. Discrimination remains the rule rather than the exception, albeit more covert than in the past. The lives of minorities are controlled by a pervasive Eurocentrism that imposes restrictions in defining what is acceptable and desirable. Pressures to succeed are formidable, yet the appropriate skills, training, and support may be lacking. Conversely, those with overseas credentials, foreign experience, and professional status are no less marginalized—leaving little recourse for the highly skilled and educated except for menial and demeaning jobs. With such pressures, it is not surprising that some individuals see little option except to reject the system, preferring instead to withdraw into their ethnic enclaves or engage in lifestyles that rub up against the law.

Both minority women and men suffer exclusion and exploitation because of factors beyond their control. But minority women are doubly jeopardized as a result of their membership in yet another historically devalued category, namely, gender. Women of colour (racialized or visible minority women), immigrant and refugee women, and Aboriginal women not only face the same problems as minority men, but are additionally disadvantaged because of their gender status in a patriarchal society. In that society is organ-ized to reflect, reinforce, and advance male power and interests, **patriarchy** involves the institutionally enforced privileging of males over females and children across all domains of society, from politics to culture to family (Castells 1997). But patriarchy does not have a simi-lar impact on all women. It is experienced differently by Aboriginal women, racialized and visible minority women, and immigrant and refugee women because of differing histories, situations, and legal statuses. As a result, according to Vickers and de Seve (2000), the unique yet unequal experiences of minority women because of race, class, and ethnicity may outweigh their commonalities as women. The conclusion seems inescapable. Just as racialized differences must be taken into account in crafting a multicultural Canada, so too must the different experiences of minority women be taken seriously in a gendered society. The realities and expectations of minority women demand no less (Jiwani 2001).

Women of Colour/Racialized Women

Women of colour, or racialized women, have long endured discrimination and exclusion in Canada. As noted earlier, women of colour, especially Filipina and Caribbean women, were exploited as cheap domestic labour (Henry et al. 2000). Black women were excluded from nursing in Canada before the 1940s, and continue to experience racism and discrimination in Canadian hospitals, often at the hands of white female nurses who collaborate with management to monitor, control, and harass them (Calliste 1996; Hagey 2004). Both Canadian-born and foreign-born visible minority women continue to earn less than minority men or white women (Kunz et al. 2001). To be sure, earning differences can only measure the tip of the discriminatory iceberg. After all, earnings are conditioned by many factors, including qualifications, experiences, seniority, and number of hours, which need to be statistically controlled if labour-market discrimination is to be proved (Hum and Simpson 2000). But diverse studies using different measures and samples appear to converge and confirm that women of colour do indeed face discrimination, both systematic and systemic (Satzewich 2000). As well, racialized women who are immigrants confront additional problems because of their structural location (Jiwani 2001). They find themselves ghettoized in occupations that are dangerous or unprotected; they experience the trauma of migration including role overload because of both paid and unpaid labour; and they must endure the potential for abuse and domestic violence because of unequal power relations.

Aboriginal Women

The plight of Aboriginal women is gaining prominence. Both formal studies and personal testimonies indicate that Aboriginal women rank among the most severely disadvantaged people in Canada (LaRoque 1975, 90; see Silman 1987 for a similar assessment in the United States). They are known to experience a double oppression. As Aboriginal peoples who happen to be women, they must confront the foundational principles that govern the constitutional order of a capitalist and patriarchal society. As women who happen to be Aboriginal, they suffer from repressive practices because of sexist men or because of male governance structures imposed by the *Indian Act*. Economically, they are worse off than non-Aboriginal women and Aboriginal men in terms of income levels and employment options, with the result that the feminization of poverty bites deeply, especially for lone-parent women in cities (Williams 1997). Social hardships for these women are numerous and include reports of abusive male family members, sexual assaults and rapes, inadequate housing, squalid living conditions, unhealthy child-raising environments, and alcohol and drug abuse. Levels of violence directed against Aboriginal women and children are extremely high, as explained by the Native Women's Association of Canada in a 1991 brief (quoted in Razack 1994:910).

> We have a disproportionately high rate of child sexual abuse and incest. We have wife battering, gang rapes, drug and alcohol abuse, and every kind of perversion imaginable has been imported into our lives . . .

Depression and self-hatred among Aboriginal women is vented in high rates of suicide, alcohol dependency, and neglect of children. To that volatile mixture add the pressure of derogatory stereotypes that reinforce the marginalization of Aboriginal women (Witt 1984). For example, Aboriginal women are depicted by mass media as remote and removed. Depictions of Aboriginal women fall into two categories: the dishevelled "squaw" or the shapely Indian princess with perfect Caucasian features—a kind of Barbie in buckskins— as portrayed by Pocahontas (Fleras 2001), while Métis women are typecast by Hollywood as hot blooded but sneaky spitfires with an irresistible craving for white men (Berton 1975).

Negative images make it difficult to recognize the positive contributions of Aboriginal women. Historical and social factors also work against adequate recognition. Aboriginal women who married non-Aboriginal males were penalized through loss of status and corresponding benefits (Aboriginal men who married non-Aboriginal women retained their status). Even the repeal of the offending passage (Section 12(1)(b) of the 1985 *Indian Act*) by Bill C-31 has not eased the barriers for some women. Their status and that of their children has been reinstated to be sure, but resource-strapped bands have refused membership and residence for political and economic reasons. Even with reinstatement, women cannot pass full status to their children if a child marries a non-status Indian, with the result that status may lapse by the next generation. Efforts by Aboriginal women to do away with blatant forms of discrimination have met with resistance on the grounds that tampering with the status quo could have a domino effect by toppling conventional patterns of power and privilege (Weaver 1993). Not surprisingly, then, Aboriginal women have expressed grave concerns over the proposed entrenchment of those Aboriginal models of self-government at odds with women's equality provisions as set out in the *Constitution Act* and *Charter of Rights and Freedoms*.

Immigrant and Refugee Women

The study of immigration and immigrants has tended to ignore gender as a key variable (Willis and Yeoh 2000; Vickers and de Seve 2000). Immigrants were assumed to be gender-neutral beings who all experienced immigration in the same way. But recent research has highlighted the gendered basis of Canada's immigration policy in terms of immigration entry requirements, access to skills training and employment, and definitions of family and sponsorship (*Canadian Women Studies* 1999; also Hyndman 1999). The pervasiveness of sexism in the lives of immigrant women is graphically captured in this excerpt from Himani Bannerji, who describes the fear, anxiety, humiliation, and anger that accompanied her transition into Canada. In the final immigration interview, she faced a white and balding elderly male:

> . . . [H]e asked me—"Do you speak Hindi?" I replied that I understood it very well and spoke it with mistakes. "Can you translate this sentence for me?" he asked, and proceeded to say in Hindi what in English amounts to "Do you want to fuck with me?" . . . I gripped the edge of my chair and stared at him—silently. His hand was on my passport, the pink slip of my "landing" document lay next to it. Steadying my voice I said "I don't know Hindi that well." . . . My interview continued. I sat rigid and concluded it with a schizophrenic intensity. On Bloor Street in Toronto, sitting on the steps of a church—I vomited. I was a landed immigrant.

Immigrant women encounter additional problems because of gender and race constraints (Bannerji 2000). They often find themselves restricted to the lower echelons of the Canadian labour force where they are slotted into low-paying job ghettos such as manufacturing, service industries, and domestic work. According to Debbie Douglas (2005), executive director of the Ontario Council of Agencies Serving Immigrants and winner of the Social Action and Justice Award, many immigrant women in Toronto work in modern-day equivalents of nineteenth-century sweatshops, including 38 percent of women of colour who earn less than $10 an hour in jobs without union protection, benefits, or security. Domestic workers on two-year probationary periods are particularly vulnerable to exploitation and abuse (Macklin 1999). In a book entitled *Caregivers Break the Silence,* author Sedef Arat-Koc, a Trent University sociology professor, found that the combination of temporary work permits and the program's "live-in" requirements strips domestics of the power to complain about punishing work schedules, unpaid wages, especially for overtime work, and unlawful confinement at the hands of their employers. For immigrant women, then, Canada may be a "cage," as Melody Neufeld-Rocheleau and Judith Friesen (1987) write, because of the loneliness stemming from isolation (limited language, lack of training opportunities, child-rearing and school-related problems, racial prejudice, underemployment, lack of "Canadian" experience, and limited services to cater to their unique situations). Or as sharply put by the *Report of the Ontario Joint Task Force on Immigration and Women*, a Canadian-born woman may have difficulty reconciling the conflicting demands of homemaking and motherhood with paid employment. But immigrant women must face these same problems while having to learn a new language and adjust to a different culture, often while living in overcrowded conditions because of low earning potential.

Consider the case of temporary foreign workers in Canada. The exploitation of migrants as cheap labour to do Canada's "dirty work" applies to men and women, but only women are deliberately imported for gender-specific jobs such as the sex trade, child-rearing, and domestic labour (Macklin 1999). Nowhere are the contradictions more evident than in the system of government-sponsored labour known as foreign domestic workers (Stasiulis and Bakan 1997; Diocson 2005). In 1955, Canada established its first foreign domestic-worker policy. Caribbean women were designated as live-in domestics to provide affluent Canadian families with cheap home child-care service and domestic labour. As migrant labour, live-in domestics were granted the right to stay in Canada provided they stayed in domestic employment for at least one year after arrival (Satzewich 2000). Three trends evolved: First, an initial quota of 200 domestics per year eventually grew to 1000 annual arrivals by the mid-1960s. Second, recruitment of Caribbean women as domestic servants was gradually displaced by recruitment from the Philippines despite a historical bias against Asian immigration. As well, the 1992 Live-in Caregiver Program was tightened up by imposing tougher barriers such as stricter education and training eligibility criteria (twelve years of schooling and six months of training) for all domestic workers regardless of their country of origin. Third, by the early 1980s, domestic workers on temporary work visas were accorded the right to apply for permanent resident status from within Canada, but only upon completion of two years of live-in service (Simmie 2004). Under the terms of this seeming indentured labour, foreign domestic workers are obligated by law to live in the homes of their employers for at least two years of a three-year period. As domestic workers, they are legally classified as temporary workers and subject to deportation upon termination of their contract unless they apply for landed immigrant status. Only then can they sponsor children and partners.

In short, trafficking in women is big business (Macklin 1999). Female domestic migrants, together with sex-trade workers, are regarded by the United Nations as the most widely exploited and abused of migrant workers (Stasiulis and Bakan 1997). In Canada and elsewhere, foreign domestic workers are routinely denied citizenship status in the countries they work and reside in, in effect rendering them stateless with respect to citizenship rights. Reinforcing their status as non-citizens has had the effect of exposing them to violence and human rights violations. To be sure, although there are labour laws for protection, the vulnerability of foreign domestic workers creates an institutionalized power imbalance that puts domestic workers at risk of everything from overwork and underpay to sexual assault. Of course, not all domestic workers are exploited, but as Audrey Macklin (1999) concludes, the potential for exploitation is bolstered by the combination of unregulated work environment, the constant spectre of expulsion and deportation, and a perception among employers that they "own" the workers.

Refugee women are no less vulnerable. The 1951 Convention on the Status of Refugees clearly defined a refugee as a person who is outside his or her country, who has a well-founded fear of persecution for reasons of race, religion, nationality, political opinion, and group membership, and whom the state is unwilling or unable to protect. Definitions of persecution were typically based on male experience involving the realm of public life, with its focus on the violation of fundamental freedoms pertaining to expression, association, or conscience. Predictably, then, a refugee was typified as a male political dissident who was jailed or harassed for espousing anti-government views of a repressive regime (Ramirez 2001). The definition does not mention gender and historically has been interpreted in a way that ignores women's experiences that fall outside conventional (i.e., male) definitions of persecution—even though women and children compose around 80 percent of the world's refugees (Canadian Council of Refugees 2001). Minimal attention was directed at how refugee women faced both the risks and dangers that men confronted in flight, resettlement, and exile, in addition to threats of sexual assault and exploitation (Matsuoka and Sorenson 1999).

It has become increasingly clear that the dangers of flight experienced by women differ from that of men. Women's experiences of refugee persecution that reflect their gender status as women often take place in the "private sphere" of home and community, and may include rape, infanticide, genital mutilation, forced abortion, compulsory sterilization, sexual slavery, trafficking in women, and domestic violence (Ramirez 2001). The evidence that women use in support of their refugee claims may be more difficult to validate or quantify. To its credit, Canada in 1993 became the first country to issue guidelines on female refugee claimants fleeing gender-related persecution, including female genital mutilation. The recognition of gender-based violence is now relatively well established within Canada's refugee determination system.

Both immigrant and refugee women may be subtly yet profoundly undermined by ethnicity. Exposure to double standards is a burden for many women. Tradition may dictate a double duty for women with outside employment superimposed on traditional responsibilities of raising children. Women are expected to know their place, yet may be expected to make a contribution to the household. Actions by women that do not conform to tradition or male values may be criticized as a betrayal of the cause or the community. The family may be widely regarded as a bastion of privacy in which those who refuse to withhold unpleasant issues from the public are shunned or punished (Buckley 1996). For the sake of appearances, many women of colour are expected to defer to male authority. Such passivity may foster the facade of unity and cohesion. Yet, such submissiveness also has the effect of inhibiting the expression of skills necessary for women to excel in society at large. Not surprisingly, immigrant women may need to undergo substantial cognitive change to acquire an attitude of assertive competitiveness as part of a broader work ethic framework (Tebege 1986:6).

Female assertiveness or proclamations of freedom or equality can prove disruptive when confronting tradition-bound males (el-Tablawy 2005). Upwardly mobile immigrant women may be targets of domestic violence by those who expect servitude, deference, and submissiveness. This violence results from cultural traditions that (1) normalize male abuse of women, (2) naturalize abuse as a male right and a rite of passage for both women and men, and (3) discourage public disclosure because of family honour or community pride. The experience of domestic abuse may be further intensified because of loneliness, dependency, homesickness, lack of knowledge of English or access to services, and the threat of social ostracism. And yet immigrant women remain the "hushed-over" victims of violence. Victimized women may not know that spousal abuse is a crime in Canada or where they can go for help (Jiwani 2001). They may fear deportation if they complain or express extreme wariness toward a criminal justice system that may prove as traumatizing as domestic violence.

No one is suggesting that domestic violence is more prevalent in immigrant communities. Abuse is a display of power, and is displayed in all cultures and groups regardless of ethnicity, race, or class (Paradkar 2000). But domestic abuse impacts differently because of the unique circumstances that confront immigrant women in a foreign country without access to knowledge or resources. Few options for escape exist, and those that do often lead to more shame, physical retaliation, and isolation (Leckie 1995, Easteal 1996; Etherington 2001). Foreign-born women are told to "learn to deal with it and make sacrifices" (cited in Etherington 2001). When friends, relatives, priests/ministers, and others exert additional pressure to stay put, it becomes even more difficult to leave an abusive relationship. And when immigrant women are caught in the middle, they suffer accordingly.

| CASE STUDY | **The Politics of Hijab: Laicité vs. Diversité?** |

What is it about people's appearances that incite both provocation and perplexity? Clothing fulfills a basic human need in many climates, including Canada's, where covering up is understandably a life-affirming rule rather than a frigid exception. But clothing also possesses significant social and political functions as a non-verbal medium of ideological communication—either intended or unintended (Hoodfar 2003). The symbolic value of clothing should never be underestimated, despite our parents' admonition never to judge people by their appearances. As a marker of identity and indicator of status, clothing conveys messages that the wearer shares cultural values in common with others similarly attired, thus providing a visual means of creating community. By contrast, minor differences in clothing detail may convey individuality. Clothing as an identity and status marker may easily symbolize political expression. For the powerful, clothing is used to reinforce power; for the subdominant group, clothing can be manipulated to shift the balance of power. In contexts where visibly identifiable groups experience rejection or alienation, clothing serves as symbols of resistance in defending both individual and collective identity. Consider events in secularist Turkey. In May of 1999, a duly elected woman wearing the veil was removed from Parliament, subsequently stripped of her citizenship, and remains in exile in the United States (Kavakci 2004). Earlier in 1998, a Turkish student was barred from the medical school at the University of Istanbul because her head scarf clashed with the official dress code. The European Court of Human Rights supported this move on grounds that banning the hijab did not violate religious freedom but represented a valid countermeasure against Islamic fundamentalism (Reuters 2004).

The Controversy: A Clash of Symbols

The notion that what you wear is more important than being aware should not be taken lightly in a world where appearances count because, like it or not, approve or disapprove, people continue to judge others and be judged by how they look. The micro politics of appearances has been sharply put to the test in France, where the macro politics of robustly religious symbols clash with the priorities of a staunchly secular society. Not since the Mao jacket politicized people's appearances in the 1960s has a dress code confounded a constitutional democracy in defending its tradition of civil liberties. In enforcing the secular nature of its constitution by banning religious symbols at odds with democratic citizenship rights, France joined countries such as Turkey and the United States in keeping church separate from the state (Saunders 2004).

On the surface, the debate seems to revolve around two competing rights: the right of France to preserve its secular tradition against the religious right vs. the right of young people to wear distinctive religious symbols to public schools, including Jewish kippa and headscarves (hijab) for Muslim women. Put another way, it is the tension between the republican/liberal principle of secularism (or laicité) vs. the multicultural principle of diversity (Kastoryano 2004). In reality, the underlying issues are much deeper, and the debate especially over the hijab conceals as much as it reveals by cloaking more fundamental issues involving the interplay of race and gender with citizenship and immigration, national and transnational identities, and globalization and human rights (Resnick 2004). Not surprisingly, French reaction to the ban was mixed—seen by some as critical in preserving France's commitment to liberty, equality, and fraternity; seen by others as a blatant violation of those very principles that the French endorse. The irony is inescapable: France is a society that takes great pride in openly flaunting its sexuality as progressive and liberating, particularly in the realm of individual self-expression through haute couture. Yet, ironically, France wants to strictly regulate religious content by restricting religious symbols to the private sphere (Teitel 2004).

In short, a multicultural paradox is clearly evident: How much liberté can be advanced without jeopardizing a strong sense of égalité and fraternité (Saunders 2004)? The case study serves three purposes. It demonstrates how the politics of hijab can be differently framed, with correspondingly different interpretation. While the French authorities demonize the hijab as "back-wardness" or "aggression" (hijab as jihad), many Muslim women see it as part of their personal identity or religious conviction, without which they feel exposed (Amdur 2004). Second, the case study explores how the micro politics of veiling may play out as symbols of resistance or instruments of integration in coping with the demands of a monocultural/secular status quo. Third, the politics of hijab is situated within Canada's Multicultural framework where religious differences will sharply challenge the prospects for living together with faith-based realities (Biles et al. 2005).

The Crisis: Taking Religion Seriously in a Seriously Secular Society

In late 2003, a major French report made sweeping recommendations for regulating the relationship of religion to a secular society. The report focused on how France should balance the foundational principle of secularism with the demands of its minorities, most notably its growing Muslim population against the backdrop of escalating anti-Semitism. The report urged the passage of a law that would forbid conspicuous religious symbols in schools, including head scarves worn by Muslim girls, yarmulkes worn by Jewish boys, and large crosses worn by Christian students. The recommendations would apply to primary and secondary schools, but, curiously enough, not to students in private schools. Sanctions for refusing to obey the removal order would range from a warning to suspension or expulsion (Gainey 2004). Admittedly, the law was also aimed at Christians and Jews; nevertheless, many believed Muslim head scarves were the main target of the government's crackdown (Dobuzinskis 2004). Moreover, the frenzy over head scarves was not new, having convulsed and perplexed both French authorities and the general public for nearly two decades. Dozens of Muslim girls had been expelled over the years from schools for refusing to remove the scarf, with most schools establishing guidelines forbidding the practice, although a 1992 state ruling indicated that the wearing of scarves was permissible—unless deemed by the school to be aggressive or proselytizing. With public support firmly in favour of the proposal, the controversial ban on head scarves and other religious symbols was passed by the National Assembly on 10 February 2004 by a resounding margin, and became law when the Senate ratified it on 2 March 2004.

Neither the debate nor the fallout over the proposed ban should have come as a surprise. The symbolic power associated with the hijab lies in its ability to convey multiple meanings to both the wearer and the outsider. Two competing dynamics are at play. On one side, the presence of the veil remains a highly controversial issue because of its contested status as symbol of both oppression and resistance that masks as well as liberates (Grace 2004). Muslims endorsed the wearing of the hijab for fear of losing identity in a changing society; as a demand for privacy and protection of public honour in a world of gender violence; as a protest against Western values; and as a cutting edge of political and social change. On the other side, France has had a long history of imposing uniformity in school by suppressing difference (Amdur 2004) because of a longstanding conflict between religious and secular authorities over whose rules should rule. For nearly 125 years after the French Revolution, the Catholic Church tried everything to overthrow the Republic and replace it with a religion-friendly monarchy. A fierce strain of anti-church sentiment evolved as a result of this reaction and culminated in 1905 with the passage of a law for separating church from state. The law not only guaranteed free exercise of religious worship by ensuring a strict state neutrality toward religion, including the purging of religious symbols from all public spaces, but also sought to emancipate individuals from those religious dogmas and community constraints that precluded people from full and equal involvement in society (Kastoryano 2004). The revival of religion among Jews and Muslims reinforced the anti-clerical sentiment among those who fear the hijab as symbolizing the "thin edge of a Muslim wedge" in undermining France's secular foundations (Heneghan 2004).

Keep in mind that secularism is not synonymous with the separation of church and state. According to the separation doctrine, religious groups can discriminate against their own members (e.g., women cannot become priests in the Roman Catholic Church, which on the surface appears to be discriminatory) because the church, is seen as a private and voluntary association. As such it has its own rules, and the state cannot interfere unless overriding public interest such as safety prevails (Hurst 2005). By contrast, a secular society is one in which there is no official state religion and religion is banned from the public sphere, although permissible in the private domain (Ewing 2002).

Why France? Why now? France is a devoutly secular society whose fundamentalist secularism is anchored in a commitment to liberal universalism. France, like most liberal societies, has few problems with a pretend religious pluralism. Tolerance is tolerable when religion is seen in largely symbolic and situational terms, with practices best relegated to the private and personal. But France, like most societies, is at a loss when dealing with religious differences that want to be publicly acknowledged as a basis for identity and treatment. Problems arise when religious minorities want religion to be taken seriously as a living and lived-in reality rather than as a compartmentalized symbol that is activated on religious occasions. For many Muslims, religion is not simply an incidental marker for negotiation as seen fit. To the contrary, religion matters, because it is lived in full time—especially when under assault by unfriendly forces. Not surprisingly, Islam is emerging as a defiant element in people's identity, especially for those alienated, in hopes of restoring a moral community in which religion becomes the catalyst for internal cohesion, belonging, and distinction (Kastoryano 2004). Or as Gary Younge (2004) writes,

> [A] mosque is not just a place of worship—it is a place you won't be spat at, where you will find people who look like you and have an understanding of what you are going through.

The Debate: Freedom or Diversity?

Supporters of the ban relied on several lines of argument. The Head of Commission who produced the report argued that banning all conspicuous religious symbols embraced France's strict secular tradition. Such restrictions are deemed necessary not only for protecting French secularism from Islamic fundamentalism but also as a way of curbing Muslim demands for special privileges such as treatment of female patients by female doctors only (see Sciolino 2003). Others have argued that the head scarf itself is a symbol of Muslim patriarchy that subjugates women while hiding behind the platitudes of a religious observation. Muslim girls were seen as victims manipulated by Islamic militants, parents, and brothers in advancing political and religious agendas (Reuters 2004). In short, banning the veil not only meant breaking the chains of bondage, for example, countering the pressure imposed on unveiled Muslim schoolgirls to cover, but also preserving the core French constitutional values of a secular humanism (Heneghan 2004).

Not everyone agreed with these lines of argument. Questions were raised: Would banning the hijab help to integrate Muslim women or further isolate them? The ban could be counterproductive by virtue of excluding some Muslim girls from school—precisely the kind of exclusion the law was designed to prevent (Saunders 2004). If the hijab is seen as the "thin edge of the wedge" in destroying secularism, will the slippery slope argument be invoked to justify a host of discriminatory practices against racialized minorities? Critics of the bill criticized the proposed legislation as discriminatory as it was ostensibly aimed at the Muslim population. Restricting the hijab could spark more aggressive religious expression by driving moderates into the arms of the extremists (Contenta 2004). Besides, as Harvey Simmons argues (2004), the ban conveyed the wrong message in tarnishing those very institutions responsible for integrating people of all faiths through exposure to democratic principles of tolerance and understanding. Finally, the implementation and enforcement would prove a costly and logistic nightmare, given the vagueness of the restrictions and enforcement.

Critics also saw the ban as little more than political expediency. The government was accused of pandering to the right wing by appearing to be tough on diversity but strong on French culture and constitution while reassuring the French public by explicitly controlling the threat of a militant Islam.

Yet, the content of the ban was wildly inconsistent: Head scarves were banned in primary and secondary schools, according to the report's recommendations, but not at the university or in other public places, or in workplaces, including government offices. The report recommended that public school cafeterias cater to the dietary preferences of observant Muslims and Jews, while endorsing the public observation of Jewish and Muslim holidays on the calendar (Sciolino 2003). Interestingly, there appeared to be no mention of a ban on the wearing of the burqa—a much more conspicuous and symbolically laden item of clothing that entirely covers Muslim women. Such inconsistency suggests there is more to the ban than meets the eye.

Implications: Human Rights? Whose Rights?

Is there a right or wrong answer to this controversial ban? References to the hijab ban resonated with claims and counterclaims over conflicting notions of human rights. One side claimed human rights violation by imposing restrictions on an individual's right to religion and expression. Yes, the French state may have a right to invoke a strict secular neutrality in the public sphere. But can this right supersede the individual rights of conscience, especially when religious symbols such as the head scarf involve a divine requirement that transcends the power of secular authorities (Cochrum 2004)? The other side countered by saying that the collective rights of all French citizens must prevail over the narrow religious agendas of fundamentalist religious groups. As a sovereign state, France has a legitimate right to worry about its cultural survival within a globalizing world dominated by the English language and commercial values. France is entitled to promote strategies for securing its survival, even if this kind of nationalism raises troubling questions about the ethnic definition of citizenship in pluralistic societies. In that every society has a right to make itself safe for diversity and safe from diversity, France can legitimately claim the right to secure its internal borders by ensuring conditions for cultural minorities to co-exist with their differences—a not altogether insignificant challenge in a society where Muslims now account for nearly 8 percent of the population (or 5 million) and Jews number around 600 000. The hijab ban is also consistent with the French state's historical impulse to impose its republican value system on its increasingly diverse population, arguing that French ideals envision a uniform secular French identity as the best guarantee of national unity, equal rights, and social order (Sciolino 2004).

Perceptions of the hijab as a symbol of female oppression proved no less conflicting. Yet, proof is thin that wearing the head scarf is synonymous with backwardness or patriarchy. For young Muslim girls, the symbolic value of the hijab is not the same as that of their mothers or grandmothers who grew up in North Africa. Many are integrating quickly into French society but, paradoxically, may rely on the hijab and Islam to make the transition. The hijab allows young Muslim women to maintain connections with their parents through the more progressive aspects of religion rather than through the more archaic and repressive village traditions such as arranged marriages (Heneghan 2004). To be sure, some Muslim women are forced to wear the veil; such an imposition is to be expected of an internally diverse religion (Coleman 2006). But many Muslim women do as a matter of choice and dignity (Kavakci 2004). They choose to wear the hijab for the sake of modesty, out of religious conviction, from rebelliousness because of parental pressure, and as liberation from sexist and consumerist cultures.

As one Muslim woman put it:

> There are quite a lot of Muslims who don't classify themselves as feminists, but they are adamant that at the end of the day, the wearing of the head scarf is a way of choosing to decide who gets to see their body and who doesn't . . . And it's a matter of personal conviction rather than a form of oppression or something that's imposed on them. (Cited in Heneghan 2004)

Veiling in Canada: The Micro Politics of Identity

Canada no less than France has had to confront the challenges of religious pluralism against a backdrop of secular multiculturalism. The sharia controversy has seen to that. How, then, does Canada balance the foundational principle of secularism with the demands and rights of religious minorities to freely embrace religious practices? In the aftermath of September 11, which spotlighted Muslim dress codes and veiling, many Muslims were shocked and dismayed to find that they were "otherized" as the "enemy within" (Karim 2002; Hoodfar 2003). In theory, there should have been little to fear. The situation of Muslims in Canada may differ from that in France, in large part because many Muslim-Canadians have relatively high education levels and professional status. By comparison, Muslims in France reflect the French policy of recruiting millions of poorly skilled "guest workers" from former colonies in North and sub-Saharan Africa, who continue to arrive in large numbers but increasingly find themselves unemployed and on social assistance (Dobuzinskis 2004). Furthermore, the right to free religious expression and freedom from religious discrimination are constitutionally protected human rights issues. Not surprisingly, perhaps, a survey of 1500 adult Canadians in June of 2004 by the Centre for Research and Information on Canada indicated that two-thirds of all Canadians would *oppose* laws preventing students from wearing religious symbols or clothing in public schools, including the Islamic veil (CRIC 2004). Nor would an official Multiculturalism take issue with the hijab, as Canada's official Multiculturalism is predicated on the belief that all Canadians have a right to identify with the religious/cultural symbols of their choosing, provided that religious and cultural practices do not violate the law of the land, interfere with the rights of others, or challenge core values and institutions.

So much for the theory; how about the practice? First, Canada is not immune to pitched battles over religious symbols, including bitter debates over the feasibility of Sikh turbans in public institutions, from the RCMP to Montreal Port Authorities. Second, Canada has a history of compromising minority rights when majority interests are at stake. Restrictions on anglophones in Quebec using English as a language of public communication is one case in point (though subject to debate). Third, Canadians indicate a willingness to accommodate others if the concessions are perceived as reasonable. Canadians are much less tolerant of diversity if cultural differences are seen to threaten core Canadian values or national security, challenge widely accepted Canadian practices, or impose an unacceptably high cost (Fleras 2001). Not surprisingly, Canadian reaction to the hijab debate is mixed: On one side, especially in English-speaking Canada, the practice of veiling is tolerated as part of the multicultural mosaic. On the other side, reference to the hijab has become highly politicized in other parts of Canada—see also McDonough 2003 for controversies involving the hijab in Quebec schools—culminating in suspensions and expulsions from schools both private and public.

How does the hijab play itself out at the micro level? The veil (hijab) plays a critical role in advancing the integration of young Muslim women into Canada. By balancing the modern with the traditional (Hoodfar 2003), the veil allows Muslim women to participate in public life without compromising cultural values or rejecting religious morals, while resisting those patriarchal beliefs and practices imposed in the name of Islam. A veiled woman can defend her Islamic right to choose a spouse and reject arranged marriages without alienating family and community support. Wearing a veil allows daughters to engage in unconventional practices for Muslim women, such as going to university, mingling with men, travelling long distances, living alone, or seeking non-conventional employment. Insofar as the veil symbolizes a continued commitment to tradition within the context of Canadian society, veiled daughters may be seen as publicly asserting their Muslim Canadian identity without relinquishing their right to participate in Canadian society. To be sure, the negative portrayal of Islam and Muslims has prompted some Muslim women to openly assert the presence of a viable Muslim community in Canada. For many Muslim women, veiling symbolizes piety and spirituality, and they are clearly unhappy with its demonization as a symbol of oppression or its elevation by extremists as a symbol of Muslim identity, resistance, and even jihad (Alvi et al. 2003). Nevertheless, it is not the veil that precludes the integration of Muslim women into Canadian society, according to Hoodfar (2003). The colonial image of Muslims and the continued demonization of Islam have proven a formidable obstacle to integration and involvement.

In short, veiling and the hijab remains an indisputable symbol of Muslim identity, in addition to its status as a potent vehicle of symbolic communication (Alvi et al. 2003). Far from being a static symbol of female inferiority in Canada, the veil can mean different things in different contexts in a lived experience. It already is full of contradiction and multiple meanings (Hoodfar 2003)—ranging in scope from religious conviction, resistance to the forces of assimilation, escape from control by men and senior family members, and assertion of identity (Meshal 2003). In some contexts, veiling remains a means of controlling women's lives; in other contexts, women use the veil to empower themselves, bring about positive reforms within the community, and challenge some of those cultural and patriarchal practices that have denied, silenced, or excluded women. The decision to wear the veil also reinforces how women use Islam as a flexible resource to support their own views and practices (Predelli 2004). But while the veil may have originated in patriarchal circumstances to control women, Muslim women have appropriated the symbol in ways both empowering and subversive. Reference to the veil symbolizes a turning of the tables—of actively asserting identity and defining themselves in relationship to others as opposed to being identified and defined as different by exclusion or ostracism (Hoodfar 2003). Put bluntly, Muslim women are not passive victims; to the contrary, they increasingly assume a role as active agents who want their difference to be taken seriously in a society that claims be multicultural in principle but too often is monocultural in practice.

EXPLAINING GENDERED INEQUALITY: INTERSECTING EXCLUSIONS

Minority women are known to face sexist barriers that arise from their status as women in a predominantly patriarchal society. Patriarchy refers to a society that is organized by, for, and around men, with the result that male interests and experiences are reflected and reinforced. A system is established in which (1) the social, political, economic, and cultural are controlled by men, (2) masculinity is more highly valued than feminine values, and (3) males have preferential access to power and privilege because of their gender (Nelson 2006). Patriarchy itself consists of several interrelated constituents: **misogyny, sexism**, and **androcentrism**. Misogyny refers to hatred of women. Sexism covers that constellation of beliefs and practices that openly assert the superiority of one gender (usually men) over the other and the discriminatory behaviour that flows from such an assertion. Androcentrism reflects a male tendency to interpret reality from their point of view as natural and normal while assuming that others will think so too, and to judge others on the basis of this masculinist standard while dismissing as irrelevant or inferior those who veer beyond this framework.

Women as a group may share common experiences because of male dominance. But they also endure different patterns of control and domination because of uniquely different experiences for Aboriginal women, women of colour, and immigrant and refugee women (Gillespie 1996). Not all women are equally oppressed, given the existence of marked disparities between white women and women of colour over access to power, privilege, and resources. The allegiance of white women to white men through familial ties means that they are devalued differently than women of colour. As Hurtado (1996) observes in acknowledging how gender disparities are experienced differently, white women are increasingly striding the corridors of power whereas minority women continue to mop the floors. White women are largely concerned with projecting private sphere issues (such as accessible daycare for women in management) into the public realm. By contrast, minority women tend to focus on bread and butter issues related to racism, healthy children, and daily survival.

A conflict of interest is inevitable. Racialized women, Aboriginal women, and immigrant and refugee women confront similar issues as other women, but face them differently because these issues are filtered through the lens of racism and ethnocentrism (Jiwani 2001). Minority women experience difficulty in identifying with white feminist theories that ignore racial hierarchies, discrimination within the workplace, and oppressive patterns within their own ethnic communities. Moreover, the interlocking of gender with race, ethnicity, and class generates such a different set of outcomes that references to "sisterhood" as an all-encompassing category are both unrealistic and reductionist. As sharply put by Stasiulis (1999:355),

> Thus, to speak about or for 'women' was no longer a liberating politics but a homogenizing gesture that masked the race privilege of racially dominant women and the racial oppression and marginalization of women of colour.

Even strategies for change differ. In contrast with white women, minority women are not in a position to divorce themselves from the men of their group as neither can exist without the other in the struggle against oppression (hooks 1994, 1995). Nor are they in a position to compartmentalize their politics from broader struggles for inclusion and equality. As the O.J. Simpson trial clearly demonstrated, minority women are caught in a double bind. They may be tempted to identify with white women with whom they share gender and sexist discrimination; yet, they may have little choice except to affiliate with their sometimes sexist menfolk with whom they share a common experience of racism, ethnocentrism, and classism. To the extent that white women do not experience race, they are free to focus on sexism. To the degree that minority women must confront racism, ethnocentrism, and classism in addition to sexism, they cannot afford to privilege gender over race, class, and ethnicity as the primary site of struggle.

INTERSECTIONAL ANALYSIS: GENDER *x* RACE *x* ETHNICITY *x* CLASS

How do we account for gendered inequalities? Are they the result of innate differences or social conditioning? Should the blame lie in the structures of society or the discipline of the market? Sociologists generally discount biological theories. Psychological theories of maturational developments are best left to psychologists. Sociological theories emphasize the social as a key explanatory variable. Of those social variables most responsible for gendered inequality, the most relevant appear to be race, ethnicity, class, and gender. In the cold analytical language of sociologists, the concepts of race, ethnicity, gender, and class constitute "variables" that have had a differential impact on minority women. Race, gender, ethnicity, and class may be treated as analytically distinct dimensions of inequality; nevertheless, their conceptualization as interlocking and mutually reinforcing categories is increasingly central to social analysis (Patterson et al. 1996; Stasiulis 1999). Of course, race, class, gender, and ethnicity embody systems of inequality in their own right, with particular histories and intrinsic logic (Rothenberg 2001). Yet, each operates in conjunction with the others to construct a complex set of interlocking and overlapping patterns of domination and control (Devine et al. 2005). Recognizing the multi-faceted nature of social inequality helps to account for the dynamic interaction between different forms of subdomination and the different ways in which each is experienced in and through the other (Bottomley et al. 1991). Intersectionality is key, for taken alone, each of these barriers is painful. Taken together, however, they are unyielding yet invisible—a " . . . cage which appears light and airy, masking the fact that its occupants are trapped as completely as if they were in a sealed vault" (Rothenberg 1991:96).

Theoretical efforts to understand race, ethnic, and Aboriginal relations have come to accept the intersectionality of social relations involving race, class, gender, and ethnicity (Andersen and Collins 1998; Stasiulis 1999; Rothenberg 2001). According to Stasiulis (1999:347), feminist intersectional analysis approaches the social reality and broader contexts of women and men as " . . . *multiply, simultaneously, and interactively* [emphasis Stasiulis] determined by various significant axes of social organization." An **intersectional analysis** goes beyond an approach that sees race and ethnicity as fixed and static; that ignores diversity within groups; and that glosses over the interactive elements of social location. It provides a theoretical framework for articulating the relationship among different aspects of one's social identity (gender, class) and their interaction with different systems of oppression (e.g., patriarchy) (Krane et al. 2000). In incorporating the inseparability of race, ethnicity, class, and gender as interlocking and overlapping expressions of inequality, intersectional analysis provides an alternative analysis to (1) the reductionist tendencies that characterize Marxist/socialist thought (which emphasize the centrality of class relations in shaping dynamics and outcomes); (2) feminist thought that posits the "categorical hegemony" of gender as pivotal in explaining patterns of power and privilege over time and across space; and (3) anti-racist thought that "privileges" race and racism as the bane of minority women's existence (Stasiulis 1999).

While difficult to knit together into a coherent and accessible analysis (but see Jiwani 2001), there is much of value in promoting the multiple and simultaneous experiences of race, class, and gender as intersecting systems of privilege or inequality rather than as discrete categories that stand in a mechanistic, additive, or non-relational form (Glenn 2002). Intersectional analysis demonstrates how gender is racialized, race is gendered, and class interlocks with the logic of race and gender to create intersecting jeopardies. Thus, visible minority women experience racism differently from visible minority men, and differently among themselves depending on age, class, ability, sexual preference, and place of residence. They experience gender differently from white women because of racism and ethnicity. And the experience of ethnicity may also render minority women vulnerable to double standards, human rights abuses, and levels of subordination that are at odds with Canada's equality provisions. That makes it doubly important to focus on the different ways in which gender intersects with race, ethnicity, and class to create interlocking hierarchies of inequality in shaping the realities of minority women.

DEBATE REVISITED | **Sharia—Inclusiveness or Intersectional Exclusion?**

To date, no Western jurisdiction has formally allowed sharia religious law to settle family disputes (marriage, divorce, custody) within its secular legal system. But the Ontario government reviewed plans to institutionalize the sharia-based tribunals within the framework of the *Arbitration Act*. As long as safeguards are put in place, according to a major report by Marion Boyd, former Attorney General for the provincial NDP, there is no reason to dismiss sharia as a viable option that employs principles of faith to settle matters such as marital breakdown, spousal support, and child custody. After all, sharia tribunals are already operating informally, although their decisions are not recognized under Ontario's *Arbitration Act,* and their regulation under the Act may prevent abuses (Valpy and Howlett 2005). And yet, Quebec courts have ruled that sharia-based tribunals are inconsistent with the province's secular character—a case of multiculturalism gone mad, critics say (Gagnon 2005). In the words of Quebec's premier, Jean Charest, Quebec is an inclusive society but one that is governed by a single law and the principle that everyone is equal before the law (Greenberg 2005). Moreover, while Ontario is seriously considering an Islamic sharia court, the Muslim world appears to be deeply divided about the value of a faith-based arbitration—let alone its institutionalization into Ontario law.

On one side are the supporters: The Islamic Institute of Civil Justice has proven a prime mover in endorsing a sharia body of religious law to settle disputes within the Muslim community (see also Coleman 2006). According to the Institute, Canada's freedom of religion guarantees must go beyond a right to practise religion and, more importantly, must allow a minority's religious laws to govern all aspects of life, from the spiritual to the secular. To disallow women the right to sharia is not only condescending and controlling, not to mention a case of double standards as other faith-based groups have access to arbitration, but also contrary to Canada's multiculturalism commitments. Even those with reservations about the specifics of a sharia system continue to support the principle of faith-based arbitration—as long as the system is Canadianized, that is, secured with sufficient safeguards and checks and balances to protect the rights of those most vulnerable from internal pressure.

On the other side are groups such as the Canadian Council of Muslim Women who are concerned that the rights of Muslim women might be compromised by having to participate in male-dominated sharia tribunals without their informed consent or adequate protection. Women may be pressured by family and community to comply; those women who reject arbitration under Islamic family law may be dismissed as less than good and devout Muslims (Howlett 2005). Young immigrants and those from the Middle East and North Africa are particularly vulnerable to bullying, in part because they have known little else except sharia law throughout their entire life (Gagnon 2005). Critics of the proposal also point to foundational (patriarchal) flaws that govern sharia (which admittedly varies greatly in interpretation from one Muslim society to another). Under many interpretations of sharia law, women are viewed not as equal but as inferior to men, thus defaulting on the right to equal justice. Under sharia law, men appear to have more rights than women. They are seen as guardians of women, who must take permission from their husbands; male heirs receive more inheritance than female heirs; husbands, not wives, can initiate divorce proceedings; husbands, not wives, are generally awarded custody of daughters of puberty age in divorce cases; and in a straightforward disagreement between a husband and wife, the husband's testimony may prevail over the wife's testimony (Jimenez 2005; Hurst 2005; Evans and Hashmi 2005).

Not unexpectedly, then, many Muslim women are rejecting the sharia. As Canadians they want to live under the equality provisions of Canadian law rather than the implicit patriarchy and androcentrism embedded within sharia. Not only are sharia tribunals seen as a violation of the *Charter of Rights and Freedoms,* but their very existence makes it awkward for Muslim women to speak out against those Islamic scholars who want to impose norms of behaviour that clash with women's human rights. The relationship of sharia to Canada's official Multiculturalism is no less debated. The international rights group Women Living Under Muslim Laws has warned the government to avoid the multicultural trap of endorsing old world traditions out of a misguided notion of not being seen as anti-Muslim. There is a danger that in trying to avoid discrimination against a whole group, Canada's official Multiculturalism may inadvertently discriminate against its female members. A co-founder of the Muslim Canadian Congress is also highly critical of a process that will end up ghettoizing Muslims under the cloak of multiculturalism. According to Tarak Fatah, the fear of not offending the Muslim community's male leadership at the expense of trampling on Muslim women's rights is nothing short of racism. He writes:

> In some ways, this is the racism of lower expectations. Under the guise of empowering us and under some false notion of multiculturalism, the mainstream community is saying, well, it doesn't affect us.

Finally, there are fears that Islamic fundamentalists are utilizing sharia by stealth to impose a conservative Muslim presence in Canada. Critics believe that because of Canada's robust multiculturalism, Ontario may be targeted by extremists to entrench Islam law in Western democracy (Greenberg 2005). If it happens in Ontario, critics conclude, the precedent is set in terms of legitimacy, and sharia could happen anywhere.

In short, the Ontario government finds itself in a bit of quandary (Valpy and Howlett 2005). The path to sharia is strewn with pitfalls. On the one hand, it is only fair that Muslim Canadians have access to the kind of religious arbitration already enjoyed by Christians, Jews, and Ishmaeli Muslims. On the other hand, the government is afraid to move forward in light of the terrorist attacks in London by three British Muslims. This reluctance is based largely on fears that the public will not stomach concessions to Muslims, especially if it creates a politicized Islamic presence in Canada (Howlett 2005). Even an official Multiculturalism may prove more of a foe than a friend. The formalization of sharia under the *Arbitration Act* may appear to be logically consistent with the tolerance implicit in multiculturalism. But Canada's official Multiculturalism is clear about where to draw the line over acceptance. To the extent that differences are tolerated, Canada's official Multiculturalism will not condone a practice that runs the risk of violating the equality rights of women. In the end, however, the issue was resolved by the simple expedient of repealing the *Arbitration Act* so that faith-based mediation in Ontario would no longer be officially recognized (DiManno 2005).

CHAPTER HIGHLIGHTS

- Both minority women and men tend to be exploited or excluded because of race, ethnicity, or class. Minority women are additionally handicapped because of gender discrimination.
- Two principles underpin this chapter on gendered diversity: First, race, ethnic, and Aboriginal relations are ultimately gendered relations; second, gendered relations are in the final analysis relationships of inequality.

- Aboriginal women, racialized women, and immigrant and refugee women face similar issues, but the particular ways in which these issues are refracted through the prism of race, ethnicity, and class tends to amplify their effects.

- Gendered inequality is experienced differently by Aboriginal women, women of colour, and immigrant and refugee women because of the different demands imposed by their specific location in society.

- Intersectional analysis involves the notion that gender is superimposed on and intersects with race, ethnicity, and class to create interlocking and overlapping hierarchies of privilege/disprivilege.

KEY TERMS

androcentrism

feminism

gendered inequality

intersectional analysis

misogyny

patriarchy

sexism

REVIEW QUESTIONS

1. The concept of minority women includes Aboriginal women, women of colour, and immigrant and refugee women. Compare the different experiences, concerns, and aspirations of each of these differently located women.

2. The concepts of race, ethnicity, gender, and class are widely perceived as having a differential impact on minority women. Each of these variables is determining in its own right yet each intersects with the other to create interlocking patterns of inequality. Taken together, they create systems of gender inequality that have proven difficult to dismantle. Explain.

3. Indicate how and why the politics of the hijab (in France) and the politics of sharia have elicited such strong reactions in advancing a living together with our differences.

4. Compare the concepts of misogyny, sexism, androcentrism, and patriarchy as the basis for the unequal treatment of minority women in Canada.

LINKS AND RECOMMENDATIONS

Video

Me and the Mosque

An NFB look at how Muslim women continue to be victims of discrimination within the framework of Islamic religion.

Film

The New World

An interesting film in the tradition of *Dances with Wolves*. But while some stereotypes are reversed, Pocahontas continues to be exoticized as a "Barbie" in scanty buckskins.

Article/Report

For an extremely useful application of intersectional analysis, see "Intersecting Inequalities: Immigrant Women of Colour, Violence, and Health Care," by Yasmin Jiwani (2001). Available by "Googling" the title.

Books

Two very useful books that cover a lot of territory related to gender and diversity:

Race, Class, and Gender: An Anthology, 6th ed., by Margaret L. Andersen and Patricia Hill Collins. 2007, Wadsworth Publishing.

Race, Class, and Gender in the United States by Paula S. Rothenberg. 2001, Worth Publishing.

Random Family: Love, Drugs, Trouble, and Coming of Age in the Bronx by Adrian Nicole LeBlanc. 2003, Scribner Books, New York. A narrative look at inner city life and love as individuals' lives intersect over time, for better and often for worse. Based on ten years of reporting, the author goes behind the headlines of gangsta glamour and high-flying druggies to expose a roller coaster of poverty, disappointment, success and power, prison, betrayal, and death.

Websites

The National Action Committee on the Status of Women is Canada's largest feminist organization, and this website is a treasure trove of references to issues involving diversity and women.

www.nac-cca.ca/index_e.htm

Draws attentions to the concerns and activities of visible minority and immigrant women in Canada.

www.noivmwc.org

The official site for Aboriginal women in Canada with numerous links to issues involving identity, experiences, and opportunities.

www.nwac-hq.org

A useful clearing house of information related to gender, race, ethnicity, and the media.

www.uiowa.edu

P a r t

CANADA'S DIVERSITY MODEL: PEOPLES, NATIONS, AND MINORITIES

. . . Canada is a world leader in three of the most important areas of ethnocultural relations: immigration, indigenous peoples, and the accommodation of minority nationalisms . . . That we have managed to cope with all these forms of diversity simultaneously while still managing to live together in peace and civility is, by any objective standard, a remarkable achievement. (Kymlicka 1998:3)

Canada encompasses a rich complexity of diversity. Nearly 200 racial and ethnic groups can be identified in Canada, while Aboriginal peoples are no less internally diverse, including 50 different tribal groups (Haida, Mohawk, etc.) and over 50 different languages (INAC 2003). Such a profusion of riches poses a problem of whom to incorporate into an introductory textbook. Should the focus be on (1) Aboriginal peoples; (2) charter group members, namely the French and English; or (3) multicultural minorities, such as immigrants, refugees, members of European ethnic groups, or racialized minorities, both foreign- and Canadian-born? Should emphasis be on those who have been forcibly incorporated into Canadian society and appear anxious to "get out," or on those immigrant and multicultural minorities who have voluntarily accepted Canada as their adopted country and are anxious to "fit in"?

Efforts to "tame" this bewildering diversity by organizing it into a coherent framework have proven less than entirely successful. Of the many proposals to solve this conceptual impasse, few have met with as much success as a model that divides Canada's multi-layered and deep diversities into a limited number of categories on the basis of structural and relational similarities (Elliott 1983). *Unequal Relations* follows this format. Canada's race, ethnic, and Aboriginal composition is partitioned into three major "diversities"—Aboriginal peoples (original occupants/First Nations), charter (founding national communities) groups,

161

and multicultural minorities (immigrants and descendents of immigrants). These groups are compared on the basis of four criteria: (1) constitutional status in society, (2) major problems, (3) proposed solutions, and (4) anticipated outcomes. Each of these "diversities" is associated with a distinctive yet shared set of attributes; each also confronts a host of unique problems because of its constitutional status and structural constraints; and each is likely to espouse solutions and anticipate outcomes commensurate with its priorities (see also Roth 1998; Kymlicka 2001; Jenson and Papillon 2001). The interplay of these major diversities imparts a dynamic that transforms Canada into a contested site of competing interests. The table below provides an overview of Canada's diversity model by comparing the **three major diversities** along the aforementioned criteria: constitutional status, core problem, proposed solutions, and anticipated outcomes.

Canada's Diversity Model: The Three Major Diversities				
	Constitutional Status	**Core Problem**	**Proposed Solution**	**Anticipated Outcome**
Aboriginal Peoples	First Nations/original occupants	Internal colonialism	Self-determining autonomy	The Nations within Canada
Charter Groups	Founding national communities	Blocked sovereignty	Sovereignty without secession	Distinct society
Multicultural Minorities	Citizenship rights	Discrimination	Inclusion	Level playing field

The table clearly demonstrates how Canada's multi-layered diversities differ in terms of who they are, what they want, how they propose to get it, and where they hope to end up. Very briefly: The politics of aboriginality are inseparable from Aboriginal peoples' status as Canada's original occupants whose territorial residence on this continent preceded European colonization. The Aboriginal agenda is driven by a commitment to not only decolonize their relationship but also to construct a new (post-colonial) social contract by way of Aboriginal models of **self-determining autonomy** over land, identity, and political voice. Ottawa–Quebec relations are constructed around the constitutional status of French and English (or, more accurately, French- and English-speaking) as founding members of Canadian society. Conflicts involving Canadians/Canadien(ne)s who claim sovereign rights as national societies/communities reflect a failure to craft an innovative political order that concedes "peoplehood" to Quebecers. Finally, multicultural minorities confront a different set of challenges in staking out a place in Canada. Instead of demands for collective rights as the basis for living together separately, the concerns of minority women and men are directed at institutional inclusion through removal of discriminatory barriers. This pattern may undergo change as Canada's multicultural minorities become more politicized in defining "who gets what."

By emphasizing three broad sets of claims put forward by Canadian constituencies (Roth 1998), Canada's diversity model provides a framework for analyzing race, ethnic, and Aboriginal relations as unequal relations. Exceptions abound in this kind of typology, to be sure, including anomalous status minorities such as Hutterites and francophones outside Quebec. However, the goal of any typology is not to replicate reality in its exactitude—after all, the very nature of "ideal types" is prone to simplification or reductionism—but to render it intelligible for purposes of description or analysis. The classification of minorities into Canada's diversity model solves several problems in one swoop. Recurrent themes and predictable patterns in group behaviour can be emphasized without lapsing into a welter of detail. Specifics are sacrificed along the way; still, much can be gleaned from exploring the inner logic behind inter-group behaviour instead of getting lost in the minutiae. This "big picture" approach also reinforces a macro-sociological view of society as a dynamic of competitively different groups in ongoing struggles over power, privilege, and property.

Part 2 is organized around this macro-level analysis of Canada as a multi-layered and deeply divided diversity model of competing groups, opposing agendas, and contested challenges. Chapter 7 explores the politics of Aboriginal peoples–state relations within the context of Aboriginal peoples as political communities with an inherent right to self-determining autonomy—albeit within the framework of Canadian society. The chapter addresses the following issues: (1) the depressed socio-economic status of Aboriginal peoples, (2) the dispossession of Aboriginal peoples because of colonization, (3) government policy response to solving the "Indian problem," and (4) Aboriginal proposals for radical renewal through constructive engagement. Chapter 8 analyzes the politics of English–French (charter member) relations against the backdrop of an increasingly antiquated federalist structure. Quebec's nationalism is shown to be driven by claims to peoplehood, an aversion to being ruled by others, a commonality as a national community with a shared language and customs, and a qualified form of sovereignty around a reformulated federalism. The "language" of nationhood not only provides a rationale for advancing the demands of the Québécois, but also symbolizes the jurisdictional wrangles at the core of French–English hostilities. Chapter 9 looks at a variety of concerns that confront multicultural minorities as they cope with the challenges of "getting in," "settling down," and "fitting in." Primary attention is centred on various issues pertaining to immigration, including an overview of immigration policies, immigration patterns in the past and at present, debates over the pros and cons of immigration, and an assessment of its costs and benefits.

Part 3, on multiculturalism and inclusiveness, will deal more specifically with the politics of engaging diversity as a Canada-building challenge.

ABORIGINAL PEOPLES IN CANADA: RE-PRIMING THE RELATIONSHIP

Chapter

7

DEBATE — Nisga'a Self-Government: "More Like 'Us'" or "Less Like You"?

References to the "Indian problem" may be a misnomer, but public perception of Aboriginal peoples as having problems or creating problems will not be easily discarded. Proposed solutions to the so-called "Indian" problem are no less puzzling and provocative. On one side are those proponents who believe that assimilation is the key. According to the "assimilationists," the Indian problem reflects the isolation of Aboriginal peoples from society because of reserves, special status, **treaties**, and welfare handouts. If only they would modernize and become "more like us," that is, urban, individualistic, and private property owners, all their problems would disappear (Flanagan 1999; Fiss 2004a, b). On the other side are those who believe that less is more, and that solving the Indians' "Canada problem" lies in becoming less "like you" because "we are not you"

(Denis 1997). For "autonomists," relations repair is the key: A restructuring of Aboriginal peoples–society relations must acknowledge Aboriginal peoples as a political community, with a corresponding right to Aboriginal models of self-determining autonomy over land, identity, and political voice as part of a new social contract for living together separately (Maaka and Fleras 2005).

Not surprisingly, government policy has come under attack because of these proposed solutions. Some accuse the government of obstructing the transformation of Aboriginal peoples into "more like us" by conceding too much Aboriginal difference. Others believe the opposite is true: The government appears ruthlessly wedded to a "more like us" philosophy at the expense of a "less like you" framework. Put in a slightly different way, Is the government taking Aboriginal peoples too seriously by promoting "racially" conscious preferential treatment? Or, alternatively, not seriously enough, by insisting on ever-clever ways of fostering self-sufficient assimilation to solve the "Indian problem"?

The politics of polarization received a good working over with ratification of the Nisga'a *Final Agreement* in May 2000—the first treaty settlement in British Columbia since 1859 and the first of 50 outstanding land claims encompassing the entire province. The *Final Agreement* (the federal government prefers not to use the term "treaty") did not materialize overnight. Since 1885, the Nisga'a First Nations of Central British Columbia have looked to Ottawa for compensation for the Crown's unilateral confiscation of their land. They petitioned the British Privy Council in 1913, and in 1968 took their case to court where a Supreme Court ruling in 1973 ruled against the Nisga'a (on a technicality rather than substance). Nonetheless, the Calder decision (as it came to be known) conceded the possibility of something called **Aboriginal title** to unsurrendered land, culminating in the historic agreement. The conclusion is inescapable. The Nisga'a have come a long way since the late Pierre Elliott Trudeau denied the existence of Aboriginal rights by declaring that no country could be built on "historical might have beens."

The actual terms of the agreement are clearly articulated, but subject to diverse interpretations. The Nisga'a *Final Agreement* provides 5500 members of bands who live 800 kilometres north of Vancouver with a land base of 1900 kilometres (a fraction of the amount originally proposed). They have control over forest and fishery resources; $200 million in cash; release from *Indian Act* provisions without loss of Indian status; a supra-municipal level of government including control over policing, education, community services,

and taxes; and eventual elimination of on-reserve tax exemptions (Matas 1998). To help pay for this infrastructure, the Nisga'a will receive forest and timber cutting rights, oil and mineral resources, and a fishery-conservation trust as well as 26 percent of the salmon fishery plus $21.5 million to purchase boats and equipment. This transfer in wealth and jurisdiction is expected to alleviate community dysfunctions, including high levels of unemployment, criminal activity, and crowded homes.

A wave of reaction greeted the settlement of British Columbia's first land claims test. According to critics, an "extraordinary agreement" with the Nisga'a Nations has "raised the spectre of racially separate development across Canada" because of provisions that (1) provide the Nisga'a with more autonomy and **self-government** than it constitutionally deserves; (2) empower the Nisga'a to pass laws on any matter other than defence, currency, and foreign affairs; (3) allow specific Aboriginal rights to challenge Canadian citizenship rights; (4) confer benefits unavailable to other Canadians based solely on culture or colour; and (5) prohibit non-Nisga'a from voting for the region's administration, thus disenfranchising local residents who continue to pay taxes but lack representation. Critics charge that the Agreement has entrenched a new legislative body (Nisga'a Lisums Parliament) with constitutionally protected powers to create laws that will trump federal and provincial legislation, while greasing the slippery slide toward a patchwork of semi-sovereign states—a de facto third order of government—where citizens live by different rules than do other Canadians (Alberts 1999; Flanagan 2001; Widdowson 2003; Fiss 2004). Unlike other self-governing arrangements (the Sechelt for example) where provincial authorities prevail, the Nisga'a Agreement is shielded by a protected land claim agreement that

Parliament cannot revoke (Chwialkowska 1999). The more vociferous critics persist in playing the "race card." The Nisga'a Agreement is vilified as another apartheid in dividing Canadians from each other, nothing less than the once detested Bantustans of South Africa.

How do these accusations stand up to scrutiny? Is the Nisga'a *Final Agreement* another form of racial apartheid? Or is it about the collective and inherent rights of the Nisga'a? Is it about racial **entitlements** or about Aboriginal rights for self-determining autonomy? Is it about living apart in segregated enclaves or about living together separately through co-operative coexistence? And if not the Nisga'a, then what? How exactly do Canadians hope to live together amicably when the political space they share is informed by those mindsets and structures that created the problem in the first place (also Weisbrod 2002)?

INTRODUCTION: RETHINKING THE "SOCIAL CONTRACT"

What a difference a few decades can make. As recently as 1969, Canada's Aboriginal peoples were poised on the brink of legal extinction because of the assimilationist intent of the government's draft **White Paper**, under the then Indian Affairs Minister Jean Chrétien. Aboriginal concerns had focused on basic survival strategies, and many seemed resigned to powerful outside forces beyond their control. But Aboriginal protest mobilized over perceptions of the White Paper as predominantly a pretext for cultural genocide. By the late 1970s, a sense of revolt was mounting in reaction to government waffling over Aboriginal issues, a move that nearly derailed Trudeau's efforts at repatriating the Constitution. The constitutional entrenchment of Aboriginal and treaty rights in 1982 clearly confirmed the growing political clout of Aboriginal peoples. By 1992, Aboriginal leaders were engaging with First Ministers in Charlottetown in the hope of hammering out a workable post-Oka relationship with the government. Principles became practice when in 1995 the Liberal government leader, Jean Chrétien, acknowledged the "inherent right" of Canada's Aboriginal peoples to self-government. The ratification of the Nisga'a *Final Agreement* confirms what many suspected: Aboriginal peoples have landed as a force to be reckoned with in defining "what Canada is for" (Murphy 2003).

One of the major themes in this chapter is the distance travelled by Aboriginal peoples in reclaiming constitutional space (see also Bird et al. 2002). In a relatively short period, the status of Aboriginal peoples has leapt from that of wards of the state to self-determining peoples, from a minority with needs to a people with rights, and from the margins of Canada to robust actors at the centre of Canada's political stage. But another theme in this chapter is less hopeful, that is, the enormity of the distance that is yet to be traversed before Aboriginal peoples assume their rightful place in Canada. Canadians have been slow in taking Aboriginal differences seriously; they have been even slower in acknowledging Aboriginal realities as a basis for "living together separately." The underlying premises that inform the relationship between Canada and Aboriginal peoples have not been addressed, but embrace a largely colonial model, with the result that authority reflects a Crown prerogative instead of a power-sharing partnership. Canadians have also been reluctant to recognize the central reality that governs Aboriginal peoples–Canada relations. Aboriginal peoples have rights, both inherent and collective, and these rights not only set them apart from the mainstream in terms of entitlements, but also provide a framework for re-priming their relationship to Canada.

It is not coincidental that we begin Part 2 with an analysis of Canada's First Peoples. The term "first" in First Nations (or Peoples) is not to be taken lightly. The term "aboriginal" itself refers to the original or "first" occupants of this country. Their status as original occupants (or more accurately, descendents of the original occupants) provides **Aboriginal peoples** with the moral legitimacy as first among equals in defining who gets what. The term "first" can also be used in a less flattering way. Aboriginal peoples are "first" in those social areas that count least (unemployment, undereducation, suicide, and morbidity rates), but rarely first in realms that matter most, including wealth, power, and privilege. The colonialist structures that thwart Aboriginal aspirations have succeeded only too well in ensuring the "first" are often the "last." Yet, many Canadians are unaware of what Aboriginal peoples want, why they want it, and how they propose to achieve their goals (Ponting 1997). It is precisely this ignorance that reinforces a perception of Aboriginal peoples as "problem people" who "have problems" that cost or "create problems" that provoke (Switzer 1998). Canada's mistreatment of Aboriginal peoples has been called a national tragedy and its "hidden shame." According to Matthew Coon Come, former National Chief of the Assembly of First Nations, many Aboriginal peoples continue to be victims of state violence, policies of assimilation and extinguishment, and a racism that diminishes as it undermines. Just ponder this indictment of Canada by David Ahenakew, also a former Chief of the Assembly, who tried to justify his wilful promotion of hatred of Jewish people on grounds that Aboriginal peoples have suffered as well:

> I do not mean to trivialize the aura of the Holocaust and the pain of what happened to the Jewish people in Germany and elsewhere. However, Canadians need to honestly discuss the cultural genocide perpetuated on the First Nations in this country. We need to look honestly at the way my people have been treated since Europeans came and to have courage to recognize that the injustices against First Nations are more than equal to the horrors perpetuated against the Jewish community and the racism and ethnic cleansing that has so shocked the world in places like Rwanda and Bosnia . . . Hatred of First Nations people is rampant in our country, and it exists in the legal and justice systems, the media, and the Canadian economy. (Cited in Adam and Zachary 2005:A-1, A-2)

The international community is no less aware of Canada's shortcomings. Canada may be perennially ranked by the United Nations as one of the world's best places to live, but Canada's on-reserve Aboriginal peoples are ranked as low as number 78 on a human development index. The fact that Aboriginal peoples live 12 years less and earn about one half of the annual income of Canadians puts Aboriginal reserves on the same par as medium-developed countries such as Mexico and Thailand (Anderssen 1998). Such statistics are a stunning indictment of Canada's resolve. To Canada's embarrassment, a UN human rights committee has ruled Canada's treatment of Aboriginal peoples as a hidden shame, contrary to international law, and inconsistent with its human rights record—at least according to Rodolfo Stavenhagen, a UN special investigator into the rights and freedoms of indigenous peoples (cited in Schlein, 2005:A11).

However badly treated and maligned, Aboriginal peoples have not stood by as passive and powerless victims (Ominayak and Bianchi 2002; Ashini 2002; Samson 2003). Many have taken the initiative in re-calibrating their relationship to society, and it is these "initiatives" in moving forward rather than "inertia" from looking back that anchor the content of this chapter. But the foundational principles that govern Canada's **constitutional order** are resistant to change because of vested interests and systemic bias. The awareness that change is overdue but undervalued redoubles the need to focus on Aboriginal peoples–state relations in terms of underlying logic, hidden agendas, competing interests, and future outcomes. This chapter neither unfolds as a history nor reads as a description. Nor is it intended to obsess over social problems in Aboriginal communities as if Aboriginal peoples were the sole architects of their misfortune. Rather the chapter addresses the politics of "**aboriginality**" by analyzing the increasingly contested relationship of Aboriginal peoples to Canadian society. To what extent is the Canadian model for relations with Aboriginal peoples of utility or beyond repair (Strauss 2006)? Also addressed are the paradoxes of restructuring the relationship away from colonial practices toward a new post-colonial future, while coping with the realities and consequences of the neo-colonialism in play at present (Abele 2004).

Many have said that two narratives capture the reality of Aboriginal peoples in Canada at present (Fraser 2004). One tells of the growing recognition of Aboriginal rights, court decisions that uphold Aboriginal peoples' claims to self-determining autonomy, and constitutional changes to the political architecture for framing the relationship (see Abele 2004). The other narrative speaks of dispossession, disempowerment, degradation, and despair at individual and community levels. In acknowledging the reality of both narratives, the chapter begins with a brief overview of Aboriginal peoples with respect to their legal and socio-economic status. This is followed by an examination of policy changes that have historically shaped the fortunes of "**the nations within**." Aboriginal policy is shown to have generated as many problems as it set out to solve, partly because of faulty premises that induce negative outcomes and partly from privileging "national interests" over Aboriginal concerns. Aboriginal proposals for renewing relations between Aboriginal peoples and the government are discussed at three levels of engagement: (1) taking Aboriginal difference seriously, (2) recognizing Aboriginal title and treaty rights, and (3) promoting Aboriginal models of self-determining autonomy. Finally, the concept of "**constructive engagement**" is explored as a model for establishing a new social contract for living together separately without drifting apart.

A few words of warning to the reader. First, neither of the authors is of Aboriginal ancestry, so we cannot speak from an Aboriginal perspective by tapping into Aboriginal experiences. Such an outsider status can be a strength or weakness, but invariably necessitates a certain deftness in approach—if only to avoid the trap of treacly sentimentality, over-generalization, indignation, or defensiveness (see also Weisberger 1999). Second, limitations of space cannot be ignored. With over 600 First Nations comprising 60–80 nation groups and more than 50 languages, it is impossible to compress into a single chapter all there is to know about Aboriginal peoples, either in the past or at present. Nor can we conflate the diverse concerns of Aboriginal peoples into a coherent statement, especially when differences within Aboriginal communities may be as striking as differences with non-Aboriginal Canadians. Priorities vary widely. The political aspirations of Aboriginal "elites" may be widely endorsed in principle within Aboriginal communities, but are sharply at odds with more pragmatic local concerns for healthy children and indoor plumbing (EKOS 2004). The necessity to be selective focuses on the macro-dimension of Aboriginal realities, namely, the evolving political relationship of Aboriginal peoples with the Canadian state (or government) as reflected and reinforced through the prism of official policy and Aboriginal assertiveness.

Finally, our discussion of Aboriginal peoples is confined to general terms. Such a level of generality increases the risk of glossing over the historical and cultural specifics of different Aboriginal communities. Aboriginal peoples constitute an extremely diverse constituency, with numerous tribes of varying size, access to resources, development levels, ecological adaptations, and social health. Politically speaking, Aboriginal peoples are legally divided into status, non-status, Métis, and Inuit, each with a specific set of priorities and aspirations. The diversity is amplified by ecological adaptations to unique physical environments, in addition to individual differences based on age, education levels, location, and socio-economic status. The importance of women to Aboriginal communities is widely recognized, yet gender issues continue to be glossed over because of colonialist legacies (Monture-Angus 2002). In short, there are numerous traps in discussing Aboriginal peoples as if they were a relatively homogeneous entity with a shared sense of community and commitment. Common sense will dictate they are as heterogeneous as non-Aboriginal Canadians in political outlook, socio-economic status, and personality types. To admit this internal diversity is not to diminish the value of broad brush strokes. Nevertheless, readers must be insulated against the perils of imposing a one-size-fits-all explanatory framework on a field of astonishing complexity.

CANADA'S ABORIGINAL PEOPLES: DIVERSITY IN INEQUALITY

Indian, Native, Status Indian, Aboriginal, Treaty Indian, Non-treaty, Registered Indian, C-31s, Non-status, Inuit, Métis—about the only thing these different terms have in common is the unilateral manner in which they were imposed on the original inhabitants of Turtle Island, resulting in one of the most arbitrary yet oppressive classifications ever devised by a government to categorize and control (Sawchuk 1998). Rather than reflecting cultural or historical distinctions, each of these terms is a legalistic concept for political and bureaucratic reasons. Political authorities have reacted accordingly. While the Inuit and First Nations on reserves have entitlements and rights, those who live off reserves and the Métis are perceived as having needs. While the Métis are served by the health care system like other Canadians, the First Nations and Inuit Health Branch oversees an annual expenditure of $1.1 billion in providing a customized service for First Nations and Inuit communities (Abele 2004). These divisions make it difficult for Aboriginal peoples to speak with one voice. They also are likely to lead to legal challenges, internal conflicts, intergovernmental disputes, and difficulties in the administration of Aboriginal self-governance structures (INAC 2004). Not surprisingly, perhaps, different national organizations have been established that promote the interests of specific Aboriginal peoples, reflect their distinctive world views, and reinforce their historical experiences.

The term "Aboriginal peoples" in the Constitution describes the descendants of the original occupants. Their constitutional status can be further subdivided into the categories of status Indians, non-status Indians, Métis, and Inuit. According to the 2001 Census, 976 305 people self-identified as Aboriginal, including 608 850 North American Indians (a label that groups individuals from some 60 different First Nations), 292 310 Métis, and 45 070 Inuit (INAC 2003). With the Métis accounting for about 30 percent of the Aboriginal population, North American Indians at 62 percent, and Inuit at 5 percent, the overall figure is 22 percent higher than in 1996, compared to a growth rate of only 3.4 percent for the general population. Close to 1.3 million individuals (or 4.4 percent of Canada's population) reported having Aboriginal ancestry in 2001, up 41 percent since 1986, in part because of fertility rates, reinstatement of C-31 Indians, greater willingness to acknowledge Aboriginal origins, and different methods of counting (White et al. 2003). For example, a report by the Department of Canadian Heritage indicated an Aboriginal *population* in 2001 of 1 066 500 based on results from the 2001

Census, but adjusted upwards to offset inconsistencies with the data collection (Statistics Canada, *The Daily*, 28 June 2005; also Guimond et al. 2004). Regional differences are noticeable: The highest concentrations of Aboriginal peoples are in the Prairie provinces, including Manitoba at 12 percent of the province's population, Saskatchewan at 11 percent, and Alberta at 5 percent. Aboriginal peoples may compose only 1 percent of Ontario's population, but at 140 000 are the most numerous in absolute terms, followed by British Columbia. Less than half of those who identified as North American Indians in 2001 lived on an Indian reserve in 2001 (Guimond et al. 2004). Aboriginal peoples continue to move from reserves into urban centres, with the most dramatic increases in Winnipeg (56 000 in 2001), Edmonton (41 000), and Saskatoon (20 000) (Statistics Canada, *The Daily*, 23 June 2005).

Constitutional Status

The *Indian Act* of 1876 defined the criterion for an Indian. This criterion did not reflect the realities of race or culture but invoked the principle of patrilineal (on the male side) descent (Sawchuk 1998). Not until 1951 did the *Indian Act* define an Indian as "a person who, pursuant to the *Indian Act,* is registered as an Indian or entitled to be registered as an Indian." The current definition of Indian embraces the rank of "status" or "registered" Indian. The federal government acknowledges responsibility for providing services and programs but only for registered (status) Indians and the Inuit (Peters 2001). Status Indians are further divided into treaty versus non-treaty Indians depending on whether their ancestors signed a treaty with the federal government. C-31s constitute yet another category involving Aboriginal women who lost their Indian status because of marriage to non-Aboriginals, but now have reinstatement as status Indians. With reinstatement, many have returned to their reserve communities, including full access to housing and services; others, however, have been less fortunate. In that the Bill C-31 amendment to the *Indian Act* also redefined membership codes (i.e., transmission of registered Indian status from one generation to the next), several classes of Indians now exist, including (1) those with registered Indian status and band membership , (2) those with registered status but no band membership, (3) those without status but band membership, and (4) descendents of registered Indians but entitled to neither status nor membership (INAC 2004).

With some exceptions, membership of status Indians is defined by (1) registration in a general registry in Ottawa, (2) affiliation with one of 633 bands, (3) entitlement to residence on band reserve lands, and (4) jurisdiction under the *Indian Act* (Frideres and Gadacz 2005). Responsibility for status Indians rests with the federal government, which targets around $9 billion per year for spending on Aboriginal programs and administration in part because of treaty and fiduciary responsibilities. The current population of status Indians stands at 608 850, up from 230 902 in 1967, with a projected total of 940 000 by 2021, led by large increases in Manitoba, Alberta, and Saskatchewan (INAC 2003). Status Indians reside on one of 2567 reserves across Canada, ranging in population size from less than a dozen to nearly 20 000 at the Six Nations Reserve near Brantford, Ontario. But while status Indians may be entitled to live on reserves created by one of 61 treaties signed with the Crown, the numbers are slipping despite incentives to stay, although the actual figures are imprecise because of the circular fluidity in rural–urban migration patterns (Dosman 1972; Monture-Angus 2002). The interests of status Indians are represented by the band chiefs who comprise the Assembly of First Nations.

Non-status Indians comprise another category of Aboriginal peoples. Persons of Aboriginal ancestry are classified as non-status if their ancestors failed to register under the *Indian Act,* never signed a treaty with federal authorities, or lost their Indian status in exchange for the right to vote, drink alcohol off the reserve, or (in the case of women) marry a non-Indian. Unlike status Indians, non-status Indians are exempt from provisions of the *Indian Act,* but fall under the definition of Indian in the *Constitution Act.* The exact numbers are unknown, but estimates range from 75 000 to 125 000. Non-status Indians do not live on reserves (only status Indians are entitled to reserve life and band inheritance), but are scattered in small towns and large cities across Canada. Despite this formal estrangement from their roots, many non-status Indians continue to self-identify as Aboriginal peoples because of shared affinities. Nevertheless, relationships between non-status and status Indians remain fraught with tension because of competition over limited federal resources. Currently, non-status Indians are represented by the Congress of Aboriginal Peoples.

The third class, the Métis, constitutes a contested category comprising the descendants of mixed European–Aboriginal unions. The Métis peoples initially were restricted to those inhabitants of the Red River Settlements in Manitoba who identified with the Métis nation. But reference to the Métis may also include those of mixed heritage who live in Métis communities, in effect connoting a hybrid culture that cannot be associated with a particular culture or language but a "cultural, linguistic, and territorial mosaic" with which a population has identified and continues to evolve (Guimond et al. 2004; also Sawchuk 1998). Without much land base for developmental growth, the Métis remain hampered by difficulties in defining "Métis-ness." Even if officially regarded as a distinct Aboriginal people with constitutional protection and corresponding guarantees, the lack of judicial recognition on par with status Indians undermined their legal authority to negotiate claims over traditional lands. The assumption was that the constitutional rights of 1982 belonged to those who could prove original occupancy, claim an exclusive relationship to the land, possessed an authentic culture, and exercised Aboriginal title rights (Chartrand and Peeling 2004). But the Ontario provincial court has ruled that the Métis have as much right as status Indians to hunt and fish for food without a licence (Blackwell 2000). The ruling also confirmed the Métis as full-fledged Aboriginal people with constitutionally protected rights to self-determining autonomy because of a shared culture, collective identity, and communal life (Harty and Murphy 2005). The Métis National Council provides national representation and a lobby voice at the federal level.

The Inuit constitute the final category. The 45 070 Inuit enjoy a special status and relationship with the federal government despite never having signed any treaty arrangements or registered under the *Indian Act.* A Supreme Court ruling in 1939 defined the Inuit to be Indians for purposes of federal jurisdiction and entitlements, although the federal government subsequently revised the *Indian Act* to exclude the Inuit (Cudmore 2001). At local levels, the Inuit are governed by municipal councils, with various committees to discharge responsibilities for health and education. Inuit interests at national levels are represented by the Inuit Tapirisat (an association of various Inuit leaders) of Canada. The Inuit have concluded successful land claims settlements with Ottawa for control over their homeland in the Eastern Arctic. The territory of Nunavut, which came into being in 1999, shows great promise in self-determining growth, but confronts numerous problems.

Socio-Economic Status

Nearly four hundred years of colonial contact have plunged many Aboriginal peoples into disarray and despair. The relationship between the colonizers and the colonized can be crudely captured by this blunt aphorism: "you got it, we want it, and we are going to get it and keep it by hook, crook or the book" (see also Adams 1999). The colonizers sought to subordinate and eliminate Aboriginal peoples through a gradual yet forced assimilation into "civilization"—resulting in the "taming" and "caging" of the indigenes by way of internalized limitations that proved every bit as restraining as physical constraints (Churchill 2004; Porter 2005). In some cases, government policies deliberately undermined the viability of Aboriginal communities in the relentless quest to divest Aboriginal peoples of their land, culture, and tribal authority. In other cases, the demise of Aboriginal peoples came about through unobtrusive but equally powerful assimilationist measures like education and missionization. In still other cases, the often unintended consequences of possibly well-intentioned but ultimately misguided government policies and programs such as reserve relocation or the residential school system have had a controlling effect in marginalizing the original inhabitants (Miller 1999; Shkilnyk 1985; Canadian Press 2005).

No matter how evaluated or assessed, Aboriginal peoples as a group remain at the bottom of the socio-economic heap (Bird et al. 2002; Frideres and Gadacz 2005; Wotherspoon 2003). Housing is inadequate or overcrowded on many reserves, failing to meet basic standards of amenities and structure, including shortage of sewer or water connections (Frideres and Gadacz 2003). The awkward location of many reserves and their limited resources remain key problems for employment or developmental purposes (CBC News 2005). Nevertheless, many residents are reluctant to abandon them for fear of losing reserve entitlements, resulting in what critics call "subsidies-to-stay" whose perverse effects have proven as distorting for status Indians as they have been for Atlantic Canada (Flanagan 2001; Fiss 2004a). Of particular concern are Aboriginal peoples who live off-reserve in prisons, with Aboriginal offenders accounting for 19 percent of provincial admissions to custody and 17 percent of federal admissions (Roberts and Melchers 2003). Equally worrying is the demographic time bomb that is ticking away in many Aboriginal communities. The combination of a relatively high birth rate and extremely young population is exerting even greater pressure on limited reserve resources such as housing (Winsor 2001). With rates nearly three times the national average, unemployment is a major cause of poverty and powerlessness (Terry 2005). For example, while the jobless rate of non-Aboriginals was 5.3 percent in 2005, the Aboriginal unemployment rate stood at 13.6 percent, down from 16.7 percent in 2001. According to the 2001 Census data, only 42 percent of Aboriginal peoples 15 years and over were employed, with an average annual income of $15 994, compared to 66 percent of non-Aboriginals with an average annual income of $26 914 (*The Globe and Mail*, 17 June 2003). Even these figures are misleading. On some reserves, up to 95 percent of the population subsists on welfare or "employment" benefits.

To add insult to injury, Aboriginal peoples are increasingly pitted against one another. Disparities in wealth and power within communities may be as gaping as the gulf between Aboriginal peoples and non-Aboriginal Canadians ("No Tolerance for Incompetence" 2001). On one side is a division involving on-reserve communities who receive much of the federal funding despite an Aboriginal exodus into cities (Murphy 2003). On the other side are internal class divisions. A new class of senior managers and business elites has emerged who reward their own, control a powerful network of patronage or nepotism, or divert cash into their pockets. Those on the wrong side of the political tracks do without all these (see Blackduck 2001; Fontaine 2003). To be sure, the degree of fiscal mismanagement may be exaggerated by critics. According to the Auditor General as reported in John Ibbitson's column in *The Globe and Mail* (2 February 2005), not only are Aboriginal communities overaudited (an average of one report every second day), but, of the 557 bands audited in 2002–03, only 16 required reme-dial action. Still, the lack of transparency in and accountability for decision-making can-not be lightly brushed off (Fiss 2004a, b).

The demise of Aboriginal cultural values has compounded the difficulties of identity and adjustment. Numerous Aboriginal languages are currently under threat of disappear-ing because of pressure from English (and French) in the schools and media, with only three (Ojibwa, Cree, and Inuktitut) on a relatively solid footing (Fleras 1987). The psycho-logical effects of powerlessness, alienation, and irrelevance have been no less detrimental (Shkilnyk 1985). As noted by David Courchene, a former president of the Manitoba Indian Brotherhood, one hundred years of patronizing submission and paternalistic servitude have instilled psychological barriers that amplify material poverty (Buckley 1992:24; also Adams 1999; Alfred 2005). This interplay of powerlessness and poverty may be transferred into expressions of inner- and outer-directed violence, including violent death rates at four times the national average. Domestic abuse is so endemic within Aboriginal communities, accord-ing to some observers (Drost et al. 1995), that few Aboriginal children grow into adulthood without firsthand experience of interpersonal violence. With a suicide rate of six to eight times the national average for certain age-specific groups, Aboriginal peoples represent one of the most self-destructive groups in the world at present.

Health indicators continue to spiral downward—a scandalous state of affairs for a coun-try that trumpets its much-vaunted health care system (National Aboriginal Health Organization 2004). To no one's surprise, health care is perceived by Aboriginal peoples as the most important federal issue, although Aboriginal youth see education as a more press-ing priority (EKOS 2004). Aboriginal peoples experience heart problems at twice the rate of non-Aboriginals, are twice as likely to have cancer, and are five times more likely to have diabetes. Infectious diseases such as tuberculosis are prevalent, and an AIDS epidemic is wor-rying (Brady 2001). Infant mortality rates are about 60 percent higher than the national average. Alcohol and substance abuse is widely regarded as the foremost problem on most reserves, with alcohol-related deaths accounting for up to 80 percent of the fatalities on some reserves (Buckley 1992). But not all indicators are distress signals. In 1975, the life expectancy for a Canadian male was 11.1 years higher than for a status Indian male. This gap had closed to 6.3 years in 2000, and is expected to reach 5.3 years by 2020 (INAC 2003). Figures for Aboriginal women are also encouraging.

Of course, not all Aboriginal peoples are destined to fail—even when measured by main-stream standards. Aboriginal peoples are accessing substantial sums of money and resources because of successful land claims settlements. Communities across Canada are riding the crest of an entrepreneurial wave by cashing in on energy, forestry, and mining resources at twice the national average (Howes 2001). There are currently 20 000 Aboriginal-owned businesses (about half on reserves), 50 financial institutions, and an Aboriginal trust company and bank. Enrolments in postsecondary education have escalated as well, according to Indian and Northern Affairs Canada, from about 200 in the 1960s to 14 242 in 1987, with a doubling since then to 27 487 in 1999/2000. Nor should success be evaluated on Eurocentric grounds alone. There are individuals who possess secure and satisfying prospects and exceptionally enriched lives without rejecting one or both cultures. Not all communities should be seen as dys-functional, despite media coverage that conveys this image, but rather as viable and vibrant (Strauss 2005). As a group, however, most Aboriginal peoples live under punitive condi-tions that evoke images of grinding developing-world poverty and powerlessness.

Aboriginal Peoples in the Cities: Empowerment or Despair?

What a difference a shift in perception can make. Reserves were once stigmatized as tools of colonialism, sites of assimilation, and sinkholes of poverty and despair. Increasingly, however, they are endorsed as life-affirming enclaves of Aboriginal identity, locales for cultural protection, catalysts for self-government, buffers against a hostile world, refuges for personal renewal, and engines of development. Even with punishing levels of unemployment and dilapidated living conditions—for example, a widening gap in resources between Ontario's provincial schools and federally funded Aboriginal schools on reserves (Brown 2005)—reserves continue to be embraced as oases of spirituality, security, and community. This mixed message points to a striking ambiguity. The isolation of these reserves makes them unattractive for investment, with next to no realistic prospects for economic growth (Flanagan 2001). Nevertheless, their very remoteness fosters a context for aboriginality to flourish. The push and pull of this contradiction is unmistakable: The reserve-o-centric focus of government spending may create all kinds of incentives for staying put, yet Aboriginal peoples are abandoning reserves in droves because of impossible conditions.

Aboriginal peoples are highly mobile (INAC 2003). According to Indian and North Affairs Canada (INAC 2004), of the 976 305 people who self-identified as Aboriginals in 2002, 29 percent lived on reserves while 71 percent lived off reserves. About one-fifth of urban Aboriginals live in seven cities: Regina, Winnipeg, Calgary, Edmonton, Saskatoon, Vancouver, and Toronto. Between May 2000 and May 2001, 22 percent of the Aboriginal population had moved, compared to 14 percent for the non-Aboriginal peoples. This high level of mobility may generate problems when planning and implementing programs in housing, education, and social services, especially in urban areas. Yet, it does reaffirm the centrality of city life to many Aboriginal peoples—not just as anomalies, threats, or individuals who lacked legitimacy because they traded city lights for cultural authenticity, but as individuals and communities with interests, goals, unique experiences, and strategies. As aptly phrased by Newhouse and Peters (2003:5):

> Relationships with urban landlords, searching for employment in urban economies, making spaces for Aboriginal cultures and languages in city places, interacting with neighbours from different cultures and building urban Aboriginal programs and institutions is as much part of Aboriginal realities as are land claims, conflicts over logging, hunting, and Treaty rights, and rural economic development.

Reasons for migrating to cities are numerous, but often reflect a combination of "push" factors (lack of resources, opportunity, or excitement) and "pull" forces related to employment, education, and lifestyle. Structural (band size, proximity to urban centres), social (poor housing, unemployment), and cultural (socialization) factors influence the decision to leave—or return. People leave because of misguided reserve policies or because of fiscal mismanagement involving ruling factions who dole out favours to relatives and supporters. Imbalances in the city and on the reserve have led many Aboriginal migrants to accept dual residence (see Dosman 1972): Home in the winter may be the city, where services and heated accommodation make life bearable; summer, in turn, sees an exodus back to the reserve for the company of relatives and rural lifestyles (Comeau and Sandin 1990). Except for the very young or very old, the divide between reserve and city is increasingly fluid, flexible, and circular, with the promise of urban potential offset by a powerful sense of return to recharge batteries or soothe disappointments (Monture-Angus 2001).

For some, the move to cities is positive. There are many Aboriginal lawyers, teachers, nurses, and successful entrepreneurs who earn high incomes, the respect of peers, and are actively involved in the community. For others, the demands of a large urban centre are daunting and life destroying (Frideres 1998). Off-reserve life is beset with missed economic opportunities, abysmal living conditions and homelessness, exposure to substance abuse, discrimination and lack of cultural awareness, and repeated brushes with the law. For still others, the urban Aboriginal experiences are one of loss and opportunity: loss, as in culture and sense of community; opportunity, as in employment and education (Royal Commission 1996; Newhouse and Peters 2003).

Too often Aboriginal peoples in cities are ignored in debates over "who gets what" (Cairns 2003). Not surprisingly, government institutions are poorly equipped (both in terms of resources and needs assessments) to offer culturally sensitive services to Aboriginal clients. Many Aboriginal-run voluntary agencies have been established to address a wide range of issues related to health care, traditional healing, shelter, education and training, and criminal justice (Abele 2004). These programs incorporate a strong cultural dimension; they also range widely in funding and outreach, from Aboriginal head start incentives to assistance for Aboriginal mothers. The federal government, for its part, disdains the provision of services to off-reserve Aboriginals, citing jurisdictional problems with the provinces as a stumbling block. Although the federal government has jurisdiction and responsibility for "Indians and Lands reserved for Indians" (*Constitution Act,* 1867), the combination of increased costs for providing social programs and a growing exodus of Aboriginal peoples into cities puts pressure on the federal government to restrict social services and programs to reserve residents only—even if the federal government's inability to address poor housing and education opportunities on reserves may have paradoxically precipitated the urbanization in the first place (Stokes et al. 2004).

CASE STUDY	The Kasechewan Water Crisis: First Nations or Third World Nation?

Who would have thought of Canada as home to a crisis of third world proportions? Canadians watched in stunned disbelief upon learning that many in a remote Aboriginal community of 1900 along the shores of James Bay were suffering ill effects from polluted tap water. Despite a water-boil advisory that had been in effect for two years, the residents of the Kasechewan (or Kashechewan) Nation found themselves afflicted with serious skin infections including impetigo (a bacterial skin infection) and scabies (a nasty parasite) because of impurities in the drinking water. Painful skin rashes were further aggravated by shockingly high levels of chlorine that were added

to purify the putrid water from a federally funded water treatment plant that was built only a decade ago. The treatment plant was 135 metres *downstream* from the reserve's sewage lagoon, but incapable of servicing a growing population, resulting in overuse and breakdowns. The end result? Sewage water that flows from residential drinking taps as contaminants from the sewage plant flow past the intake valve that feeds raw water into the purification system. Compounding the problems were fears of an outbreak of *E. Coli*—the potentially lethal bacteria that killed seven people and sickened thousands of others in Walkerton, Ontario, in 2000—prompting an emergency medical evacuation of vulnerable residents to safety in Sudbury or Timmins.

Kasechewan Nation is not the only reserve in crisis. Poor water quality is endemic to many Aboriginal communities across Canada. About three quarters of the 858 Aboriginal communities experience levels of water quality that pose a "risk," according to an Indian Affairs report in 2001 as well as the Federal Auditors' report in September of 2005. To add insult to injury, Health Canada statistics reveal that 95 of these communities, including 50 in Ontario, were under a water-boil order, including seven communities with water-boil warnings for five years or more. Not surprisingly, despite federal initiatives to address the issue, a 2003 report by the Ontario Clean Water Agency concluded that some reserves were literally "Walkertons-in-waiting." And it is not a case of out of sight, out of mind. Parts of the Six Nations reserve near Brantford have reputedly been under a boil-water order for two years because of contamination by *E. Coli* and fecal coliform.

As often happens, a turf war erupted over responsibility for the tainted water crisis. The Cree of Kasechewan fall through the cracks between federal responsibilities as articulated in the Constitution and provincial capacity for program delivery. Predictably, federal authorities blame Ontario for the deplorable conditions, while Ontario claims that federal authorities have a fiduciary obligation to look after reserve Aboriginal peoples, including health care and water standards. Apart from scoring political points at each other's expense, neither the federal nor provincial authorities took much notice until intense media coverage blew their cover. Evidence suggests that both governments knew about the problem, but waffled and dithered, until publicly embarrassed into action by a slick media campaign. That said, what else but callous political indifference to the plight of Aboriginal peoples could possibly have

accounted for this explosive cocktail of jurisdictional wrangles, intergovernmental buckpassing, and inexcusable neglect that put people's lives in danger?

To be sure, the government has responded to this public relations nightmare by airlifting thousands of 18-litre bottles of water into the stricken community, in addition to promises to relocate residents of the flood-prone community onto higher ground. The decision to send in the Canadian Forces mobile water filtration machine—often used for emergencies in countries such as Pakistan or Sri Lanka—should provide a measure of instant relief, even if the process itself inadvertently reinforces an image of Kasechewan as remote and removed. And, yes, there is much to commend in federal promises to upgrade and rebuild. As the Kasechewan chief Joe Friday observed, "This is a precedent for Indian Affairs to start listening to the people that have problems in other communities." With the federal government announcement of a $4 billion cash injection to raise Aboriginal living standards, this place the local residents call "Kash" (how ironic: a package of wieners costs over eleven dollars while a mickey of bootlegged booze can fetch upwards of $80) may well prove the tipping point that galvanizes governments to move.

For Canadians, the bitterness and squalor that has afflicted the "Kash" peoples has been deeply disturbing. Many Canadians have little difficulty in intellectualizing the "Indian problem" in abstract ways, but nothing could prepare them for searing media images of the third world in their own backyard, including overcrowding, derelict housing conditions, non-existent hygiene and sanitation, garbage and liquor bottles strewn about, and punishing levels of unemployment with estimates as high as 90 percent. As one journalist put it in linking the water crisis in post-Katrina New Orleans with Kasechewan, it's as if a stake was driven into the collective hearts of Canada's national smugness, once it was learned government actions were driven not by compassion and rights, but by a shame-induced damage control. And, yet, uncomfortable truths must be addressed that go beyond the quick fix. Stronger medicine than a commitment to fix the cesspool engulfing Kasechewan must confront the core problem of any isolated Aboriginal community: namely, too many people chasing too few resources in a resource-poor region too far removed from the Canadian economy (also Howard and Widdowson 1999). Even stronger medicine will be needed to erase the stench of racism that lingers throughout this odious process. In the end, the Kasechewan crisis has done to Canada what Hurricane Katrina inflicted on the United States: exposed deep divisions of race and class in societies that deny both. One can only wonder if the governments would have responded any differently if it were white folk who had to bathe their babies in chlorinated sewage water.

In sum: The impoverishment that confronts Aboriginal peoples is a scathing indictment of the status quo. Aboriginal peoples tend to score poorly on those indicators that count, but rank high on those that don't, with few indications of immediate improvements. Poverty and powerlessness will not disappear with better opportunities or increased expenditures. A "throwing of money at a problem" approach works well in the short run, largely because it downplays the structural (and more costly) roots of Aboriginal problems, namely, the lack of power and resource control. But significant improvements will materialize only when Aboriginal peoples secure control over institutions, including access to power-sharing, an equitable share of revenue from reserve resources, and Aboriginal title to land—as aptly captured by Matthew Coon Come, then Grand Chief of the Grand Council of Crees in Quebec:

> But without adequate access to lands, resources, and without the jurisdictions required to benefit meaningfully and sustainably from them . . . no number of apologies, policies, token programs, or symbolic healing funds are going to remedy this fundamental socio-economic fact. (Cited in Barnsley 1999:1)

A review of social problems in Aboriginal communities underscores the magnitude of the challenge. Positive trends notwithstanding, poverty and powerlessness continue to plague many Aboriginal families and communities both in rural and urban areas (Abele 2004). But focusing exclusively on Aboriginal peoples as having or creating problems is not without its consequences. "Framing" Aboriginal peoples as a problem people tends to gloss over the broader context of colonization and its legacy as contributing factors (George 1997). A lose–lose situation prevails: Bigots have no qualms about stereotyping Aboriginal peoples as lazy layabouts who soak up billions of welfare dollars at the expense of the taxpayer, yet Aboriginal peoples are demonized as "uppity" if they challenge the status quo (Maaka and Fleras 2005).

Finally, the underlying logic of a problem approach may have to be rethought. The problems confronting Aboriginal peoples are the direct legacy of colonialism (Green 2003). Aboriginal peoples did not ask to be "bent, folded, spindled, and perforated" by a European colonization that sought to transform Canada into a "white man's country." And yet Aboriginal peoples continue to suffer the consequences of being forcibly incorporated into Canadian society. The conclusion seems inescapable: The "Indian problem" is really a

"Canada problem," or more accurately "the Indian's Canada problem," and any solution must begin by challenging those (neo)colonialist arrangements that spawned the situation in the first place. But solving the problem of colonialism must move beyond dismantling the physical barriers. According to Taiaiake Alfred (2005), solutions must focus on decolonizing those Aboriginal mindsets that have been conditioned to think like the colonizers. The hurting will stop only when people begin to move beyond the colonial box by asking the question: What is it about Canadian society that makes it so problematic for Aboriginal peoples?

CANADA'S ABORIGINAL POLICY: "NO MORE INDIANS"

Do government Aboriginal policies promote Aboriginal interests? Or are they more likely to undermine Aboriginal efforts at self-determining autonomy over land, identity, and political voice? Can even seemingly progressive policy initiatives end up having a marginalizing or controlling effect on Aboriginal communities (Abele et al. 2005)? Some would say yes: Inequality is inevitable by creating race-based rules that isolate Aboriginal peoples and expose them to different sets of laws and incentives (Gibson 2005). For the assimiliationists, the solution points to absorption into Canadian society: That is, to abolish the collectivist mindset that underpins these special provisions and preferential status, while exposing Aboriginal peoples to the balm of assimilatist values pertaining to individualism, competition, and private property rights (Flanagan 2001; Fiss 2004). Others say no, and that transforming Aboriginal peoples into "white-o-centric" clones will intensify alienation, poverty, and disempowerment. Government policy must play its part in securing the inherent and treaty rights of Aboriginal peoples, according to the autonomists, in effect pressuring the federal government into honouring its fiduciary responsibilities, protecting the legitimacy of Aboriginal difference, and upholding Aboriginal sovereignty and models of self-determining autonomy (Alfred 2005).

History has not been kind in exonerating the politics of policy. Government policy and its (mis)administration by state bureaucracy in marginalizing Aboriginal peoples have been amply documented. Little more can be gleaned by rehashing the negative consequences of even well-intentioned actions by government officials more interested in careerism and empire-building than in doing their job (Ponting and Gibbins 1980; Shkilnyk 1985). What more can be added to the sorry legacy of official Aboriginal policy that advanced "national interests" at the expense of Aboriginal empowerment? Harold Cardinal captured a sense of outrage in his 1969 book *The Unjust Society*:

> Generations of Indians have grown up behind a buckskin curtain of indifference, ignorance, and, all too often, plain bigotry. The history of Canada's history is a shameful chronicle of white man's disinterest, his trampling of Indian rights.

The fact that parts of this mindset prevail at present is unconscionable. For example, consider how the government's attempt to compensate residential school victims of physical and sexual abuse has induced a nightmare of Orwellian proportions. The survivors are dying at a much faster rate than rates of compensation (50 settled claims out of 12 000 since 2003, yet Aboriginal claimants may be dying at the rate of five per week). To add insult to injury, the government spends $4 on administration for every $1 paid to victims in an atmosphere that many see as adversarial, litigious, and bereft of any compassion or healing (Travers 2005). The First Nations Summit in Kelowna, B.C., in late 2005 promised to reverse this sorry state of affairs.

Still, the verdict in assessing state performance and government actions is proving ambivalent. Both the government and the state are capable of progressive policies that enhance indigenous rights; they are equally capable of regressive measures that may exclude, deny, or exploit (Spoonley 1993). Policies of disempowerment tend to circumscribe the actions and options of indigenous peoples, whereas enabling policies provide a window of opportunity for empowerment (Hinton et al. 1997). Policies have proven double-edged regardless of intent or impact, thus the policy domain underpinning relations between Aboriginal peoples and the state is properly viewed as a contested and highly politicized domain of competing agendas, endless tensions, and contradictory dynamics (Maaka and Fleras 2005).

A similar assessment can be applied to Canada. Aboriginal relations with Canada have long been mediated by progressive-sounding policy yet marred by duplicity and expediency. The Aboriginal affairs policy may have evolved through a series of overlapping stages, but has never wavered from its assimilationist logic: to solve the "Indian problem" by ensuring "no more Indians." An initial period of co-operation and accommodation morphed into a paternalistic policy of assimilation, with its underlying racist assumptions of white superiority as a basis for control and coercion. A shift from assimilation to integration and "ordinary citizenship" gathered momentum after the late 1940s. Yet, federal moves toward integration by "normalizing" its relations with Aboriginal peoples had the perverse effect of galvanizing Aboriginal peoples into protest and politics. Federal policy discourses shifted accordingly. A commitment to principles of **devolution** emerged, in part to defuse both mounting Aboriginal resentment and growing international disapproval over Canada's treatment of Aboriginal peoples. Recent policy initiatives revolve around the policy principles of a **conditional autonomy** model. The scope of Aboriginal rights as set out in the *Constitution Act* is being explored, including a collective and inherent right to self-governance within the constitutional framework of Canadian society.

In short, the message is mixed. The policy dimension of Aboriginal peoples–Canada relations has zigged and zagged from one of patron–client relationship to that of a government-to-government relationship—from that of Aboriginal peoples as allies, to that of threats, then to children, to citizens, to minorities, and to peoples. That alone speaks volumes about how far Aboriginal peoples–government relations have evolved, yet also the distance to travel before a partnership is a reality rather than a platitude.

Accommodation

Aboriginal policy in the broadest sense began with the *Royal Proclamation* of 1763. The *Proclamation* sought to establish the principle of Crown sovereignty over the unexplored interior of Turtle Island. But it also acknowledged that Aboriginal interest in land was a pre-existing sovereign right because of traditional use and ancestral occupancy rather than a Crown bestowal (Slattery 1997):

> And whereas it is just and reasonable, and essential to our interests, and the security of our Colonies, that the several Nations of Tribes of Indians with whom We are connected, and who live under our protection, should not be molested or disturbed in the Possession of such Parts of Our Dominions and Territories as, not having been ceded to or purchased by Us, are reserved to them or any of them, as their Hunting Grounds. (*Royal Proclamation*, 1763)

Those vast tracts of land encircled by the Thirteen Colonies, Rupert's Land, and the Mississippi River were subsequently designated as Aboriginal hunting grounds and closed to European trespass. The Act prohibited individual purchase of these lands without express approval of the authorities, so that only the Crown could purchase Aboriginal land as one way of underwriting the costs of colonizing Canada (Rotman 1996). In acknowledging that Aboriginal peoples could not be unilaterally dispossessed of their lands and that they had a right to control the westward expansion of whites onto their ancestral lands, the *Royal Proclamation* bore resemblance to treaties of peace and friendship in other parts of the British empire (such as New Zealand's Treaty of Waitangi in 1840) (Fleras and Spoonley 1999).

The *Royal Proclamation* is widely seen as a blueprint for framing Aboriginal peoples–Crown relations (Hall 2000:130). But interpretations are rarely consistent. Some have argued that the *Proclamation* acknowledged Aboriginal tribes as "sovereign nations" under Crown protection with jurisdictional rights over land and resources (Clark 1990). According to the Act, the principles of partnership, mutual recognition, and non-interference would inform the Crown's relationship with Aboriginal peoples (Breton 2001). The Supreme Court of Canada has ruled to this effect, arguing that British protectorate status did not extinguish Aboriginal orders of government, but reinforced their status as distinct political communities with exclusive authority over internal jurisdictions. Others disagree with that assessment. Under the *Proclamation* the British Crown asserted its sovereignty over the people and the land, with proprietary rights to Aboriginal land by virtue of the prevailing doctrines of the time: "terra nullius" and "first discovery" (Boldt 1993). Crown objectives were purely pragmatic in establishing control over settlers and property interests. The Act hoped to enlist Aboriginal nations as allies to curb American territorial expansion, minimize the outbreak of costly Indian Wars, and establish paramountcy over the newly acquired colony of Quebec (Rotman 1996). To the extent that the *Royal Proclamation* may have embraced a bracing mix of ideals with pragmatism as well as progress and stalemate, its ambiguity cannot be discounted. Such ambiguities and conflicting perspectives continue to inform the policy paradoxes that animate relations between Canada and its Aboriginal peoples.

Assimilation

> Our objective is to continue until there is not a single Indian in Canada that has not been absorbed into the body politic, and there is no Indian question, and no Indian department. (Duncan Campbell Scott, Deputy Superintendent of Indian Affairs, 1920)

An initial period of co-operation characterized post-*Proclamation* relationships. Encounters involving Aboriginal peoples, French and British explorers, missionaries, and traders revolved around the goals of mutual coexistence, involving reciprocal trade and practical accommodation. Expediency prevailed: The British were few in number and militarily weak, thus reinforcing their dependency on Aboriginal allies for survival in a harsh land (Rotman 1996). Imperial interests were furthered by the forging of military alliances with powerful tribes. From 1755 to 1812, the British Indian Department (forerunner of the Department of Indian Affairs) implemented the key tenet of British policy, namely, to blunt American and French imperial aspirations by forging alliances with Aboriginal tribes (Allen 1993).

But once the British assumed control as the premier European power in Canada, this symbiosis unravelled (Purich 1986). The end of the War of 1812 with the United States eliminated the need for Aboriginal allies, thus rendering them irrelevant and expendable. Treaty commitments and trust responsibilities were now displaced by covetous Crown interest in land, minerals, and settlement at the expense of Aboriginal peoples. To achieve these objectives, the Crown unilaterally asserted sovereignty over people and lands. Aboriginal consent was simply assumed or deemed irrelevant (Jhappan 1995). Aboriginal tribes may have had "natural title" to land by virtue of prior occupancy; however, their seemingly uncivilized status allowed the British to rationalize acquisition in the name of civilization and Christianity (Allen 1993). The post-1815 era was dominated by a commitment to pacify Aboriginal tribes through acculturation or, alternatively, displacement into increasingly remote locales.

The Dominion of Canada operated as the colonizing arm of the British Colonial office. It assumed the rights and responsibilities of the Imperial colonizer with passage of the *British North America Act* (or *Constitution Act*) of 1867. The 1867 Act enshrined state responsibility for Aboriginal peoples by establishing federal jurisdiction over Aboriginal lands and affairs (Ponting and Gibbins 1980; Kulchyski 1994). The federal government refused to acknowledge Aboriginal peoples as political communities, preferring, instead, to see them as wards of the state with limited civil rights but fully entitled to federal custodial care (this trust relationship was subsequently transformed into a fiduciary responsibility) (Jhappan 1995). The theme of assimilation defined a framework for solving the "Indian problem." In the pithy phrasing of Sir John A. Macdonald in espousing a "no more Indians" national policy: "The great aim of our civilization has been to do away with the tribal system and assimilate the Indian people in all respects with the inhabitants of the Dominion, as speedily as they are fit for the change" (cited in Miller 1989).

Government integrity left much to be desired in light of racist and evolutionary philosophies that disparaged Aboriginal peoples as inferior impediments to progress (Weaver 1984). The concept of guardianship reinforced the stereotype of Aboriginal peoples as childlike wards of the state who were unfit to look after themselves except under the tutelage of Crown-appointed guardians (Ponting and Gibbins 1980; Ponting 1986). Aboriginal languages, cultures, and identity were suppressed—ruthlessly at times—while band communities were locked into patterns of dependency and despondency that proved a personal and collective affront. Legislation served as an assimilationist tool in controlling Aboriginal peoples (Rotman 1996). The *Gradual Enfranchisement Act* of 1869 sought to eliminate "Indian" status through enfranchisement and exposure to the ". . . white race in the ordinary avocations of life" (quoted in Allen 1993:202).

Of particular note in hastening the goal of "no more Indians" was the *Indian Act*. The passage of the *Indian Act* in 1876 may have been intended to protect and civilize Aboriginal peoples; nevertheless, an emasculating rather than empowering effect had a more lasting impact. The *Indian Act* defined who came under its provisions, what each status Indian was entitled to under the government's fiduciary obligations, who could qualify for disenfranchisement, what could be done with reserve lands and resources, and how local communities were to be ruled. Traditional leadership was stripped of its authority as a legitimate political voice (Dickason 1992). Local **governance** took the form of elected band councils, many of which were perceived as little more than federal proxies, with limited powers of administration rather than self-rule (Webber 1994). Status Indians could not vote in federal elections until 1960, unless they ceded their status and rights in exchange for Canadian citizenship. Aboriginal women were not allowed to run for office until 1961 (Harding 2005). Even economic opportunities were curtailed. Under the *Indian Act*, Aboriginal peoples could not possess direct title to land or private property; they were also denied access to revenue from the sale or lease of band property. Punitive restrictions not only foreclosed Aboriginal property improvements but also forestalled the accumulation of development capital for investment or growth, since Aboriginal land held in Crown trust could not be mortgaged or used as collateral and was immune to legal seizure. To work off the reserve required a permit from the resident Indian agent.

The imposition of the *Indian Act* bestowed sweeping state powers to invade and regulate the minutest aspect of reserve life, even to the point of curbing constitutional and citizenship rights (Morse 1985). In that the *Indian Act* was an essentially repressive instrument of containment and control, its role in usurping Aboriginal authority could not have been more forcefully articulated. To the extent that the *Indian Act* continues to divide and rule 130 years after its inception, the words of Donna Isaac of Listuguj, Quebec, (1997) are sharply resonant:

> The *Indian Act* system of government imposed on us so long ago has created such divided communities. We are immobilized by internal political strife. Half of the community often gets ahead at the expense of the other half. Hurt leads to contempt, division brews, and co-operation becomes impossible as hatred grows.

Not surprisingly, given the underlying logic of the *Indian Act,* government relations with Aboriginal peoples fluctuated wildly—at times protected, at times ignored, and at times actively oppressed, but never fully embraced as equal members of Canadian society (Abele 2004).

Integration

Neither assimilation as policy nor the reserve system as practice brought about the policy goal of "no more Indians" (Smith 1993). Rather, this dubious experiment in social engineering proved disruptive in undermining the social and cultural foundations of Aboriginal society (Frideres and Gadacz 2003; Aboriginal Institutes' Consortium 2005). Failure to bring about the intended results exerted pressure to rethink the Aboriginal affairs policy agenda, especially after World War II, when the concept of fighting for freedom overseas contradicted the denial of basic human rights at home. An official commitment to assimilation merged with the principles of integration as a blueprint for reform. Strategies to desegregate once-isolated Aboriginal enclaves for re-entry into the mainstream proved increasingly attractive. Aboriginal services were costly to maintain, their effectiveness was questionable, and they caused international embarrassment. Besides, the isolation of Aboriginal peoples because of reserves and legislation contributed to inequality, exacerbated negative social conditions, and pre-empted Aboriginal participation in society.

A discussion paper to solve the "Indian problem" was tabled by then Minister of Indian Affairs Jean Chrétien. The White Paper proposed to terminate the special relationship between Aboriginal peoples and the Crown, thus eliminating the status of Aboriginal peoples as a legal entity (Weaver 1981). By the simple expedient of doing away with Aboriginal peoples as a legal construct, there would be "no more Indians"; better still, no more "Indian problem." The key planks of the White Paper were unmistakably "assimilationist": Federal responsibility over Aboriginal peoples would be transferred to the provinces; both the *Indian Act* and the Department of Indian Affairs were to be dismantled; Aboriginal assets (including lands) would be liquidated, then divided on a per capita basis for individual owners to do as they saw fit; and the eventual abolition of Aboriginal treaty privileges and special status would facilitate the "normalizing" of Aboriginal individuals into Canadian society. With integration, then, the solution to the Indian problem focused on removing the barriers to make them more like "us."

But the government badly miscalculated Aboriginal aspirations. What the government endorsed as progressive and inevitable was roundly condemned as regressive and expedient by Aboriginal elites and leaders. The White Paper stood accused of everything from cultural genocide to callous expediency in offloading federal costs and reneging on Crown responsibilities. Controversy over the White Paper reflected competing visions of Aboriginal peoples and their relational status in Canadian society. The government saw Aboriginal peoples as Canadians whose progress into the future was shackled by tradition and the past. Salvation lay in removing these barriers, elimination of Indians as Indians, and their normalization as Canadian citizens. By contrast, Aboriginal peoples envisioned themselves as self-governing political nations with rights to self-determining autonomy (Brooks 1998). Central authorities were chastened by a collective show of resistance to these oppositional visions, especially following the establishment of the National Indian Brotherhood (now Assembly of First Nations), leaving the government with little option except to rethink the Aboriginal policy agenda in hopes of reclaiming control.

Devolution

A general commitment to the principles of devolution eventually replaced the policy void created by the White Paper fiasco. This shift was preceded by a period of impasse—even paralysis—as government responses lurched from crisis to crisis without a vision of how to bridge the cultural divide. With its qualified support for the idea of Aboriginal rights and title, the Calder decision in 1973 proved a starting point for reassessment. The *Constitution Act* of 1982 parlayed Canada into the world's first country to constitutionally entrench Aboriginal and treaty rights. Enshrinement of Aboriginal rights from common law to constitutional principle established a blueprint for potentially innovative arrangements—albeit within a constitutional framework that secured the legitimacy of Canadian jurisdiction over all people and lands (Bell 1997). Additional developments underscored the political shift. A series of First Minister Conferences between 1983 and 1987 may have yielded few concrete results; nevertheless, they did sensitize decision-makers to Aboriginal demands for **self-determination** through self-government as part of a new social contract (Brock 1991).

Many applauded government initiatives to expand Aboriginal jurisdictions over matters of local relevance. A shift toward devolution resulted in increased Aboriginal input over local affairs, including greater control over service delivery, administration of departmental programs, and localized decision-making. A devolutionary framework secured some impressive gains. In 1986, the government announced a devolutionary program of community-based, municipal-style self-government, to be pursued on a band-to-band basis and outside any federally imposed blueprint. The Sechelt of British Columbia capitalized on this federal legislation by establishing municipal-level self-governance structures that transcended the provisions of the *Indian Act*. For others, a commitment to devolution proved fruitful: Aboriginal peoples received all the social provisions available to non-Aboriginal Canadians—albeit through Aboriginal-specific institutions—while the First Nations on reserves increasingly assumed local responsibilities over health, education, and social assistance (Abele 2004).

Developments within the Indian Affairs Department dovetailed with the shift toward devolution. The Department had moved away from a control-and-deliver mentality that had prevailed as a blueprint since 1876. Reorganization of the federal department into decentralized service delivery through direct band involvement drew its inspiration from three assumptions: first, the need to establish Aboriginal rather than federal control over community affairs; second, a perception that properly resourced and self-sufficient communities were better equipped to solve local problems; and third, a suspicion that centralized structures were ineffective for problem-solving across a geographically dispersed and culturally diverse people. The Department of Indian Affairs and Northern Development (DIAND) repositioned itself as a developmental and advisory agency for the transfer of federal funds to community-based self-government structures in the same way that provinces receive federal block funding for programs and services (Fleras 1996). Service delivery on a program-by-program basis was replaced by more flexible funding arrangements to improve the quality of service delivery, develop long-term expenditure plans, reduce administrative burdens, emphasize local accountability in spending, and foster transparency in decision-making. Over 80 percent of the Department's program expenditure was eventually administered by Aboriginal governments under comprehensive funding arrangements—even if some of the Aboriginal communities were poorly prepared to assume such responsibility.

But policy advances were matched by political stagnation. Impressive gains in establishing jurisdiction over land, identity, and political voice could not disguise the fact that aboriginality as a principle continued to be undefined and excluded from the national agenda. Devolution as a strategy for decentralizing service delivery along community development lines could hardly address the increasingly politicized demands for restructuring the relationship. If anything, a commitment to devolution could be interpreted as an excuse to off-load government responsibility by transferring the administration of state services. Nor was there any urgency on the part of government to restore Aboriginal rights by crafting a new social contract for living together. That indifference was abruptly shattered by the 78-day Oka crisis, which sharply refocused attention on the Aboriginal agenda.

Conditional Autonomy

Recent developments have redefined the constitutional place of Aboriginal peoples. A shift in policy focus toward the principles of conditional autonomy began in the aftermath of the Oka crisis, with the inception of four policy pillars, namely, accelerated land claims settlement, improved socio-economic status on reserves, reconstruction of Aboriginal peoples–government relations, and fulfillment of Aboriginal concerns. A continuing commitment to explore Aboriginal people–state relations was further anchored around four general themes—renewing the partnership, strengthening Aboriginal governance, improving the quality of life, and supporting strong communities through sustainable development at economic, cultural, social, environmental, and political levels (also INAC 2004). Ottawa officially endorsed a parallel Aboriginal constitutional process that culminated in full assurances of their historic right to negotiate on a government-to-government basis. Their status as a distinct tier of government was approved (at least in principle), despite the defeat of the Charlottetown Accord, with corresponding rights to sit with Canada's First Ministers and debate constitutional reform.

The principles of conditional autonomy were further advanced by publication of the much-anticipated yet often delayed *Report of the Royal Commission on Aboriginal Peoples* in 1996. The report contained a heady brew of progressive and controversial ideas about the place of Aboriginal peoples within a re-constitutionalized Canada. Compared to the White Paper, the conclusions and recommendations of the Royal Commission on Aboriginal Peoples could not be more different (Brooks 1998). While the White Paper had rejected any notion of Aboriginal difference as a basis for solving the "Indian problem," the Royal Commission concluded that Aboriginal peoples were First Nations whose sovereignty must be respected and restored. The report called for the establishment of an Aboriginal order of governance that acknowledged an inherent right to self-government as a treaty right under Canada's Constitution. Also proposed was the concept of dual citizenship for Aboriginal peoples as Canadian citizens by way of membership in First Nation communities.

To date, the government has been slow in responding to the spirit of the Royal Commission. Nevertheless, the report's recommendations secured a blueprint for a new social contract that persists into the present as a standard to measure, compare, and criticize. A threshold in restructuring Aboriginal peoples–Canada relations had been scaled. This baseline would henceforth represent the minimum starting point for future negotiations, and the Liberal government took advantage of this momentum by acknowledging Aboriginal peoples as having an "inherent" right to self-government as a basis for new partnership. Terms of an inherent self-government arrangement, as a third tier of government, were set out in a 1995 federal policy document. References to inherent self-government were based on conditional rather than absolute rights, with the result that Aboriginal self-governments must operate within the Canadian federal system, neither declare independence nor challenge Canada's territorial integrity, be in harmony with other governments, be consistent with the *Canadian Charter of Rights and Freedoms,* and enhance the participation of Aboriginal peoples in Canadian society. Given that current government policy objectives continue to explore the scope of inherent Aboriginal self-government rights, such recognition signifies an unmistakable departure from even the immediate past when governments were opposed to concessions that might challenge Canada's sovereignty.

To sum up: Historically, Canada's Aboriginal policy can be described as a contested and evolving site, involving conflicting agendas, competing priorities, and divided loyalties whose cumulative effect has had a negative impact on Aboriginal peoples (Long and Dickason 2000). Consider this disclosure by Jane Stewart, a former Minister of Indian Affairs, from the document entitled "Statement of Reconciliation: Learning from the Past" (*The Globe and Mail*, 8 January 1998):

> Sadly, our history with respect to the treatment of Aboriginal people is not something in which we can take pride. Attitudes of racial and cultural superiority led to a suppression of Aboriginal cultures and values. As a country we are burdened by past actions that resulted in weakening the identity of Aboriginal peoples, suppressing their languages and cultures, and outlawing spiritual values. We must recognize the impact of these actions on the once self-sustaining nations that were disaggregated, disrupted, limited or even destroyed by the dispossession of traditional territory, by the relocation of Aboriginal people, and by some provisions of the *Indian Act.* We must acknowledge that the result of these actions was the erosion of the political, economic, and social systems . . .

Admittedly, overt policies of integration and assimilation have been shelved in favour of those that recognize Aboriginal rights for purposes of entitlement and engagement. Sections 25 and 35 of the 1982 *Constitution Act* have expanded areas of jurisdiction that once were denied or constrained under the colonialist era. Reform is increasingly structural, collaborative, and co-operative, producing a shift in focus from welfare to self-government; from dependence to self-determining autonomy; from government assistance to power-sharing; from paternalism to partnership; and from perception of Aboriginal peoples as a minority with needs to a peoples with rights. Yet, the process remains uneven because a commitment is neither a sign of conviction nor a signal for action (Bird et al. 2002). Moves forward are matched by steps back or sideways as governments balk, duck, and elude. Rhetorics of change rarely match the realities of implementation. For some, everything has changed because governments have taken Aboriginal demands too seriously: Critics have pounced on the so-called Aboriginal orthodoxy that currently informs official government policy because of its misguided notion that Aboriginal peoples are—or were once—nations with justifiable claims to difference, institutional parallelism, and sovereignty (Editorial, *National Post*, 19 July 2001; Flanagan 1999, 2001). But for others, nothing has changed in terms of goals. Attainment of Aboriginal self-sufficiency on government terms continues to under-pin official Aboriginal policy—a situation that some find insulting and paternalistic. As a participant in an EKOS focus group study (2004) observed:

> The Government is telling us that we need to be self-sufficient! Who is it that introduced drugs and alcohol to us? Who is it that told us that our beliefs and language were something to be ashamed of? Who is it that abused us in residential schools? Now we have to be self-sufficient? Maybe, but they have no right to tell us this . . .

In short, while most Canadians dismiss colonialism as an unfortunate relic of the past, colonialistic attitudes and practices continue to be a reality for Aboriginal peoples at present. Only the means have changed, according to Aboriginal critics (Green 2003; Alfred 2005), with open assimilation strategies giving way to more covert strategies that reinforce a neo-colonialist framework.

RETHINKING THE RELATIONSHIP: TOWARD A NEW SOCIAL CONTRACT

Aboriginal peoples do not like to see themselves as a social problem (without denying the many challenges that confront Aboriginal communities). Material poverty, they contend, is not necessarily responsible for Aboriginal marginalization in Canadian society. Powerlessness associated with (neo)colonization and denial of Aboriginal rights is far more worrying (Adams 1999). Equally demoralizing are stereotypes that portray Aboriginal peoples as hopeless welfare dependants or helpless slaves of customs whose cultures preclude a secure and satisfying coexistence in Canadian society. Contrary to popular perception, Aboriginal peoples have struggled to halt the vicious cycle of exclusion and demeaning clientelism that has historically entrapped them (Porter 2005 for overview). Collectively and individually, they have explored ways to survive by asserting control over their lives. Increasingly rejected are those political and social arrangements that once colonized and controlled. Endorsed instead are arrangements that not only advance Aboriginal interests, but also challenge and transform those foundational principles that govern Canada's constitutional order (Maaka and Fleras 2005). In other words, it is not a case of fixing the Aboriginal problem as a basis for living together separately, but of fixing the relationship. Three key planks secure the foundation for a new social contract: (1) taking aboriginality seriously, (2) promoting self-determining autonomy through Aboriginal models of self-governance, and (3) acknowledging Aboriginal title and treaty rights.

Taking Aboriginal Differences Seriously

Aboriginal peoples define themselves as different and deserving of differential status and treatment (Macklem 2001). They categorically reject the view of themselves as Canadian citizens who happen to live on reserves. Nor do they like the idea of being labelled as just another ethnic or immigrant minority. Aboriginal peoples claim to be a *de facto* sovereign political community (peoples) whose inherent and collective rights to self-government (nationhood) are guaranteed by virtue of aboriginality (ancestral occupation) rather than because of need, disadvantage, or compensation. Claims to sovereignty are defended either by reference to natural law or on spiritual grounds (Ahenakew 1985). As the original occupants whose inalienable rights have never been extinguished by treaty or conquest, Aboriginal peoples do not seek sovereignty per se. Rather, they *are* sovereign because of ancestral occupation and *have* sovereignty because of Aboriginal and treaty rights. All that is required are appropriate arrangements to put this principle into practice for purposes of recognition, reward, and relationships.

Crucial to any debate over sovereignty is the centrality of **Aboriginal ("indigenous")** **rights** (Kymlicka 1999). Aboriginal rights encompass those entitlements that ensure their survival as peoples, including the right to ownership of land and resources, the right to protect and promote language, culture, and identity, the right to political voice and self-governance, and the right to Aboriginal models of self-determination (McKee 1996). Aboriginal rights are regarded as *sui generis*, that is, they differ from ordinary citizenship rights by virtue of Aboriginal peoples as the original occupants (Borrows and Rotman 1997). These *sui generis* rights are collective and inherent: *collective*, in that Aboriginal communities can exercise jurisdiction over the individual rights of members of these communities; *inherent*, in that they are not delegated by government decree, but intrinsic to Aboriginal peoples because of first principles. Inherency suggests that the legitimacy of Aboriginal governance does not flow from sources such as the Crown, Parliament, or the Constitution. Legitimacy is derived instead from original occupancy, is bequeathed by the Creator, reflects the consent of the people, complies with treaties or international law, and may never be extinguished even with explicit consent (Bell 1997). According to Elijah Harper,

> Self-government is not [something] that can be given away by any government, but rather . . . flows from Creator. Self-government . . . is taking control and managing our own affairs, being able to determine our own future and destiny . . . It has never been up to the governments to give self-government. It has never been theirs to give. (Royal Commission on Aboriginal Peoples 1992:19)

Underlying this notion of Aboriginal rights is the concept of aboriginality (Maaka and Fleras 2005). Strictly speaking, the word "aboriginality" is the nominalization of the adjective "Aboriginal" (it refers to a thing or process rather than a modifier). The relationship of aboriginality to aboriginal parallels that of ethnicity and ethnic. Both aboriginality and ethnicity refer to the process of a "shared awareness of ancestral commonalities as a basis for entitlement or engagement" (Fleras 2004). In the case of aboriginality, this difference is legitimated by the primacy of original occupancy and corresponding rights that flow from this status. More broadly, the principle of aboriginality expresses a statement about power. Aboriginality asserts a special relationship between Aboriginal peoples and the state, together with a complementary set of unsurrendered rights and unextinguished powers that inform this relationship. Aboriginality, in other words, encapsulates a politicized set of claims and entitlements against the state beyond the reach of non-Aboriginal Canadians. Programs and policies that apply to other Canadian minority groups are dismissed as inapplicable—even counterproductive—in light of Aboriginal differences as peoples and as nations.

What, then, do Aboriginal peoples want? The most direct response is, the same things as all Canadian citizens. Aboriginal peoples want to live in a just and equal society where they have the same rights as all citizens, they can empower themselves, instill pride in their culture, reclaim identities, and take charge of their lives (Fontaine 2005). But while equal opportunity or equality before the law may be necessary, it is insufficient. Put bluntly, equal standards (treating everyone the same) cannot be applied to unequal situations without perpetuating the inequality by freezing the status quo. Not surprisingly, Aboriginal peoples have insisted on recognition of their differences to complement citizenship rights. The constant that underpins Aboriginal aspirations are the following claims: (1) Aboriginal peoples are different, constitutionally speaking, (2) their differences must be protected in constructing a new social contract, (3) these differences must be taken seriously as grounds for living together separately, and (4) differences must be taken into account as the basis for rewards, recognition, and relations-repair (Macklem 2001). Without difference, Aboriginal peoples have no more moral authority than other Canadians to challenge and transform the constitutional order. Predictably, then, moves to abolish Aboriginal difference are a constant in government policy. Taiaiake Alfred (2000) writes to this effect:

> Let us understand that it is Canada's goal, advanced through policy and the co-optation of our people, to undermine the strength and the very existence of our nations by taking away . . . everything that makes us unique and powerful . . . Historically, and into the present day, it's clear the Canadian government believes that by forcing us or enticing us into the legal, political, and cultural mainstream, every bit of distinction between us and them will disappear. Then, in the future, with all the differences erased, there will no longer be any moral or political justification for laws that support special rights and separate lands for Indian people. Indian problem solved!

INSIGHT   What Will Keep Us Together: Assimilationism? Autonomism? Or Inbetweenism?

Canada's colonialist approach to Aboriginal affairs is no longer acceptable. Yet, there is no consensus as to what should replace the paternalism of a patronizing past (Brooks 1998). The debate revolves around the question of what constitutes a just society. Is it one that treats everyone the same regardless of differences? Or is it one that takes differences into account as a basis for equitable treatment? But how do we live together in a divided society without falling into the trap of dismemberment by diversity? Is it possible to promote Aboriginal difference at political levels, yet ensure some degree of shared belonging and commonality? Which of these approaches— *assimilationism* or *autonomism*—is better equipped to address the challenge of co-operative coexistence in contested political space?

At one extreme are those who endorse assimilationist principles as the only realistic solution to the problem of Aboriginal

marginality (Flanagan 1999; Fiss 2005a, b). The entire edifice of laws, arrangements, and programs for Aboriginal peoples (from reserves to the Indian Affairs department) is criticized as racially discriminatory, counterproductive, and dependency-inducing, and should be shelved in favour of equality of all before the law because all Canadians are fundamentally alike (Gibson 2005). After all, it is claimed, treating one group of Canadians preferentially on the basis of race is morally wrong, bad policy, and socially divisive (Fiss 2004b). Besides, the critics argue, the Canadian government spends up to $9 billion per year on Aboriginal affairs, with little to show for the expenditure except third world living standards, a glaring lack of accountability and transparency in the spending (apparently 984 allegations of criminal and non-criminal wrongdoing on reserves between 2002 and 2004; Fiss 2005b), and Aboriginal demands for more funds (Fiss

2005b). Finally, signing new de facto third order of self-governing arrangements such as the Nisga'a *Final Settlement* can only lead to inequality, favouritism, balkanization, and racism (Fiss 2004b). The solution to the "Indian problem": a municipal level of government that generates income from taxation on individualized property rights rather than relying on federal transfers for self-government (Fiss 2005b).

At the other extreme are the autonomists. By definition, they endorse Aboriginal peoples' claims as sovereign political nations with inherent and collective rights to Aboriginal models of self-determining autonomy over land, identity, and political voice. The logic behind the claim is consistent with the principles of dependency theories: that is, sustained contact with the West, with its corresponding pressures to assimilate, creates more problems than solutions. An emphasis on Aboriginal difference as the basis for recognition, reward, and relationships secures a degree of political space to ensure autonomous self-development.

In between these positions are those compromises that endorse Aboriginal difference but within the wider framework of Canadian society (see Parkin 2001, Cairns 2005). Consider the intermediate position by Alan Cairns in his book *Citizens Plus: Aboriginal Peoples and the Canadian State*. The term "citizen plus" was first articulated in the *Hawthorne Report* of 1966 (Cairns worked on that report). The report emphasized how Aboriginal peoples have the same rights as all Canadians but also additional

rights because of their historical and treaty status (Hawkes 2000). According to Cairns, a commitment to citizen plus provides the framework for solving complex Aboriginal problems without destroying Canada in the process. It provides a middle ground that recognizes both Aboriginal differences (thus rejecting assimilation) and the need for citizenship in Canada (thus rejecting autonomy) (2000:86). For Cairns, Aboriginal self-determination and self-government as a third order of government cannot be about separation but about incorporation—about "getting in" rather than "getting out" in hopes of completing the "circle of confederation" (cited in Hawkes 2000:142).

There is much to commend in the proposal to recognize Aboriginal difference and rights without forsaking a sense of common belonging to a single political community. Putting the ideal of citizen plus into practice may prove a stickier challenge. Critics argue that the principle of citizen plus is already in place but implementation is delayed by a dearth of the political. Or as Patricia Monture-Angus puts it, "The relationship has already been defined, it is *just not lived*" (2001:10). In other words, Aboriginal peoples already claim to be sovereign, including having the right to a nation-to-nation relationship. What they now require is the appropriate structure to implement this reality. Criticism aside, there is little doubt that Cairns's thesis has stimulated a debate by articulating a compromise model that pleases some and angers others.

In sum, Aboriginal peoples have claimed the right to be different as well as the right to be the same. Equality of treatment (formal equality) is critical; so too is the demand for group-differentiated rights (equality of outcomes) because of their unique constitutional status as original occupants. Demands go beyond the symmetrical notion of diversity implied by multiculturalism (all differences are equally different). Such equality suppresses Aboriginal difference by glossing over their unique status, history, culture, and relationships

(Kernerman 2005). Aboriginal peoples do not see any contradiction in insisting on a "first among equals" status. As far as they are concerned, this status is compensation for the loss of land, lives, and livelihood. Canadian politicians and policy-makers rarely dispute the validity of Aboriginal rights for self-determining autonomy. What are disputed are the magnitude and costs of these rights.

SELF-DETERMINING AUTONOMY THROUGH SELF-GOVERNANCE

Canada's Aboriginal peoples are in the midst of a drive to regain control over their lives and life chances. Central to this reconstruction process is the notion of an Aboriginal right to self-determining autonomy over land, identity, and political voice. The powerful expression of Aboriginal aspirations rejects the legitimacy of existing political relations and mainstream institutions as a framework for living together. Also rejected is the relevance and moral authority of those structures that once colonized Aboriginal peoples. Proposed instead is the restoration of Aboriginal models of self-determining autonomy that sharply curtail state jurisdiction while enhancing Aboriginal control over relevant domains. Key elements of this self-determination project include control over the process and power of local governance, the attainment of cultural sovereignty, and a realignment of political relations around a nation-to-nation format in key jurisdictional areas related to power, privilege, and resources (Mercredi and Turpel 1993).

Aboriginal leaders have endorsed the principle of self-determining autonomy. Its value lies in breaking the cycle of deprivation and dependency, in moving beyond the colonialist mentality of the *Indian Act*, and in its embrace of an Aboriginal renaissance as a spearhead for renewal and reform. Aboriginal models of self-determining autonomy will vary and are expected to evolve in line with community needs (social, economic, cultural) and local circumstances (rural or urban). Some will reflect a government model, others an Aboriginal model, and still others will combine elements of both, with differences being contextual rather than categorical, that is, in accordance with community levels of local development rather than ideology. A few Aboriginal models are looking for complete independence; others want a fundamental restructuring of their relationship within a reconstituted Canada; many want some kind of accommodation within the existing federal system because they lack any viable alternatives; and most may well be content with a limited autonomy involving negotiated agreements that are mostly administrative in nature, that is, delegation of government power to manage local services (Kulchyski 2003).

Four models of self-determination can be discerned: (1) statehood, a sovereign country with absolute independence, no external interference, and a final say over both internal and external affairs; (2) nationhood, a de facto sovereignty with province-like powers and jurisdiction over all internal matters; (3) municipality-level, a community-based level of self-determining autonomy, retaining control over local affairs but limited by interaction with comparable mainstream bodies; and (4) institutional-level, having meaningful decision-making powers through institutional inclusion or parallel institutions (see also O'Regan 1994). Table 7.1 summarizes these possibilities, with respect to the type of sovereignty associated with each level of self-determining autonomy and its expression through self-governance.

TABLE 7.1	Models of Self-Determining Autonomy: Levels of Sovereignty	
Statehood	**Nationhood**
absolute (de jure) sovereignty	relative (de facto) sovereignty
Municipality-level	**Institution-level**
nested (community-based) sovereignty:	nominal (as if) sovereignty

Generally speaking, Aboriginal claims for self-determining autonomy at self-governance levels are consistent with the "nationhood" model of "domestic dependent nations" in the United States. American First Nations do not possess external sovereignty (e.g., they cannot raise an army). Nevertheless, these "domestic dependent nations" retain considerable control over internal sovereignty, at least in theory if not always in practice, subject to certain restrictions at the federal and state levels. To date, with the possible exception of the Nisga'a settlement, the Canadian government has offered a lower level of self-determining autonomy with powers that go beyond a municipality jurisdiction but less than a nation or province. Aboriginal leaders publicly endorse a model somewhere between nationhood/provinces and statehood but appear willing to compromise, depending on particular circumstances.

Self-Governance/Self-Government

Aboriginal claims for self-determining autonomy are multidimensional. Political goals are important, but only as part of a more comprehensive package of reforms that include sustainable economic development, control over language and culture, and creation of healthy social arrangements from homes to communities. But the right to self-governance prevails in recognizing Aboriginal peoples as essentially political communities with the authority to decide their collective futures (Murphy 2001; Asch 2002; Cassidy 2003, Schouls 2003).

Few should be surprised that the politics of aboriginality revolve around debates over self-governance (Fleras 2000). Canada itself is a territoriality-based sovereignty involving a principled allocation of power between federal and provincial jurisdictions, and this division of jurisdictions is being played out at the level of Aboriginal self-government. Aboriginal self-government is already an emerging reality in Canada (Hylton 1994/1999). Passage of the 1984 *Cree Naskapi of Quebec Act* inaugurated the concept of Aboriginal self-government legislation in Canada (Price 1991). Establishment of self-government in 1986 by the Sechelt of British Columbia's west coast also proved pioneering. Rather than being part of a broader land claims agreement, Sechelt involved specifically designed legislative authority to move beyond the federal *Indian Act*. But the Nisga'a *Final Agreement* confirms the arrival of a powerful new self-governance (the creation of Nunavut is not seen as self-government per se, but as public government since the non-Inuit can participate in the political process). Aboriginal governments such as Nisga'a are increasingly recognized as one of three distinct orders of governance in Canada, each of which is autonomous in its own right, yet sharing in the sovereignty of Canada by way of overlapping and exclusive jurisdictions (Dufraiment 2002).

Debates over self-governance pivot around the politics of jurisdiction. The politics of jurisdiction are open to negotiations in three dimensions: what is "mine," what is "yours," and what is "ours"—ranging from shared arrangements on the one hand to exclusive tribal control over land ownership and membership up to and including autonomy on the other. Core jurisdictions entail those matters of vital political, economic, cultural, and social concern to Aboriginal peoples (Royal Commission on Aboriginal Peoples 1996). Peripheral jurisdictions include those realms that have an impact on adjacent jurisdictions or attract federal/provincial interest. Jurisdictional matters are expected to vary from band to band; nevertheless, they are likely to include control over (1) the delivery of social services such as policing, education, and health and welfare; (2) resources and use of land for economic regeneration; (3) the means to protect and promote distinct cultural values and language systems; (4) band membership and entitlements; and (5) local expenditures according to Aboriginal priorities rather than those of the government or bureaucracy. This is not to say that all Aboriginal communities possess the developmental capacity to fully engage in self-government, as related costs and responsibilities are daunting. But many do and are casting about for ways to establish arrangements that will divest all vestiges of internal colonialism in exchange for self-rule.

The range and scope of self-governing jurisdictions has yet to be decided. Of particular concern is the question of magnitude. Should Aboriginal self-government be focused on a national organization or, alternatively, on local bodies that reflect variations in culture and levels of development (Bern and Dodds 2000)? An intermediate position is gaining favour. The right to self-government will not be vested in every community but in Aboriginal "nations," that is, a sizable body of Aboriginal peoples with a shared sense of common identity that constitutes a predominant population in a certain territory (Royal Commission on Aboriginal Peoples 1996). Aboriginal communities across Canada can be collapsed into between 60 and 80 Aboriginal historically based nations, based on economies of scale and natural ties, thus reviving the nation-way in which Aboriginal peoples once were organized. The expanding population of Aboriginal peoples in the cities poses a fresh challenge that will necessitate a new social contract for sharing political and economic power (Green 2003).

Not everyone is hopping aboard the self-governance bandwagon. A few Aboriginal leaders have sounded a note of caution; for Alfred (2005), self-government as a catalyst for political and economic change is not the answer without a corresponding decolonization of minds along traditional Aboriginal lines. Non-Aboriginal opinion is often confused and rarely enthused (Widdowson and Howard 2002). Concerns are raised over costs, feasibility, effectiveness, degree of legitimacy, and belief that self-government is not the cure to all problems. Some see Aboriginal self-government as a "recipe" for social disunity; others query the soundness of a system based on race and separate status; yet others believe Aboriginal "nations" lack the capacity to be self-determining and exercise sovereignty; and still others express concerns over the cost of implementation (Smith 1995; Gibson 1998; Anderssen 1998; Widdowson 2004). Government spending on Aboriginal peoples is already deemed to be out of control, including billions spent on provincial jurisdictions such as education and health care, but with no guidelines for what to expect or how to spend (Curry 2005).

Appeals to Aboriginal self-government are also criticized as a simplistic solution to a complex problem espoused primarily by Aboriginal elites (and their lawyers and consultants), who are removed from urban realities and out of touch with local needs. Reserves may be so rife with corruption and mismanagement, including basic transparency and accountability procedures, that even Aboriginal organizations express concern over the transfer of yet more power to already dysfunctional communities (Ayed 1999). As well, there is growing concern that some Aboriginal peoples are manipulating claims to self-governing sovereignty as a smokescreen to justify illegal activities, including the slaughter of endangered species (Jones 2005) and creation of online gambling and casinos (Hamilton 2005). No less worrying are the dangers of a new Aboriginal bureaucracy and increased dependency on federal transfers, resulting in a yet larger Aboriginal "grievance industry" that enriches a few at the expense of many (Fiss 2005a, b).

Of particular concern is the spectre of separation under **Aboriginal self-governance**. Will self-governance structures create a Swiss-cheese society in Canada, one that is full of holes but with no unifying centre to hold it together? Contrary to popular belief, however, most Aboriginal proposals are not interested in making a total break with Canadian society. With few exceptions, Aboriginal demands for self-governing autonomy rarely extend to calls for political independence or territorial autonomy. Proposed instead is a relationship of relative and relational autonomy within a framework of power-sharing and partnership (Scott 1996). This excerpt from the Royal Commission on Aboriginal Peoples (1996:xi) should allay alarmist fears about "death by dismemberment":

> To say that Aboriginal peoples are nations is not to say that they are nation-states seeking independence from Canada. They are collectivities with a long shared history, a right to govern themselves and, in general, a strong desire to do it in partnership with Canada.

In other words, neither inherent self-government nor claims to Aboriginal sovereignty are synonymous with secession or independence. Advocated instead is a functional sovereignty where Aboriginal peoples are treated *as if* sovereign for purposes of entitlement and engagement. The intent of a de facto sovereignty is not to demolish Canada, but to dismantle those components of Canada that have precluded Aboriginal peoples from their rightful place as First Nations (Borrows and Rotman 1997). Aboriginal peoples are not attempting to erect subversive enclaves within "foreign" territories; to the contrary, they want to repatriate that part of their spiritual and cultural homeland whose sovereignty was never relinquished. Admittedly, attainment of Aboriginal status as peoples or nations will require a reversal of those colonialist assumptions that historically have denied and excluded. Claims to self-governance will also have to overcome a hardening of Canadian attitudes toward Aboriginal peoples. Still, mounting pressure for new governance arrangements may prove unstoppable as Canada embraces a new social contract for living together.

Aboriginal Title and Treaty Rights

Moves toward a new social contract are anchored in the recognition, definition, and implementation of Aboriginal title and treaty rights (Russell 2005). Enforcement of federal treaty obligations is particularly important in advancing Aboriginal interests and aspirations. Treaties were seen as a fundamental component of Aboriginal diplomacy with European powers. The British in particular insisted on observing legalities. Treaties represented practical nation-to-nation relationships between European colonizers and tribes. They also provided a principled approach to determining ownership of private property, as only land that had been properly acquired (without encumbrances) could be sold, mortgaged, used as collateral, or employed in a productive manner in a free enterprise economy (Walkom 1998). Treaties continue to be regarded as ongoing and organic agreements that reaffirm the distinctive legal status of Aboriginal nations. With treaties, Aboriginal peoples possess a constitutional right to carry on traditional harvesting practices for moderate livelihood, with governments having to justify any restrictions they wish to impose on this right (Manfredi 2004). They also serve as a blueprint for realigning Aboriginal peoples–state relationships on a nation-to-nation, government-to-government basis (Rotman 1997).

Treaties proved a conflict of interest from the start (McKee 1996). For the most part, European governments saw treaties as legal surrenders of Aboriginal land. Treaties would provide the Crown with legal title to underoccupied land, foster peaceful settlement, avoid costly wars, and deter foreign annexation or expansion (Price 1991). But others see it differently: According to international law, a treaty is a formally ratified agreement incorporating a nation-to-nation equitable relationship between sovereign entities. Canada's courts have shown little inclination to see treaties as international agreements, preferring instead to define them as unique contractual agreements involving mutually binding obligations and exchange of rights (Brooks 1998). For Aboriginal peoples, however, treaties reaffirmed their autonomy as political communities. Treaties were viewed as semi-sacred and mutually binding contracts involving a reciprocal exchange of rights and responsibilities. As far as Aboriginal leaders are concerned, governments remain bound to honour the contractual obligations of these treaties—if only to preserve the honour of the Crown.

Specific Treaty Claims

Two types of treaty rights exist. One is based on specific claims to existing treaty violations, and the other involves comprehensive modern-day land claims (or regional settlements). A series of treaties was signed between 1763 and 1867 involving representatives of the Crown and Aboriginal nations. The earliest treaties resembled peace and friendship compacts to facilitate trade, secure allies, and pre-empt European rivals (McKee 1996). Later treaties involved exchanges of land for goods and services. Between 1867 and 1923, 11 numbered (1–11) treaties were signed, involving a surrender of Aboriginal interest in land to the Crown across much of the Prairies and parts of the Northwest Territories, British Columbia, and Ontario (DIAND 1997). These historical Indian treaties set out the obligations and benefits for both parties to the agreement. Aboriginal peoples surrendered title to land and resources. In return, they received reserve lands, agricultural equipment, ammunition, annual payment, access to services, and clothing. Their right to hunt and fish on ceded Crown land remained in effect as long as these lands remained unoccupied. The Crown also promised schools on reserves or teachers when requested. Consider the terms of agreement between the Crown and the First Nations of Manitoba and the Northwest Territories:

- Aboriginal tribes would relinquish all their rights and title to the great region from Lake Superior to the foot of the Rocky Mountains.
- Land would be set aside as reserves for homes and agriculture. This land cannot be sold without Indian consent and then only for their benefit.
- Indians would be granted the right to hunt and fish over these Crown lands until sold into private hands.
- An annual payment of $5 would be made for each man, woman, and child ($25 for chief, $15 for councillor). Suitable clothing, medals, and flags to the chiefs would be provided.
- To assist in agricultural endeavours, each band would receive implements, herds, and grain.
- Schools would be established on reserves.
- Sale of alcohol on reserves would be prohibited (see Price 1991).

Noble intentions were one thing; implementation proved another. The treaty process was often marred by such wilful duplicity and callous expediency that it hardly seemed worth the paper it was written on (Price 1991). Most grievances reflected failures to live up to treaty promises. Benefits were pared back or simply ignored with the passage of time. Miserly payouts proved a sore point. Another source of grievance entailed the unauthorized and uncompensated whittling away of reserve lands because of fraud, expropriation, or government theft. No less devastating was the misappropriation of Aboriginal monies from government sale of resources or mineral rights held in trust by the Crown. **Specific treaty claims** are aimed at righting historical wrongs associated with deception and double dealing. Not surprisingly, perhaps, the courts have instructed the federal government to display a "fair, large, and liberal interpretation" of treaty provisions by providing the benefit of the doubt to Aboriginal peoples. In the words of Chief Judge Beverley McLachlin, "Put simply, Canada's Aboriginal peoples were here when Europeans came, and were never conquered" (cited in Makin 2005), thus putting the onus on the "honour of the Crown" to deal generously with Aboriginal claims.

Comprehensive Land (Treaty) Claims

Comprehensive land claims consist of modern-day treaty arrangements for disputed ownership of land. To date, eight modern treaties have been negotiated, beginning with the James Bay and Northern Quebec Agreement in 1976 for most of the territorial north, most of northern Quebec, and parts of British Columbia (Abele 2004). As well, there are currently more than 1000 outstanding specific claims, ranging from expropriations for hydro lines to actual land parcels, including much of downtown Toronto (Maccharles 2005). Comprehensive claims do not deal with redressing specific claims. Rather, modern-day treaties address the need to establish treaty relationships with those Aboriginal nations that had never signed a treaty in the past (Purvis 1999). Securing certainty of control over "untreatied" land and resources is imperative: For the Crown, certainty of ownership is a prerequisite for investment and development purposes. For Aboriginal peoples, clarifying the rights of ownership secures a solid economic base for prosperity and survival. Negotiated settlements provide Aboriginal communities with constitutionally protected rights to wildlife harvests, resource management, some subsurface mineral rights, and regulated development (Aatami et al. 2004). Economic benefits can be derived by renting out lands and resources at rates that are favourable to Aboriginal interests. Benefits can also be achieved through local development (in tandem with public or private interests) at a pace that reflects community priorities and developmental levels.

The resolution of land claims settlements in Canada is predicated on the principle of **Aboriginal title**. Broadly speaking, Aboriginal title specifies Aboriginal rights of use over land and resources whose ownership (title) has not yet been legally extinguished and transferred to the Crown (Gray 1998). The principle itself focuses on the question of who occupied the land prior to the unilateral assertion of Crown ownership. If Aboriginal peoples can prove they had continuous and exclusive occupation of the land prior to European contact, they can claim Aboriginal title; otherwise, the land reverts to Crown ownership. Because it has no counterpart in English common property law, Aboriginal title is unlike other forms of property ownership, hence *sui generis:* Aboriginal title cannot be surrendered or transferred to any individual but only the Crown, is sourced in original occupancy, and is collectively held in perpetuity for the benefit of future owners.

How, then, does Aboriginal title apply to Canada? The Calder decision of 1973, which acknowledged the possibility of Aboriginal title to unceded (unextinguished) land, was silent on the matter. The Sparrow decision in 1990 gave practical effect to constitutional guarantees of existing treaty and Aboriginal rights (Rotman 2004). The Delgamuukw ruling in 1997 further advanced the cause when it overturned an earlier British Columbia Court decision that dismissed Aboriginal claims to land title as impossible to determine, even if it existed. The ruling concluded a legal campaign by 51 Gitskan and Wet'suwet'en hereditary chiefs whose ancestors had struggled since the 1880s to reclaim Aboriginal title to their lands. Delgamuukw recognized the validity of Aboriginal claims to certain lands that had never been ceded in treaties or agreements.

Under Delgamuukw, the court ruled that Aboriginal peoples have a constitutional and exclusive right of use and ownership to land they can prove was occupied by them prior to European arrival. Until Aboriginal title is settled, according to a Supreme Court ruling, not a single tree can be felled by Crown authorities without consultation, agreement, and compensation—even in cases where infringements on Aboriginal title lands are for public purposes or national interests (Matas et al. 1997). Subsequent Supreme Court rulings have strengthened the Aboriginal hand, despite some judicial backpedalling. The government has a moral and legal duty to meaningfully negotiate (not just pay lip service to consult) before permitting developmental activities on disputed land. (The reader should keep in mind that the obligation to negotiate meaningfully does not oblige the government to agree or reach an agreement; Maccharles 2005.) Nor can the government issue licences for mining or logging to private developers while the disputed land is under negotiation (Makin 2005). Moreover, rather than restricting land use to traditional hunting and foraging practices, Aboriginal claimants can use the land or resources in almost any way they wish, except in a destructive sense that may imperil future use (Gray 1997). Delgamuukw also advanced the concept of Aboriginal title by expanding the support base for proving title. To assist in proving claims, oral traditions are now as admissible as evidence as written documents in deciding Aboriginal title, in effect tipping the burden of proof from the claimants to the Crown.

SPEEDBUMPS ON THE ROADMAP FOR REMAKING CANADA

Historically, Canada and other settler societies struggled to remove the existence of the "nations within" by way of assimilation, forced migration, bureaucratic indifference, or outright suppression (McRoberts 2003; Churchill 2004). The present may be no less single-minded, albeit more subtle. In reaction, Aboriginal peoples in Canada and throughout the world have taken the initiative in politicizing their demands for a radical restructuring of society along the lines of a new social contract (Fleras and Elliott 1992; Neizen 2003). The focus of a new social contract has shifted from one that seeks survival to one that challenges the distribution of power within a new constitutional order. The terrain is increasingly contested. Aboriginal leaders have relied on various tactics and strategies to get the message across. Political authorities, ever distrustful and fearful of losing power or control, have responded with a host of delaying or defusing tactics (Sissons 2005).

Aboriginal Initiatives

Aboriginal moves for redefining their relationship to society are varied. Principles and philosophies span the spectrum from "radical" to "moderate": At one end are those who believe in revolutionary changes for advancing the political architecture to accommodate Aboriginal peoples' claims to self-determining autonomy (Mercredi and Turpel 1993; Alfred 2005). At the other are the moderates who endorse a conciliatory, incremental approach that cuts deals, enhances local autonomy, improves job opportunities, and fosters dialogue with private sectors (Fontaine 1998; also Gray 1997). In between are those who don't know, who don't care, or who are more concerned with "getting on" than with "taking a stand."

Aboriginal initiatives tend to focus on land and resources (Kulchyski 2003). Without land, any hope of economic development is seriously compromised, as is their right to protect language and culture, speak the language of nationhood, or assert self-determining autonomy in any meaningful fashion (of course, Aboriginal land continues to have spiritual and social significance above and beyond the practical [Little Bear 2004]). Whether to protect land or promote issues, Aboriginal initiatives for change are generally pursued through conventional channels of dialogue, consultation, and persuasion with central policy structures. Tactics include recourse to Parliament, the existing court system, public opinion polls, and special interest/lobby groups such as the Assembly of First Nations. Courts are preferred venues for exerting pressure on the government to honour its constitutional obligations, while securing a forum for articulating Aboriginal issues. Lacking the reach of wealth and government power, Aboriginal peoples must rely on the powers of persuasion and moral rectitude through the courts, litigation, and the law (Wilkins 2004). And court decisions from Calder to Sparrow to Delgamuukw have secured redress for historical inequities as grounds for advancing collective interests. Aboriginal leaders have also relied on international fora and agencies for assistance. They have gone to the United Nations, to Britain, even to the Vatican in the hopes of righting historical wrongs. These tactics have attained a measure of success, partly because of Canada's vulnerability to international criticism and censure.

Alternative strategies have been adopted as well. This cannot come as a surprise; after all, the use of conventional channels involves working within a framework that (1) historically colonized Aboriginal peoples, (2) is constructed in a way that unreflectively advances mainstream interests, and (3) in general is prone to protect the system against challenge and change (see Green 2003). Failure of political and constitutional channels to adequately address local grievances and national concerns has culminated in activist protest, ranging from acts of civil disobedience to threats of violence in some cases. Flamboyant and theatrically staged protests involving the mass media are particularly important in tweaking the conscience of a publicity-conscious government. By startling a complacent public, the use of negative publicity to embarrass the government has proven especially effective because of Canada's much ballyhooed commitment to human and individual rights (see Marcus 1995). Finally, there have been occasional threats to employ violence if necessary. Yet the threat of violence has rarely moved beyond rhetoric and, when employed as at Oka or Burnt Church, is often defensive in nature. How long this non-violence will persist is open to conjecture, given the urgency of Aboriginal grievances, the impatience of younger activists, and perceptions of federal foot-dragging.

Aboriginal demands are consistent with their articulated status as "nations within." Central to their aspirations is the middle way: to strike a balance between extremes. Aboriginal peoples don't want to separate from Canada in the territorial sense, yet they also reject any move toward assimilation with a corresponding diminution of their unique status as self-determining political communities. A separate country is not on the agenda. What is proposed, instead, is a consensual partnership involving a sharing of jurisdiction in some areas such as health, but exclusive jurisdiction in other areas such as culture—with just enough room to ensure Aboriginal self-determining autonomy (Erasmus and Sanders 2002). A commitment to Aboriginal models of self-governance is endorsed as a compromise between the extremes of separatism and absorption. In other words, Aboriginal peoples want to be modern, with the political and economic power critical for rebuilding strong communities, yet not at the expense of abandoning traditional values but rather by embracing the promise and practices of the past as a framework for the present (Alfred 1999; 2005; Dean and Levi 2006). Aboriginal peoples are pragmatists who wish to achieve a working balance between the cultural and spiritual values of the past without rejecting the technological benefits of modern society. They are not against development per se, unless attained at the cost of sacrificing uniqueness, authenticity, and spirituality, but insist on controlling benefits from local developmental projects.

Non-Aboriginal Responses

Many Canadians fret over the unconventional nature of Aboriginal proposals. But Aboriginal demands are not radical compared to the alternatives. Their demands rarely invoke the over-throw of mainstream values or institutions; after all, it is hardly in their best interests to destroy the fiduciary relationship that informs their existence. Few actively espouse the dis-memberment of Canadian society or the imposition of Aboriginal cultural values. Endorsed instead is a restructuring of relations to ensure (1) Aboriginal rights are taken seriously, (2) implementation of Aboriginal models of self-determination by way of self-governance, and (3) recognition of Aboriginal title and treaty rights. If these demands appear threatening to Canadians as a whole or if they seem unrealistic in light of contemporary realities, con-sider the options. A continuation of ineffectual government interference and paternalistic hand-outs is not the answer. No more effective is throwing more money at the problem or expanding the legion of experts. In short, the costs of re-priming the relationship may be formidable; even more daunting will be the costs of doing nothing different.

Central authorities for the most part have stumbled in responding to Aboriginal demands for indigenizing Aboriginal peoples–state relations. Political sectors have come under attack for caving in to Aboriginal demands while sacrificing national interests through restitu-tional expenditures and power giveaways (Smith 1995). They have also been criticized for sacrificing Aboriginal interests in pursuit of national goals (Adams 1999). The promises of lofty rhetoric notwithstanding, there remains a noticeable lack of political will for "walk-ing the talk" (Weaver 1993; Macklem 1993). Instead of a principled approach to addressing the issues, what prevails is the equivalent of a political cha-cha-cha: every step forward is matched by one step back and two steps sideways (see also O'Reilly 2005). Politics and initiatives continue to be driven by public opinion polls, despite known deficiencies in mass surveys (Ponting 1997; Purvis 1999). Canadians appear to be broadly supportive of Aboriginal concerns and sympathetic to Aboriginal problems. But public support may be superficial, ten-tative, and conditional, thus making any government fearful of moving too quickly. Inasmuch as the intent is to simply rearrange the furniture without altering the floor plan, even of a sink-ing relationship, the government's Aboriginal agenda appears more concerned with appear-ances than with substance.

Policy officials are understandably wary of dissolving the once habitual patterns of domination for the uncharted waters of Aboriginal self-determining autonomy. True, the political landscape has shifted significantly, but mixed messages prevail: Political awareness is growing that the Crown acted irresponsibly in dealing with Aboriginal peoples, in effect reneging on the trust implicit in this relationship. But a willingness to compensate Aboriginal peoples for historical wrongs does not extend to bankrupting Canada. There is growing acceptance that Aboriginal peoples (1) are a distinct society, (2) possess a threatened culture and society, (3) depend on government trust and responsibilities for survival, (4) desire more control in line with local priorities, and (5) prefer to achieve their goals in partnership with central authorities. But there is no enthusiasm for putting the principles of power sharing and partnership into a meaningful and measurable practice. The Crown is often unwilling to negotiate Aboriginal issues except when compelled to do so by the threat of unfavourable litigation (Rotman 2004). The principle of Aboriginal self-governance is endorsed not as an independently sourced inherent right but as a political concession, both contingent (qualified) and delegated on a band-to-band basis, with accountability to Parliament and the Constitution. Claims to Aboriginal self-governance may be acceptable, but only when they do not affect most Canadians, do not involve exorbitant sums, and cannot be used as leverage in neutralizing the Québécois threat of secession (Widdowson 2004). Political authorities appear receptive to Aboriginal claims—if only to avert a crisis of legitimacy and restore some semblance of political tranquility—but not if this restructuring process results in a fundamental shift in power.

In brief, aboriginality as principle and practice poses an unprecedented challenge to the balancing act in any society constructed around a series of compromises. Few politicians can afford to cavalierly dismiss aboriginality or deny the existence of Aboriginal rights. By the same token they can't afford to be seen as capitulating to Aboriginal demands. What prevails instead are debates over how to re-calibrate the relationship without destroying Canada's social fabric in the process. Yet, the debate over the place of Aboriginal peoples in Canada remains so steeped in the foundational principles of a colonial constitutional order that prospects for transformational change are sharply compromised (Alfred 2001). Contrary to popular and political belief, Canada has not discarded the colonialism of the past, only its most egregious forms (Denis 1997). The legacy of Eurocentric-based colonialism continues to shape how the legal system identifies, interprets, and enforces Aboriginal rights, proving, yet again, that Canadian law is neither neutral nor impartial, but an instrument for advancing dominant values under the guise of neutrality and fairness (Asch 1997). The words of Noel Lyons (1997) are especially timely in emphasizing the contradictions of working within the system:

> As long as the process continues to be defined by rules and standards set by the dominant society, no measure of real self-government is possible because the process itself is a denial of the inherent rights of self-government of Aboriginal peoples. In other words, we cannot de-colonize peoples by relying on the rules and standards that were used to colonize them in the first place . . .

How is this neo-colonial relationship manifested (Denis 1996; 1997; Maaka and Fleras 2005)? Neo-colonialism works on the assumption that people appear to be free. But this is an illusion, as hidden agendas continue to control and contain, albeit in an indirect manner (Adams 1999). For example, Delgamuukw may acknowledge Aboriginal title as an exclusive and collective right to land and its use, but not unless or until Aboriginal communities prove title to land—an often expensive and lengthy undertaking (Christie 2005). An extraordinarily high level of proof is required. According to Chief Justice Beverley McLachlin (2005), Aboriginal claimants must prove exclusive physical possession, establish a substantial connection to the land, demonstrate direct lineage with the original inhabitants of the land, and avoid claims that do reflect a "logical evolution" of activities from traditional times. As a result, a right to fish or hunt for moderate livelihood may be acceptable because of its traditional nature, but not logging on Crown land (Toughill and Gordon 2005).

Or consider how Aboriginal peoples–state relations remain rooted in the colonialist assumption that the Crown owns all the land outright. Even the courts are complicit in upholding unilateral Crown assertion of sovereignty over Aboriginal peoples and their territories. Yet, on what grounds can Canada define Aboriginal title as a legal burden on the Crown? Could it not be the case that the Crown imposes a burden on un-surrendered Aboriginal land, thus necessitating some kind of process by which to substantiate Crown claims to land ownership? As Sharon Venne (1998) points out, there is no legal proof for ascertaining the legality of the Crown's unilateral assertion over Aboriginal jurisdictions. Such neo-colonial arrogance, Venne asserts, is nothing more than a "political statement" dressed up in "hocus pocus" rules and regulations designed by the colonizers to dispossess Aboriginal peoples of land and resources.

To be sure, the courts have conferred on Aboriginal peoples a "quasi-national *sui generis* legal status" based on their occupation of Canada prior to the Crown's unilateral assertion of sovereignty over Canada (Murphy 2001:110). The courts have also ruled to reinforce Crown fiduciary obligations and to restrict Crown infringement on Aboriginal rights, and have insisted that court decisions are not a substitute for Aboriginal policy but provide a principled basis for negotiating Aboriginal peoples–Crown relations (Harty and Murphy 2005:39). But the courts are not prepared to challenge the colonialist assumptions that privilege the undisputed primacy of the Crown's claims to absolute sovereignty while diminishing Aboriginal title to little more than an inconvenience on the Crown. How could it be otherwise? Court judges tend to be middle-class non-Aboriginal persons who are by training, personal history, and inclination more in tune with mainstream rhythms, ordering principles, and institutions rather than Aboriginal realities, resulting in decisions that have a way of advancing mainstream interests (Wilkins 2004:293).

In short, the foundational principles of a creaky colonial social contract are doing a disservice. This social contract for living together is based on a brand of liberal universalism that leaves little room for taking differences seriously, distrusts the notion of self-determining autonomy for Aboriginal communities, and privileges individual rights to choose over collective rights to survive (Peach 2005). The pervasive Eurocentrism that informs a neo-colonial political architecture has had the effect of (1) dismissing Aboriginal rights, values, or traditions as irrelevant or inferior; (2) normalizing Eurocentric ways of seeing and doing as natural and inevitable; and (3) asserting the superiority and dominance of conventional patterns and institutional structures. The framing of issues from a Eurocentric perspective draws attention to some aspects of reality as normal and necessary, but others as not; defines some aspects of reality as acceptable and desirable, but not others; and imposes a preferred reading of reality by emphasizing commonalities and similarities at the expense of deep differences (Maaka and Fleras 2005). But for Aboriginal peoples to be equal, they must be different and their differences must be taken seriously as a blueprint for relationships, rights, and recognition (see Denis 1996). Otherwise, there is a risk of being muscled into agreements that say more about securing a neo-colonial status quo rather than a new post-colonial social contract (Venne 1998).

UNBLOCKING THE IMPASSE: CONSTRUCTIVE ENGAGEMENT

Aboriginal struggles to sever the bonds of colonialist dependency and underdevelopment are gathering momentum. Several innovative routes have been explored for improving Aboriginal peoples–state relations, including constitutional reform, indigenization of policy and administration, comprehensive and specific land claims, constitutional reform, *Indian Act* amendments, devolution of power, decentralization of service delivery structures, and, of course, self-government arrangements (Prince 1994). An Aboriginal "wish list" is varied, as might be expected in light of diverse constituencies and specific histories, but typically involves demands for jurisdictional control at local and national levels. Yet, the politics of jurisdiction are not without costs and typically engender consequences that may inadvertently reinforce the very colonialisms that Aboriginal peoples want to escape.

Pressure is mounting to transcend confrontational models as blueprints for framing Aboriginal peoples–Canada relations. Proposed is a more flexible approach that emphasizes negotiation over litigation, engagement over entitlement, relationships over rights, interdependence over opposition, co-operation over competition, reconciliation over restitution, and power-sharing over power conflict (Maaka and Fleras 2005). Advocated, too, is a principled approach that acknowledges the importance of working together by standing apart as grounds for belonging separately. Emergence of a **constructive engagement** model may provide a respite from the interminable bickering over "who owns what" while brokering a **post-colonial social contract** for co-operative coexistence. The following foundational principles secure a new framework for constructive engagement.

1. De facto Sovereignty: Aboriginal peoples do not aspire to sovereignty per se. Strictly speaking, they already have sovereignty by virtue of original occupancy, having never surrendered their sovereignty by explicit agreement. The fact that Aboriginal peoples are sovereign for purposes of entitlement or engagement would imply only the creation of appropriate structures for its practical expression.

2. Relations Repair: Aboriginal peoples are not looking to separate or become independent. Except for a few ideologues, appeals to sovereignty are largely about establishing relationships of relative yet relational autonomy (Young 1990; Scott 1996). Reference to sovereignty is not about a boundary to defend but a set of relationships to be nurtured. In acknowledging that "we are all here to stay," as former Chief Justice Antonio Lamer once observed, is there any other option except to nurture a partnership?

3. Rightsholders: Aboriginal peoples are neither a problem to be solved nor a need to be met. They are societies with an inherent right to Aboriginal models of self-determining autonomy. Nor should they be considered a competitor to be jousted, but rather a partner with whom to work through differences in a spirit of partnership.

4. Political Communities: Acceptance of Aboriginal peoples as a fundamentally autonomous political communities is critical in crafting a constructive engagement. Unlike ethnic and immigrant minorities who are looking to settle down, fit in, and move up within the existing social and political framework, Aboriginal peoples must be seen as wanting to "get out" of political arrangements that deny, exclude, or oppress.

5. Power-sharing is pivotal in advancing co-operative engagement and coexistence. Deeply divided societies that have attained some degree of stability endorse a level of governance that involves a sharing of power that is constitutionally or statutorily entrenched (Linden 1994). Precise arrangements for rearranging power distributions are varied, of course, but predicated on the principle of giving and sharing rather than taking and monopolizing.

6. Living Together Separately: Concerns over jurisdiction cannot be taken lightly. Control and power must be allocated along clear lines by carefully calibrating what is mine, what is yours, and what is ours. In advocating a problem-solving exercise in which

both sides have a stake in the outcome, parties must enter into negotiations not on the basis of jurisprudence but on the grounds of justice, not by cutting deals but by formulating a clear vision, and not by litigating but by listening.

7. Self-determination vs. state determination: The principle of Aboriginal self-determining autonomy over jurisdictions related to land, identity, and political voice is key. But government-imposed models of self-determination for self-sufficiency may reinforce the very colonialisms Aboriginal peoples are seeking to abolish. What is required are challenges to the rules upon which governance is based, rather than simple changes to the conventions that refer to those rules.

8. Belonging as Citizenship: Innovative patterns of belonging such as dual citizenship are critical when two peoples share the same political and territorial space but neither is willing to be dominated by the other (Oberschall 2000). Aboriginal proposals for belonging to society are anchored in primary affiliation with the group rather than as individual citizens, thus implying that Aboriginal peoples can belong differently to Canada (through group membership rather than as individual citizens) without necessarily rejecting citizenship or loyalty.

9. Partnership: Placing partnership at the centre of a relationship entails a fundamental rethink in living together separately—not just in the narrow sense of consultation between a senior partner and a junior partner, but within the framework of two peoples sharing the land as co-equals.

10. Aboriginal Difference: Constructive engagements are anchored in the notion that Aboriginal difference must be taken seriously. A settler constitutional order tends to endorse a pretend pluralism that has had a controlling effect in distorting Aboriginal peoples–state relations. Aboriginal peoples *are* different because of their constitutional status, and these differences must be incorporated as a basis for recognition, reward, and relationships.

11. Conciliation at the Centre of Relations Repair: An expression of regret for the deplorable acts of a colonial past is not meant to humiliate, embarrass, or extract reparations. A commitment to reconciliation is meant to exorcise the pain and humiliation endured by Aboriginal peoples. The atonement is intended to create the basis for the healing and restoration of Aboriginal pride and dignity (Maaka and Fleras 2005).

In sum: An adherence to constructive engagement transcends the legalistic (abstract rights) or restitutional (reparations)—however important these concerns are in identity-building and resource mobilization. Increasing reliance on contractual relations for sorting out ownership may have elevated litigation to a preferred level in resolving differences (Spoonley 1997). But this reliance on the legalities of rights and reparations tends to emphasize continuities with the past at the expense of the situational and evolving (Mulgan 1989). By contrast, a new social contract based on the constitutional principles of constructive engagement goes beyond restitution or cutting deals. Emphasis is focused on advancing a relationship on a principled basis by taking into account shifting social realities in sorting out who controls what in a spirit of give and take. Policy outcomes based on a post-colonial social contract cannot be viewed as final or authoritative any more than they can be preoccupied with "taking" or "finalizing," but must be situated in the context of "sharing" and "extending." That is, wisdom and justice must precede power, rather than vice versa (Cassidy 1994).

TOWARD A POST-COLONIAL CANADA

Canada is a test case for a grand notion—the notion that dissimilar people can share lands, resources, power, and dreams while respecting and sustaining their differences. (*A Word from the Commissioner's Highlights of the Report of the Royal Commission on Aboriginal Peoples* 1996:ix)

Canada is struggling to recast its relationship with Aboriginal peoples. Growing awareness of massive disparities has combined with mounting resentment and emergent political realities to improve Aboriginal outcomes by moving forward together (Canada 2004). The need for structural change is broadly acknowledged by Aboriginal and non-Aboriginal leaders alike. Nevertheless, approaches vary on how to hasten this transformation of Aboriginal peoples from colonized subjects to self-determining nations in ways that are workable, necessary, and just.

A sense of perspective is useful. A generation ago, most Canadians would have been ashamed to discover Aboriginal ancestry; at present, they are scouring their closets in hopes of discovering an ancestor they can claim as their own (Kulchyski 2003). Not long ago Canada believed it had moral authority and developmental progress on its side; now, however, it is Aboriginal peoples who claim the historical moment is in their grasp, because only they can hug the high moral ground that was once occupied by those who justified their superiority by reference to "white" or "might" (Cairns 2003). The distance travelled has been impressive. In the space of just over three decades, Aboriginal peoples have recoiled from the brink of dependency and disappearance to reclaim a pivotal role in the reconstruction of Canadian society. Such a reversal originated and gained legitimacy when the "costs" of excluding Aboriginal peoples from the national agenda proved unacceptably high in social, political, and economic terms (Fleras and Krahn 1992).

But while the rhetoric of transformation may be compelling, it may also be premature. Despite the collapse of the most egregious colonialist structures, Aboriginal moves to redefine their relationship with the people of Canada are fraught with ambiguity and deception because of competing paradigms, hidden agendas, and entrenched interests. The very notion of a nation-state continues to rest on principles that suppress Aboriginal demands and challenges, namely, one legal and sovereign political authority in a given territory with a single nationality and universal citizenship that acknowledges differences as having equal weight before the law. (McRoberts 2003; Harty and Murphy 2005). Not surprisingly, political authorities continue to call the shots by endorsing the foundational principles of a settler constitutional order, while Aboriginal values and aspirations are overwhelmed by the priorities and constraints of the majority "whitestream" (Denis 1996). The fundamental objective of Aboriginal affairs policy agendas—to eliminate the Aboriginal "problem" by fostering European-style self-sufficiency—has barely budged with the passage of time (Ponting 1986). Only the means have changed, with crude assimilationist strategies conceding ground to more sophisticated channels that not only co-opt Aboriginal discourses for self-serving purposes but also have the effect of advancing a corporatist agenda.

Recent developments are pointing to yet another paradigm shift in Aboriginal peoples–Canada relations. A proposed paradigm shift is gathering momentum, partly in response to escalating Aboriginal pressure, partly to deflect a growing crisis in state legitimacy. But rather than a paradigm shift, what we have is a paradigm "muddle." On one side are the "old rules of the game," many of which appear to be drawing to a close, but not without a struggle (Borrows and Rotman 1997:31). On the other, a new post-colonial paradigm lacks the critical mass of support to take hold. Proposals for change are imbued with an air of ambivalence as colonialist paradigms grind up against post-colonizing realities, as the old collides with the new without displacing the other. Metaphors borrowed from plate tectonics and continental drift are helpful in visualizing the optics, as perspectives slide into each other, past each other, around each other, and over or under each other. Each of the "plates" tends to "talk past the other" by using the same words but speaking a different language. Neither paradigm is strong enough to dislodge its conceptual counterpart, with the result that the renewal process is pervaded by discordant amalgams of the progressive with the regressive. Such a state of tension and conflict is likely to persist until such time as conventional thinking accepts a unifying "vision" of Canada as a multi-layered partnership of two founding peoples—Aboriginal and non-Aboriginal (French and English colonizers)—each sovereign in its own right yet sharing in the sovereignty of post-colonial Canada.

DEBATE REVISITED	Living Together Separately: Inclusiveness or Apartheid?

How potent are the powers and authority of the Nisga'a nation? Critics tend to overestimate the aura attributed to the Nisga'a. True, Nisga'a self-governing powers may be constitutionally protected—a status that no municipality can claim at present. Nor are Nisga'a laws subject to override except by mutual agreement with federal and provincial authorities (Walkom 1998). The Nisga'a government will have exclusive jurisdiction in matters related to language and culture in addition to citizenship and property, even when these conflict with federal/provincial laws.

Yet, appearances are deceiving. Nisga'a powers are circumscribed and considerably less than those implied by federal recognition of Canada's First Nations as "peoples" with an "inherent right to self-government." These powers are restricted to those of a super-municipality, including authority over policing (but not the federal *Criminal Code*), education, taxes, and community services, with a few provincial bits thrown in for good measure. The *Canadian Charter of Rights and Freedoms* still applies; so do federal and provincial laws, although any conflicts or inconsistency will have to take

into account Nisga'a sovereignty. Health, education, and child welfare services must meet provincial standards. In short, Nisga'a governance will reflect a "concurrent jurisdiction"—that is, shared and overlapping jurisdictions rather than watertight compartments—as both Nisga'a laws as well as federal and provincial jurisdiction will continue to apply to communities, citizens, and lands (Gosnell 2000).

It is true that voting in Nisga'a will be restricted to Nisga'a citizens. According to critics, a government based on race is wrong and contrary to Canada's territorially based federal system where individual voting rights are acquired by residence; that is, if you live in Toronto, you can vote in Toronto (Fiss 2004b). In contrast, rights in the Nisga'a nation are based on aboriginality, with the result that only the Nisga'a can claim rights of citizenship or vote for government. But, Nisga'a will not be the only jurisdiction in Canada to restrict voting rights. The proposed Tlicho Land Claim and Self Government Act is also restrictive in who can hold office (Ivison 2004). And nearly 2600 reserves across Canada also restrict voting to membership in one of 608 bands.

Besides, what is the point of self-government if "others" can vote and undermine the very point of self-rule (Peach 2005)?

Even more disconcerting is critics' penchant for "racializing" the Nisga'a pact. Nisga'a is not about racially separate development or race-based governments in the mould of apartheid (Fiss 2004a, b). Apartheid was forcibly imposed on South African blacks to exclude, deny, and exploit. By contrast Nisga'a is about *Aboriginal rights* rather than entitlements by race, including the right of Aboriginal peoples to construct self-governing models because of their constitutional status and treaty settlements (Fontaine 2005). It is about the rights of six generations of Nisga'a who, since the late nineteenth century, have tried to establish Aboriginal title to ancestral land that had never been surrendered to European powers (Dufraiment 2002). It is about shifting the yardsticks for advancing Canada-building—away from a monolithic project with a singular culture and identity to engaging constructively as a basis for living together separately (see also Saul 2003).

Canada is widely renowned as a country constructed around compromises. The Nisga'a settlement is but another compromise in crafting an innovative political order in which each level of government—federal, provincial, and Aboriginal—is sovereign in its own right, yet shares in the sovereignty of Canada as a whole by way of multiple and interlocking jurisdictions. A settlement of such magnitude is not intended to be divisive or racial. The objective is to find some common grounds for constructive re-engagement between founding peoples. The challenge is formidable: How exactly to construct a balance that reconciles Aboriginal rights to self-determining autonomy with the legitimate claims of the Crown to govern and regulate? How to reconcile seemingly valid but mutually exclusive claims without eroding a commitment to Canada? Is it possible to construct future Nisga'a-like arrangements that are safe for Canada yet safe from Canada? Answers to these postcolonial conundrums rarely elicit agreement. But then nobody said that living together separately would be easy.

CHAPTER HIGHLIGHTS

- Canadians may perceive Aboriginal peoples as a "social problem" or as having problems in need of solution through government intervention. Yet, the depressed social and economic conditions that confront many Aboriginal communities may be a Canada problem insofar as Aboriginal peoples were forcibly incorporated into a system that continues to deny, exclude, or exploit.

- Aboriginal policy has evolved through several stages: reciprocity, assimilation, integration, devolution, and conditional autonomy. Perceptions of Aboriginal peoples as allies, children, citizens, minorities, and peoples appear to coincide with this evolution.

- Aboriginal resistance has shifted from a focus on cultural survival and formal equality to a highly politicized demand for radical renewal based on recognition of Aboriginal title and treaty rights, Aboriginal models of self-determining autonomy at self-government levels, and taking Aboriginal difference seriously.

- Efforts to decolonize the Aboriginal agenda are widely anticipated as necessary and overdue; nevertheless, proposals for reconstitutionalizing the foundational principles of Aboriginal peoples–state relations must contend with political and bureaucratic interests, both of which resist fundamental change for fear of destabilizing the status quo.

- The concept of constructive engagement provides an ideal model for establishing a new set of foundational principles to govern Aboriginal peoples–Canada relations. Still, it remains to be seen if creation of a more positive relationship for remaking Canada can overcome the foundational planks of a colonial constitutional order.

KEY TERMS

Aboriginal ("indigenous") rights
aboriginality
Aboriginal peoples
Aboriginal self-governance
Aboriginal title
comprehensive land claims
conditional autonomy
constitutional order
constructive engagement
devolution

entitlement
governance
nations within
postcolonial social contract
self-determination
self-government
specific treaty claims
treaties
White Paper

REVIEW QUESTIONS

1. Outline the current demands of the Aboriginal peoples with respect to improving their relational status in Canadian society. How do Aboriginal demands compare with the solutions proposed by the federal government?

2. Demonstrate how and why the assimilationists differ from the autonomists in defining and solving the so-called "Indian problem."

3. The concept of the "nations within" is slowly gaining acceptance in Canada as the basis for a new social contract for living together separately. What is meant by this concept? How is it justified? What does it propose to accomplish? How does it differ from government proposals for remaking Canada?

4. Briefly discuss the shifts in Canada's Aboriginal policy, and how these shifts have contributed to the muddles in Aboriginal peoples–government relations.

5. How do the foundational principles of constructive engagement provide a principled approach in creating a post-colonial contract for living together separately?

6. To borrow a phrase from Charles Dickens, for Aboriginal peoples in Canada, this is both the best of times and the worst of times. Indicate how this applies to the current status of Aboriginal peoples–Canada relations.

LINKS AND RECOMMENDATIONS

Films

Dances with Wolves—The film that really disrupted conventional stereotypes of Native Americans and the American Cavalry during the taming of the Wild West.

Once Were Warriors—A gritty and disturbing look at inner city life among the indigenous peoples of New Zealand. To offset the harshness, try *Whale Rider,* which is also New Zealand–based but addresses some of the challenges confronting rural Maori as they move into the twenty-first century.

Two Worlds Colliding—An interesting National Film Board study of the crisis that happened in Saskatoon when frozen Aboriginal bodies were discovered on the outskirts of the city, raising the possibility that police services may have been responsible for the deaths.

Books

Poison Stronger Than Love by Anastasia Shkilnyk, 1985, Yale University Press. An unflinching indictment of the destruction inflicted by well-meaning government initiatives on an Aboriginal community in Northern Ontario—in the process giving credence to the expression "the banality of evil."

"Urgent Need, Serious Opportunity: Towards a New Social Model for Canada's Aboriginal Peoples," by Frances Abele, *Canadian Policy Research Networks, Research Report F/39*. April 2004. A useful guide to the current and emerging status of Aboriginal peoples in Canada.

The Politics of Indigeneity by Roger Maaka and Augie Fleras. 2005. Otago University Press. Provides an overview of indigenous peoples politics by comparing the politics of indigeneity in Canada and New Zealand.

Magazines

Windspeaker. Monthly newspaper highly recommended as a source of information about Aboriginal peoples from an Aboriginal perspective.

Websites

Indian Affairs and Northern Development. A useful site providing a government-based overview of its relationships and responsibilities with the First Nations.
   www.inac.gc.ca

Assembly of First Nations. A perspective from a status Indian viewpoint.
   www.afn.ca

Congress of Aboriginal Peoples. Represents the view of off-reserve and Métis peoples.
   www.abo-peoples.org

Native Women's Association. Aboriginal women's perspectives are emphasized.
   www.nwac-hq.org

Chapter

THE QUEBEC QUESTION, A CANADA QUANDARY

8

DEBATE   Official Bilingualism: Society-Building or Yet More Solitude?

Canada can be described as officially bilingual, with national language policies that are simultaneously a source of unity and disunity, of pride and dismay. Problems in communication and cohesion can be expected in a country of two major languages, with over three-quarters of the population speaking one language and one-quarter the other. The problem is compounded by a geographic divide. Nearly 4 million Quebec francophones are largely monolingual. If the island of Montreal is excluded, the vast majority of Quebecers do not speak English. English Canadians are no less monolingual, including about 90 percent of those outside the National Capital Region, New Brunswick, and the Nickle Belt in Ontario. Such a communication breakdown not only fosters the "solitudes within," but also enhances a need for bridging devices if we hope to cobble together a Canada.

Some readers believe that Canada is the world's only officially bilingual country. Others might think that all language dualities are modelled after Canada. Both are wrong because bilingualism itself comes in different configurations. Under **individual bilingualism**, each person is expected to become proficient in two or more languages of the country. Minorities in many countries have little choice but to learn the dominant language besides their native tongue if they hope to prosper. **Territorial bilingualism** is another option; it reflects a division of language use along geographical lines. For example, Belgium and Switzerland are divided into regions where an official language predominates (Linden 1994). Finally, there is **institutional**

bilingualism that focuses on incorporating official languages at organizational levels, including the use of dual language workplaces and delivery of services.

All three models of bilingualism are found in Canada. There exists a territorial bilingualism, namely, the division of Canada into two language heartlands—Quebec and the rest of Canada—with a limited number of bilingual districts adjacent to Quebec, such as the National Capital Region (Ottawa) and New Brunswick. Individual bilingualism also exists in Canada. Nearly 18 percent of the total population in the 2001 Census possesses a degree of fluency in both languages, up from 13 percent in 1971, including 38 percent of the residents in Quebec, 33 percent in New Brunswick, and 12 percent in Ontario. Officially, however, Canada endorses an institutional bilingualism: Passage of the *Official Languages Act* (1969/1988) acknowledged the equal and official status of French and English as languages of communication in federal institutions across the country. How, then, does the theory stack up to reality? And does it make a difference?

Canada's experiment with federal bilingualism began in the 1960s (Annual Report 2005). Efforts to strengthen French language rights in exchange for social peace culminated in a quintessential Canadian compromise: recognition of the right of federal public servants in 1966 to conduct business in either French or English. In acknowledging the conclusions of the Royal Commission on Biculturalism and Bilingualism, the passage of the *Official Languages Act* in 1969 formalized linguistic duality as a fundamental principle of Canadian society. Provisions of the Act acknowledged the presence and legitimacy of both French and English as Canada's official languages. The courts and Parliament were designated as bilingual, in addition to the central offices of all federal government institutions. Bilingualism was expressed in federal documents, signs in national parks, parliamentary proceedings, court cases, and federally chartered passenger vehicles from Air Canada planes to shuttle buses at Point Pelee National Park.

The *Official Languages Act* of 1988 further expanded Canada's language rights. The 1988 Act (1) confirmed the right of Canadians to use French or English as the language of work in federal organizations in designated bilingual regions (viz., the National Capital Region, Montreal, New Brunswick, and parts of the Gaspé, Eastern Townships, and Ontario); (2) confirmed the right to receive federal services in either language at designated federal institutions; (3) granted the protection of official language minority rights (English in Quebec, French outside of Quebec) in areas where numbers warranted or demand was significant; and (4) granted equal opportunities for French and English speakers in the public service (at present, 25 percent of positions excluding those institutions where the Treasury Board is not an employer) (Annual Report 2005). The Act also strengthened official language minority control over education and school boards in contexts where they constitute a viable population. Parents who speak one of the official languages have a right to educate children in either language, provided, of course, both numbers and demand suffice (Annual Report 2004).

Canada is officially bilingual in name and commitment. Polls routinely indicate that Canadians are supportive of bilingualism, since ". . . living in a country with two official languages is one of the things that really defines what it means to be a Canadian" (cited in Annual Report, 2004:16). But despite a sea-to-sea commitment, shortcomings are clearly evident. The reality of bilingualism is restricted to (1) federal institutions designated as bilingual,

(2) communities with a high proportion of French-speaking residents such as Eastern and Northern Ontario, (3) the delivery of some essential provincial services, and (4) select schoolchildren in larger urban centres. The unveiling of the government's Action Plan for Official Languages in 2003 also confirmed the need for more official languages funding and promotion to offset (1) recent government cutbacks in spending ($750 million in extra funding was promised), (2) the offloading of government responsibility to provinces and municipalities, and (3) a diminishing of political vision and leadership in this area (Annual Report 2005). And, yet, federal services continue to fumble their language responsibilities. With a network of 7000 offices across Canada, Canada Post is the institution that deals most often with the Canadian public. Nevertheless, a sample of designated bilingual offices exposed glaring deficiencies in staffing, questionable services in person or by telephone, and the entrenchment of an inward-looking organizational culture that compels citizens to adapt to the bureaucracy rather than vice versa (Annual Report 2004).

At the provincial level, only the province of New Brunswick is officially bilingual. Even here, hostilities have erupted between French-speaking Acadians, who want to expand French language services, and the English-speaking majority who prefer the status quo. Language policies in the Territories also capture the spirit of the *Official Languages Act*. The Northwest Territories has acknowledged French and English as official languages, in addition to six Aboriginal languages, for a total of eight official languages. Nunavut is home to three official languages—English, French, and Inuktitut. Outside of New Brunswick and Quebec, English remains the de facto language of communication in the delivery of service, commerce,

administration, and provincial court activities, including British Columbia and Newfoundland/Labrador, neither of which have laws or policies regarding official languages. The English-speaking provinces have wavered in their commitment to implementing minimal concessions to **official language minorities**, despite constitutional guarantees to that effect (Annual Report 2005). For example, Ontario provides limited French language services. Passage of the *French Language Services Act* (Bill 8) in 1986 enshrined the delivery of French language services when warranted by numbers (viz., where the French-speaking population stands at 5000, or represents 10 percent of the population). Yet, Ontario refuses to formally guarantee bilingual rights across the province, citing economic (too costly), political (too undemocratic), cultural (too confusing), and social (too divisive) factors. Finally, Quebec, too, is officially unilingual. With the passage of the ***French Language Charter*** (Bill 101) in 1977, French became the primary language of commerce, education, and public communication. Nevertheless, Quebec's anglophones are guaranteed access to English language services in health, universities, and education—an equivalent that is rarely extended to francophones in other provinces (Seguin 2001).

How, then, to assess **official bilingualism**—as a success or failure? As benefit or cost? Given the difficulties in defining the criteria for assessment, answers to these questions will be politically charged. On the one hand, there is much that is endearing about official bilingualism. A 2004 UN Development Programme Report cited the global potential of Canada's unique federalism as a model for protecting minority language rights. On the other hand, debates over the coexistence of federal and Quebec language policies have infuriated and divided the country as few other issues have. Quebecers dismiss official bilingualism as a plot of appeasement, bereft of any moral legitimacy or of any relevance to them. English Canadians appear equally unhappy over Canada's language duality because of the inherent inconvenience and costs. Underlying this impasse is a clash of principles: Whereas an official bilingualism reinforces the language rights of individuals to choose, a right many English-speaking Canadians can readily identify with, Quebec's French-only policies advance the collective language rights of a (threatened) community who comprise the majority in a given territory. The courts have acknowledged the inherent conflict between these competing rights. Quebec may have a right to protect French, even with unorthodox methods to achieve this goal, the courts have ruled, but must do so in compliance with the Charter's individual equality rights (Annual Report 2005). How, then, are these compromises working out?

INTRODUCTION: TWO SOLITUDES OR SCORPIONS IN A BOTTLE?

Canada is widely regarded as one of the world's best places to live. According to a United Nations quality of life ranking, Canada's lofty position is secured by a combination of tangible measures such as income and less quantifiable dimensions such as tolerance and equal opportunity. Yet, for all its resources and resourcefulness, Canada stands in danger of splintering along ethnic fault lines. Canada is not alone in this predicament. Around the world, the forces of ethnicity (as well as language, region, and religion) pose a greater threat to territorial **sovereignty** than does the danger of external invasion (Taras and Ganguly 2002). Ethnic upheavals from within have displaced traditional cross-border wars involving the forcible capture of coveted territory. Nor is there any evidence that ethnic conflicts diminish when countries modernize or become globally connected. No matter how much effort is expended in securing a common citizenship, traditional loyalties and reassuring identities rarely vanish, while multicultural add-ons or inclusive initiatives never seem to satisfy ethnic activists. The potential for conflict is further sharpened in those contexts where "national" minorities have been forcibly incorporated into a society perceived as non-responsive to their collective concerns.

The proliferation of ethnic-based conflicts may well pose a definitive challenge for the twenty-first century. Nevertheless, existing states appear seemingly immobilized by this challenge because many are structurally wired for fostering uniformity and consensus rather than for taking ethnicity seriously. But political indifference or state resistance to minority demands may well have the opposite effect of intensifying ethnic conflicts. As Walker Connor (2000) points out:

> Unfortunately, central authorities have tended to perceive any demand for a significant increase in autonomy as tantamount to, or an important step toward, secession. Governments have been inclined to guard their prerogatives zealously . . . In doing so, they often further the very result that they ostensibly wish to avoid, for there is an inverse relation between a government's willingness to grant meaningful autonomy and the level of separatist sentiment.

The challenges of living together with differences are sharply grounded in Canada. French–English relations (or, more accurately, French- and English-speaking relations) have coexisted uneasily since 1841, when Upper and Lower Canada combined into an incipient nation-state, a tinderbox aptly described by Lord Durham as the equivalent of "two nations warring in the bosom of a single state." Interaction since then has been captured by a series of metaphors—from stretches of sullen isolation (two solitudes) to periods of convulsive social change (the Quiet Revolution), with occasional bursts of violence in between (two scorpions in a bottle). In between are positions of indifference or incomprehension, a stance stunningly captured by Alice Simard, mother of former Quebec Premier Lucien Bouchard, when she admitted: "I've never met an English-speaking Canadian, but I'm sure they're as nice as any other foreigner" (cited in *Report on Business*, January 1996). She is hardly alone in her solitude. Many Canadians cannot even communicate with each other outside of a bilingual belt that runs from Longlac to Ottawa to Montreal to Sherbrooke to Moncton. Both acrimonious failures and bitter debates have contributed to an impasse so profound and defiantly deep that bridging the Quebec–Canada divide may prove impossible (Gibbins and Laforest 1998).

Points of conflict are varied and numerous. They range in scope from pitched language battles to twisted debates over collective versus individual rights, with plain old provincial–federal squabbling in between. But the sharpest clashes tend to coalesce around Quebec's sovereign aspirations as a "nation" or "peoples." The Québécois constitute a powerful political community (a **distinct society**) who claim sovereignty by virtue of a common history, a collective vision, shared grievances, and a distinctiveness because of traditional ancestry. Even if not explicitly secessionist, the language of sovereignty typically elevates nationhood as the primary goal. Participation within Canada is acceptable, but often conditional and contingent on advancing Quebec's interests (Kymlicka 1998). Independence may not be the preferred option under these conflicting circumstances, except as a benchmark by which other options are measured. Failure to foster a *rapprochement* between these conflicting perspectives has propelled Canada perilously close to the brink (see *Economist,* 3 December 2005). Moreover, moves to repair the rift are plodding along without much passion or sense of urgency, despite the aftershocks of the October 1995 referendum with its razor-thin endorsement of the status quo (see Jedwab 2005a).

The antagonism appears to be mutual: Quebecers perceive English-speaking Canada as a remote, even unfriendly place, with its own set of priorities and preoccupations, few of which apply to Quebec (Gagnon 1996; Conlogue 1997). English-speaking Canadians are also perceived as callously insensitive to Quebec's language aspirations—in part because they are seen as lacking a distinct cultural identity. While Québécois know who they are, according to this line of argument, English-speaking Canadians are dismissed as bereft of a common culture, except in opposition to something else, thus inhibiting their receptivity to Quebec's differences. Worse still, it is argued, English Canadians do not even constitute a people in the sociological sense, but a site of convenience, in effect relinquishing any moral authority to deny "real peoples" the right to sovereignty (see McRoberts 1998; Seguin 1998). Or in the words of the former premier of Quebec, Lucien Bouchard, "Canada is divisible because Canada is not a real country. There are two people, two nations, two territories. And this one is ours."

English-speaking Canadians are no less dismissive of Quebec's claims and criticisms. Quebecers are dismissed as narrow-minded ideologues whose rabid jingoism represses as it excludes. The sometimes absurd zeal of Quebec's language police confirms a suspicion that French is wielded as a weapon to slay the English rather than a resource to protect. English Canada interprets Quebec's demands for more power and autonomy as little more than political blackmail and economic extortion (see Donolo and Gregg 2005). *Globe and Mail* columnist Jan Wong (1998:A29) conveys a sense of this entitlement:

> Quebecers don't really want to separate. They just want to keep getting pregnant so they'll receive a bigger welfare cheque from the rest of Canada . . . Quebec is like a madman who keeps taking himself hostage. Every year or so he whips out a gun and shouts, Give me all your money or I'll shoot myself!

Not surprisingly, the demonization of Quebec's claims to nationhood ("distinct society") has contributed to a siege (or fortress) mentality that boxes Quebecers into a perpetual defensive stance (Seguin 2001).

The conclusion seems inescapable: Both sectors are locked into seemingly unflattering images of the other as racist and rigid. Each regards its counterpart as the "problem" because of divergent models of Canada and Quebec's place within the constitutional order (McRoberts 1997). English Canadians tend to support a Trudeau-inspired model of Canada, with its focus on a strong central government, equality of provinces with no special status for Quebec, a commitment to multiculturalism and official bilingualism, and primacy of individual rights (**Canada as a contract**). Such a model has less currency in Quebec, where a bicultural commitment prevails, including a strengthened cultural homeland, protection for French, assimilation of immigrants, and special arrangements for Quebec within a more flexible federalism (**Canada as a compact**). These conflicting models respond differently to the question "What is Canada for?" For English Canadians, a kind of liberal universalism where everyone is equal before the law must prevail, and for the Québécois, the focus is on a communitarian liberalism that sees Canada as a space for Quebec to flourish (Taylor 1993; Kernerman 2005). A deepening of the divide creates yet more confusion: English-speaking Canadians cannot understand why Quebec "wants out"; hardline Quebecers can't comprehend why anyone would force them to "stay in."

This chapter focuses on the Quebec question against the backdrop of a Canada quandary. Quebec may want to stay in Canada, but on its own constitutional terms, while English Canada wants to dictate the terms of the staying, in effect exposing deficiencies in Canada's federalism as grounds for *rapprochment* (see Gagnon 2003). The chapter examines the constitutional crisis that imperils Canada's national unity by exploring the politics of French–English relations in Canada. The politics of bilingualism and bi-nationalism are framed within the broader context of Canadian federalism on the one side, the process of Canada-building on another, and the competing nationalisms of Quebec and Quebec's Aboriginal peoples on yet another. Prospects for arriving at a mutually satisfactory solution remain elusive because of radically different visions for defining Quebec's place within the constitutional framework. The emergent notion of a "**sovereignty without secession**" as a preferred constitutional option in redefining French–English relations is analyzed in light of "what Quebec wants" and "what English Canada is willing to concede." Signs are pointing to the inevitability of constitutional reform on grounds that a reinvention of a federal Canada along asymmetrical lines may be this country's only realistic hope for survival (see Ignatieff 2005).

A note on terminology: The chapter addresses the relationship of French-speaking Canadians in Quebec (the Québécois or Quebecers) with the English-speaking Canadians who live in the rest of Canada but are symbolically centred in Canada's capital of Ottawa. Within Quebec itself there are additional solitudes, such as Québécois of "old stock" on one side, anglophones on the other, and allophones (neither French nor English) on still another. Nearly one million racialized minorities who live in Montreal find themselves outside the Québécois mainstream despite efforts by the government toward inclusiveness. The nearly 2 million French-speaking persons outside of Quebec are no less isolated, including the 500 000 Franco-Ontarians and 300 000 Acadians in New Brunswick who occupy a different legal status (official language minorities) from the Québécois. A reluctance by Quebec to endorse the struggles of francophone communities attests to divergences of outlook and aspirations.

The term "English-speaking" also requires some clarification. Rather than a conventional ethnic group with a shared history and attributes, this category provides a label of convenience to describe those Canadians who reside primarily outside Quebec, rely on English as the primary language of communication, and generally subscribe to the Charter principles and principles of an official Multiculturalism. English-language minorities who live in Quebec are often called anglophones. Allophone is the term for those immigrants and refugees in Quebec whose first language is neither French nor English. Finally, references to English–French relations (or Ottawa–Quebec relations or Quebec–Canada relations) are employed as a proxy in referencing the relationship between French-speaking Quebec and English-speaking Canada.

QUEBEC: PROVINCE OR PEOPLES?

Quebec is historically a part of Canada's federalist system. But many of Canada's constitutional conundrums reflect competing views of federalism (Kymlicka 1998). The *Constitution Act* (formerly known as the *BNA Act*) of 1867 established federalism as a framework for balancing conflicting interests. On one side were those who wanted a centralized system as a bulwark against American might; on the other side were proponents of a decentralized arrangement who acknowledged the fundamental duality of two peoples. The political compromise established a federal system that folded Quebec's linguistic, legal, and social distinctions into the constitutional fabric, in effect confirming Quebec's status in Confederation without undue interference from Ottawa, except in cases involving (inter)national concerns (Burgess 1996). This arrangement also set the stage for one of Canada's longest running debates: How much unity does Canada really need? How much diversity can it handle (Kernerman 2005)?

The seemingly opposed forces of centralization vs. decentralization have coexisted uneasily in Canada. Much of the tension reflects different interpretations of federalism as it applies to Quebec (Harrison and Friesen 2004). Is the federal system properly envisaged as a "**contract**" between central authorities and the provinces? According to this "federalist" interpretation, Quebec is a province like the others, with no special status or privileges. Or is Canada better seen as a "**compact**" between the French and English? Quebec's status is then akin to a nationhood or peoples rather than a province. Or should the relationship be reframed as a "**coalition**" involving an alliance that incorporates Aboriginal peoples alongside both the French and English? Under a tri-national model of Canada, Quebec is but one of several national communities within a multinational arrangement. The interplay of these competing perspectives—contract, compact, and coalition—animates the dynamics that propel and perplex French–English relations.

Canada as Contract

A contract model envisions Canada as a federalist system of ten equal provinces under a central authority in Ottawa. A contract exists between the provinces (of which Quebec is one) and the federal government. The provinces (including Quebec) as well as the central authority in Ottawa are sovereign within their own jurisdiction as set out in the *Constitution Act* of 1867. Neither can usurp the authority or powers of the other as also specified. Not surprisingly, the defining narrative behind Canadian history can be interpreted as a struggle between the provinces and Ottawa over control of jurisdictions, with the balance of power in recent years tilting toward the provinces.

Two variations of the contract thesis exist. First, provinces are equal to each other (including Quebec), but subordinate in status and power vis-à-vis the federal government. The privileging of Ottawa as "first among equals" is justified because of its responsibility for advancing Canada's national interests both at home (comprehensive social programs) and abroad through diplomatic or military initiatives. Second, **federalism** is defined as an arrangement of relatively autonomous provinces that have freely entered into accord with the federal government. Under the terms of the agreement, Ottawa has assumed those duties and responsibilities that go beyond the interests and capacities of the provinces. As a result of this freely agreed-upon division of power, all 11 jurisdictions are equal in status, with an attendant alignment of power and authority as outlined by constitutional decree. Quebec is perceived as equivalent to the other provinces in legal status even if some minor concessions may be invoked to promote Quebec's distinctiveness in Canada (in The Calgary Declaration, 1997, cited in Kernerman 2005:46).

Canada as Compact

A second vision interprets **Canada as a compact** between English-speaking and French-speaking Canadians. The "two founding nations" see federalism as a pact between the French and English, a pact that was generally endorsed by English political elites under the prime ministership of Lester B. Pearson (Harty and Murphy 2005). This view is also strongly endorsed by the Québécois, who reject definitions of themselves as ethnic minorities or as mainstream Canadians who happen to speak French but live in Quebec. Even the notion of Quebec as a province in the conventional sense is dismissed. Proposed instead is a vision of Quebec as a peoples or a "distinct society" with inherent rights to nationhood by virtue of popular sovereignty. Charles Taylor captures this ethos:

> ... Quebec is not a province like the others. As a jurisdiction at the heart of the French zone in convergence, it has responsibilities and challenges unlike those of other provinces ... This is not to say that each and every province is not also different from others in its own way. But only Quebec is different in this way: that it sustains a society converging on French within a continent in which English massively predominates. (Cited in Chambers 1996)

According to the compact thesis, Canada is not a union of one central authority with 10 equal provinces, including Quebec. Yes, there should be equality among provinces, but Quebec is fundamentally different from the others because its province-hood is infused by its status as a nation, in effect requiring moves toward a flexible (or asymmetrical) federalism (Harty and Murphy 2005). Accordingly, Canada represents a compact, or "covenant," between the French and English, one that is rooted in constitutional law and long-standing political agreement. Quebec entered into Confederation with assurances that it would retain its status as a nation and entitlements as a **charter member**. Quebecers continue to see themselves as a "peoples" with a shared language, culture, and homeland rather than another province with equal rights or an ethnic group whose differences are charming but irrelevant. They claim to constitute a "nation" as well, not only deserving of recognition of their differences but also entitled to those self-governing powers equivalent to that of English Canada (Harty and Murphy 2005). Predictably, then, the language of nationhood remains critical in advancing

Quebec's interests because (1) it provides a standing and legitimacy within the international community, (2) it distinguishes Quebec's claims from those of ethnic minorities, (3) it imparts a sense of history and authenticity to Quebec's demands, and (4) it equalizes the bargaining power between Quebec and Ottawa (Kymlicka 1998).

Canada as Coalition

A new and more inclusive vision of Canada is slowly gaining ground. According to this line of rethinking, Canada is neither a contract between a centre and the provinces nor an exclusive compact between Ottawa and the French. Instead, Canada consists of a coalition comprising a tri-national partnership of the French, the English, and Aboriginal peoples, each of whom is sovereign in its own right yet sharing in the sovereignty of Canada as a whole (Kymlicka 2001; Royal Commission on Aboriginal Affairs 1996). As a result, Canada is envisaged as a community of distinct collectivities who see themselves as territorially grounded "nations" and as culturally specific "peoples," with claims to nationhood and meaningful autonomy.

To be sure, a radical restructuring of Canada along the lines of a three-nations state has yet to be formulated (McRoberts 2001). At minimum, this coalition will require a highly decentralized framework for three national communities to exist in a loose but mutually productive alliance that acknowledges relative autonomy yet has mutual interdependence (Laforest 1998; Gibbins 1998). Under such a confederal arrangement, most of the functions performed by Ottawa would be transferred to Quebec and to Aboriginal nations, except for those pertaining to foreign affairs, currency, and defence. And while their jurisdiction would transcend that of a province, neither Quebec nor Aboriginal nations would be sovereign in the conventional sense of territorial autonomy. The key to making this work is predicated on the principle of severing the link between nation and state as a framework for national self-determination (Reynolds 1996; Kymlicka 1998). Peoples within a **multinational federation** do not need sovereign state status to flourish; rather, they require a meaningful self-determining autonomy over jurisdictions under their control. But cobbling together such a coalition may prove infuriating when interests diverge and jurisdictions blur—as the next case study reveals.

CASE STUDY	**Duelling Nationalisms/Intersecting Sovereignties**

As an ideology of national identity based on ethnicity, ethnic nationalisms threaten the territorial integrity of many societies (Lane and Ersson 2005). Central authorities fear the balkanizing effect of ethnic nationalisms, with their capacity to fractionalize the country like pieces of a jigsaw puzzle. But from the vantage point of ethnic nationalisms, a centralized system that craves control by standardizing differences is no less divisive. Quebecers may be politically divided, according to this line of thinking, but many are unhappy with federalist arrangements that deny or demean. But Quebecers are not alone in advocating a fundamental rethink of their sovereign status. The indigenous peoples of Quebec have also claimed sovereign rights as a fundamentally autonomous political community with controlling ownership over much of Quebec's land and resource base. These competing nationalisms clash over the question of who is more sovereign than the other. Whose sovereignty trumps the other in terms of priority and power? Or does the territorial integrity of a sovereign Canada supersede all counter claims? Can contending visions of sovereignty and nationalism be reconciled when two different peoples lay claim to the same territory (Turpel-Lafond 1996; also Shipler 2001)?

The peoples who compose the 60 000-strong First Nations in Quebec (including the Cree [Eeyouch], Inuit, Mohawk, Huron, and Algonquin) are adamant in rejecting Quebec's legal claim to their lands. They see themselves as no less sovereign as nations, with as much right to remain in Canada as Quebec has a right to secede. Aboriginal leaders also argue that up to 80 percent of Quebec remains under Aboriginal control because lands have never been ceded while other land claims have yet to be resolved through treaty settlements. The unsettled claims to land that Quebec had slated for resource development, combined with Cree claims that they have as much right to leave Quebec as Quebec has to leave Canada, have firmed Cree resolve to reject forcible confinement in an independent Quebec (Harty and Murphy 2005).

Clearly then, Quebec's Aboriginal peoples argue that if Canada can be divided, so can Quebec. If Quebec can unilaterally leave Canada, the Cree can leave Quebec if the original occupants exercise their indigenous right to remain in Canada (Grand Council of Crees 1995). The 1996 Cree document, *Sovereign Injustice*, reinforced their refusal to be unwillingly absorbed into an independent Quebec, arguing that their fiduciary relationship with the Crown cannot be extinguished or unilaterally transferred from Ottawa to Quebec. After all, the federal government is obligated to protect Aboriginal interests because of the special trustee relationship between Aboriginal peoples and the Crown. Any unilateral secession on the

part of Quebec would terminate constitutionally protected Aboriginal and treaty rights; hence any constitutional amendment on Quebec independence is contingent on Aboriginal consent. To think otherwise is both offensive and insulting. Aboriginal peoples are not simply assets and liabilities for negotiation as part of any divorce settlement, but a peoples with an inherent right to self-determination over where they belong and how they relate.

> The Cree people are neither cattle nor property, to be transferred from sovereignty to sovereignty or from master to master. We do not seek to prevent the Québécois from achieving their legitimate goals. But we will not permit them to do so on Cree territory and at the expense of our fundamental rights, including our right to self-determination. (Matthew Coon Come, Chief, James Bay Cree Nation, quoted in *This Magazine*, June 1994)

The Quebec government disagrees. Quebec's boundaries are inviolate, as far as the Québécois are concerned, and its territoriality is sovereign and beyond negotiation or division. As far as Quebec's leaders are concerned, Aboriginal rights to Quebec's land no longer exist. They were extinguished when the Canadian state transferred Ungava (the northern half of Quebec) to provincial jurisdiction at the turn of the twentieth century. The James Bay Agreement in 1975 also signed away Aboriginal "interests" (although a federal act in 1977 also said that the Cree and the Inuit would retain the "benefits and rights of all other [Canadian] citizens"). In short, Quebec's territorial integrity is not on the agenda, even with recent provincial initiatives to address, on a nation-to-nation basis, Aboriginal groups' concerns involving development- and revenue-sharing plans, comprehensive land claims, and initiatives toward self-government (Harty and Murphy 2005). Quebec's reaction is understandable: It can hardly afford to capitulate to Aboriginal peoples (and indirectly to Ottawa) for fear of losing those untapped reserves of surface and subsurface resources that would underscore Quebec's credibility as a sovereign society.

What does international law have to say about the legitimacy of these contested claims? Under international law, colonial peoples (those who live in a defined territory but under an overseas power) have the right to secede. But this right to independence and self-determination does not apply to either Quebec or the Cree—despite both having co-opted the language of nationhood in pressing forward their claims. Only "saltwater" (overseas) colonies have the right to unilaterally seek independence under international law. Such a restricted reading should come as no surprise. Both international law and the United Nations are constructed around the inviolability of sovereign states. There is little enthusiasm for compromising state interests by extending secessionary rights to Aboriginal peoples. Yes, there remains an obligation to respect minority rights, but within limits. Yes, a "people" may have the right to self-determining autonomy, but not the right to secession except under exceptional circumstances, and even then only through negotiation and compromise *(United Nations Declaration on the Rights of Persons Belonging to National or Ethnic, Religious and Linguistic Minorities).*

How, then, does federal Canada reconcile competing nationalisms within a single state? The inclusion of Aboriginal peoples as a founding peoples and a foundational member may complicate an already complex balancing act involving the two charter members. But the clash of these duelling nationalisms may yield new possibilities and alliances (Whitaker 1997). The federalist strategy rests with playing one group off the other in the hopes of neutralizing the combined impact. Ottawa sees the Cree as allies and a negotiating chip in bargaining with Quebec (Widdowson 2004), even if the government generally rejects any constitutional recognition of Aboriginal peoples as sovereign "peoples." But Canada may have no choice but to close ranks with Quebec because neither side wants to transfer vast tracts of disputed land over to Aboriginal ownership. In other words, dangers await whatever course of action is chosen by federal authorities. Siding with the Québécois against the Cree could spark an Aboriginal backlash that might make Oka seem a light-hearted romp. Yet, playing off one against the other might play into Québécois hands; after all, if the federal government can recognize Aboriginal peoples as "peoples" with an inherent right to self-government, why not Quebec?

Nevertheless, there is room for optimism. The politics of the past may no longer be applicable. Perceptions of Canada as two founding nations not only complicated the goals of compromise and accommodation, but also undermined the possibilities for coalition-building (Schmitt 1997). The potential for conflict increases when policy issues revolve around a zero-sum game of winners and losers. But the addition of another key player enhances the possibility of new patterns, including strategic alliances, policy tradeoffs, coalition shifts, and negotiated settlements. Or as Georg Simmel once observed in analyzing the power of numbers, there is a lot more you can do with three than with two. If several nations are competing for power, it becomes possible to compromise, deflect demands, co-opt allies, or conceal disadvantages by allowing each party to be part of a winning coalition on particular issues. How ironic: Quebec's First Nations' demands for autonomy may yet prove to be the buffer that blunts Quebec's separatist aspirations and secures national unity.

THE POLITICS OF BRINKMANSHIP: BLUFF OR REALITY?

French–English relations remain as brittle as ever. On one side, there are signs that debates from the past are just that. Young Québécois and new Quebecers seem less obsessed with issues such as a distinct society, the language wars, and more flexible federalism. According to Gilles Gagné, professor of sociology at Laval University, "Young people today have no use for the old arguments. They don't hate the English; they don't care about the latest fight with Ottawa," preferring, instead, to talk about the environment, the distribution of wealth, and issues of social justice in a global market economy (cited in Gordon 2005). To be sure, a lot of Quebecers both young and old may support independence in the abstract, but few have the appetite for yet another round of turmoil that convulsed Quebec during the referenda crises (*Economist,* 3 December 2005).

On the other side, however, the old guard persists. A politically charged environment is filled with suspicions and threats, but remarkably little dialogue, and what little there is may be more accurately described as a *dialogue des sourds* (of the deaf), as both sides continue to talk past each other in a spiral of barely concealed indifference (McRoberts 1997; Conlogue 1997). The unthinkable—the spectre of Quebec separating from Canada—is actively contemplated in the aftermath of the referendum that nearly dismembered Canada a decade ago. According to a Léger Marketing poll (cited in *Economist*, 3 December 2005), 55 percent of respondents would say "yes" in response to the question: "If a referendum was held today on the sovereignty of Quebec, and an offer of political and economic partnership with the rest of Canada, would you be for or against the sovereignty of Quebec?"—up from 40 percent in 2003.

Three scenarios can be projected: First, we are presiding over a turbulent period of profound social change from which Canada will emerge a strengthened and restructured union. Second, we are witnessing the transformation of Canada into a "Swiss cheese" federalism of relatively autonomous political entities without much centre or rationale. Third, it will be back to business once all the bluff and bluster subside. Of course, no one can predict which scenario will prevail, but questions remain: What, then, do the Québécois want; conversely, what is English-speaking Canada willing to concede in addressing these demands? Admittedly, we could just as easily reverse the question by asking what English-speaking Canadians want, and what the Québécois are doing to accommodate these demands, but space limitations are a factor. We should also remember that the intent behind the question "What does Quebec want?" can be misinterpreted. There is a bullying inference that Quebec has no reason to complain as it occupies an enviable position in Canadian society with a freedom to express what in other countries might be ruthlessly suppressed as treason. No such slight is intended here.

What Does Quebec Want?

It is unfair to imply that the Québécois have a uniform set of expectations and aspirations—at least no more so than English Canada can speak with one voice and vision. Like English-speaking Canada, Quebec too has been buffeted about because of challenges to its identity and legitimacy (Venne 2000; Harrison and Friesen 2004). Quebecers have lost those certainties and securities of a world defined by rigid Catholic-dominated social orders of religion and class. The shock waves created by the Quiet Revolution continue to reverberate, prompting many Québécois to cast about for a fixed reference point.

Quebec's sense of nationhood has continued to evolve. Quebec is moving from a defensive, inward-looking community to an increasingly open and cosmopolitan society (Salée and Coleman 1997). Its emergent nationalism is more liberal and tolerant than ever, and couched in secular and universalistic terms, without abandoning its commitment to French language, culture, and interests both in Canada and abroad (Harty and Murphy 2005). Unlike conventional ethnic nationalisms, Quebec's more civic-oriented nationalism reflects a willingness to integrate immigrants into society with full democratic citizenship rights. Such a transition is not without glitches. Debates in Quebec vacillate between democratic impulses for inclusiveness and universal citizenship on one side, and anxieties over losing its distinctiveness, identity, and political relevance on the other side. Quebecers' dual status, as a majority in their homeland but a minority within the broader North American context, may account for their ambivalence in seeking a new social contract yet demanding retention of the past, of refusing to assimilate yet fearing exclusion, and of identifying with Quebec without relinquishing attachment to Canadianness (Venne 2000). Rather than a sign of confusion or indecision, such ambiguity underpins Quebecers' perception of themselves as a majority in their homeland but a minority in Canada, and those who misread these mixed signals run the risk of miscalculating the nuances of Quebec nationalism.

Responses to what Quebec wants vary widely, ranging from those who endorse the status quo or moderate changes within the existing framework, to those who advocate a radical restructuring of Quebec's relationship with Canada, up to and including the point of outright secession (Gray 2001; Letournoux 2001). Polls conducted since the referendum of 1995 paint an inconclusive picture. A majority of Quebecers endorse some form of renewal within the present federalist system according to the 2005 edition of Portraits of Canada, the annual tracking poll conducted by the Centre for Research and Information Canada (CRIC). For example, when asked questions on constitutional choices for Quebec, 49 percent would vote "yes" in a referendum on sovereignty-partnership while only 34 percent would say "yes" to Quebec's independence (CRIC 2005). In short, neither maintenance of the status quo nor a complete break with Canada like outright independence are preferred options for a new relationship in living together.

Contradictions abound: A sizable minority want Quebec to be sovereign; an overwhelming majority want Quebec to remain in Canada (Gagnon 1996). Quebecers are attached to Canada, but this attachment comes with strings attached. Opinions and responses depend on how survey questions are asked: When asked to choose between complete independence and the status quo, a majority of Quebec respondents prefer the status quo. When offered more choice than these two extremes, the majority opt for some kind of renewed federalism or sovereignty association (Greenspon 1998). Ambiguities often reflect situational circumstances, such as the decline in support for sovereignty following the 11 September 2001 terrorist attack (Mackie 2001a). Consider the shift in Quebecer identity as measured in a Léger poll involving a representative sample of 1016 Quebec residents conducted between 18 October and 22 October 2001. The following responses to the question "Do you consider yourself to be . . ." proved instructive. Responses to similar questions in 2005 (CRIC 2005) are reproduced as well:

	Feb. 2001 (%)	Oct. 2001 (%)	Aug. 2005 (%)
Solely a Quebecer	24	15	19
A Quebecer first, then a Canadian	25	32	43
Both a Quebecer and a Canadian	26	32	21
A Canadian first, then a Quebecer	15	13	11
Solely a Canadian	8	7	5

Finally, there is evidence that many Quebecers believe in the advantages of belonging to Canada (CRIC 2005). Nearly 67 percent agree that being part of Canada allows Quebec to benefit from Canada's international stature, 65 percent believe that protection of rights under the Charter represents an advantage for Quebec, 64 percent acknowledge the benefits of transfer payments, 62 percent the protection from terrorism, and 46 percent even feel that being part of Canada is beneficial for the protection of Quebec's language and culture.

In short, Quebecers appear to have two loyalties, and this dual allegiance may not be captured by reference to either Canadian federalism or Québécois nationalism (Webber 1994). Despite the breathing space of a decade since the near death experience of the 1995 referendum, Quebecers are just as divided over independence as they were then, based on a Strategic Counsel poll of 1000 Canadians (500 in Quebec) in October of 2005, although most would vote to stay in Canada if the question were put to them clearly and directly (Lahgi 2005). Québécois attachment to Canada may be real and powerful, but is conditional on Canada's acceptance of Quebec as a homeland of last resort. Quebecers may not want to leave Canada, but neither do they want to appear weak or vacillating by caving in to federalist demands. Responses also reflect a fundamental ambivalence toward Canada: Canada may be my country, it is said, but Quebec is my homeland. Or as quipped by Yvon Descamps, a French-Canadian comedian, in pinpointing the contradiction: "They want an independent Quebec inside a united Canada" (cited in *The Globe and Mail*, 18 June 1994). In that ambiguity is at the core of Québécois aspirations and opinions, those leaders who intuitively grasp the politics of ambivalence will reap the spoils, and those who don't, won't (Gibbins and Laforest 1998).

Broadly speaking, all Quebecers appear anxious to maintain the French character of their society. Envisaged here is a set of arrangements, both political and economic, to preserve Quebec's distinctiveness as the homeland of last resort in North America. But agreement about goals does not always translate into consensus over means (Fournier 1994). On the one side are the moderates who generally prefer accommodation within the framework of Canada. Proposed is a strengthening of Quebec's position within a modified federalist system, in large part by reinforcing its presence in Ottawa while expanding Quebec's access to power and resources. A new constitutional division of jurisdiction is also proposed to ensure that each level of government controls what it does best. Moderates may even define themselves as "soft" sovereigntists, but disagree with the principle of separation, preferring instead a kind of flexible federalism that ensures power, autonomy, and identity.

Radical perspectives espouse a sovereign status for Quebec. Even here there is little consensus over the concept of sovereignty. Meanings are bandied about without much regard for precision, with the result that references to sovereignty or distinct society continue to generate more heat than light. Is it a desire to be left alone, or for Quebec to leave Canada, or vice versa, or a new social contract for rejoining Canada (Walkom 2001)? For some, sovereignty is defined as a final authority that brooks no external interference over internal matters; for others, sovereignty refers to arrangements between fundamentally independent political communities involving patterns of relative autonomy within a context of relational interdependence (Maaka and Fleras 2000; also Scott 1996). The distinction between separation and sovereignty is subtle but real. Sovereignty is what the Québécois already possess, as far as many are concerned, because of constitutional guarantees that uphold Quebec's status as a founding nation. Secession, by contrast, may be advocated by a small but vociferous segment of the population. Secessionist moves come in different packages, ranging from outright separation to sovereignty association, with most proposals entailing some degree of political autonomy without loss of close economic ties such as free trade and common currency.

Thus sovereignty is not merely a softer version of separation. Nor is it a sign of confusion in the minds of the Québécois, but a nuanced reading of Quebec's rightful place in the Canadian federal system.

The call for separation is not without foundation. Separatists believe Quebec is poised to go it alone. It has a broad industrial base for wealth creation (Quebec's economy is the thirtieth largest in the world), a healthy government structure, a shared sense of culture and community, and autonomous sources of revenue. Federalism does not pay; rather, staying in Canada exacts a heavy economic cost because of needless duplication and jurisdictional gridlock. Besides, many *indépendantistes* are tired of being stigmatized as a costly or inconvenient minority. They prefer a space to call their own, where they are the majority and call the shots. Quebecers want to be in the big leagues—a nation within a state—not just an outmanoeuvred administrative subunit of Canada (Latouche 1995). Or, as put by Louise Beaudoin of the Parti Québécois in acknowledging how Quebec wants to be treated as independent because it feels it is, "I want to be a majority in my own country" (Editorial, *The Globe and Mail*, 1 March 1995). To be sure, sovereignty will come with economic and social costs, yet ethnicities everywhere have shown a willingness to pay for heroic ideals. Besides, if grievances alone drove Quebec's nationalism, Quebec's spirit of independence might have faded by now, thanks to a vibrant economy, a French-speaking business sector, and a healthy language and culture (*Economist*, 3 December 2005). Nor will sovereignty solve all of Quebec's problems, conceded former Quebec premier Jacques Parizeau (1996), but it will normalize an awkward situation by creating a new political framework for living together separately.

What Is English-Speaking Canada Willing to Concede?

In August 1998, Canada's longest-running political drama took a twisted turn in the aftermath of the1995 referendum (Rocher and Verrilli 2003). To avert the possibility of yet another separatist scare, the federal government put three issues to the Supreme Court test: (1) Can Quebec legally and unilaterally secede from Canada? (2) Does international law regarding the right of self-determination condone the right to unilateral secession? (3) Which body of law would take precedence in case of conflict between domestic and international interpretation? The verdict was differently interpreted: To the delight of federalists, Canada's Supreme Court ruled unanimously in rejecting Quebec's claims to unilaterally secede from Canada. Any decision to declare Quebec's independence must be balanced by the realities of a federal system within the framework of Canada as a tri-national society. But the ruling was hardly a victory for federal forces. To the Québécois delight, the nine judges also made it clear that if a majority of Quebec voters embraced secession, the federal and provincial governments must negotiate the complex process of divorce. This ruling has also confirmed the Parti Québécois credo that Quebec people have the inalienable right to freely decide the political and legal status of Quebec in or out of Canada.

Not all Quebecers shared this enthusiasm (Rocher and Verrilli 2003). The *Clarity Act*'s focus on legal procedures and the workings of the referendum gloss over the key problem: that is, a redefining of Quebec's relational status with the rest of Canada. It also glosses over the crux of the conflict between the French and English: Why do claims to sovereignty continue to appeal, and what can be done to address these concerns and aspirations? Criticism aside, however, the *Clarity Act* provides an example of the compromises that constitute the balancing act called Canada. The government's *Clarity Act* suggests the possibility of a negotiated divorce. That is, the federal government will enter into negotiations for separation if a clear majority of Quebecers decide to leave in response to a clear question. In amending the country's basic governing charter for engineering its own partition, Canada would represent one of the few countries in the world to orchestrate its own demise. In conceding that Canada is divisible, albeit on shifting ground rules established by the federal government (what will determine what constitutes a clear question or clear majority, and on what grounds?), a major constitutional crisis is looming. To the extent that Canada is exploring the possibility of balancing unity with diversity against a backdrop of differentiated citizenship, Canadians are once again rewriting the rules for living together differently across a deeply divided society.

TOWARD A FLEXIBLE (ASYMMETRICAL) FEDERALISM

What is wanted is a larger bed (more space for each partner), maybe even twin beds. But there is definitely a desire to continue sharing the bedroom. This is a marriage not of passion but of reason and convenience—a fine arrangement based on common history, shared interests, and mutual respect. (Lysiane Gagnon, 27 July 1996)

Tension between Canada's French- and English-speaking communities is as old as the country itself (Kernerman 2005). French Canadians have complained of second-class status ever since the British defeated the French forces on the Plains of Abraham outside Quebec City in 1759. Many Canadians believe Canada is forever hovering on the brink of self-destruction despite an abundance of riches that is the envy of many. None other than Trudeau once pounced on this skepticism and negativity when he said "We peer so suspiciously at each other that we cannot see that we Canadians are standing on the mountaintop of human wealth, freedom, and privilege" (cited in Porter 2005). Admittedly, the picture at present is transitional, yet there is room for a guarded optimism. Canada's federal system is remarkably flexible and adaptive in endlessly tweaking the balance of power between self-rule and shared rule (Chrétien 1999; Cairns 2000). De facto arrangements have been in place since 1995 that recognize the uniqueness of Quebec as a distinct society with wide-ranging powers of self-determining autonomy (Dion 2005). Quebec has its own pension plan, its own system of private law and civil code, levies its own income tax, and exercises a degree of control over immigration that is unprecedented for any federal system (McRoberts 1996). According to Stéphane Dion (2005), a former constitutional adviser for the federal Liberal government, in many ways Quebec resembles a quasi-state, with controlling powers for setting provincial priorities and negotiating jurisdictions. In other words, with or without constitutional guarantees, Quebec is acting as if it were a distinct society by exercising a range of sovereignty-like powers.

Reaction by the rest of Canada is ambivalent. Canadians are not set against ad hoc arrangements that cater to Quebec's demands and needs. The stumbling block resides in moves to *legally* recognize Quebec as a people with a distinct society status. As Charles Taylor (1993) explains, English-speaking Canadians may be willing to accept negotiated and pragmatic arrangements that recognize Quebec's special place in Confederation (Editorial, *The Globe and Mail*, 16 September 1997). But many balk at the idea of formalizing any arrangements that (1) oppose conventional views of Canada (as a social contract), (2) violate certain values related to formal equality (the principle of equal provinces), (3) involve a massive transfer of power to Quebec, (4) create imbalances within Canada's federal system because of preferential treatment, and (5) contravene core constitutional values related to individual versus collective rights. Too much formal recognition may give Canadians more political unity than they really want (in the words of Professor John Richards). Or as David Cameron of the University of Toronto explains, the ongoing drama in French–English relations should be seen as a tension to be played out rather than a problem to be solved. Besides, one way of "solving" a complex problem is by ignoring it—in large part by acknowledging the propensity of Canada's media to twist everything into a unity problem, thus overdramatizing the normal disagreements of any functioning democracy (Dion 2005).

What now? For some, the national unity dilemma is the consequence of secessionist forces that have influenced the public agenda by propagating misconceptions about Quebec's place in Canada (e.g., English Canada is unsympathetic to Quebec's aspirations) (Musto 1997). Effective communications may solve the problem without the need for constitutional change. For others, however, a workable accommodation between Ottawa and Quebec is unlikely without a major reappraisal of governance in Canada. Relations repair is the key. On the one hand, Quebec is demanding more autonomy as a distinct society, and on the other, Canadian provinces (especially those from the west) want more power-sharing at the federal level—in effect reinforcing a need for a more flexible federalism (Taylor 1993; Kernerman 2005).

Flag-waving or finger-pointing will not solve what many perceive to be a structural problem rather than a simple case of mutual pigheadedness. That is, can two relatively autonomous political communities, each claiming sovereignty, learn to share a common political space over a shared homeland without self-destructing in the process (see Shipler 2001)? Perhaps Canada's current governance structures cannot cope with the deeply divided demands of a tri-national society. Just as the idea of provinces may be antiquated and irrelevant (Diamond 1997), so too is a federal political process designed for a small agricultural unitary state (Gillies 1997). This should come as no surprise: The prospect of uncritically relying on a nineteenth-century political framework for solving the twenty-first-century problems of a multination state is hardly a realistic option, especially in the face of free-wheeling global forces and inward-looking identity politics. Engin Isin of York University writes of the need to reconsider the Quebec question within the shifting parameters of the new world order:

> [P]olitical boundaries no longer represent the social and economic realities facing Canadian provinces today. Loyalties of Canadian citizens and their sense of belonging are divided along other lines than the nineteenth century territorial boundaries represented by the provinces. There are many other territorial identities and regions that are articulated into the different spheres of the global economy, rendering provincial loyalties and identities increasingly not only banal but counterproductive. (1996:6)

In other words, the Quebec question is really a Canadian quandary—in part because Canada's governance structures are saddled with ideological baggage from the Victorian era. Federalism as a system for engaging diversity may have worked in the past. But the emergence of Quebec nationalism and the vibrancy of indigenous nationalisms have exposed flaws in a provincially organized federal system (Gibbins 1998; Kymlicka 2001). As long as Canada is defined as a provincially (or territorially) based federalism rather than a multinational federation, a jurisdictional gridlock will persist. The challenge lies in advancing a multination concept of Canada, one in which the constituent units include peoples or nations in addition to provinces or regional entities (Resnick 2000; McRoberts 2001). The need to reorganize around national communities instead of provinces—to acknowledge that the Québécois and Aboriginal peoples are Canadian through membership in their groups (Kernerman 2005)—is captured by Kymlicka (1998:20), who writes

> So we must accept as given both that there will be minority nationalisms in Canada, and that these national loyalties will be territorially defined. We need to accept, in other words, that Canada is and will remain a *multination* state—a federation of peoples, if you will—in which people's national identity differs from, and may conflict with, their identity as Canadian citizens.

Constitutional impasses will lead to gridlock without transformative change to the foundational principles that govern Canada's constitutional order. Rather than complying with a British model of a single culture, language, and society (Rimmer 1998), a new social contract must provide a political covenant for the twenty-first century, one that reflects, reinforces, and advances the governance structures that underpin French–English partnership (Gibbins 1998). Perhaps, then, the "solitudes within" will come to realize that this regrettable necessity called Canada is not such a bad arrangement after all.

DEBATE REVISITED | **Official Bilingualism: A Canadian Covenant?**

The jury is still out. Over 35 years of official bilingualism have proven inconclusive as a tool for national unity. Has official bilingualism contributed to Canadian unity by keeping Quebec in Canada? Or is linguistic duality little more than an open sore, with biculturalism as the scab that people keep picking at? Are the costs justified in light of seeming paltry returns in advancing national unity? Or should its worth be measured in less tangible terms, such as in improving Canadian awareness of French–English relations?

References to success or failure will depend on how these terms are defined, by whom, and on what grounds. Responses will vary with the criteria employed for evaluation; with the social location of the respondents in terms of age, socio-economic status, gender, and ethnicity; and finally with the phrasing of questions on (and timing of) national surveys. When linguistic duality and bilingualism are couched in terms of responsiveness and inclusiveness rather than government decree, a majority of Canadians appear to support Canada's language duality, the principle of bilingualism, and the provision of bilingual government services as key features of Canadian identity and its collective personality—in effect shaping how we see ourselves and how the world sees Canada (Annual Report 2005). The extension of French language social services into areas of high francophone concentration is also endorsed, while highly motivated parents have enrolled their children in language immersion programs across Canada. Yet a backlash is ever present, especially the farther west one moves from Ontario and Quebec.

Both political and public responses involve a mixture of support, rejection, expediency, and indifference. Critics tend to exaggerate the magnitude and costs of official bilingualism; supporters prefer to inflate its benefits. A broad spectrum of opinion is evident. On one side, Max Yalden, a former Commissioner of Official Languages, has praised the *Official Languages Act* as one of the most innovative social reforms in a democratic society.

An official bilingualism may not be the perfect answer, but it may yet prove its worth in managing those tensions that simultaneously divide yet unite Canadians. On the other, bilingualism is chided for failing to unite Canadians or to avert a constitutional crisis (Reid 1993). In between are the critics who pounce on official bilingualism for not making Canadians more bilingual—in contrast with Quebec's success in advancing French in the province by way of admittedly controversial legislation (Auger 1997). Others applaud the expansion of bilingualism across Canada, but are concerned that the costs may not justify the results. Despite massive annual outlays, the number of bilingual speakers in Canada outside Quebec has remained relatively constant (Annual Report 2005).

Does official bilingualism contribute to or detract from Canada-building? Much depends on how Canada is defined: as a multicultural or bicultural (or bi-national) society. Those with a more multicultural slant on Canada have a positive spin. Official bilingualism originated in large part to counter the surge of nationalism in Quebec by offering Quebec the promise of participation and opportunity throughout all of Canada. Those who endorse a bicultural view of Canada see bilingualism as little more than a "conflict management" strategy for defusing the threat of separatism. Bilingualism may also be differently evaluated by those who subscribe to a compact or contract view of Canada and Canadian federalism. For those who see Canada as a pact between founding peoples, the *Official Languages Act* is dismissed as a dangerous irrelevancy: irrelevant, because it doesn't address the real issues; dangerous, because it distracts from the issues at hand. The national unity question is addressed, not by making Quebec more distinctive or by power-sharing, but by the simple expedient of making the rest of Canada more like

Quebec while making Quebecers feel more at home across Canada.

Put baldly, Ottawa tried to dilute Quebec nationalism by dispersing it across Canada, most obviously in the form of official bilingualism. According to this strategy, Ottawa would deny Quebecers additional powers in their own province in exchange for additional rights in Ottawa and all the other provinces. This Trudeau-inspired national unity strategy reflected an abrupt reversal of political trends in Canada (at least according to the elite consensus and its expression in the Royal Commission on Biculturalism and Bilingualism). Proposed instead of Pearson's equal partnership was a redefining of Canada along the lines of multiculturalism, individual rights, and the equality of all provinces. However acceptable for English-speaking Canada, Quebecers have criticized this constitutional reordering for erasing historical differences, ignoring collective rights, and compressing a founding people into yet another tile in the Canadian mosaic.

But, while Trudeau's efforts to transform Canada's foundational principles appealed to many Canadians, his efforts at re-constitutionalizing Canada badly miscalculated the depth of Quebec's nationalism. The end result may have transformed how English-speaking Canadians think of Canada, but this national unity strategy failed to dampen Quebec's nationalism. If anything, Kenneth McRoberts (1997) notes, it has solidified Quebec's resolve to see itself as a people by relying on the language of nationhood to fan in-group solidarity.

Failure to integrate Quebec into the national political community by way of language policies rather than power-sharing makes it abundantly clear. Official bilingualism may be a useful but ultimately insufficient component of a national unity strategy unless supplemented by power-sharing arrangements in advancing the

Québécois as *maîtres chez nous*. The irrelevance of official bilingualism is conveyed by political philosopher Charles Taylor (1993), who dismisses the question of being served in French by focusing on whether or not there will be enough francophones in the next generation. A meaningful autonomy is required, in other words, one that secures for Quebec those powers of decision-making over matters that matter (Connor 2000).

CHAPTER HIGHLIGHTS

- Canada represents a multicultural and bilingual society whose French–English duality constitutes a defining yet contested characteristic.

- Official bilingualism does not appear to have been a resounding success in improving Quebec–English Canada relations. Official bilingualism is widely viewed within Quebec as appeasement without power. Still, under official bilingualism all Canadians have a right to work or receive services at the federal level in the official language of their choice.

- A central question in this chapter is "What is really going on in terms of Quebec–Ottawa relations?" Answers to this question suggest the usefulness of seeing Canada from a variety of diverse perspectives, including Canada as a contract, a compact, and a coalition.

- What do the Québécois want? While answers are varied and reflect a certain degree of ambiguity, emphasis points to a new social contract that will enhance the distinct and sovereign character of Quebec's identity, language, and culture.

- Competing ethnic nationalisms continue to complicate politics in Canada. Quebec's First Nations argue for the right to stay in Canada if Quebec decides to secede. International law appears to be siding with the Canadian state in denying Quebec the right to unilaterally leave. The *Clarity Act* suggests the possibility of a negotiated divorce.

- The Quebec question is really a Canadian conundrum. That is, existing federal arrangements cannot handle the nationalist aspirations of Quebec, suggesting instead a redesigned multinational federalist system for solving the Canada problem.

KEY TERMS

bilingualism (individual, territorial, and institutional)

Canada as a coalition

Canada as a compact

Canada as a contract

charter member

distinct society

federalism

French Language Charter (Bill 101)

multinational federation

official bilingualism

official language minorities

Official Languages Act

sovereignty

sovereignty without secession

REVIEW QUESTIONS

1. Compare and contrast the differing visions of Canada with respect to English–French relations. Which do you think is the most correct reading of Canadian society?

2. The Quebec question may be a Canadian quandary. For some, Canada is the problem that Quebec is trying to solve. For others, Quebec is the problem with Canada as the solution. How would you respond to each of these assertions?

3. If someone were to ask you what you thought Quebec wants, how would you respond?

4. Indicate the nature of the sovereignty debate that is going on in Quebec between Quebec nationalists and Aboriginal peoples. Whose argument do you support and why?

5. Has an official bilingualism contributed to or detracted from national unity? Discuss.

LINKS AND RECOMMENDATIONS

Films

There are many films that provide insight into Quebec. One of the most recent and best is *The Barbarian Invasions*, a film that simultaneously celebrates the Quebec character while satirizing government and societal shortcomings.

Books

Michael Venne (ed.). *Vive Quebec!: New Thinking and New Approaches to the Quebec Nation* (James Lorimer & Sons, 2000).

Roger Gibbins and Guy Laforest (eds.). *Beyond the Impasse: Toward Reconciliation* (Institute for Public Policy and Information, 1998).

Alain-G. Gagnon, Montserrat Guibernau, and François Rocher (eds.). *The Conditions of Diversity in Multinational Democracies.* (Montreal: IRPP, 2003).

Websites

For information on Canada's official languages and official bilingualism, click on Official Languages Act or Office of the Commission of Official Languages.
   www.pco-bcp.gc.ca

To see arguments in favour of Quebec independence:
   www.expansionistparty.org/ForQCsep.html

For arguments against separatism:
   www.libertarianthought.com/smalltexts/antiseparatism.html

To follow a timeline for the Parti Québécois, which represents the political wing of the province's separatist movement:
   www.cbc.ca/news/background/parti_quebecois

IMMIGRANTS AND IMMIGRATION: GETTING IN, SETTLING DOWN, FITTING IN, MOVING UP

DEBATE The Refugee Determination Process: Is It Working?

Debates over **refugees** have provoked Canadians as few other issues have. Debates over who they are, how we find out, and whether the current system is workable and fair should come as no surprise, given the magnitude of this global problem and its implications for world peace. There are currently 35 million people who have fled their homes in war-torn countries, according to a report by the U.S. Committee for Refugees (Kenna 2000). Of the 35 million in flight, 21 million were internally displaced because of conflict (uprooted but remaining in their country

of origin for return to their community). Another 14 million had abandoned their home countries in search of safety (more recent figures put the number at 21 million). Palestinians accounted for nearly 4 million refugees, while the number of Afghani refugees stood at 2.5 million. A more conservative tally by the UNHCR (United Nations High Commissioner for Refugees) puts the figure at just over 10 million refugees in 2003, in addition to nearly 21 million "persons of concern." Disparities in number notwithstanding, the conclusion seems inescapable: The refugee crisis is real, its impact on countries and the global order is inestimable, and the crisis is unlikely to dissipate in the foreseeable future.

Canada is no less exempt from coping with the crisis. On the surface, establishing a system that is fair, fast, and final would appear a simple enough challenge (Showler 2005). Yet, the refugee determination question remains complex and contested. How can an overburdened system possibly address the principles that were established to process a handful of Cold War dissidents (Spencer 2003)? Can the refugee determination system distinguish genuine cases from bogus applicants? Or is the refugee determination system subject to abuse and breakdown, resulting in a safe haven for terrorists and a quick-fix channel for queue jumpers? Has the system proven effective in balancing national interests with the rights of refugees? Why should Canadians even accept refugees, as some critics ask? After all, unlike many immigrants who are pre-selected for their potential contributions to Canada, refugees rarely are in a position to directly contribute (see also Adelman 2004).

Canadians appear to be of mixed minds when it comes to refugees. Acceptance of Vietnamese refugees in the 1970s stands in sharp contrast to the blistering attacks on the 600 Chinese "boat people" who landed on the British Columbia coast during the late 1990s. Ambivalence runs deep: An Ipsos-Reid poll in 2004 indicated that 71 percent of respondents believe that Canada's refugee system requires "a major rethink" (Jimenez and Den Tandt 2005). Support is overwhelming for refugees who are seen as legitimate victims of state oppression, but many Canadians balk at those who appear to be shopping around for the best deal. The welcome may be less inviting for refugees who are smuggled in, arrive unannounced without documentation, and whose racial and ethnic characteristics are most removed from a Canadian norm of "whiteness." Issues of control are no less important. As long as they are in charge and under control of the process, Canadians see themselves as generous patrons to genuine victims, but bristle at the prospect of being duped by the unscrupulous.

Canada's refugee debate swivels around two philosophical axis points (Plaut 1989). One mindset wants a generous acceptance of as many refugees as possible because of Canada's humanitarian commitments. The objective is to cast as wide a net as possible for refugees, then dispose of those who don't fit. According to this line of logic, all refugees should be assumed innocent by giving them the benefit of doubt until proven guilty. Moreover, there is no such thing as illegal migrants because all asylum seekers are within their rights by international law to ask for the right to stay upon entry into a country. Admittedly, proof of authenticity may be awkward without identity papers, but standing in queue is not an option for most refugee claimants. Such is the nature of any flight from persecution that few can afford the luxury of asking permission for papers in a context of chaos (Rico-Martinez 1999).

The other perspective imparts the worst possible spin on refugee claims by arguing for measures to thwart their entry into Canada while facilitating their exit out of Canada (Gallagher 2004; Collacott 2006). **Refugee claimants** are criticized as a potential threat to the safety and prosperity of Canada. Loopholes in the determination process are exploited by refugees, while the system itself is subject to abuse by opportunistic lawyers, ruthless smugglers, gullible refugees, scheming refugee and ethnic organizations, and bungling **Immigration and Refugee Board (IRB)** members (Bauer 1994).

Three options are possible: Detain undocumented asylum seekers until proof of person is established; establish a firewall that excludes as many refugees as possible, then deal with genuine cases as they arise; or redesign Canada's refugee program by selecting (sponsoring) only those from refugee camps around the world (Stoffman 2002).

What is it about the refugee determination system that provokes such perplexity? A 1986 Supreme Court decision ruled that everyone who landed in Canada had the right to due process when claiming refugee status. In theory, defining a refugee seems straightforward. According to the United Nations Human Rights Convention of 1951 (to which Canada is a signatory), **refugees** constitute a class of individuals who have left their country and cannot return because of a well-founded fear of persecution for reasons of race, religion, nationality, group membership, or political opinion. Signatories are under obligation not to send asylum seekers back to highly unstable countries where they may face persecution.

But defining who is a refugee has become a lot more complex (Kumin 2004). Unless they have been explicitly singled out for persecution, those who have fled famine or civil wars, endured atrocities, or suffered the death of family members may not qualify as **convention refugees** under international law. Even the distinction between refugee (political persecution) and **immigrant** (economic opportunity) is getting fuzzier all the time as the threat of political persecution may dovetail with economic hardship. For example, is it possible to distinguish between outright persecution and ordinary discrimination, between individual harassment and generalized violence? Is a refugee a victim of state hate, or can a person be a refugee if the state fails to protect her from public scorn or institutional harassment? Can the

term "well-founded" be operationalized, that is, defined in concrete terms or converted into measurable values? Can reference to refugees include people who are forced to flee because of civil wars or environmental disasters? Or consider how some so-called refugees are not really refugees, as was the case with Kosovo in 1999, but are part of an emergency evacuation program with the option of either returning home once hostilities subside or applying for permanent resident status in Canada (Chakkalakal 1999).

In keeping with Canada's humanitarian commitments, the refugee net is being cast more broadly. There is growing acceptance of certain groups who do not strictly comply with refugee law, including those who experience refugee-like conditions, such as political oppression or environmental disaster. In May 1997, Canada expanded its definition of refugee status to include people who have been internally displaced because of war or terrorism and are in need of temporary protection from a dangerous situation (Stoffman 1997; Waldie 1998). The new ***Immigration and Refugee Protection Act*** (2002) has opened the doors to those asylum seekers who need protection because they fear becoming victims of crime (from gangs to lawlessness) in their homeland (Freeze and Jimenez 2004). Refugee status may be granted to minorities such as the Roma ("gypsies") who fail to receive state protection from public discrimination. Gender is also proving to be grounds for refugee status, reflecting patterns of persecution that affect women only, including cases of abusive domestic situations, exposure to mutilation, or forced marriage and sterilization (Kumin 2001). Finally, even rejected claimants or those who commit a serious crime may escape deportation if they risk being abused in their home country or if children born in Canada would suffer from their absence (Freeze 2005).

How far can the refugee determination net be stretched before it unravels? Two projections prevail: Those who are highly critical of government policy are predisposed to see hidden agendas behind every move to expand or justify. Those who endorse government policy in this area are reluctant to tamper with success. Yet, even those who are highly supportive concede that Canada cannot possibly accept all refugees without paying a price. The sovereignty and prosperity of Canada depend on securing its boundaries against the random flow of those asylum seekers who may pose a national security risk (Crepeau and Nakache 2006). Canada is hardly alone in confronting this challenge. Similar fears and concerns prevail throughout the Western world—too many refugees, too few resources, too slow a system, too inefficient a process, and too few deported (Showler 2005). Global dynamics have overwhelmed Canada's capacity to deal with the global movements of peoples, with the result that the process is inundated with excess capacity, refugee workers are overworked, claimants encounter lengthy delays, and the system itself is subject to abuse because of political patronage in staffing the IRB (Collacott 2006).

The movement of people into Canada is not the problem. More than 100 million people enter Canada annually. Most of these cross-border movements are seen as desirable (tourism or business) but others are not, making it more important than ever to separate the desirable from the undesirable (Showler 2005). Key questions arise: How workable and fair is Canada's approach to the entry and acceptance of refugees? Is the refugee determination system capable of doing the job it was designed to do or is it largely ineffective in carrying out its functions? Is the system too strict or not restrictive enough? On what grounds? Who says so, and why? The Debate Revisited box, "Refugee Determination Process: System or Dysfunction?" at the end of the chapter will provide some additional insight into a highly charged issue.

INTRODUCTION: THE PARADOX OF IMMIGRATION

[A]ll of us are migrants or descended from migrants—it's just a question of how many generations. (Editorial, *Christchurch Press*, 21 October 2001)

Ours is a species on the move (Castles and Miller 1998). People from around the world are in a constant quest to improve their lives, to flee from political repression, and to escape from natural and social disasters. In this era of human uprootedness and migration, interest in the study of immigration has expanded accordingly (Ucarer 1997; Abu-Laban and Li 1999; Hiebert 2000). This is notably true of Canada, where immigrants have long proven instrumental in building a Canadian society (Li 2003). On the whole, Canada has become a more vibrant and dynamic society because of immigrants (Ibbitson 2005). Immigrants have contributed to Canadian society without unravelling its social fabric in the process (Dyer 2001). Immigration remains a pivotal dynamic in boosting the Canadian economy, both domestically and abroad (Halli and Driedger 1999). Immigration has emerged, by default if not by intent, as Canada's de facto population policy (Ley and Hiebert 2001). Immigrants may provide a solution to the problems of an aging population, shrinking birth rate, declining support/dependency ratio, and skills shortage in a global and information-based economy, while re-energizing Canada's economy by virtue of their consumer spending, optimistic outlook, and entrepreneurial spirit.

Canadians for the most part have embraced immigration with the kind of civility and open-mindedness that is becoming a national trademark (Siddiqui 1998; Adam 2003). While many countries are turning against immigration, including Australia, Britain, America, and Germany, Canada continues to maintain historically high levels. Canadians appear favourably disposed to immigration, with only 21 percent saying it is "a very big problem" compared to 37 percent for Americans and 46 percent for Britains, according to a 2002 poll by the Washington-based Pew Research Center for People and the Press. Canada routinely ranks first among countries with the highest rate of immigrants on a per capita basis. It has signed a number of international human rights protocols that safeguard the human rights of all asylum seekers, regardless of where they come from or who they are (Canadian Council of Refugees 2000). For its work with international refugees, Canada received the UN Nansen medal in 1986—the first and so far the only country to ever receive such an accolade. The conclusion seems inescapable: Canada remains a country of choice for those fleeing to improve fortunes, to reunite with family and relatives, and to escape political repression. And for many, the choice has proven to be a wise one.

Yet, there is a darker side to this bucolic picture. Canada may be a land of immigrants that is in deep denial about immigration. Debate over immigration has proven divisive. Those on the right complain of too many, those on the left of not enough, and those in the middle may be confused over what is right. Canada's immigration program is deemed unfair and inefficient and in need of a major overhaul: (1) Immigration rules are thought to be unjust, prone to abuse, and difficult to enforce, e.g., the reckless issuing of ministerial permits in exchange for favours or to facilitate entry or stay (Francis 2005); (2) the rules are subject to crass political considerations rather than national interests, e.g., the proposed increase of elder immigration to offset mounting pressure for the sponsorship of (grand)parents (Collacott 2005); and (3) the bureaucratic ineptness of an overburdened Immigration Department is regularly exposed (Ibbitson 2005; Thompson 2005). Aspects of Canada's immigration program are accused of being sexist and racially discriminatory—not necessarily explicitly or deliberately but through application of seemingly neutral rules that negatively impact on the most vulnerable (Canadian Council of Refugees 2001). And Canada's much vaunted tolerance has been put to the test in the aftermath of 11 September 2001 amidst fears that lax enforcement of loose immigration regulations fosters a haven for terrorist groups (Thompson 2001).

This chorus of criticism has muscled its way into the national consciousness. Paradoxes prevail. Immigration may be inseparable from the quality of life in Canada because its standard of living will depend on immigration to offset an aging population and declining birth rate (Ibbitson 2005). Yet, the promise and productivity of immigration are lost in a welter of debates over fiscal uncertainty, corporate downsizing, job losses, economic restructuring, and political expediency (Abu-Laban, McIrvin and Li 1999). Up to 30 percent of new immigrants may possess a B.A. or better, but a large percentage have fewer than 13 years of education, speak neither French nor English, with many consigned (and resigned) to a lifetime of un- or underemployment (O'Reilly 2000; Monitor 2005). True, by "talking the walk," many institutions have intellectualized the issue of diversity by supporting it in principle, according to the Conference Board of Canada (2004), but they are unable to "walk the talk" by putting principles into practice. Immigration may have facilitated a robust consumer economy in Canada's gateway cities of Vancouver and Toronto, yet associated costs cannot be discounted, including congestion, shortage of affordable housing, and strains on social service delivery (Ley and Hiebert 2001). Immigrants are expected to contribute to Canada's social and economic fabric, yet are roundly condemned as too ambitious or too assertive if they do. They are rebuked for stealing jobs from "real" Canadians, yet rejected as "free-loading parasites" if unemployed. Put bluntly, Canadians remain "reluctant hosts" who appear welcoming at times and obstructionist at other times, but whose ambivalence—even hostility—toward certain foreign-born individuals is palpable beneath a folksy veneer of tolerance.

"Getting in" is one thing. "Settling down," "fitting in," and "moving up" have proven even more of a challenge. Immigrants and refugees come to Canada with the best of intentions for making a positive contribution to Canada and for themselves (Isajiw 1999). Yet, Canada has not always proven the haven that many had expected. True, both immigrants and refugees possess the rights of citizenship and the multicultural right to inclusiveness; nevertheless, many continue to encounter obstacles that may serve to concoct a dangerous and disruptive cocktail (also Biles and Burstein 2003). Formidable barriers exist in a society whose welcome mat is yanked out from underneath at the slightest provocation. Admittedly, the introduction of government policies and programs has facilitated the process of integration (Halli and Driedger 1999). Entrenchment of official Multiculturalism provides a collective platform for articulating issues of relevance to this sector. But in a country whose national agenda is dominated by Aboriginal politics and Québécois nationalism, the exclusion of immigrant and **multicultural minorities** from meaningful national dialogue over "why," "who," "what," and "how" poses a concern, including:

- Why should Canada accept immigrants?
- Who should be encouraged to come to Canada?
- How many immigrants (if any) should be accepted?
- From what countries should Canadians accept immigrants?
- Which category of immigrant is preferred: family, economic, or refugee?
- What kind of diversity should immigrants bring with them?
- In what way do immigrants contribute to or detract from Canada-building?
- What is the best way of integrating immigrants—by focusing on differences or emphasizing commonalities?

Answers to these questions require careful deliberation that must go beyond political slogans or public posturing. Responses often elicit intense emotions—even levels of hysteria—that defy rational discussion. Yet, some kind of consensus will be necessary for living together with our differences.

A focus on the negative is no more helpful than concentrating exclusively on the positive. Nor should response or assessment be based entirely on utilitarian terms. The importance of immigration to society goes beyond the question of demography or economy. Immigration has proven a defining feature of Canada and Canada-building (Halli and Driedger 1999; Ibbitson 2005). Evolving patterns of immigration have irrevocably altered the very concept of Canada by transforming a British colony into a cosmopolitan kaleidoscope of cultures, colours, and connections. By playing down the historical duality that once defined "Canadianness," immigration has resculpted the political contours of Canada's social landscape, with striking implications for national unity and identity. For better or worse, immigrants continue to fuel the spark for rethinking this adventure called Canada. As former minister of citizenship and immigration Sergio Marchi once commented in connecting immigration with national identity: "Immigration is fundamentally about nation-building—about deciding who we are as Canadians and who we want to become . . . We need a clear and practical vision of the kind of nation we want to build" (Annual Report 1994:iii; also *Immigration* 2003).

It is within the context of concern and criticism, of progress and stalemate, and of costs and benefits that this chapter explores the politics of immigration. By looking at the relationship of Canadian society to immigrants and multicultural minorities, and vice versa, the chapter examines the social dimension of immigration in terms of its impact on and implications for Canada-building. The chapter begins with an overview of Canada's multicultural minorities in terms of demographic composition and geographical distribution. It continues with a closer look at the laws, policies, and programs that have governed the movement of immigrants into Canada. Of particular note are historical ambiguities implicit in defining "entry" as this category has evolved over time—even if the need for immigrants to fuel Canada's capitalist expansion has never wavered (Bolaria and Li 1988), thus reinforcing the ambivalence that many Canadians harbour toward immigration and refugees. Also discussed are many of the controversies associated with immigration, including who gets in, on what grounds, from where, what for, and at what level of acceptance. Criticism of Canada's refugee determination process poses awkward questions, including, Who is a refugee? How do we find out? Is the system fair? Is the system working? The difficulties endured by immigrants in adjusting to Canadian society—that is, settling down, fitting in, and moving up—confirm what many suspect: have Canada's immigration policies outlived their usefulness?

A chapter on immigration, immigrants, and multicultural minorities could not possibly address all topics without stretching its resources to the point of superficiality and gloss. Emphasis is focused primarily on the needs and concerns of migrants and minorities from so-called non-conventional countries of origin. Attention is directed at immigrants of colour (racialized immigrants) in terms of their adjustment to Canadian society under a bewildering array of policy circumstances, institutional barriers, and social pressures. Specific groups are not dealt with per se. Our intent is to provide a comprehensive overview of immigrants and refugees *as if* they constituted a relatively uniform category for analytical purposes. This ideal–typical stance runs the risk of oversimplification, reductionism, or essentializing (treating everyone in a category in a fixed, homogeneous, and deterministic fashion). Others might argue that immigrant voices are being silenced by relying too excessively on analysis. There is some validity to these charges, insofar as the diversity and depth of the immigrant experience cannot be underestimated (Harvey et al. 1999). Still, there are benefits in focusing on the big picture while holding constant the range of internal diversity because of age, gender, culture, socio-economic status, length of residence, sexual preference, and country of origin.

A note on terminology: Canada's multicultural diversity is not conducive to simple labelling. There is no one term that adequately encapsulates all Canadians who do not fit the category of Aboriginal peoples or charter members. Expressions such as "immigrants," "ethnic group," "**people of colour**," "racial or ethnic minorities," and "racialized minorities" may be inadequate because, paradoxically, they are too broad or too narrow. Other expressions, such as visible minorities, are widely accepted as administrative labels, albeit with limited emotional appeal. We have tried to resolve this dilemma by categorizing immigrants and descendants of immigrants as multicultural minorities. In general, multicultural minorities consist of those Canadians of colour, both foreign- and Canadian-born, who are not of (or who choose not to identify with) British, French, or Aboriginal ancestry. This descriptive category includes those whose legal status is derived from their rights as immigrants or descendants of immigrants rather than as founding peoples or first principles. Their interests as a collective do not comprise part of the national agenda, but reflect their status as citizens with no agenda-setting rights except through conventional channels. Collectively, they look to official Multiculturalism as the framework for articulating their grievances and mediating their relationship to society, hence the expression "multicultural minorities."

DIVERSITY IN CANADA

Canada embraces a diverse tapestry of immigrants and refugees from different parts of the world. Because of a robust immigration program, Canada also represents a staunchly heterogeneous society whose reputation as a multicultural mosaic needs little fanfare or praise (Jaimet 2005). Canada's ethnic composition has undergone a radical transformation since the passage of the *British North America (Constitution) Act* of 1867. Only 8 percent of Canada's population was neither of British nor of French ancestry at the time of Confederation (Palmer 1975). Between 1896 and 1914, the balance began to shift when up to 3 million immigrants—many of them from Central and Eastern Europe—arrived to domesticate the West. Immigration increased substantially prior to and just after World War I, reaching a peak of just over 400 000 in 1913, followed by an all-time low of just 7600 immigrants in 1942. The post–World War II period resulted in yet another "exodus" from the war-devastated countries of Europe, but sources of immigration since the 1980s have shifted as well—in the process rekindling controversy over the politics of "who gets in."

Over 5 million immigrants (foreign born) live in Canada, representing about 18 percent of the total Canadian population—a figure that has remained relatively constant since the early 1950s. With a population of about 32 million and an annual intake of around 220 000 immigrants over the past 15 years, Canada's acceptance rate stands at 0.7 as a percentage of the total population—a ratio of one legal immigrant for every 140 residents, making Canada one of the largest per capita immigrant-receiving countries in the world. Immigrants in 2001 accounted for just under 60 percent of Canada's population growth, including nearly 20 percent of Canada's labour force. By 2025 immigrants will account for all of Canada's population increase (natural increases based on birth will be offset by death as Canadian women continue to reproduce at levels below the replacement rate).

Both the numbers and scope of Canada's immigration program have contributed to its diversity, including the following ethnic breakdowns (as tabulated in Statistics Canada 2002). Nearly 39 percent, or 11.7 million (single and multiple responses), reported "Canadian" as their ethnic origin (most of these respondents were Canadian-born and indicated either French or English as their mother tongue). The most frequently reported non-Canadian ethnic origins were English (20.2%), French (15.8%), Scottish (14%), Irish (12.9%), German (9.3%), Italian (4.3%), Chinese (3.7%), Ukrainian (3.6%), and Aboriginal peoples (3.4%).

In 1966, about three-quarters of all immigrants to Canada arrived from Europe or the United States. Since 1981, the proportion has reversed itself with about three-quarters of all immigrants coming from Asia, Africa, the Caribbean, and Central America. Just over 13.4 percent of Canada's population was identified as visible (persons other than Aboriginals who are non-Caucasian in race and non-white in colour) minorities in 2001. Those of Chinese origin are the most populous, accounting for 26.9 percent of the **visible minority** population, followed by South Asians (23%) and African-Canadians (16%). This trend is expected to continue. With immigrants continuing to arrive primarily from China (16.3 percent in 2003), India at 11.1 percent, and Pakistan and the Philippines at about 5.4 percent, visible minorities are projected to comprise about 20 percent of Canada's population by 2017.

Canada remains one of the most urbanized countries in the world. Immigration has contributed greatly to the cosmopolitan mix in which migrants and minorities coexist within a shared urban space (McIsaac 2003). Regional and municipal variations in ethnic composition are clearly evident. Nearly three-quarters of all immigrants live in Toronto, Vancouver, and Montreal, as do 90 percent of all visible minorities, with many increasingly residing in ethnic enclaves—partly from choice, partly from constraints (Hiebert 2003). Both absolute numbers and relative percentages make Toronto and Vancouver more diverse than provincial or national averages, according to the 2001 Census data, with the foreign-born or immigrants accounting for 43.7 percent of Toronto's population and 37.5 percent of Vancouver's. Nearly one half of Canada's visible minorities live in Toronto, or 37 percent of its population—the same as Vancouver—reflecting 169 different countries and about 100 different languages, and prompting the United Nations to designate Toronto as the world's most ethnically diverse city. Richmond, B.C., with 59 percent and Markham, Ontario, with 55.5 percent have the highest percentage of visible minorities per municipal population.

That immigrants and refugees are drawn to large urban regions is understandable (Hiebert 2000). Cities provide the networks, supports, and resources that facilitate the adjustment and integration of immigrants and refugees. This, in turn, proves irresistible as a magnet for incoming immigrants and refugees. For example, about one half of all immigrants to Toronto cite family and community as the chief reason for selecting that city (only about a quarter cite economic or work reasons). By contrast, immigrants are reluctant to settle in the Atlantic provinces because the cities lack a critical mass of their "own kind" (Ibbitson 2004). Not surprisingly, urban planners confront challenges in creating more inclusive urban environments not only to improve the participation of all Canadians in city life, but also to capitalize on diversity as a basis for innovation and prosperity (Urban Nexus 2003; Sandercock 2003). To date, debates over creating a more geographically balanced distribution of migrants and minorities across Canada have proven futile, despite proposed government incentives to do so, with some arguing that such a move would be contrary to Canada's constitutional mobility rights even if new Canadians proved receptive to the idea (Editorial, *National Post*, 29 August 2002; also Biles and Burstein 2003).

GETTING IN: CANADA'S IMMIGRATION LAWS, POLICIES, PROGRAMS, AND PRACTICES

With up to 175 million people on the move outside of their homeland, it is safe to say that few countries have been untouched by international migration or are immune to its effects (Papademetriou 2003). Despite its centrality to contemporary existence, however, few societies have acknowledged the reality and importance of immigration, in part out of fear of disrupting national identities, exposing weaknesses in national governance and security, and undermining state capacity for enforcing unpopular laws.

Canada is one of the few countries in the world that can be defined as an immigration society (Ucarer 1997). The United States and Australia are two notable immigration societies, as are Brazil and Argentina, several Latin American countries, and, most recently, New Zealand (Hiebert et al. 2003). An immigrant country can be defined as one that takes a principled and proactive approach to immigration and immigrants. Four characteristics distinguish immigration countries from non-immigration countries:

- Policies and programs exist to regulate the entry of immigrants into the country.

- Programs are in place to assist in the integration and settlement of immigrants.

- Immigrants are entitled to all rights and privileges, including the right to full and equal citizenship.

- Immigration is viewed as an asset or resource in advancing society-building and national identity construction.

Compare these attributes of an immigrant country with non-immigration countries like Germany whose agenda historically kept out immigrants. Immigration in non-immigration societies was perceived as an anomaly that did not contribute to national identity or society-building. Policies were devised to stabilize inflows, limit long-term stays, discourage permanent residence, label newcomers as guest workers, and withhold citizenship and attendant rights (Ucarer 1997). Foreigners and their children were generally excluded from citizenship even if born and raised in Germany, while, paradoxically, those of German parentage (ancestry) were automatically granted citizenship regardless of where they lived (Modood 2003a). To be sure, this mindset is changing as Germany and other non-immigrant countries (which historically were emigrant countries) have little option except to embrace immigration and citizenship as means to offset the effects of an aging population, a plummeting birth rate, costly welfare programs, and EU membership (Munz and Ohliger 2002).

Canada is frequently praised—or pilloried—as a society of immigrants (Foster 1998). With the possible exception of Aboriginal peoples, all Canadians are immigrants or descendants of immigrants. Immigration has played a pivotal role in Canada's national development and will continue to do so in the foreseeable future (Ibbitson 2005). The increasingly unfettered movements of people, ideas, labour, and investment because of globalization will see to that. Yet, Canadians seem curiously ambivalent about immigration and immigrants, despite a longstanding reliance on immigrant labour as a catalyst for development. Antipathy toward new Canadians borders on the xenophobic at times, with calls for rigorous screening procedures including DNA testing and vigorous deportation procedures. Debate revolves around the questions of "how many," "where from," "what sort," and "what for." Yet, the sensitivity of the topic can provoke hostility because the management of immigration may challenge national unity and identity, requires difficult political decisions and tradeoffs, and exposes weaknesses in a society's governance structures (Papademetriou 2003).

Early Practices

The content and direction of Canadian immigration practices have not stood still, but have evolved since Confederation (Foster 1998; Boyd and Vickers 2000). Initial attempts at immigration control (rules governing the admission of foreign individuals) were moulded by a combination of ideological considerations, political expediency, international obligations, and the colonialist requirements of a hinterland economy. Outcomes were decided by an interplay of factors, including racism and ethnocentrism, the agricultural bias of Canada's early immigration policies, the pivotal role of private and business interests, Canada's Commonwealth commitments as part of the British Empire, and high levels of out-migration to the United States. Historically, the Canadian state has grappled with conflicting interests, that is, how to preserve its whiteness while securing an adequate supply of migrant labour (Thobani 2000a). This conflict of interest transformed immigration policy and practice into a kind of contested site, with competing interests jockeying to impose their agenda in defining entry.

Until the 1860s, immigration into most receiving countries including Canada was largely unrestricted (Meyers 2002). But initial practices regarding who to let in and who to keep out could be described as essentially racist in orientation, assimilationist in objective, nativist in content, and exclusionary in outcome (Abu-Laban 1999). Three factors combined to define who was admitted, how many, and where from: the state of the economy, a commitment to admit only British types, and compliance with Commonwealth obligations and international laws. Immigration was based on a distinction between preferred versus non-preferred "races" (Thobani 2000a; Elabor-Idemudia 1999). A preference for more assimilable whites contrasted with the dismissal of inferior "races" as contrary to Canada's climate or cultural values (Simmons 1999). As much energy was expended in keeping out certain "types" as was in encouraging others to settle. The 1869 *Immigration Act* and subsequent amendments including the 1910 *Immigration Act* excluded certain types of undesirables, such as criminals, the mentally unfit, the diseased, nationalities unlikely to assimilate, and those whose occupations would lure them to cities. Strict limitations were imposed on the Japanese, Chinese, and East Asians, in part through head taxes or regulations such as Continuous Journey (this required all immigrants to travel directly from their country of origin or citizenship with a through ticket purchased in the home country). Both the courts and the legal system were profoundly implicated in Canada's racist treatment of immigrants prior to entry and upon settlement (see Backhouse 1999).

A "racial pecking order" of preference quickly emerged (Lupul 1988; Walker 1998). In keeping with a dominant perception of Canada as "a white man's country," preferred categories of immigrants were drawn from the so-called superior stock of Western Europe. This category was virtually exempt from entry restrictions except for certain formalities (Abella and Troper 1991). At the bottom of this pecking order were black people and Asians, both of whom were seen as inherently inferior and ultimately unassimilable. The Irish, too, were deemed to be culturally and economically dangerous people—a poor, ignorant, and knavish people with "papist" religious convictions and prone to crime and joblessness. In between these two poles were the non-preferred classes, consisting of immigrants from Eastern and Middle Europe and Russia. While admiring them for their brawn and industry, Canadians also harboured a degree of suspicion toward these "dangerous foreigners," particularly those Bolsheviks who dared to challenge the principles of free enterprise (Avery 1995). A special "restricted" permit class controlled the entry of Jews and Mediterranean peoples.

Once preferred sources dwindled, other Europeans began to look better. Canada's first immigration minister, Clifford Sifton, made virtue of necessity in 1896 when he encouraged immigrants from Eastern Europe to settle the west, despite a chorus of criticism over compromising national interests. Sifton resolutely opposed the import of urban factory workers, many of whom were seen as degenerate, susceptible to economic unrest, or fodder for radical agitators. Most immigrants were expected to settle, to farm, and to secure a rural economic base for Canada (Pendakur 2000). The agricultural bias of early immigration was eloquently expressed when Sifton mused about "stalwart peasants in a sheepskin coat, born on the soil, whose forefathers had been farmers for ten generations, with a stout wife and a half-dozen children." But not all immigrants saw themselves as tillers of soil. Over time, migrants shifted from agriculture to wage employment in labour-intensive industries such as railroad construction, mining, and construction work (Avery 1995). Nor did all immigrants look to Canada as the promised land. It took a lot of convincing to get people to come; even more inducements were required to make them stay. Many new Canadians promptly emigrated to the United States—between 1851 and 1948, almost as many left for the United States as immigrated to Canada (Isajiw 1999; Beaujot 1999) while during the 1971 to 1981 decade, there were almost half as many long-term departures (636 000) as permanent arrivals (1 429 000)—in effect reinforcing a perception of Canada as little more than a transfer point between America and Europe (Whitaker 1991). This trend persists into the present, according to a Statistics Canada study, including the departure of one-third of all mature male immigrants within 20 years of arrival (Thompson 2006).

Promotion of immigration from across Europe provoked debate over two related problems: the need for cheap labour and a means for rapid removal of immigrants when no longer required (Walker 2001). Political parties engaged in endless polemics over who was desirable or assimilable, preferred or non-preferred (Thobani 2000a, b). But all agreed that Canada's survival depended on excluding those workers who were perceived as unsuitable to Canadian conditions, who were thought to be incapable of assimilating into prevailing norms of decency and democracy, and who were demonized as a menace at odds with Canadian values and institutions. Non-preferred immigrants were tolerable as long as they quietly toiled away in remote regions and at tasks deemed too demeaning, and demanding, for white Canadians (e.g., railways, mines, lumber camps, domestic work). The *Immigration Act* of 1910 defined a series of prohibited classes, including the physically, mentally, and morally unfit. Asian "guest workers" or "sojourners" such as the Chinese and Indians were tolerated as "fodder" for Canadian capitalist expansion—a tap to be turned on when needed, turned off when not, as the following case study reveals.

CASE STUDY	**Chinese Immigration to Canada: Yellow Peril or White Xenophobia?**

Canada's reaction to early Chinese immigration exposes an embarrassing face that many Canadians would prefer to ignore or forget (Baureiss 1985; Li 1998). Canadians may be upset to learn that, historically, racism was openly and ruthlessly directed at non-whites. They may recoil at discovering how racism was routinely institutionalized within the justice system to the detriment of new Canadians (Walker 1998). For example, courts ruled that preventing Chinese from hiring white women to work in laundries was not deemed discriminatory because the injunction applied to all Chinese males. Even more dismaying is an awareness of how Canada-building was built upon and inseparable from institutionalized racism. In that racism persists into the present, albeit in a more subtle manner, the adage of "continuity in change" is confirmed.

Few groups were more subject to racism and discrimination than the Chinese. The earliest Chinese migrants came to Canada in 1858 to take advantage of the gold rush. The second cohort arrived as virtually indentured labour for building the Canadian Pacific Railway, with nearly 17 000 arrivals from the China mainland between 1882 and 1885 (the total population in British Columbia was 53 000 in 1891) (Xiao-Feng and Norcliffe 1996). Chinese migrants were seen as cheap and exploitable workhorses for the most hazardous sections of the railway, but expendable once the task was completed (Lee 1997). A split labour market quickly appeared: Chinese labourers were employed for $1 a day (only 80 cents if they did not buy provisions from the company store), compared to $2 a day for Canadian workers or $3.50 for American labourers (Faces 1996).

From the time of their arrival in Canada, Chinese immigrants were subjected to legislation that sought to destroy the community, restrict political activity, and inhibit healthy social growth (Vasil and Yoon 1996). According to Xiao-Feng and Norcliffe (1996), virtually every industry in British Columbia depended to some extent on Chinese labour. Nevertheless, the Chinese were targets of prejudice and discrimination, exploited as cheap labour, and manipulated as strike-breakers in defiance of labour union relations. Various exclusionary mechanisms were directed at those who gained entry and remained in Canada (Bolaria and Li 1988; Satzewich 2000). They were denied the right to vote, prohibited from working on government projects or in coal mines, excluded from holding hand-loggers' licences, prevented from settling on Crown land, barred from the professions of law or pharmacy, and banned from hiring white women to work in Prairie restaurants or laundries. Numerous tactics were deployed for restricting their entry in Canada, but they proved ineffective because of the demand for cheap labour during the railway construction period.

Public antipathy was openly palpable. Federal plans to import an additional 5000 Chinese for the construction of the Grand Trunk Railway elicited a sharp editorial rebuke from the September 1906 issue of *Saturday Night*:

> We don't want Chinamen in Canada. This is a white man's country and white men will keep it so. The slant-eyed Asiatic with his yellow skin, his unmanly humility, his cheap wants, would destroy the whole equilibrium of industry . . . We cannot assimilate them. They are an honest, industrious, but hopelessly inferior race. (cited in Fraser 1989:12).

Upon completion of the railway, many returned to China with their savings. Others were stranded in Canada because of insufficient funds, with few options except unskilled employment in laundries and gardens. The Chinese were increasingly exposed to caricature and abusive treatment by the general public and provincial politicians. In the same year the railroad was completed, the British Columbia government passed the 1884 *Chinese Regulation Act*, arguing that Chinese "were not disposed to be governed by our laws; are useless in instances of emergency; and desecrate graveyards." The demonization of the Chinese knew no limits. They were frequently subjected to racial invectives by organized labour, who demonized them as strike-breaking "scabs." Others vilified them as a kind of "yellow peril" that would undermine the purity and integrity of a "white man's country." The exploitation of the Chinese as a political football or as electoral scapegoats played into white xenophobia. Even the withdrawal of Chinese into their own communities for protection had little effect in dampening public hostility and suspicion.

With no political voice or representation, the Chinese were unable to adequately defend themselves. This is not to say that all passively accepted these injustices. Protests, strikes, and lawsuits were often employed in reaction to negative government legislation and discriminatory practices (see Ip 1998). But resistance proved somewhat futile. Under public pressure, successive governments imposed financial disincentives to deter entry. The first federal *Chinese Exclusion Act* in 1885 imposed a head tax of $50 on Chinese immigrants; this amount was increased by increments until it reached a total of $500 in 1903—a sum equivalent to two years' wages or the cost of a new home in Vancouver. An additional $200 was required in 1910 as landing tax for all Asian immigrants. Between 1886 and 1923, more than $22 million was collected in head tax payments. Admittedly, the first *Immigration Act* of 1869 had imposed a head tax of $1.50 per person on everyone, while a 1914 landing fee of $250 was universally applied, but only the Chinese were singled out for special taxation.

Although the head tax temporarily derailed the flow of Chinese migrants, it did not curb it (Xiao-Feng and Norcliffe 1996). The federal government curtailed Chinese immigration in 1923 following passage of the *Chinese Immigration Act;* as a result, the Chinese became the only people to be specifically prohibited from entry to Canada because of race. This exclusionary injunction also forced the separation of Chinese men from their wives and partners, in effect curbing population growth. Only 44 Chinese were granted permission to enter Canada between 1923 and 1946 (Xiao-Feng and Norcliffe 1996). This now politically embarrassing ban was lifted in 1947 with repeal of the *Chinese Exclusion Act* and passage of Canada's first *Citizenship Act.* Yet, until 1962, only spouses and unmarried children of Chinese in Canada were allowed admission, in contrast to relatively unrestricted immigration from Europe and the United States. The introduction of the point system in 1967 facilitated ease of entry for Chinese immigrants, either from Hong Kong or Taiwan, but none from the mainland following the Communist revolution in 1949.

The status of Chinese-Canadians has improved in recent years. Successive generations of Chinese have moved from relative social isolation to active involvement in staking a rightful claim to their status as Canadian citizens. Chinese-Canadians are increasingly seen as model minorities because of their hard working habits. But prejudicial and racist attacks persist (Li 1998). Instead of being labelled inferior or unassimilable, Chinese-Canadians are criticized for cultural practices, which are denounced as "un-Canadian." They are chided for creating a host of social problems, from monopolizing spaces in medical schools to driving up real estate prices in Vancouver. And they are taken to task for establishing ethnic enclaves in the Greater Toronto area. These attacks are less direct than in the past. Nevertheless, the undercurrent of thinly veiled dislike is no less disconcerting, suggesting that racism in racialized societies never disappears, but reappears in a variety of different disguises. *Plus ça change, plus c'est la même chose.*

Three insights can be gleaned from this case study. First, diverse interests tended to sway public and political reaction to immigrants and immigration. For example, business and powerful transportation companies supported immigration on the grounds that a prosperous local economy required a steady supply of migrant labour. By contrast, organized labour and public sentiment generally favoured a restriction of those immigrants who depressed wages, increased job insecurity, and threatened to "lower [the] Canadian standard of living" (Avery 1995; also Stoffman 2003). The government found itself sandwiched in between, sometimes hugging the high ground, other times capitulating to private or public interests as the circumstances dictated. Moreover, membership in the Commonwealth and eventually the United Nations meant that Canada could no longer maintain an overtly discriminatory immigration policy (Basran and Zong 1998).

Second, early immigration practices reflected practical considerations that coincided with Canada's economic needs. Immigrants were selected on the basis of their ability to fill slots in the expanding economy. When Chinese migrants were required for railroad building, the taps were turned on; when they were no longer required, the taps were turned off. The resulting taps-on and taps-off approach reinforced a cautious estimate of Canada's absorptive capacity. Western settlement required large numbers, with immigration peaking at 400 870 in 1913; wars and Depression conditions resulted in lower figures, bottoming out in 1942 at 7576 immigrants. This stop-and-go mentality exposed Canada to criticism that it was merely operating a guest-worker system; that is, foreigners were welcome when the economy boomed, but unwelcome otherwise.

Third, the acceptance of immigrants was driven by a hard-boiled pragmatism. Canada "needed" workers and settlers for the backbreaking task of taming wilderness. To an extent that few would care to admit, the practical aspects of Canada's immigration policy remain in effect. Canada wants immigrants for largely self-serving reasons, including to (1) offset the effects of an aging population and declining birth rate, (2) ensure a sufficient tax base to underwrite increasingly costly services, (3) expand the size of the domestic market, and (4) stimulate sustained economic activity. Emphasis is on economic or skilled migrants. Those immigrants who are willing to invest in Canada through creation of employable industries are also actively courted. The need for cheap labour is critical as well; the importation of agricultural migrant workers and domestic live-in caregivers are but two instances of how Canada creates conditions that cause people to migrate in the first place, then capitalizes on this process to establish a pool of disposable workers (Grzejszczak and Gordon 2005). Canada, of course, is not the only country whose immigration practices reflect political calculation and economic expediency. European countries have demonstrated all too readily their eagerness to accept immigrants as guest workers to feed a labour-starved economic boom, but an equal disdain for them during the downturn.

Overhauling the System

Canadian immigration remained expansionist until World War I. But depressed rates of immigration following the Depression and World War II lasted until Canada's post-war boom economy. Canada's new immigration policy in 1947 articulated who could get in: (1) British subjects and American citizens if meeting standards of health and character, (2) those who were qualified to work in labour-starved primary industries, (3) sponsored relatives from those European countries like Greece or Italy with strong family connections, and (4) refugees and displaced persons under international supervision. Compare this with entry criteria that in 1931 embraced British subjects, American citizens, dependants of permanent residents in Canada, and agriculturalists, while discouraging migrants from Southern and Eastern Europe and prohibiting entry of Asians between 1923 and 1947 (Castles and Miller 1998). Both self-interest and guilt over Canada's heartless denial of sanctuary for Holocaust victims during the war helped to fuel the immigration boom (Thompson and Weinfeld 1995). But in continuing to distinguish between preferred and non-preferred races, immigration was locked into a context of exclusion that privileged whiteness (Gwyn 2000).

The Department of Immigration and Citizenship was established in 1950. Immigration reforms related to the reunification of families and entry of skilled non-agricultural workers were introduced, but with orders to maintain a strict eye on Canada's absorptive capacity. To be sure, post-war immigration continued to reflect a preference for "preferred" Europeans. Quotas still applied for most non-Europeans. But a rethinking of who "got in" was prompted by the politics of availability. An expansionist immigration policy in the 1950s and 1960s reflected a growing demand for skilled and unskilled labour (Weinfeld and Wilkinson 1999). By 1962, Canadian immigration laws experienced a major shift when Canada became one of the first countries in the world to announce that "any suitable qualified person from any-where in the world" would qualify for entry, based primarily on personal merit. Canada's im-migration selection process was deracialized by shifting the selection criteria from national origin and ethnicity to those of skills, education, and experience (Mackey 1998; Hawkins 1974; Gwyn 2000). Class rather than race emerged as the pivotal criteria for entry once economic necessity overwhelmed restrictions based on racist ideology and national origins (Ralston 1999). Regulations were introduced emphasizing labour market needs and fam-ily relations, while independent-class immigrants were admitted on the strength of their technical/professional qualifications.

The criteria for entry to Canada underwent further reform in 1967. Canada's expanding economy required educated and skilled labour. But economic recovery in Europe had sharply usurped Canada's favourite taproot. Skilled immigrant labour could be found only in those quarters of the world that historically fell outside the "preferred categories" (Foster 1998). To fuel Canada's expanding economy, immigration pipelines tapped into non-conventional sources, including countries in Asia, Africa, and South and Central America. Criteria for entry were justified on four major immigrant classes: family, assisted relatives, independents, and refugees. A points system of evaluation was introduced: both independent and assisted-relative applicants were numerically assessed against the demands of occupation, educa-tion, and language expertise. Establishing a formally colour-blind immigration policy reduced the risk of race as criteria for entry. Still, the system was not free of systemic bias. A points system continued to favour class-advantaged male applicants with access to educational institutions (Abu-Laban 1999). This bias continues into the present (Thompson 2006).

Contemporary Policy

Canada has rarely engaged in a national debate over immigration and its relationship to society-building (Knowles 1992). For the most part, Canada's immigration program has been largely reactive in responding to domestic realities and international pressures. But passage of the *Immigration Act* of 1978 formalized a shift in thinking. The Act not only cod-ified the grounds for admission into Canada, but also articulated the core themes that sought to balance the goals of (1) family reunification, (2) protection of legitimate refugees, (3) enhancement of Canada's prosperity and global competitiveness, and (4) preservation of Canada's integrity. Immigration policy and programs focused on protecting national inter-ests, ensuring sufficient immigrants for Canada's economic growth, reuniting families, and providing a safe haven for those in need of protection (Citizenship and Immigration 2001). The federal government retained primary responsibility for the selection of immigrants and setting of policy. Nevertheless, it increasingly engages in consultation/negotiations with the provinces over policy agenda, immigration levels, and settlement measures, while sev-eral provinces like Manitoba and Quebec have taken advantage to exercise control over provincial nominees (Taylor 2005).

In short, immigration policy proposed to balance the enlightened with the practical to ensure fairness without loss of control. Political compromise focused on balancing the humanitarian goals of family reunification and refugee protection with labour market needs and economic contri-bution of immigrants (Grant and Oertel 1999). On one side, a commitment to humanitarian values is reflected in the relatively high numbers from the refugee and family reunification classes, even in the face of mounting criticism. On the other side, a reliance on high immigration totals reflects a commitment to moderate and controlled intake as grounds for economic growth. Prior to the late 1980s, immigration policies tended to respond to shortages or surpluses in the labour market. This "taps-on, taps-off" approach was challenged by focusing on immigration as integral to sustainable economic growth. Immigrants did not just serve the needs of labour; they also represented consumers and investors with the "critical mass" and "connections" to improve Canada's economic performance. Such a shift in thinking may help to explain the relatively high and constant rates of immigration during the 1990s despite recessionary pressures and public disgruntlement. Consider how Canada has averaged around 220 000 immigrants per year since the early 1990s, including 256 000 in 1993, compared to an average of 126 000 per year in the 1980s, 144 000 in the 1970s, and 137 000 in the 1960s.

A new immigration era began with the passage of the *Immigration and Refugee Protection Act* in 2002. As the first major change to Canada's immigration program since 1978, the Act sought to tighten up the immigration program by (1) imposing more restrictions on entry, (2) focusing on the recruitment of immigrants who can integrate quickly into the workplace and society, (3) shifting from a strict points system tally to an emphasis on labour market contribution and income-generating potential, (4) insisting on knowledge of an official language, and (5) firming up sponsorship rules to ensure that family-class immigrants assumed a greater burden of the costs in resettlement. In the words of Dennis Coderre, former minister of Citizenship and Immigration (2003:5), in defending a new immigration law:

> Our strategy is designed to strike a balance between attracting workers with flexible skills, reuniting families and being tough on those who pose a threat to Canadian security, all the while maintaining Canada's humanitarian tradition of providing a safe haven to people in need of protection.

Of particular note are proposals to redefine the economic category by shifting the emphasis from one of occupation to that of flexible and transferable skills in line with Canada's growing knowledge-based economy. But not everyone is happy with the focus on human capital attributes rather than occupational demand. Critics charge that the system is now clearly elitist, resulting in a shortage of skilled tradespeople (including a large number of truck drivers) and a surplus of foreign-trained professionals who cannot crack a highly regulated job market (Goar 2004). Changes to the processing of refugees have been introduced as well, with the result that the fate of refugees may be determined by a one-step process involving single-member panels with limited avenues of appeal (Dauvergne 2004). The introduction of a safe third country agreement with the United States may compromise the status of refugee claimants, critics argue, in part because the United States offers less protection than Canada, frequently detains asylum seekers without identity papers, does not recognize refugee criteria such as gender persecution, and withholds social assistance or work permits to claimants for the first six months (Maccharles 2004). Based on projections from the first half of 2005, Canada will receive 17 300 refugee claims for the calendar year, down from the post-1989 average of 29 680, including a high of 44 714 in 2001, in part because of the Safe Third Country agreement, tightening of border security, and interception measures by Canadian officials overseas (Keung 2005). Finally, in this age of insecurity, security issues have leapt to the forefront of immigration issues (Collacott 2006; Crepeau and Nakache 2006). Passage of Bill C-36 and the issuing of security certificates enable the government to detain, arrest, and deport immigrants or refugees based on suspicion of terrorism or secret evidence that suspects cannot access (Beare 2003).

Immigration into Canada: A Paradigm Shift

The dynamics of contemporary immigration differ from those of the past. Immigration into Canada is influenced by global labour shortages in key economic sectors, competition on the global markets, demands of an aging population, a shrinking labour force, shifts in source countries, and improvements in communication and transportation networks (Citizenship and Immigration Canada 2001). The logic governing immigration differs as well in terms of focus, rationale, underlying assumptions, and anticipated outcomes. The nature of immigrants with respect to origins, requisite skills, and expectations has shifted as well. No less evident are changes in immigration patterns—both more transient and complex than in the past—with periods of sojourning increasingly more common in a world of circular migration, dual citizenship, and transnational communities (Willis and Yeoh 2000). Comparing past patterns with present-day practices reveals the following trends (also Boyd and Vickers 2000):

- From a focus on immigration as short-term labour supply (taps-on, taps-off) to that of sustainable economic growth (plug and play), thus shifting the emphasis from matching immigrants with worker shortages to that of attracting newcomers with education, skills, and language who can quickly integrate into a knowledge-based economy (Beach et al. 2003; Weber 2005).

- From a focus on immigration as a program to be administered to a recruiting agency for expediting the entry of the world's brightest and best (Volpe 2005). The focus on bringing into Canada those highly-skilled knowledge workers is consistent with the government's sustainable economy agenda.

- From a loosely monitored administration with relatively open borders to a tightly regulated and politically charged system involving different levels of government, including the provinces.

- From a focus on whom to keep out to an emphasis on whom to let in, including a greater emphasis on relatives and workers from wealthier countries who do not require costly resettlement services.

- From rural-based agricultural/primary industry workers to urban-based skilled professionals.

- From an emphasis on racial and national origins as criteria for selection to that of colour-blindness in attracting the best and brightest.

- From a reliance on European sources to those from Asia and other so-called non-conventional origins.

- From a purely pragmatic focus for advancing national interests to a balancing of the practical with the compassionate without reneging on the "big picture."

Despite these shifts in trends, two themes appear to be constant. First, immigration remains a response to capitalist demands for labour (see Li 2003). The prime objective has never wavered: to supply a labour pool, first for agriculture and settlement, then for industrialization, and currently for the professionally skilled. The fact that the preferred requirements have varied from one historical context to the next does not invalidate this underlying commitment. Second, much of the discourse behind reform reflects an unspoken assumption that immigrants are a burden on Canadian society whose costs must be minimized for ongoing acceptance. To be sure, there are "good" immigrants who are economically productive, readily self-sufficient, and can easily integrate without draining public resources (Abu-Laban 1999). But "bad" immigrants are increasingly tarred as problems rather than assets who don't do much for Canada. Such a polarization does not auger well for establishing a co-operative framework for living together with our differences.

IMMIGRATION PROGRAMS: WHO GETS IN?

- A total of 235 808 people immigrated to Canada in 2004, well within the planning target range of 220 000 and 245 000.

- Fifty-seven percent of immigrants were from the economic class (including both principal applicants, spouses, and dependents), 27 percent from the family class, and 14 percent from the refugee class (both conventional and claimants). In 1993, both economic and family class accounted for 44 percent of all immigrant totals. A numerical breakdown is shown in Table 9.1.

- Immigrant landings by classes can vary from region to region. For the Waterloo region, 38.8 percent of the immigrants between 1996 and 2002 were economic (skilled workers), 34.7 were sponsored relatives (family), and 26 percent were refugees. For Toronto, 60.5 percent of immigrants between 1995 and 2002 were economic, 28.4 percent were sponsored relatives, and 9.5 percent were refugees.

- A total of 9762 individuals arrived under the economic subcategory of business class (including investors, self-employed, and entrepreneurs). This figure includes spouses and dependants.

- Live-in caregivers (spouses and dependants) totalled 4291, including spouses and dependants.

- Provinces including Manitoba and Quebec are exerting growing control over the selection of immigrant candidates, thereby bypassing the backlogged pool of permanent resident applications under Ottawa's jurisdiction (Taylor 2005). Typical processing time for Canadian visa classes is 32 months but for provincial nominees, 7 months.

- Sixty-nine percent of immigrants come from Asia, the Middle East, and Africa. The top four countries of origin (country of last permanent residence) were China (15 percent or 36 410), India (11 percent or 25 568), the Philippines (5.5 percent or 13 299), and Pakistan (12 796). The United States was a distant fifth. China and India have held the top two positions for seven consecutive years.

TABLE 9.1 Immigrants by Landing Class and Totals, 2004	
Family class	62 745
Economic class (principal applicants)	55 579
Economic class (spouses & dependants)	77 764
Refugees/Protected persons (conventional)	10 525
Refugees/Protected (claimants/asylum)	22 158
Other	6637
Total	235 808

- Over half of all immigrants (53 percent) settled in Ontario. Quebec at 19 percent and British Columbia at 16 percent followed. About 1.5 percent settled in the four Atlantic provinces.

- More than 90 percent of immigrants who arrived during the 1990s lived in a metropolitan area. Of recent immigrants, Toronto had the largest proportion at 23 percent, followed by Vancouver at 21 percent and Montreal at 9 percent. Kitchener, London, and Windsor received about 7–8 percent.

- Thirty-eight percent of immigrants between 25 and 64 years of age were university graduates.

- Just over 37 percent of new immigrants declared no knowledge of either French or English on landing. Twenty-nine percent were children less than 10 years old.

- Refugees account for about 17 percent of all newcomers. The five leading countries for refugees were Pakistan, Columbia, China, Afghanistan, and Sri Lanka. The refugee backlog declined from a high of 56 000 to 28 000 at the end of 2004.

- Foreign worker flows increased to 90 661 in 2004, with seasonal agricultural workers forming the largest group.

- Foreign student flows totalled 56 529 in 2004, with 43 percent from China, Japan, and South Korea.

Classes of Immigrants

Canada's immigration program defines three categories of entry into Canada: family, economic, and refugee. The family class recognizes the need for families to stay together to improve their integration into Canada. Families can employ two basic entry strategies (Thomas 2001). They can migrate as a unit by relying on the skills and resources of the principal applicant to qualify for admission under the point system (see below). Or some members might migrate first, then send for the remaining members once permanent residency is established. Under this strategy, immediate members of the family—a spouse (or fiancé), parents, grandparents, dependant and unmarried children under 19 years of age, and orphaned brothers, sisters, nieces, nephews, and grandchildren—are allowed automatic entry into Canada provided, of course, they are of good health, pass security checks, and are without a criminal record. To ensure family relationships are authentic, individuals may be asked to prove identity through DNA testing, especially for those from Africa, the Caribbean, India, and Pakistan (Jimenez 2004). Non-immediate nuclear-family relatives such as aunts and uncles must rely on points for entry.

The economic class (including skilled workers and business people, viz., entrepreneurs, self-employed, and investors) has emerged as a major source of landing for immigrants. In contrast to the period between 1980 and 1995 when most immigrants entered Canada on the strength of family relations, the current situation is much different with nearly 60 percent of immigrants defined as economic. As Canada increasingly looks for those immigrants with higher skill levels whose costs of training and education are borne outside this country, this trend is likely to continue (Weinfeld and Wilkinson 1999). Keep in mind that, strictly speaking, the totals for the economic class include spouses and dependents who are not preselected on a skills basis, with the result that in 2004 just over 23 percent of immigrants from the economic class were processed as principal applicants under the point system (see Table 9.2).

A point system is applied that assesses the principal applicant on the grounds of job-related skills, age, official-language knowledge, and education. The candidate also

TABLE 9.2	The Skilled Worker Point System
Maximum Points Allowed	**Criteria for Points**
Education—25 points	25 points for education (maximum for PhD or MA, 5 points for high school dip)
Language skills—24 points	24 points for language proficiency (up to 16 points for first official language—reading, writing, speaking, understanding; up to 8 points for the second official language)
Work experience—21 points	21 points for work experience (top points for 4 years of experience in a highly skilled occupation, 15 points for one year)
Employment status—10 points	10 points for arranged employment in Canada
Age—10 points	10 points for age (maximum points for those between 21 and 49; 2 points less each year over 49 or under 21 years of age)
Adaptability—10 points	10 points for adaptability (5 points for full-time job experience in Canada; 5 points for full-time study in Canada; 5 points for having a close relative in Canada, 5 points for a spouse with a university degree)

Source: Citizenship and Immigration Canada.

undergoes an assessment for adaptability. The number of points required for entry varies, with 67 points for skilled workers and the self-employed. Applicants from the business class (both investor and entrepreneur) can earn up to 35 points for their commercial experiences and connections. Assisted relatives also receive credit as nominated immigrants (5 points), but require additional points elsewhere to qualify. Everyone in this category must pass the usual health and security clearances. Each adult applicant must also pay a $500 application fee ($100 for children), in addition to a $490 right-of-landing fee (until recently, $975) to a maximum of four members per family. The landing fee was waived for refugees in 2000.

The economic class includes the business subcategory—namely, investor, entrepreneur, and self-employed. Both the investor and entrepreneur subcategories entail a transfer of funds as a precondition for entry into Canada. The "entrepreneurial" program selects immigrants with an ability to establish or buy a business that will create at least two full-time jobs for non-family members. The amount of investment varies across Canada, but to qualify, an entrepreneur must hold at least 33.3 percent of the equity of a Canadian business. Under the "investor" program, applicants must meet the usual immigration criteria, with a demonstrated net worth of $800 000. In exchange for investing $400 000 in a Canadian fund for five years, a business applicant receives permanent resident status (Jimenez 2004). Nearly 20 000 immigrants have taken advantage of this program since its inception in 1986, with a total investment of $4.3 billion (Jimenez 1999). But the program has also been plagued by charges of fraudulent abuse, cumbersome delays (up to five years to have files processed), and gross mismanagement that provides little of benefit to Canadians (Mitrovic 1999; also Ley and Hiebert 2001). As a result, the number of investor and entrepreneur immigration applications dropped to 1961 in the first eight months of 2004, from 6851 in 2000 (Jimenez 2004). There is talk of transferring more responsibility to the provinces for the monitoring of investment funds.

The refugee category is the third category of landing. Refugees are accepted as part of Canada's humanitarian and legal obligations to the world community. Since 1951, or more accurately 1969 when it signed the 1951 UN Convention on Refugees, Canada has performed admirably in protecting **asylum seekers**, especially by comparison with countries that perfunctorily deny entry or routinely deport (Walkom 1999). Since World War II, Canada has officially admitted over half a million refugees, with recent annual intakes ranging from 20 000 to 35 000. In 2004, according to the UNHRC, Canada was the 5th largest destination country for asylum-seekers, just behind France, United States, United Kingdom, and Germany (Crepeau and Nakache 2006). Two categories of refugees are "recognized," neither of which require points for entry. One category consists of convention or sponsored refugees who are selected abroad. These "assisted" refugees are preselected either by government officials (Government Assisted Refugees) or by private agencies, individuals, clubs, or church groups (Privately Sponsored Refugees), with private sponsors obligated to provide support for up to 10 years. Both government and privately sponsored refugees acquire landed immigrant (or permanent residence) status before arriving in Canada, and assistance through government programs once they arrive. A second category consists of refugee claimants (Landed in Canada Refugees) who arrive unannounced by foot, boat, or plane, often without documentation such as passports, and claim refugee status from within Canada (Dempsey and Yu 2004). In contrast with convention refugees, refugee claimants are not entitled to some of the benefits and social services that Canadians enjoy until they receive their permanent residence status.

Clearly then, refugees are admitted along two opposing paths. Those stranded in refugee camps tend to be selected on their ability to establish themselves in Canada rather than on a genuine need for protection. By contrast, refugee claimants are selected on the basis of protection from state persecution. In 1980, convention refugees (approved from abroad) outnumbered refugee claimants (announced at arrival) by 39 992 to 718. By 1992, refugee claimants outnumbered convention refugees by 37 152 to 14 726. In 2000, Canada accepted 26 708 refugees, of which 12 955 were successful refugee claimants (arrived unannounced), 7367 were government assisted, 2905 were privately sponsored, 3481 were dependants abroad, and 3258 consisted of Kosovar refugees, who received permanent resident status in 2000 (Citizenship and Immigration Canada 2001). But difficulties in processing refugee claimants have created a crisis that shows few signs of easing.

INSIGHT	**Processing Refugee Claimants**

Arrival at Canada's borders activates a set of refugee determination protocols. The current system consists of a so-called simplified procedure that purports to balance fairness with efficiency. On entry into Canada, an asylum seeker can claim to be a refugee. Within 72 hours of entry, this refugee claimant is interviewed and assessed by a senior immigration official. To avoid the possibility of false claimants entering Canada, the government insists on proper documentation to prove identity. Without documents, refugees can be temporarily detained until proof of identity is established. But unless they pose a serious criminal or health risk, or have been previously deported, refugee claimants are simply interviewed, photographed, and fingerprinted, then allowed to circulate freely. This perceived laxity, critics argue, provides an open invitation for refugees with terrorist links to evade detection or deportation. Once identity has been established and forms completed, refugee claimants must attend a more detailed hearing by the Immigration and Refugee Board (IRB).

| **FYI** | **Immigration and Refugee Board** |

The IRB constitutes a quasi-independent tribunal whose primary (but not exclusive) function is to hear refugee protection claims. Created in 1989 following a scandal involving political and diplomatic interference in the refugee determination process, this administrative tribunal is less formal than its judicial counterparts, thus allowing claimants to present their case in a simpler manner (Fleury 2004). The 210 members of the IRB who are paid between $87 000 and $103 000 are political appointees appointed by Order in Council for a period of seven years.

Following extensive training and access to the refugee documentation centre for assistance in making decisions, board members are charged with determining whether asylum seekers (refugee claimants who arrive unannounced) are genuine (fleeing persecution) or in need of protection because of dangers to their lives if returned to their homeland (Jimenez 2004). The difficulty of the job should not be underestimated. Many of the claims are complex, allegations are often difficult to document or verify, and many claimants must speak through an interpreter.

Those claimants who are almost certain of entry receive an "expedited hearing" to hasten the process and prevent a backlog. If the claimant is not given expedited treatment, another hearing is convened with a two-member IRB panel (now, one member). Endorsement by one of two panel members was sufficient for entry into Canada, although under some circumstances—for example, destroying identity documents—the claimant would have had to satisfy both board members. Once cleared, the claimant can then apply for permanent residency. Successful claimants are also issued a social insurance number and a record of landing (identity papers) which allows them to open a bank account, find proper employment, and travel freely within Canada.

Of course, not all claimants are successful. If the IRB says no (a unanimous decision in writing is required for a rejection), the claimant must leave within 30 days or face arrest and deportation. Claimants may

also appeal by applying for a review in the federal court within 15 days but only on matters of procedure (mistakes in law), not on the merits of the case. The entire process may take between six months and a year, but much longer if all appeal avenues are pursued (Fleury 2004) Those who have exhausted all appeal routes are ticketed for deportation, but few ever are, partly because of compassionate grounds, partly because of administrative bungling, and partly because of the dangers in extraditing failed claimants to their homeland (assuming, of course, the countries in question will allow failed claimants to re-enter) (Jimenez 2005). Unless the deportees voluntarily indicate their exit plans, Immigration Canada has no way of confirming who leaves or who stays. Finally, even failed refugee claimants may have a convincing argument for staying in Canada because of the length of time involved in processing individual cases (Gallagher 2004).

COSTS AND BENEFITS OF IMMIGRATION: PROBLEM OR SOLUTION?

Immigration has been a defining characteristic of Canada (Ibbitson 2005). From our earliest days as a nation through to the global transformations of recent decades, immigration has been vital to Canada's social, economic, and cultural development. Canadians have reacted to immigrants and immigration in different ways, ranging from enthusiasm and endorsement on the one hand to resentment and hostility on the other, with a combination of indifference, resignation, and indecision in between. For some, Canada's immigration and refugee programs are positively endorsed as model of success, reflecting both the epitome of Canadian values and Canada's maturity as a nation. Immigrants and refugees built this country, thanks to their industry and enthusiasm, and Canada's prosperity and identity will continue to depend on the perpetual movement of people. Others disagree, and point out how arguments cited in defence of immigration neither stand up to empirical scrutiny nor have a logical basis (Francis 2001; Stoffman 2003). For critics, immigration is essentially an investment option for Canada, to be measured in cost–benefit terms, and evaluated accordingly (see also Amiel 2000). If the costs are too high, pare back or bail out. Still others don't know or don't care or don't know where to start. Canadians in general are divided almost evenly in assessing whether Canada has too many immigrants, although opinions about their impact on the economy vary proportionally with the health of the economy (see Keung 2001). A step back from the fray can remind us that immigration *is* a benefit that comes *with* a cost depending on the context, consequences, and criteria for evaluation.

Increased immigration into Canada has been justified or vilified on various grounds. Studies in other parts of the world, such as Australia, New Zealand, and the United States, confirm that, on balance, immigrants are a net contributor to society—demographically, socially, culturally, and economically (Castles and Miller 1998; Fleras and Spoonley 1999; Hiebert et al. 2003). The same conclusions apply to Canada (Halli and Driedger 1999). The following benefits are most commonly cited: Immigrants create more jobs than they take; as consumers they provide markets for Canadian goods; they are more likely to start businesses than other Canadians; they are better qualified in terms of education; they provide the demographics by offsetting the effects of an aging population and declining birth rates; and they pay more in taxes than they accept in social services. Immigrants not only do the drudge work that Canadians disdain, but also ease labour shortages during phases of capitalist expansion (it is estimated that all new labour market growth by 2011 will come from immigrants; Taylor 2005). Immigrants tend to possess drive and vitality, with boundless energy and optimism, and a willingness to take entrepreneurial risks by capitalizing on international links to improve Canada's competitive position in a global economy. Finally, despite financial and social costs related to initial settlement in Canada, immigrants are the same people who will keep the economy afloat so that Canadians can retire comfortably (Ley and Hiebert 2001).

In general, then, rather than crippling the economy, immigrants inject a much-needed kick-start because of their commitment, connections, and cash. To be sure, economic benefits are not distributed equally; some regions and sectors receive a disproportionate share of both costs and benefits. Some parts of the economy (real estate or immigration lawyers) benefit from immigration, others such as manual workers suffer (Stoffman 2003), but the average person may be largely unaffected. Certain immigrants provide immediate benefit (especially economic-class immigrants), some may not (refugee class) because of their circumstances, and others do so indirectly or over time (family-class immigrants) (Li 2003).

Such an assessment makes it doubly important to appreciate how immigration is both beneficial and costly.

Not surprisingly, Canadians tend to hold competing views of immigrants. On one side are images of immigrants as rich and pampered who buy their way into Canada. On the other side, immigrants are seen as poor people who have fled their homes and are now struggling to survive through minimum wage employment or illegal activities (Kazemipour and Halli 2003; also Montreuil and Bourhis 2004). Canadians tend to be comfortable with immigrants who are poor, appear to be grateful for the opportunity, and are willing to start at the bottom as cooks, labourers, and farmhands. Immigrants are "acceptable" if (1) their cultural practices are compatible with Canada's; (2) they know their place by acknowledging their status as "guests" in Canada and fit in accordingly; and (3) they appreciate that immigration policy must advance national interests rather than cater to minority demands. Canadians are less sure of how to "cope" with those immigrants who are affluent, confident, assertive, and highly qualified; unwilling to put up with slights or slurs as the price of admission or staying; and, as professional transnationals, are willing to shop their talents wherever the global economy will take them (Siddiqui 1999).

This ambivalence is reflected in different ways. Many people are supportive of immigrants and refugees as hard-working and positive contributors to society. But Canadians are openly critical of immigrants who do not add "value" to Canada or, worse still, prove a drain on its resources (Blackwell 2004). Others dislike what they see as threats to Canada's economy; for example, immigrants may depress wages by creating more supply than demand in the labour market (Stoffman 2003). The "problems" that immigrants are *thought* to bring to Canada are a sticking point for many. These include allegations that immigrants are using their ties abroad to establish illegal international distribution systems for contraband drugs, loan-sharking, extortion rackets, prostitution, and smuggling of "human cargo" into Canada. Long-term gains may be undeniable, but short-terms costs may sting, yet often are offloaded by Ottawa to provinces, municipalities, and institutions (Simpson 1999; Francis 2001a, b). Canadians may not be unduly upset over immigration when the economy is booming, but concerns mount when the economy cools and (1) competition intensifies for good jobs and scarce resources, (2) immigrant labour becomes a permanent underclass, and (3) imbalances appear in education, welfare and service demands, and income distribution (Goldsborough 2000). The changing ethnic mix is endorsed as enriching the Canadian landscape; yet fears mount over the potential for social friction or diminution of core Canadian values (Isbister 1996). Canadians may resent the presence of refugees who jump the queue to get in, but approve of their availability as cheap and disposable labour in factories, restaurants, fields, and homes (Canadian Council of Refugees 2000).

In short, a backlash is inevitable because of these ambiguities, and any reaction may be fuelled by perceptions that immigration policy has conceded too much power to ethnic communities, that skilled immigrants are given preference over educated Canadians, that symbols of Canada will disappear because of immigration cultures, and that uncontrolled immigration will unravel Canada's social fabric. Canadians may in principle accept the necessity or inevitability of immigrants and refugees, but bristle at legislative loopholes and unscrupulous stakeholders, especially when dysfunctional government policies dovetail with a vested interest in preserving the status quo (Stoffman 2002). Also palpable is a moral quandary: Canadians do not want Canada to become a haven for terrorists because of misplaced generosity or inadequate screening procedures, but squirm at the prospect of sending people back to torture or death. Canadians are unhappy with refugees or immigrants who prove to be a social or medical burden, particularly those refugees who arrive in Canada without proper identification (SES 2003), yet balk at the prospect of deporting them to a cruel fate (Duffy 1999).

Let's be realistic: No person, no matter how opposed to immigration in principle or practice, is without some sympathy for the plight of the world's poorest. Similarly, no person regardless of pro-immigrant sympathies is without some concern over the negative impact of immigration on some sectors of society (Millman 1997). Somewhere between the "yeas" and the "nays" are those who see the interplay of costs and benefits. The in-between sector takes a practical outlook on immigration. With an intake of approximately 220 000–250 000 new Canadians each year, many with radically different cultures, experiences, and expectations, a degree of friction and annoyance is inevitable. So too is the likelihood of crowding, pressure on existing services, inflated markets, crime surges, and congested roads. Costs cannot be ignored: A country cannot expect to have a policy of immigration-driven sustained economic growth without some social and economic repercussions. Cultural clashes are inescapable as well. A sense of proportion is badly needed. If Canadians value the cultural and economic benefits associated with immigration, they must be prepared to shoulder the costs.

For the in-betweens, then, immigration is neither a sacred cow immune to criticism nor a convenient scapegoat to blame for Canada's problems. People who occupy an informed middle ground acknowledge the partial validity of arguments, both for and against. They acknowledge that costs come with benefits; for example, there is much of value in Canada's principled (rule-based, transparent, and accountable) approach toward immigration; nevertheless, a proliferation of rules can create bureaucracy, red tape, and inflexibility because of high volumes, in the process eliminating room for discretionary decisions except at political levels where such interference can prove costly (Thompson 2005). In other words, answers to questions about the costs and benefits of immigration are rarely right or wrong, but both right and wrong, depending on the context, criteria, and consequences. Few responses to the value of immigration are of an either/or variety but rather reflect the possibility of both/and, with the result that inflated claims on both sides of the debate often conceal whatever truths they contain.

| INSIGHT | **Immigration to Canada: Keeping the Dialogue Open** |

Canada's immigration program is subject to constant scrutiny and endless criticism. Nowhere is this more evident than in debates regarding who gets in. The key question is "What kind of immigration program do Canadians want?" (Thompson 2005). The current system appears incapable of coping with the volume of applicants who qualify under Canada's rules to apply as economic migrants. The end result: a frustrating and dangerous backlog because of insufficient resources for processing applicants who bounce out of an inflexible system and seek ministerial permits for entry. Even those who make it into Canada often fail to provide what the economy needs, where it is needed, and who is needed (Travers 2005). In that Canada's current immigration policies aren't working but are starting to fray at the edges, a dialogue cannot come too soon, revolving around four key questions: how many immigrants, from which sources, which class is preferred, and what for (why does Canada need immigrants)?

1. *What for: Does Canada need immigrants?*

   Why does Canada accept immigrants and refugees? Canada may want more immigrants because of tradition, openness, obligation, or compassion for the less fortunate. But does Canada need more immigrants (Stoffman 1998)? Some say no: Immigration policy appears to be driven by the well-intentioned but possibly mistaken belief that size matters, that is, increasing the size of Canada's population will make it bigger and better (Denley 1998; Collacott 2001a). Others say yes to controlled immigration. Immigrants and society-building are strongly linked and of proven benefit. Immigrants provide economic benefits; they enrich Canadians through diversity, replenish emigrants lost to the United States, bolster international reputations, and forge global linkages. And others still want a wider window of opportunity. After all, does Canada have a moral right to create laws for barring those less fortunate because of an accident of birth (Coyne 1998)? On what grounds can we justify securing our privilege while others suffer and perish?

2. *Does Canada accept too many immigrants?*

   Critics say that Canada is stretching its "absorptive capacity" by accepting too many immigrants and refugees. Immigration into Canada is currently in the 225 000–235 000 range. Some argue for an increase in numbers to about 300 000 (reflecting about one percent of Canada's population—a figure the Liberal government continues to endorse [Clark 2005]); others propose 150 000 as the preferred annual total— a figure that brings Canada in line with its post-war average and with worldwide proportions. Others suggest that Canada should allow an unlimited number of immigrants; after all, immigration controls are racist, inefficient, and costly and tend to perpetuate a kind of global apartheid (Richmond 1994; Hayter 2001). Which answer is acceptable? What is "too much" or "not enough,"and how can we determine an acceptable figure (one that can be operationalized, i.e., converted into measurable values)? On what grounds? When is the absorptive capacity stretched to the limit? Is there a principled way to justify any proposed levels?

3. *Does Canada take in too many "non-conventional" immigrants?*

   Since the 1980s, the largest percentage of immigrants to Canada has been from the so-called non-conventional countries, including about 60 percent from Asia. Should Canada seek more European or American immigrants or is that pipeline largely closed? What is the proper proportion, and can any ratio be justified or attained, keeping in mind that Canada no longer has the luxury of cherry picking who it wants from where? Not only is Canada in competition with other industrialized countries for the brightest and best, but immigration is increasingly controlled by powerful global forces that are difficult to regulate with national policy initiatives (Suarez-Orozco and Suarez-Orozco 2001).

4. *Does Canada recruit the wrong "class" of immigrants?*

   Canada's immigration quotas are unevenly divided among the family-reunification class, the economic class, and refugees. Some argue for more immigrants with the social and economic skills to contribute directly to Canada. But does Canada really need highly skilled personnel whose foreign qualifications are not readily accepted or are in direct competition with professional bodies and Canadian-born university grads (Stanford 2001; Collacott 2001a)? Can Canada justify skimming off the best and the brightest from the developing world, to that world's detriment and cost, without cautioning immigrants about the obstacles in finding employment consistent with their skills, experience, and credentials (Siddiqui 1999; Bragg 1998)? Perhaps the focus should be on immigrants who are willing to do (from service jobs to manual labour) what many Canadian-born disdain. Others believe that integrity of the family is uppermost in building a strong Canada, yet are concerned that Canada cannot control the quality of immigrants under family reunification. What about refugees who are most in need of Canada's protection? Why even take

refugees, critics argue; after all, unlike immigrants they are not pre-selected on the basis of making a direct contribution to Canadian society, but are perceived as imposing a heavier demand on Canada's health, welfare, housing, social assistance, and public sector programs; having less education and lower employment earnings; less likely to speak an official language; and experiencing more turmoil-related stress (Dempsey and Yu 2004; see also Adelman 2004). How do you sort out who is right or wrong? What is the proper mix of categories? On what basis does one justify an answer?

These questions go to the very heart of immigration debates in Canada. Answers are plentiful but agreement is in scarce supply, with the result that dialogue and debate over immigration remain as contested as ever.

"SETTLING DOWN, FITTING IN, MOVING UP"

Every act of immigration is like suffering a brain stroke: One has to learn to walk again, to talk again, to move around the world again, and, probably most difficult of all, one has to learn how to re-establish a sense of community. *(Vivian Rakoff, cited in Fulford 2003)*

Migration involves more than a movement of people with economic overtones. Rather, migration needs to be seen as a complex and drawn-out transformational process, involving a host of political and social factors and economic and cultural consequences for both the sending and receiving country (Castles and Miller 1998). Immigrants and refugees are being "pushed" from their homeland because of political oppression, ethnic conflicts, demographic pressure, and economic stagnation. They also are "pulled" to another country to take advantage of opportunity and freedom—and excitement.

The same is true for Canada: Immigration policy and practices go beyond the simple process of importing labour for Canada-building. The relationship (or "social contract") between immigrants and Canada embraces a two-way process of mutual accommodation (Parekh 1997; Frith 2003; Spencer 2003). Canada expects immigrants to identify with core cultural values, make a positive contribution, participate through involvement, and abide by the laws of society. Immigrants, in turn, expect equitable treatment through removal of discriminatory barriers, conferral of citizenship rights, and the right to identify with the cultural tradition of their choice. In short, coming to Canada activates a social contract in which immigrants trade talents for responsibilities while Canada exchanges safety and security for rights.

Canada's immigration policy continues to emphasize the integration of new Canadians. In hopes of equipping migrants with the tools to settle down, both the governmental and non-profit sector offer language training, employment counselling, and translation services. Provincial variations are noticeable: Ottawa provides Quebec with $3806 per immigrant for settlement services, although Ontario receives only $819 per each new arrival, with the result that while Ontario attracts about 55 percent of all new immigrants, it gets just 34 percent of the federal funding for their settlement. (The federal government promised more funding for Ontario in late 2005). For some immigrants, the settling down process is filled with hope and opportunity; for others it is fraught with danger and disappointment (Suarez-Orozco and Suarez-Orozco 2001). The immigrant experience may prove less gratifying than originally anticipated, including a sense of social dislocation as elders drift apart from the junior generation, as younger women chafe over traditional roles and pervasive paternalism, and as educated elites become estranged from the community at large (Handa 2003). Andrei Codrescu (1995:47) writes of the bittersweet, near death experiences of his Romanian mother:

> Most people come here because they are sick of being poor. They want to eat and they want something to show for their industry. But soon enough it becomes evident to them that these things are not enough. They have eaten and they are full, but they have eaten alone . . . This time they are lacking something more elusive than salami and furniture. They are bereft of a social and cultural milieu . . . Leaving behind your kin, your friends, your language, your smells, your childhood, is traumatic. It is a kind of death. You're dead for the home folk and they are dead to you.

For others, the "clash of cultures" creates constant tensions and worries:

> Many of us were greeted with a myriad of challenges when we arrived, but we decided to take things one day at a time. We missed our home countries but then we find opportunities here that we may not have had back home. There are some values here that we appreciate and would like to add to the values back home that we still hold on to. On the other hand, many of us still cannot help missing home because there are certain values over there that we just cannot find here. Sometimes acceptance and closeness become very limited to us. We have friends here but even when you get close, it does not feel like the closeness back home. This makes you wonder if it is your imagination or whether you are unconsciously holding back, apprehensive about giving your all. We try hard to make adjustments taking on the values here that we like and at the same time holding on to some values from home, trying to have the best of both worlds. (Peprah 2005)

To be sure, many new Canadians appear to be relatively satisfied with the quality of life in Canada. There is appreciation for the opportunities and services available to them and their children, the promise of human freedom, and sufficient market transparency to succeed. Nevertheless, many will confront a series of problems that have accompanied them into Canada or encounter problems upon entry and settlement. Problems may arise because of personal shortcomings related to culture shock, lack of political power, loss of economic well-being, personal isolation, and discriminatory barriers that preclude entry or acceptance. The persistence of immigrant enclaves has raised questions about Canada's "welcome mat." To what extent are these enclaves the result of racist and exclusionary practices such as housing discrimination? Or do they reflect an immigrant preference for familiar community (Novac 1999; Yelaja 2005)? The host society may prove unhelpful as well. Immigrants may not be second-class citizens under the law, but remain so in public perception and national discourses (Siddiqui 2000).

Generally speaking, the primary concerns of new Canadians are practical and survival related. In contrast with the more political demands of Canada's founding peoples for self-determining autonomy, immigrants and refugees are more concerned with the issues of equality, participation, and acceptance. Foremost is the desire to "put down roots" by "settling down" and "fitting in" to Canadian society, without necessarily severing ties with their cultural tradition. More specifically, immigrant needs can be itemized as follows:

1. A workplace without discrimination, racism, and exploitation.

2. The expansion of opportunities in the labour and education markets as well as improved access to housing, government institutions, social services, and mass media.

3. Conferral of full citizenship rights, including the right to move, participate, and criticize, without undue bureaucratic meddling.

4. Access to the best Canadian society has to offer without diminishing their children's sense of cultural identity.

5. The capability to express themselves in terms of their identity without paying a penalty in the process.

6. Respect for their differences as a legitimate and valued part of society.

Taken together, immigrants and multicultural minorities want the best that both worlds have to offer. They want to be treated as individuals by being accepted for what they do rather than being denied because of who they are. Conversely, they also want appreciation for who they are culturally speaking, without sacrificing meaningful involvement in society. Full citizenship rights are important, but so too is recognition of their cultural worth as a people with a meaningful past—yet no less Canadian.

But what might be regarded as the best of times may also prove the worst of times. Models of immigration settlement that were based on the European experience may no longer apply (Suarez-Orozco and Suarez-Orozco 2001). The European model saw immigration settlement as an upwardly mobile journey, that is, the longer immigrants lived in their adopted country, the greater the likelihood of success. But new patterns of immigration experience are emerging (Pendakur and Pendakur 2004). Some immigrants are primed for success; others are being painted out of the picture because of discrimination, racism, and prejudice, and still others are just muddling through. Immigrant qualifications continue to be dismissed, education degrees devalued, and overseas experience discounted as next to worthless (Finnie and Meng 2002). Foreign education counts for about half of the value of Canadian schooling in terms of earning power, while foreign experience has little market value in Canada. Not surprisingly, highly skilled Canadians find themselves segregated in menial and unskilled occupations with little in the way of security or prospects for promotion. Even those immigrant women and men who have "made it" experience ambivalence. Many continue to feel undervalued and underappreciated, patronized by the dominant sector, and torn between the cross-cutting pressures of affirming their distinctiveness while accepting middle-class norms (see also Shipler 1997). Refusal to recognize the credentials of new Canadians costs Canada $55 billion in lost revenue (Conference Board of Canada 2004).

Despite the much-hyped reference to Canada as a land of opportunity, thousands of immigrants can't find work in Canada because the closed-shop mentality of licensed occupations, from medicine to dentistry, continues to impose restrictions and deny accreditation. A 2004 study of 829 immigrant engineers in Ontario (cited in the 18 April 2005 issue of *The Globe and Mail*) found that 55 percent were unable to find jobs and 29 percent were underemployed or working at non-engineering jobs. This bottleneck that prevents professionals from gainful employment may reflect a fundamental disconnect: The federal government controls immigration, but the provinces control the licensing, while the professional bodies control who gets in. And the crisis involving foreign-born doctors is drawing even closer scrutiny and criticism.

CASE STUDY	**Being Discredited/Getting Accredited**

You can't get a job in your field without Canadian experience, and you can't get that experience without a job. (Naomi Alboim, School of Policy Studies, Queen's University. Cited in Taylor 2005:34)

Much is made of Canada's *brain drain* into the United States. Canadians are less likely to acknowledge that Canada is a recipient of a *brain gain*, thanks to an immigration policy that poaches the "best" from those countries that can scarcely afford to lose their "brightest." Paradoxically, however, Canada practises its own version of a brain drain by rejecting immigrant skills once they are in Canada (Conference Board of Canada 2004). Canada's inability to effectively integrate professionally trained immigrants into the regulated-professions labour market is of growing concern (PROMPT 2004). To ensure public safety, professional and regulatory bodies (including 400 in Canada) were established for the licensing and certification of professionals and recognition of international credentials (Hagopian 2003). But foreign-trained professionals are poorly informed about accreditation procedures prior to entry into Canada, including the lack of a national body for recognition of foreign degrees and credentials, with each province setting a different standard for certification. Many have to repeat the educational requirements and undergo costly and time-consuming retraining. Risk-averse Canadian employers are reluctant to hire them because of perceived gaps in their professional knowledge or lack of language skills (Taylor 2005). Not surprisingly, many are trapped by a vicious catch-22 cycle of systemic bias, or as John Samuel (2004)

contends: "Employers do not hire foreign-trained people unless they have attained membership in appropriate professional associations while professional associations do not grant membership unless the individual applicant has some proven amount of Canadian work experience." In other words, without Canadian experience, many cannot get certified even with extensive retraining; without a certificate, they cannot get the Canadian experience to secure employment or peer acceptance (Van Rijn 1999).

How many times have we heard this refrain: New Canadians with professional and medical degrees who are driving taxis instead of designing buildings or delivering pizzas instead of delivering babies? The proverbial immigrant taxi driver with a Ph.D. from a developing country reflects a key contradiction in Canada's immigration trends: Immigrants may be increasingly skilled and highly educated, yet many can't get a break because they are penalized by the qualifications that gained them entry in the first place (Kunz 2003). And yet, despite this untapped potential of underutilized labour, Canada is experiencing a skills shortage that in some regions is bordering on the scandalous. For example, while thousands of foreign-trained doctors cannot gain accreditation to practice in Canada, including an estimated 4000 in Ontario alone, hundreds of thousands of Canadians are suffering from gaps in health-care delivery, including one in seven Canadians who cannot find a family doctor but must rely on emergency services. Foreign-trained doctors encounter frustrating roadblocks on the road to accreditation, ranging from costly retraining programs to a restricted number of residencies (from two to seven years of training in hospitals upon graduation).

To be sure, the Ontario government has doubled to 200 the number of residency positions for foreign doctors, as well as aiming to streamline the licensing process. But a licensing bottleneck persists because accrediting institutions like the Ontario College of Physicians and Surgeons say they lack the resources to inform, assess, and provide additional training or spaces (Urbanski 2004; but see Williamson 2005 for critique).

Consider the path to Licensing for International Medical Graduates in Ontario, according to the Association of International Physicians and Surgeons of Ontario:

Step 1 An acceptable medical degree

Step 2 Equivalency Exams—Must pass the Medical Council of Canada Evaluating Exam

Step 3 Post Graduate Training—Entry into one of the 200 residency training spots

Step 4 Licentiate of Medical Council of Canada. Must pass qualifying exam

Step 5 Specialty certification. Upon completion of residency, must pass certification

Step 6 Ontario registration. Must be registered by College of Physicians and Surgeons

To be sure, not all foreign-trained doctors have to jump the hoops to practise in Canada. For example, foreign-trained doctors from the so-called Category 1 countries (New Zealand, Australia, South Africa, England, and the United States) are allowed to bypass the internship requirement and practise medicine immediately after an evaluating exam. By contrast, foreign-trained doctors from elsewhere have to pass equivalence and evaluating exams before applying for a limited number of positions in the mandatory internship program (Bains 1999). But foreign-born doctors are not the only ones who must undertake a gruelling period of pre-internship

and internship training designed to evaluate and upgrade clinical skills (PROMPT 2004). Even Canadian-born students who have trained abroad may be considered foreign-trained medical graduates in Ontario, with the result that they too must compete with the foreign-born for those coveted residency spots at university teaching hospitals (Carey 2004). The situation is no less stressful for foreign-trained dentists who, to obtain a certificate to practise in a particular province, must pass a taxing certification exam before attending a two-year qualifying program at one of five Canadian dental schools that accept foreign-trained dentists (Nazir 2004). Similarly, foreign-trained lawyers must return to school for up to two years, article with a law firm, then enter a provincial bar admission program. Engineers of "non-accredited" universities must demonstrate a fixed period of satisfactory practical experience and completion of exam requirements before consideration for accreditation (PROMPT 2004).

The exclusion created by this discrediting process does not bode well for the future of Canada. Admittedly, the federal government has unveiled an internationally trained workers initiative to facilitate the entry of new Canadians into the job market (Jimenez 2005). As well, business leaders have vowed to hear more immigrant recruits because, as put by the CEO of the Royal Bank of Canada, "Governments can attract skilled immigrants to Canada but, once they arrive, businesses have to pick up the ball. And to date we have not. In fact, we are dropping it" (cited in Abraham 2005). Let's be honest: to encourage the highly skilled to Canada, then deny them access to good jobs, is an inexcusable waste of human talent. Soon the word will get out that Canada's welcome mat is not what it seems to be, that Canada is big on seducing immigrants into Canada but then leaving them stranded to fend for themselves. In the end, the inevitable is inescapable: Canada's underutilized brain gain will become yet another brain drain (Keung 2004).

No less demanding are the challenges in moving up (Ruddick 2003). Immigrants once spent several years earning less than the average Canadian, but over time would achieve or surpass the average (Ley and Hiebert 2001). Now immigrants spend up to 10 years matching Canadian-born incomes (Citizenship and Immigration Canada 2001; *The Globe and Mail*, 25 June' 2001). For example, immigrants who came to Canada before 1981 earned more upon arrival and took less time to catch up; by contrast, those who arrived after 1981, especially visible minorities, tend to have higher unemployment rates and lower employment incomes, despite higher education levels (Harvey et al. 1999; Ley and Hiebert 2001; Pendakur and Pendakur 2004). The situation in the Waterloo region is instructive: Immigrants who arrived between 1996 and 2001 were better educated than the Canadian-born (33.2 percent with university degrees compared to 14.7 for those 15 years and over), but were more likely to be unemployed (9.4 percent for immigrants compared to 3.6 percent for Canadian-born), while earning less money ($23 413 for immigrants compared to $33 871 for the Canadian-born) (2001 Census, cited in the *Kitchener-Waterloo Record*, 5 March 2005).

Immigrant poverty is a growing concern. A study by Statistics Canada demonstrated how the low income cut-off line (poverty rate) for new Canadians stood at 35.8 percent in the year 2000, an increase from 24.6 percent in 1980, and more than twice the average than for Canadian-born families (Dunphy 2003). Clearly, then, structures and systems for resettlement are key to reducing poverty: The better the reception models in terms of integration into social and economic networks, the greater the success in adaptation (Abu-Laban et al. 2004). Yet, governments continue to slash funds for immigration settlement, including equity programs, ESL, adult education, legal aid, and bridging funds to trades and professions (Siddiqui 1999).

How do we account for these disparities? According to Jeffrey Reitz, a professor of sociology with the Centre for Industrial Relations at the University of Toronto, lower entry-level earnings are determined as much by institutional structures as they are by prejudicial attitudes and lack of human capital (Reitz 1998). Foremost among structural factors is the changing composition of immigrants, the attendant racism that comes with diversity, and an inability of employers to evaluate foreign credentials and educational degrees, resulting in a corresponding discounting of these skills, communication problems for non-English and non-French-speaking immigrants, and changes in the labour market because of economic globalization and knowledge-based economies (Biles and Burstein 2003). As well, management may find their hands tied in hiring skilled workers with overseas experience because of collective agreements' seniority rights that insist on recruiting from within the bargaining unit when filling positions (James 2005). As a result of these expanding disparities, writes John Anderson, the Director of Research for the Canadian Council of Social Development, there are two kinds of Canadians: those who were born here and those who were born there, and the gap between the two is growing (cited in Carey 2003).

Finally, there are problems of fitting in. Immigrant and refugee schoolchildren are subject to a host of conflicting demands and pressures. Some may perform poorly because of racial stereotyping, low teacher expectations, curricula and textbooks at odds with minority experiences, and lack of positive role models among school staff (Brown 2005). A study by York University sociology professor Paul Grayson, involving 5830 students who attended York between 1996 and 2000, concluded that university achievement drops for those new Canadians who must learn English or for whom English is a second language (Duffy 2004 b). Other studies indicate that ESL students tend to have higher dropout rates and lower academic performance—a figure that is masked by the high performance in some subjects such as math or science among students from China or Korea (Duffy 2004a). For immigrant youth, the pressures may be punishing: They must adjust to a new country, become involved with routines and friendships, and learn a new language quickly enough to finish high school and compete with the Canadian-born for places in postsecondary education (it generally takes five to seven years to develop English language equivalency for success at school).

Intergenerational family tensions are inevitable as parents and offspring struggle to find a workable balance between the permissiveness of Canada and the more conservative traditions of new immigrant groups (Handa 2003). While immigrant parents feel alienated from a language and culture that confuse them, immigrant children assimilate rapidly, enabling them to assume an assertiveness and independence that inverts conventional roles (Lupa 1999). Parents are forced to strike a Faustian bargain: All parents desire a better future for their children, but attainment of this success tends to undermine parental authority and family cohesion (Suarez-Orozco and Suarez-Orozco 2001). Thousands of new Canadians, especially women, are living in quiet desperation and depression, suffering in silence behind walls of social alienation, financial pressure, family turmoil, and cultural mores that isolate and foreclose avenues of help (Reinhart and Rusk 2006).

For refugees, the situation is decidedly grimmer. Traumatized by emotional and psychological abuses en route to Canada, refugees are still expected to adapt to Canada's unique social, cultural, and geographic climate with only minimal outside assistance. Refugees may have complex needs with widely varying educational and literacy levels, with much to learn in a relatively short period of time—about everything from awareness of community support agencies to issues of abortion, contraception, same-sex relations, domestic violence, child supervision, divorce, and child custody (Etherington 2005). The impact of cultural shock may be unsettling because of exposure to radically different lifestyles, mixed messages and conflicting expectations, rapid social change, and an inhospitable climate. The transitional stresses that accompany refugee claimants are compounded by their language difficulties, shame at their inability to work, and low self-esteem due to loss of control over destiny. As expressed by one refugee from Central America who fell into an abusive relationship, "I was from a country where I was the daughter of a middle-class professional. Here, I was no one. Refugee is such a negative word. People saw me as garbage" (cited in White 1999).

Prospects: Living Together with Differences

How, then, do we assess Canada's record as an immigration country? Few countries have demonstrated the same degree of generosity, inclusiveness, and tolerance that Canada has, especially with the introduction of the *Canadian Charter of Rights and Freedoms* and official Multiculturalism. Canada's commitment is reflected in the positioning of immigration within the context of Canada-building. Canada's record may not be perfect in this regard, but surely it is less imperfect than other countries in living up to an ideal, as articulated by this 1862 pamphlet to entice prospective German settlers:

> Canada is the land of peace, order, and abundance . . . The immigrant when he arrives is protected and guided by government officials . . . Canada is about the only country in which the . . . immigrant practically as well as before [the] law is seen as immediately equal to the native born. (Cited in Avery 1995:239)

There is another dimension, however. Canadians for the most part have not yet fully confronted the reality and challenges of immigrant integration as a two-way process involving giving on both sides (see Modood 2003b). Reluctance to endorse measures that encourage inclusiveness and accommodation is but one sign of this denial. Another sign is a belief that some immigrant groups are making demands that are culturally, socially, and politically unacceptable, although Tariq Modood (2005) argues that these groups are only seeking social space and respectful endorsement of their cultural heritage—a right that is implied in an official Multiculturalism. Growing anti-immigrant sentiment is yet another, even though any backlash will be constrained by (1) human rights codes that prohibit the public articulation of racist views, (2) a pervasive liberalism within the political culture, and (3) a lack of institutional power to fortify racist exclusion. There is not much likelihood of reverting to an openly racial basis for either the selection of immigrants or their treatment once in Canada. Still, immigrants continue to experience barriers that deny or exclude. Such denial and exclusion reflects badly on Canada's much vaunted reputation as an immigrant society that abides by the principles of multiculturalism.

DEBATE REVISITED | **Refugee Determination Process: System or Dysfunction?**

Globalization comes with a paradox. On the one hand globalization has created the conditions for the relatively free movement of information, goods, and capital; on the other hand the politics of deterrence has hobbled the movement of peoples especially. Consider the obstacles confronting refugees: preboarding detection barriers, passport and visa control systems, carrier sanctions and fines, internment in some cases, and often flawed systems for processing claimants, including finding and deporting those that slip through the process (Kumin 2004; Adelman 2004). Many believe that Canada's refugee determination system is a shambles. Critics pounce on it as one of the most inefficient and self-serving organs of the Canadian government because of its tendency to pander to the vested interests of politicians, bureaucrats, and lawyers (Gwyn 1999). Others are so contemptuous of the system that they would slough it off as a bad joke were it not life threatening and society destroying; costly, ineffective, and inefficient; prone to excessive gaffes that create security risks; and subject to abuse (Francis 2001a, b).

Are these criticisms accurate, who says so, and on what grounds can we evaluate the effectiveness of the system? Is Canada's relatively accommodative refugee determination system deserving of pride or shame? Responses will depend on how the relationship between Canada and refugees is defined. Does Canada have an obligation to be as generous as possible when dealing with refugees? Or should priority be assigned to protecting Canada's security and sovereignty? Are refugees essentially honest and of benefit to Canada? Or are they dishonest manipulators to be turfed out without any qualms of guilt?

Many, including the United Nations' High Commissioner on Refugees, believe Canada's refugee determination process to be one of the world's most generous. For some this generosity is to be celebrated as a source of pride (Mawani 1997); for others, it proves Canadians are being taken for a ride (Collacott 2006). Those who think the system is excessively generous point out that Canada accepts refugee claimants at six times the international norm—even accepting claims from citizens of democratic societies such as Israel, the United Kingdom, and the United States. Even more galling to some is how fraudulent refugees can clog up the process. In what was jeeringly referred to as the "Buffalo shuffle," rejected refugee claimants had to spend only 90 days in the United States before re-entering Canada to reactivate the costly process (Editorial, *The Globe and Mail*, 2 January 2001). The loophole was closed in late 2004 when Canada and the United States signed a "safe haven agreement" which prohibits refugees from shopping around for the country of their choice.

Refugee totals can be read in different ways. Of the 95 500 refugees who made claims to the IRB between 1993 and 1997, 42 percent were accepted (down from the 84 percent in 1989), 33 percent were rejected, and 25 percent were neither finalized nor ineligible. In 2003, the figure for acceptance remained at 42 percent, with 42 percent rejected and 18 percent abandoned, but reinforcing critics' view that refugee claimants are using the refugee system as a backdoor entry into Canada (Jimenez 2004). For some countries, such as Afghanistan with its now once repressive Taliban regime, the acceptance rate of 92 percent is considerably higher. There are currently in excess of 41 575 claims to be processed (Adelman 2004). With numbers continuing to grow, there are fears that the system may self-implode from taking on too much with too little.

The worst spin suggests that Canada's refugee determination system is absurdly dysfunctional. According to critics, unlike most countries that weed out "fake" asylum seekers, everyone who lands in Canada is entitled to have their case heard by IRB (Gallagher 2004). Numerous loopholes and vulnerabilities are exploited that can prove costly once legal, welfare, and administrative costs are factored in (Stoffman 1997). Operating an asylum-processing system and processing refugees does not come cheaply. That being the case, critics argue, why not accept all refugee claimants and dispense with the costs involved in deporting the few who fail to comply? The savings, time, and energy could then be used to improve settlement.

Others, including refugee lawyers and advocacy groups, accuse Canada's refugee policy of being racist and discriminatory—in consequence rather than intent (Canadian Council of Refugees 2000). Practices with an inadvertent yet negative impact on refugees may include an insistence on documentation, a narrow definition of family, racial profiling in selection processes, and skewed distribution of visa posts. For example, refugee claimants are required to produce "satisfactory identity documents" for permanent residence in Canada. Yet, this requirement negatively affects those refugee groups who come from countries that do not establish identity by way of official documents, where no government authority exists to issue such documents, where certain groups such as women or rural residents are unlikely to access such documentation, and where simply asking for such documentation could land you or your family members in trouble (remember: it is the refugees' identity that put them at risk of persecution in the first place; Canadian Council of Refugees 2000). And despite moves toward improving training, eliminating political patronage, and strengthening the criteria for appointment (Safieddine 2005), arbitrariness remains a problem, including a publicized case wherein one of two nearly identical Palestinian brothers was accepted by one board member and the other rejected by another board member. Or consider this stunning revelation: Refugee approval rates not only vary from city to city but also from board member to board member, with some having approval rates of 81 percent, while five members have a zero percent approval rate (Jimenez 2004).

Not surprisingly, the practice of refugee determination appears to be dictated more by political objectives and personal politics than by humanitarian concerns, a tendency to treat refugees as a social problem rather than as humans in distress (Dench 2005).

An intermediate position is echoed by those who contend that the current system is ensnared in a paradox. However well intentioned, the Singh decision of 1985 resulted in the clogging up of the refugee determination process. Instead of being efficient and fair, the system has become legal limbo with numerous avenues of appeals and lengthy administrative backlogs that invariably raise public ire (Simpson 2000). Contradictions are at play: Canada's refugee determination processes may not respond quickly enough to those in genuine need of protection (the victims of war and oppression in camps)—in the process encouraging a vast and profitable underground migrant smuggling system (Bell and Jiminez 2000). Conversely, it may respond too generously to those who lie and cheat to get in, with the result that a beleaguered refugee determination system may appear helpless in discrediting those who neither require nor deserve Canada's protection. However generous and compassionate, such a perverse dynamic will invariably generate bottlenecks in a system designed to be efficient and fair over matters of life and death, without compromising Canada's national interests.

Yes, there is much to commend in Canada's refugee determination system; nevertheless, there is also much room for improvement if Canada is to maintain its status as the true north strong and free. The challenge is no longer how to design the perfect refugee determination system that balances the real with the ideal, but to create one that is politically, socially, and ethically acceptable (Kumin 2004). After all, as Janet Dench (2004) points out, refugees are people who have no choice except to flee. Canadians by contrast do have a choice: to treat refugees as human beings in need of protection or to abandon them by pulling up the drawbridge.

CHAPTER HIGHLIGHTS

- Canada is sociologically regarded as an immigrant society. Currently, immigrants comprise just over 18 percent of Canada's population while visible minorities account for 13.4 percent of Canada's total.

- Immigration currently averages about 220 000 people per year, with the majority arriving from Asia, Africa, and South and Central America. Most immigrants prefer Ontario and British Columbia, while both Toronto and Vancouver are major immigrant targets.

- In the past, immigration practices were highly racist in terms of who got in. At present, Canada's immigration policy can be described as relatively colour-blind, with a focus on sustaining economic growth.

- Immigrants can enter on three grounds: family reunification class, economic class (which includes both business class and is based on the point system), and refugee class.

- Canadians continue to debate issues such as how many immigrants, from where, what kind, and what for.

- Canadians appear divided in their reaction to immigration, with some seeing it as a problem; others as a solution; and still others as both a problem and a solution depending on the context, consequences, and criteria.

- Immigrants to Canada come with benefits and costs. Benefits are numerous but differently impact different sectors of society and the economy. The costs are no less real for some Canadians.

- Immigrant needs and aspirations have been misportrayed. Most want to put down roots in their adopted country, contribute to its growth, receive benefits that all Canadians are entitled to, and get the best for their children without losing their distinctiveness.

- Refugees continue to be seen as a problem, especially those who are unsponsored. Canada may have a relatively high rate of acceptance of refugee claimants. But most agree that the refugee determination system is overworked and underresourced.

KEY TERMS

asylum seeker
Canadian Charter of Rights and Freedoms
convention refugees
immigrant
Immigration Act, 1978
Immigration and Refugee Board (IRB)

Immigration and Refugee Protection Act, 2002
multicultural minorities
people of colour
refugee claimants
refugees
visible minority

REVIEW QUESTIONS

1. Briefly compare the concept of immigration in the past with the post-1978 immigration policy in terms of underlying assumptions, goals, methods, and outcomes.

2. Discuss the benefits and drawbacks of increased immigration to Canada.

3. Discuss the aspirations of multicultural minorities in terms of needs and goals. What kind of barriers exist that preclude attainment of these goals?

4. Critics of immigration point out that Canada has too many immigrants that are derived from the wrong classes and come from the wrong countries. Respond to these criticisms.

5. Point out the issues that contribute to a "refugee crisis" in Canada.

LINKS AND RECOMMENDATIONS

Websites

Canada's official site for immigration
www.cic.gc.ca

Access to immigration laws in Canada
http://fedpubs.com

For various issues relating to immigration in Canada, the United States, and abroad
http://immigration.about.com

For a not so positive portrayal of the immigrant experience in Canada, see
www.NotCanada.com

Books

Useful sources include:

Peter S. Li, *Destination Canada: Immigration Debates and Issues*. Oxford University Press, 2003.

Valerie Knowles, *Strangers at Our Gates*. Rev. Ed. Dundurn Press, 1997.

Journal

Immigration: Opportunities & Challenges, the April 2003 issue of *Canadian Issues*, published by the Association for Canadian studies (ACS).

Films

Who Gets In. 1991. A National Film Board documentary about immigration into Canada—somewhat dated, but still packs a wallop.

Dirty Pretty Things. 2002. A searing look at what undocumented refugees in London, England must sometimes do to survive.

P a r t

3

MULTICULTURALISM
AS CANADA-BUILDING

The upsurge of racial pride and ethnic affiliation in Canada and abroad is well documented (Isajiw 1997; Fleras and Spoonley 1999). Central authorities have responded to this unprecedented surge in a variety of ways, ranging from indifference or rejection on the one hand to tolerance or acceptance of it as a society-building asset on the other (Willett 1998; Kobayashi 1999). Countries such as Australia (May 2004) and New Zealand (Pearson 2001; Spoonley 2005) have implemented varying strategies for coping with the (1) influx of immigrants, (2) proliferation of identity politics, (3) politicization of ethnicity as a social force, (4) challenges of anti-racism movements, and (5) ascendancy of ethnic and indigenous nationalisms. Alternatives for redefining majority–minority relations have evolved, in large part because traditional formats such as assimilation no longer provide a moral compass for addressing the challenges of living together with differences.

Historically, nation-states have bolstered their political legitimacy through various society-building strategies (UNDP 2004). Central to the society-building agenda was the need to secure territories and boundaries, to expand the bureaucratic reach of their institutions, and to instill a sense of loyalty and conformity in their sometimes unruly constituents. Strategies to bolster national unity and identity were varied, but invariably included centralization of political power to ensure mainstream control; imposition of a dominant legal tradition and judicial system; official language laws; nationalized system of compulsory education; adoption of state symbols for celebrating the dominant group's history; seizure of so-called empty lands in the name of progress or national interests; and restriction of immigration to those who resembled the majority sector. The presence of cultural diversity was widely perceived as a threat. Recognition of these differences could culminate in social fragmentation, block the creation of a cohesive and stable society, and jeopardize the attainment of national identity and unity. Not surprisingly, state authorities tended to either ignore or suppress differences in the hopes of slotting both immigrants and indigenous peoples into a pre-existing hierarchy of cultural power (Jakubowicz 2005). Besides, it was widely assumed that diversity was doomed with the onset of modernization. Government policy was adjusted accordingly, that is, to foster assimilation into modern society.

Many have claimed that multiculturalism has largely displaced this monocultural framework for managing diversity (Glazer 1997). In acknowledging that national unity and identity do not require a singular identity or denunciation of diversity—after all, people are known to have multiple identities and affiliations—a commitment to multicultural principles prompted a host of government programs to assist in the settlement of migrants, to acknowledge their contribution to society, and to educate the general public about the realities and benefits of a pluralistic society (May 2004). Of those societies at the vanguard for multiculturally "engaging" diversity, few can match Canada's blistering pace (Fleras 2002). With the emergence of Toronto and Vancouver as dynamically cosmopolitan cities, Canada has transformed itself into one of the world's most ethnically diverse societies without collapsing into a welter of inter-ethnic conflicts. Under the banner of multiculturalism, Canada has embarked on a seemingly bold yet unprecedented strategy for securing a society of many cultures, both united and distinct as well as diverse and equitable. Entrenchment of multiculturalism at constitutional and statutory levels has further reinforced its legacy as Canada's foremost contribution in advancing the cause of world peace (James 2005; Foster 2005).

Thirty-five years of official Multiculturalism have confirmed what many now routinely endorse: the right of people to identify with the cultural tradition of their choice without sacrificing full and equal participation in society because of cultural differences (UNDP 2004). Canada's official Multiculturalism has served admirably as a conflict management device for defusing inter-group tensions by promulgating the once unthinkable idea that people have multiple and complementary identities, that cultures are never fixed but evolving, that equitable outcomes can be achieved without denying cultural differences, and that culturally diverse people can coexist without conflict provided an overarching vision prevails. With multiculturalism, Canadians are accepted as racially or ethnically different yet no less Canadian, with a corresponding package of citizenship rights and entitlements regardless of origin, creed, or colour. To be sure, Canadians are not nearly as multicultural as our collective pride would imply; in some ways we are less diversity-driven than our melting pot neighbours to the south (Reitz and Breton 1994; Jedwab 2002; Abu-Laban and Gabriel 2002). Still, the promotion of multiculturalism has prompted a reshaping of Canada in ways that have evoked international acclaim, in effect reinforcing Canada's lofty ranking as a pacesetter in the art of living together with differences.

It is one thing to promote a multiculturalism policy that endorses diversity as a legitimate component in Canada-building. It may be something altogether different to transform these principles into institutional practice that make an appreciable difference. If the goal of an official Multiculturalism is to improve the conditions for the integration of minorities, a commitment to inclusiveness is critical. But those who remain indifferent to the challenges of inclusiveness are punished accordingly. Personal careers may be stalled; organizational reputations suffer; and bottom lines dip. In short, unless institutions move over and make institutional space for *all* Canadians, our much-vaunted multicultural mosaic will shatter into fragments too numerous to re-tile. The challenge is twofold: how to create an inclusive society in which minority women and men can maintain their identities without foreclosing hard-fought rights within the framework of a functioning society, and how to create an inclusive Canada that is both safe for diversity and safe from diversity without trampling on the rights of all Canadians.

This final section responds to these questions by exploring the politics of multiculturalism within the context of Canada-building. Multiculturalism is acknowledged as a bold but ambiguous social experiment for engaging diversity in ways that purport to be both constructive and integrative, yet may prove fractious and controversial. The first chapter in this section, Chapter 10, examines official Multiculturalism as a formal strategy for proactively engaging diversity as "different" yet "equal." Attention will focus on conceptual issues related to multiculturalism as policy and practice for improving the integration of minorities and migrants. The chapter also situates multiculturalism within the broader framework of inequality in Canada. If race and ethnic relations are ultimately unequal relations, what role does multiculturalism play in creating and maintaining inequality as well as in challenging and transforming it? Chapter 11 emphasizes the practice of multiculturalism in terms of the challenges of putting diversity to work at institutional levels. Barriers created by organizational structures and individual mindsets are shown to have precluded moves toward institutional inclusiveness at the level of policing, media, and education. The final chapter, Chapter 12, looks at the broader relationship of diversity to Canada-building. A commitment to Canada's Diversity Model has contributed to a transformation of Canada into what many see as a post-national society—at least in principle if not always in practice. The concept of an inclusive citizenship for all Canadians regardless of race or ethnicity provides a fitting reminder. Canada is by no means a perfect society when it comes to managing race, ethnic, and Aboriginal relations; nevertheless, it may well qualify as one of the least imperfect.

MULTICULTURALISM IN CANADA: "LIVING TOGETHER WITH DIFFERENCES"

| DEBATE | The Politics of Multiculturalism: Drawing the Line |

One of the best things about living in Canada is our general willingness to abide by the principle of agreeing to disagree. A commitment to **Multiculturalism** involves "accommodating" diversity by acknowledging the legitimacy of disagreements as long as people play by the rules. But there is a hitch: A willingness to agree to disagree is simple enough when the differences are superficial and choices are easy. Shall we order Szechuan tonight? How about a falafel? Anyone care for perogies? But tensions get more complex when people disagree over what is acceptable. Consider how the logic of multiculturalism is stretched to the limit when illiberal practices clash with core liberal values and women's constitutional rights. Even more perplexing are situations in which values not only clash, but one set

of values also disagrees with the principle of agreeing to disagree. True, a tolerance for those who are intolerant may be logically consistent with the precepts of multiculturalism. But putting this theory into everyday reality may erode the prospects of living together with differences (Gregg 2006).

The gap between principles and practice raises a number of awkward questions: Should Canada's **official Multiculturalism** reject those cultural practices at odds with Canadian society, even if the very act of doing so exposes the hypocrisy of unilaterally imposing Eurocentric standards on a society that advocates multicultural tolerance? Does the logic of Multiculturalism tolerate even those cultural traditions incompatible with Canada's constitutional values, ranging from compulsory arranged marriages to wife beating to female clitoridectomy (Kostash 2000)? Is there a danger that an "anything goes" multiculturalism will become the Trojan horse that erodes the very principles of freedom and equality upon which multiculturalism is based (Biles et al. 2005)? A dilemma of such perplexity raises the issue of what is tolerable in a multicultural society. Are there limits to tolerance or can immigrants import illiberal practices at odds with the principles of Canadian Multiculturalism? If so, where do we draw the line between what is acceptable and what is not? Who decides? And on what principled grounds can a line be drawn?

Incidents involving minority conflicts with the law expose the politics behind drawing the multicultural line. The concept of **"cultural defence"** is increasingly employed as an excuse for people's law-breaking behaviour. According to a cultural defence line of argument, people may be ultimately responsible for criminal behaviour, but these deviant actions do not occur in a cultural or social vacuum. If true, the criminal justice system must take cultural differences into account when sentencing minorities for unlawful actions inconsistent with Canada's legal and cultural traditions. Reaction to this course of action is mixed because of the problems involved. For some, the recourse to "cultural defence" to explain and justify criminal actions is consistent with the logic of multiculturalism. For others, however, this strategy of using culture as a defence is nothing less than a rationalization by those who hide behind the smokescreen of multiculturalism to justify law-breaking or human rights violations.

Consider the controversy that came to light when two Haitian-Canadian males were found guilty of sexually assaulting a young adult Haitian-Canadian woman in July 1996. The two received what many regarded as a "slap on the wrist," including

an 18-month sentence, to be served at home, in addition to 100 hours of community service and a 10:00 p.m. curfew for one year. Many were shocked—even outraged—by the leniency of the sentence for a crime that normally is punishable by jail. According to the judge, Monique Dubreuil, mitigating circumstances justified the leniency, including the age of the victim (she was an adult), the status of the rapists (one was at university, the other had a job), and lack of previous conviction for a similar crime. That the men "behaved like two young roosters in need of sexual pleasure without caring about the young woman" (*Toronto Star*, 28 January 1998:A-26) may have confirmed their guilt, ruled Dubreuil, but left open the questions of motive and personal responsibility. Of greater interest was the judge's willingness to invoke the disclaimer of "particular cultural context," primarily because of the lack of remorse shown by the Haitian men over their actions (*The Globe and Mail*, 29 January 1998:A-1). In the words of Dubreuil, "The absence of regret of the two accused seems to be related more to the cultural context, particularly with regard to relations with women, than a veritable problem of a sexual nature" (*Kitchener-Waterloo Record*, 28 January 1998:A-3).

This ruling and its implications did not sit well across Canada. Many argued that the decision (1) was racist and sexist, (2) sent out mixed messages about Haitians as insensitive to violence and victims of violence, (3) insulted Haitian women by suggesting their complicity in rape, (4) further deterred women from seeking justice in court, (5) played "fast and loose" with so-called cultural values that did not necessarily exist, and (6) conveyed a grossly misleading impression that Haitian-Canadians are less than human. Even the logic proved baffling: It was not an instance of arguing that "culture made me do it." Rather, the cultural defence was based on inferential deduction: that is, if men behave badly and reveal no remorse, it must be culture. The underlying subtext was clear: Haitian culture dictates how men relate to women, and if Haitian males are not contrite about their actions, it must be culturally "normal" for them to gang rape.

It is not our intent to second-guess either the ruling or its rationale; rather, we need to explain the reasoning behind such a decision within the broader framework of an official Multiculturalism. Do cultural defence arguments stand up to scrutiny in a society based on multicultural principles (see Okin 1999)? Should Canadian Multiculturalism draw a relatively narrow line by tolerating only those cultural practices commensurate with constitutional values and mainstream institutions? Or should Canada's commitment to an official Multiculturalism tolerate a broad range of culturally diverse practices? The continuation of this debate will provide some possible answers to the politics of drawing the multicultural line.

LIVING TOGETHER WITH DIFFERENCES: PUZZLES AND PROSPECTS

> Based on the dual ideals of peace and *multiculturalism* (emphasis, mine), Canada is one of mankind's greatest achievements. It is comparable to the notable civilizations of the past, and indeed exceeds most of them in terms of stability, living standards, and civil liberties. (Cowen 1999)

People overseas marvel at two dimensions of Canadian society. First, how can Canada maintain its independence and integrity despite proximity to the world's most powerful economic and military machine? That Canadians have retained their distinctiveness and autonomy under the shadow of this colossus is remarkable. That they have managed to secure an enviable standard of living as well is yet more astonishing. Second, how does Canada remain united and prosperous when confronted by the politics of a multi-layered diversity? Consider the pushes and pulls: English-speaking Canadians seem to be perpetually embroiled with the Québécois over language issues; Aboriginal assertiveness has profoundly challenged the very notion of "what Canada is for"; and Canada annually accepts thousands of culturally diverse immigrants and refugees. And yet, despite the tripwires of balancing diversity with unity, Canada has managed to cobble together a society that now ranks as the world's third oldest federalism (after the United States and Switzerland).

There are no simple responses to either of these questions; nevertheless, a commitment to multiculturalism may prove the common denominator. Canada represents one of several democratic societies to have capitalized on multicultural principles as a principled basis for living together with differences. Originating in part to harmonize competing ethnicities without losing control of the overall agenda, official Multiculturalism has been perpetuated for a variety of political and economic considerations involving state functions, private interests, and electoral survival. Multiculturalism continues to challenge the relational status of minority women and men by transcending either assimilation or segregation as a normative framework for "managing" diversity. A combination of demographic and political upheavals in recent years has further reconfigured the government's multicultural agenda in ways inconceivable even a generation ago (Ujimoto 2000; Hiebert et al. 2003).

However much revered or vilified, an official Multiculturalism is prone to paradoxes. On the one hand, Canadians believe that all citizens are equal before the law; on the other hand, should the cultural rights of minorities be respected when their cultural practices clash with core mainstream values (*Globe and Mail* Editorial, 15 September 2005)? On one side, a multicultural governance is inclined to accommodate different ways of life; and on the other, how can it do so without compromising the common values that bind Canada (Cardozo 2005)? How does Canada's Multiculturalism balance the rights of minority groups without violating the rights of those within these communities (Campbell 2005)? Is Multiculturalism about integrating immigrants into the mainstream or about their right to maintain distinctiveness by standing apart from Canada (Khan 2005)?

In short, the central paradox lies in grappling with the question of how to make Canada safe "for" diversity, yet safe "from" diversity, while, at the same time, making diversity safe from Canada yet safe for Canada (see Schlesinger Jr. 1992; Samuel and Schachhuber 2000; Pearson 2001). At the core of this paradox is a proposed balancing act between unity (commonality) and diversity. Put bluntly, too much diversity and not enough unity may destabilize a society to the point of dismemberment, and too little diversity but too much unity can create a one-size-fits-all leviathan that stifles as it standardizes (Fish 1997). Yet, in the absence of measurable values for balancing "unity" with "diversity," where exactly is the balance situated, who says so, on what grounds, and how can we find out? The challenge for Canada-building appears straightforward enough: to establish a rules-based framework and normative standards that can engage diversity as different yet equal, without eroding the goals of national unity, identity, and prosperity in the process. But what sounds simple in principle may prove difficult in practice.

Implementation of official Multiculturalism may help to solve one of the riddles of contemporary governance: How to live together with differences without sacrificing the unity of the whole and integrity of the parts? Yet, robust support for Multiculturalism as a blueprint for living together with differences has not congealed into any consensus over definition, attributes, or applications. Both championed yet maligned, idealized as well as demonized, the term itself has absorbed such a mélange of meanings that many despair of any clarity or consensus (Caws 1994). References to multiculturalism simultaneously evoke a two-edged preference for consensus as well as criticism and change; of conformity yet diversity; of control yet emancipation; of exclusion yet participation; of compliance yet creativity (see Vasta 1996).

The impact of multiculturalism has proven double-edged as well. Multiculturalism may advance the society-building goals of cultural identity, social justice, citizenship, national unity, societal integration, and equality. But while multiculturalism may have the sincerest intentions of creating a just and inclusive Canada, it can end up doing the opposite by inadvertently fostering inequality, ethnic separatism, and intergroup friction (Kostash 2000). Its promise of ethnic diversity is laudable, but critics attack multiculturalism as a new racism because of its tendency to equate a group's identity, experiences, and behaviour with race or a rigidly defined ethnicity (Berliner and Hull 2000). This paradox—multiculturalism as progressively inclusive yet regressively exclusionary—strikes a key chord in this section. To what extent does multiculturalism contribute to or detract from Canada-building, and how do we weigh the evidence for either position?

Some regard multiculturalism as the world's most powerful social force at present— for better or for worse (Savard and Vignezzi 1999). Others prefer to dismiss it as a modernist anachronism in a postmodern world of fluidity, multiplicity, and change—including a perception that a commitment to multiculturalism is dead or dying (Duncan 2005). Still others recognize both its potency and impotence in addressing the challenges of balancing unity with diversity and vice versa. In acknowledging the partial validity of each interpretation, this chapter theorizes multiculturalism by providing a working definition, examining it at different levels of meaning, analyzing the diverse perceptions and critical reactions, and evaluating its role in Canada-building. Emphasis is directed at unpacking the different levels of meaning, including multiculturalism as (1) fact (what empirically is); (2) ideology (what ought to be); (3) policy (what is about to be); (4) process (what really happens); and (5) critical discourse (what must be) (Fleras 2002). Particular attention is devoted to a historical analysis of multiculturalism as official policy, followed by a comparison of Canada's official Multiculturalism with the more critical multicultural discourses in the United States.

The central argument provides a unifying theme. In advancing national interests while addressing issues of social justice and cultural identity, official Multiculturalism has emerged as the quintessential strategy for Canada-building through the more equitable integration of migrants and minorities. In helping to construct what is known as Canada's Diversity Model (see Chapter 12), Multiculturalism is endorsed as an approach based on high moral principles of justice yet grounded in the honest pragmatism of doing what is workable, necessary, and fair (see Tsai 2003). Nevertheless, the relationship between Multiculturalism and equality is plagued by ambiguity and contradiction. Insofar as race and ethnic relations are fundamentally unequal relations, how does an official Multiculturalism create and reinforce this inequality while, at the same time, challenging and changing it? The chapter concludes by pointing out that continued misunderstanding of official Multiculturalism does not bode well for advancing a framework for living together differently.

THEORIZING MULTICULTURALISM

Pluralistic societies confront a dilemma in grappling with the question of how to make society safe for diversity yet safe from diversity (see Schlesinger Jr. 1992). A fundamental contradiction is at play. On one side is a liberal commitment to the individuality of autonomy and equality; on the other side is a society-building imperative to impose a uniformity of language, culture, and identity over a heterogeneous population (Baubock 2005). A principled framework must be established for building viable communities out of culturally diverse populations without compromising a commitment either to common values or cultural diversity in the process (Sellers 2005). In response to this challenge, white settler dominions such as Australia and Canada have endorsed multicultural principles as a blueprint for taking advantage of diversity's benefits without sacrificing unity (Pearson 2001; May 2004).

Yet, staunch support for multiculturalism is not the same as agreement over its nature and characteristics (Biles 2002). References to multiculturalism have revealed instead an uncanny knack of meaning different things to different people, of meaning everything yet nothing, and of meaning whatever the context allows (Fleras 2002). For some, multiculturalism is synonymous with Canada's official version; not surprisingly, alternative readings are simply unthinkable. For others, multiculturalism is a transformative discourse invoking a critical challenge to the cultural status quo (Goldberg 1994). For others still, multiculturalism goes beyond a political or cultural project to embrace crossings and connections as individuals routinely transverse cultural borders by way of multiple affiliations and hybridic identities (Handa 2003). For others yet, multiculturalism refers to the coexistence of diverse cultures in society, either in territorially separate spaces or sharing the same space, and its implications for unity and interactivity (Gwyn 2001).

Consider the range of models that fall under a multicultural umbrella (Fish 1997; Sandercock 2003). At one end are conservative models of multiculturalism. According to a conservative multiculturalism, a culture-blind assimilation is the key. With its well-intentioned view of everyone as equal regardless of historical circumstances or economic injustices, a society of many cultures is possible as long as cultural differences are rejected as grounds for recognition and reward; after all, if everyone is equal before the law, then everyone must receive the same treatment. Stronger models point to a liberal multiculturalism, with its lukewarm endorsement of diversity, commitment to integration and institutional inclusiveness, and an adherence to the principles of liberal universalism. To the extent that cultural differences are tolerated under a liberal multiculturalism, support is largely superficial or in the abstract—that is, differences are acceptable, but only if they are consistent with mainstream values, do not demand special reward or recognition, do not block the rights of others because such intolerance is intolerable in a tolerant democracy, and as long as everyone "agrees to disagree" by being different in the same way. Even stronger models include critical multiculturalism. With its commitment to challenge and transform relations of power, privilege, and hierarchies of oppression, critical multiculturalism exposes the struggles between the constructions of a national culture and those who have been traditionally excluded from this input because of race and ethnicity. Finally, robust models of multiculturalism endorse a no-holds barred allegiance to radical diversity. Differences must be taken seriously under a radical multiculturalism even if these differences result in different group rights, differential citizenship, illiberal outlooks, separate institutional development, and hermetically sealed communities. It remains to be seen if any society can be constructed around such a radical relativism: As the controversy and violence over the cartoon crisis in early 2006 clearly revealed, survival would be at best provocative; at worst, non-existent.

Canada is routinely labelled as a multicultural society because of its principled stand for managing diversity. In general, references to a multicultural society involve a belief that a society of many cultures is better than monoculturalism, preferred over assimilation as policy alternative, and can prevail as long as certain ground rules are in place. Inasmuch as multiculturalism engages diversity by challenging society to move over and make space without losing the interconnectedness that binds everything together, multiculturalism indeed represents a bold if somewhat flawed experiment in advancing the goal of co-operative coexistence. Yet, the concept of multiculturalism remains poorly theorized because of competing discourses, hidden agendas, and different levels of meaning (Hiebert et al. 2003; Sandercock 2003; Ley 2005).

1. Is multiculturalism about culture-conscious pluralism or culture-blind participation? Is a society of many cultures possible only by ensuring that people's cultural differences do not get in the way of full and equal participation? Or is a society of many cultures possible only when taking cultures seriously, promoting a group's cultural rights up to and including independent ethnic enclaves, and taking cultural differences into account as a basis for special treatment (UNDP 2004)?

2. Is multiculturalism about society in diversity or diversity in society? Does multiculturalism endorse a particular vision of the good society and then ask how much diversity can be incorporated within the limits of this vision? Or does multiculturalism accept the legitimacy and desirability of cultural diversity as a priority, then redesign the good society accordingly (Sandercock 2003)?

3. Is multiculturalism about diversity or disadvantage? Does multiculturalism celebrate differences as ends in themselves? Or does it emphasize the removal of discriminatory barriers to ensure equality and inclusiveness for those whose cultural differences have proven disadvantageous?

4. Is multiculturalism a radical policy departure or more of the same with fancier labels? Does multiculturalism involve a new normative framework for integrating minorities into society on more equitable terms? Or is multiculturalism a kind of assimilation in slow motion, that is, a deceptively unobtrusive tactic for absorbing minorities in the mainstream, albeit more indirectly?

5. Is multiculturalism about promoting cultural identity or social equality or national interests? Is the issue one of fostering a social climate conducive to the retention of cultural identity? Should the focus be on social equality by ensuring that everyone is equal before the law regardless of race or ethnicity? Or should multiculturalism be concerned primarily with advancing national interests by way of unity and prosperity?

6. Is multiculturalism good or bad for women? Do versions of multiculturalism embrace an androcentric tendency to condone practices at odds with a woman's gender equity rights?

7. Is multiculturalism about universality or particularity? Does a multicultural society endorse the universality principle that what we have in common as rights-bearing individuals is more important—at least for purposes of entitlement and recognition—than what divides us into culturally distinct groups? Or does multiculturalism reject the universality of liberalism by emphasizing the primacy of race and ethnicity as a basis for belonging and governance (Hall 2000)?

8. Is multiculturalism about "us" or "them"? Should multiculturalism focus on addressing the concerns of minority women and men? Or should it focus on empowering the mainstream mindset in hopes of removing prejudice and discriminatory barriers that preclude minority integration?

9. Is multiculturalism relevant or irrelevant? Has multiculturalism outlived its usefulness as a twentieth-century modernist project? Do we need to rethink multiculturalism in light of new post-national realities such as global diasporas and transnational migrations (Duncan 2005)?

10. Is it possible to create a more "religion-friendly" model of multiculturalism by engaging with religion as a valid diversity category? Or is such a shift too much to expect because of Canada's commitment to secularism and separation of church and state (Kymlicka 2003; Modood 2003b; Bramadat and Seljak 2005)?

To the extent that no consensus prevails, disagreement is inevitable. Multiculturalism may be seen as a blueprint for facilitating the integration of minorities. Yet, there is no agreement over the role of multiculturalism in promoting integration, whether multiculturalism fosters or obstructs the integration process, and how much each side needs to concede as part of the process (Jedwab 2005b). There is even less agreement regarding what multiculturalism is doing, should be doing, and is capable of doing in a liberal-capitalist society (Duncan 2005). Responses will vary with the frame of reference (official Multiculturalism versus popular multiculturalism), the level of analysis (micro versus macro), a proposed vision of society (**mosaic** or kaleidoscope), and the contribution of minorities in achieving this vision (positive or negative).

The conclusion is inescapable: multiculturalism can mean whatever people want it to mean—a kind of "floating signifier" in which many meanings can be absorbed without much fear of contradiction (Gunew 1999)—and it is precisely this ambiguity that is proving both a strength and a weakness in theorizing multiculturalism (Willett 1998; Modood 2005). Any theorizing must begin by distinguishing the general (multiculturalism as the informal, the interpersonal, the contextual) from the specific (Multiculturalism as the formal, the official, the principled). The protean quality of multiculturalism yields diverse definitions. At the general level, multiculturalism can be defined as a belief that people can live together with their differences at personal, institutional, and national levels. A society of many cultures is possible as long as rules are in place for *engaging diversity as different yet equal.* More specifically, Canada's official Multiculturalism can be defined as a package of policies and programs for managing diversity by integrating minority women and men into the institutional framework of society. A social contract is established under an official Multiculturalism, based on three largely unstated assumptions: (1) our similarities as individuals outweigh our differences because of race or ethnicity, (2) nobody should be denied or excluded because of racial and ethnic differences, and (3) within reasonable limits and rule of law, differences are helpful in crafting an inclusive society. With Multiculturalism as a model for integrating minorities and migrants, a principled framework is established for promoting full and equal participation through removal of discriminatory and prejudicial barriers. To date, Canada has performed admirably in advancing a society in which differences are seen as legitimate without undermining the integrity and connectedness of the whole. Time will tell if this "success" story can handle the more politicized demands of newer Canadians.

MULTICULTURALISM IN CANADA

How would you respond to the question: "Is Canada a multicultural society?" A multicultural society is one that minimally subscribes to the following attributes: Diversity is defined as an asset and opportunity; minorities are deemed critical to society-building; policies and programs supporting the inclusion of diversity are in place at institutional levels; governments not only endorse diversity as part of the national identity but take an active role in facilitating the integration of migrants and minorities into society; and sufficient resources are available for putting diversity ideals into daily practice. Reference to these criteria would define Canada as a multicultural society. Yet, the degree to which Canada is a multicultural society will also vary with how multiculturalism is defined, with definitions varying with the level of meaning employed, including multiculturalism as (1) *empirical fact* (of what is), (2) an *ideology* (what ought to be) with a corresponding array of ideas and ideals, (3) an explicit government *policy* and programs (what is proposed), (4) a set of *practices* for promoting political and minority interests (what really is), and (5) a *critical discourse* that invites challenge and change (what must be). Failure to separate these different levels of meaning should not be underestimated. Misunderstanding because of miscommunication may result because people talk past each other by using the same words but speaking a different language.

As Fact

As fact, multiculturalism makes an empirical statement about "what is." It may be stating the obvious, but the obvious is sometimes overlooked for precisely that reason, that is, most countries are ethnically diverse, composed of people from a variety of different backgrounds who speak, think, worship, and act differently (Connor 2000). Nearly all countries comprise different race and ethnic groups whose identities are stoutly defended and demanding of recognition or resources. Many of these minority groups wish to remain culturally distinct, yet are equally anxious to enjoy the benefits of full societal involvement. Employed in the descriptive sense of the term, few would dispute the notion of Canada as a multicultural society. The existence of Aboriginal, charter, and multicultural minorities attests to this empirical fact (Elliott 1983). Adding to this multi-layered variety is the realization that Canadians have been drawn from 170 different countries and speak over 100 different languages (Kalbach and Kalbach 1999). Recent immigration patterns suggest a continuation of this diversity trend.

As Ideology

Unlike its descriptive counterpart, multiculturalism as an **ideology** refers to a prescriptive statement of "what ought to be." It prescribes a set of beliefs about creating a society of many cultures in which people live together with differences without capitulating to chaos. Canadians have long prided themselves on being a tolerant society, with numerous national polls demonstrating consistent public support for Canada's multicultural mosaic over the American melting pot. To be sure, this endorsement varies with time and place, often lacks enthusiasm, is conditional, and is easily revoked when costs outstrip benefits. Nevertheless, multiculturalism is endorsed as a defining characteristic, an embodiment of "Canadianness," and proof that living in a pluralistic society allows for a more varied and richer experience than in a monocultural society (Kymlicka 2005). Ideally an ideology of multiculturalism implies that no society is perfect and beyond criticism or self-reflection: To the contrary, any society can benefit from a critical dialogue as basis for advancing a co-operative coexistence that combines respect for diversity within a framework of shared values (Runnymede Trust 2000). This idealization is captured by this passage from the noted British ethnicist, Bhikhu Parekh:

> Multiculturalism doesn't simply mean numerical plurality of different cultures, but rather a community which is creating, guaranteeing, encouraging spaces within which different communities are able to grow at their own pace. At the same time it means creating a public space in which these new communities are able to interact, enrich the existing culture, and create a new consensual culture in which they recognize reflections of their own identity. (Cited in Giroux 1994:336)

Several assumptions underlie a multicultural ideology. First and foremost is a belief that people are social beings whose well-being depends on a shared identity with ethnically similar others. Minority cultures constitute living and lived-in realities that are valued in their own right while imparting meaning and security during times of stress or social change (Kymlicka 1995). Ethnocultural affiliation does not imply an element of mental inferiority, stubbornness, or lack of patriotism. Rather, these differences are important and of benefit to both individuals and society at large if properly "managed." Second, multiculturalism does not dismiss diversity as contrary to the goals of national unity or societal progress. Cultural differences are endorsed instead as integral components of a national mosaic, a reflection of the Canadian ideal, and a source of unity and strength. Third, a multicultural ideal builds upon the principles of **cultural relativism.** This doctrine holds that all cultural practices are relative to a particular time and place, take their meaning from this context, and must be understood accordingly. That is not to say that everything *is* equally good; nor is anyone espousing the philosophy that "anything goes." To the contrary, a critically informed relativism approaches diversity *as if* it were an equally valid expression of the human experience.

Fourth, a commitment to multiculturalism is predicated on the premise that those confident in their cultural background will concede a similar tolerance to others (Berry et al. 1977). Or as Trudeau explained back in 1971, if national unity is to mean anything in the deeply personal sense, it must be anchored on confidence in one's own identity, for it is out of this respect for others that a sharing of ideas and assumptions is fostered. This notion that if people are respected for who they are, they, in turn, will be loyal to the state was put to the test when the so-called ethnic vote in the 1995 October referendum derailed (for the time being) Quebec's separatist aspirations (see also Cardozo and Musto 1997).

There is another ideological spin to multiculturalism. For some, multiculturalism is not a "happy face" ideology for embracing the virtues of tolerance and celebration of differences. Rather it constitutes a discourse in defence of dominant ideology. On one side, the ideas and ideals implicit within an official Multiculturalism tend to create consensus, conformity, and control in securing the status quo behind the smokescreen of national interests. Too much of what passes for multiculturalism is little more than an exercise in conflict management whose primary goal is to "cool out" those troublesome constituents who are problems or create problems. On the other side, an official Multiculturalism embraces an ideology that promotes the interests of vested groups at the expense of the population at large. For Marxists, the ideological aspect of multiculturalism reflects its status as false consciousness. Multiculturalism not only dulls the public senses to the continuing marginalization of migrants and minorities—a kind of opiate of the masses—but also lulls people into a false sense of security by conveying the impression of minority improvement. To the extent that nothing of substance happens, although many are convinced that something does, no one should underestimate the ideological role of official Multiculturalism as a device for preserving patterns of power, privilege, and property (for discussion, see Ley 2005).

As Policy

Policy considerations are central to any official Multiculturalism (Magsino 2000). Governments throughout the world have embarked on official strategies for controlling immigration, managing ethnic relations, accommodating differences, and integrating ethnocultural minorities into the mainstream. Policy frameworks that may have worked in the past, like assimilation or segregation, have proven inadequate in addressing contemporary minority demands. By contrast, multiculturalism represents an alternative policy option that secures an innovative blueprint for living together with differences. Of course, not everyone agrees. Instead of being praised as an authentic policy alternative, Multiculturalism is rejected as little more than an interim measure for absorbing minorities—an "assimilation in slow motion" behind a facade of diversity intentions.

Two policy levels can be discerned with respect to official Multiculturalism. One, multiculturalism consists of specific government initiatives for transforming multicultural ideals into official programs and practice. An official Multiculturalism may be aimed at preventing discrimination or, alternatively, positively promoting differences as legitimate and integral to national interests. Two, competing rights are in play: (1) the right to be different with a corresponding right to having differences recognized and respected, and (2) the right to be the same with full and equal participation based on a shared commitment to a political community (Sandercock 2003). With Multiculturalism, a new symbolic order is projected, one that addresses the integration of migrants and minorities through removal of discriminatory barriers and protection of ethnic diversity. Multiculturalism can also be interpreted within a broader normative framework that justifies the promotion of diversity programs without fear of inciting public concern over yet more government intrusion. This normative framework may not be openly articulated; nevertheless, it supplies the "underlying agenda" that legitimizes policy initiatives under a Multiculturalism umbrella.

To say that Canada is officially Multicultural is stating the obvious. Yet, the irony is improbable. From its inception in 1971, when it barely garnered a paragraph in Canada's national newspaper, official Multiculturalism has evolved to the point where it constitutes a formidable component of Canada's national identity, having profoundly altered how Canadians think about themselves and their relationship to the world. Thirty-five years of official Multiculturalism have been instrumental in orchestrating a national consensus around majority acceptance of minority participation. Multiculturalism as a policy originated around the quest for integrative society-building functions; it continues to persist for precisely the same reasons, namely, the settlement of migrants and minorities by modifying the rules of integration (Kymlicka 2001). The goal of multiculturalism has never wavered from its underlying commitment, namely, the possibility of living together with differences, without the differences getting in the way of equal involvement or social order. Only the means for achieving unity within diversity have changed, evolving in response to demographic upheavals and political developments, with ethnicity-based solutions giving way to equity-grounded reforms and, more recently, the promotion of citizenship and participation. For the sake of simplicity these shifts can be partitioned into three overlapping policy stages: *ethnicity*, *equity*, and *civic* which, in turn, correspond with the three dimensions of official Multiculturalism, namely, the cultural, the social, and the national.

Canada's official Multiculturalism arose in the aftermath of the publication of the *Report of the Royal Commission on Bilingualism and Biculturalism* in 1969. Various ethnic minority groups, especially the Ukrainians and Germans, had lobbied vigorously in arguing that their language and culture were as vital as Quebec's to Canada-building (Jaworsky 1979). Admittedly, the findings of the Royal Commission concluded that Canada comprised a multicultural commonwealth of many nationalities but within the bicultural (or binational) framework of two founding peoples (biculturalism). Yet, ethnic lobby groups rejected the two founding nations concept, with its implication that some Canadians were more deserving than others. Proposed instead was a descriptive ideal that captured the contribution of the "other ethnics" to the cultural enrichment of a bicultural Canada. Pressure to create a symbolic multicultural order was further heightened by the forces of Québécois nationalism in the aftermath of the Quiet Revolution (Breton 1989). The multicultural nod to ethnic minorities was envisaged as a potential counterbalance to neutralize (or depoliticize) Canada's bicultural focus (Webber 1994). Finally, with "Britishness" losing its saliency in Canada and elsewhere (see Jakubowicz 2005), Multiculturalism emerged as an ideological glue to hold Canadians together by forestalling a conflict of one against all while offering a unique way of looking at Canada. A new national unity strategy evolved, based on a vision of Canada as a multicultural mosaic of equality-seeking individuals rather than a bicultural partnership of nations (McRoberts 1997).

A commitment to multiculturalism within a bilingual framework was subsequently articulated by the Liberal government when then–prime minister Pierre Elliott Trudeau rose in Parliament on 8 October 1971 and declared his government's intentions to embrace "multiculturalism within a bilingual framework." As many have noted, multiculturalism originated in response to Trudeau's disdain of both British and French nationalism, whose ethnocentric tyrannies compromised individual rights and right of choice. By abolishing culture and rootedness as justification for superior entitlement while putting all Canadians on equal footing regardless of their culture or immigrant status, Trudeau's goal was a Canada in which members of different nationalities intermingled as neighbours on a common territory without discarding their distinct cultural identities if they chose to do so (Cameron 2004). In the words of Trudeau, the linking of individual rights with equal status under multiculturalism would "strengthen the solidarity of the Canadian people by enabling all Canadians to participate fully and without discrimination in defining and building the nation's future." Four major principles secured this commitment to re-sculpt Canada along multicultural lines:

- *Equality of status:* Canada does not have an official culture; all cultures are equal.
- *Canadian identity:* Diversity lies at the heart of Canadian identity.
- *Personal choice:* The right to identify with the cultural tradition of their choice.
- *Protection of individual rights:* Individual rights to be free of discrimination.

To put these principles into practice, the government proposed initiatives to (1) assist those cultural groups that demonstrated a commitment to develop, share, and contribute to Canada; (2) assist the members of all cultural groups to overcome cultural barriers to full participation in Canadian society; (3) promote creative encounters and exchanges among all Canadian cultural groups in advancing national unity; and (4) assist immigrants to acquire at least one of Canada's official languages to ensure full and equal participation.

The conclusion is inescapable: official Multiculturalism was not about celebrating cultural differences; if anything, it hoped to eliminate those cultural prejudices that denied or excluded. By encouraging an understanding and sharing of ethnocultural traditions, the goal of Canada's **integrative multiculturalism** focused on improving minority and migrant integration into society (Donaldson 2004). A commitment to cultural preservation was not high on the multicultural agenda—at least not beyond an initial commitment when powerful ethnic lobbyists prevailed. (It is fair to say that Canada's multicultural discourses remain rooted in an almost essentialized understanding of ethnicity as primordial and immutable rather than flexible, dynamic, and relational, in which membership and participation in the mosaic locks individuals into hermetically sealed groups whose culture is authentic, known, and practised by its members, providing a source of pride, and serving as powerful shapers of attitudes and behaviour [Kurien 2004].) According to an ethnicity-based integrative multiculturalism, a society of many cultures was possible, provided cultural differences did not preclude full citizenship rights and equal participation. Conditions applied, of course, including: (1) all new Canadians should have primary commitment to Canada, (2) all new Canadians must accept Canada's fundamental structures, principles, and values, and (3) all new Canadians have a right to identify with the culture of their choice (within limits) and to share this with other Canadians (McRoberts 1997; Cardozo and Musto 1997). And to the extent they are tolerated, cultural differences cannot violate people's rights, break the law, or contravene core constitutional values.

The focus of official Multiculturalism shifted noticeably by the early 1980s. Instead of emphasizing the centrality of ethnicity, Multiculturalism discourses shifted toward the more equity-driven concerns of racialized immigrants. The often different requirements of European "ethnics" compared to visible minority immigrants proved more perplexing as visibility complicated the process and prospect of minority integration. Migrant and minority concerns shifted accordingly under an *equity Multiculturalism*. For new immigrants, the need for dismantling racial barriers to opportunity was more important than the celebration of their cultural differences

(McRoberts 1997). The earlier emphasis on ethnicity and identity as keys to integration was subsequently replaced by a commitment to equity, social justice, and institutional inclusiveness (Agocs and Boyd 1993; Donaldson 2004). Funding allocations were adjusted. Rather than simply doling out money to ethnocultural organizations or events as had been the case, authorities channelled multicultural spending into equity goals related to anti-racism, race relations, and removal of discriminatory barriers at institutional levels.

Subsequent developments further advanced the political profile of official Multiculturalism. The *Charter of Rights and Freedoms*, which came into effect in 1985, constitutionally entrenched Multiculturalism as a distinguishing feature of Canadian life. The emergence of Multiculturalism as a tool of interpretation at the highest levels of constitutional decision-making reinforced its status as a fundamental characteristic of Canada. Its prominence was further advanced when Canada became the world's first and only official Multiculturalism with the passage of the *Multiculturalism Act* in 1988. Passage of the Act sought to promote cultures, reduce discrimination, and accelerate institutional inclusiveness through the "preservation and enhancement of Canadian multiculturalism." In a sense, then, the *Multiculturalism Act* completed the Canada-building project associated with the passage of the *Official Languages Act* of 1969, the Statement on Multiculturalism in 1971, and its enshrinement in the *Constitution Act* of 1982. The significance cannot be understated. Each of these initiatives converged to create a distinctly Canadian society based on the integrative principle that each individual as a self-defining agent should be able to participate fully and equally regardless of differences (Breton 2001).

Official Multiculturalism continues to acknowledge the importance of cultural identity. Its commitment to social equality is no less important, and is manifest in the mainstreaming of diversity to ensure minority access, representation, and equitable treatment at institutional levels. Equally evident at present is a more explicit commitment to national interests by equating multiculturalism with citizenship, a relationship that was consummated under the short-lived Department of Multiculturalism and Citizenship. Multiculturalism remains aligned with the Citizenship and Canadian Identity portfolio, albeit as a program within the broader superministry of Canadian Heritage. In light of growing criticism from the left and the right, a civic orientation to the multiculturalism agenda began to emerge. A repackaging was formalized in 1996, when the Multiculturalism program was renewed around three strategic goals: civic participation (full and equal involvement), social justice (equitable treatment), and identity (advancing cultural diversity to ensure belonging and attachment). A civic commitment was subsequently consolidated in 2002 when the Multiculturalism program identified four priority objectives: fostering cross-cultural understanding; combating racism and discrimination, promoting shared citizenship, and developing more responsive and representative institutions (Dept. of Canadian Heritage 2005).

A **civic multiculturalism** is oriented toward Canada-building by promoting a commonly shared citizenship (Canadian Heritage, Multiculturalism, 2003/04; Abu-Laban 2001). Emphasis is on fostering a sense of belonging, a civic engagement, an active involvement in community life, and a shared awareness of Canadian identity against the broader backdrop of Canada's national interests. In eschewing a Multiculturalism that was aimed only at minorities, the scope of civic multiculturalism is directed at a shared national unity by "break[ing] down the ghettoization of multiculturalism," according to Hedy Fry, former minister for Multiculturalism (1997):

> As a national policy of inclusiveness, multiculturalism's activities aim to bring all Canadians closer together, to enhance equal opportunities, to encourage mutual respect among citizens of

diverse backgrounds, to assist in integrating first-generation Canadians, to promote more harmonious inter-group relations, and to foster social cohesion and a shared sense of Canadian identity.

A recent minister of state for Multiculturalism, Raymond Chan (2005), was equally enthusiastic about a Multiculturalism for integrating all Canadians into one happy family:

> Ideally, I would like to get to the point I think where multiculturalism is associated with our shared interests, as Canadians, in institutional inclusion and equality of opportunity. The idea is that we need to be able to respect diversity and at the same time recognize one another as equal citizens. We want to achieve full contribution of people of all backgrounds to Canadian society where multiculturalism, as policy and program, supports the integration while at the same time fostering communities that strengthen this integration.

To sum up: Official Multiculturalism must be interpreted as a complex and contested policy that has evolved over time in response to social and political changes (Seiler 2002). A multicultural commitment to diversity and disadvantage provides more equitable terms for the integration of migrants and minorities (Kymlicka 1998; 2001). A two-way process of adjustment is implied under an integrative multiculturalism, that is, you adapt, we adjust. And yet working through a multicultural model of integration reveals contradictory strands. On one side, Multiculturalism appears to reject the legitimacy of diversity for fear of isolating minorities into self-contained enclaves with their own separate power bases. On the other side, Multiculturalism appears to endorse the need to take differences into account to ensure full participation and equal citizenship rights. But a constant across all Multiculturalism discourses is a commitment to integrate minority women and men through removal of prejudice and discriminatory barriers. Only the means to achieve these goals have changed, with an ethnicity focus giving way to an equity focus, and currently emphasizing a civic dimension. Table 10.1 compares and contrasts the different stages in the evolution of Canada's integrative multiculturalism, keeping in mind the inevitability of simplification when comparing ideal–typical categories.

As Practice

Glowing reviews about celebrating and sharing cannot disguise what many have long suspected: The implementation of multiculturalism as ideology does not always translate into practices consistent with policy principles. Multiculturalism as practice refers to its application

TABLE 10.1 Canada's Integrative Multiculturalism: Policy Shifts			
	Ethnicity Multiculturalism (1970s)	**Equity Multiculturalism (1980s)**	**Civic Multiculturalism (1990s–2000s)**
Focus	Celebrating differences	Fostering equality	Living together
Reference Point	Culture	Structure	Society-building
Mandate	Ethnicity	Race relations	Citizenship
Magnitude	Individual adjustment	Institutional inclusion	Community participation
Problem Source	Prejudice	Systemic discrimination	Exclusion
Problem Solution	Cultural sensitivity	Employment equity	Inclusiveness
Key Metaphor	"Mosaic"	"Level playing field"	"Belonging"

for advancing goals, agendas, and ambitions. Politicians and bureaucrats look upon multi-culturalism as a resource with economic or political potential to be exploited at national or international levels for practical gain. Hardly a surprise, given that Canada's official Multiculturalism originated as a political program to achieve political goals in a politically astute manner (Peter 1978). The governing apparatus of the Canadian state relied on Multiculturalism to fulfill a variety of legitimating functions involving national unity, economic prosperity, and electoral survival (see also Bharucha 2000). Inception of official Multiculturalism hoped to formulate a new founding myth of Canada as a land of opportunity and equality, thus uniting all Canadians at a time of political turmoil, yet doing so without any fundamental redistribution of power (Helly 1993). It also sought to shore up electoral strength in urban Ontario, to counterbalance Western resentment over perceived favouritism toward the Québécois, to pre-empt the encroachment of American cultural values, and to thwart inter-group strife because of competing priorities. In short, an official Multiculturalism parlayed a potential weakness into strength without sacrificing a commitment to social cohesion, national identity, domestic peace, economic advantage, and global status (Kurthen 1997).

References to the politics of multiculturalism tend to dwell on party politics. From nomination struggles to ethnic coalitions, multicultural politics at the crassest level revolve around a belief in ethnic support as relevant for (re-)election. The vast majority of Canada's multicultural minorities are concentrated in the MTV centres of Toronto, Montreal, and Vancouver—a trend likely to be amplified by future immigration patterns (e.g., the percentage of immigrants in Ontario ridings based on 2004 electoral boundaries included Scarborough Rouge River at 66.8 percent and Scarborough Agincourt at 64.5 percent [Jedwab 2004b]. Or consider how 37 of the 44 ridings in the Toronto region voted Liberal in the 2003 federal election [repeated again in 2006], thanks in part to the immigrant vote.) The continuing heterogeneity of Canada's population will further prompt political parties to pursue the multicultural vote through promises of increased representation, funding, and Employment Equity at federal levels.

Also widely touted is the commercial potential of multiculturalism. The then–prime minister Brian Mulroney promoted a business model of multiculturalism rooted in economic rationality and self-interest in his "Multiculturalism Means Business" speech at a Toronto conference in 1986. The commercial value of multiculturalism remains stronger than ever because of the demands of a global economy. Diversity and the market are closely intertwined because capitalizing on differences is seen as good for the economy, especially when 40 percent of Canada's GDP is export-based.

> The ethnocultural diversity of Canada's population is a major advantage when access to global markets is more important than ever to our economic prosperity. Protecting this advantage means that steps to eradicate racism are essential. Canada cannot afford to have any of its citizens marginalized. As a knowledge-based economy in an increasingly global marketplace, every mind matters. All Canadians must have the opportunity to develop and contribute to their full potential. (Canadian Heritage 2001)

Multiculturalism continues to be promoted as a valuable export just as staple products were in the past (Abu-Laban and Gabriel 2002). By enhancing Canada's sales image and competitive edge in a global economy—particularly by cultivating and tapping into the lucrative Asian market—references to multiculturalism are touted as having the potential to harness lucrative trade contracts, establish international linkages and mutually profitable points of contact, attract members of the transnational elite, and penetrate export markets (Multiculturalism/Secretary of State 1993). By playing the "ethnic harmony card," the promotion of Multiculturalism as an ideology of racial harmony and worldly cosmopolitanism provides reassurance for nervous investors and fidgety capital (Mitchell 1993). As the globalization of capitalist market economies continues to expand, Multiculturalism may well provide the networking for confronting the challenges of a shifting and increasingly borderless reality that may be the twenty-first century norm (Woodley 1997). In that multicultural priorities will continue to be driven by an economic agenda more interested in improving Canada's competitive advantage than in securing institutional inclusiveness, the business side of Multiculturalism should never be discounted.

Multicultural minorities are no less inclined to adopt Multiculturalism as a resource for attaining practical goals (Burnet 1981). Minority needs are basic. They as a group want to become established, expand economic opportunities for themselves and their children, eliminate discrimination and exploitation, and retain access to their cultural heritage without loss of citizenship rights. Multiculturalism is employed as a tool for meeting these needs by opening up avenues through elimination of discriminatory barriers in employment, education, housing, and criminal justice. With Multiculturalism, minority women and men are empowered with a tool for staking out their claims while articulating their demands alongside those of the first and second force. Multiculturalism empowers an otherwise powerless sector with the leverage to prod or provoke central policy structures by holding them accountable for failure to connect multicultural ideals with everyday results. Appeals to official Multiculturalism are thus calculated to extract public sympathy and global scrutiny—in the same way as Canada's Aboriginal peoples have relied on international fora (such as the United Nations) as leverage in negotiating with the federal government. For minorities, then, the driving force behind Multiculturalism is equality not nationalism, integration not isolation, and inclusion not separation. There is no inclination for separate homelands or autonomous states. Emphasis instead is on acceptance as equals and to be respected as different without sacrificing the right to full and equal participation (Cardozo and Musto 1997).

As Critical/Transformative Discourse

An integrative multiculturalism is not the only multicultural game in town (May 2004). Different multicultural discourses can be discerned that challenge, resist, and transform rather than advocate consensus, conformity, and control. As a transformative discourse of resistance, **critical multiculturalism** challenges the authority and legitimacy of the status quo by contesting the prevailing distribution of power and privilege. A critical multiculturalism transcends the simple construction of identities, celebration of differences, or commitment to tolerance. It goes beyond a United Colors of Benetton pluralism with its corporate-orchestrated tastes, appearances, sensations, and colours—a consumer-driven approach to ethnic diversity that does little to transform institutional inequalities (May 2004). As a philosophy of criticism and protest, critical multiculturalism approaches cultural institutions as fundamentally racist in privileging Westocentric values at the expense of minority struggles, identities, and aspirations (Early 1993). Criticism is directed at the legacy of European ethnocentrism, with its cramming of diversity into a single paradigm, its positing of Europe as the apex of evolutionary progress, its self-appointed right to do what it pleases, and its sanitizing of Western exploitation and human rights abuses (Stam and Shohat 1994). Differences do not merely exist under critical multiculturalism; they are a critical part of the struggle to create a new public culture. There is explicit recognition that society comprises citizens of different backgrounds whose identities and cultures must be publicly recognized, respected, and rewarded rather than relegated to the private and personal (Kurien 2004). Inasmuch as minority interests are openly contesting the shaping of institutional knowledge from education to media, the politics of critical multiculturalism are transformative in content and style (Frederickson 1999). To be sure, critical multicultural discourses exist in Canada (Thobani 2000a, b). But transformative multiculturalisms receive much more publicity in the United States, where challenging the "dominant silencing of diversity" (Eisenstein 1996; 2004) fosters a framework by which new identities are (re)formulated, new communities are constructed, knowledge and power are contested, and Eurocentric universalisms are exposed for what they are: self-serving discourses in defence of dominant ideology. In contrast with Canada's **consensus multiculturalism,** the postmodernist discourses that animate America's critical multiculturalism subvert as they resist. Critical multiculturalism transcends the constraints of official policy initiatives, unhampered as it is by the compromising demands of political process or electoral pandering. Unlike an integrative multiculturalism that espouses a diversity devoid of historical context and inter-group power relations, the transformative discourses of critical multiculturalism oppose Eurocentricity by relativizing the white capitalist patriarchy with its exclusionary designs on the "Other" (Giroux 1994; Eisenstein 1996).

In short, Canada's official Multiculturalism is essentially a society-building exercise that seeks to depoliticize differences through institutional accommodation. This integrative multiculturalism is grounded in the liberal universalist credo that our commonalities as rights-bearing, equality-seeking individuals are more important than what divides us through group membership. As a discourse in defence of ideology, the logic of integrative multiculturalism is concerned with drawing people into the framework of an existing Canada rather than in bringing about transformative social change. Compare this integrative model with a critical multiculturalism model where group differences and identity claims are politicized by challenging the prevailing distribution of social power. That is, while critical multiculturalisms often focus on group-based rights with an emphasis on the politics of recognition and identity politics, an official Multiculturalism establishes an individual right to choose and to have choice, with a focus on equality and (dis)advantage to ensure an inclusive society. A "playful" inversion is called for in evaluating these duelling discourses. Rather than making diversity safe from society as well as safe for society, as is the case with critical multiculturalism, official Multiculturalism purports to make society safe from diversity yet safe for diversity.

PUBLIC PERCEPTIONS / CRITICAL REACTIONS

Of the conceptual tripwires and cultural landmines strewn across the Western landscape in recent years, few have triggered as much vitriol or controversy as multiculturalism (Possner 1997; Gilroy 2004). Timing in particular has played politics with a modernist project that many regard as passé for the post-9/11 (and 7/7 in London) realities of the twenty-first century. Inception of multiculturalism as a popular and political discourse may have originated in an era of optimism and reform but is badly listing at present because of concerns over security (Rex and Singh 2004; also Gregg 2006). What started out as a society-building idea with noble intentions (to assist newcomers into Canada) has evolved into a flashpoint for tension. On one side are those advocates who continue to worship at the altar of multiculturalism; on the other side are those who recoil at the very prospect of foisting yet more diversity on an unsuspecting public; on yet another side are those critics who sneer at something so irrelevant or counterproductive. By virtue of fostering ethnic segregation, however unintentionally, multiculturalism has outlived its usefulness, despite the unavoidable uncertainty of growing cultural diversity (see Ley 2005).

Not surprisingly, public perception of multiculturalism in Canada is varied. Some Canadians are vigorously supportive; others are in total rejection or denial; still others are indifferent; and yet others are plainly uninformed (see Cardozo and Musto 1997; Cameron 2004). The majority appear to be caught somewhere in between, depending on their reading of multiculturalism and its contribution (or lack thereof) to Canadian society. Variables such as age, income, level of education, and place of residence are critical in gauging support, with higher levels of approval among the younger, more affluent, better educated, and urban (Anderssen and Valpy 2003). To the extent that most Canadians are unsure of what Canada's official Multiculturalism is trying to do, and why, the prospect of living differently together is compromised.

Public support for official Multiculturalism is open to debate. Opinion polls are known to provide different answers depending on the kind of questions asked. Nevertheless, national surveys on Multiculturalism suggest a solid base of support often in the 60 to 70 percent range (Angus Reid 1991; Berry 1993; Musto 1997; ACS/Environics 2002; Jedwab 2005b; Dasko 2005). Yet, support for Multiculturalism is not as transparent as the data would suggest. First, Canadians may be supportive of Multiculturalism, but support may reflect confusion over its many dimensions. Respondents may endorse multiculturalism in principle or as a demographic fact, yet reject Multiculturalism as official policy or mistakenly conflate Multiculturalism with unpopular government programs like Employment Equity. Second, support is not the same as enthusiasm. Canadians appear to embrace multiculturalism as a reality to be tolerated rather than an ideal to be emulated. The idea of multicultural tolerance is widely supported; after all, a mix of cultures is perceived to make Canada a more interesting place, but there is little passion for its implementation. Third, support or rejection tends to be selective and inconsistent. Most Canadians support some aspect of multiculturalism, but are conflicted over issues of accommodation, with significant numbers believing that Multiculturalism deters new Canadians from integrating into society (Jedwab 2004; Collacott 2006). Worse still are fears about its unintended consequences, including worries over fostering conditions that breed terrorism or encouraging ghettoization, including cultivation of hostile differences (Friesen 2005; Baubock 2005). Fourth, support is conditional: Canadians are prepared to accept Multiculturalism if costs are low and demands are reasonable, such as assisting new Canadians to settle in, removing discriminatory barriers, learning about others, and promoting tolerance (Gwyn 1996). Support is withdrawn when endorsement is seen as eroding Canada's sense of national unity and identity, challenging authority or core values, curbing the integration of cultural communities, criticizing the mainstream, or acquiescing to the demands of particular groups (Simpson 2005).

CRITIQUING MULTICULTURALISM

Official Multiculturalism is unevenly supported across Canada (Duncan 2005). Residents of Ontario and western Canada appear receptive, but the Québécois and Aboriginal peoples have demonstrated widespread rejection (Ignace and Ignace 1998; Breton 2000; Kymlicka 2001). For the "nations within" and national minorities, their concerns go beyond those of disadvantage or diversity but focus on the injustices and disempowerment foisted on them because of Canada's society-building project (Baubock 2005). Instead of self-defining themselves as immigrants in need of integration and equality, both Aboriginal peoples and the Québécois prefer the language of nationalism over that of multiculturalism for justifying claims to self-determining autonomy over jurisdictions of land, identity, and political voice (Murphy 2005; Maaka and Fleras 2005). An official Multiculturalism cannot possibly address the demands of fundamentally autonomous political communities who claim they are sovereign in their own right yet sharing in the sovereignty of Canada by way of shared jurisdictions. With its roots in consensus and control, an integrative multiculturalism is poorly equipped to handle the highly politicized discourses of challenge and transformation (McRoberts 2001).

Many observers of Canada's political scene have criticized government initiatives in this area (see Fleras 2002 for review). Multiculturalism is seen as divisive because of its tendency to tolerate practices incompatible with Canada's central core, yet also of being hypocritical in offering the illusion of tolerance while punishing behaviour at odds with core values (Stoffman 2002). No other than the current governor general of Canada, Michaëlle Jean (2005), has accused multiculturalism of creating a ghetto nation in a speech in Montreal before becoming Canada's viceroy:

> Citizenship means living together . . . But does 'multiculturalism' really propose us living together? We are even given money so that we will stay in our own separate enclosures. There's a kind of proposition of ghettoization that is there, and that is financed.

Some dismiss Multiculturalism as a bad idea that is doing badly as predicted. For Robert Fulford (1997), a multiculturalistic classification of citizens according to race and ancestry was a bad idea from the beginning and may prove a colossal public policy blunder. Others are no less dismissive of Multiculturalism as a good idea gone bad: Gina Mallet (1997:D-2) captures a sense of this self-implosion when she writes

> Although the drive to honour diversity through official multiculturalism was originally undertaken in order to promote tolerance, it is accomplishing the opposite. By setting Canadians against one another and emphasizing our differences rather than the many things we have in common, diversity has, in fact, gone too far.

Still others pounce on Multiculturalism regardless of what it does or doesn't do. Multiculturalism has been accused of being too radical or too reactionary, of promoting too much or not enough change, of promising more than it can deliver (a sheep in wolf's clothing) or delivering more than bargained for (a wolf in sheep's clothing). And while Multiculturalism may be embraced by many as a strength to be admired, it is dismissed by others as a weakness to be condemned or exploited, as noted by Irshad Manji (2005:A19):

> As Westerners bow before multiculturalism, we anesthetize ourselves into believing that anything goes. We see our readiness to accommodate as a strength—even a form of cultural superiority . . . Radical Muslims, on the other hand, see our inclusive instincts as a form of corruption that makes us soft and rudderless. They believe the weak deserve to be vanquished. Paradoxically, then, the more we accommodate to placate, the more their contempt for our "weakness" grows. And the ultimate paradox may be that in order to defend our diversity, we'll need to be less tolerant.

Academic opinion is mixed. For some, Multiculturalism is not perfect but remains the option of choice for Canada (Kymlicka 2005). Criticism is twofold: whether Multiculturalism fosters or hinders the integration of minorities and migrants and how much must be given up by those doing the integration and those being integrated (Jedwab 2005b). For others, the paradoxes and ambiguities implicit within Multiculturalism justify the criticism

(Bannerji 2000; Cameron 2004). Critics on the Left have pounced on Multiculturalism as ineffective except as a mantra for politicians to trot out for publicity purposes. Multiculturalism is criticized as a colossal hoax perpetuated by vested interests to ensure minority co-optation through ideological indoctrination (false consciousness) (Thobani 1995). Or to put it more bluntly, multiculturalism represents a clever device by ruling elites to control unruly ethnics (Hage 1998). As a capitalist plot to divide and distract the working classes, Multiculturalism ghettoizes minorities into occupational structures and residential arrangements, thereby preserving the prevailing distribution of power and wealth behind a smokescreen of well-oiled platitudes (Dei 2000; Bannerji 2000).

Those on the right repudiate Multiculturalism as a costly drain of resources that runs the risk of eroding national unity. Worse still, Stewart Bell writes in *Cold Terror: How Canada Nurtures and Exports Terrorism Around the World* (2004), the openness of Multiculturalism makes Canada vulnerable to infiltration by terrorists (Collacott 2006). Moderates may be unsure of where to stand. Official Multiculturalism may sound good in theory, but implementation may falter because of difficulties in balancing unity with diversity. For example, while its intent may be to facilitate the integration of immigrants and secure their loyalty, Multiculturalism may have a perverse effect by strengthening immigrants' attachment to their homeland and giving rise to diasporic nationalisms (Kurien 2004). Conversely, while Multiculturalism may provide minorities with a platform for promoting distinctiveness, the very act of participation may have the effect of absorbing minorities into the dominant culture (Pearson 2001). Or alternatively, Multiculturalism is long on principle and promise, but has proven short on delivery except to convey an air of mutual indifference in which Canadians share geographic and political space but little else (Ignatieff 2001).

The conclusion seems inescapable: In its role as the self-appointed catalyst for social engineering, multiculturalism has attracted its share of criticism—even in the country where first enunciated and most fully institutionalized (Ley 2005). National shortcomings for some reason tend to polarize around the multicultural management of minority relations. But while much of this criticism may be true, it is not entirely true. Criticism of Multiculturalism may not reflect a backlash any more than silence is proof of its acceptance. To the extent that criticism is vocal, the disgruntlement may arise from growing discontent among the already disenchanted rather than a new legion of malcontents. And it is difficult to determine what exactly people dislike about Multiculturalism—the principle, the policy, the practice? A sense of perspective is helpful: In that both critics and supporters gloss over the underlying logic of Multiculturalism, those who stoutly defend Multiculturalism at all costs are as ideological as those who disparage it for lacking any redeeming value whatsoever. In that there are many publics, with different expectations and needs, the impact of official Multiculturalism is neither all good nor all bad; rather, it may be either good or bad depending on context, criteria, and consequences. More importantly, Multiculturalism may be both good *and* bad simultaneously, both liberating yet marginalizing, unifying yet divisive, inclusive yet exclusive, with benefits yet costs.

Consider the following paradoxes: On one side, an official Multiculturalism may be divisive by undermining the basis of Canadian unity and identity. Yet, Canada's integrative Multiculturalism is unifying by creating a blueprint for an inclusive Canada. Emphasizing the virtues of sharing, interaction, and participation points to Canada-building by improving the terms of integration for minorities rather than condoning the creation of segregated ethnic communities with separate power bases (Kostash 2000; McRoberts 2004). On one side,

Multiculturalism may be seen as regressive in ghettoizing or stigmatizing minorities. Neil Bissoondath (1994) has castigated a Multiculturalism that aids in the containment and control of migrants and minorities while essentializing their identities in some frozen past. Yet, Multiculturalism has proven progressive in reversing discrimination by creating a commitment to institutional inclusiveness. In building bridges rather than erecting walls, Canada's Multiculturalism encourages minority women and men to become involved, construct productive lives, and contribute to society (McGauran 2005). By incorporating efforts to remove discrimination, nurture civic engagement, foster cross-cultural understanding, and promote responsive institutions, Multiculturalism connotes a process for making the mainstream more inclusive rather than making minorities more multicultural (also Chan 2003/2004). On one side, Multiculturalism is criticized for not taking differences seriously because of preference for a pretend pluralism. Yet, Multiculturalism is not about diversity but about addressing disadvantage by removing discrimination because of perceived differences. Still, Multiculturalism provides a social climate that not only encourages an individual to affiliate with the cultural tradition of their choice, but also ensures that cultural differences do not interfere with getting along, settling down, and fitting in. And finally, Multiculturalism may be accused of being a symbol without substance—a frivolous diversion with no power to challenge or transform. Yet, Multiculturalism has presided over a radical remaking of Canada from an exclusionary British monoculture to a cosmopolitan society of many cultures and colours in part by incorporating the symbols of diversity into the narratives of Canadian "nationhood" (Will Kymlicka in Gregg 2006).

In short, Canada's official Multiculturalism is double-edged in impact and implications. In the same way that ethnicity can empower or divide depending on a particular frame of reference, so too can a commitment to Multiculturalism serve to enhance yet detract. Positive and negative effects coexist uneasily. On the one hand, the benefits of Multiculturalism cannot be discounted, thus reflecting the ability of the powerless to convert the very tools for controlling them into levers of resistance and change (Pearson 1994). On the other hand, recourse to official Multiculturalism can de-politicize the potency of diversity by channelling it into the private or personal. Far from being a threat to the social order, Canada's official Multiculturalism constitutes a discourse in defence of dominant ideology. Depending on where one stands on the political spectrum, this is a cause for concern or contentment.

A sense of perspective is useful. Multiculturalism is not the cause of Canada's problems, any more than it can be the cure-all. There is no risk of Canada unravelling because of Multiculturalism: The politics of "distinct society" and the "nations within" will see to that first. Nor should we get worked up over the absence of a common culture—as if Multiculturalism destroyed what never existed except, perhaps, within the context of British colonialism. Perhaps Canada's core value is the absence of any common culture except those shared values pertaining to a basic decency, a respect for rule of law, a commitment to individual equality, and a constant quest for identity (see Sajoo 1994). Diversity, not uniformity, is Canada's strength, and to expect otherwise is unrealistic in a multi-layered and deeply divided society organized around overlapping citizenships of the First Nations, the Québécois, and multicultural minorities. Disagreement and conflict are inevitable in such a deeply divided context. Just as shared ethnicity does not entail a unanimity of vision, as Bissoondath (1994) reminds us albeit in a different sense, so too can a multicultural society survive on a multiplicity of voices and visions—provided that, within limits, we agree on the principle of agreeing to disagree.

Europe's Retreat from Multiculturalism and Immigration Versus Canada's Continued Acceptance

References to Multiculturalism as policy and philosophy have come under intense scrutiny not only in so-called complete societies (those in Europe) but also in immigrant societies (such as Australia) (Gregg 2006). Policies and ideologies that once embraced multiculturalism as a basis for living together with differences (by removing discriminatory barriers and celebrating diversity) are now dismissed as irrelevant or inferior, a failure or a threat. In the aftermath of 9/11, the Madrid and London bombings, and the murder of Dutch filmmaker Theo van Gogh, multiculturalism in Europe has come under criticism for everything from the spate of terrorist attacks to the fostering of cultural separatism, political fragmentation, and social ghettoization. A resonant note of dismay is captured by Trevor Phillips, chair of Britain's Commission for Racial Equality, when he contends "We focused far too much on the 'multi' and not enough on the common culture"—thereby allowing tolerance to solidify into isolation rather than insisting on sharing common values without losing a sense of uniqueness. In other words, multiculturalism may have reigned supreme in Europe for 20 years, but no more, and a commitment to multicultural governance has proven much more unnerving than many would have imagined—more of a deadly liability instead of an empowering solution.

Europe's love affair with multiculturalism may be in retreat, but the situation in Canada differs. Canada's multiculturalism appears to be relatively untouched by criticism or backlash, while support for immigrants and immigration remains at an all-time high. For example, in a survey by the Centre for Research and Information on Canada involving a representative sample of 2032 randomly selected Canadians who were interviewed in August of 2005 (with a margin of error of plus or minus 2.2 percent 19 times out of 20), Canadians clearly value multiculturalism as a defining characteristic of Canada, while large majorities link immigration with a host of positive social, economic, and cultural advantages (also Dasko 2005). Nor is Canada victimized by the race riots in European cities or the intensely segregated ethnic neighbourhoods that breed suspicion and isolation, although concern is mounting over some 250 neighbourhoods in Canada with relatively high concentrations (30 percent of the neighbourhood populations) of a single ethnicity—an increase from six in 1981.

How do we account for differences (also Hiebert et al. 2003)? Why is Canada seemingly immune to calls for retrenchment of multiculturalism or immigration, whereas European jurisdictions are circling the proverbial wagons against what is perceived as excessive (read, Muslim) immigration and politically correct multiculturalism? Should we see this anti-immigration/multiculturalism backlash for what it really is? Should we look at it as a code for anti-Muslim hate, which is prompted by a combination of fear of Muslim terrorism, concerns over core Muslim values pertaining to gender and gay rights at odds with dominant ideology, and worries that the EU will be "swamped" by Muslims should Turkey enter it? How reasonable are these reactions in Europe? Should Canada be worried as well, and begin to reassess its much-ballyhooed commitment to multiculturalism and immigration? Is there something about the Canadian Way and Canada's Diversity Model that transforms immigration and multiculturalism into low-risk options for living together with our differences? Or is Canada just plain lucky because of geography and distances?

A bit of context might help: Multiculturalism in European societies tended to disengage immigrants from full and equal citizenship rights. On one side is the French model that extols the virtues of a single national culture and citizenship regardless of differences. Yet, the torching of 7000 cars in late 2005 in the outer suburbs of Paris by disaffected European-born youth with dark skin and non-European-sounding names suggests that principle is one thing, practice quite another (Ghitis 2005). On the other side is the German model. Immigrants were rarely seen as potential permanent residents, but rather as guest workers who would eventually return upon completion of their work. Europe's embrace of multiculturalism was predicated on a separatist logic: that guest workers and their families required retention of their cultural and language skills for readjustment upon return to their home countries. For example, children in Dutch schools learned Turkish or Berber in primary schools, while many lived in ethnic enclaves that encouraged an inward-looking isolation rather than creative encounters. Furthermore, the benign neglect of immigrant communities was justified on the grounds that European countries did not see themselves as immigrant societies; therefore, they had minimal responsibility to actively integrate immigrants (guest workers) into the social fabric.

The end result? The segregation of differences culminated in a visionless coexistence of separate groups with little or no inter-ethnic interaction (much less creative encounters) among them. Without an overarching vision for living together with differences, the social and economic integration of migrants and minorities stalled. Worse still, far too many immigrants found themselves marginalized with an underclass status

because of this segregationist approach. For instance, Muslims in Britain have three times the unemployment rates of the population as a whole, including 16 percent who have never worked or are among the long-term unemployed. Rootless and restive, alienated from their communities and shunned by society, young Muslims (whom *Time* magazine in its 3 October 2005 issue refers to as Generation Jihad) have increasingly embraced religious extremism—further reinforcing public fears that multiculturalism has been co-opted by radical politics for the dismantling of liberal–democratic values (Hurst 2006).

The situation in Canada differs. Canada defines itself as an immigrant society. As an immigrant society, immigrants are seen as assets rather than burdens, crucial to Canada-building rather than a national liability, and as potential citizens rather than a permanent underclass. Multiculturalism, in turn, is defined as a tool to facilitate the integration of new Canadians by improving their chances of settling down, fitting in, and moving up. Ontario Premier Dalton McGuinty capitalized on the province's rich multicultural heritage in his 12 October 2005 Throne Speech to attract highly skilled immigrants—the first time a government has linked the province's cultural diversity with its economic prosperity. Not unexpectedly, as Will Kymlicka, the noted Queen's University political philosopher points out, both immigration and multiculturalism are more likely to enjoy public support when immigrants are seen as bona fide permanent residents with access to full and equal citizenship rights. Support is also more likely when there are principled rules regarding the acceptability of immigrant cultural practices. To the extent that cultural diversity is encouraged under Canada's integration multiculturalism—the 1988 *Multiculturalism Act* sought to integrate new Canadians into the mainstream through their ethnic identity rather than offer unqualified preservation of their differences—this commitment is conditional: Cultural differences cannot break the law, violate individual rights, or contravene core constitutional values.

In short, immigration and multiculturalism are seen by many Canadians as a low-risk option (Kymlicka 2005). The Canadian state has multicultural protocols in place to manage the risk by ensuring immigration that is legal, skilled, and unthreatening. Compare this situation with European countries, many of which are in close proximity to poor, unstable countries from North Africa or the Middle East whose young inhabitants are anxious for opportunities, whether as legal migrants, illegal workers, guest workers, or asylum seekers. Predictably, then, a disconnect emerges in public support of multiculturalism when immigrants are associated with illiberal practices at odds with mainstream norms and values, when immigrants are viewed as illegal by entry or unwelcome for the long haul, and when they are perceived as ill-equipped for coping with the demands of contemporary society. Under these circumstances, it is doubtful that even the most robust multiculturalism could have staved off the sense of alienatior and despair. Finally, Canada's advantage may lie in its geography. By making it difficult for the poor from Africa or the Middle East to migrate, the luxury of distance allows Canada to select who it wants and how to integrate them, in effect reinforcing public perception of immigration and multiculturalism as relatively safe options for engaging with differences as different yet equal.

MULTICULTURALISM: DOING IT THE CANADIAN WAY

Societies have different options in responding to the growing presence of immigrant minorities (Rex 1998). Options include (1) exclusion and expulsion, (2) tolerant indifference toward the culturally distinct, (3) non-recognition of guest workers as persona non grata, and (4) the inclusion of minorities in the institutional fabric of society under the banner of multiculturalism. A commitment to multiculturalism has contributed to Canada's image as a progressive society. Some measure of proof is gleaned from accolades by high-flying personalities, including Bono of U2, who claims the world "needs more Canadas," and the Aga Khan, who extols Canada as the most "successful pluralist society" in the world (see Biles et al. 2005:25). Canada's lofty status as an enlightened multicultural society with an enviable standard of living is further confirmed by several UN panels. Finally, when compared with others Canadians themselves seem to express markedly more positive attitudes toward immigration, multiculturalism, and diversity, while taking pride in Canada's reputation as an open and inclusive society (Jedwab 2005b).

Canada's worldwide reputation as a beacon of tolerance in an intolerant world is largely deserved. The fact that Canada has escaped much of the ethnic strife that currently convulses many countries speaks well of its stature in proactively working through differences. The majority of Canadians, especially the younger and the well-educated, are relatively open to diversity and proud of Canada's multicultural heritage, despite undercurrents of fear and resentment and a general reluctance to transform good intentions into transformative change (Anderssen and Valpy 2003). But even whole-hearted support is no excuse for glossing over its imperfections. Compared to a utopia of perfect harmony, Canada's multiculturalism falls short of the mark; in contrast with the grisliness of reality elsewhere, it stands as a paragon of virtue. But compared to the ideals enshrined in multiculturalism, we could be doing better in the art of living together with differences. Furthermore, everyone agrees that there are enough loopholes in federal multiculturalism to dishearten even the most optimistic. Few would deny its vulnerability to manipulation by politicians and minority leaders. And when carelessly bandied about, fewer still would dismiss its potential to deter, divide, diminish, or digress.

But in any evaluation carping criticism is no more helpful than unstinting praise. For in the final analysis, evaluating multiculturalism is not simply a case of either/or, but both/and. Moreover, criticism is one thing; proposals for alternatives to multiculturalism are quite another. Critics may be relentless in their attacks on multiculturalism as regressive or irrelevant. But most critiques rarely offer constructive criticism in proposing positive alternatives that are workable and fair. If a commitment to multiculturalism is dead or in retreat because of the incompatibilities of living together with differences, what other options are there? Our stand is unequivocable: Multiculturalism is hardly an option in a modern Canada because of its defiant diversities, robust immigration programs, and competing citizenships. Neither assimilation nor isolation stands much chance of survival in our politicized era. A much-touted return to traditional values for cementing Canadians into a unified and coherent whole sounds good in theory (Bibby 1990; Bissoondath 1993, 1994). In reality, such wishful thinking may camouflage a wistfulness for a golden age that never existed.

Thirty-five years ago Canada blazed a trail in the art of living together with differences. Has it been worth it? On balance, yes. Multiculturalism has resulted in the establishment of a national agenda for engaging diversity that strikes many as consistent with Canada's liberal–democratic framework. A social framework has evolved that to date has managed to balance diversity with unity—even if that balancing act is a bit wobbly at times. Such an endorsement may not sound like a lot to those with unrealistically high expectations; nevertheless, the contributions of multiculturalism should not be diminished by unfair comparison with utopian standards. A sense of proportion is required. Just as multiculturalism cannot be blamed for everything that is wrong in Canada, so too excessive praise should be avoided. The nature of its impact and implications falls somewhere between the poles of unblemished good and absolute evil. Multiculturalism is neither the root of all Canada's problems nor the all-encompassing solution to problems that rightfully belong elsewhere. It is but one component—however imperfect—for improving the integration of migrants and minorities by balancing the competing demands of diversity with unity.

Multiculturalism, in short, remains the governance of necessity for a changing and diverse Canada (Ley 2005). As a skilful blend of compromises in a country built around compromises, multiculturalism symbolizes an innovative if imperfect social experiment for living together with differences. Multiculturalism has excelled in extricating Canada from its colonialist past to its much-ballyhooed status as a trailblazer for engaging with diversity. Under the circumstances, it is not a question of whether Canada can afford multiculturalism. More to the point, Canada *cannot* afford to *not* embrace multiculturalism in advancing political unity, social coherence, economic prosperity, and cultural enrichment. That is not to say that the coast is clear or that we can rest on our laurels. Still, the entrenchment of multiculturalism has elevated Canada to the front ranks of society—not a perfect society by any stretch of the imagination, but possibly one of the least imperfect societies in the world.

DEBATE REVISITED	**Cultural Defence or Multiculturally Offensive?**

Traditions deserve respect only insofar as they are respectable—that is, exactly insofar as they themselves respect the fundamental rights of women and men. (Amin Maalouf, French-Arab novelist, cited in Manji 2005)

Does the logic of multiculturalism compel us to tolerate those cultural practices that themselves are intolerant of others? Or does a commitment to official Multiculturalism include the option of banning practices that offend, violate, or interfere? Where does Multiculturalism draw the line over so-called offensive cultural practices? Is there a principled method for dividing the acceptable from the non-acceptable? Does a cultural defence strategy provide an excuse to condone behaviour at odds with Canada's normative frameworks? Answers to these questions will become increasingly more important as Canada diversifies, while diversity, in turn, becomes increasingly politicized in the competition for recognition and rewards.

Canada is not alone in confronting these conundra. A Communitarian Network (2002) has emerged in the United States whose stated goals are to create a workable society by addressing the challenge of balancing diversity within unity. According to the Communitarians, the politics of diversity require a principled response that explores the middle ground between unity (assimilation) and diversity (anything goes multiculturalism). For Communitarians, individuals are free to maintain their distinct cultures as long as (1) cultural values do not clash with the shared cultural core (e.g., gender equality), laws of the land and democratic institutions,

or UN-defined human rights, (2) loyalty to society supersedes loyalty to the homeland should these loyalties come into global conflict, (3) all minorities (including Aboriginal peoples) are equal before the law and cannot expect special treatment (e.g., territorial autonomy), rights, or exemption, and (4) people are free to challenge conventional ways of balancing unity with diversity, but must do so through conventional channels. Clearly, then, the Communitarian Network espoused a liberal universalism position, one in which denying differences may violate a person's equality rights; conversely, however, singling out people's differences for special treatment is equally wrong because of our commonalities as individuals.

Similarly, Canada's official Multiculturalism provides a principled response for engaging diversity. According to an official Multiculturalism, a person's cultural differences cannot be allowed to stand in the way of equality before law, full institutional participation, and equal democratic citizenship rights. Under Multiculturalism, each individual has the right to abide by the cultural tradition of his/her choice as long as the corresponding practices do not contravene the laws of the land, interfere with individual rights, or reject core constitutional values. If the behaviour in question falls within the parameters of these limits, it is acceptable; if not, then not, although there are democratic channels in place to contest the line by challenging the Eurocentric convention of acceptance. Canada is not alone in setting limits: Australia's Multicultural policy also requires all Australians to accept the basic structures and principles of Australian society (from parliamentary democracy to

English as the national language), to acknowledge obligations as well as rights, including the right of others to express their views and values, and to ensure all Australians have an overriding commitment to Australia, its interests, and its future (McGauran 2005; Jakubowicz 2005). And more recently, in response to the 7/7 bombings in London, England, Prime Minister Tony Blair confirmed how acceptance into British society is conditional on becoming British:

> That duty is to share and support the values that sustain a British way of life. Those who break that duty and try to incite hatred or engage in violence against our own country have no place here. (Cited in Manji 2005)

What can we infer from these examples? Put bluntly, reference to culture cannot trump human rights. This logic can be applied to our case study on Haitian-Canadians: Yes, the judge was correct in finding the defendants guilty. Neither Canada's laws nor its official Multiculturalism condone the violation of the woman's rights. But yes, the judge was also multiculturally correct in reducing the punishment to acknowledge the importance of culture as a key variable in influencing people's behaviour, although the severity of the punishment is open to debate. As cultural defence arguments contend, culture is so ingrained within individuals that it predisposes them to act in ways that may bring them into conflict with the law. Furthermore, to withhold recognition of a people's culture is tantamount to robbing them of the symbolic order necessary for survival or to make informed choices (Taylor 1994; Kymlicka 1995). Not surprisingly, judges in Canada are under strict instructions to take cultural differences into account when sentencing, in part to acknowledge Canada's multicultural commitments, in part to trim the skyrocketing costs of incarceration.

To be sure, the cultural defence argument can be taken too far. Critics argue that a cultural defence position may condone the oppression of vulnerable groups, put tradition on trial, reinforce stereotypes, constitute a form of cultural racism in the guise of cultural sensitivity, and ignore the dynamic nature of culture by reifying particular customs (Okin 1999). In other words, there is a regrettable tendency to essentialize (treat something as a singular, fixed, and homogeneous entity by freezing it in time and space) what increasingly is fluid and flexible, dynamic and variable, and situationally relevant (Kurien 2004). Culture may provide a blueprint for behaviour, but this conceptual map is provisional, contextual, socially constructed, and, more often than not, consulted after the fact to justify or excuse actions. With cultural defence, moreover, there may be a tendency to promote the rhetoric of grievance and victimhood, in which every minority is oppressed, every white is a racist (consciously or unconsciously), every institution is discriminatory, and no government program is to be trusted (Wente 2002). Despite these caveats and concerns, if official Multiculturalism is about constructing a Canada of many cultures, Canadians will have to become a lot more attentive to taking culture seriously as a basis for living together with differences in our increasingly testy times.

CHAPTER HIGHLIGHTS

• This chapter emphasizes the politics of official Multiculturalism as a politically moti-vated framework for living together with differences within the context of Canada-building.

• Is Canada a multicultural society? Responses to this question vary with different lev-els of meaning implicit within multiculturalism, that is, as a sociological fact, an ideo-logical system of beliefs and values, a set of policies involving government–minority relations, a renewable resource in serving political and minority interests, and a crit-ical discourse that challenges as it resists.

• Canada's integrative Multiculturalism is based on the principle of mutual adjustment: i.e., you adapt, we adjust. According to this integrative model of multiculturalism, a society of many cultures can exist as long as people's cultural differences do not get in the way of equality, participation, and citizenship. To the extent that cultural dif-ferences are tolerated, individuals are permitted to identify with the cultural tradition of their choice, provided this affiliation does not violate human rights, laws of the land, or core constitutional values.

• Canadian Multiculturalism has historically been concerned with improving minority equality and participation in society, initially through elimination of ethnocentric biases (ethnicity), then through removal of discriminatory barriers and institutional accommodation (equity), and currently through enhancing a sense of belonging and cit-izenship (civic).

• At once an asset as well as a hindrance, multiculturalism has been regarded as a source of social tension in addition to an innovative means for minority conflict manage-ment. Neither a problem nor a solution, its influence exists somewhere in between—but is one component for engaging diversity in a complex yet unequal context.

• Multiculturalism is usually criticized as being divisive, regressive, or incompetent. Multiculturalism can also be shown to be unifying, progressive, and effective. The degree of criticism or praise may vary with diverse visions of Canadian society and the role of multiculturalism in fostering this vision.

• The multicultural paradox is self-evident: Too many differences can create anarchic conditions that inhibit the effective functioning of a social system, while too many restrictions make a mockery of multicultural principles. Nevertheless, the question arises: Where do we draw the line? Who says so, and why?

KEY TERMS

civic multiculturalism	ideology
consensus multiculturalism	mosaic
critical multiculturalism	multiculturalism
cultural defence	*Multiculturalism Act,* 1988
cultural relativism	official Multiculturalism

REVIEW QUESTIONS

1. Indicate how multiculturalism differs from other blueprints for managing race and ethnic relations (consult Chapter 1).

2. Compare and contrast the different phases in the development of Canada's multiculturalism policy in terms of objectives, assumptions, means, and outcomes.

3. Is Canada a multicultural society? "Yes," "no," "maybe," "it depends"? Be sure to focus on the different levels of meaning associated with multiculturalism.

4. Demonstrate some of the benefits and costs associated with multiculturalism. Defend whether or not you believe multiculturalism is a solution to the problem of unequal relations or more of a problem rather than a solution.

5. Multiculturalism is about knowing limits and drawing lines as a basis for living together with our differences. Explain, and provide an example to illustrate how much diversity a multicultural society can tolerate before self-destructing.

6. On the basis of the text of the chapter, discuss each of the following commonly voiced assertions over Canada's official Multiculturalism:

   multiculturalism is not working?

   multiculturalism is experiencing a backlash?

   multiculturalism ghettoizes minorities?

   multiculturalism is about celebrating diversity?

   multiculturalism is only for ethnic minorities?

   multiculturalism tolerates an anything-goes mentality?

   multiculturalism promotes group rights?

   multiculturalism is eroding Canadian society?

   multiculturalism forces people to choose between Canada and ethnicity?

   multiculturalism is irrelevant?

LINKS AND RECOMMENDATIONS

Books

The most insightful of all academics on issues of multiculturalism is Will Kymlicka of Queen's University. His 2001 book, *Politics in the Vernacular* (Oxford), is a must read.

Also recommended is Richard Day's *Multiculturalism and the History of Canadian Diversity* (2000, University of Toronto Press).

For more about the multicultural backlash in Europe, check out the *Journal of International Migration and Integration*, vol. 3, no. 3/4,. 2002.

Another interesting take on multiculturalism is Cecil Foster's *Where Race Does Not Matter* (2005, Penguin).

Pardon the bias, but also recommended is Augie Fleras, *Engaging Diversity: Multiculturalism in Canada* (2003, Nelson).

Websites

The official website for Canada's official Multiculturalism provides a lot of information, albeit from a government slant.

www.canadianheritage.gc.ca

A broader website also published by the Department of Canadian Heritage but dealing with the history and current status of multiculturalism in terms of respecting Canada's differences.

www.canadianheritage.gc.ca/progs/multi/respect_e.cfm

Another comprehensive overview of multiculturalism, including the Annual Report on the Operation of the Canadian Multiculturalism Act 2003/2004.

www.pch.gc.ca

Wikipedia provides useful insights into multiculturalism, including comparisons and criticisms of multiculturalism in the United States and Australia.

www.wikipedia.org

Chapter

PUTTING MULTICULTURALISM INTO PRACTICE: POLICING, MEDIA, AND EDUCATION

11

Processing Aboriginality: Criminal Injustice System

What passes for justice in parts of Canada is a travesty (Hylton 2002). A white judge sits at the front of a nondescript community centre room, surrounded by several white lawyers, a Crown prosecutor, some legal aid workers, and several burly white RCMP officers. In the back of the room sits a row of grim-faced Aboriginal youth in ski jackets and track shoes. Over the next three days, up to 150 accused will be processed and sentenced, with most being charged with alcohol- and solvent-related assaults, break and enter, domestic abuse, and public disorder. Many of those charged with property crimes rarely do much damage. They are just as likely to break into stores for snacks or pop—just for something to do or perhaps to get caught for a ticket out. The goal is imprisonment in a comfy "southern" jail, which provides at least temporary respite from the bleak combination of boredom, despair, and cold.

Court workers fly in from Yellowknife every other month. After several days of proceedings, they shift to other outposts in Northern Canada. Sessions are assembled in a gym or community centre, on plain folding tables, with most of the town turning up to watch. In contrast to the measured pace of southern courts, court proceedings move rapidly to accommodate a packed docket of backlogged cases. Legal aid workers spend only a few minutes with the accused before cases are called. Stock arguments are routinely circulated about the defendant seeking counselling or conflict management therapy. Community reaction to the court proceedings is muted regardless of the severity of the crime or sentence. Most youth appear only vaguely aware of their legal rights, nor do they show much interest in the court processes. Many plead guilty because they do not understand the issues at hand or prefer taking the path of least resistance (CCJA 2000). Emotions are rarely expressed, with most youth speaking in a flat emotionless style to describe even traumatic events, which the court then interprets as indifference or guilt. Those who are sentenced fly out with the judge to a Yellowknife jail or a detention centre in Hay River (adapted from Nolen 2000).

Aboriginal peoples may have high expectations of the criminal justice system (La Prairie 1999). But the criminal justice system continues to miscalculate Aboriginal realities and cultural needs by squeezing them into a Eurocentric box (CCJA 2000). The statistics speak disapprovingly. Compared to the general population, Aboriginal accused are more likely to be denied bail and to spend more time in pre-trial detention, less likely to have adequate legal representation, and more likely to be incarcerated for even minor offences. Not surprisingly, while Aboriginal people represent only 3–4 percent of Canada's population, they comprise around 18 percent of the inmates at federal prisons. No less disturbing are regional differences: Aboriginal inmates constitute 64 percent of the federal penitentiary population in western Canada, according to Statistics Canada, but only 12 percent of the Prairie population. Who can be surprised to find that most Aboriginal males will have been incarcerated in a correctional centre at some point in their lives by the age of 25? Admittedly, some degree of cautiousness must be exercised. Statistics may be misleading as offenders may be convicted for petty offences and serve time for offences that require only a fine, or the numbers may be inflated by a small number of individuals who repeatedly get into trouble with the law (Buckley 1992). Nevertheless, the revolving door of incarceration and recidivism has stripped many Aboriginal peoples of their self-esteem, in effect leading to self-spiralling cycles of despair and destructiveness.

Efforts to improve the relationship of the criminal injustice system to Aboriginal peoples have taken several routes. Proposed changes for improving effectiveness range from reform of existing arrangements to those radical alternatives that challenge foundational principles. Questions about the relationship of Aboriginal peoples to Canada's criminal justice system remain sharply contested: Should there be one set of rules for all Canadians, or should justice be customized to reflect diverse Aboriginal realities? Should attention focus on reforming the existing criminal justice system or overhauling it by establishing parallel or even separate structures that take Aboriginal differences seriously? Should all crime be punished equally, or must Aboriginal social and cultural differences be taken into account when processing Aboriginal offenders? Is it racist and paternalistic to imply that a racial or ethnic background merits special consideration in sentencing? Is it just as racist not to do so? The Debate Revisited box, "Restoring Justice," will comment.

INTRODUCTION: PUTTING MULTICULTURALISM TO WORK

As noted in previous chapters, Canada's historical track record on race relations has left much to be desired. Prejudice and discrimination reinforced a dismissive belief in diversity as inimical to society-building. Ethnic minorities were expected to blend into the existing institutional framework as the price of admission into Canada. With the inception of multiculturalism, however, institutional response to diversity has improved. Diversity is currently promoted as an integral and legitimate component of Canada's social fabric, with untapped potential for improving national wealth and international standing. Multicultural differences are no longer dismissed as a bothersome anomaly, of no redeeming value outside a personal or private context. To the contrary, the ongoing reconstruction of Canadian society is now primed for putting multiculturalism to work at institutional levels (Zachariah et al. 2004).

There is much to commend in institutions' becoming more multiculturally responsive. At a time when both the workforce and the community at large are increasingly diverse and demanding, only the pace or scope of adjustments remains open to debate (Diller 2004). Public and private institutions are increasingly anxious to enhance overall effectiveness by including all Canadians who have something to contribute. For service organizations, a commitment to multiculturalism can reap institutional dividends by easing workplace tensions, generating creative synergies, and facilitating community access by improving the quality of service delivery. For private companies, the inclusion of diversity is tantamount to money in the bank. Corporations increasingly rely on the language skills, cultural knowledge, life experience, and international connections that people of diversity bring to the workplace. Diversity connections can also provide the catalyst for internationalizing domestic businesses, thus improving competitive advantage in global markets.

However valued and overdue, preliminary efforts at putting multiculturalism to work at institutional levels have proven uneven. The commitment may be there, but not necessarily the political will or the resources for implementation, in effect leaving a slippage between rhetoric and reality. Of particular note are service-oriented institutions such as media, education, and policing, each of which is under pressure to move over and make institutional space. This is not surprising: Their mandate as agencies of socialization and social control not only strikes at the hub of social existence, but also influences the degree to which we are in harmony with our communities or alienated from them. Media and education furnish the "blueprint" for acceptable behaviour; the police, in turn, control the limits of unacceptable behaviour by enforcing the rules. Failure of each of these institutions to bridge the gap runs the risk of marginalizing untapped talent, shortchanging the delivery of services, and compromising both institutional effectiveness and efficiency.

The theme of putting multiculturalism to work at institutional levels is analyzed in this chapter. The chapter examines how major institutions are responding to the challenges of engaging diversity in ways that balance multicultural responsiveness with organizational realities. It explores those programs and policies for fostering **institutional inclusiveness** both internally (in terms of organizational procedures and workforce) and externally (with respect to service delivery and community relations). Emphasis is on how the institutions of policing, media, and education have addressed the challenges and paradoxes of implementing multiculturalism, in the process revealing both the pitfalls and promises of institutional inclusiveness as well as the complexities and contradictions. Each institution is analyzed on the basis of those barriers that complicate the attainment of inclusiveness, what has been accomplished to date in accommodating diversity, and what still needs to be done for improving patterns of inclusiveness. The conclusions should come as no surprise. Institutions have responded differently to the demands of diversity. Progress intermingles with stagnation to create a confusing picture that speaks volumes about the challenges of putting principles into practice at institutional levels. Institutions may have come a long way from the indifference of the past; nevertheless, they still have a long way to go before inclusiveness becomes a reality.

INSTITUTIONAL INCLUSIVENESS: PRINCIPLES AND PRACTICE

The emergence of inclusiveness as a popular buzzword poses a key question: What do we mean by the term "inclusiveness"? Is it about diversity or disadvantage; about culture-blind or culture-conscious initiatives; about reform or radical change (Mittler 2000; Winter 2001; Ratcliffe 2004)? Inclusiveness is not about being nice to minorities. It goes beyond switching white personnel with minority hires and promotions along the corporate ladder. And it most certainly is more than simply celebrating differences to enliven a dull corporate culture. Instead, as a form of institutional accommodation, inclusiveness involves a process by which institutions adjust institutional design, operation, and outcomes to make them more multiculturally responsive to, and reflective of, diversity (Keung 2004). Inclusiveness is about establishing a new relationship with minority women and men that improves access, representation, and equity—both within the workplace and outside in terms of service delivery. With inclusiveness, an embracive institutional environment is proposed in which both workers and clients feel recognized and respected (culturally safe) rather than excluded or at risk (Fleras and Spoonley 1999). Finally, inclusiveness is about rethinking the value of diversity—not as a problem to solve or surmount but as an asset to nurture for improving the bottom line and enhancing the workplace climate and the delivery of social services.

The politics of inclusiveness can be tricky. Consider the conundrums: Underemphasizing the relevance of differences when required may be as discriminatory as overemphasizing diversity when uncalled for. Excluding minorities from full and equal involvement can generate conflict, yet including diversity can be equally disruptive to those who prefer the status quo. Fostering an inclusive workplace climate requires a careful reassessment of rules, procedures, and outlooks; nevertheless, changes of this magnitude may imperil the bottom line. The adjustment process must occur not only at the level of institutional structure and individual mindsets but also concentrate on the relationships within (the workplace environment) in addition to relationships without (clients). According to Navdeep Singh Bains, MP (2005), institutions must balance legitimate employment and equity concerns with an equally legitimate Charter-right requirement that institutions make reasonable accommodation to meet employer and worker needs. Such varied demands confirm the complexities of working together with differences, especially when sharply different cultures are involved.

Having good intentions is one thing, putting them into practice another. Institutions are complex, often baffling landscapes of domination, power, and control, often pervaded by prejudice, nepotism, patronage, and the "old boys" network. Moves to inclusivize are rarely simple or straightforward but fraught with ambiguity and tension because of individual resistance, structural barriers, and institutional inertia. Conservatives confront progressives in a struggle for control of the agenda. Conventional views remain firmly entrenched as vested interests balk at discarding the tried and true. Newer visions are compelling but lack the critical mass to scuttle traditional ways of "doing business." The interplay of these juxtapositions can be disruptive as institutions evolve into a "contested site" involving competing world views and opposing agendas.

What defines an inclusive institution? Five dimensions prevail: *workforce representation, organizational rules and operations, workplace climate, service delivery, and community relations*. First, an institution's workforce should be representative, that is, relatively proportional to the composition of the regional labour force, acknowledging, of course, both extenuating social and cultural factors to account for discrepancies. Such a numerical accommodation applies not only to entry-level jobs but also across the board to include all managerial levels. Second, institutional rules and operations cannot hinder the recruitment, selection, training, promotion, and retention of minority personnel. This commitment to rooting out both open and systemic discrimination demands a careful scrutiny of company policy and procedures. Third, the institution must foster a working climate conducive to minority well-being and success. At minimum, such a climate cannot tolerate harassment of any form; at best, diversity is actively promoted as normal, necessary, and beneficial to effective functioning. Fourth, an inclusive institution ensures a delivery of its services that is community-based, culturally sensitive, and multiculturally responsive. This multicultural commitment to culturally sensitive services entails an institutional willingness to engage as partners in genuine dialogue with the community at large. Outcomes must be based on bilateral decision-making rather than being unilaterally imposed to secure a culturally safe service (Fleras and Spoonley 1999). Fifth and finally, institutions do not operate in a social or political vacuum. Some degree of community input, power-sharing, and public account-ability is critical if open and productive lines of communication are to be secured.

Numerous barriers intrude on the inclusion process (Conference Board of Canada 2004). To some extent, these barriers coincide with those dimensions that constitute an inclusive institu-tion, and include *people, hierarchy, bureaucracy, corporate culture,* and *occupational subcul-tures.* People as institutional actors are a prime obstruction especially when their self-interest is threatened because of preferential treatment to others (Thomas et al. 2004). That revelation should come as no surprise. Unless convinced or compelled, few individuals are inclined to relinquish power or share privilege, especially with those once perceived as inferior or irrelevant. Inclusiveness may be derailed by institutional structures such as hierarchy. Those in higher echelons may "talk the walk" of inclusiveness, but fail to "walk the talk" when it comes to practice or implementation. Middle and lower management may be less enthusiastic about changes, preferring instead to cling to traditional authority patterns. Those at the bottom of the corporate pecking order may be least receptive to institutional change, and act accordingly to sub-vert or ignore (see Kanter 1977). Bureaucracy can also inhibit institutional inclusion. Larger sys-tems operate on bureaucratic principles of rational control to ensure standardization and regulation. Such a controlling imperative is not conducive to inclusiveness, especially if diver-sity is perceived as disruptive, imposed, and irrelevant. Barriers are implicit within corporate cul-tures as well. Corporate cultures may recoil from adjustment when posing a threat to the bottom line or the "way we do things around here." Institutions instead reveal an all too common ten-dency to become ends in themselves over time by satisfying only their own criteria for excel-lence at the expense of consumer interests and concerns. Finally, occupational subcultures may derail the best of intentions. Those informal groupings that characterize all organizations not only exercise control over members' behaviour because of common values and shared experiences, but also resist the implementation of inclusiveness initiatives.

Several models of inclusiveness can be discerned (Humpage and Fleras 2001). Each is based on the assumption that mainstream institutions are not neutral in terms of design, process, or rewards, but constructed by the dominant group to advance majority interests, either deliberately or systemically (Harris 1995). The *reform* model attempts to ensure equal treatment for all by modifying existing arrangements through removal of discriminatory bar-riers. The goal is a level playing field where all can participate equally regardless of race or ethnicity. A *minority-ization* model involves the incorporation of diversity into institutional rules, agendas, and priorities. Initiatives range from including more minorities at all levels of the institutional ladder to the incorporation of minority symbols and concerns in redefining "how we do things around here." The creation of *parallel institutions* reflects a need for minorities to work apart by constructing structures modelled after mainstream institutions, but operated entirely by minority women and men. Examples include the establishment of native policing, black-focus schooling, or ethnic presses. Proposals for *separate systems* entail the creation of a separate institution or systems of institutions, based on the principle that certain minorities have the right to construct self-determining structures that reflect their realities, reinforce their priorities, and advance their interests (Chung 2005). The "Schooling with a Difference" case study on Islamic schools in Toronto provides an example, as does the Debate Revisited box on restoring Aboriginal justice.

POLICING IN A MULTICULTURAL MILIEU

The criminal justice system should be at the forefront of moves toward institutional inclusiveness. People's lives depend on it, and mistakes because of miscalculations are not always measured by inconvenience but in deadly consequences. For this reason, the slow and erratic nature of its response has proven cause for concern. Such an indictment is especially evident at the level of policing minority communities. The police have been accused of underpolicing (i.e., slow response rates), of overpolicing (i.e., excessive and unnecessary coverage), and of mispolicing (i.e., prejudicial and discriminatory enforcement) (Holdaway 1996; Fridell et al. 2001; CRRF 2003; MacDonald 2003). The consequences of this interactional breakdown have had the unintended but real effect of racializing crime while criminalizing minorities (Henry and Tator 2006). The breakdown also raises the question of whether policing in a multicultural society should treat everyone in exactly the same way regardless of differences, or whether differences should be taken into account when appropriate.

Reaction to the criminal justice system exposes a profound perceptual rift between minorities and the mainstream. White people tend to accept the criminal justice system as a pillar of civilized society. Children are taught that the police are their friends and protectors, with the result that white experiences with the law have proven generally satisfactory, even if occasional miscarriages of the law have tarnished the "badge." By contrast, minority experiences along all dimensions of the criminal justice system have proven distressful. The criminal justice system is particularly harsh on young black males who, compared with others, are disproportionately stopped, charged, and arrested (Neugebauer 2000; Wortley 2005) (see also case study on Racial Profiling). They are also more likely to be locked up, to be denied bail, and to receive unfavourable treatment in detention (*Report of the Commission on Systemic Racism* 1995; see also Carey 2000). Rather than a friend to be trusted, the police are more apt to be vilified as a menacing symbol of white power establishment over communities of colour. Not surprisingly, black parents are in the habit of teaching their children how to survive interactions with police, especially as even inappropriate body language may prove deadly. As one black youth phrased this dilemma:

> Any normal reaction is taken as an over-reaction, any quietness of temperament is taken to be arrogance. You see a black person as being, for lack of a better term, "cool," under the circumstances, it's taken to be arrogance. So you can't win. You either say something and be termed violent or you say nothing and be termed arrogant. (cited in Britton 2000:704)

Both internal and external pressures have exposed anomalies in police–minority relations. An increasingly fractious policing environment is evolving because of changing demographics, new legislation, racialized communities, minority activism, and public demands for account-ability. A looming crisis in police–minority relations appears to be eroding minority confi-dence in aspects of Canadian policing. Police have responded to this crisis in credibility by redefining patterns of interaction (Cryderman et al. 1998). Police authorities have cast about for ways to ease the tension, calm troublesome constituents, patch up the trouble spots, and improve community dialogue without impairing police effectiveness in the process. In that police–minority relations leave a lot to be desired, can a style of policing be established that addresses the needs and wants of minority communities in a multicultural Canada (see also Fitzgerald and Hough 2002)?

On the surface the assessment looks bleak. Police–minority relations continue to reflect an awkwardness that leads to miscommunication at best, but crisis and chaos at worst. Police in the Greater Toronto Census Metropolitan Area have been accused of being trigger-happy in preferring to shoot first, talk later. During the 1990s, young black males were shot at and killed by police at rates disproportional to their numbers in the total population (see Neugebauer 2000). The cumulative effect of this mispolicing is predictable. The legitimacy of the police in certain multicultural communities is withdrawn, the community closes ranks, lawlessness flourishes, constables in cruisers reflect a reluctance to police minority com-munities, and the estrangement spirals out of control. That this scenario is repeated else-where, including the United States (Koring 1999), Britain (Modood and Berthoud 1997; Fitzgerald and Hough 2002), Australia (Chan 1996), and New Zealand (Fleras and Spoonley 1999), suggests the primacy of structural over attitudinal roots to the problem.

Accusations fly in both directions because of this interactional gridlock. Minority par-ents and community leaders contend that mispolicing is not an isolated case, but reflects an institutional pattern of police harassment, brutality, or indifference. Police are accused of being preoccupied with the belief that minorities are predisposed to crime, yet underoccu-pied in their attention to ethnic communities when their services are needed (Kivel 1996; Neugebauer 2000; Di Matteo 2001). The police would dispute this assessment of their rela-tionship with targeted minority communities. To the extent that police harass youth, such pro-filing is dismissed as isolated and coincidental, reflecting the growing menace of guns, gangs, and drugs. Racially motivated profiling may exist, they concede, but excesses reflect a small number of "rogue" officers rather than any institutionalized pattern. Besides, the police argue, the apprehension of minority youths is not a case of discriminatory policing, but a response to those burgeoning street crimes that necessitate police attention. Moreover, as far as police are concerned, minority communities have only themselves to blame if they refuse to co-operate with the police in solving crimes.

Who is right? Or wrong? Are some minorities stopped more often because they commit more crime or because police *think* they do, and act accordingly? Are the police just doing their job in apprehending disaffected youths behaving irresponsibly? Or are police just a bunch of racist and trigger-happy uniforms whose primary objective is protecting their turf against intruders? Is police misconduct an isolated act, or is it pervasive and structurally rooted? Is policing marred by a few "bad apples," or is it institutionalized, that is, rotten to the core? What is it about policing that creates "bad" officers? Does the "badness" reside in (1) the recruitment and selection process, (2) the nature of police work, (3) the organizational frame-work, (4) negative work experiences, or (5) the type of personality supposedly attracted to policing? The fact that the questions are difficult to answer is worrying enough. The fact that neither side can understand the other—much less engage in co-operative actions—only magnifies the potential for crisis and confrontation. The result is a strained mutual avoidance. Minority youth stake out their patch by challenging the legitimacy of the police. The police, in turn, encircle the wagons even more securely against what they perceive as unwarranted attacks by aggressive youths, community activists, an unsympathetic press, opportunistic politicians, a revolving-door court system, and the forces of political correctness.

| INSIGHT | Crisis in Policing Minority Youth |

That urban police and certain sectors of the minority community do not mix well is an established fact (Ungerleider 1993). To some extent, conflict is inevitable; after all, the police are perceived as the most visible embodiment of a white establishment that criminalizes people on the basis of colour, in effect racializing "them" as the undeserving "other" (Ungerleider 1995; Holdaway 1996). As cited in Charles Smith (2003:2):

> The police in all societies are charged with maintaining public order and protecting public safety [and crime fighting], and that generally means conserving the status quo in whatever form it may take. The police are inherently conservative in both their actions and predispositions. They represent the vested economic and political interests and values of the societies in which they perform their policing duties. Where countries are changing and adding cultural and ethnic multiplicity, the police are most likely to be aligned with the old cultural and ethnic guard, or they may be perceived as such by new or newly empowered constituents.

Police attitudes are condemned by the powerless as controlling and obstructing service delivery that minorities would define as "safe" (Ramsden 1995). Crimes by the poor are more likely to attract police attention, in contrast with white-collar crime, which is neither as visible nor as easily detected. Such selective enforcement would suggest that minorities are not more criminal but more likely to be criminalized because of their visibility in the public domain.

Police–minority encounters tend to augment stereotypes and prejudices on both sides of the interactional divide (Henry and Tator 2006). The police employ styles of communication, both verbal and non-verbal, that inadvertently reinforce negative stereotypes about themselves as aggressive defenders of white privilege. Conversely, black interactional styles may confirm police perceptions of male youth as surly, defiant, unco-operative, disrespectful, deceptive, deviant, and deserving of increased surveillance. With such mutually contemptuous views of each other, who can be surprised by the schism in police–minority youth relations?

At the core of this interactional breakdown are stereotypes, none of which flatter the other side (Forcese 2000). Black youth see police as racist for enforcing the law in a discriminatory and insensitive fashion. Police are accused of double standards. Black people believe they are harassed, charged, arrested, and convicted more often than white people; and that a higher number of stops result from police preconceptions and preoccupations with highly visible street activities that inflate charge and arrest rates. The police tend to reject these accusations as unwarranted. As far as they are concerned, their job is to enforce the law evenly and without prejudice. Higher crime rates can only reflect greater criminal activity among black people, in turn justifying special police attention.

Not unexpectedly, the police are seen by some sectors as the "enemy," as a Toronto race relations consultant once reminded us, whose status is that of an "occupying army" and who are not to be trusted (see also Modood and Berthoud 1997). By mandate and by action, police are perceived as agents of coercive control in contexts both unequal and dominating. They are also seen as overzealous in policing black youth because of preconceived notions that make it easier to racialize minority encounters. In other words, the police are likened to just another gang in the city, black youths argue, with uniforms, patches, weapons, and an internal code of ethics. Only the legal right to wield force in staking out their "turf" distinguishes the police from the "hood."

Police stereotypes are equally one-sided. The police tend to see black people as problem people whose frequent brushes with the law must be quashed before chaos appears. Black people are rarely viewed as normal and adjusted, but labelled as criminals, drug pushers, pimps, welfare cheats, or malcontents, even if evidence suggests the actions of a small proportion of youth are blowing things out of proportion, in effect demonizing an entire community for the actions of a few (Henry 1994). Black teens are seen as criminally inclined with a predisposition toward guns, gangs, and drugs, along with a taste for violence imported to some extent from the violent street cultures of the Caribbean. Rarely is much consideration given to perceptions of black youth as alienated and underprivileged, without much stake in a system where few seem to care if they live or die. Black activists are also denounced as self-serving malcontents whose loose rhetoric and grandstanding tends to inflame public resentment toward the police. And ironically,

they argue, while minority communities want the police to fix the guns--drugs–gangs problem, they are just as likely to accuse the police of racial profiling when steps are taken to solve the problem.

Many of the stereotypes on either side of the profiling divide are subculturally driven. By positioning themselves in opposition to a white society and everything that it symbolizes (Henry 1994), animosity toward the police may be part of defining a young male identity (Neugebauer-Visano 1996), what Elijah Anderson (1994) calls an oppositional culture that reflects the code of the street with its craving for respect, power, bravado, and deference. As one 19-year-old male youth acknowledged in his interview with University of Toronto professors Scot Wortley and Julian Tanner (2004):

> I like the respect. I like the power. You walk into a place with your boys, and people notice you, ladies notice you. You got status, you can swagger. People know you aint no punk.

Desmond Ellis, a York University professor, suggests that black youth reject society's standards of success or status, preferring instead to adopt street values where status is based on respect, where disputes are settled directly and violently, and where the mildest "diss" can lead to confrontation (*The Globe and Mail,* 2 November 2002). In the absence of real job prospects (except flipping burgers), with little in the way of education, and where easy access to guns and drugs transforms every indiscretion into a confrontation, status and respect among their peers is all that matters (Slinger 2005). Because making their mark is the only way they know how, few are willing to back down from a challenge for fear of being seen as a "punk" or as "weak," especially when group colours or personal honour are at stake (Wortley and Tanner 2006). This assertiveness is given a menacing edge because of the growing presence of guns and drugs. Complicating the relationship is a fatalistic perception that life is cheap, even disposable—at least judging by the 52 handgun deaths in Toronto in 2005, most of which were gang-related. According to a 24-year-old Toronto male,

> If I thought I could get out and get a real job that pays good, I would. But I'm not some spoiled kid. . . . My mom don't have no money to send me to university. See, I got no chance. So I do what I have to do. At least I have my pride. I can be brave and fight and make some real money . . . but really I've just kind of given up. (Cited in Wortley and Tanner 2006)

In other words, the very masculinities that evoke deference and respect among peers often bring minority youth into conflict with the law (Gillborn 1998).

Police occupational subcultures are also concerned with the virtues of toughness, assertiveness, and control (Desroches 1998; Fitzgerald and Hough 2002). Subcultural values are organized around a perception of police as the "thin blue line" between the civilized "us" and the hordes of "them." Core values within the occupational subculture include the following: deference to police authority and control, respect for the badge, a dislike of uncertainty or disorder, an endorsement of even extreme police tactics, a limited tolerance for deviance, a relatively rigid definition of right versus wrong, and a suspicion of those who criticize police authority (Ungerleider 1995). To be in charge and in control at all times is pivotal for enforcing law and maintaining order (James and Warren 1995). To no one's surprise, the police fiercely resent those segments of the community that defy

police authority or resist arrest for any offence. Police overreaction is likely in those situations that (1) challenge police conception of normalcy and order, (2) invoke disrespect for their status as legitimate authority, or (3) involve those who are perceived as deviant, dangerous, complaining, and discredited (James and Warren 1995). Thus patterns of police abuse are often triggered by interactions that influence the manner in which everybody is policed—black or white.

Put bluntly, both police and minority youths display stereotypical perceptions of each other. However inaccurate and unrealistic, these misconceptions do not make them less real in terms of their consequences. Perception *is* reality where interaction and communication are involved. Failure of police to go beyond stereotypes may take a toll by marginalizing minority youths' lives and life chances. The criminalization of minority street behaviour amplifies the labelling of youth as potential troublemakers, while the racialization of crime has the effect of perpetuating the criminal injustice cycle. Interactional patterns are further hampered by ineffective race-awareness training. Few police services have the resources—or the political will—to conduct anti-racist training for uprooting the racist and discriminatory aspects of police behaviour. What little most officers receive has been conducted by poorly trained, sometimes unmotivated, officials. On some occasions diversity training is perceived as a punishment to discipline unruly officers. Much of the education has been geared toward cultural sensitivity rather than race relations. Rather than improving police–minority relations such a focus may have the effect of reinforcing stereotyping by essentializing differences or rationalizing away deviant behaviour (Kivel 1996). Even in those contexts that foster dialogue and learning, the question remains: How do police transfer this knowledge to the street and apply it to crisis situations (Lopez 2001)?

In short, police in Canada have come under pressure from different quarters. In urban police work under already stressful conditions, split-second decisions have to be made over matters of life and death in environments that rarely appreciate the pressures of contemporary policing. The combination of low police morale, high suicide rates, and increased attrition rates may reflect the costs of incorrectly reading the situation. Police appear to be alienated from both minority youth and minority communities, according to Clayton Ruby (2004), who writes of the problems that confront a predominantly white police service who live far from race-related gang land contexts:

Witnesses in these communities are reluctant to assist the police—because they rarely see the police except when officers drive around in their big cars, and because the communities feel too threatened to help.

Police are accused of losing the fight against crime because of outdated workplace styles. Allegations of harassment, brutality, double standards, intimidation, abuse, corruption, and racism have fuelled the fires of criticism toward the police. Additional questions arise over police effectiveness and efficiency in a diverse and changing society. The concept of community-oriented policing may provide a solution to this legitimacy crisis by restoring public confidence in the thin blue line.

BRIDGING THE GAP: COMMUNITY POLICING

Police throughout Canada have long sought to avert deterioration of their credibility in multicultural communities. Recruitment of minority police officers is widely heralded as a first step in restoring community confidence in law enforcement. Proactive recruitment strategies have been designed and implemented to secure a proportion of visible minority officers commensurate with their numbers in the local population. Of those initiatives at the forefront of multicultural policing, however, few have achieved the profile or the notoriety that community policing has (Fleras 1998). Broadly speaking, community policing represents a reaction to those limitations in conventional policing styles that had distanced the police from community involvement (Bayley 1994). More specifically, community policing is about redefining the nature of police work via a more responsive relationship between police and communities as partners in crime prevention (Jain et al. 2000).

In general, policing can be defined as any activity that is expressly intended to make society safe by establishing and enforcing a normative order for living together (Murphy and Clark 2005; Hermer et al. 2005). A social contract is evident. Individuals surrender certain liberties to the state to promote public order; the state, in turn, promises to ensure these restrictions are exercised in an impartial, equitable, and transparent manner, while safeguarding those remaining liberties that have not been surrendered. But **community-based policing** differs in principle from conventional policing (Cryderman et al. 1998). Professional crime-fighting models promoted a view of police as a highly trained and mechanized force for crime control and law enforcement. Police work could be described as incident driven and complaint-reactive, and its effectiveness was measured by random car patrols, rapid response rates, and high conviction and clearance rates. Structurally, police were organized into a paramilitaristic model of bureaucracy involving a top-down chain of command and control. Rewards and promotions were allocated on the basis of the big catch or unswerving loyalty to the force.

By contrast, community policing is about transforming the police from a "force" to a "service." Community policing is concerned with establishing a more meaningful partnership with the local community as part of a broader collaborative strategy in preventing crime through proactive efforts in problem-solving. The partnership is reciprocal. The community is defined as an active participant in crime prevention rather than a passive bystander. The police, in turn, discard their "crime-buster" image for proactive styles that embody a willingness to communicate and co-operate (see Shusta et al. 1995). To date, virtually all police services in Canada (from the RCMP to provincial and regional) have endorsed the principles of community-based policing. Four principles define the idea of community policing:

1. *Partnership*: A partnership is committed to the ideal of police working with the community to prevent crime. A working partnership rejects the view of the police as experts with exclusive credentials for crime control. In its place is an image of police as "facilitators" and "resource personnel" who co-operate by working alongside citizens.

2. *Problem-solving*: Many have criticized the futility of much police work because of its preoccupation with repeated responses to recurrent incidents in the same area by a small number of repeat offenders. A strategy is proposed that diagnoses the underlying causes rather than just responding to symptoms (Rossmo and Saville 1991). A problem-solving strategy seeks to (1) isolate and identify the underlying causes of recurrent problems, (2) evaluate alternative solutions, (3) respond by applying one or more solutions, (4) monitor the impact, and (5) redesign solutions if feedback is negative.

3. *Prevention/Proactive*: Arguably, all policing is concerned with crime prevention. Whereas conventional policing endorsed law enforcement as the main deterrent to criminal offending, community policing endorses prevention through collaborative problem-solving as the preferred alternative.

4. *Power-sharing*: A commitment to power-sharing with the community is essential to community policing. Without a sharing of power, community policing is simply tokenism or calculated expediency to offload responsibilities for burdensome tasks.

BARRIERS TO COMMUNITY POLICING

Interest in community policing has expanded to the point where it adorns the mission statement in each of Canada's policing jurisdictions. This commitment to community policing has focused on transforming the police from a professional crime-fighting force to a customer-inspired and customized service that is community responsive, culturally sensitive, problem oriented, and "user-friendly." But good intentions notwithstanding, initiatives in community policing are fraught with perils and pitfalls. Not everyone is supportive of this shift in priorities from crime fighting and law enforcement to public service, collaboration, and peace-keeping. Principles clash with personal self-interest, structural barriers, entrenched interests, established values, and organizational inertia (Fleras 1998). Expediency prevails: More police are being put back into cruisers as resources dwindle, demands increase, and priorities shift (Di Matteo 2001).

Resistance is to be expected: Community policing principles appear to be at logger-heads with conventional police work. Many perceive community policing as inconsistent with long-standing police practices, contrary to "real" police work, a threat to cherished values and images, an impediment to career enhancement, and an erosion of police powers and autonomy. Its endorsement by senior administration simply reinforces rank and file resent-ment over a management out of touch with reality and beholden to political rather than police interests (Gillmor 1996). The warning signs are all too clear. Implementation of com-munity policing will invariably challenge vested interests; it will also encounter resistance from bureaucratic structures and occupational subcultures (Chan 1997).

People who work in a similar occupation may develop distinctive ways of perceiving and responding to their social environment (Chan 1996). The grounds for a police occupational subculture are not difficult to uncover. Most police officers in Canada are male, white, able-bodied, French or English speaking, and of working-class origin. This homogeneity in gen-der, social class, ability, and ethnicity is reinforced by similar socialization pressures related to common training and peer group influence. Such inward solidarity not only reflects but also reinforces patterns of exclusion from the ethnic community (us versus them). Perception of the public as ignorant and unsupportive of law enforcement activities is fostered as well. Suspicion of those outside the profession compounds the tendency toward isolation, mutual distrust, and alienation. Police solidarity and estrangement from the community are further reinforced by the requirements of the job, including shift work and patterns of socializa-tion outside the workplace (Desroches 1998).

The gap between the principles of community policing and police occupational sub-cultures could not be more striking (see Eck and Rosenbaum 1994). Community policing cul-ture endorses the virtues of trust, familiarity, co-operation, and respect. The community is perceived as a "resource" with unlimited potential for dealing with local issues. Opposing this is the occupational subculture of the police with its disdain of community involvement. The community is dismissed as uninterested in social control work, indifferent and passive (waiting to be policed), incompetent to carry out even simple tasks, disorganized to act in uni-son, and misinformed about the pressures and demands confronting the police. It is per-ceived as irrelevant—even an impediment—for effective policing except as a source of informants. (Only a small number of crimes—possibly as low as 4 percent—are solved by police without community involvement [Bayley 1994]. Gun-related gang slayings are even harder to solve because the killers are ruthless, leave few clues or scientific evidence, and often intimidate witnesses into not co-operating with the police [Powell 2005].) This clash of visions—community as problem vs. community as solution—makes it difficult to envis-age a situation more conducive to "anti-community" policing.

No less inhibiting of institutional inclusiveness is the pervasiveness of police bureaucracy. The police as an institution are organized around bureaucratic principles whose paramilitar-istic overtones rarely coincide with community-based initiatives. Police organizations are gov-erned by a central command and control structure, with a ranked hierarchy, complex division of labour, impersonal enforcement of formal rules, carefully stipulated procedures, and the provision of a rationally based service. These bureaucracies exist to control a large number of persons (both internally and externally) without displaying favouritism or making any excep-tions. This control function is attained through a combination of rational control procedures, stan-dardization, conformity through rule-following, and accountability to the organizational chain of command. The police may not deliberately set out to control, but the nature of their mandate as bureaucratic "functionaries" has had a controlling effect when discharging their obligations.

The principles of bureaucracy and community policing appear diametrically opposed. The partnership ethos inherent in community policing clashes with the imperatives of bureaucratic control. Community policing emphasizes collaboration, creativity and thinking outside the box, joint problem-solving, answerability to clients, and co-responsibility for crime control and order maintenance (Normandeau and Leighton 1990). Bureaucracies by contrast are destined to be remote, isolated, and case-oriented; they are also bound by standardization, strict organizational procedures, and a stifling hierarchy. A fundamental reorientation is called for that de-bureaucratizes roles, status, functions, reward structures, operational styles, training programs, and objectives. But talking of change is one thing, and doing it is another. How can creative problem-solving techniques flourish under organizational conditions that expect obedience and compliance while discouraging questioning, self-motivation, and innovation (Tomovich and Loree 1989)? Can innovative—even possibly risky—solutions be reconciled with a managerial mindset based on "not rocking the boat" or "shut up, and do as you're told"?

In the final analysis, community policing will succeed only as part of an incusiveness package. Isolated strategies will not work, according to the Canadian Association of Chiefs of Police, nor will simply adding a box to the organizational chart. The commitment and will must come from the top. The success and failure of community policing will also depend on its capacity to convince front-line officers of its vision of an "inclusive blue line." Community policing will miss its mark unless police are convinced of its credibility and effectiveness. Nor will it make much of an impact until the goals of community policing are shown to be attainable, realistic, and rewarding. As long as individual officers believe they have nothing to gain from community policing because rewards lie with "kick-ass policing," the prospect of commitment is remote.

And yet a commitment to diversifying policing cannot be taken lightly. Policing from top to bottom must become better acquainted with the multicultural community in terms of its varied needs, entitlements, demands, and expectations. A commitment to diversity encourages police to approach members of a community as a resource of potential value in preventing crime. The principles of community policing appear to offer the best multicultural option for doing what is workable, necessary, and fair. But until there is a collective mindset shift toward acceptance of multicultural communities as partners in pre-empting crime before it starts, the crisis in police–minority relations will persist.

MEDIA AND MINORITIES: A CONTESTED SITE

With the possible exception of schools and police agencies, few institutions have attracted as much criticism and concern as the mainstream media (Henry and Tator 2006).The media have been singled out as visibly negligent in responding positively to Canada's evolving diversity (Fleras and Kunz 2001). The passage of the *Multiculturalism Act* in 1988 has obligated all government agencies, such as the CBC, to improve minority access, equity, and representation. But media treatment of minorities in Canada remains mixed at best, deplorable at worst (Kunz and Fleras 1998). Criticism applies across the board, from a dearth of employment opportunities to negative media portrayals of minorities. The media have been reproached for biased and inaccurate coverage of Aboriginal peoples and racialized minorities, many of whom continue to be insulted, stereotyped, caricaturized, ignored as irrelevant, or "miniaturized" as inferior. The cumulative impact of this dismissive treatment is unmistakably clear: all the talk of inclusiveness will go for nought unless mainstream media are brought on board.

Why should the media be under such scrutiny? To say the media are powerful and pervasive is merely stating the obvious. This potency lies in the media's ability to articulate who is important, what is acceptable in society, and whose voices shall be heard (Fleras 2004). This agenda-setting function is referred to as "reality construction" (see Harris 1993). The media construct those images that define acceptability, importance, or desirability, then confer legitimacy on the constructed reality through selective exposure and positive reinforcement. The ideological basis of reality construction is doubly articulated. The media are ideological insofar as they not only reflect but also advance the ideas and ideals of the dominant sector in ways that eventually reinforce prevailing discourses (Abel 1997). Alternative perspectives are dismissed as inferior or irrelevant as minority realities are refracted through the Eurocentric prism of a white-controlled media. The end result is that majority interests rather than minority needs are served by these discourses in defence of dominant ideology.

The consequences of being ignored or trivialized by the media should not be underestimated. In a world where firsthand experiences of diversity may be uncommon, mainstream media may constitute the only or primary source of information about minority women and men (Orbe and Harris 2001; Children Now 2001). To the extent that this information is glossed over or distorted, our ability to understand social reality is sadly compromised. Admittedly, the media do not tell us what to think, but what to think about, in the main by drawing attention to some aspects of reality and away from others. Rather than directly determining attitudes or behaviour, media impacts are indirect. Public discourses are generated by media messages in which certain persons or objects are "normalized" as acceptable and desirable, whereas others are demonized as problem people. Nor do media necessarily set out to control; nevertheless, the cumulative impact of negative images and messages has had a controlling effect on those victimized by unflattering portrayals. The consequences of mismanaging media images reflect poorly on Canada. If the media represent a mirror that reflects an image of society, Canadians still have a long way to go in achieving a multicultural "looking-glass self."

PORTRAYING MINORITY WOMEN AND MEN

The world we inhabit is pervaded and transformed by images. The control of knowledge and its dissemination through media images is fundamental to the exercise of power in society. These images not only assist in the identification and construction of ourselves as social beings but also serve as "windows" in defining what it means to be a Canadian and who is entitled to claim Canadianness (Bullock and Jafri 2001). For minority women and men, the circulation of images has proven both enabling yet disempowering.

> Visual images in that sense are congealed social relations, formalizing in themselves either relations of domination or those of resistance. The politics of images is the same as any politics; it is about being the subjects not the objects of the world that we live in. (Bannerji 1986:20)

With images as powerful as they are, the representational basis of media–minority relations has come under scrutiny (Fleras and Kunz 2001). How do the media portray Aboriginal peoples and racialized minority women and men? In what ways do media images of minorities say more about the mainstream and its fears or fantasies? Are prevailing images the result of conscious or unconscious decisions? What, if anything, can be done to improve this level of representation (Jakubowicz et al. 1994)?

Media (mis)treatment of minority women and men appears to fall into four categories, reflecting recurrent images of minorities as invisible, stereotyped, problem people, and adornments (Fleras and Kunz 2001; Fleras 2003). This assessment would appear true for all mainstream media processes, including newscasting, advertising, and TV programming.

Invisibility: Numerous studies have confirmed what many regard as obvious. Canada's multicultural diversity is poorly reflected in media processes and outcomes. Visible minorities are reduced to an invisible status through underrepresentation in programming, staffing, and decision-making. Even substantial representation in the media may be misleading if minority women and men are pigeonholed into a relatively small number of programs or into a limited number of roles like entertainers or athletes. Consider the plight of African-Americans on television. Shows whose casts include black people are common enough, especially in shows involving workplace dynamics such as *ER,* yet rarely are dramas constructed around black stories in the belief that there is no sizable demographic audience for this kind of material. TV sitcoms tend to be segregated into all-white casts and all-black casts, while minorities such as Latinos/as, Asians, and Aboriginal peoples are under-represented compared to their numbers in real life (Kalamipour and Carilli 1998).

It would be inaccurate to say that the news media ignore minorities. Rather, a "shallows and rapids" treatment is a more accurate appraisal. That is, under normal circumstances, minorities are ignored or rendered irrelevant by the mainstream press (shallows). Otherwise, coverage is guided by the context of crisis or calamity, involving natural catastrophes, civil wars, and colourful insurgents. When the crisis subsides or persists too long, media interest wanes. Conflicts and calamities occur in minority communities, of course, but the absence of balanced coverage may distort perceptions of minority experiences and aspirations. This distortion may not be deliberately engineered. Rather, the misrepresentation reflects media preoccupation with readership and advertising revenues. The flamboyant and sensational are accorded disproportionate coverage to satisfy audience needs and sell copy, without much regard for the effects on the lives of those sensationalized. The media may shun responsibility for their discriminatory impact, arguing they are reporting only what is newsworthy. Nevertheless, such an exclusive focus has had the effect of portraying minorities as "troublesome constituents" who are less than Canadian (Fleras 2004).

Stereotypes: Minorities have long complained of stereotyping by the mainstream media (Azam 2000; Stam and Miller 2000). Historically, people of colour were portrayed in a manner that did not contradict prevailing prejudices. Liberties taken with minority depictions in consumer advertising were especially flagrant. In an industry geared toward image and appeal, the rule of homogeneity and conservatism prevailed. Advertisers wanted their products sanitized and bleached of colour for fear of lost revenue. People of colour were rarely depicted in the advertising of beauty care and personal hygiene products, so entrenched was the image of "whiteness" as the preferred standard of beauty (Bledsloe 1989). Elsewhere, images of racial minorities were steeped in unfounded generalizations that accentuated the comical or grotesque. This stereotyping fell into a pattern. People from the Middle East continued to be portrayed as tyrannical patriarchs or crazed fanatics with a bent for linking terrorism with religion (Elmasry 1999; Karim 2002). Asians have been typecast either as sly and cunning or as mathematical whizzes; Latinos/as as hot-blooded salsa-lovers. Black people in prime-time shows remain stuck as superheroes/athletes or sex-obsessed buffoons surrounded by a host of secondary characters such as hipsters, outlaws, and "gangstas."

Consider how the media have historically portrayed Canada's Aboriginal peoples as the "other," a people removed in time and remote in space. This image of Aboriginal peoples has filtered through Eurocentric lenses, ranging in scope from their eulogization as "noble savage" and "primitive romantic" to their debasement as "villain" or "victim" or "comical simpleton," with the stigma of "problem people" or "menacing subversives" sandwiched in between (see also Blythe 1994). Images of tribalism continue to resonate with a spicy mixture of meanings, from backwardness to spiritual mysticism to ecological custodians (Jakubowicz et al. 1994). Most portrayals embraced a mythical image of an imaginary warrior who occupied the Plains between 1825 and 1880 (Francis 1992). The standard for the generic North American Indian could be packaged with ingredients from a so-called Indian Identity Kit (Berton 1975), which consisted of the following items, few of which were even indigenous to Aboriginal peoples prior to European settlement: wig with hair parted in the middle into hanging plaits; feathered war bonnet; headband (a white invention to keep the actor's wig from slipping off); buckskin leggings; moccasins; painted-skin teepee; and a tomahawk and bows and arrows. This one-size-fits-all image applied to all First Peoples, regardless of whether they were Cree or Salish or Ojibwa or Blackfoot. These images could be further broken down into a series of recurrent stereotypes, in effect reinforcing a "seen one Indian, seen them all" mentality.

Collectively, these images reinforce the notion of Aboriginal peoples as a people from a different time and place, whose histories began with the arrival of white people, and whose reality makes sense only with settler interaction. Collective resistance to their colonization is rarely depicted, in effect depoliticizing Aboriginal concerns and contributions to Canada, although individual acts of protest may be valorized. Aboriginal activism is portrayed as a departure from established norms while protestors are reduced to dangerous militants or irrational ideologues. News stories involving Aboriginal assertion are framed as a narrative involving a conflict of interest between the opposing forces of mayhem and stability (Abel 1997). The subsequent demonizing of Aboriginal activism marginalizes the legitimacy of dissent, trivializes Aboriginal issues, and distracts from the issues at hand. To be sure, the media have begun to invert conventional stereotypes between white people and First Peoples, with much greater emphasis on their courage or compassion compared to the rapacious greed of white settler colonization (think *Dances with Wolves*). Nevertheless, there is a long way to go, as Maurice Switzer, a member of the Elders' Council of the Mississaugas of Rice Lake First Nations, at Alderville, Ontario, writes in *Windspeaker* (1997:21–22):

> The country's large newspapers, TV and radio news shows often contain misinformation, sweeping generalizations and galling stereotypes about natives and native affairs. Their stories are usually presented by journalists with little background knowledge or understanding of aboriginals and their communities . . . As well very few so-called mainstream media consider aboriginal affairs to be a subject worthy of regular attention.

Why such stereotyping? Stereotyping simplifies the process of representation. A pool of Aboriginal stereotypes provides a convenient shorthand that audiences can relate to because of shared cultural codes. Reliance on these simplistic and reductionist images creates readily identifiable frames (tropes) that impose a thematic coherence for story lines, plot twists, or character development. Over time, these stereotypes solidify into definitive statements about "reality," and, while not "real" in the conventional sense, stereotypes are real in their social consequences. In other words, rather than an error in perception, stereotyping constitutes a system of thought control through the internalization of negative images. Stereotypes are employed to keep Aboriginal peoples out of sight and out of mind, thus sanitizing the colonization of First Peoples by assuaging white guilt (Churchill 1999). The racially coded discourses that compose stereotyping not only fan public fears but also feed public demands for tougher measures of social control. Such stereotyping may also contribute to the construction of white identities (Davis 1996). Imaginary Indians are filtered through the prism of European prejudice and preconceptions, in the process projecting whiteness onto the Aboriginal "other." To the extent that white people have long resorted to fantasies or anxieties about the "other" as a basis for collectively defining who they are in relation to the world around them, media images really do say more about the "us" than the "them."

Problem People: Minority women and men are frequently singled out by the media as troublesome constituents who "are problems," "have problems," or "create problems" and are in need of political attention or scarce national resources (Fleras 2004). As "problem people" they are taken to task by the media for making demands at odds with Canada's unity or national prosperity. Portrayal of Canada's Aboriginal peoples is instructive, especially when they are depicted as (1) a threat to Canada's territorial integrity or national interests (Nisga'a *Final Settlement)*; (2) a risk to Canada's social order (from Oka to Caledonia); (3) an economic liability (the costs associated with massive land claims settlement or compensation for victims of residential schools); and (4) a problem for the criminal justice system (possible cover-up in the killing of Dudley George) or an unfair player (cigarette smuggling or contraband alcohol). Compounding this negativity are repeated reports of Aboriginal reliance on welfare, a dependency on alcohol and substance abuse, a perceived laziness and lack of ambition, and an inclination to mismanage what little they have. The combined impact of this negative reporting paints a villainous picture of Canada's First Peoples as "troublesome constituents" whose demands for self-determining autonomy are society-destroying. Success stories are rarely reported, and the few exceptions simply confirm the rule.

Non-Aboriginal minorities are also problematized by the media. People of colour, both foreign and native-born, are targets of negative reporting that dwells on costs, threats, and inconveniences. Media reporting of refugees usually refers to illegal entries and the associated costs of processing and integration into Canada. Canada's refugee determination system is repeatedly criticized for allowing entry of refugees who pose a security threat (Francis 2001). Immigrants are routinely cast as potential troublemakers who steal jobs from Canadians, cheat on the welfare system, take advantage of educational opportunities, lack commitment to Canada, engage in illegal activities such as drugs or smuggling, and imperil Canada's unity and identity by refusing to discard their culture. This negativity is reinforced when stories are framed around minority challenges to conventional assumptions about who is entitled to power and privilege in Canada (Jiwani 2001). These slanted portrayals have had the cumulative effect of racializing the "them" as a problem "other."

Trivialization: The media tend to diminish minority women and men. They are portrayed as little more than adornments that are meant to amuse, distract, or embellish. This decorative aspect is achieved by casting minorities in stereotypical roles. Minorities are associated with the exotic and sensual, portrayed as congenial hosts for faraway destinations, enlisted as superstar boosters for athletics and sporting goods, or ghettoized in certain marketing segments related to rap or hip-hop. Most minority roles on television consist of bit parts, either as background scenery or as foils to sharpen white characters and characteristics. Black people on television are locked into roles as entertainers or athletes. Rarely is there any emphasis on intellectual or professional prowess, much less recourse to positive role models to which youth can aspire outside athletics or entertainment (Edwards 2000). Such a restriction may prove inherently satisfying to mainstream audiences who historically have enjoyed laughing at black people when cast as breezy entertainment. Yet, the laugh-tracking of minorities is not without consequences. The depoliticizing of black people as "emasculated" cartoons ("playing 'em for laughs") has the effect of reassuring audiences that minorities still know their place (see Farhi 1995).

To sum up: Minority women and men are rendered invisible through underrepresentation in areas that count. Conversely, they are visibly overrepresented in areas that count for less, including tourism, sports, international relief, and entertainment. Double standards prevail and loop into a cultural Catch-22: Minorities are criticized by media for being too different yet may be chided for not being different enough; they are taken to task for aspiring to be the same yet denounced when trying too hard. Media portrayals lean toward minorities as the *other*. Minorities complain of being treated as "foreigners" or "outsiders" whose lives seem to revolve around their "defining" status of race or religion to the virtual exclusion of other attributes. Minority concerns are also compromised by a pervasive Eurocentrism that slots cultural differences into a single perspective while Westocentric accomplishments provide the standard by which others are judged (Shohat and Stam 1994). Ethnocentrism and white superiority may not be openly articulated by media "whitewashing," but are assumed and normalized as the unquestioned norm. The fact that media bias exists is not the problem; after all, bias is inevitable because all social constructions reflect the values and agendas of those who create them. The problem is twofold: media coverage that is systemically biasing because of its one-sidedness (Fleras 2006) and a media that is so steeped in bias that it cannot admit to this ethnocentrism, preferring instead to hide behind claims to objectivity and neutrality (Maracle 1996).

ACCOUNTING FOR THE PROBLEM

Neglect of minorities in the media may occur for a variety of reasons. These may span the spectrum from hard-boiled business decisions that reflect the realities of market forces to a lack of cultural awareness to deep-seated prejudice among media personnel. Does media mistreatment of minorities imply the presence of personal prejudice or overt discrimination? Is it a case of unwittingly cramming minority realities into Eurocentric categories as a basis for description or evaluation? Or does it reflect a preference to act out of self-interest by kow-towing to the dictates of the marketplace, especially during economic uncertainty and periods of corporate restructuring? Confusion and uncertainty are the rule rather than the exception. Key personnel may be unsure of how to integrate Canadians of colour into the media without being accused of paternalism or tokenism. Even sensitive presentations must grapple with dilemmas as varied as the following: (1) how to portray other cultures at odds with Canada's democratic principles; (2) whether it is best to emphasize the positive features of minorities rather than the problems that many confront; and (3) whether cultural differences can be presented without reinforcing stereotypes or polarizing the world into us versus them (see McAndrew 1992). Unsure of what to do or how to do it, TV programmers and advertising personnel may avoid cultural topics for fear of career-curbing mistakes.

Media executives concede the importance of improving the quantity and quality of minority representations. The combination of a growing ethnic market and an increased competition for consumer loyalty and dollars has sounded the death knell for monocultural media. But moves to convey a positive image of minorities have tended to misfire. Media efforts to improve minority representation may be greeted with disdain or coolness. Positive portrayals and inclusive programming may be dismissed as window-dressing, condescending, tokenistic, or "politically correct." A no-win situation may prevail. Portrayals of minorities in high status and stable relationships (such as the *Cosby Show*) are rebuked for creating unrealistic and unattainable expectations that can only foster resentment. Benetton ads that prominently display minorities in a variety of controversial situations are praised by some as progressive; others see them as exploitative and insulting. Such an apparent dichotomy puts the media in a double bind; that is, in a lose-lose situation where they are damned if they do, damned if they don't. Bewildered and taken aback by criticism for either action or inaction, the media recoil from fear of detonating yet another cultural landmine that could impede corporate profits or implode on personal careers.

Studies in this area suggest that the representational basis of media–minority relations is tainted by discrimination and racism—at times deliberate, at other times inadvertent. Systemic biases are especially powerful in shaping what we see or hear. At the core of systemic bias is an unswerving Eurocentrism—a set of beliefs about the superiority of Westocentric values and practices that is so pervasive as to escape detection. Under Eurocentrism, reality is automatically interpreted from a mainstream point of view as natural and normal; minority perspectives are also refracted through the prism of "whiteness" and dismissed accordingly. Yet, the unspoken nature of these tacit assumptions is powerful in privileging the West at the expense of the rest (Shohat and Stam 1994). Take the news media (Herman and Chomsky 1988), which are ideological in that they privilege (or normalize) "pale male" points of view as normal and acceptable whereas minority viewpoints are discredited as inferior or irrelevant. News media are also ideological in that they themselves are loaded with ideological assumptions that influence how news stories are "framed." The framing of news provides a handy reference point for quickly defining issues around a preferred reading (Guerrero 1997). Incidents are squeezed into conflict formats or given a racial "spin" to generate interest or play up an angle (e.g., "race-profiling"). But this "framing" experience is not neutral; it reflects the interests of those who own or control the media. That kind of hegemony for controlling thought without our awareness of what is happening reinforces the status of news as a yet another discourse in defence of dominant ideology.

In short, media constitute systems of "soft" propaganda (Fleras and Kunz 2001). Media do not set out to do propaganda; nevertheless, propaganda is the inevitable consequence of creating one-sided messages that consistently support one point of view to the exclusion of others. Of course, mainstream media are not propaganda in the conventional sense of deliberate and organized brainwashing. Rather, media propaganda in a democratic society tends toward a systemic propaganda. How is this systemic (or soft) propaganda expressed? In that news media invariably frame minority women and men as "troublesome constituents" in opposition to the Canadian norm, propaganda is at play. To the extent that media routinely portray Aboriginal women and men as having problems or creating problems, this one-sided depiction constitutes propaganda. To be sure, mainstream media do not go out of their way to control people's thoughts, given the realities of doing business in a liberal–democratic society. But the cumulative impact of largely negative portrayals of minority women and men has had a controlling effect in shaping mainstream perceptions of who is important, acceptable, and a true Canadian.

MULTICULTURALIZING THE MEDIA

The media in Canada are under scrutiny to make appropriate adjustments (Fleras 2006). Multicultural minorities and Aboriginal peoples have asked some tough questions of the media regarding their commitment to inclusiveness. Proposed demands include the incorporation of minority perspectives into the media process, more multicultural programming, balanced and impartial newscasting, and sensitivity training for journalists and decision-makers (Abel 1997). Other changes include the creation of separate ethnic and Aboriginal media.

To some extent, many changes are already in progress. The government Task Force on Broadcasting Policy, co-chaired by Gerald Caplan and Florian Sauvagneau in 1986, singled out the need to include Aboriginal peoples and racial minorities (Raboy 1988). The 1988 *Broadcasting Act* has come out in favour of "cultural expression" by expanding air time for ethnic and racialized minorities. Reforms include sensitivity training for program and production staff, language guidelines to reduce race–role stereotypes, and monitoring of on-air representation of historically disadvantaged people. Rules are in place to deter abusive representations of individuals on the basis of race or ethnicity as well as age, gender, religion, or disability. In advertising too, racial minorities are appearing more frequently across a broader range of products and services. Companies that utilize diversity are now perceived as sophisticated and cosmopolitan compared with their all-white counterparts who come across as staid and outdated. Demographics may be pushing the changes: When people of colour compose over 30 percent of the populations in Vancouver and Toronto, the media have to acknowledge that diversity is "cool."

In Southern Ontario, CFMT, the multicultural channel, delivers a much-needed service. Serving 18 cultural groups and 15 languages, CFMT is unique in the world, not only in producing 23 hours of original programming per week, but also because 60 percent of the programming is non-French or non-English (Quill 1996). Vision TV also hosts about 30 programs largely about different religious faiths and practices. Inroads are also evident in the private sector, where multicultural issues since 1984 have been addressed by Toronto's Citytv station through two large blocks of non-English, non-French programming produced by CHIN on Saturdays and Sundays. On-air programming such as the racially acclaimed series *North of Sixty* also explored the frontier of acceptance by showing Aboriginal peoples as individuals living in a community of problems and solutions where culture is anchored in history but not stuck in the past (Wortley 1998; Alia 1999). Finally, the establishment of the Aboriginal Peoples Television Network in 1999 promises to counteract miscasting by promoting a positive portrayal of Canada's First Peoples across a broad range of topics (Brioux 1999; Molnar and Meadows 2001).

Despite changes, institutional inclusiveness does not come easily to the media (Fleras 2005). A conflict of interest is proving a stumbling block. The commercial media do not see themselves as reform agencies to promote progressive change or to accommodate, even if they may have a social responsibility to do so. They are a business whose *raison d'être* is simple: to make money by connecting audiences to advertisers through ratings. Institutional practices that once worked to generate revenues (e.g., stereotyping) will be retained; those that don't will be discarded. Such a bottom-line mentality will invariably be at odds with minority demands for balanced and contexted coverage, given media preference for morselization over context, conflict over co-operation, and personalities over issues (see Atkinson 1994). For example, all media storytelling, from news and weather to TV programming, is framed around conflict format (We Interrupt the News 2001). But this one-sidedness has a negative impact on those minorities who rarely have positive images to counterbalance the negative. The irony seems inescapable. The very changes that minorities want of the media (responsible coverage of minority interests, less sensationalism, more context, toned-down language, and less stereotyping) are precisely the tools that media use to sell copy or capture eyeballs (Fleras 2001).

The expansion of the ethnic or "third media" (minority presses and broadcast programs) is a prime example of minority empowerment. Minorities now publish up to 250 papers (about half in Toronto) in their language on issues of relevance to them, both in Canada and abroad (Siddiqui 2001). In British Columbia the Indo-Canadian *Punjabi Times* competes with three English-language weeklies and four Punjabi weeklies that address Indo-Canadian issues. As the diversity hub in Canada, Toronto too is well served by eight non-English dailies, three in Chinese, two in Korean, and one each in Spanish, Polish, and Italian. Toronto is also served by six ethnic radio stations, one black-owned FM station, two closed-circuit audio services, an ethnic television station, three ethnic specialty services, and another six non-English or -French channels accessible with special receiving equipment (Zerbisias 1999). Finally, one of the more successful stories in the third media is located in Northern Canada, where Aboriginal communities have wrested control over the local media in large part by appropriating satellite technology to meet cultural needs (Molnar and Meadows 2001).

COUCHED IN COMPROMISE

The media play an influential role in defining what is socially desirable or normal. This agenda-setting function is largely accomplished by defining a specific cultural framework that provides a reference point for acceptance or validity. Their role in shaping public discourses is staggering: As dominant meaning-making machines, mainstream media have the potential to articulate a powerful statement about the legitimacy of diversity in our society. But as machineries of meaning they appear to be sending mixed messages about a responsiveness to diversity (Mahtani 2002). Minorities continue to be played for laughs; stereotyping remains as rampant as ever in advertising or programming; newscasting continues to portray minorities as problem people or in conflict; and invisibility remains a problem. Prime-time television continues to be overwhelmingly white despite promises by the four major networks to increase minority representation, according to a study entitled "Fall Colours 2000–2001" by the San Francisco–based advocacy group Children Now. Sitcoms remain as segregated as ever, with only 14 percent having racially mixed casts. Dramas, especially those in the 10 p.m. slot, are three times as likely to have mixed casts (see also Steinhorn and Diggs-Brown 1999).

In other words, advances are interposed with stagnation. In theory, both the quality and quantity of media representations have improved. In reality, however, the picture remains as exclusive as ever, with modest improvements in numbers undermined by continuing misrepresentations in quality (Kunz and Fleras 1998). This suggests that media representations of minority women and men are couched in compromise. It also suggests the media will continue as a contested site for control of the agenda, with advocates of the economic, political, and social status quo in competition with the forces of change (Pritchford 2001). At the core of this contestation process is power. Until the issue of power is resolved—in terms of who owns it, who has access to it, and whose values will dominate— the representational basis of media–minority relations will remain riddled with ambiguity and frustration.

MULTICULTURAL AND ANTI-RACIST EDUCATION

Some of the most interesting advances in inclusiveness are found in the educational system. This commitment to **multicultural education** represents a significant shift from the past. Schooling and education have for the most part reflected a fundamental commitment to monoculturalism. The schooling of children was inseparable from the absorption of diversity into the mainstream (Alladin 1996). This can come as no surprise; after all, Canada (like Australia and New Zealand) was historically seen as a local version of British cultural expansion, with its goal to assimilate both the indigenes and immigrants into the pre-existing hierarchy of cultural power (Jakubowicz 2005). All aspects of schooling, from teachers and textbooks to policy and curriculum, were aligned with the principles of angloconformity. Anything that veered outside this anglocentric framework was ignored as irrelevant or dangerous and punished accordingly. Special curricula and references to other languages or cultures were rejected as inconsistent with the long-term interests of Canada-building.

But the demographies are changing. About 20 percent of students in public, elementary, and secondary schools are of visible minority or immigrant status—with projections of a majority of students by 2017 (Areepattamannil 2005). The figures for Toronto are even more impressive, with racial and ethnic minorities constituting nearly 50 percent of secondary students. But because teachers and administrators of colour continue to be grossly underrepresented, fears are mounting that schools are failing to provide a positive learning environment that fosters and values cultural diversity. In addition, children of economically deprived immigrant and racialized minority groups are not doing as well in school as their Canadia-born peers, with lower achievement in test scores, grades, graduation rates, and college applications. Such underachievement comes with a hefty price tag: When children leave school without the basic tools for job success or learning skills the underachievement affects everything, from quality of life to social inclusion to self-esteem. The blot this has on Canada's democratic and egalitarian reputation puts the underachievement into perspective, that is, the educational system must become more representative of and responsive to the diversity that informs a changing Canada (Areepattamannil 2005).

Not surprisingly, the explicit assimilationist model that once prevailed within educational circles no longer prevails, even if assimilation remains an unspoken but powerful ethos at all schooling levels (Banks and Banks 1997; May 1999). The site encompassed by schooling and education has been transformed into a contested space, involving the struggles of those who endorse the status quo versus the historically excluded who are seeking to multiculturalize the agenda (Giroux 1994). A dual dynamic is apparent: Education plays both a conservative and a progressive role in society. On one side, there is an explicit commitment to innovations such as child-centred curricula, with their focus on self-esteem and personal growth, encouragement of informed debate as a basis for progressive change, and embracing of diversity as necessary, normal, and beneficial. On the other side, however, a tacit commitment to assimilation remains a central objective: not assimilation in the openly monocultural sense of wilful indoctrination, but through the logical consequences of schooling in a liberal-capitalist society.

The impetus for multicultural education constitutes a departure from conventional ways of doing things. Its introduction has not only challenged how schools should relate to diversity but also raised questions about the dynamics of formal education in a changing and diverse society. The extent to which multicultural education seeks to accommodate diversity is eminently worthwhile. But what sounds good in theory may falter in practice because of entrenched interests and structural barriers that blunt, deflect, absorb, or crush any significant move toward meaningful inclusiveness. A more radical extension of multicultural education known as anti-racistm education has been proposed instead to challenge the limitations of multicultural education as well as the inequities that continue to persist both within and outside the education system.

MONOCULTURAL EDUCATION

Both the media and education are secondary agents of socialization whose social functions are often at odds with formal mandates. The following functions of education are widely acknowledged: (1) socialization, or transmission of culture; (2) self-actualization and individual self-development; (3) preparation for the workplace, consumerism, and citizenship; (4) improvement in Canada's competitive edge; and (5) reproduction of the social order. Central to the logic of public education is the centrality of social control, particularly when involving students from different cultural backgrounds. From daily routines to decision-making at the top, education is organized to facilitate cultural indoctrination and societal assimilation of minority students. These reproductive functions can be accomplished in a direct manner by way of Eurocentric course content, pedagogical styles, and methods of evaluation. Indirect and largely unobtrusive measures are also employed. The school system screens out certain information by projecting certain types of knowledge as necessary and normal, others as inappropriate. Issues are framed in a way that gives prominence and confers cultural legitimacy to some, but ignores others. Through schooling, the reproduction of the ideological and social order is realized without much public awareness or open debate. The widely accepted practice of grading students may have the effect of reinforcing competitive individualism at the expense of culture or co-operation. This "hidden curriculum" is nicely described by Alok Mukherjee (1992:73):

> Traditionally, the school has been a conservative institution. Its function, on the one hand, is to legitimize the dominant social, political, economic, and cultural ideas of society and, on the other, to perpetuate existing relations. The ownership, organization, and activities of the school reflect this dual role.

In linking power with culture, schooling and education have evolved into a site for the reproduction of social inequality by denying equal opportunity and fostering outcomes at odds with certain minority students (Dei 1996). This disempowerment is accomplished in different ways, including (1) school policies and politics; (2) school culture and organization; (3) lack of community involvement; (4) bureaucracy and red tape; (5) assessment, testing procedures, and program tracking; (6) instructional materials; (7) the formal and "hidden" curriculum; (8) the ethnic composition of the teaching staff; and (9) teacher attitudes, values, and competency.

The assimilationist dynamic imposes constraints on expanding a multicultural agenda. A commitment to diversity and change may be fundamentally compromised in a context where monoculturalism prevails. Rarely do schools seriously contemplate the magnitude of commitment needed for inclusiveness to infiltrate everything from curriculum to language, culture programs for children, placement and assessment, employment and promotion, teacher training, and relations with the community (McAndrew 1992). Ad hoc adjustments are more common than radical restructuring. Nor does there appear to be any wholesale move to reject the assimilationist ethos of the school system. Discriminatory structures are not easily dismantled given entrenched interests and ideologies, many of which are unlikely to tolerate transformative changes without considerable resistance. Reforms may be relegated to the cosmetic realm, and away from the key domains of decision-making, agenda-setting, and power-sharing. These impediments should warn against any excessive expectations regarding the potential of multicultural education. For in the final analysis, multicultural education occupies a contested status: If race, ethnic, and Aboriginal relations are fundamentally unequal relations, does multicultural education contribute to the creation and maintenance of inequality or is it a forum for challenge and change? The answer to date is hopeful, but not very promising. Still, the fact that inclusiveness initiatives have materialized at many schools suggests a stronger commitment to multicultural education in Canadian society.

MULTICULTURAL EDUCATION

Multicultural education strives to be inclusive of diversity. It encompasses a variety of policies, programs, and practices for engaging diversity within the school setting to ensure that differences do not disadvantage students. It also seeks to incorporate all students by modifying existing content and protocols to ensure better involvement and success. Different styles of multicultural education can be observed, ranging in scope and comprehension from "moderate" to more "radical" approaches (Moodley 1999; van Driel 2000). Three of the more common moderate approaches are enrichment, enlightenment, and empowerment. An anti-racism approach is constitutive of a fundamentally different logic.

Enrichment Model: An enrichment multicultural education is aimed at all students. Students are exposed to a variety of different cultures to enhance knowledge of and appreciation for cultural diversity. For example, the Ontario government has introduced a First Nations perspective into grades one to twelve as part of a revamped social studies curriculum, including social studies, history and geography, and Canadian and world studies courses (Brown 2005). The curriculum is enriched with various multicultural add-ons. Special days are set aside for multicultural awareness; projects are assigned that reflect multicultural themes; and specific cultures are singled out for intensive classroom study. Additional perspectives include a focus on healthy identity formation, cultural preservation, intercultural sensitivity, stereotyping awareness, and cross-cultural communication. A desirable side effect of the enrichment process is greater tolerance, enhanced sensitivity, and more harmonious intercultural relations. A less beneficial consequence is a failure to initiate sweeping institutional changes, much less challenge the racism within and outside the school.

The enrichment model is widely accepted because of its non-threatening nature. Yet, this very innocuousness has brought it into disrepute with critics. Enrichment styles have been criticized as too static and restrictive in scope. The style tends to focus on the exotic components of a culture that everyone can relate to, rather than to more substantive issues such as values and beliefs, and when taught by uninspired teachers may inadvertently trivialize or stereotype (Henry et al. 2000). Diverse cultures are studied at the level of material culture, stripped of their historical context, and discussed from an outsider's point of view (Mukherjee 1992). There is also a danger of over-romanticizing minorities by focusing on a timeless past or, alternatively, of crippling them as social problems when dwelling on the present. That these questions have yet to be answered to everyone's satisfaction is indicative of the elusiveness in pinpointing the right balance.

Enlightenment Model: A second approach that is compatible with the first is an enlightenment model of multicultural education. This approach is similar to the enrichment model insofar as both seek to modify people's attitudes by changing how they think about diversity. Enlightenment models are less concerned with celebrating differences as a basis for attitudinal change. The focus is on enlightening students about race relations in society. Enlightenment models go beyond description of specific cultures; endorsed, instead, is a broader, analytical approach toward diversity not as a "thing" but as a relationship, both hierarchical and unequal. Attention is directed to how minority–majority relations are created and maintained as well as what would be required to challenge and transform these predominantly unequal relationships. Stronger versions may expose students to Anglo-European complicity in crimes of racism, dispossession, and imperialism and the corresponding concentrations of power in white hands. Specific group victimization may be included, for example, genocide against First Peoples, while emphasizing the achievements of indigenous and immigrant peoples as a corrective to their marginalization in history, society, and culture.

Empowerment Model: Both the enrichment and enlightenment styles of multicultural education concentrate on the needs of non-minority pupils. In contrast is a third model, called empowerment multicultural education, which is directed essentially at the needs of minority students. The minority-focus empowerment model is predicated on the belief that monocultural school systems are failing minority pupils. Minority students do not see themselves represented in a Westocentric curriculum that rarely acknowledges minority achievements and contributions to society. What minority students require is an inclusive curriculum that incorporates the values they bring to school for improving successful learning outcomes (Dei 1996); a school context that capitalizes on minority strengths and learning styles as a basis for achievement; and a platform for minority stories to be told in their own voices, while repudiating the white-centredness of school knowledge as the only legitimate form of culture (Mukherjee 1992; McCaskill 1995).

Empowerment models come in different shapes. On one side of the empowerment model is the creation of culturally safe places within the existing school system. On the other side is the creation of separate schools for minority pupils, such as Aboriginal youth or youth at risk (Brown 2005). A minority-centred school provides an alternative learning environment that caters to students for whom mainstream schools are inappropriate even with thoughtful reforms (Dei 1996; Duffy 2004). For example, an Africentric or African-focused school arrangement seeks to improve academic and social achievement for students at risk by emphasizing the centrality of black experiences in social history and cultural development for those minority students who are alienated and disengaged from a Eurocentric educational system. These empowerment models—largely exemplified in proposals for black-focus schools with more black staffing and black studies—have proven controversial, as not everyone necessarily shares in the assumption that separate but equal is the appropriate multicultural path (McGuinty 2005, but Dei 2005). The next case study amplifies this point.

CASE STUDY	**Schooling with a Difference**

Islamic schools are testing the boundaries of multicultural education in Canada (Sampson 2000). Certain tenets of Islam may prove incompatible with the secular liberalism of Canada's education system. This disjunction exposes a multicultural conundrum. How can Islamic beliefs be incorporated into the school system without collapsing into chaos? How valid is a commitment to the multiculturalism in multicultural education if Islamic beliefs and practices are rejected? Does the creation of separate Islamic schools pose more of a problem or a solution for the integration of Muslim Canadian youth into Canadian society (see also Tolson 2005; Pipes 2005)?

To accommodate the religious practices and beliefs of Muslim students, some schools in Toronto have already made a number of adjustments. These include an acknowledgment that (1) students must dress modestly and cover their heads; (2) depictions of human and animal figures are inappropriate; (3) special dietary restrictions must be observed; (4) the playing of stringed instruments is prohibited; and (5) boys and girls should not be in close contact, even on group projects (Scrivener 2001). Yet problems arise when moves toward inclusiveness clash with the stricter interpretations of Islamic tenets. Equity policies on sexual orientation have proven a flashpoint for those Muslim parents who see these policies as encouraging a gay lifestyle that many perceive as contrary to their beliefs.

The dilemma is clearly evident: How does one reconcile two competing constitutional values, namely, the rights of Canadians to similar treatment because they are equal before the law versus the right to be different as implied by Canada's multiculturalism commitments? For Muslim parents, there is a double dilemma. The school system is *not* *inclusive* enough to take their differences seriously. At the same time, it is proving *too inclusive* by accommodating practices that contravene their beliefs. Islamic schools have arisen as one way of circumventing this awkward situation. According to the website **TorontoMuslims.com,** there are currently 30 Islamic schools in Toronto. Waiting lists continue to swell even though these schools tend to be short of equipment, staffed by underpaid and sometimes uncertified teachers, and supported by annual fees and volunteer help rather than government funding. As with all independent schools (in 2001, Ontario boasted about 725 independent schools, the vast majority Christian based), each school must register with the Ministry of Education, but unless they confer high school diplomas, independent schools are exempt from regulation or inspection. Teaching certificates are not required by law, though the most well-established schools may require them as a matter of policy (Scrivener 2001).

The popularity of Islamic schools reflects their demanding educational standards (see Tolson 2005). Their popularity also arises from the perception among parents that they provide a "cocoon" of safety for Muslim pupils. In providing both containment and protection within the context of an Islamic environment, the cocooning serves a dual purpose (Meadows/Bridgeview 2005). First, Muslim students are insulated from a public school system that is widely perceived as excessively secular and undisciplined. Second, by providing a cultural and religious sensitivity not available elsewhere, Islamic schools emphasize a God- and prayer-centred curriculum focused on an interplay of religion, morality, discipline, and Muslim family values.

Public reaction to these schools is mixed. For some, Islamic schools represent multiculturalism in action. They can play a critical role in fostering a new Muslim identity, one that combines being a good Muslim and a good citizen in a multicultural society (Tolson 2005). By preparing Muslim youth for their future roles as responsible citizens, the schools encourage success in mainstream society without compromising their values (Meadows/Bridgeview 2005). For others, they are contrary to the principles of multiculturalism. The point of an official Multiculturalism is not to isolate communities but to encourage sharing, exchange, and interaction. Both reactions may be right, but for different reasons. To the extent that Islamic schools are responding to a need, they exemplify a pattern of inclusiveness. To the extent that they appear to divide and separate, they run counter to the goals of an official Multiculturalism. To the extent that these schools may represent a new kind of belonging together by staying apart ("I will become a Canadian through my Islam"), they may signal the future of a multiculturalism that must take religious differences seriously as a basis for living together.

Another example of empowerment education can be seen in the struggle by Aboriginal peoples to gain control of Aboriginal education. Since the early 1970s, Aboriginal peoples have sought to implement a variety of reforms involving the need to (1) decentralize the educational structure, (2) transfer funding control to local authorities, (3) devolve power from the centre to the community, and (4) empower parents to assume increased responsibility for their children's education. Aboriginal grievances and concerns over education are understandable. Federally directed native education sought to disrupt the cultural patterns of Aboriginal children, then expose them to the values and priorities of the West, often in schools off the reserve and away from community, friends, and relatives. The rigid assimilationism and abusive consequences of residential schools have been amply documented (Miller 1999). Other consequences are less direct but no less real in denying Aboriginal experiences, as the Métis scholar Paul Chartrand (1992:8–9) says:

> It is easy to assert power over others if they are made to feel they have no identity, they have no past, or at least no past that matters.

As a corrective to these historically imposed disadvantages, the aims of Aboriginal-controlled education are bicultural. First, it seeks to impart those skills that Aboriginal children will need to succeed in the outside world. Second, it hopes to immerse children in an environment that is unmistakably Aboriginal in content, style, and outcome. The key is to produce children who possess a strong sense of who they are and where they come from, without forsaking the skills to compete in the dominant sector (Rushowy 2001).

To sum up: The introduction of multicultural education has transformed schools into much more inclusive places than in the past. Yet, multicultural education has been criticized from all sides. The right denounces it because the celebrating of differences is contrary to the goals of a "real" education that prepares children for citizenship and the marketplace. The left attacks multicultural education as hegemonic nonsense that does nothing to challenge structural inequalities. Both criticisms may be correct. However, each ignores how multicultural education has the potential to shift the very foundations of both education and society by transferring diversity to the centre of the agenda (Gay 1997). Table 11.1 provides an ideal–typical comparison of enrichment, enlightenment, and empowerment models of multicultural education along diverse criteria.

TABLE 11.1	**Styles of Multicultural Education**		
	Enrichment	**Enlightenment**	**Empowerment**
Focus	Celebrate	Analyze	Empower
Objective	Challenge prejudice	Remove discrimination	Achieve success
Goal	Celebrate diversity	Eliminate disparity	Build self-esteem
Outcome	Lifestyle ("heritage")	Life chances	Biculturalism
Means	Cultures	Race relations	Cultural renewal
Style	Experience	Understand	Immerse
Target	Students	Institution	Minority students
Scope	Individual	Interpersonal	Collectivity

ANTI-RACIST EDUCATION

Multicultural education revolves around a philosophy of diversity. It consists of activities and curricula that promote an awareness of diversity in terms of its intrinsic value to minorities and/or society at large. The aim of multicultural education is largely attitudinal, that is, to enhance sensitivity by improving knowledge about cultural differences (enrichment) and race relations (enlightenment). But there is no proof that enriched or enlightened attitudes will lead to behavioural changes.

By contrast, **anti-racist education** takes its cue from anti-racism in general: that is, a commitment to challenge, resist, and transform through direct action. Emphasis is on the identification and removal of racially discriminatory barriers at interpersonal and institutional levels both within education and outside. Anti-racist education begins with the assumption that minority underachievement is not necessarily caused by cultural differences. Nor will cross-cultural understanding contribute to any fundamental change in uprooting the structural roots of inequality (Kivel 1996). Cultural or communicative solutions are unlikely to solve structural problems. Improving minority status is contingent on removing the behavioural and structural components of racial inequality both within and outside the education system, along with the power and privileges that sustain racism through institutional policies and procedures. Sweeping changes are needed rather than tinkering with multicultural concessions.

Anti-racist education can be defined as a proactive and process-oriented approach that balances the value of difference with a sharing of power (Dei 2000). Four processes are involved: (1) critical insight into those intersecting disadvantages that students bring into the classroom; (2) an informed discourse that focuses on race and racism as issues of power and inequality rather than matters of cultural difference; (3) an interrogation of existing school practices to uncover the structural roots of monoculturalism and inequality; and (4) challenge to the status quo by fostering engagement through political and social activism (Dei 1996). Finally, anti-racist education questions the foundational principles of education. It calls into question the constitutional framework of schooling by politicizing the very basis of what passes for knowledge. The pedagogy becomes political (Giroux, 1999) when it addresses how the production of knowledge, social identities, and social relations has historically privileged some and disprivileged others. Under an anti-racist education, both students and teachers are offered the opportunity to see how culture is organized, who is authorized to speak about different forms of culture, and which

TABLE 11.2	Multicultural and Anti-Racist Education: Comparisons and Contrasts	
	Multicultural Education	**Anti-racist Education**
Focus	Culture	Structure
Objective	Sensitivity	Removal of discriminatory barriers
Concerns	Ethnocentrism	Systemic racism
Scope	Student	Institutions
Style	Accommodative	Challenge/Resist
Outcome	Understanding Equality	Promoting Equity

cultures are acceptable and which are unworthy of public esteem. They also come to understand how power operates in the interests of dominant social relations and how these unequal relations can be transformed to create an inclusive Canada. Taken together, the goal of anti-racist education is to delegitimize those Eurocentrisms and white privilege at the heart of contemporary society by "interrogating" the system of power relations that continue to deny or exclude.

In short, anti-racist education differs sharply from multicultural education. While multicultural education is merely intolerant of racism in principle, anti-racist education is resolutely opposed to racism even as a matter for debate. Anti-racist education explores how racism is historically created, symbolically expressed, and structurally sustained. It also addresses what needs to be done to challenge and transform those racist assumptions and systemic biases that inform schooling and education. These systemic biases are most apt to occur at the level of mission statement, culture and subculture, power and decision-making, structures (including rules, roles, and relationships), and distribution of financial and human assets. The table above provides a quick summary and comparison.

DEBATE REVISITED | **Restoring Aboriginal Justice**

To say that Canada's criminal justice system has experienced a profoundly troubled relationship with Aboriginal peoples is surely an understatement (Royal Commission 1996; Green 1998). For some, being processed through the criminal justice system is an intimidating and terrifying experience. Emphasis on incarceration as punishment has had a detrimental effect on those Aboriginal offenders for whom confinement is embarrassing or awkward (CCJA 2000). For others, however, their level of indifference to white justice stymies the deterrent value of prisons

(Waldram 1997). Rather than a stigma, prison time represents a badge of honour and resistance.

To circumvent this impasse, Aboriginal peoples have endorsed an alternative criminal justice system. As far as they are concerned, Canada's largely retributive criminal justice is organized around the process of determining blame and administering pain in a contest between lawyers and the state along procedural lines (Blumenthal 1999). Only the rights of the accused are involved within the context of an adversarial system where offenders are coaxed to look out for themselves by creating distance from the consequences of their actions. Both the victim and the community are largely ignored in this contested battle as crime is defined as an offence against the state. The result is a no-win situation for many. Victims and their family are deeply scarred, the offender's family is in a turmoil, the community is angered and frightened, and the social fabric is irreplaceably frayed.

Aboriginal justice initiatives have much in common with a restorative model (LaPrairie 1999). The central premise of both is a belief that crime is a violation of a relationship, and that the goal of the justice system should be to restore harmony by repairing the breach (Clairmont 2001). A punitive and adversarial style is superseded by holistic approaches that embrace the principles of community, relationships, healing, recovery, reparations, reconciliation, and atonement. Under Aboriginal justice, the victim is incorporated into the overall process, offenders take responsibility for their actions, the community closes ranks around the disruptive, and community resources are brought to bear on restoring community equilibrium. Community participation is encouraged in sentencing and supervision by way of innovative alternatives that divert the offender from courts and jail (Green 1998). Consider how sentencing circles as a sentence diversion can include the following stakeholders: the accused, their family and members of the community, community elders, and victims (Cobban 2005). The victim can express his or her pain, the group encourages the offender to understand the seriousness of the violation and the need to make some reparation to the victim, and all participants take responsibility for monitoring the follow-through. The key is simple: Aboriginal people dealing with Aboriginal people in culturally appropriate ways that may get through to the offender in ways that the court system cannot.

Differences between Aboriginal and criminal justice could not be more striking—at least in theory. These differences are captured in this pithy aphorism: With its focus on crime as violation of the law, Canada's criminal justice system asks three basic questions of a criminal act: What law was broken, who did it, and what penalty should be handed out? An Aboriginal justice approach asks: Who was harmed, what harm was done, and whose responsibility is it to make things right? Yet, despite impressive-sounding principles for healing the hurt, critics are not convinced of its effectiveness, especially in reducing the number of Aboriginal peoples in correctional institutions (La Prairie 1999; Daly 2000). On one side, Aboriginal initiatives are criticized as politically expedient strategies for conveying the impression of improvement without diminishing state control over criminal justice (Tauri 1999). On the other, Aboriginal justice principles sound good in theory but may not be effective in dysfunctional communities. Without adequate resources, in other words, specific justice programs are nothing more than quick-fix solutions to complex problems with a risk of aggravating the situation. Still, no matter how flawed Aboriginal justice is as principle or practice, compared to the travesty that exists today, almost anything would be an improvement.

CHAPTER HIGHLIGHTS

- The concept of putting multiculturalism to work is concerned primarily with engaging diversity through institutional inclusion. The media, education, and police services are but three of the institutions that must respond to a changing and diverse society.

- Institutional inclusiveness is concerned with modifying institutional structures and values to ensure the full and equal participation of all Canadians. It is also concerned with improving an organization's representation, workplace climate, operational procedures and rules, and service delivery in a multicultural society. The most common barriers to institutional accommodation are people, hierarchy, bureaucracy, corporate culture, and occupational subculture.

- Models of inclusiveness can range from those that work within the existing system (reform and minority-ization) to those that posit alternative institutional solutions (parallel and separate).

- Police–minority relations are currently experiencing a crisis. The sources of the problem are varied but invariably include problems of perception, communication, lifestyle differences, and authority patterns.

- Community-based policing is riding a popular wave at present. The principles are widely accepted, including partnership, prevention, problem-solving, and power-sharing, but have proven difficult to implement because of bureaucratic structures and occupational subcultures.

- Canada's media industry has been remiss in responding to the challenges of diversity and institutional inclusiveness. Such an omission creates problems, as the media possess the capacity for defining public discourses regarding what is acceptable, normal, and necessary.

- Recent initiatives to create an inclusive and multicultural media are to be applauded. But accommodation is slow and gradual because of numerous points of resistance at individual and institutional levels.

- Three types of multicultural education are shown to exist. Enrichment multicultural education is concerned primarily with celebrating differences. Enlightenment education is focused on informed understanding of Canadian race, ethnic, and Aboriginal relations. Empowerment education is geared toward the empowering of racial minorities and Aboriginal peoples by taking steps to overcome the monoculturalism of conventional schooling.

- Anti-racistm education differs from multicultural education. It is concerned with isolating and challenging expressions of racism and racial discrimination at personal and institutional levels through direct action.

KEY TERMS

Aboriginal justice

anti-racist education

community-based policing

institutional inclusiveness

multicultural education

REVIEW QUESTIONS

1. Compare and contrast the different models of multicultural education in terms of assumptions, objectives, and intended effects.

2. Compare and contrast anti-racist education with multicultural education with respect to focus, objectives, concerns, scope, and outcomes.

3. How are multicultural minorities and Aboriginal peoples portrayed by the media? Why? How does this present a problem in Canada's multicultural society?

4. Indicate what, if anything, can be done to improve media images of multicultural minorities and Aboriginal peoples. Keep in mind both the commercial and organizational context in which changes must occur.

5. What are the basic problems underlying police–minority relations in Canadian metropolitan regions? What steps have been taken to alleviate these problem areas?

6. What do we mean by institutional inclusiveness? What are the components of an inclusive institution? What barriers exist that may preclude the institutional inclusion of diversity?

LINKS AND RECOMMENDATIONS

Film

Two Worlds Colliding (2005). An interesting documentary by the National Film Board that focuses on the mistrust between the Saskatoon police services and the local Aboriginal community when frozen Aboriginal corpses begin to appear on the outskirts of the city.

Websites

Many of the websites listed in Chapter 10 are applicable here. Here are several other recommendations.

For media, two sites are outstanding in providing insights into how mainstream media (mis)represent minorities:

Diversity Watch
   www.diversitywatch.ryerson.ca

Media Awareness Network
   www.media-awareness.ca

For multicultural and anti-racist education, a useful overview of activities in this area is provided by the following website (click on "What's New").
   http://schoolfile.com

For community policing issues, see the COPs website sponsored by the US Department of Justice.
   www.usdoj.gov/cops

Issues of community and restorative justice for Canada's Aboriginal peoples are found at
   www.aboriginalcanada.gc.ca

THIS ADVENTURE CALLED CANADA

Rethinking Citizenship: Universal or Differentiated?

Canadians take quiet pride in themselves as citizens of a truly progressive society. Every year about 150 000 immigrants—including about 84 percent of all immigrants who eventually come to Canada—take the oath of **citizenship** as a rite of passage into this exclusive club, putting Canada at the forefront of citizenship sweepstakes (Kymlicka 2003; Tran et al. 2005; *Hamilton Spectator* 2005). But until the passage of the ***Citizenship Act*** in 1947, there was no such thing as a Canadian citizen apart from a Commonwealth context. All persons in Canada were defined as British subjects who happened to be living in Canada and who had an obligation to conduct themselves in a manner consistent with the language, culture, and identity of England. But passage of Canada's first *Citizenship Act* announced that Canada would no longer serve as

another British outpost. A new kind of belonging was proposed that reflected the realities of Canada rather than those of the United Kingdom.

The *Citizenship Act* was one of the world's first to ignore the distinction between native-born and foreign-born. Citizenship was directed at the integration of all Canadians in the hope of fostering a sense of loyalty and community among the unconnected. The boldness of this universalistic embrace cannot be underestimated. In an era when differences usually implied inferiority or exclusion, passage of the *Citizenship Act* conferred the right of inclusion to all citizens regardless of who they were or where they came from. The Act also redefined what it meant to be a Canadian, who could belong, and how they could contribute to Canada-building. Or as Paul Martin Sr. (father of former prime minister Paul Martin) said in introducing the Act, "Citizenship is the right to full participation in the fortunes and future of the nation."

Broadly speaking, citizenship entails membership in a legally constituted political community (Delanty 2000). It may be defined as a legal-social contract involving a transaction of mutual benefit between individuals/groups and the state (Hebert and Wilkinson 2002). Two dimensions inform this legal-social contract. The first is a reciprocal exchange of rights and duties. Individual citizens rely on the state to protect their rights and freedoms, while the state, in turn, expects certain obligations and responsibilities from the individual citizens. For citizens of Canada, these rights and freedoms include equality rights, democratic rights, legal rights, mobility rights, language rights, a right of return to Canada from overseas travel, freedom of religion, freedom of expression, and freedom of assembly and association. In return, Canadian citizens are obliged to obey Canadian laws, participate in the democratic process, respect the rights and freedoms of others, and recognize Canada's linguistic duality and multicultural heritage. Second, citizenship involves an explicitly defined relationship of belonging. The debate over belonging is based on who belongs, who can belong, and how citizens should belong.

Citizenship as belonging can be assigned in several ways: by blood or geneology, citizenship is restricted to those who share a common descent (Germany); by soil or territory, citizenship is open to all who were born in a certain territory (United States); by ideology, citizenship is offered to those who share values or a commitment to the rule of law (Canada); and by colonialism, citizenship is open to members of a former Empire

(Great Britain) (Castles and Miller 1998; Bell 2004). But a feature common to most citizenship regimes is its universality. A **universal citizenship** can be defined as one that treats each person the same. Each individual is entitled to the same benefits and rights—and stands in the same relation to the state—regardless of who the person is. People's differences cannot be used to exclude; by the same token their differences do not entitle them to special privileges. In privileging the priority of individual rights, a universal citizenship rejects any type of entitlement rooted in collective or group rights as contrary to the principle of equality before the law. Promotion of group differences on racial or ethnic grounds—even in the spirit of inclusiveness and progress—can only distract from the functions of citizenship, namely, to foster loyalty, unity, and identity. To be sure, special treatment may be invoked for the historically disadvantaged but only if the measures are temporary, specific to the problem, and based on need rather than race or ethnic grounds.

However enlightened for the times, the concept of universal citizenship has come under attack (Bosniak 2000; Kernerman 2005; Harty and Murphy 2005). Frameworks that may have worked in the past have proven cumbersome in addressing the highly politicized and collective claims of national minorities and indigenous peoples. In a world of migration and multiple identities, the idea of a common national citizenship seems obsolete, although others argue that increased ethnic diversity makes it more important than ever (Kymlicka 2003). Because of political, demographic, and global changes, there is growing interest in rethinking the concept of citizenship, as Hebert and Wilkinson (2002:1) write:

Citizenship is in transformation, its meaning is expanding, and interest in the subject is exploding. Citizenship has moved from being closed to being opened, from exclusion to inclusion. Once having had a unitary meaning, citizenship is now diffuse, multiple, and ever-shifting. Originally defined clearly by geographical borders and a common history, citizenship is increasingly in question . . . the transformation of citizenship is important, for it concerns who we are, how we live together, and what kind of people our children are to become.

This transformational crisis raises some provocative questions about the politics of citizenship in Canada. Is it possible to balance the particularistic demands of diversity with the unifying framework of universal citizenship? How do societies that are long accustomed to the virtues of homogeneity create a citizenship in which differences are taken seriously without sacrificing an equality before the law? Should Canada's citizenship be customized to reflect its deep diversities, or will this differentiation run the risk of rupturing national unity? Should citizenship rights be allocated to individual citizens or to members of culturally defined groups? Can a dual-type citizenship be established that incorporates different identities without dividing loyalties? Is it possible to create a citizenship (or belonging)-in-space in a global world of transnational communities and diasporic migrants (see also Kernerman 2005; Harty and Murphy 2005)? Or is Canada destined to become a space of travelling cultures and people with varying degrees of attachment and ports of convenience (Sandercock 2003)?

Responses vary. For some, everyone should have the same rights and obligations regardless of their differences. Only a unitary (universal) citizenship can perform the twin tasks of protecting Canada's national interests while ensuring protection of the fundamental rights of all loyal Canadians. For others, this one-size-fits-all unitary citizenship is not good enough for Canada's multi-layered and deeply divided context (Hebert and Wilkinson 2002; Redhead 2003). Entitlements under a "universal" citizenship often fail certain marginalized minorities because they privilege individual rights over group differences, thus ranking all individuals as similar for political purposes at the expense of their circumstances within a broader context (Schouls 1997). As well, citizenship rights need to be customized not only to accommodate differences in constitutional status, but also to acknowledge different ways of belonging to Canada. For still others, the challenge lies in creating a broader-based citizenship that incorporates the best a universal citizenship has to offer regardless of circumstances with the best a differentiated citizenship offers in addressing group differences and historical disadvantages (Kymlicka 1995, 1998, 2001).

A formidable challenge looms at present. Is it possible to redefine and expand citizenship rights so that they reflect group-specific experiences and collective aspirations without precluding a belonging to Canada? Some say yes, some say no. As a result, citizenship has evolved into a complex and multi-dimensional site of contestation with a corresponding rethinking of "what Canada is for." The Debate Revisited box, "Toward an Inclusive Citizenship: Belonging Together Differently," will provide answers.

INTRODUCTION: NEW GAME, NEW RULES, NEW ADVENTURES

[1]**Adventure, n.** daring enterprise *(Concise Oxford Dictionary)*

That we live in a period of convulsive social change is surely beyond dispute. Canada is currently in the midst of a social and demographic revolution so profound in its impact and implications that it threatens to overwhelm the moorings that formerly secured a tightly scripted society. Everything is changing so quickly that nothing is certain or predictable except a pervasive sense of confusion or uncertainty. What once were endorsed as universal truths are no longer accepted as morally valid. In rejecting traditional notions of deep diversities as incompatible with good governance, a new constitutional design based on the principles of identity, equality, and democracy is emerging that offers a principled approach to accommodating different ways of managing diversity (Magnet 2004). What once were vices are now embraced as virtues; strengths, in turn, have morphed into weaknesses as the politics of difference scuttle traditional assumptions about right and wrong. Not unexpectedly, rules of the established order do not always apply in an age of defiance and change while new rules are resisted by those whose vested interests coincide with the status quo.

The impact of this transformation has proven both disruptive and dismaying, yet liberating and empowering. In reshaping the context for living together with differences, these transformative changes require a sense of perspective. Compared to societies that are plagued by human and natural misery, Canada's relentless inspection of itself reflects the indulgence of a country that by any measure is a "solution in search of a problem." The challenge of **Canada-building** may pale in comparison to that of India with its one billion people divided into 16 official languages and five major religions. Or consider Indonesia with its 200 million people across 17 000 islands, representing 300 ethnic groups and 500 languages/dialects (Gee 1998). Still, the diversities and divisiveness of a deeply divided Canadian society pose a striking challenge. Canada's status as a multicultural/multinations country ensures its status as a "contested site" involving a lively struggle among those in constant competition over power, status, and resources. In having to cope with new rules, a new game, and new stakes, Canada is indeed at a crossroads with regard to its future.

To the extent that the rules of the established order are openly challenged and resisted, but the new order has yet to be formulated, Canada appears to be cresting the wave of a brave new adventure. This adventure called Canada-building (as a former governor general of Canada, Vincent Massey, once deftly put it) involves a series of interrelated but incomplete and competing national projects. First and foremost is the ongoing business of constructing a cohesive Canada by integrating Canadians into a moral community of citizens with a shared sense of core values, a common vision, a sense of belonging and commitment, a unifying citizenship, and a singularity of collective purpose. The challenge lies in transforming this sprawling but narrowly populated land mass into a community of communities to be nurtured and embraced rather than a treasure trove for plunder by self-serving individuals. Of equal importance to the national project is the sorting out of jurisdictions and entitlements around a three-nations model of Canada. Aboriginal demands for self-determining autonomy over land, identity, and political voice will dominate the social landscape for the foreseeable future. A parallel situation exists at the level of charter member groups, where English- and French-speaking relations continue to be driven by the politics of brinkmanship to see who blinks first. And the multicultural minorities of Canada are no less political in demanding their rightful place in Canada as different yet equal on their terms rather than someone else's (see Jenson 2002). Sorting through each of these different demand levels—and doing so simultaneously—may well prove to be the definitive challenge to Canada-building in the twenty-first century.

Developments in Canada-building often involve conflict or controversy. That much can be expected in a society where the politicization of diversity has profoundly challenged the very notion of "what Canada is for." The lurching about from one diversity crisis to another has left many Canadians confused over where to go next. For some, the prospect of a tri-national state within a multicultural framework may equip Canada with the flexibility to withstand the stresses of uncertainty and change. Others disagree, and continue to embrace attitudes inconsistent with renewal or reform. In trying to turn back the clock, they want to fortify Canada against the intrusions of a changing and diverse world. Still others fall somewhere in between. They are mentally predisposed for change but baffled by the prospect of dealing with tomorrow's problems by way of yesterday's solutions. There is mounting dismay that many of the initiatives that seemed so promising in the 1970s and 1980s—from multiculturalism to employment equity—have capitulated to a pessimism that nothing works and nobody cares (see also Kitaro 1997; Friesen 2005). With everything up for grabs, only one thing appears certain: Canada's **society-building** skills will be sorely tested in reconciling the often competing demands of unity with those of diversity in a freewheeling global market economy.

It would be folly to underestimate the magnitude of the problems confronting Canada. Group dynamics are being reshaped by the interplay of three major diversities, each with competing agendas, unique histories, distinct legal statuses, and different entitlements. Society-building in this "adventure called Canada" is complicated by factors as disparate as geography, history, regionalism, proximity to the United States, the presence of deep diversities, and the temperament of its population (Hiller 2000). Yet, there is hope in reformatting a deeply divided Canada along diversity lines. The Royal Commission on Aboriginal Peoples (1996) contained many insights, including its belief that Canada qualifies as a social experiment in proving that dissimilar peoples can share land, power, and resources while respecting and sustaining their differences. A preference for negotiated compromise may prove our lasting contribution to world peace. In the words of Professor Xavier Arbos, a Catalan and president of the International Council for Canadian Studies, "Canadians have reasons to be proud of a country that is balanced, democratic, a country that cares, where there is less violence . . ." Canada may not be perfect, he adds, but it looks a lot better than most.

We concur with this assessment, and this concluding chapter explores the possibilities for Canada at a critical juncture in its evolutionary development. The chapter will examine how this "adventure called Canada-building" is fraught with uncertainty and tension, yet full of promise and potential. Current debates over citizenship and **human rights** are shown to encapsulate many of the paradoxes and challenges in building Canada. A reassessment of Canada's so-called weaknesses as a post-national strength provides a basis for the rethinking of Canada in the new millennium. Finally, reference to the "Canadian Way" implicit within **Canada's Diversity Model** will be examined as a blueprint for living together with differences in a deeply divided society. Our conclusions are gung-ho: True, Canada is hardly perfect; nevertheless, it may be less imperfect than the rest. Moreover, Canada may possess the right kind of imperfections that will ensure its survival and prosperity in an increasingly post-national global order.

CANADA: A WORK IN PROGRESS

> Can a modern (European-based) constitution recognize and accommodate cultural diversity? This is one of the most difficult and pressing questions of the political era we are entering at the dawn of the twenty-first century. (James Tully 1995:1)

Canada sits among a handful of modern countries, including Australia and New Zealand, that are in the vanguard of constructing a coherent yet pluralistic society. Canada's status as a global trailblazer for "accommodating" diversity stems from the "atypical" way it has gone about solving its largely atypical problems (see Saul 1998). The canvas of Canada is gradually shifting from a predominantly monocultural system to one consistent with pluralist principles and postmodern realities. The transformation along pluralistic lines—including Canada as a bilingual and tri-national state within a multicultural framework—signals a departure from earlier eras when government agendas routinely privileged the superiority of majority values and dominant institutions (Magnet 2004). But a profound cultural and demographic shift has uprooted Canada's Eurocentric moorings, with a corresponding reassessment of those foundational principles that govern its constitutional order. As a result, minority women and men are cresting the wave of what Michael Adams (1997) calls a sea change in Canada's social values—from an authoritarian pyramid to a more horizontal "pancake" model anchored in pragmatism, flexibility, and openness.

The challenges confronting a diversifying and changing Canada should not be underestimated. A proliferation of divided loyalties has complicated the search for national unity—especially when national minorities envision their commitment to Canada as provisional and contingent, and consisting of claims that must be differently accommodated (Kymlicka 2001). Aboriginal peoples and minority groups are no longer willing to bide their time on the sidelines; they are actively and openly competing for recognition and resources as part of an ongoing reformulation of Canada's Aboriginal peoples–state relations. The proposed restructuring of Quebec–Ottawa relations within a renewed federalism has proven frustratingly elusive, and may not be resolved without a major rewiring of Canada's political infrastructure. But the two interdependent solitudes have such a vested interest in staying together that this mutual dependency may well yield the flexibility and compromise to shore up an awkwardly coherent Canada. The politics of Canada's multicultural agenda are no less potent. A commitment to the trifecta of cultural identity, social equality, and civic citizenship has catapulted official Multiculturalism to the forefront of strategies for engaging diversity, albeit not without criticism and backlash (Zachariah et al. 2004; Donaldson 2004; Folson 2004).

The politics of working through differences has profoundly transformed Canada (Parkin 2003; Magnet 2004). In ways unimaginable and yet inescapable, the Canada of today is much different from the country of even a generation ago, let alone the one that existed a century ago. Many of these changes are reflected and reinforced at policy levels, at institutional levels in terms of entitlements, at the level of the social climate that defines what is acceptable, and at the symbolic level with respect to images of being Canadian. Consider the following shifts in redefining Canada's evolving response to managing race, ethnic, and Aboriginal diversity:

- From assimilation as a framework for absorbing diversity to the principles of multiculturalism as a basis for living together with differences.

- From the exclusion of those who fell outside an Anglo-Canadian profile to a commitment to institutional inclusiveness regardless of race or ethnicity.

- From an intolerance of others because of race or ethnicity to an embrace of tolerance as central to Canadian identity at national and individual levels (Foster 2005).

- From an endorsement of inequality as inevitable, normal, and necessary to a commitment to the principle of equity, including the right to take people's differences into account (when necessary) for purposes of recognition and reward.

- From a government reluctance to get involved in managing race, ethnic, and Aboriginal relations to an increased micromanagement of Canada's diversity.

- From a focus on individual rights in confirming Canada as a community of citizens to a recognition of collective rights and a need for group-specific measures for true equality to kick in.

- From a focus on uniformity and standardization as key to Canada-building, including a unitary (universal) citizenship with similar rights and obligations, to the idea of customizing arrangements so that differences can be taken seriously.

- From a homogeneous and inward-looking rural Canada to a cosmopolitan and urban society that acknowledges the importance of diversity as an asset, especially in fostering global connections.

This list seems to confirm the adage that to be a Canadian is to be in constant change. However accurate, these changes do not materialize in a political and social vacuum. Rather, a combination of national and global changes tends to move the yardsticks along. Of the many changes to have impacted Canada's diversity landscape, few have resonated so fiercely as the emergence of a human rights agenda. At one time the concept of human rights was considered irrelevant to all humanity except for a few white elites. In its place is a focus on human rights not only in advancing the quality of life for all Canadians regardless of race or ethnicity, but also a discursive framework for eliminating racial discrimination around the world (Norton 2004). But as the following Insight box points out, the politics of human rights continue to provoke, in the process complicating those dilemmas that propel the unity-in-diversity dynamic.

| INSIGHT | **Contesting Human Rights** |

The Universal Declaration of Human Rights in 1948 established the principle of civil, political, economic, and cultural rights of all individuals. The declaration recognized the inherent dignity, equality, and inalienable rights of all human beings in hopes of creating a global safety net applicable to all persons regardless of race, ethnicity, origins, or creed. Different dimensions of rights and freedoms eventually came into play, including *freedoms to (right to life), freedom of (speech)*, and *freedom from (fear and want)*. Also included in the human rights package were legal rights, political rights, economic rights, and rights of national minorities to self-determination (Beitz 2001). Rather than a magnanimous gesture bestowed by benevolent authorities, these rights and freedoms were inextricably linked with human existence from which no one could be exempted or denied (Tharoor 1999/2000).

The inception and acceptance of human rights discourses have proven revolutionary in impact and implications. References to human rights have moved to the forefront of national and international affairs, with the result that these rights may now supersede even once-sacrosanct jurisdictions such as the right to state sovereignty. Political systems and the global order are increasingly organized around the once-unprecedented principle that each person has the right to belong and to be recognized, to speak and be heard (Ignatieff 2001). Not surprisingly, the doctrine of human rights has emerged as a moral touchstone that secures a standard of assessment, criticism, and reform over prevailing laws, institutions, and practices as they relate to individuals and groups (Beitz 2001).

But what seemed a relatively straightforward agenda at mid-century has revealed itself to be much more complex and contested (Sjoberg et al. 2001). According to Amnesty International, human rights abuses continue to prevail despite good intentions and international criticism of violators (Ward 2004). The first human rights codes were aimed at redressing specific instances of open and deliberate discrimination. Current human rights codes tend to be less specific than in the past, and focus instead on discrimination that is systemic and largely unconscious. That is, human rights abuses do not have to be motivated by discriminatory intent. Rather they may be attributed to policies that apply equally to everyone but have a disadvantaging impact for reasons beyond intent or awareness. Human rights are no longer about what is done to deny or exclude, but about what is not being done to prevent situations that harm or exploit others. Attainment of human rights increasingly revolves around the principle of equal outcomes rather than abstract appeals to equal opportunity. And human rights discourses are more concerned with modifying institutional structures and institutionalized power than simply changing people's attitudes.

In brief, the domain of human rights has evolved into a contested site, involving a struggle between opposing perspectives and powerful ideas. Three competing issues drive current debates: (1) human rights versus state rights, (2) individual rights versus collective rights, and (3) universality versus cultural specificity of human rights. Consider the first conflict: The relationship between the rights of sovereign states and human rights teeters on shaky ground because state sovereignty (final authority) is no longer immune from outside intervention. The United Nations can undertake armed intervention to secure human rights even in direct contravention of the foundational principle of national sovereignty that historically had underpinned international relations (Todorov 2001). Furthermore, states lose their exemption from international non-intervention when trampling on the human rights of citizens—thus allowing the possibility of external intervention in cases of gross violations.

What is the nature of individual rights versus collective rights, how do they relate to each other, and what is their relationship to the broader picture (Mendes and Lalonde-Roussy 2003)? On one side are those human rights discourses that focus primarily on protecting individual rights, and then define the nature of this relationship to the group. This commitment to individualism is anchored in the liberal foundational principle that what we have in common as individuals is more important than differences because of membership in a group—at least for purposes of recognition, relations, or reward. To the extent that collective minority rights exist, they are better seen as derivatives of the equality rights of an individual (Selva 2004). On the other side are those discourses that emphasize collective well-being as the first priority and set out individual rights accordingly. Individuals' rights are situated within the broader context of group membership in advancing a smooth-functioning social order. Individual autonomy is dismissed as a recipe for social disaster, as societies become unsustainable once the individual ceases to be subordinate to the group

(Franck 2001). The importance of the community to individual survival is acknowledged instead, as this passage by an African writer clearly reveals: "I am because we are, and because we are, therefore, I am" (cited in Tharoor 1999/2000:1).

To be sure, the distinction may be overdrawn. Most liberal-individualistic societies have proven to be more collective oriented than they would like to admit. Conversely, most collectivist orientations accommodate some degree of individualism, albeit within the broader context, that is, individualism is encouraged but any accomplishment must advance collective interests rather than personal gain. Not surprisingly, human societies have evolved mechanisms for acknowledging the compatibility of both sets of human rights. Nevertheless, the distinction between individual and collective rights is perceived to be real and animated by ongoing debates over "where to draw the line," as this excerpt forebodingly demonstrates:

> But let there be no mistake: the fight is essentially one between powerful ideas, the kind that shake the pillars of history. It is a deadly earnest conflict between an imagined world in which each person is free to pursue his or her individual potential and one in which persons must derive their identities and meanings exclusively in accordance with immutable factors: genetics, territory, and culture. (Thomas A. Franck 2001:204)

Are human rights universal and cross-culturally applicable (Teeple 2004)? Or are they specific to a particular time and place? Are universal human rights really universal or simply an extension of Western values, particularly those of individualism (Ibhawoh 2000)? Some argue for the universality of

human rights, insofar as they brook no cultural exception in transcending the specifics of any particular society. Thus, torture and inhumane practices can never be justified or excused by reference to religion or culture. Others deny the universality of human rights as all states have a sovereign right to self-define what is appropriate rather than having a Westocentric human rights package imposed on them. As Michael Ignatieff (2001:102) writes:

> Human rights doctrine is now so powerful, but also so unthinkably imperialist in its claim to universality, that it has exposed itself to serious intellectual attack. These challenges have raised important questions about whether human rights norms deserve the authority they have acquired; whether their claims to universality are justified or whether they are just another cunning exercise in Western moral imperialism.

A universal package of rights may be hegemonic. As the West can no longer dominate through direct imperialism, the universalizing language of human rights has emerged as a way of co-opting foreign cultures into a Western sphere of influence. Rather than self-evident, universal, culture-free, and race-neutral, the concept of human rights reflects the Eurocentric experiences and liberal aspirations of the rich and the powerful. The conclusion? Universal human rights may exist, but universality should not be confused with uniformity, nor should American exceptionalism pose as global universalism. It remains to be seen if a truly universal package of human rights can be constructed that transcends the specifics of any society while embracing the universality of all humankind.

CANADA'S DIVERSITY MODEL: THE CANADIAN WAY

Canada a good model for other countries, Chief Judge tells Israel (*National Post*, 20 December 2000).

Greeks laud Canada's multicultural success (*Toronto Star*, 13 November 2000).

Canada hailed as a model for the twenty-first century (*Toronto Star*, 10 August 1998).

We have established a distinct Canadian Way, a distinct Canadian model: Accommodation of cultures. Recognition of diversity. A partnership between citizens and the state. (Jean Chrétien, June 2000, cited in Canadian Heritage 2000)

Each of these excerpts confirms what many Canadians intuitively know yet rarely articulate. Canada is widely regarded both nationally and internationally as a world leader when it comes to constructively engaging diversity. Canada's experiment in accommodating diversity has resulted in nearly 140 years of relatively peaceful coexistence with three competing national groups and increasingly politicized multicultural minorities (Kymlicka 2004; Selva 2004; also in Bickerton and Gagnon 2004). Canada provides a model for "living together with differences" for those countries that are also grappling with issues of immigration, multiculturalism, equity initiatives, and ethnic nationalisms. Questions arise: What do we mean by Canada's Diversity Model: Is it a commitment? A process? Content? Strategy? Is reference to the Canadian Diversity Model meant to reflect reality, or does it point to a set of ideals to strive for? Despite uncertainties and confusion, Canada's Diversity Model is being promoted as a solution to the key challenge of the new millennium: How to allow for the different ways of accommodating diversity in deeply divided societies without capitulating to chaos?

Canada's Diversity Model revolves around its distinctive proposals for engaging diversity. It is modelled around Canada's willingness to recognize three mutually exclusive yet principled policy platforms for simultaneously accommodating different ways of belonging to Canada, namely, recognition of Aboriginal peoples, linguistic and cultural duality, and multiculturalism (Jenson and Papillon 2001). The Diversity Model is also forged out of the tensions and choices implicit in competing values: uniformity vs. diversity; individual rights vs. group rights; formal equality (symmetry or equal treatment) vs. substantive equality (asymmetry or special treatment); and personal freedom vs. national security. To be sure, as Jenson and Papillon observe, tensions within this model may well perpetuate inequities, discrimination, intolerance, blind spots, or perversely unintended consequences. Nevertheless, the challenge for Canada's Diversity Model is to balance these fundamental yet opposed values in a way that most Canadians find acceptable, that provide a blueprint for living together across deep differences, and that consolidate the centre without undermining the integrity of the parts (McRoberts 2003).

Canada's Diversity Model is about accommodating different ways of accommodating diversity. At one level are Aboriginal peoples' claims to be sovereign peoples with rights of self-determining autonomy over land, identity, and political voice (Anderson and Barnett 2006). A corresponding constitutional structure is proposed whose foundational principles promote a partnership based on a government-to-government relationship. To the extent that Canada is grappling with decolonizing its relationship with the First Nations, the contours of a new post-colonial social contract are taking shape. The second level addresses the concerns of the Québécois who, like Aboriginal peoples, claim to be sovereign in principle. Québécois demands pivot around putting this principle into practice in a way that acknowledges a compact view of

Canada, Quebec's status as a distinct society, and Québécois' demands to be masters of their own house (Gagnon et al. 2003). English-speaking Canada appears to be moving in the direction of a more flexible federalism, one that recognizes Quebec as more than a province but less than a separate nation-state, although there is reluctance to constitutionally entrench this shift for fears of blowing the fictions that paper over Canada's contradictions. At the third level, Canada's Diversity Model acknowledges the rights of Canada's immigrant and multicultural minorities to be different yet the same without paying a penalty in the process (James 2005; but also Abu-Laban and Gabriel 2002; Barry 2001). The combination of initiatives from anti-racism to employment equity reinforce the notion of Canada as a society of many cultures in which people's cultural differences cannot preclude full participation and equal citizenship rights as a matter of course, while still acknowledging that differences may have to be taken into account when necessary.

At the heart of Canada's Diversity Model is the concept of the Canadian Way. The Canadian Way may mean a lot of things, depending on the speaker, context, or intended audience. But certain patterns can be discerned that define the Canadian Way as a *commitment (or content)* and a *process*. First as commitment: The **Canadian Way** is commonly used to articulate a commitment to the principles of *diversity* and *inclusiveness*. The Canadian Way is based on the idea that it is possible to create a prosperous and cohesive Canada by incorporating a diversity dividend into the national agenda. A principled commitment to diversity in no way erodes an equally strong attachment to national unity and respect for core Canadian values.

> Canada's approach to diversity is based on the belief that the common good is best served when everyone is accepted and respected for who they are, and that this ultimately makes for a resilient, more harmonious, and more creative society. This faith in the value of diversity recognizes that respect for cultural distinctiveness is intrinsic to an individual's sense of self-worth and identity, and a society that encourages achievement, participation, attachment to country and a sense of belonging. (Canadian Heritage 2001)

An endorsement of diversity is synonymous with inclusiveness. References to the Canadian Way often imply the importance of inclusiveness to ensure that all Canadians participate fully and equally regardless of their racial or ethnic background. According to an inclusiveness line of thinking, people can be different without differences standing in the way of participation or equality. Differences may be important in an age of identity politics, in other words, but these differences should never be used as an excuse to deny or exclude. The inclusiveness principle includes the notion of a universal citizenship. Citizenship rights apply to all Canadians, whether foreign or native-born. Anyone can become naturalized as a citizen as long as one subscribes to a set of ideals and rules of law.

Canadians have also constructed a principled process to meet the evolving challenges of diversity (Kymlicka 2001). The Canadian Way refers to those mechanisms and arrangements that are in place to facilitate engagement and community without violating individual rights and national interests. Two ingredients are important in fostering an appropriate process. First, there must be a society-wide commitment to the principle of agreeing to disagree so that differences of opinion can be articulated, discussed, and adjusted accordingly. Second, the process of negotiated compromise requires an institutionalized structure that creates relatively open lines of communication. Or as Will Kymlicka (2000: A-15) writes in defending process as the heart of the Canadian Way:

> Canada has a legal framework for discussing issues of diversity. Policies of multiculturalism, federalism, and Aboriginal rights give the relevant groups a seat at the table and constitutional

legitimacy to their identities and interests. Many countries have no framework for the majority and minority to sit down and discuss how to live together.

Together, then, reference to the Canadian Way connotes the pragmatic ways in which Canadians go about solving the challenge of diversity in a multi-layered and deeply divided society. Canada's strength lies in working through problems rather than in having solutions unilaterally imposed by decree. Structures are in place so that working through disagreements can be resolved through negotiation and compromise instead of a rigid dogmatism. Admittedly, references to the Canadian Way tend to overstate Canada's strength in the diversity sweepstakes while understating its weaknesses in engaging diversity. The most egregious expressions of colonialism in Canada have been eradicated, to be sure, but the Canadian Way is silent about challenging the foundational principles that govern Canada's constitutional order. Despite lip service to diversity, there remains a refusal or incapacity to take differences seriously because of costs and consequences. Yes, Aboriginal self-government is in place, but not Aboriginal *models* of self-determining autonomy. Nor is there much enthusiasm about engaging aboriginality or the Québécois seriously as a fundamentally autonomous political community, both sovereign yet sharing sovereignty. The implementation of the principle of inclusion may reflect the practice of multiculturalism, but only in a very narrow sense of "non-white" faces within the existing framework of rules, structures, and priorities. Inasmuch as the foundational rules upon which conventions and practices are based remain intact, much remains to be done in creating a new Canada for coping with the realities of the twenty-first century.

TOWARD A POST-NATIONAL CANADA

The world is engulfed by two mutually exclusive yet inextricably linked forces (Nelson and Fleras 1998). On the one hand are the universalizing (and homogenizing) forces of a free-wheeling global market economy. Transnational movements of goods and services are conducted with little regard for societal boundaries. Advances in information technology tend to render national borders increasingly porous and difficult to monitor and control. On the other hand, the fragmenting forces of insurgent ethnic nationalisms are poised to dismember and destroy. Radical ethnicities and ethnic nationalisms appear to be largely indifferent to the legitimacy of the nation-state, preferring instead a commitment to challenge, resist, and transform (Ignatieff 2005). This interplay of centrifugal ("push out") and centripetal ("pull in") forces promises to reshape the political contours of societies large and small, in the process contesting the concept of "what society is for."

On balance, Canada appears to have been relatively successful in balancing these global forces with national interests and minority rights, even if the juggling act tends to be wobbly at times. Such an achievement is not to be sneered at because of the challenges for Canada-building. "Canada is not a real country," Lucien Bouchard taunted English-speaking Canadians, but a society of shreds and patches. Unlike the more **completed (or civilizational) societies** of Europe (Castles and Miller 1998), Canada *is* an idea and a set of ideals rather than a peoples with a history, language, and culture, and it is this fundamental ambiguity that underscores the contradictions in Canada-building. Others agree. Jody Berland, writing in *Border/Lines,* points to Canada as an excuse waiting to happen. There is no real political, economic, or cultural reason to justify Canadian society, nationality, or identity. Canadians have little in common—no common language, no shared ancestors or genetic pool, no origin myths, and few common rituals—except a commitment to public institutions such as universal health care. Or rephrased, Canada is not so much a mosaic as a complex matrix of defining lines and contested angles in response to the demands of multiple identities and competing sovereignties under a single polity.

This assessment of Canada as all "lines" and "angles" may not flatter. Yet, these very vulnerabilities may yield a host of possibilities for a new kind of Canada. That is, Canada may be poised on the brink of becoming the world's first post-national society. Consider the contrasts: A "national" society is based on the principles of modernism, with its commitment to a master narrative (uniformity), a coherent state identity (standardization), centrality (to ensure conformity and control), and the convergence of a nation (peoples) with the state as a basis for society-building. By contrast, a post-national society reflects the postmodernist principle of "doing things differently." By challenging the rules upon which the conventional is based rather than simply the practices that refer to the rules (Angus 2002), a post-national society incorporates those conflicting allegiances and multiple identities that transcend national boundaries or elude state attempts to standardize (Dijkstra et al. 2001). Moreover, according to the post-national camp, it is futile or repressive to aspire to modernist goals of structure, coherence, centralized authority, hierarchy, and common citizenship in an era of transnationalism and diasporic dispersion where people no longer identify exclusively with one country rather than another, preferring instead multiple and intersecting identities that are activated as the situation arises (Handa 2003). In place of uniformity and centredness is a sense of impermanence and mutability in a radically skeptical world where everything is relative and contested because nothing is absolute and definitive (Gwyn 1996; see also Bauerlein 2001).

Under a post-nationalism, then, traditional criteria for defining a nation-state are contested, including the goal of matching territory with culture, identity, a peoples, and history. Society is defined as an ongoing social construction rather than something natural or normal, a convention created by individuals and groups who make choices and take chances albeit under circumstances not of their making—as this quote nicely conveys:

> Canada is a kind of model for the 21st century, in which a nation defines itself not as a piece of geography or a race of people but as a political and cultural and existential concept. (John Gray, cited in Whittington 1998; for similar comments see Tibbetts 2000 and Canadian Press 2000)

Advocated instead is a new game with a different set of rules that often invert conventional ways of belonging, identity, and unity. Weaknesses become strengths under a post-nationalism; conversely, strengths may prove to be weaknesses in contexts of diversity, change, and uncertainty as nation-state power is eroded by global capital. Consider the restructuring of the relationship between the margins and the centre. Instead of a definitive centre that categorically defines and controls, Canada is constructed around a society-building process that is diverse and evolving, is subject to negotiation and compromise, and is sufficiently flexible to include all Canadians—at least in theory if not always in practice.

In short, a rewriting of the rules for living together allows Canada to claim status as the world's first post-national society (see also Gwyn 1994, 1996). The lightness of being that is associated with Canada's post-nationalism may provide a prototype for the ideal twenty-first century society by the simple expedient of transforming weaknesses into strengths because of shifting circumstances. This statement by a former prime minister reinforces the idea that what once was a liability is now an asset:

> Canada has become a *postnational* [emphasis added], multicultural society. It contains the globe within its borders, and Canadians have learned that their two international languages and their diversity are a comparative advantage and a source of continuing creativity and innovation. Canadians are, by virtue of history and necessity, open to the world. (Jean Chrétien, June 2000, cited in Canadian Heritage 2001)

Other inversions also contribute to Canada's post-nationality. The fact that Canada represents a political union born out of economic necessity rather than a national spirit or violent struggle may work in its favour. The endless debates over power and jurisdictions may have morphed into a kind of glue for binding Canadians together by defining who we are. To be sure, debates over Canada's unity and identity question may perplex and provoke, even infuriate those who live it on a daily basis. But the paradox of a rolling Canadian identity provides a resiliency and flexibility that avoids being locked into the rigidities of a "completed society" (see Castles and Miller 1998). This tension-to-be-negotiated-rather-than-a-problem-to-be-solved mentality may have also contributed to Canada's reputation as an open and tolerant society, with a commitment to accommodate different ways of accommodating diversity (Saul 1998).

Put bluntly, in a world of diversity, uncertainty, and change, Canada's atypicalness may be its strength. Canada's seeming vulnerability—its decentralized unity and diversity-based identity—may prove a tower of strength in a world where rigidity and authority are incompatible with the freewheeling demands of the global market economy and international movement of people and ideas (Erickson 1997). Perhaps this penchant for snatching virtue from vice defines and distinguishes Canadians in promoting post-nationalist ways of living together with difference in a deeply divided and multi-layered Canada. Canadians may well possess the kind of temperament best suited for the postmodern realities of the twenty-first century, namely, a dedication to pragmatism, a commitment to civility and tolerance, and a willingness to compromise for the sake of the whole. In a world where rules and conventions are being turned inside out, Canada's threshold for uncertainty and tolerance of ambiguity may provide just the right amount of resilience to bend, not break. In a world where a passionate attachment to homeland or culture may maim or destroy, its redemption may reside in a willingness to "cut some slack" when necessary. In renegotiating the meaning of Canadianness by way of rights, principles, obligations, and rules of engagement (MacQueen 1994), this lightness of being is quintessentially Canada, and is nicely captured by Edward Greenspon (2001):

> Increasingly, we are cultural Canadians: Canadian by willpower rather than by policy. We feel attached to Canada because we like the smell of it. It is an affair of the heart. The process is ephemeral, not mechanical, but no less real. Get used to it. We live in an age of intangibles, and our love of country is as intangible as it is profound.

The conclusion is inescapable: Canadian society remains a work in progress. It may not be a real country in the completed sense of the term, but rather an ongoing project that must be continually willed into action. As a social construction of ideas and ideals—a space of travelling cultures—Canada cannot rest on its laurels, but must always define, modify, and change in line with changing circumstances (see also Sandercock 2003). That it has managed to transform this inconclusiveness into contemporary strengths must surely say something about the people and their society. In other words, Canada is not perfect yet it appears to have just the right kind of imperfections to provide it with the resources and resourcefulness to meet the challenges of an increasingly post-national global era. The words of Adrienne Clarkson, the former Governor General of Canada, seem especially reassuring:

> It's a strength and not a weakness that we are a permanently incomplete experiment built on a triangular foundation—aboriginal, francophone, and anglophone. What we continue to create today, began 450 years ago as a political project . . . It is an old experiment, complex, and, in worldly terms, largely successful. Stumbling through darkness and racing through light, we have persisted in the creation of a Canadian civilization. (7 October 1999, cited in Canadian Heritage 2001)

| DEBATE REVISITED | **Toward an Inclusive Citizenship: Belonging Together Differently** |

The principle of unity within diversity is central to Canada's official Multiculturalism. But this multicultural mantra is not without problems. Too much unity can exclude or stifle; too much diversity can divide or dismember. This paradox is captured in debates over citizenship. Proponents of a universal citizenship square off with advocates of differentiated citizenship in defining a preferred style for belonging in Canada.

For many liberal thinkers, the promotion of universal citizenship is critical. Equality and progress stem from the renunciation of differences to ensure that everyone is equal before the law. For others, however, the opposite is true. We no longer live in a society that can be defined or understood in terms of one group, one identity, one culture, or one territory (Hebert and Wilkinson 2002). To the contrary, identities today are openly and politically plural, each person belonging to many different groups and defining themselves in terms of these multiple affiliations without necessarily placing these belongings in a hierarchical order. And just as Canada allows dual (even triple) citizenship and allegiances at the same time (Hurst 2005), so can Canadians take advantage of such crossings and connections to embrace specific affiliations without rejecting a commitment to commonalities. Moreover, recognition of group-specific special needs is central to social equality and national unity. As Iris Marion Young (1990) has argued, a universal conception of citizenship is unfair when applied to unequal contexts. The unfairness arises from treating all citizens—regardless of race, class, or gender—as individuals in the abstract rather than as disadvantaged members of real groups.

Proposed instead of a universal citizenship is a **differentiated citizenship** that addresses the varied demands of national minorities, Aboriginal peoples, and the historically disadvantaged (Harty and Murphy 2005). Four types of differentiated citizenship models can be discussed—equity, multicultural, self-determining, and post-national (or cosmopolitan)—each of which reflects a reading of Canada as a multi-layered and deeply divided diversity. According to this line of thinking, people who identify with minority groups *are* different and require a different set of citizenship rights as a basis for a respectful belonging. Both Aboriginal peoples and national minorities such as the Québécois have different needs, aspirations, status, and experience; thus citizenship rights must be customized accordingly. Similarly, those who have been historically disadvantaged because of their differences may also require an adjustment in citizenship. Finally, the emergent realities of globalization, increased mobility, and new communication technologies may define yet another pattern of belonging.

Equity Citizenship Rights: Racialized minorities are underrepresented in many parts of Canadian society. Equity citizenship rights are aimed at improving institutional access and representation while facilitating their integration into society.

Multicultural Citizenship Rights: Both racial and cultural minorities may require some degree of official protection of their ethnocultural heritage. Membership in a living and lived-in cultural reality is critical for personal well-being by providing individuals with meaningful choices to maximize freedom (Kymlicka 1992; 2004).

Self-Determining Citizenship Rights:
Another type of citizenship right applies to Aboriginal peoples and the Québécois. As peoples or nations (national communities), their demands as citizens go beyond universal citizenship to include claims upon the state for control over land, culture/language, and identity; the right to self-government and jurisdiction over matters of direct relevance; and a transfer of power from central authorities (devolution) rather than mere political representation or institutional accommodation (Kymlicka 1992).

Post-national Citizenship Rights:
Post-national citizenship refers to the possibility of dual or even multiple citizenships, both concurrently and without contradiction. The theory of a post-national (or transnational) citizenship in a global era is predicated on three realities: the eroding sovereignty of states; less constraining geography because of technology; and the capacity of people to maintain multiple links (Delanty 2000). In an age of migration where up to 170 million people may be on the move at any time and connections are a mouse click away, new patterns of belonging may reflect loyalty to the home country and the adopted country (Kymlicka 2003). Immigrants may have traditionally discarded the old by severing ties with the homeland and embracing the new, but the context for multiple identities and transnational belongings allows the maintenance of traditional ties because of return migration (Castles and Miller 1998). In short, in a freewheeling global era of diasporic communities, there are clear and unequivocal advantages to being able to operate in multiple cultural codes and traverse cultural spaces by way of post-national citizenships (Suarez-Orozco and Suarez-Orozco 2001).

However well it may be suited for the realities of the twenty-first century, a differentiated citizenship is not without its faults. First, on principle: For critics, citizenship differentiated into "this" and "that" cannot possibly fulfill its basic function of creating shared loyalty, common identity, and patriotic commitment. Without the shared values of a universal (common) citizenship, there is a danger of society splintering into a series of fractured communities, with virtually nothing to hold them together. A differentiated citizenship, with its special and collective rights, undermines a common culture and those unifying symbols for bonding citizens into a single framework. Besides, critics argue, reference to a differentiated citizenship is seen as unCanadian as it (1) treats some as more equal than others, (2) elevates special group rights over individual rights, and (3) undermines the legitimacy of the political community at large. Second, in practice: Specifying certain minorities for special citizenship entitlements raises questions about who is entitled to the largest concessions and why. Can a differentiated citizenship right be applied to groups that are dispersed or partially assimilated? Are special citizenship rights to last only as long as groups experience marginality, then removed when no longer required?

Let's put this debate into perspective by way of key questions: How should Canada respond to increased diversity and cosmopolitan citizens—by promoting more consensus through a universal citizenship or by acknowledging diversity through a differentiated citizenship (Kymlicka 2003)? Is a unitary citizenship appropriate for a country that espouses a people's right to be different yet the same? How can a universal citizenship address the key dimension of Canada's Diversity Model: that is, accommodating different ways of accommodating diversity in Canada? Can a differentiated citizenship generate sufficient "centre" to hold Canada together or will it encourage a splintering of Canada into bits too disparate to connect? Is it possible to reconcile the principle of belonging as an individual citizen (as promulgated by a unitary citizenship) with that of belonging to Canada via group membership (as implied by a differentiated citizenship)? Is it possible to construct a model of an inclusive Canadian citizenship that takes differences seriously while fostering commonalities (Hebert and Wilkinson 2002)?

The concept of an "inclusive" citizenship emphasizes the validity of both universal and differentiated citizenship rights. In visualizing citizenship as a rope of interwoven strands, one of these strands emphasizes universal citizenship rights with respect to individual equality and similar treatment. Another strand focuses on those citizenship rights that take differences seriously, and acknowledges the need to take differences into account for meaningful equality. This unity-in-diversity balancing act will prove extremely difficult, as Ruth Lister (1997:66) concludes, since neither is sufficient in its own right but requires the other to complete it:

> [R]ejecting the "false universalism" of traditional citizenship theory does not mean abandoning citizenship as a universalist goal. Instead, we can aspire to a universalism that stands in creative tension to diversity and difference and that challenges the divisions and exclusionary inequalities which can stem from diversity.

Is Canada ready for a formally articulated **inclusive citizenship**? Not every Canadian will be comfortable with the notion of citizenship as (1) overlapping and situational, (2) inclusive of differences yet united in purpose, (3) responsive to both individual and collective group rights, and (4) allowing a primary affiliation with the whole while retaining membership in subnational units without fear of contradiction. But like it or not, approve or disapprove, the future of a post-national Canada is contingent on customizing different models of belonging. This is no time to impose the modernist notion of a unitary Canadian citizenship, with a dash of multicultural colour thrown in for good measure. A one-size-fits-all citizenship is unlikely to appeal in a deeply divided and multi-tiered Canada where some want to "get in" while others want to "get out." Yes, it will take time to convince Canadians that people are alike in different ways yet different in similar ways. Yet, acceptance of this seeming paradox will prove critical in advancing the post-national goal of belonging differently together without drifting apart.

CHAPTER HIGHLIGHTS

- Canada can be envisaged as a work in progress with respect to managing race, ethnic, and Aboriginal relations. While the project remains unfinished (as one might expect of a journey with no goal), Canada has evolved from an intolerant and exclusive British colony to a post-national society based on the principles of living together with our differences.

- Conventional ways of thinking about citizenship (universal citizenship) are being challenged by the concept of differentiated citizenship rights. An inclusive citizenship seeks to combine the unitary with the customized as a basis for living together across a deeply divided Canada.

- Debates over the issue of human rights raise the question of universality versus relativism, state versus individual rights, and collective versus individual rights.

- Canada's Diversity Model and the Canadian Way are widely touted as Canada's main contribution to co-operative coexistence, in large part by acknowledging the challenges of accommodating different ways of accommodating diversity rather than relying on a single one-size-fits-all standard.

- Canadians possess a relatively high threshold for ambiguity and change because of historical precedents. Such flexibility not only allows weaknesses to be transformed into strengths but also may secure Canada's status as the world's first post-national society.

KEY TERMS

Canada-building
Canada's Diversity Model
Canadian Way
citizenship
Citizenship Act, 1947
completed (or civilizational) societies

differentiated citizenship
human rights
inclusive citizenship
society-building
universal citizenship

REVIEW QUESTIONS

1. One of the key themes in this chapter is the notion that Canada has been able to transform weaknesses into strengths. Describe what is meant by this, and provide several examples of snatching virtue from vice at the level of Canada-building.

2. What are some of the central issues at the heart of the debate over human rights?

3. Compare and contrast the different types of citizenship that are brought to bear in living together with our differences.

4. What do you think is meant by the expression "Canada's Diversity Model"? How does the notion of the Canadian Way fit into this model?

5. Evidence suggests that Canada may be advantageously positioned to redefine itself as the world's first post-national society. Comment on what constitutes a post-national society and how Canada appears to fit this model.

LINKS AND RECOMMENDATIONS

Books

Tariq Modood. *Multicultural Politics*. University of Minnesota Press, 2005.

Alan C. Cairns et. al. *Citizenship, Diversity, and Pluralism*. McGill-Queen's University Press, 2000.

S. Harty and M. Murphy. *In Defence of Multicultural Citizenship*. UBC Press, 2005.

Websites

The official website for Citizenship and Immigration in Canada
   www.cic.gc.ca

For a review of the *Citizenship Act* in Canada and for Canada's Human Rights
   http://laws.justice.gc.ca

For a general overview of citizenship and diversity and for more on Canada's Diversity Model, see Jenson and Papillon's article.
   www.pch.gc.ca

All prospective citizens of Canada must answer 20 multiple choice questions—do you think you could pass the test? Check it out.
   www.v-soul.com

The official site for Canada's Human Rights
   http://laws.justice.gc.ca

For the activities and rulings of the Human Rights Commission, see:
   www.chrc-ccdp.ca

If your interest lies in the notion of Canada as a post-national society, the *International Journal for Canadian Studies*, vol. 25, 2002, might be useful.
   www.iccs-ciec.ca

For more on Canada's Diversity Model, see Jenson and Papillon's article.
   www.pch.gc.ca

Glossary

Aboriginality   Used in a descriptive sense, aboriginality describes the principle by which a shared awareness of original occupancy provides Aboriginal peoples with recognition (identity), reward (action), and relationships (community). In a political sense, appeals to aboriginality involve the politics of transformative change that not only challenge the legitimacy of the sovereign state as the paramount authority but also advance innovative patterns of belonging that embody the post-sovereign notion of a nation-state. *See also* Aboriginal peoples, Aboriginal rights, and Aboriginal self-governance.

Aboriginal justice   Unlike conventional criminal justice systems, which tend to focus on punishing individuals through the state, Aboriginal justice embraces the need to restore harmony in the community (restorative justice) by involving all stakeholders in dealing with the problem and providing a solution.

Aboriginal peoples   Aboriginal peoples represent the descendants of the original (indigenous) occupants of Canada who have been colonized and forcibly incorporated into Canadian society, but now claim to have a right to Aboriginal models of self-determining autonomy over land, identity, and political voice. *See also* Aboriginality.

Aboriginal "indigenous" rights   The entitlements that Aboriginal peoples have by virtue of their original occupancy of the land. These rights are unique to Aboriginal peoples, secure the basis for rewards, recognition, and relationships, and include the right to Aboriginal models of self-determining autonomy over jurisdictions related to land, identity, and political voice. *See also* Aboriginal peoples, Aboriginality.

Aboriginal self-governance   Aboriginal peoples insist they have a right to govern themselves in a way that reflects their realities, reinforces their experiences, and advances their interests. *See also* Governance, Self-government.

Aboriginal title   A constitutional awareness that Aboriginal peoples own those lands and resources that they have occupied continuously for centuries. The Crown cannot encroach upon those lands that have not been lawfully surrendered by way of treaty or negotiation.

Androcentrism   A tendency for men to see the world from their point of view as normal and necessary (and superior); to assume that others are seeing the world in the same way; and to dismiss other perspectives as inferior or irrelevant.

Angloconformity   An expectation that minorities outwardly conform to the beliefs and practices of mainstream (British) society. *See also* Assimilation.

Anti-racism   A commitment to identify, isolate, and challenge racism in all its forms through direct action at individual and institutional levels.

Anti-racist education   An educational discourse and practice that seeks to challenge and transform the behaviour and structures that continue to uphold power imbalances within and outside the school system.

Assimilation   A complex and dynamic process in which minorities begin to lose their distinctiveness through absorption into dominant society. As policy or political framework, assimilation can refer to those formal government initiatives for absorbing minority populations into the mainstream. *See* Anglo-conformity.

Asylum seeker   A person who flees one country and seeks refuge and protection in another country by claiming refugee status.

Bilingualism   Bilingualism entails the coexistence of two languages at *territorial*, *institutional*, or *individual* levels. Canada is officially bilingual at institutional levels, but of the 10 provinces and 2 territories, only New Brunswick is. Approximately 16 percent of all Canadians regard themselves as bilingual speakers.

Bill 101   The Bill that became the 1977 *French Language Charter,* which made French the official language of Quebec.

Canada as a coalition   A view of Canada as a partnership involving at least three nations: the French-speaking, the English-speaking, and Aboriginal peoples.

Canada as a compact   A view of Canada as a covenant (special relation) between Quebec and the rest of Canada instead of a contract of federal and provincial subunits. According to the compact vision, the Québécois are not an ethnic minority or even a province, but a distinct people with a common homeland, culture, language, and identity whose status is equivalent to that of the English as a founding (charter) group. *See also* Charter groups/members.

Canada as a contract   A view of Canada as a contract between the federal authorities and 10 equal provinces. No province can expect more entitlements than other provinces because of this contract.

Canada-building   *See* Society-building.

Canada's Diversity Model   Widely regarded as a progressive model for managing different levels of diversity at the same time, the Diversity Model acknowledges the need for customizing policy and programs to meet the distinctive aspirations and concerns of each of Canada's three major diversities: Aboriginal peoples, the Québécois, and multicultural minorities. *See also* Canadian Way.

Canadian Charter of Rights and Freedoms When it came into effect in 1985, the Charter constitutionally entrenched the right of individuals to be free from state-based discrimination on irrelevant grounds. The concept of collective rights was also endorsed as a reasonable limitation on individual rights when taking into account both national interests and specific realities.

Canadian Way   A discourse that espouses Canada's commitment to diversity (content) and dialogue (process) as a model for living together with differences. *See also* Canada's Diversity Model.

Capitalism   An economic (and social) system organized around the rational pursuit of profit.

Charter groups/members   The 1867 *British North America Act* (now *Constitution Act*) acknowledged and enshrined the rights of the French and English settlers/colonizers as the foundational members (or **charter members**) of Canadian society, with the right to establish agendas and set priorities.

Citizenship   A contract establishing a reciprocal exchange of rights and duties between a person and the state in which he or she lives. Citizenship has historically revolved around the concept of treating everyone equally through conferral of similar rights and obligations, but awareness is growing for different kinds of belonging without sacrificing loyalty to the whole. *See also* Inclusive citizenship.

Citizenship Act, 1947   Passage of this Act in 1947 established citizenship as something distinctively Canadian in terms of identity and rights, thereby replacing the earlier notion that Canadians were British subjects.

Civic multiculturalism   The current emphasis on Canada's Multiculturalism policy focuses on the language of inclusion by way of citizenship, belonging, and participation.

Civic nationalism   A contested term usually employed to indicate state initiatives in building a cohesive society, civic nationalism is concerned with creating a society that entails a community of individuals who belong together by virtue of (1) possessing equal rights, (2) a common loyalty to shared values, rule of law, and institutions, and (3) a willingness to live together in a spirit of live and let live.

Class   An aggregate of persons who occupy a similar status or stratum in society because of similarities in power, wealth, or status. Marxists see class as the division of society because of people's relationship to the means of production and private property. Those of a Weberian bent see class as a complex interplay of factors such as wealth, power, and prestige, not all of which coincide, in effect leading to different class systems, including a division of society into the always popular categories of upper, middle, and lower class.

Collective definition   A distinct if somewhat underutilized approach to the study of race and ethnicity, collective definition endorses a view of race and ethnic relations as dynamic and contested, involving competing sectors within both the dominant and subdominant groups, each of which defines the situation differently and acts accordingly. *See also* Dualism.

Colonialism   A specific era of European expansion and settlement on so-called unused or underutilized lands. European powers forcibly exploited indigenous peoples by appropriating land and resources, extracting wealth, and capitalizing on cheap labour, while invoking racial doctrines to justify and explain the colonization of indigenous peoples.

Community-based policing   A philosophy and set of practices by which police services share power and work as partners with members of the community to prevent crime.

Completed (or civilizational) society   A term used to described the settled countries of Europe. With respect to institutions, cultural heritage, and people, European societies are defined as finished projects, with a corresponding rejection of immigration as key to society.

Comprehensive land claims   A modern-day equivalent of nineteenth-century treaty agreements in which the Crown acquired certainty of ownership over large blocks of Aboriginal land in exchange for rights to smaller sections of land, allocation of services, money, and goods, and access to Crown land resources. These newer treaties tend to include protocols for establishing Aboriginal self-governing arrangements as well as rights to co-manage arrangements and revenue-sharing from resource extraction.

Conditional autonomy   Aboriginal self-governance must be consistent with Canada's constitutional framework and *Charter of Rights and Freedoms*, cannot threaten Canada's territorial integrity, and must improve the participation of Aboriginal peoples in Canada.

Conflict theory   Based on the idea that societies are sites of inequality, with the result that confrontation, competition, and change are inevitable when diverse groups compete for scarce resources in contexts that favour some groups and not others. *See also* Internal colonialism.

Consensus multiculturalism   Canada's official Multiculturalism is not driven by the principles of challenge or change, but instead focuses on the smoother integration of new and racialized Canadians into the existing social and political framework. Also known as integrative or inclusive multiculturalism. Compare with critical multiculturalism.

Constitutional order   A tacitly assumed framework for the principled distribution of power in society. Those foundational principles that govern the social, political, and economic order of society operate at relatively high levels of generality and often are beyond examination or criticism. *See also* Governance, Aboriginal self-governance.

Constructive engagement   A new (postcolonial) social contract for redefining the relationship of Aboriginal peoples to society at large. Constructive engagement is premised on the notion of Aboriginal peoples as fundamentally autonomous political communities who are sovereign in their own right while sharing sovereignty over society. *See also* Postcolonial social contract, Aboriginality.

Constructivist explanation   A perspective that seeks to explain ethnicity by reference to its socially constructed character. That is, there is nothing real, natural, or inevitable about ethnicity; it is a social convention created by individuals who make meaningful choices, albeit not within contexts of their own making.

Convention refugees   Refugees who fulfill the UN criteria for refugees or who are selected and sponsored for entry into Canada.

Critical multiculturalism   A populist multiculturalism that promotes the need to challenge, resist, and transform those prevailing patterns of power and privilege that have marginalized minority women and men.

Cultural defence   A belief that cultural differences should be taken into account when sentencing those whose actions violate Canadian law but are consistent with their cultural background. This type of defence is perceived by many as contrary to the principle that everyone is equal before the law.

Cultural relativism   A belief that cultures are relative to the society in which they exist and that, as a result, all cultural practices should be analyzed and assessed on their own terms rather than by some arbitrarily selected external criteria. It is widely (but incorrectly) thought that, in the absence of absolute standards, cultural relativism embraces the idea that all cultural practices are good and valid— even those in violation of human rights.

Depoliticizing ("neutering") of ethnicity/diversity   A process by which the potency of ethnicity is "neutered" or rendered neutral by eroding its potential for inter-group strife. Ethnicity is relegated to the private or personal domains, thus dislodging it from competing for power and privilege in the public sphere.

Devolution   The practice of transferring responsibilities and structures (decentralization) to the local level on the assumption that those closest to the community have a better sense of addressing local concerns than do remote bureaucrats. Devolution rarely involves the transfer of power but, more accurately, the offloading of administration from the centre to the periphery.

Differentiated citizenship   The idea that the social contract implicit in belonging to society must be customized to reflect the different realities, experiences, and needs of Canada's major ethnic groups. *See also* Citizenship, Inclusive citizenship.

Discrimination   Often viewed as the behavioural counterpart of prejudice (attitudes), discrimination consists of actions that have an adverse effect (whether deliberate or not) of denying or excluding someone because of who they are. Discrimination can be expressed at different levels, ranging from the personal, intentional, and direct to the impersonal, inadvertent, and systemic. *See also* Racism.

Distinct society   The concept of distinct society is usually applied to describe the political aspirations of the Québécois. The Québécois assert that they constitute a "distinct society," that is, a historical people with a unique language, culture, and identity whose homeland of last resort is Quebec.

Diversity   Separate states of being in which different people are slotted into a pre-existing category. Diversity can also be used in a more radical sense to convey the placement of different groups along a hierarchy of power that is undergoing constant evaluation and adjustment in contexts that are unequal and constraining.

Dominant group   The collectivity of persons in society with the institutionalized authority to preserve the prevailing distribution of power, privilege, and property. The dominant sector represents that part of society with the capacity to define itself and its culture as the standard or norm by which others are judged and evaluated.

Dualism   A term at the core of collective definition perspective, the concept of dualism suggests a series of binary divisions (factions) within both the dominant and subdominant sectors of society. *See also* Collective definition.

Employment equity   This concept can be interpreted as a principle or a policy with a corresponding set of programs and practices. As a *principle,* employment equity embraces the notion of institutional inclusion by improving the hiring and treatment of minorities through removal of discriminatory barriers and implementation of proactive programs. As a *policy,* it refers to official policies such as Canada's *Employment Equity Act* of 1986, which enshrined equity principles as a formal government initiative.

Entitlement   The conferral of certain rights and privileges (who gets what) to a particular group or members of a group.

Equity   The belief that true equality is based on recognizing the relevance of context, the importance of taking differences into account, and a balancing of individual with collective rights. A commitment to equity acknowledges the primacy of equal results (not just equal opportunity) to ensure that members of a group have a fair share of scarce resources.

Essentializing   Exercising the belief in unchanging human characteristics that are uniform and stable within a certain category and impervious to social context or historical modification.

Ethnic   The identity of a group of individuals who see themselves as socially distinct because of their identification with a common language, ancestry, homeland, and historical and cultural symbols.

Ethnic cleansing   A variant of genocide involving not only killing but the forced and physical removal of a racial or ethnic minority from a particular locale.

Ethnic groups   Communities of "like-minded" individuals with a shared awareness of a common identity, language, history, and culture; a sense of group belonging; and real or imagined ancestral links.

Ethnicity   A principle by which people are defined, differentiated, and organized on the basis of a shared awareness of ancestral linkages as grounds for reward, recognition, and relationships. In addition to securing a basis for both community and identity, this shared awareness provides a rationale for organizing "like-minded" people into action for advancing social, political, and cultural interests.

Ethnic nationalism   Those who share an ancestrally based identity are mobilized into an action group (social movement) for attainment of certain goals related to the defence of the homeland rather than loyalty to society at large. They claim a right to speak the language of nationhood, and insist on their status as peoples with an inherent right to self-determining autonomy, including secession. *See also* Civic nationalism and Nationalism.

Ethnocentrism   A universal tendency to see and interpret reality from a particular cultural perspective as normal, necessary, and natural, with a corresponding inclination to dismiss or denigrate others as inferior or irrelevant. Ethnocentrism can also include a belief in the superiority of one's culture, values, assumptions, and world view when judging other practices or beliefs by one's own cultural standards. *See also* Eurocentrism.

Eugenics   A science and a social movement that attained considerable popularity during the first part of the twentieth century, eugenics is concerned with improving the quality of the human species through selective reproduction. Eugenics encouraged the creation of large families among the socially superior, while discouraging breeding within so-called inferior stock (i.e., the poor or minorities).

Eurocentric   Believing in the moral superiority of European thoughts and practices as the norm or standard by which others are judged and interpreted. Also a tendency to see and interpret the world through European eyes as natural and normal, assume others are also doing so, and dismiss those that don't as irrelevant or inferior. *See also* Ethnocentrism.

Everyday racism   *See* Normative racism.

Federalism   A political arrangement with a relatively well-defined division of jurisdiction and authority between the centre and the subunits.

Feminism   A widely varied ideology and social movement that espouses the equality and worth of women. Feminisms range from those that reject the existing system as patriarchal, racist, or classist to those that are willing to work within the system by removing discriminatory barriers to equality. Feminisms may also vary depending on whether the differences between men and women are perceived as absolute or relative.

Formal equality   An equality that is based on strict mathematical equivalence; that is, for true equality everyone should be treated the same regardless of their differences. Often associated with the principle of equal opportunity. *See also* Equity.

Functionalism   A perspective (or theory) of society that sees it as a complex and integrated whole composed of interrelated parts that individually and collectively contribute to the stability and survival of society.

Gendered inequality   A belief that inequality between women and men is embedded within the organization and design of society in ways that have the intent or effect of marginalizing or exploiting women while bolstering the interests, privilege, and power of men as natural and normal. *See also* Patriarchy.

Genocide   An orchestrated effort by members of a society to eradicate members from a devalued group within the same society. Although current debates revolve around the centrality of "intent" as crucial to any definition, genocide in a broader sense can also be indirect and not openly violent in process.

Governance   The relationship between the ruled and the rulers in terms of how authority is divided, power is distributed, and valued resources are allocated within a particular jurisdiction. The term is not synonymous with *government,* which refers to specific forms of this relationship. *See also* Aboriginal self-governance, Constitutionalism.

Harassment   A type of discrimination in which persistent and unwelcome actions (or conditions) are directed at individuals by those who ought to know better.

Hate racism   An open dislike of others because of who they are or what they do.

Human rights   The doctrine that all persons have certain inalienable (inherent) entitlements as individuals and members of a group.

Hybridic ethnic identity   *See* Postmodern ethnicity.

Identity politics   Also known as politics of recognition, identity politics acknowledges the desire of individuals and groups to ensure their distinctiveness is recognized and accorded respect *on their own terms,* rather than on the conditions espoused by central authorities.

Identity thesis   The idea that a person's ethnicity provides a buffer in coping with the demands of a changing, diverse, and uncertain world.

Ideological racism A racism based on society-wide ideas and ideals, including beliefs and values, that have a negative or controlling effect on a devalued group.

Ideology Defined in its broadest sense, ideology refers to a complex of ideas and ideals that attempts to explain, justify, and perpetuate a specific set of circumstances. Ideology can also be employed in the Marxist sense; namely, as those beliefs that rationalize the prevailing distribution of power, privilege, and resources in society by bolstering the cultural patterns of the dominant sector as natural or normal, while dismissing subdominant patterns as irrelevant or inferior.

Immigrant Persons born overseas but voluntarily residing in a new country, with a right to permanent residency on the grounds of labour market contribution or family reunification. Temporary residents such as foreign students or persons on seasonal work visas are not included as immigrants, while refugees are seen as a special category of immigrants (fleeing because of persecution fears). With the possible exception of Aboriginal peoples, all Canadians are immigrants or descendants of immigrants.

***Immigration Act,* 1978** Although superseded by the *Immigration and Refugee Protection Act* of 2002, this Act continues to provide the ideological underpinnings of Canada's immigration policies, programs, and practices. The focus is on finding a working balance between humanitarian and pragmatic concerns while protecting Canada's national interests and international commitments.

Immigration and Refugee Board (IRB) An agency of 180 political appointees who sit in single-person tribunals to determine whether an asylum seeker qualifies for entry into Canada as a legitimate refugee.

Immigration and Refugee Protection Act, 2002 This Act replaces the 1978 *Immigration Act.* Emphasis is increasingly aimed at addressing Canada's security concerns without sacrificing conventional commitments to Canada-building through immigration.

Inclusive citizenship A belief that citizenship in Canada must be customized to reflect the distinctive needs and aspirations of Aboriginal peoples, national communities such as the Québécois, and historically disadvantaged multicultural minorities.

Indigenous peoples *See* Aboriginal peoples.

Institutional inclusiveness The idea that mainstream institutions must make space for the historically disadvantaged. At one level, inclusion is about increased minority presence through removal of discriminatory barriers and introduction of proactive measures to improve minority access, treatment, and equity. At another level, however, inclusion is about redesigning institutional structures, values, and practices to ensure minority differences are taken into account when defining who gets what.

Institutional racism An explicitly condoned set of organizational policies and discriminatory practices that openly deny and exclude minorities from full and equal participation.

Instrumentalist approach The use of ethnicity to achieve goals in a competitive world through collective action.

Insurgent ethnic identity A reference to an ethnic identity involving a strong identification with one's own group, often accompanied by an intense dislike of others as inferior, irrelevant, or a threat. Also called Politicized ethnic identity.

Integration A model of race and ethnic relations as well as a policy framework for managing diversity that involves a set of policy ideals and practices that stand in opposition to the principles of segregation or separation. As policy or model, integration is concerned with incorporating minorities into the mainstream so that they can participate as equals. Integration can also refer to a process in which different cultures come together and fuse as "paints in a bucket" to create a new hue.

Integrative Multiculturalism Canada's official Multiculturalism is not about promoting differences but about ensuring inclusion of all Canadians through multicultural models of integration (and integrative models of multiculturalism).

Interactionism Symbolic interactionism (as it is often known) provides a sociological perspective that sees society as an ongoing human accomplishment, involving a dynamic process in which social reality is created and recreated by individuals who engage in meaningful interaction. Also called symbolic interactionism.

Internal colonialism A fundamentally exploitative relationship in which indigenous peoples are forcibly incorporated into a system not of their own making with a corresponding loss of land, identity, and political voice.

Intersectional analysis   A theoretical approach to the study of inequality that incorporates the interplay of race, gender, ethnicity, and class in defining outcomes. For example, gender is superimposed on and intersects with race, ethnicity, and class to create overlapping and mutually intensifying patterns of domination and exploitation.

Lived-in ethnic identity   A kind of ethnic identity that is full time and lived out on a regular basis. Compare to symbolic ethnic identity.

Marxism   A philosophy or ideology based on interpreting the work of Karl Marx. According to Marxism, both the dynamics of history and the organization of society can be understood as an ongoing and evolving clash between the ruling (capitalist) class and the working class.

Melting pot   A metaphor that is used to describe the preferred ideal in American race and ethnic relations. The concept of a melting pot suggests the fusion of minority differences to create a new and improved national culture. The ideal, however, does not match the reality for many racial minorities who by choice or circumstances remain unmeltable. *See also* Mosaic, Integration.

Merit/Meritocracy   The act of rewarding a person on the basis of credentials or achievement. Three features make a judgment meritocratic: the measurement of achievement against a commonly accepted scale is applied to all candidates; every candidate is measured impersonally, that is, on the basis of performance rather than identity; and examiners are selected on the basis of their excellence and impartiality.

Minority group   Any socially defined category of individuals who are perceived as different and inferior and treated accordingly by the majority. *See also* Subdominant groups, Visible minorities.

Misogyny   Hatred of women.

Mosaic   A metaphor to describe the ideal arrangement of unity within diversity involving various racial and ethnic groups in Canada. The proposed image is that of a patterned entity comprising disparate and distinct elements arranged into a cohesive whole. Proponents admire the positive images associated with the mosaic; detractors denounce it as a gross distortion that neither fits reality nor escapes the conceptual trap of cultural "apartheid" both fixed in time and separated by inequality.

Multicultural education   A philosophy of education that believes that schooling should reflect, reinforce, and advance the diversity of the classroom. Three major types exist— enrichment, enlightenment, and empowerment—each of which can be contrasted to anti-racist education.

Multiculturalism   A belief that a society of many cultures is possible as a basis for "living together with differences." Different levels of meaning of multiculturalism can be discerned, including multiculturalism as a statement of empirical fact; a set of ideals around celebrating diversity; an official policy, a set of practices; and a critique that challenges the prevailing distribution of power and privilege. *See also* Official Multiculturalism.

Multiculturalism Act.   *See* **Official Multiculturalism**

Multicultural minorities   Those Canadians who are immigrants or descendants of immigrants. The term is used to describe immigrants and descendants of immigrants whose priorities and interests differ from the more politicized concerns of Aboriginal peoples. *See also* People of colour.

Multinational federation   A proposed political arrangement that rejects the current system of provincial-based federalism, and favours instead a federalism that acknowledges Canada as a multi-layered coalition of different nations. *See also* Canada as a coalition.

Nation   A moral community of "like-minded" people who share a common homeland, language, identity, set of grievances, and cultural and historical symbols. This strong collectivity often is found within an existing state structure, expresses a political consciousness as a distinct peoples, and claims the right to speak the language of nationalism. Both Quebec and Aboriginal peoples prefer to see themselves as "nations" within the framework of Canadian society.

Nationalism   A belief that those peoples who claim to be nations have the right to self-rule and inherent rights to self-determining autonomy over land, identity, and political voice, up to and including independence. *See also* Ethnic nationalism, Civic nationalism.

Nations within A term normally employed to describe Aboriginal ambitions for self-determination in Canada. The "nations within" concept acknowledges the relative autonomy of Aboriginal peoples but does not advocate outright secession as an independent state with absolute control over external affairs. *See also* Self-government.

Normative racism Racism that is expressed and reinforced in the minutiae of daily life and interaction, for example, through use of certain language or images. Also referred to as Everyday racism.

Official bilingualism *See* Bilingualism, *Official Languages Act.*

Official language minorities French-speaking Canadians who live outside Quebec and English-speaking Canadians who reside in Quebec have certain rights that provide them with access to services in their language (where numbers warrant), in addition to rights to exercise control over institutions such as education.

Official Languages Act Passage of this Act in 1969/1986 established Canada as an officially bilingual society. The Act ensures bilingual services and workplaces within federal institutions across the country, while protecting the language rights of official-language minorities (French outside Quebec, English in Quebec).

Official Multiculturalism The transformation of multicultural principles into official policy began with an all-political party agreement in 1971, followed by the entrenchment of multiculturalism in the *Canadian Charter of Rights and Freedoms* in 1982, and its subsequent enshrinement with the passage of the *Multiculturalism Act* in 1988.

Patriarchy The notion of society as designed by, for, and about men so that the constitutional order (in terms of core values, key institutions, and distribution of power) reflects, reinforces, and advances male privilege and power.

People of colour *See* Visible minorities, Multicultural minorities.

Pluralism The belief that culturally different groups can coexist in society. A commitment to multiculturalism represents one variant of a pluralist society.

Polite racism A dislike of others that is indirect because it is coded in euphemistic language.

Politicization The process by which issues are taken out of the personal or private domain and situated instead within the public domain in the competition for scarce resources.

Politicized Ethnic Identity *See* Insurgent ethnic identity.

Postcolonial social contract. A proposed restructuring of Aboriginal peoples–state relations that rejects the colonial assumptions of the past in favour of a new arrangement involving the principles of partnership, power sharing, radical participation, and a commitment to respect, recognition, and restoration.

Postmodern ethnic identity A kind of ethnic identity based on a dynamic integration of past and present to create a hybridic notion of "who am I?" that is fluid, contextual, and multiple, without reflecting a sense of contradiction or confusion.

Postmodern(ism) In the sense often preferred, a discourse that rejects the modernist claim for a unified and organized way of thinking about the world from a fixed and objective point of view. Proposed instead is a position that there is no such thing as reality with a rational core of meaning in the centre, but only discourses about reality, whose truthfulness not only reflect a person's standpoint but are little more than a narrative in defence of dominant ideology. Post-modernism also espouses a mind-dependent world where there is no centre of authority, only different viewpoints where everything is relative and true because nothing is absolutely knowable, and where nothing is neutral or impartial because everything/everyone is located in time and space.

Power In everyday language, the ability to make others do what they normally wouldn't want to do. Power should not be thought of as a thing, but as a process inherent to relationships. The relational nature of power shifts from context to context, suggesting that minorities can wield power in certain situations.

Prejudice A set of biased and generalized prejudgments of others based on faulty and inflexible generalizations. Rather than being viewed as a purely psychological phenomenon involving an irrational and unfounded set of assumptions, prejudice may be interpreted in sociological terms, insofar as it originates when the dominant sector invokes negative ideas to justify and entrench its power and privilege over the subordinate sector.

Primordial explanation A perspective that explains the popularity of ethnicity by reference to some deep biological yearning (or hard-wiring) that compels people to be with their "own kind."

Profiling *See* Racial profiling.

Race Currently defined as a biologically based social construct involving the classification of persons into hierarchical categories on the basis of real or imagined characteristics. Race has no empirical validity or scientific justification; nevertheless, people continue to believe it does and act accordingly, thus reinforcing the sociological axiom that phenomena do not have to be real to be real in their consequences.

Racialization The idea that race relations do not exist (as there is no such thing as race) but with a focus on why certain relations between groups become defined by reference to race. Racialization also entails the idea that certain activities become linked with race (e.g., crime may be racialized by linking gangs with black youth).

Racialized inequality The process by which race-based (dis)advantages are embedded within society. Rather than being neutral and value free, society has evolved and is organized in a way that reflects, reinforces, and advances as normal and necessary the interests of those with the power to define or control it.

Racialized minorities This term is increasingly preferred over Visible minorities or People of colour because it acknowledges that attaching a race label to minorities reflects a socially constructed process rather than a description based on alleged biological traits.

Racial profiling Discriminatory actions by those in positions of authority that rely on stereotypes of race to target group members for reasons of security or law and order.

Racial stratification A hierarchical ranking of racial and ethnic minorities in ascending/descending order on the basis of the criteria of income, education, or social class. Think of Canada as "layered" into "strata" based on how different minorities fare in the competition for valued resources, with "whites" on top and groups such as First Nations and visible minorities near the bottom.

Racial typologies The process whereby racial groups are evaluated and hierarchically arranged in ascending and descending orders of superiority or inferiority to justify patterns of privilege and power.

Racism Generally speaking, racism refers to a relatively complex and organized set of ideas and ideals (ideology) that assert or imply natural superiority of one group over another in terms of entitlements and privileges, together with the power to put these beliefs into practice in a way that denies or excludes those who belong to a devalued category.

Refugee Defined by the United Nations as a person who flees his or her country because of a well-grounded fear of persecution based on race, national origins, religious background, or other factors largely beyond a person's control. The grounds for admittance have expanded in recent years; for example, Canada now extends the concept of refugee status to include gender-based persecution.

Refugee claimants Unlike convention refugees who are privately or government sponsored, these asylum seekers arrive unannounced and invoke their right to claim refugee status. Also called "in Canada refugees."

Resource mobilization theory Accounting for ethnicity by acknowledging how like-minded people will mobilize into action groups to improve their competitive edge in the competition for scarce resources.

Reversing discrimination In contrast to reverse discrimination, which argues that special rights for minorities are a kind of discrimination in reverse, reversing discrimination contends that special measures for minority women and men are initiatives that help to reverse (remove) the discrimination that historically has denied or excluded them.

Scientific racism The belief that racial capacities between populations could be measured and evaluated by scientific means, particularly the IQ (Stanford-Binet) test.

Segregation   The process and practice of separating groups on the basis of race or culture. This *separation* can occur voluntarily or involuntarily, can involve formal or informal measures, and may be interpreted as empowering or disempowering.

Self-determination   *See* Self-determining autonomy.

Self-determining autonomy   As fundamentally autonomous political communities that are sovereign and share sovereignty over the land, Aboriginal peoples claim to have inherent and collective rights to Aboriginal models for assuming control over jurisdictions (or domains) of immediate concern related to land, identity, and political voice. Self-determining autonomy is not the same as independence but reflects a willingness to work within the framework of a new (post-colonial) social contract.

Self-government   A term that is usually employed within the context of Aboriginal demands for Aboriginal models of self-determining autonomy. Aboriginal peoples claim self-government provides the political expression of their demand for control over internal affairs. *See also* Aboriginal self-governance.

Separation   *See* segregation.

Sexism   A belief in the superiority of men.

Situational ethnic identity   *See* Symbolic ethnic identity.

Social Contract   *See* Postcolonial social contract.

Social Darwinism   A doctrine of racial superiority that reworked some of Darwin's ideas on evolution and survival of the fittest and applied them to group relations. According to social Darwinists, the world can be portrayed as an arena where populations are locked in mortal combat over competition for scarce resources. Those with the adaptive skills survive and prosper; those without are destined for the margins.

Society-building   The ongoing process by which contemporary societies utilize policies and programs to create and re-create a political and moral community of individuals in the face of internal demands and external pressures. The term "nation-building" may also be used because most states (or societies) are seeking to become more nation-like.

Sovereignty   The exercise of exclusive and final authority over land, peoples, rules, and all legal and political matters within a strictly bounded territory. For some, sovereignty is about borders; for others, especially Aboriginal peoples, it is about establishing relations.

Sovereignty without secession   A claim by the Québécois to establish a relative yet relational autonomy with Canada based on the principle of Quebec as a distinct society.

Specific treaty claims   Refers to Crown breaches of existing treaty provisions. *See* Comprehensive land claims.

State   A political, legal, and administrative unit that claims to exercise final authority over a specific territory, monopolizes the legitimate use of force to enforce decisions and keep the peace, and is governed by authorities who purport to represent the inhabitants.

State nationalism   *See* Civic nationalism.

Stereotype   A shorthand way of classifying social reality into convenient categories on the basis of common properties. As a generalization, it provides an oversimplification or exaggerated version of the world based on preconceived and unwarranted notions that apply to all members of the devalued group.

Subdominant group   Also called subordinate, subdominant groups stand in an unequal relationship to dominant groups because of differences in power, privilege, and wealth.

Subliminal racism   A subconscious racism that reflects a conflict of interest between competing value sets. On one side, seemingly enlightened people may endorse the principle of equality; on the other side, they will reject the means to achieve that goal on principled grounds if cost or inconvenience are involved. The end result? Nothing happens, and the prevailing (and racialized) distribution of power, privilege, and property remains intact.

Substantive equity   Based on the idea that differences sometimes have to be taken into account in achieving an equality that goes beyond theory. This colour-conscious approach to equality appears to be at variance with colour-blind notions where everyone is treated the same. *See also* Equity.

Symbolic ethnic identity   (Also called situational ethnic identity) A process in which an individual retains a cognitive or emotional affiliation with a cultural past while continuing to fully participate in the wider society.

Symbolic interactionism *See* Interactionism.

Systematic racism A direct attempt by institutions, employing explicit rules and deliberate practices, to prevent the full and equal participation of minorities.

Systemic discrimination Based on the principle that bias and barriers may be inherent within the normal functioning of an institutional system. It involves a process in which the rules or practices of an institution when evenly and equally applied may exert a negative effect or consequences (rather than be based on intent or awareness) on certain minorities who are excluded or penalized through no fault of their own but because of their membership in devalued groups.

Systemic racism *See* Systemic discrimination

Tolerance Two meanings can be discerned (Forst 2004). First, a dislike of other practices, but a willingness to put up with this dislike in the name of public peace. Second, the value, validity, and acceptance of what is disliked in pursuit of social justice.

Treaties Transactions between the Crown and Aboriginal peoples involving an exchange of rights, duties, and obligations. Treaties of alliance and friendship exist, but most treaties involve a transaction in which Aboriginal peoples surrender large tracts of land in exchange for goods and services in perpetuity,

and rights of use of unoccupied or underutilized Crown land.

Universal citizenship The idea that everyone in Canada belongs in the same way, as individuals with identical rights, duties, and obligations.

Vertical mosaic A twist on the notion of Canada as a multicultural "mosaic," the term originated with the publication of the book *The Vertical Mosaic,* by John Porter, the eminent Canadian sociologist. According to Porter, Canada's multicultural mosaic is organized and aligned along a system of stratification that has advantaged some and disadvantaged others.

Visible minorities The term used to designate those Canadians who are non-white, non-Aboriginal, non-Caucasian in origin or identity, regardless of place of birth, and are defined as such by the government or have agreed to this label for purposes of employment equity or census taking. Used interchangeably with People of colour or, increasingly, Racialized minorities.

White Paper A bill tabled by the Liberal government in 1969 to do away with Aboriginal peoples as a distinct status group in Canada. The bill proposed to repeal the *Indian Act,* dismantle the Department of Indian Affairs, and then eliminate reserves by allocating land on an individual basis to Aboriginal peoples. Aboriginal leaders strongly resisted the White Paper, a move that initiated what many see as the single most important factor in redefining Aboriginal peoples' relations with Canada.

References

Abel, Allen. 2001. "P Is for Prejudice." *Saturday Night*. (June) 23/30.

Abel, Sue. 1997. *Shaping the News. Waitangi Day on Television*. Auckland: Auckland University Press.

Abele, Frances, Russell LaPointe, and Michael Prince. 2005. "Symbolism, Surfacing, Succession, and Substance: Martin's Aboriginal Policy Style." Pp. 99–121 in *How Ottawa spends*, ed. B. Doern. 99–121. Montreal/Kingston: McGill-Queen's University Press.

Abele, Francis. 2004. Urgent Need, Serious Opportunity: Towards a New Social Model for Canada's Aboriginal Peoples. CPRN Social Architecture Papers. Research Paper F/39. April.

Abella, Irving and Harold Troper. 1991. *None is too Many: Canada and the Jews in Europe 1933–1948*. 3rd ed. Toronto: Lester and Orpen Dennys.

Aboriginal Institutes' Consortium. 2005. *Aboriginal Institutions of Higher Education. A Struggle for the Education of Aboriginal Students, Control of Indigenous Knowledge and Recognition of Aboriginal Institutions. An Examination of Government Policy*. Toronto: Canadian Race Relations Foundation.

Abraham, Carolyn. 2005. "Race" *Globe and Mail,* 18 June.

Abu-Laban, B., T. Derwing, and M. Mulder. 2004. "Why Canada Should Accept Refugees." *Canadian Issues* (March): 33–36.

Abu-Laban, Yasmeen. 1999 "The Politics of Race, Ethnicity, and Immigration." In *Canadian Politics*, eds. J. Bickerton and A. Gagnon. Peterborough: Broadview.

Abu-Laban, Yasmeen, and Christina Gabriel. 2002. *Selling Diversity: Immigration, Multiculturalism, Employment Equity, and Globalization*. Peterborough, ON: Broadview Press.

Abu-Laban, Yasmeen, Sharon McIrvin, and Peter S. Li. 1998. *Canadian Immigration and Immigrant Adaptation at the Millennium*. (Introduction) *Special volume of Canadian Ethnic Studies* 30(3):1–5.

Achenbach, Joel. 2004. "Brain *Trust Can't Pin Down* 'Race'." *Toronto Star*. Oct 16

ACS/Environics. 2002. "Public Opinion Poll." *Canadian Issues* (February):4–5.

Adam, Betty Ann and Jamie Zachary. 2005. "Ahenakew Guilty of Hate, Claims He's a Victim." *National Post*. 9 July.

Adams, Howard. 1999. *Tortured People. The Politics of Colonization*. Penticton BC: Theytus Books.

Adams, Michael. 1997. *Sex in the Snow. Canadian Social Values at the End of the Millenium*. Toronto: Penguin.

Adelman, Howard. 2004. "Introduction." *Canadian Issues* (March): 3–4.

Adorno, T. S. et al. 1950. *The Authoritarian Personality*. New York: Harper and Row.

Agocs, Carol and Monica Boyd. 1993. "Ethnicity and Ethnic Inequality." Pp. 330–52 in *Social Inequality in Canada* (2nd ed.), eds. J. Curtis et al. Scarborough, ON: Prentice-Hall.

Aguiar, Luis L.M., Patricia Tomic, and Ricardo Trumper. 2005. "Racism, Hate, and Monoculturalism in a Canadian Hinterland." Pp. 163–174 in *Possibilities and Limitations*, ed. C. James. Halifax: Fernwood.

Aguirre, Adalberto Jr., and Jonathan Turner. 1995. *American Ethnicity: The Dynamics and Consequences of Discrimination*. New York: McGraw Hill.

Ahenakew, David. 1985. "Aboriginal Title and Aboriginal Rights: The Impossible and Unnecessary Task of Identification and Definition." Pp. 24–30 in *The Quest for Justice: Aboriginal Peoples and Aboriginal title*, eds. Menno Boldt and J. Anthony Long. Toronto: University of Toronto Press.

Alberts, Sheldon. 1999. "Opposition Exhausts Hopes of Stopping Nisga'a." *National Post*, 13 December.

Alfred, Taiaiake. 1999. "Racism: Federal Policy." *Windspeaker* (November).

Alfred, Taiaiake. 1999. *Peace, Power, and Righteousness. An Indigenous Manifesto*. Toronto: Oxford University Press.

Alfred, Taiaiake. 2001. "Mexico Laps Canada in Fight for Rights Recognition." *Windspeaker* (April).

Alfred, Taiaiake. 2005. *Wasase. Indigenous Pathways to Action and Freedom*. Peterborough, ON: Broadview Press.

Alia, Valerie. 1999. *Un/Covering the North. News, Media, and Aboriginal People*. Vancouver: UBC Press.

Al-Kranawi, Alean and John R Graham (eds.). 2003. *Multicultural Social Work in Canada*. Toronto: Oxford.

Alladin, Ibrahim. 1996. "Racism in Schools: Race, Ethnicity, and Schooling in Canada." Pp. 4–21 in *Racism in Canadian Schools*, ed. I. Alladin. Toronto: Harcourt Brace.

Allan, Robert. 1993. *His Majesty's Indian Allies. British Indian Policy in the Defence of Canada. 1774–1815*. Toronto: Dundurn Press.

Alland, Alexander Jr., 1996. "Review: The Eternal Triangle: Race, Class, and IQ." *Current Anthropology* 37 (Supplement):151–152.

Allport, Gordon. 1954. *The Nature of Prejudice*. New York: Doubleday and Company.

Alvi, S. S., et al. (eds.). 2003. *The Muslim Veil in North America. Issues and Debates*. Toronto: The Women's Press.

Amdur, Rueul S. 2004. "French Go for Uniformity." *Echo,* (May) p. 9.

Amiel, Barbara. 2000. "Ballerinas and Immigration." *Maclean's,* 19 June.

Andersen, Margaret L. and Patricia Hill Collins (eds). 1998. *Race, class, and Gender. An Anthology*. 3rd ed. Belmont, CA: Wadsworth.

Anderson, Elijah. 1994. "The Code of the Streets." Atlantic Monthly 273 (May): 81–94.

Anderson, Robert B., and Corinne Barnett. 2006. "The Indigenous land Claims in New Zealand and Canada: From Grievance to Enterprise." Public Policy Paper no 39. SIPP. Regina, Saskatchewan: University of Regina.

Anderssen, Erin. 1998. "Nunavut to be a Welfare Case." *The Globe and Mail,* June 5.

Anderssen, Erin. 1998. "Canada's Squalid Secret: Life on Native Reserves." *The Globe and Mail*, 12 Oct.

Anderssen, Erin and Michael Valpy. 2003. "Face the Nation. Canada Remade." *The Globe and Mail*, 6 June.

Angus Reid Group Inc. 1991. *Multiculturalism and Canadians: Attitude Study, 1991. National survey report submitted to the Department of Multiculturalism and Citizenship*.

Angus, Ian. 2002. "Cultural Plurality and Democracy." *International Journal of Canadian Studies* vol. 25.

Anisef Paul and Kenise Murphy Kilbride (eds). 2003. *Managing Two Worlds: The Experiences and Concerns of Immigrant Youth in Ontario*. Toronto: Canadian Scholars Press.

Ansley, Bruce. 2004. "Stealing a March" *Listener NZ,* May 15.

Anthias, Floya. 1998. "Evaluating 'Diaspora': Beyond Ethnicity?" *Sociology* 32(3):552–580.

Areepattamannil, Shaljan. 2005. "Wanted: More Multicultural Teachers for our Rainbow Classrooms. *The Globe and Mail,* 7 September.

Asch, Michael. 1997. *Aboriginal and Treaty Rights in Canada. Essays on Law, Equality, and Respect for Differences.* Vancouver: UBC Press.

Asch, Michael. 2002. "Self Government in the New Millennium." In *Nation to Nation.* J. Bird et al. (eds.) Pp. 65–73. Toronto: Irwin

Ashini, Napes 2002 "Niassinam: Cariboo and F16s." Pp. 74–81 in *Nation to Nation*, J. Bird et al. (eds.). Toronto: Irwin.

Assante, Molefi Kete. 2003. *Erasing Racism. The Survival of the American Nation.* Amherst NY: Prometheus Books.

Associated Press. 2005. "U.S. 'Wealth Gap' Widening Along Racial Lines: Expert" Reprinted in *Toronto Star,* 18 Jan.

Atkinson, Joe. 1994. "The State, the Media, and Thin Democracy." In *Leap into the Dark. The Changing Role of the State in New Zealand since 1984.* ed. A Sharp. Auckland: Auckland University Press.

Auger, Michael C. 1997. "Two Visions, Two Results." *The Globe and Mail,* 9 Dec.

Augostinos, M. and K J Reynolds (eds.). 2001. *Understanding Prejudice, Racism and Social Conflict.* Thousand Oaks CA: Sage.

Avery, Donald H. 1995. *Reluctant Hosts: Canada's Response to Immigrant Workers 1896–1994.* Toronto: McClelland and Stewart.

Ayed, Nahlah. 1999. "Self Government a Mess, Native Coalition Testifies." *Toronto Star*, 3 March.

Aydemir, A., and M. Skuterud. 2004. Explaining the Deteriorating Entry Earnings of Canada's Immigrant Cohorts: 1996–2000. Family and Labour Studies Division, Statistics Canada. 11F0019MIE. No 225.

Azam, Sharlene. 2000. *Rebel, Rogue, Mischievous Babe: A Book about Real Girls and the Myths We Ask Teens to Believe.* Toronto: HarperCollins.

Backhouse, Constance. 1999. *Colour-Coded: A Legal History of Racism in Canada. 1900–1950.* Toronto: University of Toronto Press.

Bains, Camille. 1999. "Foreign Doctors Denied Right to Work." *National Post,* 20 December.

Bains, Navdeep Singh. 2005. "An Article of Faith for Sikhs." *Letter to Toronto Star.* 30 August.

Bambrah, Gurmeet. 2005. Canadian *'Experiments in Diversity: The Case of Immigrants with Engineering Backgrounds Who Settle in Ontario. CERIS Working Paper no 41. Toronto*: CERIS [Joint Centre of Excellence for Research on Immigration and Settlement—Toronto].

Banaji, Mahazir. 2003. "Colour Blind?" *This Magazine,* January/February.

Banks, J. A., and C. A. McGee Banks (eds) 1997. *Multicultural Education: Issues and Perspectives.* Toronto: Allyn and Bacon.

Bannerji, Himani. 2000. *The Dark Side of the Moon.* Toronto: Canadian Scholars Press.

Bannerji, Himani. 1986. "Now You See Us/Now You Don't." *Video Guide* 8(40).

Banton, Michael. 1987. *Racial Theories.* Cambridge: Cambridge University Press.

Banton, Michael. 2005. "Historical and Contemporary Modes of Racialization." In *Racialization.* ed. K Murji and J. Solomos. Oxford UK: Oxford University Press.

Banton, Michael. 2005. "Three Current Issues in Ethnic and Racial Studies." *British Journal of Sociology* 56(4): 621–631.

Barkun, Michael. 1994. *Religion and the Racist Right. The Origins of the Christian Identity Movement.* Chapel Hill NC: University of North Carolina Press.

Barnsley, Paul. 1999. "Cree Chief Slams Gathering Strength." *Windspeaker,* 1 January.

Barrett, Stanley R. 1987. *Is God a Racist? The Right Wing in Canada.* Toronto: University of Toronto Press.

Barry, Brian. 2001. *Culture and Equality: An Egalitarian Critique of Multiculturalism.* Cambridge, UK: Polity Press.

Barth, Frederick. 1969. *Ethnic Groups and Boundaries.* Boston: Little, Brown.

Basran, G.S., and L. Zong. 1998. "Devaluation of Foreign Credentials as Perceived by Visible Minority Professional Immigrants." *Canadian Ethnic Studies* 30(3):6–23

Bates, Judy Fong. 2004. *Midnight at the Dragon Café.* Toronto: McClelland & Stewart.

Baubock, Rainer. 2005. "If You Say Multiculturalism Is the Wrong Answer, Then What Was the question You Asked?" *Canadian Diversity* 4(1):90–94.

Bauer, William. 1994. "How the System Works." *The Globe and Mail,* 12 November.

Bauerlein, Mark. 2001. "Social Constructionism: Philosophy for the Academic Workplace." *Partisan Review* 68(2):228–41.

Baureiss, Gunter. 1985. "Discrimination and Response: The Chinese in Canada." in *Ethnicity and ethnic relations in Canada,* ed. Rita M. Bienvenue and Jay E. Goldstein.Toronto: Butterworths.

Bayley, David. 1994. "International Differences in Community Policing." in *The Challenge of Community Policing.* ed. D. P. Rosenbaum. Thousand Oaks, CA: Sage.

Beach, Charles, M. Alan G Green, and Jeffrey G. Reitz (eds.). 2003. *Canadian Immigration Policy for the 21st Century.* John Deutsch Institute for the Study of Economic Policy, Queens University, Kingston.

Beare, Margaret. 2003. "Policing with a National Security Agenda." Commissioned by the Department of Canadian Heritage for the National Forum on Policing in a Multicultural Society.

Beaujot, Roderic P. 1999. "Immigration and Demographic Structures." in *Immigrant Canada.* eds. S. Halli and L. Driedger. Toronto: University of Toronto Press.

Beddgood, Janet. 1997. "Pakeha Ethnicity" *Sites* (Spring): 81–100.

Bedford, David. 1994. "Marxism and the Aboriginal Question: The Tragedy of Progress." *Canadian Journal of Native Studies* XIV (1):101–117.

Behrens, G. 1994. "Love, Hate, and Nationalism." *Time,* 21 March.

Beitz, Charles R. 2001. "Human Rights as Common Concerns." *American Political Science Review* 95(2).

Bell, Avril. 1996. "We're Just New Zealanders." In *Nga Patai: Racism and Ethnicity in Aotearoa/New Zealand.* Paul Spoonley et al. (eds.). Pp. 144–158. Palmerston, North NZ: Dunmore Publishing.

Bell, Catherine. 1997. "Metis Constitutional Rights in Section 35(1)" *Alberta Law Review* 36(1):180–204.

Bell, Michael. 2004. "Tripping up on the Dual Citizenship." *The Globe and Mail,* 29 July.

Bell, Stewart and Marina Jimenez. 2000. "Canada Should Go Overseas to Select Refugees, System's Critics Say." *National Post,* 31 March.

Bell-Fialkoff, Andrew. 1993. "Ethnic Conflict." *The World and I* (July): 465–477.

Bem, Sandra Lipsitz. 1994. "In a Male-Centered World, Female Differences Are Transformed into Female Disadvantages." *The Chronicle of Higher Education,* 17 August, B1–2.

Berliner, Michael S, and Gary Hull. 2000. *Diversity and Multiculturalism: The New Racism.* The Ayn Rand Institute.

Berry, John and Rudolph Kalin. 1993. "Multiculturalism and Ethnic Attitudes in Canada: An Overview of the 1991 National Survey." Paper presented to the Canadian Psychological Association, Annual Meetings. Montreal. May.

Berry, John W., Rudolph Kalin, and Donald M. Taylor. 1977. *Multiculturalism and Ethnic Attitudes in Canada.* Ottawa: Ministry of Supply and Services in Canada.

Berton, Pierre. 1975. *Hollywood's Canada: The Americanization of our National Image.* Toronto: McLelland and Stewart.

Bharucha, R. 2000. *The Politics of Cultural Practice: Thinking Through Theatre in an Age of Globalization.* Hanover, NH: University Press of New England.

Bibby, Reginald W. 1990. *Mosaic Madness. The Potential and Poverty of Canadian Life.* Toronto: Stoddart.

Bibby, Reginald. 2002. *Restless Gods: The Renaissance of Religion in Canada.* Toronto, Canada: Stoddart.

Bickerton, James and Alain-G. Gagnon, eds. 2004. *Canadian Politics, 4th ed.* Peterborough, ON: Broadview Press.

Biddiss, Michael D. (ed.) 1979. *Images of Race.* New York: Holmes and Meier.

Biles, John and Humera Ibrahim. 2005. "Religion and Public Policy: Immigration, Citizenship, and Multiculturalism—Guess Who's Coming to Dinner?" in *Religion and Ethnicity in Canada*, eds. Paul Bramadat and David Seljak. Toronto: Pearson.

Biles, John and Meyer Burstein. 2003. "Immigration: Economics and More." *Canadian Issues.* (April): 13–15.

Biles, John, Erin Tolley, and Humera Ibrahim. 2005. Does Canada Have a Multicultural Future? *Canadian Diversity* 4(1): 23–28.

Biles, John. 2002. "Everyone's a Critic." *Canadian Issues.* (February): 35–38.

Binder, Leonard, ed. 1999. *Ethnic Conflict and International Politics in the Middle East.* Florida: University Press of Florida.

Bird, John, Lorraine Land, and Murray Macadam. 2002. *Nation to Nation: Aboriginal Sovereignty and the Future of Canada* (2nd ed.). Toronto: Irwin.

Bishop, Anne. 2005. *Beyond Token Change: Breaking the Cycle of Oppression in Institutions.* Halifax: Fernwood.

Bissoondath, Neil. 1993. "A Question of Belonging: Multiculturalism and Citizenship." In *Belonging. The Meaning and Future of Canadian Citizenship.*, ed. William Kaplan. Kingston/Montreal: McGill-Queen's University Press.

Bissoondath, Neil. 1994. *Selling Illusions. The Cult of Multiculturalism.* Toronto: Stoddart.

Biswas, Sharmila. 2003. "The Gap." Foreward to *Immigrant Youth in Canada. A Canadian Council of Social Development research program.* Available at www.ccsd.ca

Blackduck, Alison. 2001. "Dogrib Gathering a Reminder of How Nation Should Work." *Toronto Star,* 21 August.

Blackduck, Alison. 2001. "Indigenous Landscape is Looking Very Bleak." *Toronto Star,* 12 July.

Blackwell, Tom. 2000. "Judge Rules Metis Don't Need License to Hunt in Ontario." *National Post,* 21 January.

Blackwell, Tom. 2004. "Ontario Cracks Down on Migrant Sponsors." *National Post,* 26 November.

Blank, Rebecca M, Marilyn Dabady, and Constance Citro (eds.). 2004. *Measuring Racial Discrimination.* The National Academies Press.

Blauner, Rob. 1994. "Talking Past Each Other: Black and White Languages." Pp. 18–28 in *Race and Ethnic Conflicts*, eds. Fred L. Pincus and Howard J. Ehrlich. Boulder, CO: Westview Press.

Blauner, Robert. 1972. *Racial Oppression in America.* New York: Harper and Row. Bloemradd, Irene. 2006.

Blumenthal, H. 1999. "Taking a New Approach to Crime and Correction" *Let's Talk.* (March): 2–4.

Blumer, Herbert and Troy Duster. 1980. "Theories of Race and Social Action." In *Sociological Theories: Race and Colonialism.* ed. UNESCO. Paris. 211–238.

Blythe, Martin. 1994. *Naming the Other. Images of the Maori in New Zealand Film and Television.* Metuchen, N.J.: Scarecrow Press.

Bolaria, B. Singh, and Peter S. Li. 1988. *Racial Oppression in Canada* (2nd ed). Toronto: Garamond Press.

Boldt, Edward D. 1985 "Maintaining Ethnic Boundaries: The Case of the Hutterites." In *Ethnicity and Ethnic Relations in Canada,* ed. Rita M. Bienvenue and Jay E. Goldstein. Toronto: Butterworths. 87–104.

Boldt, Edward. 1993. *Surviving as Indians: The Challenges of Self-Government.* Toronto: University of Toronto Press.

Bonilla-Silva, Eduardo. 1996. "Rethinking Racism: Toward a Structural Interpretation." *American Sociological Review.*

Bonnett, Alastair. 2000. *Anti-racism.* London: Routledge.

Booth, William. 1998. "New Wave of Immigrants Tests a Dream." *Guardian Weekly*, 17 April.

Borrows, John and Leonard Rotman. 1997. The Sui Generis Nature of Aboriginal Rights: Does it Make a Difference?" *Alberta Law Review* 36:9–45.

Bosniak, Linda. 2000. "Citizenship Denationalized." *Indiana Journal of Global Legal Studies* 7(2):447–509.

Bottomley, Gill, Marie de Leveranche, & Jeannie Martin. 1991. *Gender/Class/Culture/Ethnicity.* Sydney: Allen and Unwin.

Boyd, Monica and Michael Vickers. 2000. "100 Years of Immigration in Canada." *Canadian Social Trends* (Autumn):2–12.

Brace, C. Loring. 2005. *"Race" is a Four Letter Word. The Genesis of the Concept.* New York: Oxford University Press.

Brady, Margaret. 2001. "A Separate Health Crisis." *National Post*, 19 July.

Bragg, Rebecca. 1998. "Why PhDs Are Working as Security Guards." *Toronto Star,* 24 May.

Bramadat, Paul. 2005. "Beyond Christian Canada: Religion and Ethnicity in a Multicultural Canada." In *Religion and Ethnicity in Canada.* ed. Paul Bramadat and David Seljak. Toronto: Pearson Longman.

Breton, Eric. 2000. "Canadian Federalism, Multiculturalism, and the Twenty-first Century." *International Journal of Canadian Studies* 21(Spring):160–75.

Breton, Raymond. 1964. "Institutional completeness of ethnic communities and the personal relations of immigrants." *American Journal of Sociology.* 70: 103–205.

Breton, Raymond. 1989. "Canadian Ethnicity in the Year 2000." Pp. 149–152 in *Multiculturalism and Intergroup Relations,* ed. James Frideres. New York: Greenwood Press.

Breton, Raymond. 1998. "Ethnicity and Race in Social Organizations: Recent Developments in Canadian Society." Pp. 60–115 in *The Vertical Mosaic Revisited,* eds. R. Helmes-Hayes and J. Curtis. Toronto: University of Toronto Press.

Breton, Raymond, Wsevolod W. Isajiw, Warren E. Kalbach, and Jeffrey G. Reitz. 1990. *Ethnic Identity and Equality: Varieties of Experience in a Canadian City.* Toronto: University of Toronto Press.

Brezina, Timothy and Kenisha Winder. 2003. Economic Disadvantage: Status Generalization, and Negative Racial Stereotyping by White Americans. *Social Psychology Quarterly.* 66:402–418.

Brioux, B. 1999. "Birth of a Station." *National Post,* 17 February.

Bristow, Peggy (coordinator), Dionne Brand, Linda Carty, Afua A. Cooper, Sylvia Hamilton, and Adrienne Shadd. 1993. *We're Rooted Here and They Can't Pull Us Up: Essays in African Canadian Women's History.* Toronto: University of Toronto Press.

Britton, N. J. 2000. "Examining Police/Black Relations: What's in a Story?" *Ethnic and Racial Studies* 23(4):692–711.

Brock, Kathy L. 1991. "The Politics of Aboriginal Self-Government: A Paradox." *Canadian Public Administration* 34(2): 272–285.

Brooks, Stephen. 1998. *Public Policy in Canada. An Introduction.* Toronto: Oxford University Press.

Brown, David. 1989. "Ethnic Revival: Perspectives on State and Society." *TWQ* 11(4): 1–17.

Brown, Louise. 2005. "Amid Debate, Race-based School Thrives." *Toronto Star,* 15 September.

Brown, Louise. 2005. "Turning a Page in History." *Toronto Star,* 19 September.

Browne, Murphy. 2005. "Ways to Go To Equality." *Share,* 17 Mar.

Buckley, Helen. 1992. *From Wooden Ploughs to Welfare: Why Indian Policy Failed in the Prairie Provinces.* McMillian Collier: Toronto.

Buckley, Stephen. 1996. "Wife Abuse is the Norm in Africa." *Kitchener Waterloo Record,* 4 May.

Bullock, K. H. and G. J. Jaffri. 2000. "Media (Mis)representations: Muslim Women in the Canadian Nation." *Canadian Woman Studies* 20(2):35–40.

Bunzl, Matti. 2005. "Between anti-semitism and Islamophobia: Some thoughts on the new Europe." *American Ethnologist* 32(4): 499–508.

Burgess, Michael. 1996. "Ethnicity, Nationalism, and Identity in Canada-Quebec Relations: The Case of Quebec's Distinct Society." *Journal of Commonwealth and Comparative Politics* 34(2):46–64.

Burnet, Jean. 1981. "The Social and Historical Context of Ethnic Relations." Pp. 17–36 in *A Canadian Social Pyschology of Ethnic Relations*, eds. Robert C. Gardiner and Rudolph Kalin. Agincourt, Ontario: Methuen.

Cairns, Alan. 2000. *Citizens Plus: Aboriginal Peoples and the Canadian State.* Vancouver: UBC Press.

Cairns, Alan. 2003. "Aboriginal Peoples in the Twenty First Century. A Plea for Realism." Pp. 135–166 in *The Canadian Distinctiveness into the XXIst Century*, eds. C. Gaffield and K. L. Gould. Ottawa: University of Ottawa Press.

Cairns, Alan C. 2005. *First Nations and the Canadian State: In Search of Coexistence.* Kingston: Queen's University Institute of Intergovernmental Relations.

Calliste, Agnes and George Dei, eds. 2000. *Anti-Racist Feminism: Critical Race and Gender Studies.* Fernwood Publishing.

Cameron, Elspeth. (ed.). 2004. *Multiculturalism and Immigration in Canada: An Introductory Reader.* Toronto: Canadian Scholars Press.

Campbell, Murray. 2005. "Indifference to Natives Shows Again." *The Globe and Mail,* 27 Oct.

Canadian Council for Refugees. 2000. *Report on Systemic Racism and Discrimination in Canadian Refugee and Immigration Policies.* In preparation for the UN World Conference Against Racism, Racial Discrimination, Xenophobia and Related Intolerance. Montreal.

Canadian Council for Refugees. 2001. "Recommendations." The World Conference Against Racism, Racial Discrimination, Xenophobia, and Other Forms of Intolerance. Montreal.

Canadian Council for Refugees. 2001. "Refugee Women Fleeing Gender-Based Persecution." at www.web.net/~ccr/genderpers.html

Canadian Heritage. 2001. *Canadian Diversity: Respecting Our Differences.* Ottawa.

Canadian Press. 2000. "Greeks Laud Canada's Multicultural Success." *Toronto Star,* 13 November.

Canadian Press. 2005. "Canada Least Racist Nation But Problems Exist, Chan." *The Hamilton Spectator,* 16 March.

Canadian Press. 2005. "New location, same woes." *Kitchener-Waterloo Record,* 15 January.

Caplan, Gerald. 2005. "The Genocide Problem: "Never Again" All Over Again." *The Walrus,* Pp. 68–76.

Cardinal, Harold. 1969. *The Unjust Society.* Edmonton: Hurtig.

Cardozo, Andrew. 2005. "Multiculturalism vs Rights." *Toronto Star,* 15 September.

Cardozo, Andrew and Luis Musto (eds.). 1997. *Battle over Multiculturalism: Does It Help or Hinder Canadian Unity?* Ottawa: Pearson-Shoyama Institute.

Carey, Elaine. 2000. "Police 'Bias' Hits Blacks, Study Says." *Toronto Star,* 23 March.

Carey, Elaine. 2003. "Income Gap Growing Between Immigrants, Native-born." *Toronto Star,* 20 June.

Carey, Elaine. 2004. "Red Tape Deters Needed MDs." *Toronto Star.* 12 July.

Cassidy, Frank. 1994. "British Columbia and Aboriginal Peoples: The Prospects for the Treaty Process." *Policy Options,* (March):10–13.

Cassidy, Frank. 2003. "First Nations Governance Act: A Legacy Lost." *Policy Options* 24(4):46–50.

Castells, Manuel. 1997. *The Power of Identity.* Oxford: Blackwell.

Castles, Stephen, and Mark J. Miller. 1998. *The Age of Migration.* 2nd ed. London: Macmillan.

Caulfield, Timothy, and Gerald Robertson. 1996. "Eugenics Policies in Alberta: From the Systematic to the Systemic." *Alberta Law Review* xxxv(1):59–81.

Caws, Peter. 1994. "Identities: Cultural, Transcultural, and Multicultural." Pp. 371–378 in *Multiculturalism. A Critical Reader,* ed. D. T. Goldberg. Oxford: Blackwell.

CBC News. 2005. Innu strategy doing little to help: Reports. Screened 8 February. Available at cbc.ca.

CCJA. 2000. "Aboriginal Peoples and the Criminal Justice System." *Special Issue of the Canadian Criminal Justice System.* Ottawa.

Chagnon, Napoleon. 1998. *The Yanomamo.* 5th ed. New York: Holt Rinehart and Winston.

Chakkalakal, Tess. 1999. "Canada: The Moral Superpower." *This Magazine* (July/August): 30–33.

Chambers, Gretta. 1996. "Distinct Clause Needs Study, Not Merely Semantic Jigging." *The Globe and Mail,* 22 April.

Chan, Janet. 1996. "Police Racism. Experiences and Reforms." Pp. 160–172 in *The Teeth are Smiling: The Persistence of Racism in a Multicultural Australia.* eds. E. Vasta and S. Castles. Sydney: Allen & Unwin.

Chan, Janet. 1997. *Changing Police Culture. Policing in a Multicultural Society.* Cambridge, UK: Cambridge University Press.

Chan, Raymond. 2005. "Interview." *Canadian Diversity* 4(1):3–5.

Chan, Wendy and Kiran Mirchandani. 2002. "From Race and Crime to Racialization and Criminalization." In *Crimes of Colour. Racialization in the Criminal Justice System in Canada*, (eds). W. Chan and K. Mirchandani. Peterborough: Broadview Press.

Chartrand, Paul L., and Peeling, Albert. 2004. Sovereignty, Liberty, and the Legal Order of the "Freemen" (Otipahemsu'uk): Towards a Constitutional Theory of Metis Self-Government. S*askatchewan Law Review* 67(1):339.

Children Now. 2001. Fall Colors 2001–01. Cited in Greg Braxton, "TV Nets Lashed on Minority Mix." *Toronto Star*, 2 May.

Chrétien, Jean. 1999. "Federalism Reigns for Most Who Live in Democracies." *Canadian Speeches: Issues of the Day* 13(4):62–64.

Christie, Gordon. 2005. "Aboriginal Resource and Subsistence Rights After Delgamuukw and Marshall." In *Advancing Aboriginal Claims: Visions, Strategies, Directions*, ed. Kerry Wilkins. Saskatoon, SK: Purich Publishing.

Chung, Andrew. 2005. "A call for 'Separateness'." *Toronto Star*, 8 October.

Churchill, Ward. 1999. *Fantasies of the Master Race: Literature, Cinema, and the Colonization of North American Indians.* Winnipeg: Arbeiter Ring.

Churchill, Ward. 2004. *Kill the Indian, Save the Man. The Genocidal Impact of American Indian Residential Schools.* San Francisco. City Lights Books.

Churchill, Ward. 2004. *Speaking Truth in the Teeth of Power: Lectures on Globalization, Colonialism, and Native North America.* Oakland, CA: AK Press.

Chwialkowska, Luiza. 1999. "It'll Become Law, But Is It Legal?" *National Post*, 13 December.

Citizenship and Immigration Canada. 2001. *Planning Now for Canada's Future.* Ottawa: Minister of Public Works and Government Services Canada. Catalogue number Ci51–2000/2001.

Citizenship and Immigration Canada. 2001. "Pursuing Canada's Commitment to Immigration." *The Immigration Plan for 2002.* Ottawa.

Clairmont, Don. 2001. "Restorative Justice in Nova Scotia." *Isuma:* 145–52.

Clark, Bruce. 1990. *Native Liberty, Crown Sovereignty: The Existing Aboriginal Right of Self-Government in Canada.* Kingston: McGill-Queen's University Press.

Clark, Campbell. 2005. "Canadians Want Strict Security: Poll." *The Globe and Mail*, 11 August.

Closs, Bill. 2003. "Racial Profiling Guidelines Ensure Fairness For All." *Kingston Whig Standard.* 16 May.

Cobban, Helena. 2005. "Tiny New Zealand's Big Role in Restorative Justice". Available at http://www.csmonitor.com

Cochrum, Alan. 2004. "A French Fracas Over Faith." *The Sun*, February 2004.

Codrescu, Andrei. 1995. Faux Chicken & Phony Furniture. *Utne Reader*, (May/June): 47–48. Originally published in the *The Nation*, 12 Dec, 1984.

Cohen, Randy. 1999. "Cut Rate Rationale." *NY Times Magazine*, 18 July.

Cohen, Rob. 1998. *Global Diasporas. An Introduction.* Basinstoke: UCL Press.

Coleman, Isobel. 2006. "Women, Islam, and the new Iraq." *Foreign affairs* (Jan/Feb): 23–35.

Collacott, Martin. 2001. "Canada Is a Great Country—for Refugees." *National Post*, 4 August.

Collacott, Martin. 2001. "We're Not Ready for an Open-Door Policy." *National Post*, 8 June.

Collacott, Martin. 2006. "A Refugee System in Need of Overhaul." *National Post,* 9 March.

Comeau, Pauline and Aldo Santini. 1990. *The First Canadians: A Profile of Canada's Native Peoples Today.* Toronto: James Lorimer and Sons.

Conference Board of Canada. 2004. The voices of visible minorities: Speaking out on breaking down barriers. September.

Conley, Dalton. 1999. *Being Black, Living in the Red: Race, Wealth, and Social Policy in the United States.* Berkeley, CA: University of California Press.

Conlogue, Ray. 1997. "Arret! You Are Entering a French-Speaking Area." *The Globe and Mail,* 22 March.

Connor, Walker. 2000. "National Self Determination and Tomorrow's Political Map." Pp. 163–176 in *Citizenship, Diversity, & Pluralism,* eds. A. Cairns, J. C. Courtney, Peter MacKinnon, Hans J. Michelmann, and David E. Smith. Montreal/Kingston: McGill-Queen's University Press.

Cooper, Afua. 2006. *The Hanging of Angelique.* Toronto: HarperCollins.

Cornell, Stephan and Douglas Hartmann. 1998. *Ethnicity and Race. Making Identities in a Changing World.* Thousand Oaks, CA: Pine Forge Press.

Cose, Ellis. 1997. *Color-Blind. Seeing Beyond Race in a Race-Obsessed World.* NY: HarperCollins.

Cowen, T. 1999. "Cashing in on cultural free trade: Don't give us shelter: A U.S. economist sings the praises of Canadian artists." *National Post,* 24 April.

Coyle, 2004. "Racist Officer Almost Beyond Sensitivity Training." *Toronto Star,* 24 Jan.

Crepeau, Francois, and Delphine Nakache. (eds.). 2006. "Controlling Irregular Migration in Canada: Reconciling Security Concerns with Human Rights Protection." *IRPP Choices* 12(1).

CRIC (Centre for Research and Information on Canada). 2004. "ANew Canada, Revisited. July 1, 2004." Ottawa.

CRIC (Centre for Research and Information on Canada). 2005. Portraits of Canada. Backgrounder, Quebecers See Advantages in Key National Public Policies.

CRRF. 2003. *Facts About Racism and Policing.* Fact Sheet: Canadian Race Relations Foundation. www.crr.ca

Cryderman, Brian, Chris O'Toole, and Augie Fleras (eds.). 1998. *Policing, Race, and Ethnicity. A Guidebook for the Policing Services,* 3rd edition. Toronto: Butterworth.

Cudmore, James. 2001. "Inuk Accuses Ottawa of Discrimination." *National Post,* 22 March.

Curry-Stevens, Ann. 2005. *Expanding the Circle: People Who Care About Ending Racism. We Need Your Help.* Toronto: Centre for Social Justice. Available as Adobe Acrobat file from www.socialjustice.org

Curtis, Michael. 1997. "Review Essay. Antisemitism: Different Perspectives." *Sociological Forum* 12(2):321–327.

D'Angelo, Raymond, and Herbert Douglas (eds.). 2005. *Race and ethnicity: Clashing views on controversial issues.* Dubuque, Iowa: McGraw-Hill/Dushkin.

Dalmage, Heather M. (ed). 2004. *The Politics of Multiculturalism: Challenging Racial Thinking.* Albany: State University of New York.

Daly, K. 2000. "Restorative Justice in Diverse and Unequal Societies." *Criminal Justice in Diverse Communities* 17 (2):167–180.

Dasko, Donna. 2005. "Public Atttitudes Toward Multiculturalism and Bilingualism." Canadian and French Perspectives on Diversity Conference (16 Oct, 2003). Ottawa: Canadian Heritage for the Minister of Supply and Public Works.

Dauvergne, C. 2004. "Why Judy Sgro Is Just Plain Wrong—No One Is Illegal." *The Globe and Mail,* Monday, 2 August.

Davis, Kingsley and Wilbert E. Moore. 1945. "Some Principles of Stratification." *American Sociological Review* 5:242–249.

Deak, Istvan. 2002. "The Crime of the Century." *New York Review* 26 Sept. Pp. 48–50.

Dean, Bartholomew and Jerome M. Levi (eds.). 2006. *At the Risk of Being Heard: Identity, Indigenous Rights, and Postcolonial States.* University of Michigan Press.

Dei, George. 1996. "Black/African-Canadian Students' Perspectives on School Racism." Pp. 2–61 in Racism in Canadian Schools, ed. I. Alladin. Toronto: Harcourt Brace.

Dei, George Sefa. 1996. Anti-Racism Education. Theory and Practice. Halifax: Fernwood.

Dei, George Sefa. 2000. "Contesting the Future: Anti-racism and Canadian Diversity." Pp. 295–319 in *21st Century Canadian Diversity*, ed. S. Nancoo. Toronto: Canadian Scholars Press.

Dei, George Sefa. 2004. "Why I Back School Board Plan. *Toronto Star,* 26 November.

Delanty, Gerard. 2000. *Citizenship in a Global Age. Society, Culture, Politics.* Philadelphia: Open University Press.

Dempsey, Colleen and Soojin Yu. 2004. "Refugees to Canada: Who are they and how are they faring?" *Canadian Issues* (Mar): 5–10.

Dench, Janet. 2004. "Why Take Refugees?" *Canadian Issues* (Mar):11–13.

Denis, Claude. 1996. "Aboriginal Rights In/And Canadian Society. A Syewen Case Study." *International Journal of Canadian Studies* 14 (fall):13–34.

Denis, Claude. 1997. *We Are Not You: First Nations and Canadian Modernity*. Peterborough: Broadview Press.

Denley, Randall. 1998. "Its Time to Talk About the Results of Our Policy." *Kitchener-Waterloo Record,* 15 Jan.

Denton, Nancy A. and Stewart. E. Tolnay (eds.). 2002. *American Diversity: A Demographic Challenge for the Twenty-First Century*. Albany: State University of New York.

Department of Canadian Heritage. 2005. *Canada's Diversity: Respecting Our Differences*. Annual Report on the Operation of the Canadian Multiculturalism Act 2000–2004. Ottawa: Minister of Public Works and Government Services.

Desai, Sabra and Sangeeta Subramaniam. 2003. "Colour, Culture, and Dual Consciousness: Issues Identified by South Asian Immigrant Youth in the Greater Toronto Area." Pp. 118–161 inIN *Managing Two Worlds,* eds. P. Aniseff and K. M. Kilbride (eds). Pp. 118–161. Toronto: Canadian Scholars Press.

Desroches, Frederick. 1998. "The Occupational Subculture of the Police." Pp. 121–132 in *Police, Race, and Ethnicity. A Guide for Law Enforcement Officers*, eds. B. Cryderman et al. Markham: Butterworths.

Devine, Fiona, Miles Savage, John Scott, and Rosemary Crompton. 2005. *Rethinking Class: Culture, Identities, and Lifestyle*. New York: Palgrave Macmillan.

Di Matteo, Enza. 2001. "Regent Park Drive Thru." *Now*, 2–8 (August).

Diamond, Jack. 1997. "Provinces are Archaic. More Power to Cities." *The Globe and Mail,* 26 May.

Dickason, Olive Patricia. 1992. *Canada's First Nations: A History of Founding Peoples from Earliest Times.* Toronto: McClelland and Stewart.

Dijkstra, S., K. Geutjen, and A. De Ruijter. 2001. "Multiculturalism and Social Integration in Europe." *International Political Science Review* 22(1):55–84.

Diller, Jerry V. 2004. *Cultural Diversity. A Primer for the Human Services* 2nd ed. Belmont CA: Thompson – Brooks/Cole.

DiManno, Rosie. 2005. "Sharia solution a fair one, and not racist." *Toronto Star,* 16 September.

Diocson, Cecilia. 2005. "Filipino women in Canada's live-in caregiver program." *Philippine Reporter*, (March): 16–31.

Dion, Stephane. 2005. "Nothing Can Justify Secession in Canada.". *Toronto Star,* 30 October.

Dion, Susan. 2005. "Aboriginal people and stories of Canadian history." Pp. 34–57 In *Possibilities and Limitations,* ed. C. James., Halifax: Fernwood.

Doane, Ashley. 1997."Dominant Group Ethnic Identity in the United States: The Role of 'Hidden' Ethnicity in Intergroup Relations." *Sociological Quarterly* 38(3):375–397.

Dobuzinskis, Laurent. 2004. "Reasons, Reasonableness, and Reason." *Inroads* 15:80–85.

Donaldson, Ian. 2004. "Identity, Intersections of Diversity, and the Multicultural Program". *Canadian Diversity* 3(1):14–16.

Donolo, Peter and Allan Gregg. 2005. "What Regional Tensions?" *The Globe and Mail,* 22 September.

Dosman, Edgar. 1972. *Indians: The Urban Dilemma.* Toronto: McClelland and Stewart.

Douglas, Debbie. 2005. "Award Winner Battles for Immigration Workers". Cited in Debra Black, *Toronto Star*. March 9.

Dow, Steve. 2003. "Racism in the Net." Available at www.smh.com.au

Driedger, Leo. 1989. *The Ethnic Factor: Identity in Diversity.* Toronto: McGraw Hill Ryerson.

Drost, Herman, Brian Lee Crowley, and Richard Schwindt. 1995. *Marketing Solutions for Native Poverty.* Toronto: CD Howe Institute.

D'Souza, Dinesh. 1995. *The End of Racism. Principles for a Multicultural Society.* New York: Free Press.

Duffy A. 1999. "Ex-prostitute with AIDS wins deportation delay." *Windsor Star*, 20 November.

Duffy, Andrew. 2004a. "Struggle for Success." *Toronto Star,* 25 September.

Duffy, Andrew. 2004b. "Language Skills Dog Immigrants." *Toronto Star,* 11 October.

Dufraiment, Lisa. 2002. "Continuity and Modification of Aboriginal Rights in the Nisga'a Treaty." *UBC Law Review* 35(2):455–477

Duncan, Howard. 2005. "Multiculturalism: Still a Viable Concept for Integration?" *Canadian Diversity* 4(1):12–14.

Duncanson, John, Dale Ann Freed, and Chris Sorensen. 2003. "There's Racism All Over the Place." *Toronto Star,* 26 February.

Dunphy, Bill. 2003. "Immigrant Poverty Rate Soaring." *Hamilton Spectator,* 20 June.

Durie, Mason. 2005. "Race and Ethnicity in Public Policy: Does It Work?" *Social Policy Journal of New Zealand*, Issue 24 (April).

Dyer, Gwynne. 2001. "Visible Majorities." *Canadian Geographer* (Jan/Feb):45–51.

Early, G. 1993. "American Education and the Postmodernist Impulse." *American Quarterly* 45(2):220–221.

Easteal, Patricia. 1996. *Shattered Dreams. Marital Violence Against Overseas-Born Women in Australia.* Canberra: Australia National University Press.

Eck, John E. and Dennis P. Rosenbaum. 1994. "The New Police Order: Effectiveness, Equity, and Efficiency in Community Policing." Pp. 3–26 in *The Challenge of Community Policing,* ed. D. P. Rosenbaum. Thousand Oaks, CA: Sage.

Economist. 2005. "Peace, Order, and Rocky Government." 3 December.

Editorial. 2000. "The Us and the You of Quebec Nationalism." *The Globe and Mail,* 16 December.

Editorial. 2001. "No Tolerance for Incompetence." *National Post,* 2 June.

Editorial. 2001. "The Doors to Refuge." *The Globe and Mail,* 2 January.

Editorial. 2002. "How to scare away Immigrants." *National Post,* 29 August.

Editorial. 2005. "When Values Clash." *Globe and Mail,* 15 September.

Editorial. 2005. "Fighting Racism." *Share.* 17 Mar.

Editorial. 1999. "Immigrant and Refugee Women." Special Issue of Canadian Woman Studies 19(3).

Edwards, Harry. 1971. *The Sociology of Sport.* Homewood IL: Addison Wesley.

Edwards, Harry. 2000. "Crisis of Black Athletes on the Eve of the 21st. Century." In *Black and White: Race and Sports in America,* ed. Kenneth Shropshire. New York: New York University Press.

Eisenstein, Zillah. 1996. *Hatreds. Racialized and Sexualized Conflicts in the Twenty-first Century.* New York: Routledge.

Eisenstein, Zillah. 2004. *Against Empire: Feminism, Racism, and the West.* New York: Zed Books.

EKOS. 2004. "Fall 2003 Survey of First Nations People Living On-Reserve." Integrated Final Report by EKOS Research Associates. March.

Elabor-Idemudia, Patience. 1999. "The Racialisation of Gender in the Social Construction of Immigrant Women in Canada: A Case Study of African Women in a Prairie Province." *Canadian Woman Studies* 19(3):38–44.

Elliott, Jean Leonard. 1983. *Two Nations: Many Cultures. Ethnic Groups in Canada.* Scarborough, ON: Prentice-Hall.

Elmasry, M. 1999. "Framing Islam." *Kitchener-Waterloo Record,* 16 December.

El-Tablawy, Tarek. 2005. "Female-led Muslim Service Sparks Anger." *Toronto Star,* March.

Endelman, Todd M. 2005. "Anti-semitism in Western Europe Today." Pp. 64–79 in *Contemporary Anti-semitism.* D. Penslar et al, (eds.). Toronto: University of Toronto Press.

Entine, Jon. 1999. *Taboo: Why Black Athletes Dominate Sports and Why We Are Afraid to Talk About It.* New York: Public Affairs.

Entine, Jon. 2000. "Why White Men Can't Jump." *National Post,* 1 April.

ERASE. 2005. "What is Institutional Racism?" available at http://www.eraseracismny.org

Erasmus, G. and J. Sanders. 2002. "Canadian History: An Aboriginal Perspective." In *Nation to Nation: Aboriginal Sovereignty and the Future of Canada,* ed. John Bird, Lorraine Land, and Murray MacAdam. Toronto: Irwin Publishing.

Erickson, Arthur. 1997. "Our Lack of National Identity is Our Strength." *The Globe and Mail,* 10 June.

Essed, Philomena. 1991. *Understanding Everyday Racism An Interdisciplinary Study.* Newbury Park, CA: Sage.

Estes, John. 2005. *I Am A Man. Race, Manhood, and the Civil Rights Movement.* Chapel Hill, NC: The University of North Carolina Press.

Etherington, Frank. 2001. "Immigrant Women Face Double Burden if Abused." *KW Record,* 4 September.

Etherington, Frank. 2005. "Newcomers have Complex Needs." *KW Record,* 19 March.

Evans, Patrick and Sikander Hashmi. 2005. "Activists Speak Out Against Sharia." *Toronto Star,* 1 August.

Ewing, Katherine Pratt. 2002. "Legislating Religious Freedom: Challenges to the Relationship be-tween Church and State in Germany and France." Pp. 62–74 in *Engaging Cultural Differences,* ed. Richard Shweder. New York: Russell Sage Foundation.

Faces. 1996."No Labor of Love." Compiled by *Faces* staff. Spring.

Farhi, Paul. 1995. "TV 'Ghetto' has the Last Laugh on Blacks." *Guardian Weekly,* 29 January.

Farley, John E. 2005. "Race, Not Class: Explaining Racial Housing Segregration in the St Louis Metropolitan Area, 2000." *Sociological Focus* 38(2):133–150.

Feagin, Joe. 2005. "Death by Discrimination." Available at www.edchange.org.

Ferber, Abby L. 1998. *White Man Falling: Race, Gender, and White Supremacy.* Boston: Rowman & Littlefield Publishers.

Ferrante, Joan and Prince Brown Jr. 1998. *The Social Construction of Race and Ethnicity in the United States.* Don Mills, ON: Addison-Wesley.

Finnie, Ross, and Ronald Meng. 2002. "Are Immigrants' Human Capital Skills Discounted in Canada?" May. Ottawa: Statistics Canada, Business and Labour Market Analysis Division.

Fish, Stanley. 1997. "Boutique Multiculturalism, or Why Liberals Are Incapable of Thinking About Hate Speech." *Critical Inquiry* (Winter):378–95.

Fiss, Tanis. 2004. *Apartheid: Canada's Ugly Secret.* Centre for Aboriginal Policy Change. Canadian Taxpayer Federation. Calgary.

Fiss, Tanis, 2004. Westbank Self-Government Agreement (C-11). Presentation to the Senate Standing Committee on Aboriginal Peoples. Canadian Taxpayers Federations' Centre for Aboriginal Policy Change. May 4. Calgary.

Fiss, Tanis. 2005. *Dividing Canada. The Pitfalls of Native Sovereignty.* Centre for Aboriginal Policy Change. Canadian Taxpayers Federation. Calgary.

Fiss, Tanis. 2005. *Road to Prosperity: Five Steps to Change Aboriginal Policy.* Centre for Aboriginal Policy Change. Canadian Taxpayers Federation. September. Calgary.

Fitzgerald, Marian and Mike Hough. 2002. *Policing for London: Responding to Diversity.* www.policingforlondon.org

Flanagan, Tom. 1999. *First Nations? Second Thoughts.* Montreal and Kingston: McGill-Queen's University Press.

Flanagan, Tom. 2001. "Property Rights on the Rez." *National Post,* 11 December.

Fleras, Augie. 1987. "Redefining the Politics over Aboriginal Language Renewal. Maori Language Schools as Agents of Social Change." *Canadian Journal of Native Studies* 7(1):1–40.

Fleras, Augie. 1993. "From Culture to Equality: Multiculturalism as Ideology and Policy." Pp. 330–352 in *Social Inequality in Canada*, (2nd ed.) eds. James Curtis, Edward Grab, and Neil Guppy. Scarborough: Prentice-Hall.

Fleras, Augie. 1996. "The Politics of Jurisdiction." Pp. 11–143 in *Visions of the Heart,* eds. David Long and Olive Dickason. Toronto: Harcourt Brace.

Fleras, Augie. 1998. "From Force to Service: Community Policing in Canada." Pp. 94–134 in *Police, Race, and Ethnicity: A Guide for Law Enforcement Officers* (3rd ed.), eds. Brian K. Cryderman et al. Toronto: Butterworths.

Fleras, Augie. 2001. *Social Problems in Canada: Constructions, Conditions, and Challenges* (3rd ed.). Don Mills, ON: Pearson Education.

Fleras, Augie. 2002. *Engaging Diversity: Multiculturalism in Canada: Politics, Policies, and Practices.* Scarborough, ON: Nelson.

Fleras, Augie. 2002. "Multiculturalism as Critical Discourse: Contesting Modernity." *Canadian Issues* (February) 9–11.

Fleras, A. 2004. "Racializing Culture/Culturalizing Race: Multicultural racism in a multicultural Canada." In C.A. Nelson and C.A. Nelson (Eds.), *Racism eh? A critical inter-disciplinary anthology of race and racism in Canada.* Pp. 429–443. Concord, ON: Captus Press.

Fleras, Augie, and Frederick J. Desroches. 1989. "Bridging the Gap: Towards a Multicultural Policing in Canada." *Canadian Police College Journal* 13(3):153–164.

Fleras, Augie, and Jean Leonard Elliott. 1992. *Multiculturalism in Canada: The Challenge of Diversity.* Scarborough: Nelson.

Fleras, Augie, and Jean Leonard Elliott. 1992. *The Nations Within: Aboriginal-State Relations in Canada, the United States, and New Zealand.* Toronto: Oxford University Press.

Fleras, Augie, and Jean Leonard Elliott. 2003. *Unequal Relations: An Introduction to Race and Ethnic Dynamics in Canada.* Toronto: Pearson Education Canada.

Fleras, Augie, and Jean Lock Kunz. 2001. *Media and Minorities: Misrepresenting Minorities in a Multicultural Canada.* Toronto: TEP.

Fleras, Augie, and Paul Spoonley. 1999. *Recalling Aotearoa: Indigenous Politics and Ethnic Dynamics in New Zealand.* Auckland: Oxford University Press.

Fleras, Augie, and Roger Maaka. 1998. "Politicising Customary Rights: Tino Rangatiratanga as Post-Colonising Engagement." *Sites* (NZ) 35:20–47.

Fleras, Augie, and Vic Krahn. 1992. "From Community Development to Inherent Self-Government: Restructuring Aboriginal-State Relations in Canada." Paper presented at the Annual Meetings of Learned Societies. Charlottetown. June.

Fleury, Jean-Guy. 2004. "Canadian Values at Work. The Immigration and Refugee Board." *Canadian Issues* (Mar): 41–42.

Flynn, Karen. 1998. "I Prayed that the Killer Was Not Black." *Toronto Star,* 18 August

Folson, Rose Baaba. 2004. *Calculated kindness: Global restructuring, immigration, and settlement in Canada.* Halifax: Fernwood.

Fontaine, Phil. 2003. "Native Status Not an Obstacle." Letter to the *National Post,* 3 November.

Fontaine, Phil. 2005. "First Nations Rights are Contractual and Benefit Everyone." *The Globe and Mail,* 21 July.

Foot, R. 2000. "Canadians are an Ethnic Group in Their Own Right, Professor Says." *National Post,* 28 January.

Forcese, Denis. 2000. *Police: Current Issues in Canadian Law Enforcement.* Toronto: Golden Dog Press.

Foster, Cecil. 2005. *Where Race Does Not Matter: The New Spirit of Modernity.* Toronto: Penguin.

Foster, Lorne. 1998. *Turnstile Immigration. Multiculturalism, Social Order, and Social Justice in Canada.* Toronto: Thompson Education.

Fournier, Pierre. 1994. *A Meech Lake Post-mortem: Is Quebec Sovereignty Inevitable?* Montreal: McGill-Queen's Press.

Francis, D. 1992. *The Imaginary Indian: The Image of the Indian in Canadian Culture.* Vancouver: Arsenal Pulp Press.

Francis, Diane. 2001. "Canada Gets Well-Deserved U.S. Snub." *National Post,* 22 September.

Francis, Diane. 2001. "Cities Fight for Fair Refugee Policy." *National Post,* 15 May.

Francis, Diane. 2001. "Federal Policy Alarms Reader." *National Post,* 12 June.

Francis, Diane. 2002. Immigration: The Economic Case. Toronto: Key Porter.

Francis, Diane. 2005. "Immigration Issues Should be Probed." *National Post,* 28 April.

Franck, Thomas M. 2001. "Are Human Rights Universal?" *Foreign Affairs* 80(1):191–204.

Frankenberg, Ruth (ed.). 1993. *White Women, Race Matters. The Social Construction of Whiteness.* Minneapolis: University of Minnesota Press.

Fraser, Graham. 2004. "Premiers Reminded of Suicide Epidemic." *Toronto Star,* 26 Sept.

Fraser, Graham. 2005. "Racism on the Rise." *Hamilton Spectator,* 16 March.

Fraser, John. 1989. "Refugee Riddles, Dark Mirrors, and the National Honour." *Saturday Night,* 7–8 March.

Frederickson, G.M. 1999. "Mosaics and Melting Pots." *Dissent* (summer):36–43.

Frederickson, G.M. 2002. *Racism. A Short History.* Princeton, NJ: Princeton University Press.

Frederico, Christopher and Samantha Luks. 2005. "The Political Psychology of Race." *International Journal of Political Psychology* 26(6):661–674.

Freeze, Colin. 2005. "Criminals with Refugee Claims are Well-Versed on Their Rights." *Globe and Mail,* 18 April.

Freeze, Colin, and M. Jimenez. 2004. "Gangsters' Victims Seek Haven in Canada." *The Globe and Mail*, Saturday, 18 Sept.

Fridell, Robert Lunney, Drew Diamond and Bruce Kubu. 2001. *Racially Biased Policing: A Principled Response.* Washington DC: Police Executive Research Forum.

Frideres, James S. 1998. *Native Peoples in Canada: Contemporary Conflicts* (5th ed.). Scarborough: Prentice-Hall.

Frideres, James S., and René R. Gadacz. 2005. *Aboriginal Peoples in Canada*, 7th ed. Scarborough: Pearson Education Canada.

Friesen, Joe. 2005. "Blame Canada (for Multiculturalism)." *The Globe and Mail,* 20 August.

Frith, Rosaline. 2003. "Integration." *Canadian Issues* (Apr): 35–36.

Fukuyama, Frances. 1994. "The War of All Against All." *New York Times Book Review,* 10 April.

Fulford, Robert. 1997. "Observer: Do Canadians want ethnic heritage freeze-dried?" *Globe and Mail,* 19 February.

Fulford, Robert. 2003. "From Russia, with stories: David Bezmozgis captures the essence of immigrant life in his new fiction." *The National Post*, 27 May.

Gagnon, Alain-G. 1996. *Canadian Parties in Transition.* Toronto: Nelson Canada.

Gagnon, Alain-G., Monsterrat Guibernau, and Francois Rocher, (eds.). 2003. *The Conditions of Diversity in Multinational Democracies.* Montreal: IRRP.

Gagnon, Lysiane. 2005. "The Folly of Sharia in Ontario." *The Globe and Mail,* 5 September.

Gagnon, Lysianne. 1996. "Sorry to be Boring but Quebec Loves its Constitutional Contradictions." *The Globe and Mail,* 6 July.

Galabuzi, Grace-Edward. 2006. *Canada's Economic Apartheid: The Social Exclusion of Racialized Groups in the New Century.* Toronto: Canadian Scholars Press.

Gallagher, Stephen. 2004. "Canada and the Challenge of Asylum Migration." *Canadian Issues* (Mar):43–44.

Garroutte, Eva Marie. 2003. *Real Indians. Identity and the Survival of Native Americans.* Berkeley: University of California Press.

Gates Jr., Henry Louis. 1998. "The Two Nations of Black America." *Brookings Review* 16(2):4–7.

Gay, G. 1997. "Educational Equality for Students of Color." Pp. 195–228 in *Multicultural Education,* eds. J. Banks and C. Banks. Toronto: Allyn and Bacon.

Gee, Marcus. 1998. "Is this the End for Suharto?" *The Globe and Mail,* 14 Jan.

Gee, Marcus. 2001. "Debunking the Race Myth." *The Globe and Mail,* 15 February.

Gee, Marcus. 2001. "Ethnic Conflicts." *The Globe and Mail,* 8 August.

Gerstle, Gary. 2003. "Pluralism and the war on terror." *Dissent* (spring):31–39.

Ghitis, Frida. 2005. "Europe Casts Wary Eye on France." *Toronto Star,* 27 November.

Ghuman, Paul A. Singh. 2003. *Double Loyalties: South Asian Adolescents in the West.* Cardiff: University of Wales Press.

Gibb, J. T., and L. Huang. 2003. *Children of color: Psychological intervention with culturally diverse youth.* (2nd ed.). San Francisco: Jossey Bass.

Gibbins, Roger and Guy Laforest (eds.). 1998. *Beyond the Impasse? Toward Reconciliation.* Montreal: Institute of Research for Public Policy.

Gibson, Gordon. 1998. "Nisga'a Treaty: The Good, the Bad, and the Alternative." *The Globe and Mail,* 13 October.

Gibson, Gordon. 2005. "Canada's Apartheid World." *The Globe and Mail,* 15 July.

Gillborn, David. 1998. "Race and Ethnicity in Compulsory Education" Pp. 11–23 in *Race and Higher Education,* eds. T. Modood and T. Acland. Policy Studies Institute: University of Westminister.

Gillespie, Marie. 1996. *Television, Ethnicity, and Cultural Change.* London: Routledge.

Gillies, James. 1997. "Thinking the Unthinkable and the Republic of Canada." *The Globe and Mail,* 28 June.

Gillmor, Don. 1996. "The Punishment Station." *Toronto Life* (Jan): 46–55.

Gilroy, Paul. 2004. *After Empire: Melancholia or Convivial Culture?* London: Routledge.

Giroux, H. E. 1994. "Insurgent Multiculturalism as the Promise of Pedagogy." Pp. 325–43 in *Multiculturalism: A Critical Reader,* ed. D. T. Goldberg. Oxford: Blackwell.

Giroux, Henry E. 1995. "Foreward" Pp. ix–xi in *Culture and Difference: Critical Perspectives in the Bicultural Experience in the United States,* ed. Antonia Darder. Westport Conn: Bergin and Garvey.

Giroux, H 1999. "Rewriting the Discourse of Racial Identity: Towards a Pedagogy and Politics of Whiteness. *Harvard Educational Review* 67(2): 285–320.

Glazer, Nathaniel. 1997. *We are All Multiculturalists Now.* Cambridge: Harvard University Press.

Glenn, Evelyn Nakano. 2002. *Unequal Freedom: How Race and Gender Shaped American Citizenship and Labor.* Cambridge: Harvard University Press.

Globe and Mail. 2005. Editorial: "When Values Clash." 15 September.

Goar, Carol. 2004. "Immigration Report Masks Truths." *Toronto Star,* 8 November.

Goar, Carol. 2005. "Nation Ignores U.N. Criticism." *Toronto Star,* 11 November.

Goldberg, D. T. (ed). 1994. *Multiculturalism: A Critical Reader.* Oxford: Blackwell.

Goldberg, David Theo. 1993. *Philosophy and the Politics of Meaning.* Oxford: Basil Blackwell.

Goldberg, David Theo. 1994. "Introduction: Multicultural Conditions." Pp. 1–44 in *Multiculturalism: A Critical Reader,* ed. D.T. Goldberg. Cambridge, MA: Basil Blackwell.

Goldberg, David Theo. 2005. "Racial Americanization." Pp. 87–102 in *Racialization,* eds. K. Murji and J. Solomos. Oxford, UK: Oxford University Press.

Goldsborough, James. 2000. "Out of Control Immigration." *Foreign Affairs* (Sept/Oct):89–101.

Gordon, Sean. 2005. "A New Kind of Sovereigntist." *Toronto Star,* 30 October.

Gosine, Andil. 2003. "Myths of Diversity." *Alternatives Journal* 29(1):1–4.

Gosnell, Joseph. 2000. "Nisga'a Treaty Options Opens Economic Doors For Everyone." Speech to the Canadian Club. 15 May. Reprinted in the *Canadian Speeches* 14(4):10–14.

Grace, Daphne. 2004. *The Woman in the Muslin Mask: Veiling and Identity in Postcolonial Literature*. London: Pluto Press.

Grand Council of the Crees. 1995. "Sovereign Injustice: Forcible Inclusion of the James Bay Cree and Cree Territory into a Sovereign Quebec." Nemaska, QC: Grand Council of the Crees. October. Available at www.uni.ca

Grant, Hugh M. and Ronald R. Oertel. 1999. "Diminishing Returns to Immigration? Interpreting the Economic Experience of Canadian Immigrants." *Canadian Ethnic Studies* 31(3):56–66.

Gray, John. 1998. "Mining Companies Reluctant to Invest After Ruling." *The Globe and Mail,* 9 June.

Gray, John. 2001. "Separatists Have Never Agreed on the Route." *National Post,* 13 January.

Green, Joyce. 2003. "Decolonizing in the Age of Globalization." *Canadian Dimension* (Mar/Apr):3–5.

Green, Paul. 1994. *Studies in New Zealand Social Problems*. Palmerston, North NZ: Dunmore Publishing

Green, Ross Gordon. 1998. *Justice in Aboriginal Communities: Sentencing Alternatives.* Saskatoon, SK: Purich Publishing.

Greenberg, Lee. 2005. "Opposition to Sharia Courts Goes Global." *National Post,* 8 September.

Greenspon, Edward. 1998. "Sovereignty Outlook Weakening." *The Globe and Mail,* 2 April.

Greenspon, Edward. 2001. "Building the New Canadian Identity." *The Globe and Mail,* 10 November.

Gregg, Alan. 2006. "Identity Crisis. Multiculturalism: A Twentieth-Century Dream Becomes a Twenty-first Century Conundrum. Pp. 28–38 of *Walrus*, March.

Griffin, Richard. 1996. "Canada was the Testing Site for Baseball's Racial Experiment." *Kitchener-Waterloo Record*, 1 June.

Gross, Michael L. 1996. "Restructuring Ethnic Paradigms: From Premodern to Postmodern Perspectives." *Canadian Review of Studies in Nationalism* xxiii(1–2): 51–65.

Grubel, Herbert. 2005. *Immigration and the Welfare State in Canada: Growing Conflicts, Constructive Solutions.* Public Policy Sources no. 84. Vancouver: The Fraser Institute. Digital document available at www.fraserinstitute.ca/admin/books/files/Immigration.pdf no

Grzejszczak, Katherine and Todd Gordon. 2005. "Capitalism and Immigration." http://newsocialist.org

Guimond, Eric, Don Kerr, and Roderic Beaujot. 2004. "Charting the growth of Canada's aboriginal populations: problems, options, and implications." *Canadian Studies in Population* 31(3): 55–82.

Gunew, Sneja. 1999. "Colonial Hauntings: The (Post)Colonialism of Multiculturalism in Australia and Canada." *Australian-Canadian Studies* 17(2):11–31.

Gurr, Ted Robert. 2001. *Peoples Vs States: Minorities at Risk in the New Century*. Washington: United States Institute for Peace.

Gurwitz, Jonathan. 2005. "World is Ignoring War in Darfur." *San Antonio Express News.* Reprinted in the *Kitchener Waterloo Record*, 19 May.

Gwyn, Richard. 1994. "The First Borderless State." *Toronto Star,* 26 November.

Gwyn, Richard. 1996. *Nationalism Without Walls: The Unbearable Lightness of Being Canadian.* Toronto: McClelland & Stewart.

Gwyn, Richard. 1999. "Canada's Generosity an Illusion." *Toronto Star,* 17 September.

Gwyn, Richard. 2000. "A Visionary Challenges Our Policy on Immigration." *Toronto Star,* 12 March.

Gwyn, Richard. 2001. "Old Canada Disappears." *Toronto Star,* 21 March.

Gwyn, Richard. 2001. "Racism Must Be Addressed." *KW Record,* 5 September.

Hage, G. 1998. *White Nation: Fantasies of White Supremacy in a Multicultural Society.* Sydney, Australia: Pluto Press.

Hagey, Rebecca et al. 2001. "Immigrant Nurses' Experience of Racism," *Journal of Nursing Scholarship,* Vol. 33 No. 4, Pp. 389–94.

Hagey, Rebecca. 2004. "Implementing Accountability for Equity." *Directions* 2(1):59–77.

Hagopian, Susan. 2003. *Canada's skilled worker program: Speaking to the experts.* Metropolis Policy Briefs. Pp. 3–4.

Hai, Yasmin. 2003. "Sex is part of our culture now." *Guardian Weekly,* November 13–19.

Hall, Anthony J. 2000. "Racial Discrimination in Legislation, Litigation, Legend, and Lore." *Canadian Ethnic Studies* 32(2):119–37.

Hall, Stuart. 1996. "New Ethnicities." In *Stuart Hall in Critical Studies,* eds. D. Marley and K. H. Chen. London: Routledge.

Halli, Shiva S. and Leo Driedger (eds.). 1999. *Immigrant Canada: Demographic, Economic, and Social Challenges.* Toronto: University of Toronto Press.

Hamilton, Graeme. 2005. "'Sovereign' Reserve Hits the Jackpot." *National Post,* 18 July.

Hamilton, Roberta. 1996. *Gendering the Vertical Mosaic: Feminist Perspectives on Canadian Society.* Toronto: Copp Clark.

Handa, Amita. 2003. *Of Silk Saris and Mini-Skirts. South Asian Girls Walk the Tightrope of Culture.* Toronto: Women's Press.

Harding, Katherine. 2005. "Hail to Ms. Chief." *The Globe and Mail,* 2 September.

Harris, Fred. 1995. *Multiculturalism from the Margins.* Westport, CT: Bergin and Garvey.

Harris, Leonard, ed. 1999. <u>*Racism.*</u> Amherst, NY: Humanity Books.

Harris, Paul. 1997. *Black Rage Confronts the Law.* New York: New York University Press.

Harris, Scott R. 2005. "Challenging the Conventional Wisdom: Recent Proposals for the Interpretive Study of Inequality." *Human Studies* 27:113–136.

Harrison, Trevor W., and John W. Friesen. 2004. *Canadian society in the twenty—first century: A historical sociological approach.* Toronto: Pearson.

Harty, Siobhan and Michael Murphy. 2005. *In Defence of Multinational Citizenship.* Vancouver: UBC Press.

Harvey, Edward B., Bobby Siu, and Kathleen D. V. Reil. 1999. "Ethnocultural Groups, Period of Immigration and Socioeconomic Situation." *Canadian Ethnic Studies* 31(3):95–108.

Hawkes, David. 2000. "Review of Citizens-Plus." *Isuma* (Autumn):141–42.

Hayter, Teresa. 2001. "Open Borders: The Case against Immigrant Controls." *Capital & Class* 75:149–55.

Heath, A. F., and J. R. Tilley. 2005. "National identity and xenophobia in an ethnically divided society." *International Journal on Multicultural Societies* 7(2): 119–132.

Hebert, Yvonne M., and Lori Wilkinson. 2002. "The Citizenship Debates: Conceptual, Policy, Experiential, and Educational Issues" Pp. 3–36 in *Citizenship in Transformation in Canada,* ed. Y. Hebert. Toronto: University of Toronto Press.

Hechter, Michael. 1975. *Internal Colonialism: The Celtic Fringe in British National Development.* Berkeley: University of California Press.

Heinbecker, Paul, and Lloyd Axworthy. 2005. "Let's do the Right Thing in Quebec." *The Globe and Mail,* 4 June.

Helly, Denise. 1993. "The Political Regulation of Cultural Plurality: Foundations and Principles." *Canadian Ethnic Studies* XXV(2):15–31.

Helmes-Hayes, Rick, and James Curtis (eds.). 1998. *The Vertical Mosaic Revisited.* Toronto: University of Toronto Press.

Heneghan, Tom. 2004. "Muslims Say French Misunderstand Headscarf Issue." *Agence France Presse*, 9 February.

Henry, Frances. 1994. *The Caribbean Diaspora in Canada.* Toronto: University of Toronto Press.

Henry, Frances, and Carol Tator. 1993. "The Show Boat Controversy." *Toronto Star,* 28 May.

Henry, Frances, and Carol Tator. 2000. *Racist Discourse in Canada's English Print Media.* Toronto: Canadian Race Relations Foundation.

Henry, Frances, and Carol Tator. 2002. *Discourses of Domination: Racial Bias in the Canadian English-Language Press.* Toronto: University of Toronto Press.

Henry, Frances and Carol Tator. 2006. *The Colour of Democracy: Racism in Canadian Society* (3rd ed.). Toronto: Harcourt Brace/Nelson.

Herman, Ed, and Noam Chomsky. 1988. *Manufacturing Consent: The Political Economy of Mass Media.* New York: Pantheon Books.

Hermer, Joe, Michael Kempa, Clifford Shearing, Philip Stenning, and Jennifer Wood. 2005. "Policing in Canada in the Twenty-first Century: Directions for Law Reform." Pp. 22–91 in *Re-Imagining Policing in Canada*, ed. D. Cooley. Toronto: University of Toronto Press.

Hiebert, Dan. 2000. "Immigration and the Changing Canadian City." *Canadian Geographer* 44(1):25-43.

Hiebert, Dan. 2003. "Immigration and Minority Enclaves." *Canadian Issues* (April): 27–29.

Hiebert, Dan, Jock Collins, and Paul Spoonley. 2003. "Uneven globalization: Neoliberal regimes, immigration, and multiculturalism in Australia, Canada, and New Zealand." Working Paper Series No 03-05. Research on Immigration and Integration in the Metropolis. Vancouver, B.C.: Vancouver Centre of Excellence.

Hiller, Harry. 2000. *Canadian Society. A Macro Analysis,* 4th ed. Scarborough: Prentice-Hall.

Hinsliff, Gaby and Martin Bright. 2000. "Black Youth Culture Blamed as Youths Fail." *Times Higher Education Supplement,* 24 August.

Hinton, M., E. Johson, and D. Rigney. 1997. *Indigenous Peoples and the Law.* Sydney: Cavendish publishing.

Hochschild, Jennifer L. 1998. "American Racial and Ethnic Politics in the 21st Century." *Brookings Review* 16(2):43–46.

Holdaway, Simon. 1996. *The Racialisation of British Policing.* New York, NY: St. Martin's Press.

Holmes, Steven A. 2001. "Levelling the Playing Field, But for Whom?" *NY Times,* 1 July.

Hommel, Maurice. 2001. "Escaping Poisonous Embrace of Racism." *Toronto Star,* 24 August.

Hoodfar, Homa. 2003. "More Than Clothing: Veiling as an Adaptive Strategy." Pp. 3-40 in *The Muslim Veil in North America*, eds. S. S. Alvi et al. Toronto: The Women's Press.

hooks, bell. 1995. *Killing Rage.* Boston: South End Press.

hooks, bell. 1994. *Outlaw Culture: Resisting Representations.* New York: Routledge.

Horton, James O. and Lois E Horton. 2004. *Slavery and the Making of America.* New York: Oxford University Press.

Howard, Albert and Frances Widdowson. 1999. "The disaster of Nunavut." *Policy Options.* (Jul/Aug):58–61.

Howard-Hassmann, R. E. 1999. "'Canadian' as an Ethnic Category: Implications for Multiculturalism and National Unity." *Canadian Public Policy* 25(4):523–537.

Howes, Carol. 2001. "The New Native Economy." *National Post,* 27 January.

Howlett, Karen. 2005. "Islamic-law plan will Respect Rights, Ontario Says." *Globe and Mail,* 7 September.

Hum, Derek and Wayne Simpson. 2000. "Not all Visible Minorities Face Labour Market Discrimination." *Policy Options* (Dec):45–51.

Humpage, Louise and Augie Fleras. 2001. "Intersecting Discourses. Closing the Gaps, Social Justice, and the Treaty of Waitaingi." *Social Policy Journal of New Zealand* 16:37–54.

Huntington, Samuel. 1993. *The Clash of Civilizations and the Remaking of World Order.* New York: Simon and Schuster.

Hurst, Lynda. 2003. "A Critical Meaning of Bias." *Toronto Star,* 12 April.

Hurst, Lynda. 2005. "Canada Among First to Allow Dual Citizenship." *Toronto Star,* 20 August.

Hurst, Lynda. 2005. "Sharia law out of the question, Quebec government insists." *Toronto Star,* 26 March.

Hurst, Lynda. 2006. "Discontent in Eurabia." *Toronto Star,* 11 February.

Hurtado, Aida. 1996. *The Color of Privilege: Three Blasphemies on Race and Feminism.* Michigan: University of Michigan Press.

Hutchinson, John, and Anthony D. Smith (eds.) 1996. *Ethnicity.* London: Oxford University Press.

Hylton, John H. (ed.) 1999/1994. *Aboriginal Self-Government in Canada: Current Trends and Issues.* Saskatoon, SK: Purich Publishing.

Hylton, John. 2002. "The Justice System and Canada's Aboriginal Peoples: the Persistence of Racial Discrimination." Pp. 139–158 in *Crimes of Colour,* eds. W. Chan and K. Mirchandani. Peterborough: Broadview Press.

Hyndman, Jennifer. 1999. "Gender and Canadian Immigration Policy: A Current Snapshot." *Canadian Woman Studies* 19(3):6–10.

Ibbitson, John. 2004. "Why Atlantic Canada Remains White and Poor." *The Globe and Mail,* 20 August.

Ibbitson, John. 2005. "McLellan Becomes 'Minister No' to Visible Minorities." *The Globe and Mail,* 6 April.

Ibbitson, John. 2005. "Canada's Immigration Challenge." *The Globe and Mail,* 11 March.

Ibbitson, John. 2005. *The Polite Revolution: Perfecting the Canadian Dream.* Toronto: McLelland & Stewart.

Ibhawoh, Bonny. 2000. "Between Culture and Constitution: Evaluating the Cultural Legitimacy of Human Rights in the African State." *Human Rights Quarterly* 22:838–60.

Ignace, M. B., and R. E. Ignace. 1998. "The Old Wolf in Sheep's Clothing: Canadian Aboriginal Peoples." Pp. 101–132. in *Multiculturalism in a World of Leaking Boundaries,* ed. D. Haselbach. New Brunswick, N: Transaction Publishers.

Ignatieff, Michael. 1994. *Blood and Belonging: Journeys into the New Nationalism.* Toronto: Viking.

Ignatieff, Michael. 1995. "Nationalism and the Narcissism of Minor Differences." *Queens Quarterly* 102(1): 1–25.

Ignatieff, Michael. 2001. "Human Rights and the Rights of the State: Are They on a Collision Course?" Hagey Lecture. University of Waterloo, 24 January.

Ignatieff, Michael. 2001. "The Attack on Human Rights." *Foreign Affairs* (Nov/Dec):102–14.

Ignatieff, Michael. 2001. "The Hate Stops Here." *The Globe and Mail,* 25 October.

Ignatieff, Michael. 2005. "The Coming Constitutional Crisis." *The Globe and Mail,* 16 April.

Immigration: Opportunities and Challenges. 2003. Editorial. Special issue of *Canadian Issues* (April).

INAC 2003. Budget 2003. Backgrounder: Demographics.

INAC 2004. *The Landscape. Public Opinion on Aboriginal and Northern Issues.* Published under the authority of the Minister of Indian Affairs and Northern Development.

INAC. 2004. *Sustainable Development Strategy 2004–2006. On the Right Path Together. A Sustainable Future for First Nations, Inuit, and Northern Communities.* Available at www.ainc-inac.gc.ca

Ip, Manying. 1998. "Gender, Racism, and the Politics of Chinese Immigration." In *Feminist Thought in Aotearoa/New Zealand.* Auckland: Auckland University Press.

Isajiw, Wsevolod (ed.). 1997. *Multiculturalism in North America and Europe: Comparative Perspectives on Interethnic Relations and Social Incorporation.* Toronto: Canadian Scholars Press.

Isajiw, Wsevolod W. 1997. Multiculturalism in North America and Europe: Comparative Perspectives on Interethnic Relations and Social Incorporation. Toronto: Canadian Scholars Press.

Isajiw, Wsevolod W. 1999. *Understanding Diversity. Ethnicity and Race in the Canadian Context.* Toronto: Thompson Educational.

Isbister, John. 1996. *The Immigration Debate: Remaking America.* West Hartford, CT: Kumarian Press.

Isin, Engin. 1996. "Global City-Regions and Citizenship." In *Local Places in the Age of the Global City*, eds. D. Bell, R. Keil, and G. Wekerle. Montreal: Black Rose Books.

Ivison, John. 2004. *"The end of 'one country, one voice' "*? *National Post,* 26 November.

Jaimet, K. 2005. "Policy creating ghetto nation." *National Post,* 23 September, A13.

Jain, Harish C. 1988. "Affirmative Action/Employment Equity Programs and Visible Minorities in Canada." *Currents* 3–7.

Jain, Harish C. and Rick D. Hackett 1989. "Measuring Effectiveness of Employment Equity Programs in Canada: Public Policy and a Survey." Canadian Public Policy XV(2): 189–204.

Jain, Harish, C. P. Singh, and C. Agocs. 2000. "Recruitment, Selection, and Promotion of Visible-Minority and Aboriginal Police Officers in Selected Canadian Police Services." *Canadian Public Administration* 42(3):46–67.

Jakubowicz, Andrew et al.1994. *Racism, Ethnicity, and the Media.* St Leonards NSW: Allen & Unwin

Jakubowicz, Andrew. 2005. "Multiculturalism in Australia: Apogee or Nadir?" *Canadian Diversity.* 4(1): 15–18.

James, Carl. 1998. *Seeing Ourselves: Exploring Race, Ethnicity, and Culture.* 2nd ed. Toronto: Thompson Education.

James, Carl, ed. 2005. *Possibilities and Limitations. Multicultural Policies and Programs in Canada.* Halifax: Fernwood.

James, Carl, and Adrienne Shadd (eds.) 1994. *Talking About Differences. Encounters in Culture, Language, and Identity.* Toronto: Between the Lines.

James, Steve, and Ian Warren. 1995. "Police Culture." Pp. 3–13 in *Cultures of Crime and Violence. The Australian Experience,* ed. Judith Bessant et al. Bandoora VIC: LaTrobe University Press.

Jaret, Charles. 1995. Contemporary Racial and Ethnic Relations. Scarborough, ON: Harper Collins.

Jaworsky, John. 1979. *A Case Study of Canadian Federal Government's Multicultural Policies.* Unpublished MA Thesis. Political Science. Ottawa: Carleton.

Jedwab, Jack. 2002. "Melting Mosaic: Changing Realities in Cultural Diversity in Canada and the United States." *Canadian Issues* (February): Pp. 19–23.

Jedwab, Jack. 2005a. "Event that has Most Influenced English-French Relations and Quebec's Most Respected Political Leaders." Exclusive to the *Montreal Gazette* and Le *Devoir*. Week of July 25.

Jedwab, Jack. 2005b. "Neither Finding Nor Losing Our Way: The Debate over Canadian Multiculturalism." *Canadian Diversity* 4(1):95–102.

Jencks, Christopher and Meredith Phillips. 1998. "The Black-White Test Score Gap." *Brookings Review* 16(2):24–27.

Jenson, Jane. 2002. *Citizenship: Its Relationship to the Canadian Diversity Model.* Paper for the Program and Policy Officers of the Department of Canadian Heritage. Ottawa.

Jenson, Jane, and Martin Papillon. 2001. "The Changing Boundaries of Citizenship. A Review and a Research Agenda."

Jhappan, Radha. 1995. "The Federal-Provincial Power Grid and Aboriginal Self-Government." Pp. 15–186 in *New Trends in Canadian Federalism*, ed F. Rocher and M. Smith. Peterborough, ON: Broadview Press

Jimenez, Marina. 1999. "Immigration Rules Costing Canada Billions." *National Post,* 18 February.

Jimenez, Marina 2004. "Tough Refugee Rules Create Agony for Parents." *The Globe and Mail,* 16 October.

Jimenez, Marina. 2005. "Refugee Approval Rates Vary Widely." *The Globe and Mail.* 24 July.

Jimenez, Marina. 2005. Sharia Protestors Target Canada. *The Globe and Mail.* 2 September.

Jimenez, Marina. 2005. "Volpe to Reject Appeal System for Refugees." *The Globe and Mail*, 1 Nov.

Jimenez, Marina and Michael Den Tandt. 2005. "How to Repair the Welcome Mat." *The Globe and Mail,* 22 April.

Jiwani, Yasmin. 2002. "The Criminalization of "Race," the Racialization of Crime." In *Crimes of Colour*, ed. W. Chan and W. Mirchandani. Peterborough: Broadview.

Jiwani, Yasmin. 2001. *Intersecting Inequalities. Immigrant Women of Colour, Violence, and Health Care.* Available at www.harbour.sfu.ca/freda/articles/hlth04.htm

Johal, Rav. 2003. "The Internal Battle of Cultures." *Toronto Star*. November 11.

Jonas, George. 2006. "Anti-Semitism's Presentable Cousin." *National Post*. 20 January.

Jull, Peter, and Donna Craig. 1997. "Reflections on Regional Agreements: Yesterday, Today, and Tomorrow." *Australian Indigenous Law Reporter* 2(4):475–493.

Kalbach, M. A., and W. E. Kalbach. 1999. "Demographic Overview of Ethnic Origin." Groups in Canada. Pp. 3–20 in *Race and Ethnic Relations in Canada*, 2nd ed. Toronto: Oxford University Press.

Kamalimpour, Y.R., and T Carilli, (eds.). 1998. *Cultural Diversity and the U.S. Media*. New York: State University of New York Press.

Kanter, Rosabeth. 1977. *Men and Women of the Corporation*. New York: Vintage.

Karim, Karim H. 2002. *Islamic Peril. Media and Global Violence*. Montreal: Black Rose Books.

Kastoryano, Riva. 2004. "France's Veil Affair." *Inroads.* 15:62–71.

Katz, Irwin, Joyce Wackenhut, and R. Glen Hass. 1986. "Racial Ambivalence, Value Duality, and Behavior." Pp. 35–60 in *Prejudice, Discrimination, and Racism*. ed. John F. Dovidio and Samuel L. Gaertner. New York: Academic Press.

Kavakci, Merve. 2004. "Headscarf Controversy." *Foreign Policy*. (May/June): 66–67.

Kazemipur, A. and S. S. Halli. 2003. "Poverty Experiences of Immigrants: Some Reflections." *Canadian Issues*. (April): 18–20.

Kenna, Kathleen. 2000. "Refugee Numbers 'Dismal.'" *Toronto Star*, 15 June.

Kennedy, Randall. 1996. *Race, Crime, and the Law*. New York: Pantheon Books

Kernerman, Gerald. 2005. *Multicultural Nationalism. Civilizing Difference, Constituting Community*. Vancouver: UBC Press.

Keung, Nicholas. 2001. "Canadians Upbeat about Economic Impact of Immigration, Forum Told." *Toronto Star*, 1 March.

Keung, Nicholas. 2004. "A Business Case for Diversity." *Toronto Star*, 6 May.

Keung, Nicholas. 2005 "Racism Hurts Nurses, Study." *Toronto Star*, 6 May.

Keung, Nicholas. 2005. "New Policy Slashes Refugee Claims." *Toronto Star*, 19 August.

Kevles, Daniel J. 1995. *In the Name of Eugenics: Genetics and the Use of Human Heredity*. New York: Alfred A. Knopf, Inc.

Khan, Sheema. 2005. "The Sharia Debate Deserves Proper Hearing." *The Globe and Mail*, 15 September.

Khayatt, Didi. 1994. "The Boundaries of Identity at the Intersections of Race, Class, and Gender." *Canadian Women Studies*. (14)(2):6–13.

Kilgour, David. 2005. "Darfur: Tears are Not Enough." *Toronto Star*, 15 May.

Kinsella, Warren. 1994. *Web of Hate: The Far-Right Network in Canada*. Toronto: Harper Collins.

Kitaro, Harry. 1997. *Race Relations*. Englewood Cliffs, NJ: Prentice-Hall.

Kivel, Paul. 1996. U*prooting Racism: How White People Can Work for Justice*. Philadelphia: New Society Publishers.

Kivisto, Peter, and Wendy Ng. 2005. *Americans All*, 2nd ed.. Los Angeles: Roxbury.

Knowles, Valerie. 1992. *Strangers at our Gates. Canadian Immigration and Immigration Policy. 1540–1990*. Toronto: Dundurn.

Kobayashi, Audrey. 1999. "Multiculturalism and Making Difference: Comments on the State of Multiculturalism Policy in Canada." *Australian-Canadian Studies* 17(2):33–39.

Kobayashi, Audrey. 2001. *"Race" and Racism in Canada*. Race Relations Training Module prepared for Human Resources Department Canada.

Koenigsberg, Richard. 2004. "Dying for One's Country: The Logic of War and Genocide" Available at www.earthlink.net

Koring, Paul. 1999, "Human-Rights Group Lashes Out at 'Widespread' Police Brutality". *Globe and Mail*, September 22.

Kostash, Myrna. 2000. *The Next Canada: In Search of Our Future Nation*. Toronto: McClelland & Stewart.

Kozol, Jonathan. 2005. "Still Separate, Still Unequal." *Harpers* Magazine. (September):1 41–51.

Krane, Julia, Jacqueline Oxman-Martinez, and Kimberley Ducey. 2000. "Violence against Women and Ethnoracial Minority Women: Examining Assumptions about Ethnicity and 'Race.'" *Canadian Ethnic Studies*. 32(3):1–15.

Kulchyski, Peter (ed.). 1994. *Unjust Relations. Aboriginal Rights in Canadian Courts*. Toronto: Oxford University Press.

Kumar, Kartick, and Max Kelly. 2005. "Darfur. Why Canada Should Do More." *The Globe and Mail*. 24 June.

Kumin, Judith. 2001. "Gender: Persecution in the Spotlight." *Refugee* 2(123):12–13.

Kumin, Judith. 2004. "Can This Marriage Be Saved? National Interest and Ethics in Asylum Policy." *Canadian Issues.* (March) 14–17.

Kunz, Jean Lock 2003. "Social Capital: A Key Dimension of Social Integration." *Canadian Issues.* (April):33–34.

Kunz, Jean Lock and Augie Fleras. 1998. "Women of Colour in Mainstream Advertising: Distorted Mirror or Looking Glass?" *Atlantis* 13:48–73.

Kunz, Jean Lock and Augie Fleras. 1998. "Women of Colour in Mainstream Advertising: Distorted Mirror or Looking Glass?" *Atlantis* 22(2):27–38.

Kurthen, Hermann. 1997. "The Canadian Experiences with Multiculturalism and Employment Equity. Lessons for Europe." *New Community* 23(2):249–270.

Kymlicka, Will. 1992. "The Rights of Minority Cultures: Reply to Kukathas." *Political Theory 20*: 140–145.

Kymlicka, Will. 1995. "Misunderstanding Nationalism." *Dissent* (Winter):131–137.

Kymlicka, Will. 1998. "Multinational Federalism in Canada: Rethinking the Relationship." Pp. 15–50 *in Beyond the Impasse*, ed. R. Gibbins and G. Laforest. Montreal: IRPP.

Kymlicka, Will. 1998. *Finding Our Way. Rethinking Ethnocultural Relations in Canada*. Toronto: Oxford University Press.

Kymlicka, Will. 1999. "Cracks in the Mosaic." Interview in *University Affairs Magazine.* (February):8–9.

Kymlicka, Will. 2000. "An Ethnic Stitch in Time." *The Globe and Mail,* 27 December.

Kymlicka, Will. 2001. *Politics in the Vernacular: Nationalism, Multiculturalism, and Citizenship.* Toronto: Oxford University Press.

Kymlicka, Will. 2003. Immigration, Citizenship, Multiculturalism: Exploring the Links. *The Political Quarterly*: 195–208.

Kymlicka, Will. 2004. *Universal Minority Rights. The Prospects for Consensus*. Research group on nationalism, ethnicity, and multicultural citizenship. Kingston, ON: Queen's University.

Kymlicka, Will. 2005. "The Uncertain Futures of Multiculturalism." *Canadian Diversity* 4(1): 82–85.

Laforest, Guy. 1998. "Standing in the Shoes of the Other Partners in the Canadian Union." In *Beyond the Impasse. Toward Reconciliation.* R. Gibbins and G. Laforest (eds). Pp. 51–82. Montreal: IRPP.

Lane, Jan-Erik, and Svante Ersson. 2005. *Culture and Politics. A Comparative Approach.* Burlington VT: Ashgate Publishing.

Lapchick, Richard E. 2000. "Crime and Athletes: New Racial Stereotypes." In *Black and White: Race and Sports in America*, ed. Kenneth Shropshire. New York: New York University Press.

LaPrairie, Carol. 1999. "Some Reflections on the New Criminal Justice Policies in Canada: Restorative Justice, Alternative Measures, and Conditional Sentences." *Australian and New Zealand Journal of Criminology*. Special Issue.

LaPrairie, Carol. 1999. "The Impact of Aboriginal Justice Research on Policy: A Marginal Past and Even More Uncertain Future." *Canadian Journal of Criminology* 41: 249–254.

LaRoque, Emma. 1975. *Defeathering the Indian*. Agincourt, ON: Book Society of Canada.

Lawton, Valerie. 1999. "Firing Ruled Discriminatory." *Toronto Star,* 10 September.

Leckie, Jacqui. 1995. "Silent immigrants? Gender, immigration and ethnicity in New Zealand." In S. W. Greif, ed., *Immigration and national identity in New Zealand.* Pp. 50–76. New Zealand: Dunmore Press.

Lee, Edward. 1997. "Canada's Chinese Still Stereotyped." *Toronto Star,* 15 December.

Lerner, Gerda. 1997. *Why History Matters. Life and Thought.* New York: Oxford University Press.

Letourneau, Jocelyn. 2001. "Put the Future Behind Us." *The Globe and Mail*, 25 June.

Levine, Judith. 1994. *My Enemy, My Love. Man-hating and Ambivalence in Women's Lives.* New York: Doubleday.

Levitt, Cyril. 1997. "The Morality of Race in Canada." *Society* (July/August):32–37.

Ley, David and Daniel Hiebert. 2001. "Immigration Policy as Population Policy." The *Canadian Geographer* 45(1):120–25.

Ley, David. 2005. Post-Multiculturalism? Working Paper No. 05-17. Research on Immigration and Integration in the Metropolis. Vancouver BC: Vancouver Centre of Excellence.

Li Peter. 1995. "Racial Supremacism Under Social Democracy." *Canadian Ethnic Studies* xxvii(1):1–17.

Li, Peter S. 1998. *The Chinese in Canada.* Toronto: Oxford University Press.

Li, Peter S. 2003. *Destination Canada: Immigration Debates and Issues.* Don Mills: Oxford.

Lian, Jason Z. and Ralph David Matthews. 1998. "Does the Vertical Mosaic Still Exist? Ethnicity and Income in Canada, 1991." *Canadian Review of Sociology and Anthropology* 35(4):461–77.

Linden, W. 1994. *Swiss Democracy.* New York: St. Martin's Press.

Lister, Ruth. 1997. *Citizenship. Feminist Perspectives.* London: Macmillan.

Littleton, James (ed.) 1996. *Clash of Identities*: *Essays on Media, Manipulation, and Politics of the Self.* Scarborough: Prentice-Hall.

Loney, Martin. 1998. *The Pursuit of Division. Race, Gender, and Preferential Hiring in Canada.* Montreal/Kingston: McGill-Queen's University Press.

Loney, Martin. 2005. " 'Racialized' Beyond Reason." *National Post,* 6 July.

Long, David, and Olive Dickason. 2000. *Visions of the Heart: Canadian Aboriginal Issues.* 2nd ed. Toronto: Harcourt.

Lopez, Asbel. 2001. "Police against Racism." *UNESCO Courier.*

Loury, Glen. 1997. "The Conservative Line on Race." *Atlantic Monthly* (November): 144–148.

Loury, Glen C. 1998. "An American Tragedy." *Brookings Review* 16(2):38–42.

Lupa, Alan. 1999. "When Generations and Cultures Clash." *Boston Sunday Globe,* 8 August.

Lupul, Manoly R. 1988. "Ukrainians: The Fifth Cultural Wheel in Canada." Pp. 177–192 in *Ethnicity in a Technological Age*, ed. Ian H. Angus. Edmonton: Canadian Institute of Ukrainian Studies, University of Alberta.

Lupul, Manoly. 2006. *The Politics of Multiculturalism. A Ukrainian-Canadian Memoir.* Canadian Institute of Ukrainian Studies Press.

Maaka, Roger and Augie Fleras. 2000. "Engaging With Indigeneity: Tino Rangatiratanga in Aotearoa." Pp. 89–112 in *Political Theory and the Rights of Indigenous Peoples*, ed. D. Ivison et al. Cambridge: Cambridge University Press.

Maaka Roger and Augie Fleras. 2005. *The Politics of Indigeneity. Indigeous Peoples-state Relations in Canada and New Zealand.* Dunedin, NZ: University of Otago Press.

Maccharles, Tonda. 2004. "Canada, U.S. in Refugee Deal." *Toronto Star,* 15 October.

MacDonald, Heather. 2003. *Are Cops Racist?* Chicago: Ivan R Dee Publishers.

Mackie, Richard. 2001. "Sovereignty Support Near Low, Poll Finds." *The Globe and Mail,* 26 October.

Macklem, Patrick. 2001. *Indigenous Difference and the Constitution in Canada*. Toronto: University of Toronto Press.

Macklin, Audrey. 1999. "Women as Migrants in National and Global Communities." *Canadian Woman Studies* 19(3):24–32.

MacQueen, Ken. 1994. "I am a Canadian. Don't Let Me Screw Up." *Kitchener-Waterloo Record*, 23 April.

Magnet, Joseph Eliot. 2004. *Modern Constitutionalism: Identity, Equality, and Democracy*. Toronto: Butterworths.

Magsino, R. F. 2000. "The Canadian Multiculturalism Policy: A Pluralist Ideal Revisited." Pp. 320–41 in *21st Century Canadian Diversity*, ed. S. Nancoo. Toronto: Canadian Scholars Press.

Mahtani, Minelle. 2002. "Interrogating the Hyphen-Nation: Canadian Multicultural. Policy and Mixed Race Identities." *Social Identities* 8(1).

Maioni, Antonia. 2003. "Canadian Health Care." Pp. 307–326 in *Profiles of Canada*. Ed. K Pryke and W Soderland. Toronto: Canadian Scholars Press.

Mallet, Gina. 1997. "Has Diversity Gone Too Far?" *The Globe and Mail,* 15 March.

Manji, Irshad. 2005. "Not all Traditions Deserve Respect." *NY Times*. Reprinted in the *National Post,* 11 August.

Marable, Manning. 1998. "Ethnic Nationalism. Black Fundamentalism." *Dissent* (Spring).

Maracle, Brian. 1996. "One More Whining Indian Tilting at Windmills." Pp. 15–20 in *Clash of Identities*, ed. J. Littleton. Scarborough, ON: Prentice-Hall.

Marcus, Alan Rudolph. 1995. *Relocating Eden. The Image and Politics of Inuit Exile in the Canadian Arctic*. Hanover, NH: The University Press of New England.

Marger, Martin. 2001. *Race and Ethnic Relations: American and Global Perspectives*. (5th ed). Toronto: Nelson Thomson.

Martin, James G., and Clyde W. Franklin. 1973. *Minority Group Relations*. Columbus, OH: Charles E. Merrill Publishing Company.

Matas, Robert. 1998. "Nisga'a People Make History With B.C. Pact." *The Globe and Mail,* 16 July.

Matas, Robert, Erin Anderssen, and Sean Fine. 1997. "Natives Win on Land Rights." *The Globe and Mail,* 12 December.

Matsouka, Atsuko, and John Sorenson. 1999. "Eritrean Women in Canada: Negotiating New Lives." *Canadian Woman Studies* 19(3):104–09.

Mawani, Nurjehan. 1997. "Is Refugee Determination Fair." *The Globe and Mail*, 13 December.

May, Harvey. 2004. *Broadcast in Colour: Cultural Diversity and Television Programming in Four Countries*. Australian Film Commission.

May, S. (ed.). 1999. *Critical Multiculturalism*. Madison: University of Wisconsin Press.

McAndrew, Marie. 1992. "Combatting Racism and Ethnocentrism in Educational Materials: Problems and Actions Taken in Quebec. Pp. 49–60 in *Racism and Education. Different Perspectives and Experiences*. ed. Ontario Teachers Federation. Ottawa.

McCalla, Andrea, and Vic Satzewich. 2002. "Settler Capitalism and the Construction of Immigrants" and "Indians" as Racialized Others." In *Crimes of Colour*, ed. W. Chan and K. Mirchandani. Peterborough: Broadview.

McCaskill, Tim. 1995. "Anti-Racist Education and Practice in the Public School System." Pp. 253–272 in *Beyond Political Correctness*, ed. S. Richer and L. Weir. Toronto: University of Toronto Press.

McDonough, Sheila. 2003. "Perceptions of Hijab in Canada." Pp. 121–142 in *The Muslim Veil in North America,* ed. S. S. Alvi et al. Toronto: The Women's Press.

McGauran, the Hon Peter. 2005. "The Australian Government Minister for Citizenship and Multicultural Affairs." *Canadian Diversity* 4(1):6–8.

McGill University. 1994. *Anti-Racism and Race Relations*. Prepared by Monique Shebbeare. McGill's Equity Office, July.

McGuinty, Dalton. 2005. *See* Brennan and Brown.

McHugh, Paul. 1998. "Aboriginal Identity and Relations: Models of State Practice and Law in North America and Australasia" In *Living Relationships*, ed. K Coates and P. McHugh. Institute of Public Policy. New Zealand: Victoria University of Wellington.

McIntosh, Peggy. 1998. "White Privilege and Male Privilege: A Personal Account of Coming to See Correspondences Through Work in Women Studies." Working Paper No. 189. MA: Wellesley College, Centre for Research on Women.

McIntyre, Sheila. 1993. "Backlash Against Equality: The 'Tyranny' of the 'Politically Correct.' *McGill Law Journal/Revue de Droit de McGill* 38(1):3–63.

McIsaac, Elizabeth. 2003. *Nation Building Through Cities: A New Deal for Immigrant Settlement in Canada.* Ottawa: Caledon Institute.

McKee, Craig. 1996. Treaty Talks in British Columbia. Vancouver, BC: UBC Press.

McKenna, Ian. 1994. "Canada's Hate Propaganda Laws—A Critique." *British Journal of Canadian Studies* 15:42.

McRoberts, Kenneth. 1996. "Introduction (Citizenship and Rights)." *International Journal of Canadian Studies* 14(Fall):5–12.

McRoberts, Kenneth. 1997. *Misconceiving Canada: The Struggle for National Unity.* Toronto: Oxford University Press.

McRoberts, Kenneth. 1998. "Are Canadians a People? Are Quebeckers?" *The Globe and Mail,* 19 March.

McRoberts, Kenneth. 2001. "Canada and the Multinational State." *Canadian Journal of Political Science* 24(4):683–713.

McRoberts, Kenneth. 2003. Managing Cultural Differences in Multinational Democracies. Pp. 1–14 in *The Conditions of Diversity in Multinational Democracies*, ed. A-G. Gagnon et al. Montreal: IRRP.

McRoberts, K. 2004. "The future of the nation state and Quebec-Canada relations." In M. Seymour, *The Fate of the Nation State.* Montreal: McGill-Queens Press.

Mead, Walter Russell. 1993. "This Land is My Land." *New York Times* Book Review, 7 November.

Meadows/Bridgeview, Marguerite. 2005. "The Model School, Islamic Style. *Time*, 11 June. Available at http://www.time.com

Medrano, J-D, and M. Koenig. 2005. Nationalism, Citizenship, and Immigration in Social Science Research—Editorial Introduction. *International Journal on Multicultural Societies* 7(2):82–89.

Mendelsohn, Matthew. 2003 "Birth of a New Ethnicity." In *The New Canadians.* E Anderssen and M. Valpy (eds.). Pp. 59–66. Toronto: McClelland & Stewart

Mendes, Errol P. and Anik Lalonde-Roussy. 2003. *Bridging the Global Divide on Human Rights: A Canada-China Dialogue.* Burlington, VT: Ashgate Publishing.

Mercredi, Ovide and Mary Ellen Turpel. 1993. *In the Rapids: Navigating the Future of First Nations.* Toronto: Penguin Books.

Meshal, Reem A. 2003. "Banners of Faith and Identities in Construct: The Hijab in Canada." Pp. 72–104; in *The Muslim Veil in North America*, ed. S. S. Alvi et al. Toronto: The Women's Press.

Meyers, Eytan. 2002. "The Causes of Convergence in Western Immigration Control." *Review of International Studies* 28:123–141.

Miles, Robert. 1982. *Racism and Migrant Labour*. London: Routledge and Kegan Paul.

Miller, J. R. 1989. *Skyscrapers Hide the Heavens: A History of Indian-White Relations in Canada*. Toronto: University of Toronto Press.

Miller, J. R. 1996. *Shingwauk's Visions: A History of Indian Residential Schools*. Toronto: University of Toronto Press.

Miller, J. R. 1999. The State, the Church, and Residential Schools in Canada. Paper presented at a conference on Religion and Public Life: Historical and Comparative Themes, Queen's University, May 13–15, 1999. Retrieved May 4, 2006 from http://www.anglican.ca/Residental-Schools/resources/miller.htm.

Millman, Joel. 1997. *The Other Americans: How Immigrants Renew Our Country, Our Economy, and Our Values*. New York: Penguin.

Milloy, Courtland. 2001. "Racism Still Lurks in US Corporate World." *KW Record*, 10 January.

Mitchell, Alana. 1998. "Sensitivity Required in Using Race Data." *The Globe and Mail*, 17 February.

Mittler, P. 2000. *Working Toward Inclusive Education: Social Contexts*. London, UK: Fulton.

Modood, Tariq and Tony Acland (eds.). 1997. "Introduction." Pp. 1–10 in *Race and Higher Education*, ed. T. Modood and T. Acland. Policy Studies Institute: University of Westminster.

Modood, Tariq. 2003a. Muslims and European multiculturalism. Available at www.openDemocracy.net

Modood, Tariq. 2003b. "Muslims and the Politics of Difference" *The Political Quarterly*. Special Issue. 100–115.

Modood, Tariq. 2005. *Multicultural politics: Racism, ethnicity, and Muslims in Britain*. Minneapolis: U. of Minnesota Press.

Molnar, Helen and Michael Meadows. 2001. *Songlines and Satellites. Indigenous Communication in Australia, the South Pacific, and Canada*. Sydney: Pluto Press.

Montreuil, Annie, and Bourhis, Richard Y. 2004. "Acculturation Orientations of Competing Host Communities toward Valued and Devalued Immigrants." *International Journal of Intercultural Relations*, 28(6):507–532.

Monture-Angus, P. 2002. *Journeying Forward: Dreaming First Nations' Independence*. Halifax, Nova Scotia: Fernwood Publishing.

Moodley, Kogila. 1999. "Antiracist Education Through Political Literacy: The Case of Canada." Pp. 138–152 in *Critical Multiculturalism*, ed. S. May. Madison: University of Wisconsin Press.

Morning, Ann and Daniel Sabbagh. 2005. "From Sword and Ploughshare: Using Race for Discrimination and Antidiscrimination in the United States". *International Social Science Journal* 57(183): 57–70.

Morris, Barry and Gillian Cowlishaw, eds. 1997. *Race Matters. Indigenous Australians and 'Our' Society*. Canberra: Aboriginal Studies Press.

Morse, Bradford, W. (ed.) 1985. Aboriginal Peoples and the Law. Ottawa: Carleton University Press.

Mothers United Against Racism. 2005. "The Police's Fight Against Incivilities Encourages Racial Profiling and Harassment: Minority Mothers." Press release, 16 May.

Muharrar, Mikal. 2005. Cited in Ethnic Profiling and Gang and Gun Violence, by Patricia Hylton. *Pride* (October): 12–18.

Mukherjee. Alok. 1992. "Educational Equity for Racial Minorities and the School: The Role of Community Action." Pp. 73–81 in *Racism and Education: Different Perspectives and Experiences.* Ontario Federation of Students: Ottawa.

Munz, Rainer, and Rainer Ohliger (eds.) 2003. *Diasporas and Ethnic Migrants: Germany, Israel and post-Soviet Successor States in Comparative Perspective.* Portland, OR: Frank Cass.

Murji, Karim, and John Solomos. 2005. "Introduction." Pp. 1–28 in *Racialization. Studies in Theory and Practice*, eds. K. Murji and J. Solomos. Oxford UK: Oxford University Press.

Murphy, Christopher, and C. Clark. 2005. "Communities of Policing and Policing Communities: A Comparative Study of Policing in Two Urban Communities" (with C. Clark). Pp. 209–259 in *Re-Imagining Policing in Canada*, ed. D. Cooley. Toronto: University of Toronto Press.

Murphy, Michael. 2001. "Culture and Courts: A New Direction in Canadian Jurisprudence on Aboriginal Rights?" *Canadian Journal of Political Science* 34(1):109–29.

Murphy, Michael. 2005, (ed.). *Canada: The State of the Federation 2003. Reconfiguring Aboriginal-State Relations.* Published by the Institute of Intergovernmental Relations. School of Policy Studies. Queen's University, Kingston.

Murray, Charles and Richard J. Herrnstein. 1994. *The Bell Curve. Intelligence and Class Structure in American Life.* New York: The Free Press.

Muszynski, Alicja. 2000. "The Social Construction/Deconstruction of Sex, Gender, Race, and Class." In *Social Issues and Contradictions in Canadian Society.* B. Singh Bolaria (ed.). Pp. 96–131. Toronto: Harcourt Brace.

Myrdahl, Gunnar. 1944. *The American Dilemma: The Negro Problem and the Problems of Democracy.* New York: Harper.

Nagel, Joane, and Susan Olzak. 1982. "Ethnic Mobilization in the New and Old States: An Extension of the Competition Model." *Social Problems* 30(2):127–142.

Nazir, Arif. 2004. "Foreign Trained Dentists Treated Like Third Class Citizens." *Kingston Whig-Standard.* 6 July.

Nazroo, James Y., and Saffron Karlsen. 2003. "Patterns of Identity Among Ethnic Minority People: Diversity and Commonality." *Ethnic and Racial Studies* 26(5):902–930.

Negotiating Religious Pluralism: International Approaches. 2005. Vol. 4, no. 3 of *Canadian Diversity* (Fall).

Niezen, Ronald . 2003. *The Origins of Indigenism: Human Rights and the Politics of Identity.* Berkeley: University of California Press.

Nelson, Adie. 2006. *Gender in Canada*, 3rd ed. Toronto: Pearson.

Nelson, Adie, and Augie Fleras. 1998. *Social Problems in Canada: Conditions and Consequences*, 2nd ed. Scarborough: Prentice-Hall.

Neufeld-Rocheleau, Melody, and Judith Friesen. 1987. "Isolation: A Reality for Immigrant Women in Canada." *Saskatchewan Multicultural Magazine* 6(2):12–13L.

Neugebauer, R. S. (ed.). 2000. *Criminal Injustice. Racism in the Criminal Justice System.* Toronto: Canadian Scholars Press.

Neugebauer-Visano, R. 1996. "Kids, Cops, and Colour: The Social Organization of Police-Minority Youth Relations." In *Not a Kid Anymore,* ed. G. O'Bireck Scarborough: ITP Nelson.

Newhouse, David, and Evelyn Peters. 2003. *Not Strangers in These Parts. Urban Aboriginal Peoples.* Ottawa: Policy Research Initiative.

Niezen, Ronald. 2003. *The Origins of Indigenism: Human Rights and the Politics of Identity.* Berkeley: University of California Press.

Nolen, S. 2000. "The Adman's Best Friend." *The Globe and Mail*, 10 August.

Normandeau, A. and B. Leighton. 1990. "A Vision of the Future of Policing in Canada: Police-Challenge 2000." Background Paper. Policy and Security Branch. Solicitor-General. Ottawa: Minister of Supply and Services.

Novac, Sylvia. 1999. "Immigrant Enclaves and Residential Segregation: Voices of Racialized Refugees." *Canadian Woman Studies 19*(3):97–103.

Oberschall, Anthony. 2000. "Social Movements and the Transition to Democracy." *Democratization* 7(3): 25–45.

Okin, Susan (ed.). 1999. *Is Multiculturalism Bad for Women?* Princeton, NJ: Princeton, University Press.

Oliver, Melvin and Thomas M Shapiro. 1995. *Black Wealth/White Wealth: A New Perspective on Racial Inequality.* London: Routledge.

Ominayak, Bernard and Ed Bianchi. 2002. "Lubicon Cree. Still No Settlement After all These Years". Pp. 163–174 in *Nation to Nation*, ed. J Bird et al. Toronto: Irwin.

Orbe, M. P., and T. M. Harris. 2001. *Interracial Communication. Theory into Practice.* Boulder, CO: Westview Press.

O'Regan, Tipene. 1994. *Indigenous Governance. Country Study—New Zealand.* Study prepared for the Royal Commission on Aboriginal Peoples. Ottawa.

Palmer, Douglas L. 1996. "Determinants of Canadian Attitudes Toward Immigratioin: More Than Just Racism?" *Canadian Journal of Behavioural Science* 28(3):180–192.

Palmer, Howard (ed.). 1975. *Immigration and the Rise of Multiculturalism.* Toronto: Copp Clark Publishing.

Papademetriou, Demetrios G. 2003. "Managing Rapid and Deep Change in the Newest Age of Migration." *The Political Quarterly.* Special Issue. Pp. 39–58.

Papillon, Martin. 2002. *Immigration, Diversity and Social Inclusion in Canada's Cities.* Discussion Paper F/27. Canadian Policy Research Network.

Paradkar, Bageshree. 2000. "Suffering in Silence." *Toronto Star*, 24 June.

Parekh, Bhikhu. 1997. "Foreward." In *Ethnic Minorities in Britain*, ed. T. Modood and R. Berthoud. London: Policy Studies Institute.

Parekh, Bhikhu. 2000. "Preface." In Runnymede Trust. 2000. Commission on the Future of Multi-Ethnic Britain. Chair, Bikhu Parekh. *The Future of Multi-Ethnic Britain—Report of the Commission on the Future of Multi-Ethnic Britain.* London: Profile.

Parkin, Andrew. 2001. "Introduction." What Will Hold Us Together? *Centre for Policy Research in Canada.*

Parkin, Andrew. 2003. *A Changing People: Being Canadian in a New Century.* CRIC Papers (April).

Patterson, Lorraine, James E. Cameron, and Richard N. Lalonde. 1996. "The Intersection of Race and Gender: Examining the Politics of Identity in Women's Studies." *Canadian Journal of Behavioural Science* 28(3):229–239.

Peach, Ian. 2005. "The Politics of Self-Government." *SIPP News* (Spring): 4–6.

Pearson, D. 1994. *Canada compared: Multiculturalism and biculturalism in settler societies.* St. Johns, NF: Institute of Social and Economic Research, Memorial University.

Pearson, David. 2001. *The Politics of Ethnicity in Settler Societies.* London: Palgrave Macmillan.

Pendakur, Krishna. 2005. *Visible Minorities in Canada's Workplaces: A Perspective on the 2017 Projection.* Vancouver: Metropolis Project.

Pendakur, Krishna, and Ravi Pendakur. 2004. "Colour My World: Has the Majority-Minority Earnings Gap Changed over Time?" Working Paper No 04-11. Research on immigration and integration in the metropolis. Vancouver BC: Vancouver Centre of Excellence.

Pendakur, Ravi. 2000. *Immigrants and the Labour Force: Policy, Regulation, and Impact.* Montreal and Kingston: McGill-Queens University Press.

Penslar, Derek J. 2005. "Introduction" In *Contemporary Antisemitism: Canada and the World*, ed. D. J. Penslar. Toronto: University of Toronto Press.

Perkel, Colin. 2002. "No racial targeting anywhere in Ontario, police chiefs say." *The Toronto Star.* Wednesday, October 30, A3.

Peter, K. 1978. "Multi-cultural Politics, Money, and the Conduct of Canadian Ethnic Studies." *Canadian Ethnic Studies Association Bulletin* 5:2–3.

Peters, Evelyn. 2001. "Geographies of Aboriginal People in Canada." *Canadian Geographer* 45(1):138–44.

Philip, M. Nourbese. 1996. "How White is Your White?" *Borderlines* 37:19–24.

Picard Andre. 2005. Health's a black and white issue: Colour-blindness is killing minorities. *The Globe and Mail,* 12 February.

Picard, Andre (2005). "Obesity Rates Vary Across Ethnicities, Study Finds." *The Globe and Mail.* 29 June.

Picard, Andre. 2005. "Health's a Black-and-White Issue: Colour-Blindness is Killing Minorities. *The Globe and Mail,* 12 February.

Pipes, Daniel. 2005. What are Islamic schools teaching? *New York Sun,* 29 March. Available at www.danielpipes.org

Plaut, Rabbi W. Gunther. 1989 "Unwanted Intruders or People in Flight." *Perception* 13(2):45–46.

Pluss, Caroline. 2005. "Constructing Globalized Ethnicity. Migrants from India in Hong Kong. *International Sociology* 20(2):201–224.

Ponting, J. Rick. 1986. *Arduous Journey: Canadian Indians and Decolonization.* Toronto: McClelland and Stewart.

Ponting, J. Rick. 1997. *First Nations in Canada: Perspectives on Opportunities, Empowerment, and Self-Determination.* Toronto: McGraw Hill Ryerson.

Ponting, J. Rick, and Roger Gibbins. 1980. Out of Irrelevance: A Socio-Political Introduction to Indian Affairs in Canada. Toronto: Butterworths.

Porter, Henry. 2005. "It's Great Up North." *Guardian Weekly.* 2–8 December.

Porter, John. 1965. *The Vertical Mosaic.* Toronto: University of Toronto Press.

Porter, Robert Odawi. 2005. *Sovereignty, Colonialism and the Indigenous Nations: A Reader.* Durham NC: Carolina Academic Press.

Possner, Michael. 1997. "*A Battlefield Primer on Multiculturalism*": A Review, 12 July.

Powell, Betsy. 2005. "Summer's Gunmen Getting Away." *Toronto Star,* 30 August.

Predelli, L. N. 2004. "Interpeting Gender in Islam: A Case Study of Immigrant Muslim Women in Oslo Norway." *Gender & Society* 18(4):473–493.

Price, Richard. 1991. *Legacy. Indian Treaty Relationships.* Edmonton: School of Native Studies, University of Alberta.

PROMPT. 2004. In the Public Interest: Immigrant Access to Regulated Professions in Today's Ontario [unpublished policy paper]. PROMPT: [Toronto].

Purich, Donald. 1986. *Our Land: Native Peoples in Canada.* Toronto: James Lorimer.

Purvis, Andrew. 1999. "Whose Home and Native Land?" *Time*, 15 February:16–26.

Quill, Greg. 1996. "CFMT: The World in Miniature." *Toronto Star,* 19 May.

Raboy, M. 1988. *Missed Opportunities. The Story of Canada's Broadcasting Policy.* Montreal/Kingston: McGill-Queen's University Press.

Ralston, Helen. 1999. "Canadian Immigration Policy in the Twentieth Century: Its Impact on South Asian Women." *Canadian Woman Studies* 19(3):33–37.

Ramirez, Judith. 2001. "Canada at Forefront in Gender Guidelines for Refugee Status." *Toronto Star*, 4 May.

Ramsden, Irihapeti. 1995. "Cultural Safety: Implementing the Concept." *NZ College of Midwives Journal* (October):6–9.

Ratcliffe, Peter. 2004. *'Race', Ethnicity, and Difference: Imagining the Inclusive Society.* New York: Open University Press.

Rathzel, N. 2003. "Antagonistic Girls, or Why the Foreigners are the Real Germans." Pp. 40–61 in *The Social Construction of Diversity*, eds. C. Harzig and D. Juteau. New York: Berghahn Books.

Razack, Sherene. 1994. "What is to be Gained by Looking White People in the Eye? Culture, Race, and Gender in Cases of Sexual Violence." *Sign* (Summer):894–922.

Razack, Sherene. 2004. *Dark Threats and White Knights. The Somalia Affair, Peacekeeping, and the New Imperialism.* Toronto: University of Toronto Press.

Redhead, Mark. 2003. "Charles Taylor's Deeply Diverse Response to Canada's Fragmentation: A Project Often Commented On but Seldom Explored." *Canadian Journal of Political Science* 36(1):61–83.

Reid, Scott. 1993. *Lament for a Notion: The Life and Death of Canada's Bilingual Dream.* Vancouver: Arsenal Pulp Press.

Reinhart, Anthony, and James Rusk. 2006. "Immigrants Suffer in Silence Within Walls of Suburbs." *Globe and Mail.* 11 March.

Reitman, Oonagh. 2005. "Multiculturalism and Feminism. Incompatibility, Compatibility, and Synonymity?" *Ethnicities* 5(2): 216–247.

Reitz, Jeffrey, and Raymond Breton. 1994. *The Illusion of Difference: Realities of Ethnicity in Canada and the United States.* Toronto: CD Howe Institute.

Reitz, Jeffrey. 1998. *Warmth of the Welcome: The Social Causes of Economic Success for Immigrants in Different Nations and Cities.* Boulder Co: Westview Press.

Rensberger, Boyce. 1994. "The Case for One Race." *Toronto Star*, 24 December.

Report of the Commission of Inquiry into Systemic Racism in Ontario's Criminal Justice System. 1995, December. Toronto: Queen's Printer of Ontario.

Resnick, Philip. 2000. "Civic and Ethnic Nationalism: A Canadian Perspective," in, eds., *Canadian Political Thought*, ed. Ron Beiner and Wayne Norman. Toronto: Oxford University Press.

Resnick, Philip. 2001. *The Politics of Resentment. British Columbia Regionalism and Canadian Unity.* Vancouver: UBC Press.

Resnick, Philip. 2004. "Republicanism, Multiculturalism, and Liberalism." *Inroads* 15:77–79.

Reuters. 2004. "Turkey's Head Scarf Ban is Upheld by Rights Courts." *International Herald Tribune*, 30 June.

Rex, John. 1998. "The Problematic of Multinational and Multicultural Societies." *Ethnic and Racial Studies* 20(3):1–15.

Rex, John. 2004. Multiculturalism and Political Integration in the Modern Nation State. Documentos CIDOB, *Dinamicas Interculturales*. Numero Uno.

Rex, John, and Gurharpal Singh. 2004. *Governance in Multicultural Societies.* London, U K: Ashgate.

Reyna, Christine, A. Tucker, W. Korfmacher, and P. J. Henry. 2005. "Searching for Common Ground Between Supporters and Opponents of Affirmative Action." *Political Psychology* 26(5):667–681.

Richmond, Anthony. 1994. *Global Apartheid: Refugees, Racism, and the New World Order.* Toronto: Oxford University Press.

Rimmer, Alan. 1998. "PQ Win Means Return to the Referendum Debate." *Echo* (Dec) 3-9. P4.

Roberts, Bronwyn. 2000. "Gap between Rich and Poor Blacks Widens." *National Post*, 27 July.

Roberts, Julian V, and Ronald Melchers. 2003. "The Incarceration of Aboriginal Offenders: Trends from 1978 to 2001." *Canadian Journal of Criminology and Criminal Justice* 45(2):1–18.

Roberts, Lance W. and Rodney A. Clifton. 1990. "Multiculturalism in Canada: A Sociological Perspective." Pp. 20–147 in *Race and Ethnic Relations in Canada*, ed. Peter S. Li. Toronto: Oxford University Press.

Rocher, Francois and Nadia Verrilli. 2003. "Questioning Constitutional Democracy in Canada: From the Canadian Supreme Court Reference on Quebec Secession to the Clarity Act." Pp. 207–240 in *The Conditions of Diversity in Multinational Democracies*, eds. A-G. Gagnon et al. Montreal: IRRP.

Rossmo, K., & G. J. Saville. 1991. "Policing Challenge 2000: Riding the Winds of Change." *Canadian Journal of Criminology* 33: 543–549.

Roth, Lorna. 1998. "Television Broadcasting North of 60." Pp. 147–166 in *Images of Canadianess*, ed. L. d'Haenens. Ottawa: University of Ottawa Press.

Rothchild, Donald, and Alexander J. Groth. 1995. "Pathological Dimensions of Domestic and International Ethnicity." *Political Science Quarterly* 110(1):69–79.

Rothenberg, Paula S. (ed.). 1991. *Race, Class, and Gender in the United States.* New York: St Martins Press.

Rothenberg, Paula S. (ed.). 2001. *Race, Class, and Gender in the United States* (5th ed.). New York: Worth Publishers.

Rotman, Leonard Ian. 1996. *Parallel Paths: Fiduciary Doctrine and the Crown-Native Relationship in Canada.* Toronto: University of Toronto Press.

Royal Commission. 1992. Framing the Issues: Discussion Paper No 1. Ottawa: Royal Commission on Aboriginal Peoples.

Royal Commission. 1996. People to People, Nation to Nation. Highlights From the Report on the Royal Commission on Aboriginal Peoples. Ottawa: Minister of Supply and Services Canada.

Ruby, Clayton 2004. "Fix the Racial Disconnect." *The Globe and Mail*, 10 March.

Ruddick, E., 2003. "Immigrant economic performance." *Canadian Issues* 5:16–17.

Rummell, R.J. 2005. "Genocide: Meaning and Definition." Available at www.hawaii.edu/powerkills/GENOCIDE.ENCY.HTM.

Runnymede Trust. 2000. Commission on the Future of Multi-Ethnic Britain. Chair, Bhikho Parekh. *The Future of Multi-Ethnic Britain: Report of the Commission on the Future of Multi-Ethnic Britain.* London: Profile.

Rushowy, Kristin. 2001. "Native Students Return to Roots at School in the Heart of the City." *Toronto Star*, 15 October.

Rushton, P. 1994. *Race, Evolution and Behavior: A Life History Perspective*. New York: Transaction.

Rushton, P. 1995. *Race, evolution, and behavior: A life history perspective.* New Brunswick, NJ: Transaction Publishers.

Rusk, James. 2005. "Conditions on Reserve 'Atrocious' Doctor Says." *The Globe and Mail,* 24 October.

Russell, Peter. 2005. *Recognizing Aboriginal Title: The Mabo Case and Indigenous Resistance to English-Settler Colonialism*. Toronto: University of Toronto Press.

Sajoo, Amyn B. 1994 "New Dances With Diversity." *Policy Options* (December): 14–19.

Salee, Daniel, and William Coleman. 1997. "The Challenges of the Quebec Question: Paradigm, Counter-Paradigm, and the Nation-State" In *Understanding Canada*, ed. W. Clement. Montreal/Kingston: McGill-Queen's University Press.

Samson, Colin. 2003. *A Way of Life That Does Not Exist: Canada and the Extinguishment of the Innu*. St. John's, NF: ISER Books.

Samuel, J., and D. Schachhuber. 2000. "Perspectives on Canadian Diversity." Pp. 14–35 in *21st Century Canadian Diversity*, ed. S. Nancoo. Mississauga: Canadian Scholars Press.

Samuel, John. 1997. "Why Canada Should Celebrate Its Impressive Array of Languages." *Toronto Star*, 12 December.

Samuel, John. 2004. "Barriers to Attracting and Retaining Immigrants to Atlantic Canada." *National Post*.

Sandercock, Leonie. 2003. Rethinking Multiculturalism for the 21st Century. Working Paper No. 03-14. Research on immigration and integration in the metropolis. Vancouver BC: Vancouver Centre of Excellence.

Sandhu, Ravinder. 2003. "Minorities Within Minorities." *Toronto Star*, 26 August.

Sarich, Vincent, and Frank Miele. 2004. *Race: The Reality of Human Differences*. Boulder: Westview Press.

Sarick, Lila. 1999. "Serbian Community Feeling Betrayed." *The Globe and Mail*, 8 May.

Satzewich, Vic. (ed.). 1998. *Racism and Social Inequality in Canada*. Toronto: Thompson Education.

Satzewich, V. 2000. "Whiteness Limited: Racialization and the Social Construction of 'peripheral Europeans,'" *Histoire sociale/Social History* 23: 271–290.

Saul, John Ralston. 1998. *Reflections of a Siamese Twin: Canada at the End of the Twentieth Century.* Toronto: Penguin.

Saul, John Ralston. 2003. "The Inclusive Shape of Complexity." Pp. 13–28 in *The Canadian Distinctiveness into the XXIst Century*, eds. G. Gaffield and K. L. Gould. Ottawa: University of Ottawa Press.

Saunders, Doug. 2004. "Sacrificing Freedom For Equality." *The Globe and Mail*, 4 September.

Savard, P., and B. Vignezzi. 1999. *Multiculturalism and the History of International Relations from the 18th Century Up to the Present*. Ottawa: Carleton University Press.

Sawchuk, Joe. 1998. *The Dynamics of Native Politics. The Alberta Metis Perspective*. Saskatoon: SK Publishing.

Schlein, Lisa. 2005. Disparity between native and non-native Canadians highlighted in UN report. *Toronto Star,* 11 April.

Schlesinger, Arthur M., Jr. 1992. *The Disuniting of America: Reflections on a Multicultural Society*. New York: W. W. Norton.

Schoenfeld, Gabriel. 2004. *The Return of Anti-Semitism*. San Francisco: Encounter Books.

Schouls, Tim. 1997. "Aboriginal Peoples and Electoral Reform in Canada: Differentiated Representation versus Voter Equality." *Canadian Journal of Political Science* xxiv (4):729–749.

Scott, Craig. 1996. "Indigenous Self-determination and the Decolonization of the International Imagination." *Human Rights Quarterly* 18:815–820.

Scott, James C. 1998. *Seeing Like a State*. Princeton, NJ: Yale University Agrarian Press.

Scrivener, Leslie. 2001. "Islamic Schools a Safe Place." *Toronto Star*, 25 February.

See, Katherine O'Sullivan, and William J. Wilson. 1988. "Race and Ethnicity." Pp. 223–242 in *Handbook of Sociology*, ed. Neil J. Smelzer. Newbury Park: Sage.

Seguin, Rheal. 1998. "A 'Canadian People' Nonexistent, Lawyer Says" *The Globe and Mail*, 6 March.

Seguin, Rheal. 2001. "View of Language Laws Seen as Racist." *The Globe and Mail*, 26 March.

Seiler, Tamara Palmer. 2002. "Thirty Years Later: Reflections on the Evolution and Future Prospects of Multiculturalism." *Canadian Issues* (February):6–8.

Seljak, David. 2005. "Education, Multiculturalism, and Religion." In *Religion and Ethnicity in Canada*, eds. Paul Bramadat and David Seljak. Toronto: Pearson.

Sellers, Frances Stead. 2005. "Multiculturalism." *Kitchene-Waterloo Record*, 25 August.

SES Canada Research. 2003. "No Welcome Mat for Refugees Without ID. Ontarians Want Refugees with false ID Sent Home" Media release. Available at www.sesresearch.com

Shapiro, Thomas M. 2004. *Racial Inequality: The Hidden Cost of Being African-American*. New York: Oxford University Press.

Shipler, David. 1997. *A Country of Strangers: Blacks and Whites in America*. New York: Knopf.

Shipler, David K. 2001. "A Conflict's Bedrock Is Laid Bare." *New York Times*, 27 May.

Shkilnyk, Anastasia M. 1985. *A Poison Stronger Than Love*. New Haven, CT: Yale University Press.

Shohat, Ella, and Robert Stam. 1994. *Unthinking Eurocentrism: Multiculturalism and the Media*. New York: Routledge.

Showler, Peter. 2005. "Refugee Laws Are Not the Problem." *The Globe and Mail*, 29 April.

Shusta, R. M. (ed.). 1995. *Multicultural Law Enforcement: Strategies for Peacekeeping in a Diverse Society*. Englewood Cliffs, NJ: Prentice-Hall.

Siddiqui, Haroon. 1998. "Muslims Unfairly Labelled." *Toronto Star*, 10 January.

Siddiqui, Haroon. 1999. "A Mismanaged Immigration Department." *Toronto Star*, 12 August.

Siddiqui, Haroon. 1999. "Immigration Policies Hurt Torontonians." *Toronto Star*, 14 November.

Siddiqui, Haroon. 2000. "An Abysmal Record of Hiring Minorities." *Toronto Star*, 20 April.

Siddiqui, Haroon. 2001. "Linguistic Militancy Misses Target." *Toronto Star*, 8 March.

Silverberg, Christine. 2004. "After Stonechild: Rebuilding Trust." *The Globe and Mail*, 20 October.

Simmons, Alan B. 1999. "Immigration Policy: Imagined Futures." Pp. 21–50 in *Immigration Canada*, eds. S. Halli and L. Driedger. Toronto: University of Toronto Press.

Simpson, Jeffrey. 1999. "The Politics of Immigration." *The Globe and Mail*, 23 November.

Simpson, Jeffrey. 2000. "Waiting for the Right Immigration Bill." *The Globe and Mail*, 2 April.

Simpson, Jeffrey. 2005. "There's a Lesson For all of Us from the Sharia Issue." *The Globe and Mail*, 14 September.

Sirna, Tony, 1996. "Creating a 'Society of Communities'". *Communities Journal for Cooperative Living* 50–53.

Sissons, Jeffrey. 2005. *First Peoples: Indigenous Cultures and Their Futures*. London UK: Reaktion Books.

Sjoberg, Gideon, Elizabeth A. Gill, and Norma Williams. 2001. "A Sociology of Human Rights." *Social Problems* 48(1):11–47.

Slattery, Brian. 1997. "Recollection of Historical Practice." Pp. 76–82 in *Justice for Natives: Search for a Common Ground*, ed. Andrea P. Morrison. Montreal/Kingston: McGill-Queen's University Press.

Sleeper, Jim. 1997. *Liberal Racism*. New York: Viking.

Slinger, Joey. 2005. "Making Their Mark is the Only Way They Know How." *Toronto Star*, 16 August.

Smith, Anthony D. 1996. "LSE Centennial Lecture. The Resurgence of Nationalism? Myth and Memory in the Renewal of Nations." *British Journal of Sociology* 47(4): 1–16.

Smith, Charles C. 2003. "Crisis, Conflict, and Accountability: The Impact and Implications of Police Racial Profiling." Commissioned by the African Canadian Community Coalition on Racial Profiling.

Smith, Earl, and Wilbert M. Leonard II. 1997. "Twenty-Five Years of Stacking Research in Major League Baseball: An Attempt At Explaining This Re-Occurring Phenomenon." *Sociological Focus* 30(4):321–332.

Smith, Melvin H. 1995. *Our Home or Native Land?* Toronto: Stoddart.

Snyder, Jack L. 2000. *From Voting to Violence: Democratization and Nationalist Conflict*. New York: W.W. Norton.

Solomos, John, and Les Back 1996. *Racism and Society*. London: Macmillan.

Solomos, John, and Martin Bulmer. 2005. *Researching Race and Racism*. New York: Routledge.

Sowell, Thomas. 2004. *Affirmative Action Around the World: An Empirical Study*. New Haven, CT: Yale University Press.

Spencer, Martin E. 1994. "Multiculturalism." *Sociological Focus* 9(4):550–566.

Spencer, Sarah. 2003. "Introduction." *The Political Quarterly*. Special Issue. 1–24.

Spoonley, Paul. 1993. *Racism and Ethnicity in New Zealand*. Auckland: Oxford University Press.

Spoonley, Paul. 2005. "Multicultural Challenges in a Bicultural New Zealand." *Canadian Diversity* 4(1):19–22.

Stam, R., and E. Shohat. 1994. "Contested Histories: Eurocentrism, Multiculturalism, and the Media." Pp. 296–324 in *Multiculturalism: A Critical Reader*, ed. D. T. Goldberg. Cambridge, MA: Blackwell.

Stam, R., and T. Miller. 2000. "Black America Cinema." Pp. 236–256 in *Film and Theory: An Anthology*, eds. R. Stam and T. Miller. Oxford, UK: Blackwell.

Stanford, Jim. 2001. "We Don't Need No Education." *This Magazine* (July/August).

Stasiulis, Daiva K. 1990. "Theorizing Connections: Gender, Race, Ethnicity, and Class." Pp. 69–305 in *Race and Ethnic Relations in Canada*, ed. Peter S. Li. Toronto: Oxford University Press.

Stasiulis, Daiva, and Abigail B. Bakan. 1997. "Negotiating Citizenship: The Case of Foreign Domestic Workers in Canada." *Feminist Review* 57:112–39.

Stasiulis, Daiva K. 1999. "Feminist Intersectional Theorizing." Pp. 347–97 in *Race and Ethnic Relations in Canada* (2nd ed.), ed. Peter Li. Toronto: Oxford University Press.

Statistics Canada. 2002. *Canada's Ethnocultural Portrait: The Changing Mosaic, 2001 Census*. Catalogue no. 96F0030XIE2001008. Available online at www12.statcan.ca/english/census01/products/analytic/companion/etoimm/contents.cfm

Statistics Canada. 2005. *The Daily*. "Study: Aboriginal people living in metropolitan areas." Thursday, June 23. The eighth research paper in the new series Trends and Conditions in

Census Metropolitan Areas, *Aboriginal Conditions in Census Metropolitan Areas, 1981 to 2001.* Catalogue no. 89-613-MIE2005008, free. Available online. To access the series, go to the Statistics Canada home page, select *Studies* on the left sidebar, then under *Browse periodical and series*, choose *Free and for sale.*

Statistics Canada. 2005. *The Daily.* "Readmission to Saskatchewan Correctional Services Among Aboriginal and non-Aboriginal Adults, 1999/2000 to 2003/2004." June 3 Catalogue no. 85-002-XIE20050028411

Steinhorn, Leonard, and Barbara Diggs-Brown. 1999. *By the Color of Our Skin: The Illusion of Integration and the Reality of Race.* New York: Dutton.

Stepan, Nancy. 1982. *The Idea of Race in Science: Great Britain, 1800–1960.* London: Macmillan Press.

Sternberg, Robert J., and Elena Grigorenko. 1997. *Intelligence, Heredity, and Environment.* NY:Columbia University Press.

Stocking, George. 1968. *History of Anthropological Theory.* New York: Free Press.

Stoffman, Daniel. 1997. "Making Room for Real Refugees." *International Journal* (Autumn): 575–581.

Stoffman, Daniel. 2002. *Who Gets In: What's Wrong with Canada's Immigration Program – and How to Fix It.* Toronto: McClelland & Stewart.

Stoffman, Daniel. 2003. "The Mystery of Canada's High Immigration Levels." *Canadian Issues* (April): 23–24.

Stokes, J. 2003. *Demographic Trends and Socio-Economic Sustainability in Saskatchewan: Some Policy Considerations.* Public Policy Paper 19. Regina: Saskatchewan Institute of Public Policy.

Stokes, J., Peach, I., and Blake, R. 2004. *Rethinking the Jurisdictional Divide: The Marginalization of Urban Aboriginal Communities and Federal Policy Responses.* Public Policy Paper 28. Regina: Saskatchewan Institute of Public Policy.

Strauss, Julian. 2005. "Can They Build a Future?" *The Globe and Mail,* 28 October.

Strauss, Julius, 2006. "Is the Canadian Model for Relations with Aboriginals Beyond Repair?" *The Globe and Mail,* 16 January.

Suarez-Orozco, Carola, and Marcelo M. Suarez-Orozco. 2001. *Children of Immigration.* Cambridge, MA: Harvard University Press.

Sue, Derald Wing. 2003. *Overcoming Racism. The Journey to Liberation.* San Francisco: John Wiley and Sons.

Switzer, Maurice. 1998. "The Canadian Media Have Declared Open Season on Indians." Pp. 8 in *Aboriginal Voices*, (December).

Taras, Raymond C., and Rajat Ganguly. 2002. *Understanding Ethnic Conflict: The International Dimension.* Montreal: Longman.

Tauri, J. 1999. "Recent Innovation: Empowering Maori or Biculturalising the State." *Australian and New Zealand Journal of Criminology.* Special Issue.

Taylor, Charles. 1993. "The Deep Challenge of Dualism." Pp. 82–95 in *Quebec: State and Society*, (2nd ed.), ed. Alain-G. Gagnon. Scarborough: Nelson.

Taylor, Charles. 1994. "The Politics of Recognition." Pp. 25–74 in *Multiculturalism and the Politics of Recognition*, ed. Amy Gutman. Princeton, NJ: Princeton University Press.

Taylor, Peter Shawn. 2005. "Help Wanted." *Canadian Business.* (March) 14–27: Pp. 29–34.

Teelucksingh, Cheryl, and Grace-Edward Galabuzi. 2005. "Working Precariously: The Impact of Race and Immigrant Status on Employment Opportunities and Outcomes in Canada." Report for the Canadian Race Relations Foundation. Toronto.

Teeple, Gary. 2004. *The Riddle of Human Rights*. Toronto: Garamond.

Teitel, Ruti. 2004. Through the Veil, Darkly: Why France's Ban on the Wearing of Religious Symbols is Even More Pernicious Than It Appears. Available at http://writ.findlaw.com/commentary/20040216_teitel.html

Tepper, Elliot L. 1988. *Changing Canada: The Institutional Response to Polyethnicity. The Review of Demography and Its Implications for Economic and Social Policy*. Ottawa: Carleton University.

Tharoor, Shashi. 1999/2000 Winter. "Are Human Rights Universal?" *World Policy Journal* 16(4).

Thernstrom, Abigail, and Stephan Thernstrom. 1998. "Black Progress." *Brookings Review* 16(2):12–16.

Thobani, Sunera. 1995. "Multiculturalism: The Politics of Containment." Pp. 213–16 in *Social Problems in Canada Reader*, eds. E. Nelson and A. Fleras. Scarborough, ON: Prentice-Hall.

Thobani, Sunera. 2000a. "Closing Ranks: Racism and Sexism in Canada's Immigration Policy." *Race & Class* 42(1):35–55.

Thobani, Sunera. 2000b. "Closing the Nation's Doors to Immigrant Women: The Restructuring of Canadian Immigration Policy." *Atlantis* 24(2):16–29.

Thomas, Derrick. 2001. "Evolving Family Arrangements of Canada's Immigrants." *Canadian Social Trends* (Summer):16–19.

Thomas, Robyn, Albert J. Mills, and Jean Helms Mills. 2004. *Identity Politics at Work: Resisting Gender, Gendering Resistance*. New York: Routledge.

Thompson, Allan. 2001. "Minister Defends Refugee System." *Toronto Star*, 15 September.

Thompson, Allan. 2005. "Immigration in Dire Need of Overhaul." *Toronto Star*, 22 January.

Thompson, Allan. 2006. "Time to Take a Look at Selection Process Flaws." *Toronto Star*. 11 March.

Thompson, Allan, John Herd, and Morton Weinfeld. 1995. "Entry and Exit: Canadian Immigration Policy in Context." *Annals of the American Academy AAPSS*, 538 (March): 185–198.

Tibbetts, Janice. 2000. "Canada Good Model for Other Countries, Chief Judge Tells Israel." *National Post*, 20 December.

Tishkov, Valery. 2004. *Chechnya: Life in a War Torn Society*. Berkeley: University of California Press.

Todorov, T. 2001. "A Case of Right over Might." *Foreign Affairs* (February).

Tolson, Jay. 2005. "An Education in Muslim Integration." *U.S. News and World Report*, 21 November.

Tomovich, V.A., and D.J. Loree. 1989. "In Search of New Directions: Policing in Niagara Region." *Canadian Police College Journal* 13:29–54.

Townshend, Errol. 2001. "Multiculturalism Is on Its Deathbed." *Toronto Star*, 11 July.

Tran, Kelly, Stan Kustec, and Tina Chui. 2005. "Becoming Canadian: Intent, Process, and Outcome." *Canadian Social Trends* (Spring): P 8-10.

Travers, James. 2005. "Her Story Not Today's Story." *Toronto Star*, 6 August.

Tsai, Georges. 2003. "Citizenship, Inclusion, and Diversity in the Public Services of Canada." *Canadian Diversity* (Spring).

Tully, James. 1995. *Strange Multiplicity: Constitutionalism in an Age of Diversity*. Cambridge: Cambridge University Press.

Turpel-Lafond, Mary Ellen. 1996. "Oui the People? Conflicting Visions of Self-Determination in Quebec." *Public* 14:118–33.

Ucarer, Emek M. 1997. "Introduction: The Coming of an Era of Human Uprootedness: A Global Challenge." Pp. 1–16 in *Immigration into Western Societies. Problems and Policies*, eds. E. M. Ucarer and D. J. Puchala. London: Cassells.

Uitermark, J., U. Rossi, and H. van Houtum. 2005. "Multiculturalism, Urbanization, and Citizenship: Negotiation of Ethnic Diversity in Amsterdam." *International Journal of Urban and Regional Research* 29(3):622–640.

Ujimoto, K. Victor. 2000. "Multiculturalism, Ethnic Identity, and Inequality." In *Social Issues and Contradictions in Canadian Society*, ed. B Singh Bolaria. Pp. 228–247. Toronto: Harcourt Brace.

UNDP. 2004. "Cultural Liberty in Today's Diverse World". Summary: Human Development Report.

Ungerleider, Charles. 1993. "Police-minority Relations in Democratic Societies." *Currents* 8(1):3–5.

Ungerleider, Charles. 1995. "Police, Race, and Community Conflict in Vancouver." *Canadian Ethnic Studies*: 91–104.

Urban Nexus. 2003. A monthly e-bulletin of the Family Network of Canadian Policy Research Networks. Available at www.cprn.org

Urbanski, M. 2004. "What doctor shortage?" August 19. *Toronto Star.*

Valpy, Michael and Karen Howlett. 2005. "Female MPPs' Concerns Delay Sharia Decision." *The Globe and Mail*, 8 September.

van den Berghe, Pierre. 1967. *Race and Racism*. New York: John Wiley.

van den Berghe, Pierre. 1981. *The Ethnic Phenomenon*. New York: Elsevier.

van Dijk, Teun A. 1987. *Communicating Racism: Ethnic Prejudice in Thought and Talk*. Newbury Park: Sage Publications.

Van Rijn. 1999. "Canada wasting 'a valuable resource'; Expert immigrants are being left out in the cold." *Toronto Star,* 21 February.

Vasil, R., and H.K. Yoon. 1996. *New Zealanders of Asian Origin*. Institute of Policy Studies. Victoria University of Wellington.

Vasta, Ellie, and Stephen Castles. 1996. *The Teeth are Smiling: The Persistance of Racism in a Multicultural Australia*. Sydney: Allen & Unwin.

Velez, William (ed.). 1998. *Race and Ethnicity in the United States: An Institutional Approach.* Dix Hills, NY: General Hall, Inc.

Venne, Michel, ed. 2001. "Rethinking the Nation, or How to Live Together." Pp. 3–16 in *Vive Quebec: New Thinking and New Approaches to the Quebec Nation*, transl. R. Chodos and L. Blair. Toronto: James Lorimer and Co.

Venne, Sharon. 1998. "Analysis of Delgamuukw." *Internet,* 3 March.

Vickers, Jill, and Micheline de Seve. 2000. "Introduction." *Journal of Canadian Studies*. Special edition devoted to nationalism and gender.

Waldie, Paul. 1998. "More Refugees Sheltered in Canada by New Rules." *The Globe and Mail,* 14 November.

Waldrom, James. 1997. *The Way of the Pipe. Aboriginal Spirituality and Symbolic Healing in the Canadian Prison System*. Peterborough, ON: Broadview.

Walker, James W. St. G. 1985. "Racial Discrimination in Canada: The Black Experience." *The Canadian Historical Association Booklet* No. 41.

Walker, James W. St. G. 1998. *"Race", Rights, and the Law in the Supreme Court of Canada.* Waterloo: Wilfrid Laurier Press.

Walker, James W. St. G. 2001. "Routes of Diversity: Strategies for Change 1945–1970." A background paper prepared for the Multiculturalism Program, Department of Canadian Heritage.

Walkom, Thomas. 1998. "The Big Power Shift." *Toronto Star*, 5 December.

Walkom, Thomas. 1999. "Shaky Sanctuary." *Toronto Star*, 2 October.

Walkom, Thomas. 2001. "Conflict at the Core." *Toronto Star*, 13 January.

Walters, David, Kelli Phythian, and Paul Anisef. 2006. Understanding the Economic Integration of Immigrants: A Wage Decomposition of the Earnings Disparities Between Native-born Canadians and Immigrants of Recent Cohorts. CERIS Working Paper No. 42. Joint Centre of Excellence for Research and Immigration and Settlement. Toronto.

Ward, Olivia. 2004. "Battling to Understand Our Genocidal Instincts." *Toronto Star*, 5 June.

We Interrupt the News/Youth Force. 2001. *How the New York Times Frames the News*. New York: Between the Lines.

Weaver, Sally M. 1981. *Making Canadian Indian Policy: The Hidden Agenda, 1968–1970*. Toronto: University of Toronto Press.

Weaver, Sally M. 1993. "Self-Determination, National Pressure Groups, and Australian Aborigines. The National Aboriginal Conference 1983–1985." Pp. 3–74 in *Ethnicity and Aboriginality. Case Studies in Ethnonationalism*, ed. Michael D. Levin. Toronto: University of Toronto Press.

Weaver, Sally M. 1993. "First Nations Women and Government Policy 1970–1992: Discrimination and Conflict." In *Changing Patterns: Women in Canada* (2nd ed.), eds. Sandra Burt et al. Toronto: McClelland and Stewart.

Webber, Jeremy. 1994. *Reimaging Canada: Language, Culture, Community, and the Canadian Constitution*. Montreal/Kingston: McGill-Queen's University Press.

Weber, T. 2005. "Ottawa Targets Immigration." *The Globe and Mail,* 18 April.

Weinfeld, Morton. 2001. "Keep Our Door Open." *The Globe and Mail*, 22 June.

Weinfeld, Morton. 2001. *Like Everyone Else But Different: The Paradoxical Success of Canadian Jews*. Toronto: McClelland & Stewart.

Weinfeld, Morton. 2005. "The Changing Dimensions of Contemporary Canadian Antisemitism." In *Contemporary Antisemistism: Canada and the World*, ed. D. J. Penslar. Toronto: University of Toronto Press.

Weinfeld, Morton, and Lori A. Wilkinson. 1999. "Immigration, Diversity, and Minority Communities." Pp. 55–87 in *Race and Ethnic Relations in Canada* (2nd ed.), ed. P. Li. Toronto: Oxford University Press.

Weisberger, Bernard A. 1999. "Natives and Other Americans." *American Heritage* (May/June): 14–19.

Weisbrod, Carol. 2002. *Emblems of Pluralism: Cultural Differences and the State*. Princeton, NJ: Princeton University Press.

Wente, Margaret. 2002. "Black Blame, White Guilt." *The Globe and Mail*, 9 November.

Wetherell, M.. and J. Potter. 1993. *Mapping the Language of Racism: Discourse and the Legitimation of Exploitation*. New York: Columbia University Press.

Whitaker, Reginald A. 1991. *Double Standard: The Secret Story of Canadian Immigration*. Toronto: Lester and Orpen Dennys.

Whitaker, Reginald. 1997. "Canadian Politics at the End of the Millenium: Old Dreams, New Nightmares." In *A Passion for Identity: An Introduction to Canadian Studies,* ed. David Taras and Beverly Rasporich. Toronto: ITP Nelson.

White, N. J. 1999. "Beyond 2000: Home to the World." *Toronto Star*, 23 April.

Whittington, Les. 1998. "Canada Hailed as a Model for the 21st Century." *Toronto Star*, 10 August.

Widdowson, Frances. 2003. "Separate But Unequal: The Political Economy of Aboriginal Dependency." Paper presented to the Annual Conference of the Canadian Political Sciences Association, 2003 [unpublished].

Wieseltier, Leon. 1989. "Scar Tissue." *The New Republic* (June) 5:18–22.

Wilkins, Kerry (ed.). 2004. *Advancing Aboriginal Claims: Visions, Strategies, Directions.* Saskatoon, SK: Purich Publishing.

Wilkinson, Richard G. 2005. *The Impact of Inequality – How to Make Sick Societies Healthier.* Routledge.

Willett, Cynthia. 1998. *Theorizing Multiculturalism: A Guide to the Current Debate.* Malden, MA: Blackwell.

Willis, Katie, and Brenda Yeoh (eds.). 2000. *Gender and migration.* Northampton, MA: Edward Elgar Publishing.

Winant, Howard. 1998. "Racism Today: Continuity and Change in the Post–Civil Rights Era." *Ethnic and Racial Studies* 21(4):89–97.

Winland, Daphne N. 1998. "Our home and native land? Canadian ethnic scholarship and the challenge of transnationalism." *Canadian Review of Sociology and Anthropology* 35(4):555–84.

Winsor, Hugh. 2001. "The Medicine Man at Indian Affairs." *The Globe and Mail*, 27 August.

Winter, Elke. 2001. "National unity versus multiculturalism? Rethinking the logic of inclusion in Germany and Canada." *International Journal of Canadian Studies* 24:169–182.

Wise, Tim. 2005. "Race to our credit: Denial, privilege and life as a majority." Available at Tim Wise's homepage; also available at http://academic.udayton.edu.race/

Wiwa, Ken. 2001. "Black, white, and colourful." *The Globe and Mail*, 15 September.

Wiwa, Ken. 2003. "The fusion generation" *The Globe and Mail,* 12 June

Wong, Jan. 1998. "Why should I? This is my home." *The Globe and Mail,* Nov 26.

Woodward, Jonathan. 2005. "B.C. farms face crackdown over migrants." *The Globe and Mail.* 6 October

Wortley, Linda. 1998 "The Mountie and the Nurse. Cross Cultural Relations North of 60." In *Painting the maple leaf.* ed. V. Strong-Boag. Vancouver: UBC Press. 173–186.

Wortley, Scot. 2005. *Bias free policing. The Kingston data collection project. Preliminary results.* University of Toronto and the Centre for Excellence for Research on Immigration and Settlement.

Wortley, Scot, and Julian Tanner. 2004. "Social Groups or Criminal Organizations: The Extent and Nature of Youth Gangs in Toronto." Pp. 59–80 in *From Enforcement and Prevention to Civic Engagement: Research on Community Safety,* Jim Phillips and Bruce Kidd, eds. Toronto: Centre of Criminology.

Wortley, Scot, and Julian Tanner. 2005. "Inflammatory rhetoric? Baseless accusations? A response to Gabor's critique of racial profiling research in Canada." *Canadian Journal of Criminology and Criminal Justice* 47:581–609

Wotherspoon, Terry. 2003. "Aboriginal people, public policy, and social differentiation in Canada." in *Social differentiation: Patterns and processes.* ed. D. Juteau. Toronto: University of Toronto Press. 155–197.

Wrzesnewskyj, Borys. 2005. "Hell is still Darfur." *The Globe and Mail,* 31.

Xiao-Feng, Liu, and Glen Norcliffe. 1996. "Closed windows, Open doors: Geo-politics and the post-1949 mainland Chinese immigration to Canada." *The Canadian Geographer* 40(4):306–19.

Yamato, Gloria. 2001. "Racism: Something about the subject that makes it hard to name." in *Race, class, and gender: An anthology,* Margaret L. Andersen and Patricia Hill Collins, eds. Scarborough, ON: Wadsworth/Nelson. 150–58.

Yelaja, Prithi, and Nicholas Keung. 2005. "Living is where it's like home" *Toronto Star.* June.

Yinger, J. Milton. 1994. *Ethnicity. Source of strength. Source of conflict?* Albany NY: SUNY Press.

Yoshino, Kenji. 2006. "The pressure to cover." *New York Times Magazine,* 15 January.

Young, Iris. 1990. *Justice and the politics of difference.* Princeton: Princeton University Press.

Zachariah, Mathew, Allan Sheppard, and Leona Barrett.(eds.). 2004. *Canadian Multiculturalism: Dreams, Realities, and Expectations.* Edmonton: Canadian Multicultural Education Foundation.

Zhou, Min. 1997. "Segmented Assimilation: Issues, Controversies, and Recent Research on the New Second Generation." *International Migration Review* xxx1(4):975–1008.

Index

Abel, S., 318
Abele, F., 168–169, 175, 178, 182
Abella, I., 7, 239
Aboriginal difference, 166, 184, 186–189
Aboriginal justice, 332
Aboriginal orthodoxy, 186
Aboriginal peoples, 2, 10, 129, 216–218,
  302–303, 318–319, 329, 331–332
  and the constitution, 189
  and education, 329
  and genocide, 10
  and Quebec, 216–218
  constitutional status, 170–171
  criminal justice system, 302–303,
   331–332
  government policy, 178–186
  Indian Act, 190
  media and, 318–319
  population, 169–170
  socioeconomic status, 192–193
  urban, 174–175
  women, 143–144
Aboriginal policy, 178–186
Aboriginal rights, 7, 187, 194–196
  see also self–determination, aboriginality
Aboriginal self-determination, 189–193
  see also self-determining autonomy
Aboriginal self-government, 192–193
  see also aboriginal self-governance.
Aboriginal title, 165, 193–195
Aboriginal women, 143–144
aboriginality, 168, 198
  see also Aboriginal peoples
Aboud, F., 61
Abu-Laban, Y., 5, 232, 239, 244, 247, 261,
  284, 286, 345
Acadians, 210
accommodating diversity
  see multiculturalism; inclusiveness
Action Plan for Official Languages, 210
Adams, H., 172–173, 198

Adams, M., 340
Adelman, H., 230, 256
affirmative action, 19, 114–116
  see also employment equity
Afghanis, 229
African-Americans, 16–18, 125–128
  and sport, 27–28, 46–47
African-Canadians, 32–34, 236
  see also blacks
Agocs, C., 284
Aguiar, L., ix
Ahenakew, D., 167
Alexander, L., 79
Alia, V., 322
Alfred, T., 95, 108, 173, 178, 186, 188,
  192, 198
Allen, R., 180–181
allophones, 214
Alvi, S., 102, 152
Amnesty International, 342
Andersen, M., 155, 159
Anderson, R., 344
androcentrism, 153
Anglo-conformity
  see assimilation
anglophone, 214
  see also Quebec
Angus, I., 347
Anisef, P., 100
Ansley, B., 69
anti-racism, 75–78, 330–331
anti-racist education, 330–331
  vs. multicultural education, 331
anti-Semitism, 55, 148
apartheid, 66, 74, 166, 205, 255
Arab-Canadians, 62
Arat-Koc, S., 144, 274
Arbitration Act, 139
Areepattamannil, S., 324
Asch, M., 18, 191
Assante, M., 17, 42

Ashini, N., 167
Assembly of First Nations, 170, 197
assimilation, 13–14, 180–181
assimilationists, 164, 178, 188
assymetrical federalism, 223
asylum-seekers, 232, 250
  see also refugees
Aubrey, J., 220, 236
Australia, 297–298
autonomists, 164, 178, 188
autonomy, 184–185
  see also Aboriginal peoples/government
  policy; self-determination
Avery, D., ix, 45, 239
Axworthy, L., 110

Backhouse, C., 55
Bakan, A., 107, 119, 145, 259
Banaji, M., 6
Banks, J., 324
Bannerji, H., 5, 55, 144, 291
Banton, M., 8, 37,58
Barth, F., 89
Baubock, R., 276, 289–290
Baureiss, G., 7, 240
Bayley, D., 312
Beach, C., 246
Beaujot, R., 240
Bell, A., 44
Bell, S., 291
Bem, S., 74
Berton, P., 143, 326
Bibby, R., 91, 296
Bickerton, J., 344
Biddiss, M., 39
Biles, J., 91, 148, 234, 237, 261, 273, 295
bilingualism, 208–210, 213, 225–227
Bill 101, 210
  see also Quebec
Bill 178, 210
  see also Quebec
Bill C-31, 143
binationalism, 225

biology
  and gender, 141–143
    see also race
Bird, J., 166, 185
Bishop, A., viii, 54, 71, 75, 78
Bissoondath, N., 88, 291, 296
black focus schools, 45, 327
black people
  see blacks
Blackduck, A., 175
blacks, 51–52, 54, 121, 142, 310–311
  see also African-Americans,
  African-Canadians
Blair, T., 298
Blank, R., 60–61
Blumer, H., 60
B'nai B'rith, 55
Bolaria, S., 54, 241
Boldt, M., 8, 180
Bonilla-Silva, E., 31
Bono, 295
Borrows, J., 187, 193, 203
Bouchard, L., 212, 232
Boyd, M., 129, 140, 238, 246, 284
Brace, C.L., 28, 31, 35–36
Bramadat, P., 90
Breton, E., 180, 284, 289
Breton, R., 96, 117
British Columbia, 168–169
Brock, K., 184
Brooks, S., 183, 189, 194, 293
Buckley, H., 173
Bullock, H., 138
Bunzl, M., 69
bureaucracy, 314
Burnt Church, 198
Burstein, M., 234, 237, 261
Burt, S., 157

Cairns, A., 189, 203
Calder Decision, 165, 183, 196
  see also Aboriginal policy
Calliste, A., 6, 142
Cameron, D., 224
Cameron, E., 283, 289, 291

Canada, 6–8, 114–121, 164, 178, 335–353
  adventure called, 338–339
  as racist society, 72–75
  Chinese in, 62–63, 76
  citizenship, 335–337, 349–351
  ethnic diversity in, 87
  multiculturalism in, 279–288
  postnational, 346–348
  slavery in, 54
Canada's Diversity Model, ix, 7, 344–346
Canada-building, 107–109, 338–341, 346, 350
Canadian
  as ethnicity, 109–110
Canadian Council of Refugees, 63, 145, 233, 258
Canadian criminal justice system, 302–303, 307–315, 331–332
Canadian Diversity Model
  see Canada's Diversity Model
Canadian Race Relations Foundation, 54, 66, 120
Canadian Way, 295–296,344–346
capitalism, 35, 117
Caplan, G., 10
Cardinal, H., 178
Cardozo, A., 275, 281
Caribbean, 145, 248
Cassidy, F., 191, 202
Castells, M., 94
Castles, S, 83, 232, 252
Chagnon, N., 145
Chakkalakul, M., 264
Chan, J., 314
Chan, R., 285
Chan, W., viii, 30, 33
Charter groups, 165–167
  see also Quebec
Charter of Rights and Freedoms, 150, 219, 284
Chartrand, P., 171
Chinese-Canadians, 6, 128, 236, 240–242
  as immigrants
Chomsky, N., 321
church vs. state, 149
Churchill, W., 172, 196

citizenship, 335–337, 349–351
  as belonging, 336
  as contract, 336
  postnational, 350
  types of, 349–350
    differentiated, 337, 350
    inclusive, 351
    universal, 336, 349
Citizenship Act, 6, 242
Citizenship and Immigration Canada, 249
civic multiculturalism, 284–285
civic nationalism, 105–106
Civil Rights movement, 16–17
Clarity Bill, 222–223
Clairmont, D., 331
clash of cultures, 257
  see also South Asian
class, 115
  see also inequality
Closs, B., 78, 80
Coates, K., 197
Coleman, I., 139, 156
Coleman, W., 219
collective definition, 22–23
collective rights
  see Aboriginal rights; human rights
Collacott, M., 230, 233, 245, 263, 289
colonialism, 177, 199, 205, 346
colour bar
  see African-Americans
Coon Come, M., 167
Commissioner of Official Languages, 225
communitarianism, 297
community policing, 312–315
complete societies, 238, 346, 348
comprehensive land claims, 195
  see also comprehensive treaty claims
Conference Board of Canada, 54, 113, 233, 258–259
conflict perspective, 20–21, 129–130
  see also sociological perspectives
Conlogue, R., 62, 212
consensus multiculturalism, 288
Constitution Act, 5, 183, 284

constitutional order, 199–202, 205, 213, 346
  see also Quebec, Aboriginal peoples
constructive engagement, 200–202
constructivist approach, 93
contested site, 25, 315
Cooper, A., 54
Cornell, S., 90
Cotler, I., 116, 336
credentials, 259–262
  see also immigrants
Cree, 227
Crepeau, F., 232
CRIC, 220
crime and race, 32–34
criminal justice system
  see Canadian criminal justice system
critical multiculturalism, 287–288
Cryderman, B., 33, 308
cultural defense, 273–274, 297–298
cultural pluralism
  see multiculturalism
cultural relativism, 280
culture clash, 100–102
culture of poverty, 123
Curtis, J., 118

Daly, K, 332
Darfur, 10–12
Dasko, D, 289
de Seve, M., 106, 142, 144
deep diversity, 304
Dei, G.S., 30, 75, 78, 325, 327, 330
Delgamuukw, 191
  see also Aboriginal title
Dempsey, C., 256
Dench, J., 265
Denis, C., 164, 199, 203
Department of Indian Affairs, 183–184
depoliticizing ethnicity, 108–109, 282
Desroches, F., 311, 314
devolution, 183–184
Dickason, O., 181, 185
DiMatteo, E., 313

Diocson, C., 145
Dion, S., 8, 223
discrimination, 53, 62–64
  as harassment, 63–64
diversity, 236–237
  deep diversity, 304
  see also ethnic diversity
division of labour, 123
domestic dependent nations, 191
domestic workers, 145
  see also engaging diversity
Dominion Institute, 55
Donaldson, I., 283, 340
Dosman, E., 174
Douglas, D., 144
drawing the line, 272–274, 343
  see also multiculturalism, Canadian criminal justice system
Driedger, L., 97, 232, 234, 253
Drost, H., 173
du Plessis, R., 96
dualisms, 22–23
  see also collective definition
DuBois, W.E.B., 125
Dufraiment, L., 205
Duncan, H., 275, 278
Durie, M., 88
Dyer, G., 232

education, 324–331
  anti-racist, 330–331
  Islamic schools, 328–329
  monocultural, 325
  multicultural, 324–330
  multicultural vs anti-racist, 331
Edwards, H., 46
egalitarian, 136
Eisenstein, Z., 2, 288
Elabor-Idemudia, P., viii
Elliott, J.L., 165
Ellis, D., 310
Elmasry, M., 62, 317
Embracing Change policy, 113

Employment Equity, 29, 113–116,
  131–132, 134–135
  as philosophy, 114, 131–132, 134
  as policy, 114–116
Employment Equity Act, 29, 45, 114
engaging diversity, 3, 279
  see also multiculturalism, institutional
  inclusiveness
English-French relations
  see also Quebec.
equality, 111–136
  formal, 134
  rethinking, 132–134
  substantive, 134
    see also inequality
equity, 130–134
  see also inequality, Employment Equity
equity multiculturalism, 284
Erasmus, G., 198
Essed, P., 62, 68
essentializing, 30
Etherington, F., 146
ethnic
  boundaries, 90
  community, 96
  conflict, 124–125, 211
  groups, 83, 89
  nationalism, 86, 105–107, 220
  stratification, 138–142
ethnic cleansing, 10
ethnic diversity, 87, 236–237, 280
Ethnic Diversity Study, 63, 87
ethnic nationalism, 86, 105–107, 220
ethnic stratification, 118–121
ethnicity, 83–112, 130–131
  and Canada building, 107–109
  and inequality, 113–132
  and globalization, 84–85
  and language, 221–223
  and religion, 90–91
  characteristics, 90–91
  components, 89–90
  definition, 87–90
  depoliticizing, 108–109
  explaining, 91–95
  expressions , 95–96

  as community, 95–97
  as identity, 97–104
  as social movement, 104–106
  gender and, 153–154
  identity and, 96–102
  language of, 214–217
  nationalism, 105–107
  politics of, 85
  postmodern, 99–104
  revival of, 92
  situational, 97–98
    see also symbolic
  social movement and, 104–107
  stratification, 118
    see also Quebec, nationalism
  whiteness, 84–85, 107–108
ethnicity multiculturalism, 283–284
ethnocentrism, 61
ethnocide
  see genocide
eugenics, 40
Eurocentrism, 74, 321
  see also ethnocentrism

Fatah, T., 157
Feagin, J., 70
federalism, 223–225
  see also Quebec
feminism, 138, 258
Finnie, R., 119
First Nations
  see Aboriginal peoples
Fish, S., 275, 277
Fiss, T., 164, 172, 178, 188
Flanagan, T., 164, 172, 178, 188
Fleury, J-G., 251
Folson, B., ix, 340
Fong Bates, J., xi
Fontaine, N., 173
Fontaine, P., 187
Foot, D., 83
Forcese, D., 309
Foster, C., 29, 341
Foster, L., 244
Francis, D., 233, 252
Francophone
  see Quebec

Fraser, G., 168
Frederickson, G., 56, 58
Frederico, C., 28
French Language Charter (Bill 101), 210
French-and English speaking relations
　see Quebec
Frideres, J., 7, 170, 182
Friesen, J., 289
Friesen, J. W., 219, 339
Fukuyama, F., 85
Fulford, R., 300
functionalism, 19–20, 128–129

Gabriel, C., 286, 345
Gadacz, R., 7, 170, 182
Gagne, G., 219
Gagnon, L., 223
Galabuzi, G-E., ix, 45, 72, 113, 117,
　119–120, 123–124, 142
Ganguly, R.
　see Taras
Gates, H. Jr., 127
gender, 100–102, 138–158, 223–224
　Aboriginal women, 143–144
　immigrant women, 144–145
　inequality and, 141–142
　intersectional analysis, 153–155
　multiculturalism and, 138–139
　refugee women, 145–146
　South Asian women, 100–102
　women of colour, 142–142
　　see also visible minority women,
　　racialized women
genocide, 9–13, 183
Ghuman, P., 102
Gibbins, R., 106, 212, 358
Gibson, G., 178, 188
Gillespie, M., 84
Gilroy, P., 24, 74, 288
Giroux, H., 99, 280, 288, 324, 330
Gitlin, T., 286
Glazer, N., 18
globalization, 84
Goldberg, D.T., 18, 38
Gosine, A., 51
Gosnell, J., 204

governance, 175
　see Aboriginal self-government
Graydon, S., 138
Green, J., 177, 185, 192, 197
Greenspon, E., 220, 348, 357
Gregg, A., 5, 272, 288, 292
Gross, M., 111–114
Grubel, H., 124
Guimond, E., 170
Gunew, S., 279
Gwyn, R., 56, 347

Hage, G., 291
Hagey, R., 142
Hai, Y., 102–103
Haitian-Canadians, 273–274
Hall, A., 30
Hall, S., 84, 99
Halli, S., 119, 232, 234
Handa, A., 100–102, 257, 276, 347
harassment, 63–64
Harrison, T., 219
Harty, S., 171, 200, 203, 336
hate crimes, 65
hate racism, 64–65
Hawkes, D., 189–190
Hawkins, F., 244
Hayter, T., 269
head tax, 241
Hebert, Y., 212
Hechter, M., 94
Hiebert, D., 232, 237, 252, 261, 275, 339
Heinbecker, P., 110
Helly, D., 286
Helmes-Hayes, R., 118
Henry, F., 7, 43, 54, 69–70, 140, 142, 307,
　309–310, 315
Herman, E., 321
hijab, 147–153
Hill, L., 29
Hiller, H., 339
Holdaway, S., 30, 32
Hoodfar, H., 150, 152
hooks, b., 60
Howard, R., 83, 109
Hudson, M., 280
Hull, J., 175

Hum, D., 120, 121, 122, 124, 142
Human Genome Project, 34
human rights, 150, 341–343
Humpage, L., 312
Huntington, S., 86
Hurricane Katrina, 29, 176–177
Hutterites, 97
Hylton, J., 34, 191, 302

Ibbitson, J., 6, 51, 233, 251
identity, 98–99
   hyphenated, 99
      see also ethnicity
identity thesis, 93–94
ideological racism, 72–74
ideology of multiculturalism, 280–281
Ignatieff, M., 12–13, 105, 213, 291,
   342–343, 346
immigrants, 229–266
   credentials and, 259–262
   getting in, 237–256
   refugee vs., 231
   settling down, 256–263
   women, 261
   youth, 261–262
immigration, 7, 229–266
   classes of immigrants, 248–250
   cost/benefits, 252–254
   history of, 238–247
   paradoxes of, 232–236
   policy, 237–247
   provincial control, 244, 247
   refugees, 229–231, 248, 262
Immigration Acts, 239–240, 244
Immigration and Refugee Board, 230,
   251, 264
Immigration and Refugee Protection Act,
   231, 245
INAC, 169
inclusiveness, 159–160, 304–334
   see also multiculturalism
income, 12–123, 125–128
independent class, 261–262
   see immigration
Indian Act, 190
   see also Aboriginal Peoples, women

"Indian Problem", 164, 177, 182, 184
indigenous peoples
   see Aboriginal peoples
indigenous rights
   see Aboriginal rights
inequality, 113–137, 273
   by earnings, 120–128
   explaining, 128–130
   rethinking, 130–134
      see gender
institutional completeness, 96
institutional racism, 66–67
instrumentalist approach, 94
integration, 15–17, 182–183
integrative multiculturalism, 109,
   283–284, 294
   see also multiculturalism
interactionist models, 21–23
intergenerational conflict, 100–102, 262
intergroup dynamics, 9–17
   see also sociological perspectives
internal colonialism, 21, 166
   see also conflict theory
intersectional analysis, 153–155
Inuit, 171
Isajiw. W., 89, 233, 240
Isan, E., 224
Islam, 138–139, 328–329
Islamic schools, 328–329

Jain, H., 113, 312
Jakubowicz, A., 282, 298, 324
James, C., ix, 31, 45, 345
James, R., 80
Janzen, R., 60
Japanese-Canadians, 54, 62
Jaret, C., 35, 38
Jaworsky, J., 292
Jean, M., 290
Jedwab, J., 122, 124, 212, 278, 286,
   289–290, 295
Jenson, J., 108, 339, 344
Jews, 54, 67, 69
Jhappan, R., 181
Jimenez, M., 230, 249, 264, 265

Jiwani, Y., 32, 119, 142, 146, 154–155, 319
jurisdiction, 191–192, 197, 204

Kalbach, M and W., 280
Karim, K., 151, 315–316
Kasechewan, 7, 175–177
Kazemipur, A., 119, 253
Kenny, C., 140
Kernerman, G., 190, 213–215, 336
Keung, N., 96–97
Kilbride, D., 100
King, Martin L, 17
Kingston police services, 51–52
Kinsella, W., 65
Kivisto, P., 5
Knowles, C., 244
Kobayashi, A., ix, 55, 59
Kostash, M., 273, 291`
Kozol, J., 125
Ku Klux Klan, 42
Kulchyski, P., 181, 203
Kumar, S., 96
Kunz, J.L., 117, 119–121, 142, 259, 315–316
Kurosawa, A., 50
Kurthen, H., 286
Kymlicka, W., ix, 96, 105, 107, 187, 197, 278, 282, 285, 290, 292, 294–295, 336, 344–345, 350

Laforest, G., 212
La Prairie, C., 332
language
    see Quebec
Lauder, M., 65
Lerner, G., 141
Levitt, C., 72
Ley, D., 119–120, 232, 261, 277, 281, 289, 291, 296
Li, P., 6, 54, 232, 240, 242, 246, 253
Lian, J., 72
liberal pluralism, 29, 200, 203
Lister, R., 351
Little Bear, L., 197
Littleton, J., 94
Live-in Caregiver Program, 145

Loney, M., 55, 135
Long, D.A., 185
Loury, G., 121–122
Lupul, M., 4
Lyons, N., 199

Maaka, R., 15, 74, 105, 164, 177, 179, 186–187, 199–201, 290
Maccharles, T., 196, 245
Mackey, E., 44, 244
Macklem, P., 186
Macklin, A., 144–145
Magnet, J., 338, 340
Magsino, R., 281
Mahtani, M., 323
Maioni, A., 70
Maki, A, 6
Mallet, G., 300
Manfredi, C., 193
Manji, I., 290, 297–298
Marger, M., 8
Marxism, 21, 129
mass media
    see media
Matsuoka, A., 150
Matthews, R., 72
May, H., 276
McAndrew, M., 320
McCalla, A., 28, 30
McGauran, P., 292, 298
McGuinty, D., 294, 327
McHugh, P., 99
McIntosh, P., 43, 76, 110
McKee, C., 187
McRoberts, K., 196, 216, 224, 282, 291, 344
Meadows, M., 322
media, 315–323
    multiculturalizing, 322–323
    portrayal of minorities, 316–320
melting pot
    see United States
Mendelsohn, M., 86
Mercredi, O., 190
merit, 115
Metis, 171

Miles, R., 37
Miller, J.R., 172, 181
minorities
   see multicultural minorities, race,
   immigrants
minority youth
   see youth
Mirchandani, K., viii, 30, 33
misogyny, 153
Modood, T., 99, 238, 262, 278
monocultural education, 325
Montreal, 237, 248, 286
Monture–Angus, P., 169–170, 174
Moodley, K., 313
Moore, R., 68
Morse, B., 182
mosaic, 117
   see also multiculturalism, vertical mosaic
Mothers United Against Racism, 79
Mukherjee, A., 325
Mulroney, B., 286
multicultural education, 324–331
   types of, 326–331
multicultural minorities, 235
   see also immigrants
multiculturalism, 4–5, 138–139, 157, 272,
   301–302, 334
   and Canada-building, 303–305
   and diversity, 279–280
   and education, 324–331
   and media, 315–323
   as Canadian Way, 295–296
   as government policy, 281–285
   as ideology, 280–281
   attitudes towards, 5–6, 288–289
   critical multiculturalism, 287
   criticism of, 289–292
   cultural defense, 283–284, 305–306
   definition of, 279
   drawing the line, 39, 283–284,
      305–306
   in Australia, 297–298
   in Canada, 279–288
   in Europe, 293–295
   in the United States, 287–288
   policing, 315–323
   politics of, 272–274, 285–287

public perception of, 288–289
social contract, 279
sociological perspectives on, 22–23
theorizing, 276–279
women and, 273–274
Multiculturalism Act, 4, 284, 294, 315
multi–nation federalism, 216
Murphy, M., 166, 171, 200, 203, 215,
   217, 290, 336
Muslims, 138–139, 147–153, 293,
   328–329
   see also Arab-Canadians
Musto, L., 213, 234, 286
Muszynski, A., 140

Nagel, J., 92
Nancoo, S and R., 331
Nansen medal, 233
nation, 65
Nations-Within, 168
   see also Aboriginal peoples, self-
   determination
National Aboriginal Health Organization,
   173
national unity, 211–214
nationalism, 216–218
   indigenous nationalism, 199, 226–229
Nelson, A., 140, 349
neo-colonialism, 199–200
Neugebauer, R., 307–308
New Brunswick, 208
new global order, 125, 129–130
Newhouse, D, 174
Nisga'a, 164–166, 189, 191, 204–205
non-status Indians, 169, 170–171
normative racism, 68
Nova Scotia, 131–132
Nunavut, 210
   see also Inuit

Oertel, R., 259
Ochocka, J., 60
October referendum, 281
official bilingualism, 208
Official Languages Act, 209, 284
   see also Quebec

official language minorities, 209
  see also Quebec, language, ethnicity
official multiculturalism, 5, 23, 55,
  108, 272
  see also multiculturalism
Oka, 184
Okin, S., 138, 274, 298
Oliver, D., 54
Olzak, S., 92
Ominayak, B., 167
O'Regan, T., 190
Ornstein, M., 120

Palestinians, 229, 264
Papillon, M., 96, 108, 344
Parekh, B., 16, 100
Parkin, A., 189
patriarchy, 142
Peach, I., 200, 205
Pearson, D., 13, 275, 291–292
Pendakur, K & R., viii, 45, 114, 117,
  119–120, 122, 148, 152, 258
Penslar, D., 6
people of colour
  see multicultural minorities; visible
  minorities
Peter, K., 286
Peters, E., 174
Picard, A., 30, 70
Plaut, G., 230
plural societies
  see multiculturalism
pluralism, 16–19
points system, 248–249
  see also immigration
police minority relations, 309–311
policing, 307–315
  and racial profiling, 50–53, 78–80
policy
  aboriginal, 177–188
  multiculturalism, 299–305
polite racism, 65–66
politics of aboriginality, 168, 198
politics of multiculturalism, 272–274,
  285–287
Ponting, J.R., 167, 181
Porter, H., 223

Porter, J., 118
  see also *The Vertical Mosaic*
Porter R., 172
postcolonialism, 203
postmodern ethnic identity, 99–102
postmodernism, 288
postnational Canada, 346–348, 350
poverty, 123–124, 273
Povinelli, E., 286
power-sharing, 224
prejudice, 60–62
  vs discrimination, 75
Price, R., 191
primordial, 92–93
propaganda, 321
Purich D., 180

Qadeer, M., 96
Quebec, 106, 109, 156, 208–228, 282
  and aboriginal nationalism, 266–218
  see also nationalism, civic nationalism, ethnic nationalism
Quebec-Ottawa relations
  see Quebec
Québécois
  see Quebec

race, 27–48, 58
  and crime, 32–34
  and doctrines of racial supremacy,
  39–42
  and inequality, 116–124
  and sport, 27–28, 46–47
  as racialization, 31
  as whiteness, 43–45
  vs class, 126–128
race card, 166
racial profiling, 50–53, 78–80
racialized
  inequality (*see* inequality)
  minorities, 53, 282
  mosaic, 119
  see also multicultural minorities;
  inequality, race, racism
racialization, 27–28, 31–32
  see also inequality, racism

racial typologies, 36–37
racism, 50–82
  accounting for, 70–72
  anti-racism, 75–78
  constituents of, 60–64
  defining, 58–60
  explaining, 70–72
  theorizing, 56–58
  types of, 69–70
Rajagopal, I., 65
Ramirez, J., 151
Rashomon effect, 50–53, 78–80
  see also racial profiling
Razack, S., 7, 70, 143
refugee claimants, 230, 250
  see also refugees
refugee determination system, 229–231,
  250–251, 263–265
  see also IRB
refugee women, 145–146, 231
refugees, 229–231, 248, 262
  categories of, 263
  convention, 231, 250
  definition of, 241
  gender and, 231
  processing of (*see* refugee determina-
    tion system)
  undocumented (*see* refugee
    claimants)
Reitz, J., 70, 106, 261
religion, 328–329
  and ethnicity, 106, 147–153
reserves, 174
Resnick, P., 106, 147, 224
residential schools, 178
  see Aboriginal peoples
reversing discrimination, 114, 135
Rex, J., 288
Richards, J., 224
Richmond, A., 255
rights
  see also Aboriginal rights; human rights;
  collective rights
Roberts, J., 32–34, 172
Rocher, F., 222

Rothenberg, P., 140, 155
Rotman, I., 180–181, 187, 193, 196, 203
Royal Commission on Aboriginal
  Peoples, 7, 175, 184, 192, 203
Royal Commission on Bilingualism and
  Biculturalism, 282
Royal Proclamation, 179–180
Ruby, C., 312
Russell, P., 193
Rushton, P., 35–36, 42

Salee, D., 219
Saloojee, R., 101
Samuel, T.J., xi, 116, 259
Sandercock, L., 237, 277, 281, 337
Sarich, V., 36
Satzewich, V., 28, 53, 57, 117, 140, 143,
  241
Saul, J. R., 340, 348
Saunders, D., 11, 147
Sawchuk, J., 169
Schlesinger, A., 85, 285
Schouls, T., 191, 337
scientific racism, 41
Sechelt, 183
security certificates, 245
See, K., 92, 119
segregation, 14–15, 106–107
Seguin, R., 222
Seiler, T., 73, 285
self-determination
  see self-determining autonomy, self-
  government
self-determining autonomy, 189–193
self-governance
  see Aboriginal self government;
  self-governance; self-determining
  autonomy
self-government, 165, 185, 190–193
  see aboriginal self-government
Seljak, D., 90–91, 278
Selva, 342, 344
sexism, 159
Shapiro, T., 17, 122, 126
sharia, 138–139, 155–157
Shipler, D., 127

Shkilnyk, A., 172
Shohat, E., 320
Showler, P., 230, 232
Siddiqui, H., 111, 131, 214, 217, 233, 323
Simpson, J., 167
Simpson, W., 120, 121, 122, 124, 142, 277
Sissons, J., 196
sites of contestation, 25
situational ethnicity, 98
    see also symbolic ethnicity
Smith, A.D., 105, 211
Smith, C., 78, 309
social class
    see class
social contract, 186, 256, 279, 312
    see also Quebec
social Darwinism, 40
social movements, 104–107
society-building, 338–341
    and immigration, 252–254
        see Canada; Canada-building;
        multiculturalism
sociobiology, 93
Solomos, J., 8
South-Asian Canadians, 100–102, 236
    see also gender
sovereignty, 187, 191, 213, 216–218
    see Quebec, Aboriginal peoples
Sowell, T, 115
specific treaty claims, 194
Spoonley, P., 125, 180, 202, 252
Stackhouse, J., 172, 187
Stam, R., 317, 320
Stasiulis, D., 45, 99, 119, 141, 145,
    154–155, 259
state, 105, 290
Statistics Canada, 120, 122–123
status Indian, 170
Stavenhagen, R., 167
Stepan, N., 39
stereotype/ing, 61–62, 162, 318–319
Stoffman, D., 231, 242, 252
Stokes, E., 175
stratification, 119–120
    see also inequality
Strauss, J., 168

Suarez-Orozco, C., and M., 142, 258
subcultures
    see policing
subliminal racism, 68–69
Sudan, 10–12
Sue, D., 81
sui generis, 195
    see also Aboriginal title; treaty rights
symbolic ethnicity, 98–99
see situational ethnicity
systemic racism, 66–67, 342

Taras, R., viii, 85, 104
Tator, C., 7, 54, 70, 117, 140, 331
Taylor, C., 7, 43, 213, 215, 224, 272,
    306–307, 309, 315
Taylor, D., 73
Teelucksingh, C., ix, 17, 117, 119–120,
    123–124
Teeple, G., 343
temporary workers, 145, 248
Tepper, E., 117, 265
Tharoor, 343
Thernstrom, A., and S., 127
Thobani, S., 55, 140, 238, 288, 291
Thompson, A., 233, 244
Tishkov, V., 104
Toronto, 237, 248, 286, 308, 324
Travers, J., 254
treaty rights, 186, 194–196
    see also aboriginal title; self-determination
three-nations model, 338
    see also Canada, Quebec, multi-nation
    federalism
Troper, H., 239
Trudeau, P.E., 165, 213, 223, 281–282
Tully, J., 340
Turpel, M.E., 190
two solitudes, 211–214

Ucarer, E., 232, 237
Ujimoto, V., 275
Ukrainian-Canadians, 54, 62
Ungerleider, C., 309
United Nations, 228, 239–240, 303

United Nations High Commission for
Refugees, 229
United States, 121–124, 191, 297–298
and multiculturalism, 287–288, 297
see also domestic dependent nations

van den Berghe, P., 93
Vancouver, 237, 248, 286
Vasta, E., 125, 275
Vietnamese, 230
Velez, W., 18, 23, 128
Venne, M., 219
Venne, S., 200
Vertical Mosaic, The (Porter), 118–119
racialized, 119
Vickers, J., 106, 142, 144, 238
violence, 146
visible minorities, 118–119, 270–275
see also multicultural minorities

Walker, J. St. G., xi, 6, 53, 239
Weaver, S., 144, 181
Webber, J., 221, 282
Weinfeld, M., 7, 67, 69, 118, 244, 248
Wente, M., 298
westocentric, 321
see also eurocentric
Wetherell, M., 65

Whitaker, R., 241, 253
White, J., 169
white nationalism
see whiteness; *see also* white suprema-
cists, 106–107
White Paper, 169
whiteness, 43–45, 76, 83–84
Wilkinson, R., 117
Widdowson, F., 165, 192, 199
Winant, H., 58
Wise, T., 75
Wiwa, K., 29, 85, 99
women
see gender
violence against, 146
Wong, J., 213
Wortley, L., 322
Wortley, S., 32, 51, 79, 307, 310–311

Yalden, M., 225
Yamato, G., 76
Yelaja, P., ix, 96
Yinger, M., 88
Yoshino, K., 63
Young, I.M., 349
youth, 100–102, 261–262, 309–311
see also South-Asian Canadians; immi-
grants (settling down)